Economics and the Public Welfare

*A Financial and Economic History
of the United States,
1914–1946*

Benjamin M. Anderson

Liberty Fund, Inc.
Indianapolis

This book is published by Liberty Fund, Inc., a foundation established to encourage study of the ideal of a society of free and responsible individuals.

The cuneiform inscription that serves as our logo and as the design motif for our endpapers is the earliest-known written appearance of the word "freedom" (*amagi*), or "liberty." It is taken from a clay document written about 2300 B.C. in the Sumerian city-state of Lagash.

First edition published 1949 by the D. Van Nostrand Company, Inc. Second edition published 1979 by Liberty Fund, Inc., Indianapolis. This book was manufactured in the United States of America.

C   10 9 8 7 6 5 4 3 2 1

P   10 9 8 7 6 5 4 3

LIBRARY OF CONGRESS CATALOGING IN PUBLICATION DATA
Anderson, Benjamin McAlester, 1886–1949.
    Economics and the public welfare.
    Includes index.
    1. United States—Economic conditions.
    2. United States—Economic conditions—1918–1945.
I. Title
HC106.2.A62   1979   330.9'73'091   79-20911
ISBN 0-913966-68-1 (hardcover edition)
ISBN 0-913966-69-X (paperback edition)

Economics and
the Public Welfare

Contents

PART IV: THE NEW DEAL IN MATURITY, 1933–39

Foreword
by Arthur Kemp

"**M**ay you live in interesting times," is said to be an ancient Chinese curse. Whether so to live is truly a curse may be debatable, but there is little doubt that Benjamin M. Anderson, Jr., did indeed live in *very* interesting times—his adult life spanned two world wars, a decade of unprecedented prosperity, a decade of equally unprecedented depression and deflation, culminating in a postwar period that provided the groundwork for the most prolonged period of inflation the United States, and the world, has ever seen. More than that, his chosen profession—that of economist—experienced during that time a major revolution, now generally called the "Keynesian revolution," within that part of economics—monetary economics—which Anderson chose to make his own specialty.

Benjamin M. Anderson, Jr. received his Ph.D. from Columbia University in 1911. His doctoral dissertation, entitled *Social Value*, was an expansion and elaboration of an earlier monograph bearing the same title for which he had received a Hart, Schaffner, and Marx prize of $400—a monetary reward far greater then than such a dollar amount conjures up in one's mind today, to say nothing of the far more important prestige such an award carried with it at the time. Understandably, he turned first to employment in the academic world at Columbia University, which fitted well with his proclivities for intellectual pursuits. He served as assistant professor of economics at Harvard from 1914 to 1918, publishing in 1917 his best known theoretical work, *The Value of Money,* which has enjoyed several reprintings over the years.

With the advantage of hindsight, it now seems clear that he was torn between the intellectual enjoyments of academic life on the one hand and, on the other, the excitement of participating in the day to day political and economic decisions of the financial world. In 1918 he became economist for the National Bank of Commerce and editor of its publication, *Commerce Monthly.* This lasted less than two years, until he was enticed away by that prestigious institution, the Chase Manhattan Bank, where he remained until 1937 as chief economist and editor of the *Chase Economic Bulletin*. It is only fair to express the judgment that these were his most active years, observing and participating in decisions involving the most important of financial and banking problems, domestically and internationally. Although he never completely relinquished his connections with the financial community, he returned to academia in 1939 as professor of economics at the University of California at Los Angeles, where he remained until his death a decade later, in January 1949.

As the subtitle of this volume indicates, *Economics and the Public Welfare* is an economic and financial history of the United States over a period of time in which the author was not only an astute observer of, but also a frequent participant in, important events. Unlike many volumes of memoirs, however, the main thrust of this book is toward not the simple recording of events but an integrating of those events with the underlying principles. Anderson was no shrinking violet, however, so far as his own opinions, advice, and participation in decisions are concerned. He certainly does not hesitate to quote extensively from his own writings, both published and unpublished, and he frequently emphasizes his own high-level connections. Clearly he possessed a place of importance and from it endeavored to employ his own superb understanding, not only of the American banking system, but those of the major European nations as well. In this history, Anderson touches upon practically every aspect of commercial banking and, in almost every instance, he takes a position that might be called, for lack of a better name, "sound banking principles," which means he regarded the banking business as a regulated but private enterprise, not as an instrument for economic, social, and political experimentation by government. His views are, therefore, controversial.

It is only fair, both to Anderson and to his present-day readers, that one should keep clearly in mind when, and for whom, it was written. His intended audience of American readers had not yet experienced the post–World War II inflation, or much of any other inflation for that matter. Rather, most of them had lived through the rather severe deflation of the thirties. Since the book's publication in 1949, this nation has experienced an inflation completely unlike, either in intensity or duration, any of the three prior decades. Indeed, Anderson shows exceptional foresight in anticipating much of the ensuing inflationary onslaught. The reader should be cautious, however, in judging the numerical examples. Anderson intended them to shock the reader, to reinforce and emphasize the verbal argument. That they do not do so at the present time means only that the inflation we have experienced has so numbed our senses that nominal monetary comparisons involving interest rates, price levels, stock price indices, and exchange rates have been rendered almost meaningless.

Most monetary economists would agree that the Keynesian "revolution" has passed its peak; the revolution has been more or less successfully challenged by at least two counter-revolutions: one, that of the loosely labeled monetarist or Chicago school; the other, the equally loosely labeled Austrian school. Anderson really belongs to neither school, but if he leans a bit, it is in the direction of the Austrians. His criticism of Keynes (Chapter 60, titled "Digression on Keynes") is worth the price of the book. It is a first-rate critique of Keynes and the Keynesians written at the Keynesian zenith by an able, stimulating, and effective monetary economist. It could stand by itself—which, perhaps, is the reason it is labeled a digression—because it is theoretical rather than historical. Perhaps this is also why Henry Hazlitt included the chapter in the book *The Critics of Keynesian Economics* (New Rochelle, N.Y.: Arlington House, 1977). Anderson spent a great deal of time, thought, and effort analyzing Keynes' *General Theory*. He recognized it immediately as a serious and basic challenge to orthodox economic thought; and he provided one of the earliest of the cogent, persuasive critiques and one that is likely to last well into the future. Anderson also found much to criticize in the works of Irving Fisher, for example, whom Professor Milton Friedman labels the "greatest American economist," and in those of Laughlin Currie, a classic figure among the early members of the Chicago school. It is not too brazen to predict that there will continue to be substantial and substantive differences between these two schools of monetarist economic thought. In this book Anderson provides a great quantity of historical material, both empirical and theoretical, of greater value to the Austrian than the Chicago side. It should prove of great value to future authors of Ph.D. theses on monetary economics.

To present and future economic historians, this is an immensely valuable addition to the financial and monetary history of the United States, written by a distinguished scholar, historian, banker, financier, and economist. Benjamin M. Anderson, Jr., did more than record and study the historical events; he participated in many of them. Although this is not a fully satisfactory substitute for a study of the complete file of the *Chase Economic Bulletin* over the same period, it is more readily available and probably more readable. When it was first published, *Economics and the Public Welfare* did not receive the attention it so richly deserves. Such is not a unique experience for writers of economic treatises. As Keynes himself wrote, and as so many others have so frequently quoted, "the ideas of economists and political philosophers, both when they are right and when they are wrong, are more powerful than is commonly understood. Indeed the world is ruled by little else. Practical men, who believe themselves to be quite exempt from any intellectual influences, are usually the slaves of some defunct economist." Let us hope that, at least in this case, Keynes' observation may be proved correct.

Preface

This book is the outcome of studies which began in 1914 and have been carried through systematically since that date. As assistant professor of economics at Harvard University, the author taught money and banking from 1914 to 1918 and, both in his lectures and in published articles and books, recorded the significant economic and financial developments of World War I. A summary of these studies appeared in his *Effects of the War on Money, Credit and Banking in France and the United States,* published by the Carnegie Endowment for International Peace in 1919. From 1918 to 1939 he acted as economist for the National Bank of Commerce in New York (1918–20), and the Chase National Bank (1920–39). During these years he was in intimate contact with bankers, investment bankers, brokers, and industrialists throughout the country, and with bankers throughout the world, with the Federal Reserve System and with foreign central banks, with government officials and leading journalists of many countries, as well as with academic students in the United States and abroad.

He wrote down and published *at the time*—first (1919–20) in *Commerce Monthly,* issued by the National Bank of Commerce in New York, and second, in the *Chase Economic Bulletin* (1920–37), issued by the Chase National Bank of the city of New York—records and discussions of the period. And he recorded confidential memoranda for the use of his associates—many of which are still too confidential to be used except as background—the information that came to him from conferences in his own bank and from conferences as he traveled in Europe or to the leading cities of the United States. His banking contacts in the United States included not merely the chiefs of great banks, but also a multitude of American country bankers (an extraordinarily able group of men) who kept him informed regarding conditions in American agriculture and the industries of the smaller places.

As professor of economics at the University of California since 1939 he has retained close contact with American bankers and with men in public life and, to the extent that communication has been feasible during the war period, also with foreign bankers and men in public life. And he has continued to publish discussions of the developments of World War II and of postwar problems, particularly in the *Economic Bulletin* issued by the Capital Research Company, Los Angeles, the *Commercial & Financial Chronicle,* the *Hearings* of the Senate Finance Committee and the Senate Committee on Banking and Currency, and in documents issued by the Economists' National Committee on Monetary Policy.

There is a great fraternity of bankers both in the United States and in the world outside. They trust one another. They tell one another the truth regarding highly confidential matters. They go far out of their way to be of service to one another and to one another's customers. The author is grateful that they still include him in this great fraternity.

This book, therefore, represents, not the researches of a scholar remote from the field of activity, working primarily with the documents and the writings of other men, but rather, in very considerable measure, the records and recollections of a participant in the history.

The field of the drama which the present volume undertakes to present is too vast for any man to say (as Aeneas said to Dido regarding the events of the Trojan War), "All of which I saw and a great part of which I was." Certainly the present writer could make no such statement. But he does feel justified in saying, "Much of which I saw and of which I was a small part."

The volume contains a good many disclosures of information confidentially obtained, in cases where the author feels sure that no harm can be done to the sources from which he obtained the information. Where references are made to private conversations with men still living, either their names are not used or the author has reason to believe that they will not object.

The author is indebted to far too many men, for information and help, over the years, to make it possible to list them. He has tried to make such a list and has found it to be a vast catalog of names in New York, in Washington, in virtually every other major American city, and in the financial centers and capitals of Europe, Asia, and other parts of the world.

The author is deeply indebted to the president, vice presidents and junior officers of the National Bank of Commerce in New York (1918–20), who initiated him into practical banking, taking him into their intimate confidential relationships and having him sit with them in their conferences with important industrial and commercial customers and with important visiting American and foreign bankers.

His greatest debt, of course, is to the great Chase National Bank of the city of New York. For nineteen years (1920–39) this institution was his laboratory. The successive chiefs, the vice presidents, many of the directors, most of the junior officers, and men in virtually every department of the bank supplied him with information and opened their records freely to him. He could sample the routine or leave it alone. He was called into conferences where major questions of policy were to be determined. Its foreign offices also were his laboratories. He will always retain a deep affection for this great institution and for the men in it.

The author gratefully acknowledges the help of his wife, who has given a critical reading to every page of this book, through its several revisions, as she has done for virtually everything else he has written for over three decades, and who has saved him from many errors in form, tone, and substance.

He wishes to acknowledge the help of his colleague at the University of California at Los Angeles, Professor Warren Scoville, who has read critically every page of the manuscript of this book and has made very helpful suggestions regarding it, and of Melvin D. Brockie and Robert E. Smith, who, as graduate students in that institution, helped him assemble and check facts and figures. He is much indebted also to his associates in the Capital Research Company of Los Angeles and in the investment companies served by it, particularly Henry S. McKee, president of the Pacific American Investors, and Jonathan Bell Lovelace, president of the Investment Company of America, both of whom have read the manuscript and have given him the benefit of their criticisms. For the same service he wishes to thank Henry Hazlitt of *Newsweek* and Dwight W. Michener of the Chase National Bank. He thanks Dr. Ludwig von Mises, who has been good enough to give a critical reading to chapter 60, "Digression on Keynes." He is grateful also to Dr. V. Orval Watts of the Foundation for Economic Education at Irvington-on-Hudson for a critical reading of the whole manuscript and for many helpful suggestions.

It goes without saying that none of those who have given him help and information and opinions and advice is responsible for the views expressed in this book or for errors which it may contain.

Errors it must contain. Thirty-four years is too short a time in which to achieve serene perspective on the financial and economic developments of this momentous period! Serene perspective, moreover, is not easily achieved by a man who lived through this period, not merely as an observer but also as a fighting man trying all too ineffectively to alter the course of events. But the author has been well aware of his duty to be objective in his evaluation of the events that he has recorded, and his friendly critics have helped him to perform this duty.

BENJAMIN M. ANDERSON

University of California, Los Angeles
November 1948

Economics and
the Public Welfare

PART I

WORLD WAR I

1

The Prewar World, 1913

Those who have an adult's recollection and an adult's understanding of the world which preceded World War I look back upon it with a great nostalgia. There was a sense of security then which has never since existed. Progress was generally taken for granted. It was even necessary at times for scholars in addressing scholarly audiences—as, for example, Leonard T. Hobhouse in an address at Columbia University in 1910—to make the distinction between progress and evolution and to point out that evolution might not always be progressive. The theoretical distinction was recognized, but the experience of the preceding century, so far as social and economic evolution was concerned, had made the distinction seem unreal. We had had a prolonged period in which decade after decade had seen increasing political freedom, the progressive spread of democratic institutions, the steady lifting of the standard of life for the masses of men. We had even come to the point where some were asserting, incorrectly, that the problem of production had been solved, that enough was being produced, and that with better distribution everybody could be made comfortable.

In our economic life we had occasional sharp setbacks. Crises and depressions alternated with relatively prolonged periods of active prosperity. We thought of these depressions as severe, but they did not approach in length or depth the depression of 1929–39, or in depth the much less severe depression of 1921. Even in the midst of depression, moreover, it was axiomatic that revival would come again, the question being simply when the bottom would be reached and when the turn would come.

It was an era of good faith. Men believed in promises. Men believed in the promises of governments. Treaties were serious matters.

In financial matters the good faith of governments and central banks was taken for granted. Governments and central banks were not always able to keep their promises, but when this happened they were ashamed, and they took measures to make the promises good as far as they could. In the greenback period in the United States, the federal government was unable from January 1, 1862, to January 1, 1879, to make good its promise to pay gold on demand for its paper money. But it did make good its promises to pay interest and principal on the public debt in gold, and it did, in 1879, resume payment of gold in redemption of its paper money. No country took pride in debasing its currency as a clever financial expedient.

The world was incredibly shocked in 1914 when Bethmann-Hollweg, chancellor of Germany, characterized the treaty guaranteeing the neutrality of Belgium as a "scrap of paper." In retrospect, one may say that this was one of the most terrible things that has ever been said. The world is full of scraps of paper today. The reference here is not to the brazen, cynical, contemptuous attitude of Hitler toward treaties and toward promises. Hitler made many promises with no intention of keeping them when he made them. But the world united against Hitler. His level of bad faith obviously could not be tolerated. The reference is, rather, to the attitude of some of the most decent governments of the world toward many promises and treaties. Japan and Mussolini could never have started on their careers of aggression if the great democratic nations had kept faith with one another. The reference is also to the broken promise of the British government and the Bank of England in 1931 to pay gold on demand for Bank of England notes. If it be objected that England was forced to this, a view which is erroneous,[1] surely no such defense can be made for the government of the United States, when, in 1933, with $3 billion of gold in Federal Reserve banks, it suspended gold payment and when, in 1934, with $4 billion of gold in the Federal Reserve banks, it reduced the dollar to 59.06 percent of the old gold parity and repudiated the gold clause in its own bonds. In 1913 men trusted the promises of governments and governments trusted one another to a degree that is difficult to understand today.

The greatest and most important task of the next few decades must be to rebuild the shattered fabric of national and international good faith. Men and nations must learn to trust one another again. Political good faith must be restored. Treaties must again become sacred.

A world in which all men are upright and in which all nations are voluntarily decent in their international relations is, of course, too much to expect, but a world in which the ill intentioned fear the condemnation of the well intentioned we can rebuild. The same basic human nature which created the fabric of national and international good faith on which we relied in the century preceding 1914 exists today—just as we have discovered that the same human nature which animated the Assyrian conquerors and the hordes of Genghis Khan exists today. The raw stuff of human nature is immensely plastic and can be turned in many different directions, depending on the cultural influences which play upon it. There is no

---

[1] This point will be discussed at length in chapter 34.

certainty that we can re-create the fabric of good faith which we have destroyed, but there is no higher duty than to make the effort.

The economic life of the world in 1913 went on in an atmosphere of good faith. Men with liquid capital used the capital themselves confidently in business enterprises or loaned their capital at market rates of interest to others who would use it in productive operations. There were no billions of dollars of "hot money" such as characterized the decade of the 1930s, moving nervously about from one financial center to another through fear of confiscation or through fear of further currency debasement—moving from countries which their owners distrusted more to countries which they distrusted less, but finding nowhere a place which they could really trust.

Industry, commerce, and finance depend on credit. Credit was in general soundly based on movable goods which had dependable markets, on corporate securities, readily salable in dependable stock markets, and on governmental securities, usually moderate in volume, buttressed by balanced budgets.

Not all the great countries had safely balanced budgets. France, though enormously strong financially, in 1914 had had chronically unbalanced budgets for many years. The balance in Russia and in Italy was precarious.

But always the statesmen of these countries winced under criticism, and none of them boasted of their achievements in unbalancing the budgets or termed the deficit "investments."

There were protective tariffs in the United States, France, Germany, and many other weaker countries. England held to a free trade policy, as did Holland, the Scandinavian countries, and Switzerland. But the tariffs of those days were moderate in comparison with postwar tariffs. They were subject to infrequent change, and trade lines were sufficiently open so that countries under pressure to pay debts could do so by shipping out an increased volume of commodities.

The head of the Austro-Hungarian National Bank, Popovich, later the head of the Hungarian National Bank, said in 1929 that in a prewar crisis Austria-Hungary had paid her adverse foreign balance of indebtedness by shipping out an increase of timber down the Danube, through the Black Sea, into the Mediterranean, and up the Atlantic Coast to the Netherlands, at prices which made it effectively competitive with timber from the Scandinavian countries. All that it was necessary for him to do, as head of the Austro-Hungarian Bank, was to hold his discount rate high, compel a moderate liquidation of credit, and rely upon the merchants to find markets for Austro-Hungarian goods, which, sold abroad, would produce foreign cash and turn an adverse balance of payments into a favorable balance.

London was the financial center, but there were independent gold standard centers in New York, Berlin, Vienna, Paris, Amsterdam, Switzerland, Japan, and the Scandinavian countries. There were many other countries on the gold standard, with some tendency for the weaker countries to substitute holdings of sterling or other foreign bills for part of their gold, primarily as a means of getting increased earnings. For their purpose the sterling bill was quite as good as gold. They trusted it. They could turn it into gold. The gold exchange standard was the primary standard of India. But, in general, the great countries held their own gold. They relied upon themselves to meet their international obligations in gold. At times of great crisis a country under very heavy pressure would seek international coop-eration and international assistance, and would get it—at a steep rate of interest.

In 1907, for example, we eased off our own money panic by importing approximately $100 million of gold from London. At times London leaned on Paris. The Bank of France had a much larger gold reserve than the Bank of England, and Paris was always ready to accommodate London—at a price—in an emergency. But these incidents were infrequent. In general each country went its own way and made its own financial policies and money market policies, subject always to the limitation that if it over-extended itself the other great money markets would drain away its gold and force it to reverse its policies. There was no such thing in prewar days as the kind of international cooperation which we saw in the 1920s, under which a dangerous boom was prolonged and turned into an almost uncon-trollable inflation through the cooperation of the Bank of England and the Federal Reserve System of the United States.

In the United States, with our inelastic currency system, we had several unnecessary money panics. The panics of 1873 and 1893 were complicated by many factors, but the panic of 1907 was almost purely a money panic. Our Federal Reserve legislation of 1913 was designed to prevent phenomena of this kind and, wisely handled, could have been wholly beneficent. It is noteworthy, however, that the money panic of 1907 had nothing like the grave consequences of the collapse of 1929. The money stringency of 1907 pulled us up before the boom had gone too far. There was no such qualitative deterioration of credit preceding the panic of 1907 as there was preceding the panic of 1929. The very inelasticity of our prewar system made it safer than the extreme ductility of mismanaged credit under the Federal Reserve System in the period since early 1924.

The whole world was, moreover, far safer financially when each of the main countries stood on its own feet and carried its own gold. In the 1920s gold in New York was made the basis of deposits in American banks which served as the gold exchange reserve of great European banks, and over-expansion in New York did not lead to the prompt withdrawal of gold by foreign monetary centers.

The Outbreak of the War in 1914

The War Came as a Surprise to Most Informed Men. The war came as a great shock, not only to the masses of the American people, but also to most well-informed Americans—and, for that matter, to most Europeans. There had been no first-rate war since the Franco-Prussian War of 1870. Wars of limited objectives there had been, as the Spanish-American War of 1898 and the Russo-Japanese War of 1904–05. Colonial wars there had been, as the very important Boer War of 1899–1902. Intermittent fighting in the Balkans had existed, but the Balkans were looked upon as a special case. But a great war involving the major nations of Europe was looked upon as something so terrible, so catastrophic, and so dangerous to everybody involved that few expected it.

The present writer can recall only two men among those of his acquaintance for whose views he had high respect, who really anticipated that Germany would force the pace and precipitate world conflict. One of these was Dean David Kinley of the University of Illinois (later president of the university) who, in the winter of 1909–10, analyzing the tendencies in German thought and policy, expressed the opinion that these tendencies would make inevitably for war in the near future. The other was Franklin Henry Giddings, the great sociologist of Columbia University, who, a year or two later, after conversations with some visiting German professors, expressed himself as aghast at the rapid hardening of the German attitude and as feeling that an inevitable conflict was close at hand. But to most of the informed American public the outbreak of the war in 1914 was a bolt from the blue.

A Surprise to the Financial World—Premonitory Financial Phenomena. To the banking world and to the international bankers it came as a great surprise. There had been, indeed, financial phenomena which foreshadowed it. There had been accumulation of gold by Germany, Russia, and France. The first manifestation came as early as 1912, as German bankers began to take steps to increase their gold supply. In order to take gold out of the hands of the people and carry it to the reserves of the Reichsbank, fifty- and twenty-mark banknotes were issued to take the place of the gold in circulation. German agents regularly appeared as bidders for gold in the London auction rooms. Gold was shipped from the United States to Germany, and the famous Spandau Treasure was transferred to the vaults of the Reichsbank. By 1914 Germany ceased to take much gold, having presumably decided that her resources were adequate.

France and Russia made strong efforts to increase their gold reserves during the spring and summer of 1914. In the eighteen months preceding the outbreak of the war the gold holdings of the central banks of Germany, France, and Russia were estimated to have increased by $360 million. The drift of gold to these great central reservoirs led to a tightening of the money markets of the rest of the world and to an unusually large drain on the gold supply of the United States.

Recognized by A. D. Noyes. Few, however, even among informed financiers, saw in this a forecast of war. One notable exception among American observers was A. D. Noyes, then financial editor of the *New York Evening Post*. In his annual summaries at the end of 1912 and at the end of 1913, he called attention to the pulling in of gold by European central banks under the apprehension of war, and explained the mild recession in business in 1913 in the United States by this phenomenon. Europe had ceased to lend to the United States and had begun withdrawal of funds. We had been accustomed to rely on European capital for part of the funds needed for our own business expansion. We were ceasing to get it and were repaying part of it. Our industrial pace slowed down because of this fact.

The Causes of the War. There are not a few writers, overimpressed by the economic interpretation of history and especially by Marxist versions of the economic interpretation of history, who have seen the war of 1914 as the result of inevitable economic tendencies. There is no one principle of historical interpretation and there are few, if any, inevitable economic tendencies. Political, moral, cultural, and religious forces are coefficients with economic forces in the determination of historical events, and the influence of outstanding personalities in strategic positions is often far more significant than any economic determinist will concede.

Views of Munroe Smith and Veblen. The two writers who seem to have explained the outbreak of the war in 1914 most clearly are Munroe Smith, professor of Roman law at Columbia University, and Thorstein Veblen. Munroe Smith's explanation appeared in the *Political Science Quarterly* in March 1915 in an article called "Military Strategy Versus Diplomacy." Munroe Smith had previously written a very interesting biography of Bismarck. In the article referred to he begins by saying that he assumes that he will not be accused of setting up utopian standards when he judges the course of German diplomacy immediately preceding the war by the standards of Bismarck. Bismarck had always respected the "imponderables."

Bismarck had had a wholesome respect for world public opinion. He had never gone into war without first seeing to it that his alliances were dependable, that neutral relations were assured, and that world opinion was on the side of Germany. He had sometimes used devious tricks in creating a favorable world opinion, as in his falsification of the telegram at Ems, but he had had a respect for the opinion of mankind, and he had compelled his generals to wait until public opinion was on his side. In the war with Austria von Moltke had pleaded with Bismarck to let him strike at once, saying that every day's delay meant unnecessary military losses. Bismarck made him wait until the psychological atmosphere was right. By 1914, however, the diplomat in Germany was no longer in the saddle—the military strategist was in the saddle. Bethmann-Hollweg later admitted this.[1] It is not correct to say, Munroe Smith contends, that German diplomacy failed in 1914. The correct thing to say is that German diplomacy never had a chance.

Veblen's explanation came in an unpublished manuscript in 1915.[2] Veblen pointed out that modern war cannot be successfully carried on except by a highly industrialized country. Modern war calls for immense mechanical equipment and for a continuing supply of mechanical equipment. But industrialization involves the growth of great cities and the bringing together of great masses of the population, taking them away from the control of rural nobles and landlords and bringing them together under new conditions which promote the growth of democracy. Industrialization and democracy in general grow together. But democracy makes for peace. The common man has nothing to gain from war. He will fight to defend his country, but there is no glamour for him in aggressive fighting against other countries. Primitive war often meant booty and women and adventure for the common man, but highly mechanized modern war has few attractions.

With industrial power and democracy developing together, it was thus to be expected that the countries powerful enough to precipitate war would be pacific enough not to do it. But Veblen noted two dangerous exceptions to this rule. The first was Germany and the second was Japan. In each of these countries industrial power had developed without the concomitant growth of democracy. In each of these countries political power was in the hands of an oligarchy. Though the common man would gain nothing from war, the oligarchy might gain and would gain from a successful war. Germany and Japan, therefore, were two countries to which the world might look to force the pace in upsetting international peace.

These two discussions seem to me to contain the most fundamental

---

[1] Bethmann-Hollweg, *Reflections on the World War* (London, 1920), pp. 137–38, 147.

[2] I have not been able to find that this article was ever published. However, the reader will find much of it in two books by Veblen: *Imperial Germany and the Industrial Revolution* (New York, 1915); and *The Nature of Peace and the Terms of Its Perpetuation* (New York, 1917).

explanations of the rupturing of the peaceful world that came in 1914; and
Veblen's principle that industrial power in the hands of an oligarchy is a
menace to the peace of the world is startlingly prophetic of the developments that have come in the 1930s. Democracy is pacific, dangerously
pacific, as France and England and the United States demonstrated in the
four or five years preceding the outbreak of the war in 1939. Woodrow
Wilson had a profound insight when he said that we must "make the world
safe for democracy."

*Only Vienna Bourse Makes Immediate Response to Assassination at
Sarajevo, June 28, 1914.* The assassination of the Austrian crown prince at
Sarajevo on June 28, 1914, did not at once alarm the world. It alarmed
Austria. There was immediate heavy selling of securities on the Vienna
Bourse. Paris was preoccupied with her own economic and political
problems and did not take the episode seriously, although there was
recognition that the situation called for tact and decorum. Paul Leroy-
Beaulieu, in the issue of *L'Economiste Français* next following the assassination, gave editorial expression of sympathy for Austria and her
venerable ruler, Franz Joseph, with a degree of courtesy that makes one
feel that he was performing an official duty.

Bourse Panics in Berlin and Paris, July 23. On July 20 Vienna had a
further heavy decline in stocks. It was July 23 before Paris and Berlin had
real panic in the stock markets. There had meanwhile been reflexes in the
stock exchanges of London and New York. By July 25 selling in both
markets on foreign accounts was very heavy. On July 27 the Vienna
Exchange was closed. The next day Austria declared war on Serbia. Stock
exchanges were closed on July 28 in Montreal, Toronto, and Madrid. On
July 29 the Berlin Bourse discontinued. By July 30 the panic had reached
London and bourses were closed in Saint Petersburg and all South American countries. The Coulisse (curb market) was closed in Paris that day. On
the same day the Parquet, the official bourse of Paris, virtually suspended
selling, although it was not officially closed until September 3, when the
French government withdrew from Paris to Bordeaux.

London and New York Stock Exchanges Close, July 31. On July 31 the
London Stock Exchange was closed, and five hours later (the difference
between London time and New York time), at four minutes before ten—the
time for the opening of the New York Stock Exchange—the authorities of
that institution announced to the anxious brokers that it would not open.
Enormous selling orders from Europe and other frightened markets had
accumulated in their hands overnight, selling orders "at the market"
(meaning at any price obtainable); and it was clear that New York alone
could not stand the strain of the concentrated selling of a frightened world.

On August 1 Germany declared war on Russia, and late at night on
August 4 England declared war on Germany.

Danger, Uncertainty, and the Rush to Liquidity. Selling on the the stock exchanges at the outbreak of the war was an illustration of a fundamental principle in economic life. When there is general confidence in the uninterrupted goings on of economic life, confidence in the legal framework under which economic life operates and in the essential integrity and fairness of governments, men with capital prefer to have their capital employed. They want income from it. They want capital to work with, as giving additional scope to their personal efforts and their personal abilities. They are quite content to have their capital embodied in physical goods destined for future sale, in shares in industrial undertakings, in real estate which brings in rentals, or in loans to active men engaged in industry and commerce. But when grave uncertainties arise, and, above all, when unexpected war comes, men prefer gold to real estate. The man who has his wealth tied up in lands can make no shift. He must sit and take what comes. With the apprehension of war, however, the effort is made to convert illiquid wealth into liquid form as rapidly as possible, even though heavy sacrifices are involved.

London Strong vis-à-vis the Outside World. London was the center for international payments in 1914, and London, like all financial centers, was hard hit. But in its financial relations with the rest of the world London was exceedingly strong. The world owed London. London did not owe the world. Foreigners held sterling balances in British banks, but, on a vastly greater scale, foreigners owed sterling on daily maturing quick obligations to the British money market.

For example, a French coffee importer in Havre buying coffee at Santos in Brazil would arrange with a London acceptance house to finance the transaction. The coffee would be priced, not in francs or milreis, but in pounds sterling. The Brazilian exporter would draw, not on the French importer, but on the London acceptance house, a ninety-day bill of exchange, attaching to it the documents giving title to the coffee. The London acceptance house would accept the bill and turn over the documents to the French importer, who would then get the coffee. The Brazilian exporter would discount the bill in the London discount market and would use the sterling proceeds in buying milreis, because he wanted milreis at home for his next turnover.

London would no longer owe anything to the outside world on this transaction, but the French importer would still owe the London acceptance house, within ninety days, the sterling with which to pay a London bank or discount house when the bill matured.

In general, in financing international trade, London advanced cash in exchange for short-term obligations, and the world, on balance, was indebted to London on short term in large amounts. This was the situation at the outbreak of the war. All the world owed money to London on short term, and maturities were coming every day. All the world needed pounds sterling with which to pay these daily maturing debts.

But Internally Shaken—Weakness of Acceptance Houses. In the ordinary course of events new sterling in foreign hands would be steadily created by transactions similar to the one above described. But the outbreak of the war brought all these transactions to a sudden halt. First of all, with German cruisers on the seas shipments of goods were suddenly arrested. Second, with the shock of the outbreak of the war the position of the London acceptance houses, which had seemed invulnerable, suddenly showed great vulnerability. They had felt safe in giving acceptances up to several times their capital, counting on a steady inflow of funds to match their daily maturing obligations. But suddenly funds ceased to come to them. With the German armies invading France, the French importer of Santos coffee could not easily market his coffee, and even if he sold it for cash, could not certainly convert his francs into the sterling needed to send to the London acceptance house. The foreign exchange markets were suddenly demoralized. An acceptance house was certain that it could not collect the large amounts due it from Germany, and everywhere in the world disorders of one kind or another arose which placed the debtors of the London acceptance house in an awkward position. The acceptance houses were therefore entirely unable to give any more acceptance credits.

A further resource for obtaining sterling would normally be to ship gold to London, but this again, with hostile cruisers on the seas, was quite impossible. One great German ship, the *Kronprinzessin Cecelie,* had started out from New York for England and France just before the outbreak of the war with $10 million in gold, but had promptly turned back with the news of the outbreak of the war. The world owed London. The world could not pay in gold or in goods. The world could not get additional credit in London with the demoralization of the London money market. How was the world to pay?

Sterling Rises to $7.00. The first effect was a startling rise in the price of sterling. Men who had no option about paying their debts in London paid through the nose. Sterling rose from approximately $4.8668 to $7.00, though this $7.00 quotation represented only a few transactions in a nominal market.

Emergency Measures—Paris and London. Emergency measures of various kinds were employed in the principal centers. Paris was financially weak in any case. Prior to 1913 there had been many bad foreign loans placed in the French market through the great French banks: loans to Russia, loans to Latin America, loans to the Balkans. The weakness of the Balkan loans had been revealed during the Balkan wars in the two or three years preceding the outbreak of World War I. The weakness of the Brazilian loans and of Latin American loans in general had been revealed in the crisis that followed the collapse of the price of Brazilian coffee in 1913. With the outbreak of the war, moreover, France had the added complication that the German armies were beating their way into the richest of the

French industrial provinces. The great banks of France were frightened and cowardly. They rediscounted their bills with the Bank of France and hoarded cash. The French bourse was demoralized. The Bank of France showed itself courageous and intelligent. Governmental intervention seemed clearly indicated, but governmental intervention went much too far. Debtors were legally relieved by moratorium from the payment of their debts when due, on a sweeping scale. Bourse transactions ceased, the giving and taking of commercial credits very largely ceased, and governmental credit was extended in many places where private credits had previously been used.

Governmental emergency measures in England were much more moderate, though some seemed necessary. The Bank of England came to the rescue of the acceptance houses, taking over from the Joint Stock Banks, the discount houses, the bill brokers, and other holders their outstanding bills. The government later gave the acceptance houses, as a means of restoring their power to function, a clean slate on which to write, in that new acceptances would have priority over the old acceptances as a claim upon their assets.

Emergency Measures—United States. The stories of London and Paris in 1914 are interesting.[3] Chief attention is given here, however, to the way in which the shock was met in the United States.

No Government Intervention in United States. The American financial system met the shock with no formal government aid, although there was good cooperation and good understanding between New York and Washington. The closing of the stock exchange was decided upon by the stock exchange in conference with the New York clearinghouse banks. The banks had large loans made to stock exchange firms against stock exchange collateral. By informal agreement they refrained from calling these loans. These stock exchange loans the banks had ordinarily looked upon as one of their principal sources of liquidity. Any bank needing cash could call brokers' loans, and the broker must pay before the close of the banking day. The understanding was absolute, and on strict brokers' loans there was no question about it. The broker could get a loan from some other lender by paying the necessary rate of interest, or the broker could, if necessary, compel his customers to sell securities to pay off their loans to him so that he could pay off his loans to the bank. If the broker did not pay, the bank could sell the collateral on the floor of the stock exchange and turn over the difference between the face of the loan and the proceeds of the sale of collateral to the broker.

---

[3] See my book *The Effects of the War on Money, Credit and Banking in France and the United States*, Carnegie Endowment for International Peace (New York: Oxford University Press, 1919). For London, see the interesting articles by J. M. Keynes in the British *Economic Journal* in late 1914.

Frozen Stock Exchange Loans. With the closing of the stock exchange, however, these loans were frozen, and were no longer a source of liquidity to the banks. It did no good to call the loan and try to sell the collateral if there was no market. The banks contented themselves with seeing to it that the loans were properly margined. In valuing securities as collateral, the closing quotations of July 30, the day before the New York Stock Exchange closed, were taken.

The timing of the closing of the New York Stock Exchange was skillfully managed. There were some who had urged the closing a day or two before. It is the view of Professor O. M. W. Sprague and H. G. S. Noble, president of the New York Stock Exchange, that it is fortunate the exchange stayed open as long as it did. Stock prices went low, but not so low that the banks and the brokers could not stand the strain. The market was pretty thoroughly liquidated. The reopening of the exchange was then made much easier than would have been the case had stocks remained at a higher level with many sellers anxious to liquidate while the exchange was closed.[4] The control over selling outside the exchange during the period while the exchange was closed would, moreover, have been much less effective had not the market been thoroughly liquidated. As Noble makes clear in his interesting paper, the closing of the stock exchange was accompanied by a rigorous control over auction rooms, the Curb and all other outside markets, and the volume of security selling was held within very narrow limits indeed during the period the stock exchange remained closed. The break in prices was pretty drastic, as shown by the following table:

NEW YORK STOCK PRICES

	High, 1914	July 30, 1914	Decline
Atchison	100⅜	89½	10⅞
Baltimore & Ohio	98⅜	72	26⅜
Brooklyn Rapid Transit	94½	79	15½
Canadian Pacific	220½	156⅛	64⅜
Chesapeake & Ohio	68	41½	26½
St. Paul	107⅛	85	22⅛
U. S. Steel	67¼	50½	16¾

These securities were favorites with Europeans, and they were subject to special pressure of foreign selling in the period that preceded the close of the stock exchange. But the declines were really a good deal less drastic than might have been anticipated. Our stock exchange in those days was pretty tough and resilient. The declines in the averages were heavy, but

---

[4] O. M. W. Sprague: "Crisis of 1914 in the United States," *American Economic Review,* September 1915; H. G. S. Noble: "The New York Stock Exchange in the Crisis of 1914," *Garden City* (N. Y.) *Country Life Press*, 1915. These two papers are classics.

again moderate under the circumstances. Twenty-five typical railway stocks had an average price of 78.18 at the end of June 1914. They declined to 66.8 for their closing price in July. Twenty-five typical industrial stocks had a closing price of 58.19 in June 1914 and dropped to 48.76 by the end of July.

Break in Stocks Moderate in 1914 as Compared with 1937. If we contrast the break in security prices at the outbreak of the war in 1914 with the break in security prices in the governmentally regulated stock exchange of 1937, we may wonder whether governmental regulation designed to protect investors has proved itself an unqualified success. The high price for the Dow-Jones industrial average was 194.40 in the summer of 1937, and this dropped to 98.95 in the early months of 1938. The high for the Dow-Jones average of railroad stocks in 1937 was 64.46, and this dropped to a low of 18.00 in the early months of 1938. The investor was safer in the unregulated market of 1914 than when protected by the SEC in 1937.

Clearinghouse Certificates. In 1914 the New York banks, with liquidity suddenly impaired, though with assets which they trusted for the long pull, found themselves under unusual pressure to export cash. During the week ending July 31 the clearinghouse banks and trust companies of New York lost $56 million in cash reserve, of which $20 million represented withdrawals by American and Canadian banks. Resort was promptly made to the use of clearinghouse loan certificates, good between the banks, which had been used in New York also in previous extreme crises, namely, 1907, 1893, and 1873. These certificates were obtained by an individual bank through application to the Clearinghouse Committee. The Clearinghouse Committee would take the notes of the applying bank, secured by approved collateral with proper margin, and bearing interest of six percent. The clearinghouse certificate was the obligation of all the banks in the clearinghouse, and was acceptable to all of them in lieu of cash in settlement of clearinghouse balances. The bank which held the clearinghouse certificate received the interest which the borrowing bank paid. The clearinghouse certificate thus relieved the pressure on the cash resources of the weaker banks.

Aldrich-Vreeland Notes. In the three previous crises of 1873, 1893, and 1907 the New York banks had been obliged to restrict cash payments. We had in those years an inelastic currency, a currency which could not suddenly expand to meet emergencies or even to meet seasonal variations. It consisted of gold, silver dollars and silver certificates, United States notes (greenbacks), and national banknotes. Of these only gold could be increased, and a substantial increase of gold could come only through imports, impossible in the emergency situation of 1914 and slow in the crisis of 1907—at which time, however, the import of $100 million of gold from Europe did end the money stringency and permit the resumption of unrestricted cash payments.

We were fortunate in having available a further remedy in 1914. The Federal Reserve banks had not yet begun to operate, and the shock had to be met without this assistance. But the Federal Reserve Act of 1913 had wisely saved and improved upon the provisions of the Aldrich-Vreeland Act of 1908, which had been designed to enable national banks to issue notes freely in a crisis. This act was to have expired by limitation on July 1, 1914. But Carter Glass, chairman of the House Committee on Banking and Currency, had had the foresight to have it extended for another year to provide against emergencies pending the inauguration of the Federal Reserve System, and had amended it by reducing the tax on notes issued under the Aldrich-Vreeland Act from five percent to three percent during the first three months of issue, thereafter increasing it one-half percent to a maximum of ten percent.

No use had been made of the Aldrich-Vreeland Act prior to this emergency. The very term *emergency currency* had been an obstacle. But at the outbreak of the war speedy resort was had to it and the new notes were issued in large volume. Of the 7,600 national banks, 2,197 became members of the "Currency Associations," which issued these notes. The maximum amount of these notes outstanding was $386,616,990, on October 24, 1914. Redemption of this currency began as early as October 1914. By December 26 redemption amounted to $217 million and on July 1, 1915, all but $200,000 of the authorized currency had been retired.

The crisis of 1914 was unique in our history in that it was entirely due to external causes. The internal situation was liquid and solvent. The crisis may be said to have ended in November 1914 except for the cotton-growing southern states. Cotton was hard hit. There was a record crop of sixteen million bales, largely dependent on the European market. Cotton broke when stocks did, and the cotton exchange closed when the stock exchange closed, the closing price being 10½¢ per pound. The cotton exchange reopened in November 1914 with quotations at 7½¢ per pound, while cotton was being sold in the South for 5¢ to 6¢ a pound. An emergency loan fund was provided by banks in the northern states of $100 million, while southern banks provided $35 million. As it turned out, very little use had to be made of this fund. Less than a quarter of a million dollars was applied for in New York City, and one great bank took all of this. There came a sharp increase in foreign demand for cotton early in January 1915.

Gold and Foreign Exchange Problem. Perhaps the most acute problem that New York had to face with the outbreak of the war was the problem of gold and foreign exchange. There had been a drain on New York's gold for a considerable time in connection with the German, French, and Russian accumulations of gold in anticipation of war. Moreover, from March 1914 to August 1914 imports of goods to the United States had exceeded exports in unprecedented amount. Europe was depressed and had reduced its buying. Our imports were not unusually large, but our exports were unusually small. Usually our heaviest imports would come in the spring, and our heaviest exports to pay for them, agricultural commodities, would come in the autumn. It had been a long-standing practice of American bankers to tide over the period of low exports by drawing finance time bills on London in payment for imports, which they would later liquidate by documentary bills drawn on London, connected with our heavy autumn exports. Finance bills are pure credit instruments drawn by banks on banks; documentary bills represent the actual movement of goods and are accompanied by the usual shipping documents. There had been an unusually heavy volume of such finance bills drawn in the late spring and early summer of 1914, which London was entitled to collect from New York. An additional heavy volume of payments due to London grew out of the selling of securities in New York by frightened Europeans at the outbreak of the war.

A further unusual factor which complicated the situation was the fact that the government of New York City, seeking to escape the discipline which New York bankers had sought to impose in connection with the city's borrowing and their demand that expenditures be curtailed or revenues be increased, had borrowed $80 million on short term in England and France. With sterling exchange almost unobtainable the city's obligations abroad were in danger of dishonor. The New York banks came to the rescue of the city and undertook to provide the necessary sterling, but administered a spanking to the city officials which the latter accepted with due meekness.

Gold Pool—England Accepts Gold in Ottawa. A gold pool of $100 million was organized by the banks of New York and other principal cities under the guidance of the Federal Reserve Board, and arrangements were made with the Bank of England whereby shipments of gold to a depository at Ottawa would be accepted in lieu of gold shipped across the ocean, thus obviating the dangers of capture by hostile warships. Sterling exchange promptly came down to a reasonable figure.

Exports Turned Tide of Gold Toward New York by December 1914. But the exchange situation would have been quickly straightened out in any case by the great increase of foreign demand for American products for war purposes. In October the United States lost $44 million in gold and in November, $7 million, but in December the tide turned and the United States gained $4 million net excess of imports over exports of gold. The explanation is the very heavy shipment of commodities on European account. From December 1914 to May 1917 (we entered the war in the middle of April), the United Stated gained gold at a rate never dreamed of before. In 1915 the excess of imports over exports of gold was over $420 million, in 1916 over $520 million, and in the first four months of 1917, over $180 million—a net gain of $1,111,000,000 in gold. The problem of exchange ceased to be how to protect the dollar, but rather, how to protect the pound and other foreign exchanges. The war crisis in the United States was over by November 1914 and in early 1915 the war prosperity began.

The War Prosperity

Our *Export Balance, 1915–17.* The outstanding fact from the standpoint of the economic life of the United States from November 1914 until our entrance into the war in April 1917 was a great and ever growing volume of exports from the United States to Europe, unmatched by a return flow of imported goods—a great and ever growing export balance of trade. Measured in dollars, the increase is shown by the following table:

	U.S. exports	U.S. imports	U.S. export balance
1913	2483.9	1792.5	691.4
1914	2113.7	1789.4	324.3
1915	3554.7	1778.5	1776.2
1916	5482.6	2391.6	3091.0
1917 (4 months)	2164.8	965.5	1199.3

How Paid for—Gold. This immense unbalance in trade created, of course, a special financial problem. In some way these goods had to be paid for. They were paid for in four principal ways. One was gold. We received gold to the extent of approximately $1,100 million net, from the end of November 1914 to May 1917. This obviously solved only a minor part of the problem.

Return of American Securities—Loans in America. The second major means of payment was by the return of American securities held abroad by foreign investors and especially by British and French investors. The British and French governments both undertook to control this and to make the sale of securities orderly. They corralled American securities held by their own nationals, compensating them by giving them government securities, and disposed of them on the New York Stock Exchange in such a way as not to break prices and to get the best return possible.

The third major source was the placement in the American market of foreign government loans through investment banking syndicates, usually headed by J. P. Morgan & Company (which house acted as fiscal agent for the governments of both Great Britain and France). The largest of these loans was the so-called Anglo-French loan of $500 million. There were two great loans to the United Kingdom of Great Britain and Ireland, one for $300 million and one for $250 million. There was one great loan of $94.5 million, collateraled by American securities. There was a loan to the French Republic of $100 million. There were loans of various amounts to various French cities. There was a $25 million loan to the imperial Russian government. The Dominion of Canada borrowed $175 million, much of which was made available to the British government.

Finally, there were unfunded credits of substantial amounts, revolving, but nonetheless growing, as great American banks gave credits to European importers on the guarantee of great European banks, especially British banks, and as American business houses gave long credits to trusted European customers. By the time we entered the war in 1917 the credit of the European belligerents was under very heavy strain.

Few Credits to Germany. It may be said that the overwhelming bulk of the credits thus extended were to the Allies opposed to Germany in the war. There were no public loans floated for Germany. Germany undoubtedly received substantial private credits during the first two years of the war. At the beginning of the war we were, of course, strictly neutral, and so far as governmental policy was concerned, Germany could have had credits here. The great practical obstacle was the fact that Germany promptly lost control of the sea and so could not buy goods here, though she did receive during the first two years of the war a substantial volume of American goods through neutral countries, notably Sweden, Denmark, and the Netherlands—and for that matter, during the first year of the war, through Italy. As the British blockade against Germany became effective, there was a sharp increase in American exports to Sweden and other Scandinavian countries. This was interpreted at the time as representing goods sent to Germany via the Scandinavian countries. But only part of this increase represented American goods going to Germany. Before the war the German free port of Hamburg had been a great distributing point for the whole Baltic region, and a good many American goods regarded as going to Germany in 1912 and 1913 were in fact destined for Sweden and other Baltic countries. With our trade to Hamburg stopped by the war, American goods went directly to Sweden and other Baltic countries instead of via Hamburg.

Cheap Money, 1915–17—Gold. The role of the incoming gold in making these payments is a great deal more important than the foregoing figures would indicate. Relatively small in itself, the incoming gold nonetheless facilitated the placement of foreign loans and the absorption of American securities returned. It made an easy money market. It was easier for bank credit to expand. Speculative purchasers could more easily borrow at the banks the funds that they needed to carry the American securities returned and the foreign securities purchased. In fact, there were occasions when shipments of gold seemed to have been deliberately timed so as to make an easy money market in the United States as a favorable condition to the placement of a large foreign loan.

During the period when the stock exchange was closed late in 1914, the call rates on stock exchange loans were held at eight percent, though favored customers were charged only six percent. These loans were not, of course, really call loans. Banks could not sell collateral, and it was impossible to call the loans. They were, in fact, undated time loans. With the turn of the tide of gold in December, however, and with the reopening of the stock exchange, the rates dropped rapidly, and for over a year, from January 1915 to May 1916, New York enjoyed a period of extraordinarily easy money. The "high" on call rates at the money post on the stock exchange was two and one-fourth percent, the low was one percent, and the general range was from one and three-fourths to two percent. It was not until the heavy financial operations of the government in the summer of 1917 that call money got as high as five percent again.

Reduced Reserve Requirements. At the same time that we had this vast addition through incoming gold to the cash reserves of the banks of the country, we had a decrease in the reserve requirements of the banks through the operation of the new Federal Reserve Act, which had lowered reserve requirements for the central reserve cities from twenty-five percent to eighteen percent on demand deposits, with a corresponding lowering of reserve requirements in reserve city banks and country banks. Bank credit was easy. It was easy to float new securities. It was easy for businesses to expand if profits were in sight.

Profits were in sight. Britain and France and their Allies were buying the products of American farms and mines and industries—buying all that they could get and find transportation facilities for. Our own industries were making a great transformation as they turned to the production of munitions, and the easy money market facilitated this.

The response of American industry to this extraordinary stimulus, facilitated by abundant financial resources, was very impressive. The production-construction table on page 39 tells the story.

Wartime Prices. The first effect of the great increase in demand from Europe for our goods with the great inflow of gold was, not a rise in prices, but rather a great quickening of industry. The annual averages for the Bureau of Labor Statistics Index of Commodity Prices for the United States, taking 1913 as a base, show:

100 for 1913
99 for 1914
100 for 1915

PHYSICAL VOLUME OF PRODUCTION AND
CONSTRUCTION, 1914–22*

Year	Total volume of production	Total volume of construction
1914	100	100
1915	113.7	97.9
1916	120.6	111.3
1917	125.5	93.8
1918	124.5	64.9
1919	116.7	88.7
1920	124.5	48.5
1921	103.9	91.8
1922	121.6	139.2

* Frederick C. Mills, *Economic Tendencies in the United States* (New York, 1932), pp. 188, 191. Bases changed from 1913 to 1914.

At quarterly dates for 1915 the figures show:

January	98
April	99
July	101
October	101

By November and December of 1915, however, industrial slack in the United States had disappeared, and our labor and resources were fully utilized. Additional production of one kind of commodity could come only as labor and supplies were pulled away from other kinds of production. The pull and haul among competing uses for labor and supplies began, and a great rise in commodity prices came. Prices rose sharply from 100 in September 1915 to 112.8 in January 1916 to 152.9 by January 1917 and to 182.6 by May 1917. The peak for the year 1917 was in July, at 187, after we had entered the war; and from then on to the end of the year the price curve flattened out and even reacted a little. Our great increase in prices came before we ourselves got into the war, before the great expenditures of the United States government, before the vast public loans.

This rapid rise in commodity prices caught the country wholly by surprise. Retailers were asleep. In the summer of 1916 one purchased silver spoons in a small Connecticut town for less than the price of bar silver in New York the same day, and purchased cotton batting in the same small town for less than the price of raw cotton on the New York Cotton Exchange.

Wages and Prices. Commodity prices at wholesale rose a good deal more rapidly than wages per hour during the war boom, though wages caught up

THE WHOLESALE PRICE INDEX OF THE DEPARTMENT OF LABOR, 1913–27*
(Wholesale Index Numbers, 1913 average = 100)

Year	Yearly average	Jan.	Feb.	Mar.	Apr.	May	June	July	Aug.	Sept.	Oct.	Nov.	Dec.
1913	100	98	99	99	99	100	99	100	100	100	102	104	108
1914	98												
1915	101												
1916	126.8	112.8	115.1	118.5	121.1	122.4	122.6	123.2	126.3	129.6	135.6	145.8	148.8
1917	177.2	152.9	156.8	162.4	172.9	182.6	185.5	187.6	189.4	187.1	182.7	183.1	182.4
1918	194.3	184.3	185.7	186.6	190.0	190.1	191.4	196.1	199.7	204.0	201.9	202.9	202.2
1919	206.4	198.8	193.4	195.9	198.7	202.2	202.8	212.0	215.9	210.3	211.3	217.1	223.4
1920	226.2	233.2	232.4	234.4	244.6	246.7	243.3	240.7	231.4	226.2	211.3	196.4	179.2
1921	146.9	169.8	160.1	155.4	147.9	145.5	141.6	141.0	141.5	141.5	141.6	140.7	139.8
1922	148.8	138.3	141.4	142.2	142.6	147.6	149.6	154.9	155.0	153.3	154.1	155.5	156.2
1923	153.7												
1924	149.7												
1925	158.7												
1926	151.0												
1927	146.8												

* The figures for the first three years were from *Statistical Abstract of the United States* (1924), p. 299, while the figures for the remaining years were from *Statistical Abstract of the United States* (1928), p. 317.

with commodity prices in the postwar boom and remained far above commodity prices in the crisis and depression which followed in 1921 and 1922. The following table exhibits this.

INDEX NUMBERS OF WAGES PER HOUR AND WHOLESALE PRICES IN THE UNITED STATES*

Year	Wages per hour (exclusive of agriculture)	Wholesale prices (all commodities)
1914	100	100.0
1915	101	102.1
1916	109	125.6
1917	125	172.5
1918	159	192.8
1919	180	203.5
1920	229	226.7
1921	214	143.3
1922	204	142.0

* *Chase Economic Bulletin*, April 13, 1937, p. 30

Security Prices, 1914–18. Prices of securities, on the other hand, began to rise long before the average of commodities began to rise. The stock market broke badly in July 1914. Taking the *Annalist's* list of twenty-five industrials and twenty-five rails (closing price of each month), we find it at 145 in January 1914, dropping to about 116 at the end of July when the stock exchange closed. When the stock exchange reopened in December, the opening prices (partly pegged) averaged 120, and they averaged 120 again in February 1915. Then began a very rapid rise in the boom of the "war babies," led by Bethlehem Steel, and this average reached 185 in October 1915. The stock market was reactionary until July of the following year, 1916, when another strong upward move led up to the peak price of October 1916, this time under the leadership of General Motors. The peak price for the fifty stocks was 195 in the closing prices of September and October, though in between higher levels were reached.

This was the top of the stock market for the whole war period. The level broke to 162 as the closing price of February 1917, and after our entrance into the war it declined rather sharply to 127 for November 1917, rallying thereafter to 150 as the closing price of October 1918. The decline in stocks from the October peak of 1916 came long before the rise in commodity prices was ended and well before any decline had manifested itself in general business profits.

Profits of industrial corporations were very great in 1915, 1916, and 1917. War taxes cut into them in 1918, but they were still impressive. Dividends were increased but the corporations, in general, prudently recognized that they were in an extraordinary situation, that war profits could not be expected to last, and that it was well to provide for contingencies. A very large proportion of their profits was therefore retained and added to corporate surpluses, as shown by the following table.

ADDITIONS TO CORPORATE SURPLUSES*
(In millions of dollars)

Year

1913	1,400
1914	585
1915	2,117
1916	4,939
1917	4,732
1918	1,986
1919	4,330
1920	1,397
1921	−2,685
1922	1,676

* From *America's Capacity to Consume* (Brookings Institution), p. 109.

The stock market, in the course of World War I, kept its head amazingly well. Businessmen and men dealing in securities were constantly asking themselves how long the war would last; how much value a new plant that had been created to meet war demands would have after the war; how permanent the higher level of commodity prices was; what kind of losses would have to be incurred in readjustment after the war. And by October 1916 they concluded that prices of stocks had gone high enough.

Money Market and Capital Market. There was, further, despite the continuance of cheap call money due to the abundant gold in the United States, a progressive pressure on the supply of real capital in the form of investors' savings; there was a disposition to capitalize earnings on a higher yield basis. It is to be observed, however, that stock prices in 1916 yielded before bond prices did, contrary to previous experience in the movements of American securities prices. The best prices of standard bonds during the whole war period were reached in December 1916, nearly three months after the peak of stock prices.

Stock Prices and Corporate Profits. It may be noticed, also, that the general average of stock prices had declined a great deal before any real difficulties appeared for any great industry. In 1917 stock prices had a sharp decline late in the year as railroads came under heavy pressure from rising costs unaccompanied by rising rates, and an acute crisis was relieved by President Wilson's proposal in December 1917 that Congress put the government behind the railroads. But none of this was in evidence in October 1916, when stock prices reached their peak and turned down.

Part of the extraordinary war profits was undoubtedly due to the fact that wages, as shown by our table above, lagged behind wholesale prices in their rise.

Wages and Prices in World War II. In World War II wages rose far faster than wholesale prices, and corporate profits and additions to corporate surpluses were far more moderate in relation to the national income. In World War I the thing was left to the natural play of the markets. In World War II we had elaborate governmental policy designed to hold down corporate profits and to encourage wage increases.

4

Our War Economic Policy

The United States entered the war on April 6, 1917. Our war economic policy had to be rather rapidly improvised. Basic in it was the belief in a free economy and a determination to maintain sound money and sound public finances. There was, however, recognition that the ordinary market forces, left to themselves, would not suffice to bring as speedy a shifting from peace activities to war activities as the emergency called for. And there was recognition that if the government merely added a great increase in expenditure to existing civilian expenditure and competed against the people for goods and supplies and services, there would be an inordinate further rise in commodity prices. Goods were already very scarce, as we had been pouring out great quantities of exports to Europe and as our own people, with money incomes increased by the war prosperity, had been resisting the export of goods by bidding up prices.

Taxes and Loans—Sprague's Proposal. The traditional policy of the American government in financing a war had been by war loans, with enough increase in taxes to provide for the interest and amortization of the war loans. We had financed the Spanish–American War on this basis. But there came a speedy realization that, for the war on the scale which we were about to engage in, this procedure would be quite inadequate. One of the most influential figures in bringing this forcibly to the attention of the Congress and the President and the country was Professor O. M. W. Sprague of Harvard University, who wrote an article calling for an all-tax policy which had the significance of a great state paper. Sprague had been watching developments in England and other belligerents closely. He had seen how an immense increase in government spending, based on government borrowing and especially government borrowing from the banks in those countries, had generated a great rise in prices, wages, and profits, which in turn had led to a further rise in prices, wages, and profits as the people spent their unusual income competing with the government. He urged, correctly, that except as goods could be brought in from the world outside the country, the war must in any case be fought with the current production of the country. If we had full production, the government's increased consumption and utilization of commodities must in any case come out of the current real income of the people. We could not save ourselves current sacrifice by creating loans for future generations to pay, though by borrowing we could easily enough leave a burden of debt for the future. He proposed that we should forthwith impose taxes equal to the government's expenditure, so that the people might by taxes be forced to relinquish their ability to compete with the government.

The proposal was overly drastic, but in the compromise that came out of it we adopted the definite policy of heavy and growing taxes and the further policy of borrowing from the people instead of borrowing from the banks, to the full extent this could be done. If the people gave up their income to the government through the purchase of government bonds out of current income, we should similarly hold down their ability to buy and to compete with the government. Bank credit was to be used in moderating the transition and in softening the shock. Men might borrow from the banks on a margin to buy bonds and pay off the loans in installments, in effect giving to the government part of their income before they got it, but the savings would come in subsequent months and be paid to the banks.

Federal Reserve bank credit likewise was to be used in this process, but the government was not to borrow directly from the Federal Reserve banks. Rather, the Federal Reserve banks were to rediscount for other banks against government war paper.

To an amazing extent the policy was successful. The facts are well brought out in a chart issued by the board of governors of the Federal Reserve System.[1]

The commercial banks at the peak of the government borrowing held over $4 billion in government bonds, but they had had over $700 million to start with in bonds to secure national banknotes. Investors held over $18 billion, mutual savings banks held substantial amounts, Federal Reserve Bank holdings were very small indeed. At the peak of the government borrowing in 1919 it was estimated that the commercial banks held altogether about $6.5 billion of government war paper, of which about $3 billion were loans secured by government bonds and $3.5 billion were war bonds owned (including, of course, short government notes). We actually got the current savings of the people with taxes and with bonds on a tremendous scale.

The Role of the Federal Reserve Banks in Government Finance. The Federal Reserve banks had reduced their earning assets to well below $200 million by the time of the outbreak of the war, getting ready for the war

---

[1] *Federal Reserve Charts on Bank Credit, Money Rates and Business*, February 11, 1941, p. 20.

emergency. Their great asset was the nonearning asset, gold. They expanded credit greatly during the war, when viewed in the perspective of that time, though in terms that look very modest indeed when we consider their history in the period since 1932 and, above all, in the period of World War II.

The following table exhibits the extent of Federal Reserve Bank expansion almost to the time of the Armistice, which was November 11, 1918. It stops with October 25. It was prepared late in 1918 by Dr. M. Jacobson, statistician of the Federal Reserve Board. It is not altered nor are the dates altered, because changes in accounting methods since the inauguration of

PRINCIPAL RESOURCE AND LIABILITY ITEMS OF THE FEDERAL RESERVE SYSTEM ON SELECTED DATES
(In thousands of dollars)

Resources	Nov. 26, 1915	Dec. 22, 1916	Oct. 25, 1918
Total gold reserves.....................	492,063*	728,445*	2,045,132*
Total cash reserves.....................	529,375*	734,470*	2,098,169*
Bills discounted:			
Secured by government war obligations			1,092,417
All other.............................	32,794	32,297	453,747
Bills bought in open market	16,179	124,633	398,623
U. S. government long-term securities	12,919	43,504	28,251
U. S. government short-term securities		11,167	322,060
Total earning assets...................	89,200	222,158	2,295,122
Total resources...................	637,261	1,009,852	5,270,785**
Liabilities			
Capital paid in and surplus..........	54,846	55,765	80,324
Government deposits.................	15,000	29,472	78,218
Member banks' reserve deposits ..	397,952†	648,787†	1,683,499
Other deposits, including foreign government credits			117,001‡
Federal Reserve notes in actual circulation...........................	165,304	275,046	2,507,912

* Includes amounts of gold and other lawful money deposited with Federal Reserve agents against Federal Reserve notes issued.

** Includes clearinghouse exchanges and other uncollected items formerly deducted from member bank deposits.

† Net amount due to member banks.

‡ Exclusive of deferred credits on account of uncollected checks and other cash items.

the system, partly due to changes in law, would make it difficult for anyone not intimately versed in Federal Reserve statistics to make the changes correctly.[2]

Limited Government Security Purchases by Federal Reserve Banks. In this table, particular attention is called to two items showing the United States government securities held by the Federal Reserve banks. Of long-term securities they held twenty-eight million on October 25, 1918, and of short-term securities they held 322 million. The second of these figures was temporary, growing out of the exigencies of the fourth liberty loan. It was promptly reduced to 118 million in a few days.

In general, the Federal Reserve banks gave credit only against rediscounts, and direct holdings of government securities remained very small, with four exceptions of a few days each.

Temporary Holding of Government Securities During Liberty-Loan Drives. They had learned from British experience the trick of easing off the money market by the purchase of government securities while a loan was being floated. With each of the four liberty loans they did this. With the first liberty loan the sum was a few tens of millions. With the fourth liberty loan the increase was over $200 million. When they bought government securities, they paid for them with checks on themselves. These checks came into the hands of member banks. The member banks then deposited them in the Federal Reserve banks, building up their reserve accounts. This eased the money market and facilitated the great transactions in the placing of billions of dollars of liberty loans. When the loan was over the Federal Reserve banks sold the government securities, withdrawing the money from member bank reserves and tightening the money market again, usually forcing member banks to rediscount in the process.

Money Market Tightens as War Goes On. The money market during the war grew progressively tighter. Both capital and money market funds grew increasingly scarce. Bank credit expanded, but at progressively higher rates of interest. The call rate—which had dropped low in 1915 and to the middle of 1916, averaging less than 2 percent and dropping to 1 percent for one month in May 1915—had already tightened sharply in the second half of 1916. With our entrance into the war it began to move very sharply higher. It touched 7 percent in September 1917, dropped momentarily to 4 percent in October, and then moved up to 6 percent by January 1918, at which figure it was pegged—the pegging being accompanied by a rationing of call money by a clearinghouse committee.

Bond yields went up. It was a firm money situation. The pressure of firm money rates undoubtedly did a great deal to retard bank expansion and to hold it down to necessary things.

---

[2] The table first appeared in my book, *The Effects of the War on Money, Credit and Banking in France and the United States,* Carnegie Endowment for International Peace (New York: Oxford University Press, 1919).

The Treasury in its borrowing policy made rates of interest which were reasonably attractive to investors. The first liberty loan was at the rate of 3.5 percent, fully tax-free. The second liberty loan was at 4 percent, partially tax-free. The fourth liberty loan was at 4.5 percent, partially tax-free. There were, moreover, provisions that holders of one loan might convert into a later loan if the rate were higher. The government did not rely upon the rate alone to attract investors' money. It counted also on patriotism, and on the wonderfully organized system of drives under which a good many men who were reluctant to buy bonds found themselves under such pressure from their neighbors that they bought them. Social pressures were used as well as rates. But the rates were well above the rates at which government bonds had been selling before the war began, and were rates which an investor could feel would give a good bond, selling at par if he carried it through the period of war pressure.

Rediscount Rates Below the Market, but Rising with the Market. The Federal Reserve banks, to facilitate the loan policy of the government, put their rediscount rate below the market. The New York Federal Reserve discount rate was placed at 3 percent in 1917, was raised to 3.5 percent at the end of the year, and to 4 percent in early 1918, remaining below the market, but following the market up. But our experience with the Federal Reserve System has shown that while a rate below the market is undesirable, it does not in itself create bank expansion, nor does it by itself create cheap money. Banks usually are prudent in rediscounting. They do not like to be in debt to the Federal Reserve banks.

In 1919 and early 1920 the banks did borrow to relend at a profit, but expansion of bank credit which took place in those years was in the face of rapidly rising rates of interest and was due to the inordinate demands of borrowers in a boom. The rates below the market permitted expansion to go further than it would have gone, but did not permit it at low rates of interest. Our experience with the Federal Reserve System, taking all the years since it has been in existence, would show that the decisive instrument for cheapening money is open market purchases rather than discount rate.

Wartime Reduction in Reserve Requirements. The legislation of 1917 reduced the reserve requirements to thirteen percent, ten percent, and seven percent for demand deposits in central reserve cities, reserve cities, and country banks, respectively, and to three percent on all time deposits.[3]

Bank Expansion Slows Down During War. The extremely low reserve requirements set by the legislation of 1917 did no harm in the period of the

---

[3] In my evaluation of this legislation at the time, I made, I think, my worst mistake in economic analysis. I welcomed it as amounting to practically the abolition of legal reserve requirements, and as a measure which would put American bankers in the position of bankers in other countries who had no legal reserve requirements to reckon with—a position in which the American banker would be free to use his own judgment as to the reserves he needed. See

war. The fact that these low reserve ratios make possible a tremendous multiple expansion on the basis of *excess reserves* was not operative,[4] because there were no *excess* reserves to work on.

The expansion of bank credit was slowed down sharply during the war as compared with the preceding years 1915, 1916, and the first part of 1917. For the period June 30, 1914, to June 30, 1918, bank deposits expanded year by year as follows:

TOTAL DEPOSITS OF ALL COMMERCIAL BANKS
(In millions of dollars)

Call date	Total
1914—June 30	17,390
1915—June 23	17,993
1916—June 30	22,079
1917—June 20	25,885
1918—June 29	28,011

For the period of our actual participation in the war, the expansion was as follows:[5]

DEPOSITS OF COMMERCIAL BANKS

December 31, 1918	$26,541,039,000
April 6, 1917	20,705,588,000
Increase	$ 5,835,451,000

LOANS, DISCOUNTS, AND INVESTMENTS OF COMMERCIAL BANKS

December 31, 1918	$29,354,214,000
April 6, 1917	22,297,775,000
Increase	$ 7,056,439,000

---

my *Effects of the War on Money, Credit and Banking*, pp. 169–70. It never occurred to me that the banking community would let its actual reserves run down to these low legal limits and stay there. But very speedily under war pressure it did, and after the war it almost continuously did down to 1931, competing with one another in the effort to get rid of any excess reserves and building a multiple expansion of bank credit on the basis of excess reserves. The point was simply that for two generations American bankers had been used to having the law tell them what to do about reserves, and that they had no judgment with respect to the matter, such as foreign bankers had. In banks in other countries there had been well-developed financial traditions with respect to this matter. Banks had watched one another. Our bankers had the tradition of obeying the law with respect to reserves.

[4] The process of multiple expansion on the basis of excess reserves is explained in chapter 17.

[5] The figures of all the state and national banks and trust companies appear only once a year in the comptroller's report as of approximately June 30. For dates other than June 30, it is necessary to make estimates. During the war period these estimates are made on the basis of variation in the national bank figures.

This is a remarkable exhibition of restraint in the employment of bank credit in a great war. We had to finance the government with its four great liberty loans and its short-term borrowing as well. We had to transform our industries from a peace basis to a war basis. We had to raise an army of four million men and send half of them to France. We had to help finance our Allies in the war, and, above all, to finance the shipment of goods to them from the United States and from a good many neutral countries. We had an immense shipbuilding problem.

Private Financing of War Production—War Finance Corporation Unimportant. Commercial bankers and investment bankers, moreover, had to finance the industrial expansion that took place for war purposes. There were no great government loan organizations replacing private finance. There was, to be sure, the War Finance Corporation, a government corporation with a capital of $500,000,000, which was to extend new credits to essential industries and to savings banks and public utilities which had been suffering under the war pressure. But in practice the War Finance Corporation down to October 15, 1918, had extended credits of only $43,202,592. The most important extension of credits made by that date was $20,000,000 to the Bethlehem Steel Corporation, $17,320,000 to the Brooklyn Rapid Transit Company, $3,235,000 to the United Railways of St. Louis, and $1,000,000 to the Northwestern Electric Company. All the rest of the credit given to industry in the great war effort was made by the commercial banks and the investment market. Private finance was adequate, and private finance did an immensely efficacious job. To repeat the figures, in doing this job commercial bank credit expanded only $7,000,000,000 in loans, discounts, and investments, and only $5,835,000,000 in deposits. (The gap on the liability side of these bank figures is filled by rediscounts at the Federal Reserve banks and by an increase in banking capital funds.)

The Rationing of Credit. One important factor in holding down the expansion of bank credit was the rationing of credit, and the denial of credit to nonessential industries. The first organized step in this direction was taken on September 17, 1917, by a subcommittee on money rates of the New York Liberty Loan Committee, composed of the leading bankers of the city. It undertook to limit the funds available for the stock market, providing funds, on the other hand, when necessary for the protection of the stock market, and, above all, for the protection of the liberty loans. It pegged the call rate at six percent to the brokers, but it held down the supply. They could have what they had to have and what could be spared after giving precedence to the needs of the government and to the needs of the commercial borrowers. The committee also made a ruling that banks should require a margin of thirty percent on collateral loans made to stockbrokers where an average of twenty percent had previously been required. The stock market ceased to be a very effective competitor for loan funds, though it was not strangled, and continued to function effectively.

In addition, early in 1918 the Capital Issues Committee of the Federal Reserve Board, semiofficial in character, was organized, whose function it was to pass on proposed new issues of securities. Only essential industries were to be allowed access to the investment market. It lacked power to prohibit such issues, but it met such loyal and effective cooperation from bankers throughout the country that it was virtually able to boycott all issues of which it disapproved. Connected with it were local Capital Issues Committees in each of the twelve Federal Reserve districts. This committee surrendered its function upon the organization of the new War Finance Corporation in May 1918 to the Capital Issues Committee of the War Finance Corporation, though in part the personnel of the two committees remained the same.

There was apprehension in Washington that the competition of the bankers might prevent an effective policing of the loan situation and that with many thousands of independent banks it would be impossible to hold down nonessential loans. The proposal was once made that the Capital Issues Committee of the War Finance Corporation should pass on all loans made by banks exceeding $100,000, but this naive suggestion was promptly dropped when a great New York bank showed its loan transactions of a single day, which included one $5,000,000 loan to an essential industry made in fifteen minutes as a necessary part of meeting a rush order by the government. The great banks did scrutinize loan applications with respect to their essentiality with great rigor, and the smaller banks over the country were rapidly educated in the matter.

Of course a great deal of ordinary activity was precluded by the enormous cost of such activity. Construction, for example, dropped to a very low level in 1918. The Index of Construction stood at 111.3 in 1916. It dropped to 64.9 in 1918, and of the 64.9 a very high percentage indeed was essential construction for war purposes.

Commodity Control and Price Fixing. But we did not rely upon financial restraints only in holding down the volume of nonessential production, consumption, and construction. Construction itself was directly controlled by the denial of essential materials and by the requirements of a license for any building costing more than $500.

Price fixing we engaged in cautiously. There was a pretty clear recognition of economic fundamentals. Prices have work to do. Prices have the important function of accomplishing priorities, allocations, and rationing. That is their regular work. It is the work of free prices and freely moving wages to determine whether labor and supplies shall be drawn to the production of commodity A or of commodity B. Rising prices mean more production. Falling prices mean less production. Rising prices mean less consumption. Falling prices mean more consumption. With freely moving prices, commodities are divided among consumers in accordance with the relative urgencies of demand. With freely moving prices and freely moving wages, the goods in most urgent demand are produced, and the production of the less urgently demanded goods declines.

When prices are fixed by government, the government should step in to do directly the work that free prices would otherwise do. The government should allocate commodities. The government should give priorities. The government should ration commodities. If wages are fixed, the government should take steps to divert labor from less urgently needed production to more urgently needed production. Price fixing by itself tends to derange perversely the control of production and consumption. Holding prices down and doing nothing else encourages the depletion of supplies which would last longer if their prices were higher.

It follows from this that price fixing ought not to be pushed in advance of the development of machinery for commodity control.

In World War I we knew these things very well. Proposals for the fixing of all prices met very little sympathy from President Wilson, who was a good economist. We established a pretty comprehensive system of commodity control of scarce essentials needed for war or for the life and health of the people. We had priorities. We had allocations. We had rationing. We denied coal and freight cars and raw materials and capital to nonessential industries, or we restricted sharply the amounts of these things that they could get.

As part of this we had price fixing. We had no price fixing without priorities, allocation, and rationing. We had a great deal of priorities, allocations, and rationing without price fixing. We did not try to fix the price of luxuries. We simply denied the luxury industries the materials and supplies they needed.

We did very little about retail prices: "The great bulk of regulation over prices administered by the federal government during the war pertained to producer or wholesale prices. There was no real attempt save in food and fuel to control prices at retail. The task of controlling retail prices was undertaken in a comprehensive manner by the Food Administration after its wholesale control was well under way."[6]

Seeing the problem primarily as a problem of commodity control rather than of price control, we did not try to do it by one comprehensive organization which would do all the price fixing. Rather we had separate boards for different industries. We had a separate grain and flour administration and a separate fuel administration, for example. These handled both price fixing on the one hand, and allocations and rationing on the other, in their particular fields.

---

[6] Paul Willard Garrett, assisted by Isador Lubin and Stella Stewart, *Government Control over Prices,* War Industries Board Price Bulletin No. 3 (Washington: Government Printing Office, 1920), p. 550.

The need for having the good will and cooperation of the industries was in general recognized. And the need for using the brains of the industries and for having administrators trusted by the industries was in general recognized. As far as possible we used the existing machinery of the markets.[7] The one serious failure in price fixing came in bituminous coal, where this principle was not recognized in 1917, where the knowledge of the men in the trades was not used, where prices were fixed arbitrarily on the basis of imperfect knowledge, where production was as a consequence radically curtailed, and where a great deal of unnecessary disorder arose.

The Fuel Administration in 1917 apparently did not know that there were such things as differentials based on quality of coal, and apparently had never heard of British Thermal Units. The result was, in certain cases, that companies with both high-quality mines and low-quality mines and scarce labor shut down the high-quality mines and produced only coal with high ash content.

When Harry Garfield took charge of the Fuel Administration, he recognized these difficulties, called in the skilled men of the industry, softened the animosities that had arisen, radically improved the machinery and the practices, and finally made the fuel control successful.[8]

Wages we did not try to fix in World War I. Efforts were made to reduce the competition for labor, particularly interstate competition for labor, by the industries. Nonessential industries were made ineffective competitors for labor by being denied coal, freight cars, and capital. But wage fixing was not attempted. Wages continued to rise during the war, even though the general average of commodity prices was held down.

Price fixing was thus a factor, but not the dominant factor, in controlling the level of commodity prices during World War I. As previously shown, the curve for commodity prices at wholesale flattened out after July 1917, reacting slightly from 189 percent of 1913 prices in August to 182 in December, and then gradually, under very heavy pressure, rising slowly to a peak of 204 in September 1918, after which it again receded. This was an amazing achievement. It was accomplished by four main policies. First, there was a sudden imposition of very heavy taxes, taking up a great part of the income of the people. Second, the Treasury's borrowing policy got

---

[7] Herbert Hoover, in particular, did a superb job in bringing the grain and milling interests into the service of the country. I shall later find occasion to criticize his policies as President, but I wish to pay high tribute to his work in feeding the Belgians before we entered the war, to his work in food control at home during the war, to his postwar work in feeding stricken countries, and to his work under President Truman along similar lines after World War II.

[8] See my "Value and Price Theory in Relation to Price Fixing and War Finance," address before American Economic Association, printed in papers and proceedings, *American Economic Review,* supp., March 1918; reprinted in *Economic Bulletin* (issued by Capital Research Company of Los Angeles), December 6, 1940, and in hearings of Senate Committee on Banking and Currency on the Price Control Bill, December 16, 1941. See also my testimony of December 16, 1941, before this committee.

investors' money, got the current savings of investors. The banks took some of the bonds, but every effort was made to keep the banks from doing much. Third, we had a progressively firm money market, with tightening interest rates, which held down bank expansion. Fourth, we had price fixing for scarce essentials. There was a great deal of functional control of prices. There was very limited direct control of prices. There was a great deal of *direct control of commodities* and a great deal of wartime planning of production and consumption.

The Verdict of Charles Evans Hughes. Governmental economic planning in World War I was highly intelligent and very honest. There were blunders made. One blunder was in the cost-plus contracts, which made it to the advantage of a corporation that had such a contract with the government to incur unnecessary expenses, since the profit was a fixed percentage of the outlay. There were many blunders incidental to the haste and confusion. The army, in its haste, ordered unnecessary goods. Thus, among the surgical instruments sent to the front line hospital bases there were a large number of obstetrical instruments—an inexcusable and incredible thing, but readily enough explained when it appeared that the order for surgical instruments had been based on the standard supply of surgical instruments at an army post in the United States at which there had been a good many officers' wives.

There were some cheating and some gouging. But on the whole the record was amazingly clean and efficient. And when charges of great abuses were made after the war, President Wilson called upon his opponent in the 1916 election, the Honorable Charles Evans Hughes, later chief justice of the United States Supreme Court, and one of the most highly respected lawyers in the country, to make a thorough investigation, giving him carte blanche, access to all records, and adequate assistance. Hughes made a very thorough investigation and came out with a report that sweepingly vindicated the War Administration.

We were concerned in World War I with profiteers. It troubled us that certain companies should make a great deal of money out of war. But we were more concerned with getting results. We imposed very heavy taxes on excess profits and very heavy taxes on war profits, and we felt that it was better to let them make the profits and to tax them heavily than to slow them down by trying to prevent their making profits in the first place.

We did not look upon a great war as primarily an opportunity for accomplishing sweeping social reforms or for reconstituting the basic principles of economic life. We looked upon the war rather as something that had to be done and to be got through with as quickly as possible. We believed in economic freedom. During the war we submitted to drastic, needed economic restraints and controls. But we had no love for them, and we got rid of them as speedily as we could when the war was over. Most of them we dropped immediately—including price fixing.

5

The Federal Reserve System, 1914–18

The Federal Reserve System, as we have seen, was not in operation when the Great War broke out at the end of July 1914. The Federal Reserve Board was not organized until August 12, 1914, and the Federal Reserve banks were not open for business until November 16, 1914. It was the Aldrich-Vreeland notes, and the close cooperation of existing banks, clearinghouses, stock exchanges, and the Treasury which met the first shock of the war.

Limited Rediscounts and Earnings Till April 1917. The flood of gold which came to us beginning with December 1914 made one of the easiest money markets in the history of Wall Street down to that time, and made it largely unnecessary before April 1917 for the banks generally to have recourse to rediscounting at the Federal Reserve banks. Certain of the Federal Reserve banks, notably those in Dallas, Kansas City, and Atlanta, started to rediscount substantially soon after they began business, particularly as the rise in agricultural prices and the revival of agricultural prosperity made increasing demands on the loan funds of the member banks in those districts. But the Federal Reserve banks in the great financial centers were not rediscounting enough to enable them to pay dividends through practically the whole period prior to the entrance of the United States into the war.

At the beginning of 1917 the Federal Reserve banks had earning assets of $221,896,000, including rediscounts for member banks, bills of exchange bought in the open market, various government securities, state and municipal warrants, and the like. Their chief asset, however, was the nonearning asset, gold. Foreseeing war from the beginning of 1917, the Federal Reserve banks sought to strengthen their position by reducing their earning assets, and when the war broke out their earning assets amounted to only $167,994,000. With decks cleared for action, they were prepared to rediscount on an enormous scale as the burden of war finance should compel the other banks to have recourse to the Federal Reserve System.

Rediscount Rates Above Market. The Federal Reserve banks began to function on the basis of very orthodox central banking principles. They kept their rediscount rates above the market (meaning by the market the rate of interest charged by great city banks to prime borrowing customers). They started in November 1914 with rates at 6 percent in New York, Boston, Chicago, Philadelphia, Cleveland, St. Louis, and Richmond, and at 6.5 percent in the five other Federal Reserve banks. They engaged to a limited extent in open market operations. The law allowed them to buy United States government securities in the open market, and state and municipal tax anticipation warrants with six months or less maturity, but the supply of both of these was very limited. The federal public debt was less than a billion dollars, and approximately $700 million of this was already used as collateral for national banknotes. A substantial part of the rest was tied up in trust funds, and the floating supply was small.

We had an immense expansion of bank credit in the period from the beginning of 1915 to April 1917, but Federal Reserve policy made no contribution to this expansion. The expansion was based (a) on the incoming gold, and (b) on the reduction in reserve requirements which the Federal Reserve Act of 1913 had provided.

Concentration of Gold in Federal Reserve Banks. The Federal Reserve authorities were much impressed with the danger of the great influx of gold, and took measures to get the gold concentrated in the Federal Reserve banks. The original theory involved in this was perhaps not very clear, but in 1916 and in early 1917 there was a very definite practical consideration that we might be involved in war, and that it was important that the gold of the country be concentrated in a central reservoir as a basis for war finance. The procedure was cumbersome.

Awkward Process of Exchanging Federal Reserve Notes for Gold. The original Federal Reserve Act did not provide for the simple issue of Federal Reserve notes against gold. Incidentally, it did not provide for the issue of Federal Reserve notes by the Federal Reserve banks. The Federal Reserve notes were issued by the government to the Federal Reserve banks against collateral, and then by the Federal Reserve banks to the member banks. The government was represented in each Federal Reserve bank by the Federal Reserve agent. The Federal Reserve agent could issue notes against commercial paper, sixty percent, and gold, forty percent. The Federal Reserve banks had very little commercial paper. In converting a great deal of gold into Federal Reserve notes, therefore, it was necessary to use the same commercial paper a good many times. The president of the Federal Reserve bank would turn over to the Federal Reserve agent gold and commercial paper, receiving Federal Reserve notes. He would then turn over an additional sum of gold in redeeming the commercial paper, so that the notes had now 100 percent gold collateral. He would then use the same commercial paper with additional gold in getting more notes, and repeat the operation many times. A very substantial part of the incoming gold was by this means concentrated in the hands of the Federal Reserve agent as collateral for Federal Reserve notes.

Wartime Amendments. In the summer of 1917, after our entrance into the war, important changes were made in the Federal Reserve Act. One change eliminated this cumbersome process of issuing Federal Reserve notes against gold. Federal Reserve notes were allowed to be issued directly against gold alone, as well as against commercial paper and gold. Another provision reduced the reserve requirements of member banks to thirteen percent on demand deposits in the central reserve cities, ten percent in the reserve cities, and seven percent in the country banks, with three percent on time deposits for all classes of institutions. At the same time the member banks were required to carry all of their legal reserves as deposits with the Federal Reserve banks, their own gold and lawful money held in their own vaults no longer counting as legal reserves. This made it possible for the member banks to turn over all their gold to the Federal Reserve banks, receiving in return either deposit credits or Federal Reserve notes, depending upon their own and their customers' needs.

Great State Institutions Enter System. The main objectives in this legislation were to encourage the concentration of gold and gold certificates in the Federal Reserve banks, and to encourage banks which had remained outside the Federal Reserve System to come in. When the system was first inaugurated, all national banks were obliged to come in or to surrender their national charters, but many powerful institutions with state charters, including the great trust companies in New York City, remained outside the system. On October 13, 1917, President Wilson issued an appeal to the state banks and trust companies to enter the system as a wartime measure. The response was gratifying. The great state banks and trust companies of New York City entered rapidly and readily. And this was true in other major cities. Much the larger number of the banks with state charters remained outside, but very speedily the major part of the banking resources and banking capital of the country had entered the Federal Reserve System.

Great Technical Services During War. The Federal Reserve System performed great and distinguished services for the government and the country in World War I. It is difficult, indeed, to see how we could have handled the financial problems of the war without it. It made possible a smoothness and simplicity in handling huge financial transactions that would have been incredible under the old system. In the summer of 1918, for example, the federal government collected around $4 billion in taxes in a few weeks. In connection with the first liberty loan in 1917, $2 billion were paid into the federal Treasury in a short time. Financial transactions of this magnitude would have led, under the old system, to drains, falling primarily on the New York banks, which would have forced the banks almost instantly to suspend cash payments. Had the old subtreasury system remained in full vigor, under which all payments to the federal government were placed in cash in the vaults of the government itself, the mechanism would have broken down with the first liberty loan. Under the Federal Reserve System, however, these huge financial transactions were largely accomplished by bookkeeping entries. The Federal Reserve banks and the Federal Reserve Board at Washington, moreover, developed an extraordinary finesse in balancing debits and credits. They studied in advance the probable demands to be made on banks in various localities, and made an effort to route collection items through them in such a way as to give them funds which would break the shock of the heavy withdrawals. They provided in advance for rediscounting paper for these banks, and suggested to the Treasury the best places where government deposits might be made to offset heavy drafts. The policy was also developed of having each Federal Reserve bank rediscount with the others in such a way as to keep the gold reserve ratios of the twelve Federal Reserve banks approximately equal.

Gold Settlement Fund. Shortly after the inauguration of the Federal Reserve System, the Federal Reserve Board required the Federal Reserve banks to create a gold settlement fund in Washington, designed to lessen the physical transfer of gold from one Federal Reserve district to another in connection with interregional settlements. On July 1, 1918, daily settlements among the Federal Reserve banks were inaugurated, reducing in general the amount of gold that had to be transferred from one to another at any given date, and making it possible for the Federal Reserve Board at Washington to keep in constant touch with the reserve situation of each bank and to keep reserve percentages equalized by rediscounting. Daily settlements did not mean daily shipments of gold to and from Washington. "Suspense accounts" kept by the various Federal Reserve banks with the gold settlement fund obviated this. We went far during World War I in the direction of making one central bank out of our twelve Federal Reserve banks.

PART II

THE POSTWAR BOOM, CRISIS, AND REVIVAL, 1919–23

6

The Postwar Boom, 1919–20

The Armistice, November 11, 1918, was followed by a sharp reaction in business and in commodity prices at wholesale. The general average of commodity prices fell from 204 in September 1918 to 193 in February 1919. The first symptoms of this reaction came to the bankers' attention in New York about the middle of November, when currency—$1 bills, $5 bills, $10 bills, as well as subsidiary coins—was pouring into the New York banks from correspondent banks in many parts of the country, especially from the Pittsburgh region. There were not enough clerks in the currency departments of the banks to count this money, despite overtime work, and the cashiers were going around from department to department to find additional clerks who could be spared to help.

The Brief Postwar Reaction. With the Armistice there was immediately a cessation or sharp reduction of a great deal of production for war purposes. Payrolls were falling off, retail trade in manufacturing centers was falling off, cash was piling up in the interior banks, and they were sending it to their New York correspondents to build up their balances or to reduce their loans. A very substantial liquidation of bank credit took place as businesses, no longer needing large loans for current purposes, proceeded to reduce them or to pay them off. The money market eased. The rate to prime borrowing customers in the great New York banks dropped to 4 percent in the early part of 1919, though customers' loans in general remained well above this, and though bankers' acceptances stood at about 4.25 percent. The Federal Reserve rediscount rate meanwhile held at 4 percent.

Commodity Price Reaction. Certain commodities broke sharply in price. There had been during the war a suspension of the antitrust law, accompanied by price fixing, rationing, and allocation. The government controls promptly relaxed, but in a good many cases prices remained fixed by informal agreement among producers. In one such case the fixed price was held to despite a drastic reduction in demand.[1] One great smelting company had a contract to take and refine all the lead that a number of important mines could produce. It was being overwhelmed by the lead which they were producing and which it was unable to dispose of at the fixed price. The company thereupon notified the other interested firms that the next morning, beginning at nine o'clock, it was going to sell lead, and was going to make a price that would move the lead. What that price would be it did not know. The other companies felt that the great smelting company was very decent to give them advance notice and stood aside and watched the procedure. The next morning lead was down ¼¢, down another ¼¢, down another ¼¢, the reduction finally amounting to 4½¢ with no increase in buying. Another ¼¢ reduction met some speculative buying. The selling company promptly raised its price ¼¢ and then encountered trade buying. It raised its price another ¼¢ and the trade buying fell off. It dropped its price ¼¢ and the trade buying was resumed. Then the other companies got into the game and began to sell lead, and a free and open competitive market was established at which lead moved within a range of ½¢ at about 4½¢ below the previously prevailing fixed price. The reduced price discouraged lead production. Supply and demand were equated. Right prices are prices that move goods. Right prices cannot be foreseen in advance. They must be found out experimentally in the open market.

Business and Prices Turn Upward in Late March 1919. There was a drop in employment and there was a great deal of apprehension as to what would happen to employment as the soldiers in the army on our side of the water were released. The apprehension was short-lived. The tide turned in late March and early April. The average of commodity prices at wholesale stiffened and began to advance again. Businessmen began to report a great increase in orders.

Heavy Exports. The export and import figures for the early months of 1919 showed a continuance and even a growth in the volume of exports and in the size of the export balance. The month of January showed an export surplus exceeding $400 million. Foreign orders for goods, first of all European orders, came in increasing volume.

The expectation had been that with the end of the war, Europe would resume her manufacturing activities, and that, while she would need a great deal of food and raw materials from the United States, she would reduce very sharply her buying of manufactured goods. But orders from her for manufactured goods continued on a great scale. The export trade went on and business revived rapidly in the United States on the basis of this export trade.

Continued Government Loans to Allies. An explanation of the financial

---

[1] My attention was called to this at the time by W. R. Ingalls, a well-known mining engineer and editor of *Engineering and Mining Journal*.

basis of this export trade was readily at hand. The United States government had been authorized by Congress to lend $10 billion to our Allies in Europe during the war. The war was not yet technically over and the loans continued to be made. Something like $7 billion had been loaned down to the time of the Armistice. In the post-Armistice period, down to the end of June, nearly $3 billion more was loaned. The burden put upon the foreign exchanges by the heavy shipments of goods to Europe was offset by purchases made in the foreign exchange market, with dollars provided by these loans. J. P. Morgan & Company acted as the principal agent to the British and French governments in these exchange transactions.

The purpose of these continuing loans was to give our Allies in England time to set their houses in order to meet the shock of demobilization and to feed their people while the process of demobilization was being put through. A further purpose was to enable them to meet their commitments to American manufacturers and others on canceled war contracts.

The 1919 Bretton Woods Experiment—Morgan Unpegs Sterling, March 20. On March 20, 1919, the announcement was made that J. P. Morgan had unpegged sterling and would cease to make the purchases needed to sustain the rate. Sterling promptly broke, and all the other European exchanges broke. This was the end of the first phase of our Bretton Woods experiment following World War I. From the Armistice on November 11, 1918, to March 20, 1919, we did precisely what the International Monetary Fund under the Bretton Woods legislation is expected to do, namely, we stabilized the exchange rates of our European allies with funds drawn from the United States Treasury.

The second phase following March 20, 1919, represented continued support, though not absolute stabilization of these exchange rates with funds drawn from the United States Treasury until the loans ceased with June 30, 1919, and for a little time further until the proceeds of these loans were exhausted. The exports went on and the exchange rates went lower. But there came no backflow of goods from Europe. The continent of Europe had been so shattered by the war that it was not going back to work. It was living on imports received from the outside world. Public finances were out of hand, fiscal deficits were growing. The Continental governments were relying increasingly on loans from the central banks of issue, which were printing banknotes to cover governmental expenditures. Currencies were in disorder. As long as the outside world would take these currencies, Europe could buy imports and live upon them. Weak finance ministers had no incentive to tax the people or to place funding loans while the outside world was giving them such generous credits.

In the autumn of 1919 Frank Vanderlip, then president of the National City Bank of New York, returned from Europe where he had made a rapid but pretty fundamental survey, and, in an address at a public dinner in New York, gave an explanation of what was happening on the other side. His diagnosis was correct. His prescription was very inappropriate. His proposed remedy was that we should loan the European governments a billion dollars. But we had just loaned them nearly $3 billion since the Armistice and it had done little or nothing toward rehabilitating them. Much more fundamental remedies were needed. It is the duty of a lender to an embarrassed debtor to see to it that the debtor mends his ways and reorganizes his affairs so that the loan may be a good loan. We were lending to Europe overgenerously, but we were not performing the duty of a lender with respect to these other matters. Had we from the beginning insisted that the governments of Europe which received the loans from us should set their financial houses in order and straighten out their currencies as a condition for the loans, we should have accomplished a great deal with the loans. The governments later had to do it under much less favorable conditions and after the financial disorders had progressed much further.

The month of June 1919 represented the climax of our exports. In that single month we exported over a billion dollars' worth of goods. In that single month we had an export balance of $635 million, of which $601 million represented our excess of exports with Europe alone. The exports continued, however, month after month in enormous volume. Goods were going not only to England, which was solvent and strong, but also to France, Belgium, and Italy, which were slipping badly financially, and in great volume also to Germany, which was going to pieces financially. How were they being paid for? Who was standing the risk of these shipments? Who was providing the money?

Sterling Goes Down with the Continental Exchanges. A clue came in one strange fact—England alone among the European belligerents had her financial home in order. England alone was showing industrial revival. And yet sterling exchange was weakening rapidly along with the other exchanges. That the foreign exchange markets should reflect the internal financial weakness of France, Belgium, Italy, and Germany was reasonable. But that sterling also should be going low, despite the strong financial and industrial position of England, called loudly for explanation.

London Stands Between United States and Continent. A careful study of the actual operations in foreign exchange in the late summer and autumn of 1919 revealed the fact that while there were enormous holdings of sterling in New York, there were very small holdings of francs, lire, and Belgian francs and of the other Continental exchanges, except for German marks. German marks were being bought by a great many speculators in the United States, by a great many people who had never before speculated in foreign exchange. But there were small accumulations of the other Continental exchanges. The market in New York for these Continental exchanges was narrow. Large sums could not be sold in New York without a break in price. The good market was in London, and New York banks and other exchange dealers buying francs, lire, Belgian francs, Greek drachmas, and so on, promptly resold them in London.

London had long been the center for international speculation. In the days before the war there were always active speculative markets in London for practically anything: elephants, ships, beeswax, carved ivories from China, paintings of old masters, to say nothing of standard commodities, foreign exchange, stocks and bonds, and the like. A large body of London speculators stood ready to buy virtually anything at a concession in price. London banks, relying on the active speculative markets which made all manner of things liquid, were ready to finance, and did finance, these speculative transactions. London was usually safe in this, since London was full of experts who knew where the proper outlets were for all manner of unusual commodities, securities, or bills of exchange. After the Armistice London revived this speculative activity, so far as foreign exchange was concerned, on a great scale.

The Dove from Noah's Ark. Ordinarily such speculation had been safe because the London speculators knew their outlets. In 1919 and 1920, however, there were no outlets for any large quantity of Continental exchanges. The outside world did not owe money to France, Italy, or other belligerent countries of the Continent on net balance and consequently had little need for Continental exchange. London was thus placed in a difficult position. She could keep the mass of Continental exchanges moving through active speculation. She could move them about through Switzerland, Paris, New York, and other centers. But, like the dove that Noah sent out from the Ark, they found no resting place for their feet, and they returned to London.

The magnitudes grew, moreover, as London found it necessary steadily to buy the new exchange continuously being created in order to protect the price of what she already held.

New York–London Rate Becomes New York–European Rate. The explanation of the decline in sterling along with the other exchanges is thus to be found in the fact that the London–New York rate had in effect become a Europe–New York rate. London was interposing her vast financial strength and prestige between the stricken Continent and the United States. In part, as suggested in the foregoing, this was unintentional, but in large part it was intentional. London was not merely buying Continental exchanges and holding them in growing volume, she was also making great extensions of credit to the continent of Europe and she was buying from the United States in order to sell on credit to the continent of Europe.

On a great scale strong business houses, particularly export and import houses in England, were borrowing from New York banks on the guarantee of British banks, and British banks of first rank and undoubted solvency were large direct borrowers from New York banks and, for that matter, from large banks in other great American financial centers.

Exports Go on Unfunded Credits—Bank Expansion, 1919–20. The exports were going on the basis of unfunded credits. Government credits had ceased. Private credit took its place. Long-term credits had ceased. Unfunded credits took their place. American exporters were giving long credits to European buyers, were selling on undated open accounts. They were tying up their working capital in the process and borrowing from their banks to replenish it. The reflex action of all this on the American money market was very great. In the single year, from April 11, 1919, to April 9, 1920, the loans and investments of the reporting member banks of the Federal Reserve System increased 25.4 percent.

This expansion of bank credit occurred despite the fact that there was a reduction during this period in the holdings of government securities by the American banks. It was not government borrowing which did it.

Even Greater Rate of Bank Expansion in London, 1919–20. A similar story, intensified, appeared in England. From June 1919 to June 1920 there was an expansion of forty-one percent in "bills discounted" and "advances" of the twenty leading banks of the United Kingdom, despite the fact that their holdings of Treasury bills during this period were reduced. We were expanding to export to Europe, relying primarily on the credit of England. England was expanding bank credit in an even greater percentage as part of the same process, and also for the purpose of exporting British goods to the Continent.

The $3.5 Billion Unfunded Debt of Europe to Private American Creditors in September 1920. The unfunded debt of Europe to private creditors in the United States grew to an astounding total. The present writer estimated in October 1920 that on the fifteenth of the preceding September this unfunded debt stood at $3.5 billion. The following table, prepared at that time,[2] shows the elements that entered into the growth of the unfunded debt.

GROWTH OF UNFUNDED DEBT OF EUROPE TO PRIVATE AMERICAN CREDITORS*
January 1, 1919, to September 15, 1920

(In millions of dollars)

Europe debtor		*United States debtor*	
Commodity trade balance (Europe vs. United States), Jan. 1, 1919–July 31, 1920	$6,350	Relevant government advances, 1919	$2,665
Commodity trade balance (Europe vs. United States), Aug. 1, 1920–Sept. 15, 1920 (est.)	250	Government advances, 1920, to Sept. 16	155
		Credits granted by United States Grain Corporation	60

---

[2] See *Chase Economic Bulletin*, October 5, 1920, p. 70.

Europe debtor	
Net silver imports from U. S., Jan. 1, 1919– Aug. 31, 1920	30
Net balance on shipping, 1919	73
Net shipping balance, 1920	52
Ships purchased, 1919	20
European securities maturing, 1919	466
European securities maturing in 1920, to Sept. 15	5
Net interest to private creditors, 1919	79
Net interest to private creditors, 1920, to Sept. 15	135
Interest actually paid to U. S. Treasury, Jan. 1, 1919–Sept. 9, 1920	177
Repayment of principal to U. S. Treasury, Jan. 1, 1919–Sept. 9, 1920	114
Anglo-French 5's approaching maturity	500
Argentine maturity of May 15, 1920, met by Great Britain	50
	$8,301
	$4,528.6
Growth of the Unfunded Debt of Europe to the United States, Jan. 1, 1919–Sept. 15, 1920	$3,772.4

United States debtor	
Credits by United States Shipping Board for sales of ships	3.6
United States tourists	75
Immigrants' remittances	450
Insurance balance (small and uncertain)	000
New loans to Europe, 1919	265
New loans to Europe, 1920, to Sept. 15	216
American securities repurchased	200
Internal European securities purchased	155
Net gold brought in from Europe, Jan. 1, 1919– Aug. 31, 1920	50
Japanese and Argentine securities purchased from Europe	89
Other securities purchased from Europe	12
German gold held in custory by Bank of England for account of Federal Reserve bank	111
Gold from Hong Kong on British account, May 1920	22
	$4,528.6

---

* The explanation of the items in this balance sheet will be found in *Chase Economic Bulletin*, October 5, 1920.

Europe had, as the result of loans made by the United States Treasury before January 1, 1919, a small credit of $200 or $300 million on current account. The actual credit in bank balances was larger, but a very substantial part of it was needed for meeting canceled war contracts. Subtracting $272 million from the figures for the growth of the unfunded debt January

1, 1919, to September 15, 1920, gives the actual amount of the unfunded debt, namely, $3.5 billion.

Europe Current Account Debtor to Rest of World Also. Under ordinary conditions it would be pointless to compute relations of this kind between Europe and the United States alone. Under ordinary conditions Europe would have been building up credits in countries other than the United States, against which she could draw in settling her debts here. But in 1919 and 1920 this was not true. Europe was increasing her open account debt to all parts of the world, and nowhere was she building up credits with which to meet debts here. She was even drawing on us to meet some of her current debts in the outside world.

Our Adverse Trade Balance with Non-European Countries—Paid for with Cash. With the rest of the world the United States had an adverse trade balance. We were sending less goods to the non-European world than we were bringing in from it, and we were having to pay for these, not by drawing on European balance, but by sending out cash. The following table, covering a somewhat longer period, exhibits our trade relations with the world outside Europe.[3]

UNITED STATES TRADE BALANCE WITH COUNTRIES OUTSIDE EUROPE, GOLD AND SILVER SHIPMENTS INCLUDED
From January 1, 1919, to December 13, 1920

Commodities	Exports	Imports	Balance
1919	$2,732,759,627	$3,153,836,543	−$421,076,916
1920	3,762,104,551	4,051,556,066	− 289,451,515
Total	$6,494,864,178	$7,205,392,609	−$710,528,431
Gold			
1919	$ 329,590,927	$ 71,552,305	$258,038,622
1920	321,737,629	97,943,352	223,794,277
Total	$ 651,328,556	$ 169,495,657	$481,832,899
Silver			
1919	$ 212,412,896	$ 89,268,551	$123,144,345
1920	108,603,566	86,709,641	21,893,925
Total	$ 321,016,462	$ 175,978,192	$145,038,270
Grand total	$7,467,209,196	$7,550,866,458	−$ 83,657,262

---

[3] *Ibid.*, February 28, 1921, p. 5.

From this table it is clear that we met almost all of our adverse trade balance with the non-European world with shipments of gold and silver. We more than made up the rest by shipments of Federal Reserve notes, chiefly to Cuba, although Federal Reserve notes also went to Santo Domingo, some to the northern parts of South America, and in minor amounts to other countries.

7

The Causes of the Crisis
of 1920

The Quantity Theory of Money Stops Analysis of Causes. With the turn in the tide of commodity prices in the spring of 1919 there came into vogue a ready-made explanation which gave great comfort and confidence to the speculators and to the business community as the boom of 1919–20 proceeded. It was the explanation afforded by the quantity theory of money. Money in circulation and bank credit in the United States were enormously expanded as compared with the prewar situation. Commodity prices were enormously higher. But the prices, according to this theory, were higher *because* of the expansion of money and credit, and the prices were consequently safe, and adequately explained. Professor Irving Fisher was the leading advocate of this view in the United States. The formula of the quantity theorists is a monotonous "tit-tat-toe"—money, credit, prices. With this explanation the problem was solved and further research and further investigation were unnecessary, and consequently stopped— for those who believed in this theory. It is one of the great vices of the quantity theory of money that it tends to check investigation of underlying factors in a business situation.[1]

---

[1] This theory was accepted even by the Harvard *Review of Economic Statistics,* which in the middle of 1919 set a new level for Bradstreet's index of commodity prices at 191 percent of 1913 prices and for the Bureau of Labor Statistics index of commodity prices at 194 percent of 1913 prices (*Monthly Supplement,* June 1919, esp. p. 10). The *Review of Economic Statistics* then assumed that deviations from these levels in the following period would be of a magnitude comparable to deviations from the linear trend of prewar prices which, on the basis of twelve-month moving averages, had had a maximum deviation of 6.6 percent above the line of trend in May 1907 (*ibid.,* p. 10, n. 1). The study concludes (p. 11) with the following qualification: "This conclusion is based on that assumption that there will be no European debacle to destroy the monetary and credit structure supporting present prices. Although such a debacle is not an impossibility, we believe it is improbable and consequently should not be a ruling consideration in present calculations." The deviations from this new level in the two years which followed, both up and down, were of enormously greater magnitude!

The quantity theory of money is invalid.[2] It was clear as early as May 1919 that the boom was thoroughly unsound, that the commodity prices prevailing were dangerously high and very precarious, and that the longer the boom lasted, the more violent the reaction would be.[3] The basic cause of the boom was in the factors which we have previously considered, notably, the one-sided export trade to Europe first financed by the government, and, second, the going on the basis of unfunded private credits. We cannot accept a predominantly monetary general theory either for the level of commodity prices or for the movements of the business cycle.

Money and credit have their place in the explanation of both of these problems, but they are only a part of the explanation and often are a very minor part. The role of bank credit in particular is very frequently secondary and passive. Bank credit usually adapts itself to the underlying factors, rather than forcing the pace. Very notable exceptions, as we shall see, appeared in the period 1922–29, and in the period 1897–1903. The monetary forces provide the primary explanation of our Civil War prices, when our currency was the irredeemable greenback. Monetary forces may well dominate our price situation following World War II. The inflowing gold and the resultant ease with which the expansion of bank credit could go on were contributory factors of great importance in the rise of commodity prices in 1916 and the first part of 1917.

Money and Credit as Factors in the 1919–20 Boom. The factor of money and bank credit was not the dominating factor in the postwar boom, 1919–20, despite the fact stated above, that bank loans and investments in the United States expanded 25.4 percent between April 11, 1919, and April 9, 1920. This expansion was, on the whole, a reflex rather than a cause of the other phenomena. We were losing gold from April 1919 through April 1920. Our gold stock stood at $2,890,000,000 in April 1919 and at $2,554,000,000 in April 1920, a decline of $336,000,000, or 12 percent. Interest rates rose steadily and to very great heights. Open market commercial paper which had sold at 5.5 percent at the beginning of 1919 sold at a 7 percent rate in early 1920, reaching a peak of over 8 percent in the third quarter of 1920. Prime customers' loans at the great city banks did not rise as high as this, but they rose steadily, and 7 percent was a very common rate for strong corporations before the boom was over.

Federal Reserve Rediscount Rates Below the Market. It must be recognized, however, that the handling of the Federal Reserve rediscount rate permitted the expansion to move faster and to go further than would otherwise have been the case. That rate was held at 4 percent through the greater part of 1919 despite the rising rates of interest in the money market.

---

[2] See my *Value of Money* (New York: Macmillan, 1917; R. R. Smith, 1936).

[3] This writer and the late A. Barton Hepburn interchanged letters in late May 1919 agreeing on this proposition.

The explanation appears to be that the Federal Reserve authorities did not wish to raise their rate until the government had got over the peak of its borrowings. That peak was reached, however, in August 1919, whereas the rise in the Federal Reserve rate was delayed until November 1919. The New York Federal Reserve Bank suddenly found itself with a reserve deficiency and was thus obliged under the law to raise its rate. The rate went to 4.75 percent on November 4, 1919, to 6 percent on January 23, 1920, and to 7 percent on June 4, 1920. The other Federal Reserve banks followed New York in these moves, though only three of them went to 7 percent in June. It is thus true that down to January 23, 1920, it was definitely profitable for a member bank to rediscount at a Federal Reserve bank and relend to its customers. Too many of them did this, and too many of them found themselves heavily indebted to the Federal Reserve banks when the crisis came. The head of one great trust company, early in January 1920, put this question to an economist: "How much longer is it safe for me to go on borrowing at the Federal Reserve bank to relend at a profit?" He was shocked and startled when the economist replied that he had already gone much too far, that he had borrowed twice his reserves, and that it was essential for him to pull up. He did pull up and let some profitable business go to some other institutions, and took good care of his customers when the crisis came in autumn 1920.

The great New York banks in general were very reluctant to borrow from the Federal Reserve bank when the system was first inaugurated. Banks in general were disposed to feel that it was a sign of weakness if they rediscounted with the Federal Reserve banks, though banks in the Dallas district, where there is an immense pressure in the cotton-moving season, very early learned to do so. But it was not until the coming of war finance or shortly before this that the great New York banks rediscounted. They did so at the request of the Federal Reserve bank, which wished them to give an example to the other banks in the country.[4] However, the great banks got used to it during the war, and in the postwar boom they overdid it.

The Federal Reserve System should have held to the orthodox rule of keeping the rediscount rate above the rate to prime borrowing customers at the great city banks.[5]

Discounts at the Federal Reserve banks increased from the beginning of 1919 to the middle of 1920 about $750 million. Offsetting this in its effect on member bank reserves was the loss of gold of $336 million mentioned

---

[4] I know this from conversations with bankers at the time, and at a period a little later, but I can find no published statement regarding the matter.

[5] One of the ablest members of the Federal Reserve Board wrote to me early in 1919 asking if I did not think that the rate should be raised. At the time he wrote, liquidation was still going on, and I advised against the raising of the rate in a period of liquidation. Later I was very sorry that I had given this advice.

above, and the increase of money in circulation, which amounted to $534 million between May 1919 and May 1920. The net result of these conflicting forces was a steady increase in pressure on the money market, with rapidly rising interest rates. On balance the monetary factor was a restraining influence through the whole of 1920, and it was not the primary influence in causing the boom in 1919.

It may be observed here that following the postwar boom and crisis, the great city banks resumed their tradition that they did not rediscount except in unusual circumstances, even though it was profitable to do so. They were very reluctant to show bills payable to the Federal Reserve bank in their published balance sheets. This tradition held very strongly until 1928. When the Federal Reserve banks in 1928 began to tighten the money market by selling government securities, the member banks in New York began to rediscount again, not for the purpose of increasing their reserves or increasing their loans, but for the purpose of maintaining their reserves. Their loans and deposits did, in fact, go down in 1928, as we shall see later when we study the brokers' loan episode. But the Federal Reserve System ought not to rely upon such a tradition on the part of the banks. They ought to keep their rediscount rates above the market.

The Equilibrium Theory. The general body of economic theory which guides the interpretations given to the more than three decades of the economic history covered in the present volume, and which finds its verification in that history, is based on the notion of economic equilibrium.[6] This concept includes many elements. It includes the equilibrium of the industries among themselves. It includes the price and cost equilibrium. It includes the relation of international debts to the volume of international

---

[6] See this writer's "Static Economics and Business Forecasting," in *Economic Essays Contributed in Honor of John Bates Clark* (New York, 1927). See also "Equilibrium Creates Purchasing Power," *Chase Economic Bulletin*, June 12, 1931, and my refutation of Keynes' attack on the doctrine that aggregate supply creates aggregate demand in the *Commercial & Financial Chronicle* of January 25, 1945, reproduced in the Twentieth Century Fund's *Financing American Prosperity: A Symposium of Economists* (1945), pp. 63–70. See also my application of the equilibrium principle to long-run business forecasting in "A World Afraid of Production," *Chase Economic Bulletin*, August 24, 1925, in which (esp. p. 16) I forecast the troubles which finally came in 1929. See also chap. 60, "Digression on Keynes," in the present volume.

I think that even today the best single book dealing with the business cycle is that of Wesley C. Mitchell, *Business Cycles* (Berkeley: University of California Press, 1913). This book as a whole has long been out of print, but a new edition containing the theoretical part was recently made available. This book could not have been written by a man who was not deeply learned in equilibrium economics. It takes account of the whole business picture, and all the changing factors. The reader acquainted with this book will see that I am very much indebted to it in the analysis given of the causes of the crisis of 1920 which follows. I think this is a much better book than Professor Mitchell's later studies, produced when statistical materials were more abundant and consequently, perhaps, more confusing. I regard the book as enormously more valuable than such one-sided studies as have come from the monetary school, Keynes, Hawtrey, and their followers.

trade. It includes the position of the money market. It includes, not merely the quantity of money and credit, but also the quality of money and credit. It includes consideration of wages, rentals, and taxes, as well as interest, in the costs of production. It centers on the question of whether economic forces are working away from balance or toward balance. It is a flexible conception which puts emphasis at different times upon different factors of the situation, depending on which ones are doing unusual things.[7]

The Growing Economic Unbalance. The situation in 1920 was shot through with abnormalities, stresses and strains. The movement was in almost every case away from equilibrium.

1. *Our export balance.* The most striking abnormality from the standpoint of ordinary economic laws was that the United States, a creditor country, should have an enormous export balance. The world as a whole was heavily indebted to us, and under normal conditions this would have involved an excess of imports to the United States as foreign countries paid their debts to us with goods.

2. *Gold movements.* The second great abnormality of 1919–20 was that despite our tremendous export balance of trade we were losing gold heavily. The extent of this is indicated in the foregoing tables, and the reasons for it have been stated. We had an export balance with Europe only, and we could not draw on Europe for payments to the non-European world to pay for our import surplus from them.

3. *Prices and gold.* The net result of our foreign commerce during 1919–20 was that we lost both goods and gold. The loss of goods raised prices and encouraged speculation. The loss of gold tightened the money market.

4. *Government expenditure.* In the two years following the Armistice the government spent practically as much money as it had spent during the war itself. A large part of this was in liquidating canceled war contracts and in meeting other unavoidable expenses of postwar readjustment. But part of this governmental expenditure was for financing the shipment of goods to Europe, while the continuance of government shipbuilding after the Armistice created a surplus of unneeded ships at the same time that it led to shortages in other lines where the labor and resources could have been advantageously employed.

5. *Industrial efficiency.* One of the most striking abnormalities was to be found in the fact that the return of nearly four million men from the army and navy to industry in 1919 was accompanied by an actual decline in the physical volume of goods produced in 1919 as compared with 1918.

---

[7] With the general equilibrium conception in mind I wrote in the spring of 1920 a memorandum for private, limited use, an analysis of the existing situation, forecasting the crisis of 1920. The substance of this analysis is published, as history, in explaining the crisis of 1920 in the *Chase Economic Bulletin,* February 28, 1921, under the title "The Return to Normal."

Professor E. E. Day[8] gave figures showing an increase in agriculture of 3.3 percent, a decline in mining of 18.3 percent, and a decline of manufacturing of 8.8 percent, with a decline in production generally of 5.5 percent. Professor Walter Stewart[9] estimated the decline in the physical volume of production of 1919 as compared with 1918 at four percent. There was a great decline in the efficiency of labor in 1919 and 1920 accompanied by a rapid rise in wages. This usually comes toward the end of a boom. In a boom certain "marginal" or inefficient labor is employed which would have difficulty in finding employment in dull times, and is taken on often at full wage rates. A great deal of overtime work is engaged in, and overtime rates increase labor costs. Moreover, overtime beyond forty-eight hours a week, over a series of weeks, leads to a weariness on the part of labor. Shop discipline is increasingly difficult in boom times. The turnover of labor, moreover, is very rapid in such a period. Labor costs per unit of output were mounting rapidly.

6. *Managerial efficiency.* Toward the close of a boom managerial efficiency always goes down. Managers are harassed by rush orders, by a high labor turnover, by difficulties in getting materials in on time, and by a multiplicity of details which do not press them so hard in dull times. Moreover, profits look large and managers have less incentive for close economies. They find it easy to add increased expenses to selling prices. They are, moreover, easily persuaded by enterprising promoters with "ideas to sell," to incur extravagant overhead expenses for advertising and other items from which the return may be doubtful. They cease to watch small economies.

7. *Raw materials.* Ordinarily prices of raw materials rise faster than prices of finished products in a boom time. Imported raw materials did not rise as fast following the latter part of 1919 as did the prices of finished products, but raw materials in the cases where foreign competition was absent rose very rapidly, and this was particularly true of building materials. In some cases local monopolies were able to push building prices to outrageous levels.

8. *Money and interest rates.* The year following April 1919 saw a steady rise in money rates and in long-time interest rates on investments, with a resultant sharp increase in the interest element in the cost of production. Businesses which had maturing bond issues were especially hard hit by this development, and there was a great increase in the volume of short time notes in this period, as businesses were unwilling to tie themselves up with long-time contracts to pay existing interest rates. Gold was leaving the

---

[8] *Review of Economic Statistics,* January 1921.

[9] "An Index Number of Production," American Economic Association, December 1920, in *Papers and Proceedings* (March 1921).

country and undermining bank reserves at the same time that bank loans were expanding, as we have seen, at a rapid rate.

9. *Rentals.* In all growing cities, in view of the shortage of housing, rents rose rapidly during 1919 and most of 1920. As business leases expired during this period, new leases had to be taken on at much higher rentals, leading again to marked increases in costs of business production.

10. *The railroad situation.* The war had subjected our railroad system to a very great strain. Traffic was dislocated and equipment had got into bad condition. Railway wages were high and the efficiency of railroad labor was low. The postwar boom caught the railroads in such a position that it was not easy for them to bear the strain. More traffic was offered than they could handle, and railroad congestion grew at many points. This was one of the worst elements of the industrial disequilibrium. It led to interferences with production and marketing, created a coal shortage, increased factory costs, and led, moreover, to the tying up of goods in transit with a consequent freezing of bank credits and commercial credits based on goods in movement. Freight cars and bank loans were direct competitors. This situation was in evidence in 1919 and became acutely critical in the early part of 1920.

Railroad congestion was complicated by the fact that railroad rates were lower than they should have been. The railroads were not paying their way and the United States Treasury was standing the loss. This meant that more traffic was offered to the railroads than would have been the case had the rates been high enough to enable the railroads to pay their way. Economic abnormalities arise whenever costs and prices get out of proper relation to one another. This is the case almost equally where prices are lower than costs or where prices are higher than costs.

11. *Rising costs, and vanishing profits.* From many causes, then, costs of production rose with startling rapidity during the second half of 1919 and the first part of 1920. As costs rose businesses which were unable to advance their prices faced declining and vanishing profits. With the decline in profits in a sufficiently important minority of businesses, a boom must come to an end. The businesses facing losses contract their operations to cut their losses. If they fail to do this voluntarily, their creditors force their hands. Credits are based on earning power. As earning power diminishes creditors grow nervous and begin to press for collection, liquidation is forced, and reaction and crisis come.

The heart of the business movement is not money, is not credit, is not commodity prices. The heart of the business situation is the outlook for profits. The heart of the credit situation is the *quality* of credit and the quality of credit rests on the outlook for profits.

12. *Industries.* Especially hard hit were those industries where prices were fixed by law or custom or necessity, but where costs nonetheless rose. Typical of these were gold mining, railroading, public utilities, and the

like. The years 1919 and 1920 saw difficulties multiplying rapidly for all of these industries.

13. *Competition.* Very commonly in boom times competition functions imperfectly or disappears, and this was strikingly true in 1919–20. The legislation of the Wilson administration in 1913, in the Clayton Act, and administrative policy down to our entrance into the war in 1917 had made substantial progress in restoring competition to American business. During our own participation in the war, however, the government, for war purposes, temporarily reversed this policy and encouraged businessmen in most industries to get together, to pool their resources, and to pool their business secrets.

As a temporary war policy this was necessary and desirable. It was accompanied by price fixing, by rationing of materials and supplies, and by other restraints of an authoritative character which took the place of free competition in regulating prices and production. The end of the war saw the rapid disappearance of price fixing and authoritative controls, but did not see an adequate restoration of competition. One may add that never since the early years of the Wilson administration has there been any consistent effort to enforce antitrust legislation. Of course the whole theory of the NRA was contrary to the spirit of the antitrust laws and, indeed, the antitrust laws were suspended by the National Industrial Recovery Act.

14. *Speculation.* The great strain in commodity markets and the shortage of goods created by the abnormal growth of our export balance led to rapidly rising prices of commodities. This rise in commodity prices led to and was greatly accentuated by an appalling speculation in commodity prices. This speculation created shortages where shortages would not otherwise have existed. The year 1919 saw also a stock market boom of disquieting proportions, culminating in November. Speculation in farmlands and other real estate went dangerously far in many sections, while there was a great deal of exceedingly ill-informed and dangerous speculation in foreign exchange as well.

15. *Conditions abroad.* Our great export trade was based, not on revival in Europe, but on the failure of Europe to revive. Industrial revival in complicated modern industry must rest on sound currency and sound public finance. Public finance of the belligerents of continental Europe grew steadily worse. Monetary depreciation in Europe moved rapidly. Europe was buying goods in enormous quantity on credit from every part of the world, and building up throughout the world a fictitious prosperity similar to that which we had in the United States. Reaction and collapse were inevitable. The collapse came first in Japan with a violent break in silk prices early in 1920. Troubles came in India. Collapse came in Cuba as sugar plunged from 22.56¢ a pound in May 1920 to 3.63¢ in December.

16. *The Unbalance Among the Industries.* Leaving aside the disorder in credits and finance brought about by European troubles, there was a

fundamental disturbance in the equilibrium of the world's industries due to the great reduction in Europe's output of manufactures. The normal functioning of industry and commerce rests upon a proper balancing of various industries. Manufactures, foods, and raw materials must be produced in proper proportion.

We saw such a disequilibrium in the United States in 1893–96—it was not our only problem, for fears regarding our standard of value were very acute then, as a result of the Sherman Silver Act of 1890 and the strong agitation for bimetallism. The production of raw materials and foods due to the rapid exploitation of the Mississippi Valley had outrun the development of manufactures. As a consequence the prices of raw materials and foods fell very low, and the buying power of the producers was cut so much that they could not give full employment even to the relatively scarce manufacturing capacity of the country.

The world as a whole faced a similar problem in 1920. Europe had been the great manufacturing center, drawing in foods and raw materials from all over the world, working up the raw materials, and sending out finished manufactures in payment. The most unmistakable revival in continental Europe following 1918 was in agriculture rather than in manufacturing. City industry calls for good money. Agriculture has far fewer financial problems. There had been a drastic change in our exports and imports from prewar conditions as a consequence of this fact. Before the war only thirty percent or our exports were manufactures ready for consumption. This percentage rose very high during the war, and even as late as November 1920 we were still sending out virtually forty-two percent of our exports in the form of manufactures ready for consumption. Raw materials constituted thirty-four percent of our prewar exports. They averaged only twenty percent of our exports during 1919 and 1920. On the other hand, on the import side there had been a marked diminution during and since the war in the proportion of manufactured goods imported, with a very substantial increase in the proportion of raw materials brought in. We had been trying to take over Europe's job of supplying the world, including Europe, with manufactured goods, and of buying from the world its surplus raw materials. Our manufacturing capacity was not adequate to carry this work, and the result was so great a collapse in the price of raw materials, with a resultant decline in the purchasing power of the producers of raw materials, that our own factories could not keep active at prevailing prices.

There were many false theories accepted during this extraordinary postwar boom. One of the most remarkable was the theory offered in 1919 that there was a worldwide scarcity of raw materials. This was presented as an argument for extensive American investments in Siberia, South America, and other outlying regions, and served as a foundation for the fantastic commodity speculation in which the world engaged. But the fact was that the war had been fought chiefly in manufacturing countries and that, barring Russia, the sources of raw materials had been stimulated, rather than depressed, during the war.

Raw materials broke first and broke violently, and then all prices yielded.

8

The Crisis—1920–21

The crisis came with extraordinary suddenness. I symbolized it at the time in these terms. We have been stretching a rubber band. Europe holds one end, we hold the other. The tension in the rubber band represents the high prices of commodities. The tension has been growing. Suddenly Europe turns loose her end. Commodity prices drop in thirteen months from 248 to 141!

Europe turned loose her end, not because she did not continue to desire commodities, but because of the growing doubt all over the world as to her ability to pay, and also because of a growing exhaustion of the credit resources of those who wished to sell to her on credit.

Wholesale and Retail Prices. One of the first episodes, anticipating the general fall in raw materials and in the general average of wholesale commodity prices, was a cut of twenty percent in retail prices at John Wanamaker's in New York on May 3, 1920. Wanamaker, moving first, cleaned out his inventory at high prices, and put himself in a strong financial position. Some other retailers followed. But the first *general* break was not in retail prices. Wanamaker's acted in response to what was called a "buyers' strike." Public resistance to rising prices became a general subject of discussion, though it was probably more talked about than real.

Wholesale Prices Break from 248 to 141. The decline in commodity prices at wholesale was extraordinarily rapid. A peak had been reached in May 1920 at 248 percent of the 1913 prices according to the contemporary Bureau of Labor Statistics Index. By August 1921 this index had dropped to 141. In a single year, August 1920 to August 1921, the drop was one hundred points. American industry met this shock amazingly well. American agriculture suffered a great deal because of it. Agriculture in outlying countries, like Cuba and South America, was prostrated by it. Twenty-five-cent sugar ruined Cuba. Two-and-a-half-dollar wheat did grave damage to American agriculture. But the boom and the high prices and the great collapse left the general industrial situation in the United States pretty well intact.

Industry Stands Shock—Agriculture Badly Shaken—Different Financial Techniques. The explanation is to be found in the difference in financial technique between industry and agriculture. Industry rather generally was distrustful of the boom during the war and to a considerable extent even after the war. Industry used the boom as an opportunity to accumulate additional capital funds and to increase liquidity. The United States Steel Corporation, for example, increased its cash in banks, increased its holdings of marketable securities, and reduced its debt during the war, as well as increased its surplus and undivided profits very greatly out of earnings. It did not pay out all of its profits in dividends. The United States Steel Corporation was stronger in the summer of 1921 after the grand smash than it had been in the summer of 1914 before the war began.

Agriculture, on the other hand, to a great extent, had used the extraordinary wartime earnings as a foundation for rising prices of agricultural lands and increased mortgage debt on agricultural lands. This in part grew out of the conservative wisdom of agricultural communities. A wise investor will ordinarily buy the kind of thing that he knows and understands. The farmers knew land. With windfall profits they bought more land. Ultraconservatism in agricultural communities, on the part of old farmers who did not wish to expand, consisted in taking a first mortgage on some other man's land where he knew the land and could watch it. Ordinarily such practices had proved wholesome and sound, but when widely practiced for several years of high profits, they inevitably made for a great rise in land values and a great growth in debt based on land values.

Land Speculation—Iowa. The center of the boom in agricultural lands was Iowa. Land values had long been unduly high in Iowa as compared with land in other states with the same earning power. In 1919 and 1920 they soared extravagantly.[1]

Temporarily Embarrassed Businesses. A great many industries were temporarily very hard hit and embarrassed. Inventory shriveled in value. A great many accounts and bills receivable proved to be difficult to collect. Industry itself, however, had accounts and bills payable, including notes due at the banks, which were maturing. Liquidity decreased with great rapidity. The banker giving credit is accustomed to attach high importance to the "current ratio," that is to say, the ratio between quick assets and quick liabilities. Quick assets are cash in bank, accounts and bills receiv-

---

[1] This writer recalls a conversation with a banker in Iowa City as late as December 1920. The banker was showing me a very fine farm and he said, "I know that you economists say that land is only worth what it will produce, but it does look like some of this land around here is worth a thousand dollars an acre." In the disillusionment, Iowa suffered more than any other state.

able, and inventory. Quick liabilities are accounts and bills payable. The ratio required in different industries will vary with the general liquidity of the business and special circumstances connected with the business, but in general the banker likes to have a current ratio of 2 or 3 to 1. Current ratios declined with startling rapidity. One important company had a current ratio of 5 to 1 on December 31, 1919, and only 1 to 1 on December 31, 1920. Under such circumstances it became necessary for the banker to "look below the line," that is to say, to consider the fixed assets and the fixed liabilities of the corporation as well as its quick assets and quick liabilities; to consider whether, taking all assets and all liabilities into account, the concern was solvent even though it might be temporarily frozen. Credit policy came to be centered on the question of solvency. Business policy for a great many corporations ceased to be concerned primarily with profits and came to be concerned primarily with solvency.

There were many strong corporations which rode serenely through this trouble without needing to call upon their banks for anything but routine loans, and some, like the United States Steel Corporation, which needed no loans at all. But most businesses needed to go to their bankers, and many of them came in fear and trembling.

Banking Policy, 1920–21. The main lines of bank credit policy pursued in this great crisis were admirable and very clean-cut. The banks themselves had taken advantage of the unusual profits of the war and the postwar boom to add to surplus and even to capital on a great scale. And they had, for the first time in a great crisis, the Federal Reserve banks to lean upon.

The trouble came, in general, to concerns which could give the banks commercial paper eligible for rediscount at the Federal Reserve banks. The Federal Reserve banks were in a strong position and extended credit, at a steep rate, to enable the bankers to meet borrowing demands. The first point in bank policy was that it was the business of the banks to extend credit to enable solvent customers to protect their solvency, but that if the customer were really insolvent, there was no use in throwing good money after bad. The second main point was that if the customer was to be helped at all he was to be helped adequately. If $50,000 was needed to save him he should receive a loan of $50,000 or else nothing at all. He should not be given an inadequate $30,000 loan. There was always the qualification in cases of this sort that if the customer were accustomed to borrowing from several banks he should not expect any one of the several to give him all that he needed, but should expect the banks rather to get together and divide up the burden, but in such a way that he would have adequate funds to protect his solvency. It was the business of the banks to enable their customers to mobilize their slow assets to meet their quick liabilities. It was no part of the duty of the bankers to validate the unsound assets of a really insolvent business.

Bank Creditor Committees. Solvency in many cases was a question of degree and a question of opinion. The bank credit men amassed in an extraordinarily short time all relevant information regarding virtually every business in the United States. And through the interchange of credit information this was available to all interested bankers. It became clear that there were many cases of well-managed businesses which, caught in the great disorder, would not be saved by temporary loans, but needed long-time help and would need it for an indefinite period. In some of these cases it could be seen that given time and unusual consideration, the business would finally pay out. In other cases it seemed probable that the business could never pay in full, but might in time work out at ninety or eighty or seventy-five percent. What was to be done?

The banks in this crisis developed a new technique designed to avoid the slow and wasteful process of the bankruptcy courts with the liquidation of "going businesses." Bank creditor committees were formed. The businesses put themselves in the hands of the banks informally. Creditor banks agreed with one another to defer collection of the loans, insisting, as they did so, upon drastic economies in the debtor businesses. In cases where management was good, the banks knew very well that the management was one of the great assets of the business and that the management could handle things for the banks much better than the banks themselves could. In cases where the management was of doubtful integrity or had proved itself incompetent, the credit committees would insist on a change of management as a condition for extending the loans. Sometimes the banks would scale down the loans so as to put the businesses in a position to get new credits from purveyors of raw material. Sometimes the banks would even advance some new money to keep a business functioning, knowing very well that a functioning business might pay out ultimately, while a business that had ceased to function would rapidly disintegrate and dissipate what assets it had. It was a superb piece of credit work.

New York Aid to Rural Banks. Banking policy had many angles, and banking policy in the great financial centers had to overlook the whole country. The great New York banks had correspondent banks in every part of the nation which turned to them for help and to which they gave help, lending against whatever assets the local banks had, including the small receivables of their local customers. In the portfolio of the Chase National Bank of New York there was a note for $104, signed by John Wilhite and Lizzie his wife, secured by a chattel mortgage on Mollie—Mollie being a mare mule sixteen hands high, five years old, and broken to single and double harness—resident in the state of North Carolina. This note had come as part of the collateral to a loan for $100,000 made to a North Carolina banker.

In the first half of December 1920 the old chief of the Chase National Bank, A. Barton Hepburn, stated that he was getting very disquieting reports from the Panhandle of Texas and from Montana regarding the cattle situation. The farmers, under pressure to pay debts, were shipping out their cattle—not merely the fat cattle but also the lean cattle and the she-cattle, breaking up the flocks and herds. And these cattle sold under such stress were obtaining ruinously low prices in the market in Kansas City. Hepburn said, "Now I am going to scurry around and get some money out to the Texas and Montana banks so that they can lend enough to those farmers to keep the flocks and herds together." But he wished a speech made about it which would outline a general policy that might be useful to the banks in this situation.

The speech was made in Iowa City to the bankers of Iowa late in December. After describing the situation to them, the speaker said, "If you have farmer debtors who have fat cattle which they are holding in the hope of higher prices, call their loans, make them sell. They won't get the higher prices. If you have farmer debtors who have corn that they are holding for higher prices, call their loans. Make them sell. They won't get the higher prices. But if you have farmer debtors who have corn and who know how to feed cattle, lend them additional money to enable them to buy these extraordinarily cheap cattle in Kansas City so as to get the lean cattle and the corn together. We must keep agriculture a going concern."

Privately he told the country bankers individually that the Chase National Bank would make them additional loans to help them in carrying out this policy.

Hepburn's Stock Market Pool, December 1920. At approximately the same time Hepburn revealed the existence of a pool that had been organized to engage in some operations in the stock market. There have been no references to this pool in print, and the existence of it was not widely known even in Wall Street at the time. It was a closely guarded secret. The stock market had had a boom in 1919 which culminated in a very sharp break late in the autumn. During 1920 it had been left to its own devices, struggling against tight money, liquidating its debts, but holding without violent breaks and gradually sagging until the fourth quarter, when a sharp break came. Brokers' loans had been $1.75 billion at the end of 1919, and they had been reduced to under $700 million by the end of 1920. Hepburn said that the market was getting discouraged, and that he and a number of other men who felt responsible for the situation had decided that it needed a little support. They were not going to do much. They were going to buy 10,000 shares of United States Steel, and they were going to buy some shares of other pivotal stocks. The point was simply to steady the market. They did not expect to make any money in the pool operations, but they hoped to avoid losses. He said that the pool would begin operation the following morning, namely, December 22, 1920, and that it might be interesting to watch what the market did. The next day the market did turn up, and it continued a gradual rise into the following May, though the pool ceased to operate after a few weeks. It was interesting to see the explanations given by the financial writers in the New York papers, none of whom apparently had any suspicion that a pool was operating. The action of the stock market put new heart and courage into the financial community. The term *pool* is one which suggests a great deal of iniquity, but the present writer is unregenerate enough to believe that this was an act of financial statesmanship,

Organized Commodity Exchanges Met Shock Amazingly Well. The industrial and mercantile community met the shock with extraordinary resourcefulness. The great exchanges, the organized markets in commodities, the New York Cotton Exchange, the Liverpool Cotton Exchange, the Chicago Board of Trade, and others showed extraordinary resourcefulness in diffusing losses. The brokers kept their solvency and paid their debts. On the Liverpool Exchange, Egyptian cotton had been at a very high premium over middling cotton, and middling cotton had been at a very high price. Suddenly the basic price of middling cotton broke violently, and simultaneously the differential for Egyptian cotton practically disappeared. Information at the time was that there were no failures among the Liverpool cotton brokers.

Hedging Protected Millers and Spinners. Cotton spinners and millers normally protect themselves by short sales of the cotton or grain which they buy to work up into cloth or flour—short sales which they cover when the cloth or the flour is ready to market. If the price of wheat goes down, the price of flour will go down. The miller does not care. If the wheat and flour go up, he makes a profit on the wheat he has bought to grind, but he loses on his short sale. If the price of wheat and flour come down, he loses money on the wheat he is grinding, but he makes money on his short sale. He gives his attention to his main business, which is to get a profit out of the differential between the price of wheat and the price of flour, and avoids speculative risks by imposing on some speculator the burden of carrying the risk. But the speculator who has bought wheat for future delivery is not a philanthropist and is not a static person. He may sell the next day, and the man who buys from him may sell a few minutes later. A loss of forty cents a bushel, instead of ruining a miller, may be diffused among fifty to a hundred speculators, each of whom may lose a fraction of a cent. It is rarely necessary to waste tears over the highly organized centers of commodity speculation. They know how to take care of themselves. And they know how to take care of the industries which use them for hedge purposes.

Weak Spots Mapped and Charted by Spring 1921. Businessmen and bankers both did a very thorough job in cleaning up the weak spots and in making readjustments in prices, costs, methods, and the proportions of industrial activity. By early spring 1921 the credit weak spots were mapped and charted. The banks knew what businesses could survive and what businesses must go under or at all events have a readjustment of their financial setup. It was clear that the general credit situation was impregnably strong, and that the credit system would survive the shock.

Costs Rapidly Readjusted. Costs were rapidly readjusted. Raw materials, of course, had fallen drastically. Rentals were in many cases readjusted, often by voluntary negotiations. Sometimes a bank creditors' committee in showing leniency to an embarrassed business would call into the discussion the landlard from whom the business was leasing property and make the general settlement contingent upon the landlord's reducing the rent—a thing which was to the landlord's interest under the circumstances. In some cases it was necessary to put a concern into bankruptcy in order to get rid of losses by impossibly high rentals. The stronger businesses, of course, carried out their contracts until the leases expired.

High Interest Rates Provided Insurance Against Losses. Very often the banks in dealing with embarrassed businesses would reduce interest rates or even waive interest for a time. But the year 1921 remained a year of high interest rates. In this was one of the elements of strength in the situation. It was definitely recognized that there was a very substantial element of insurance in interest rates. The banks could stand a substantial loss on some of their loans in view of the general interest rates prevailing.

Moderate Decline in Wages. Wages declined, although nothing like so much as commodity prices. The following table compares wages and wholesale prices for the years 1914–22 inclusive:

INDEX NUMBERS OF WAGES PER HOUR AND WHOLESALE PRICES IN THE UNITED STATES*

Year	Wages per hour (Exclusive of agriculture)	Wholesale prices (All commodities)
1914	100	100.0
1915	101	102.1
1916	109	125.6
1917	125	172.5
1918	159	192.8
1919	180	203.5
1920	229	226.7
1921	214	143.3
1922	204	142.0

* United States Bureau of Labor Statistics—bases changed.

The year 1921 shows a drop in wage rates per hour of a very moderate sort. The figure was 229 in 1920 and 214 in 1921. Wholesale prices, on the other hand, dropped from a 1920 average of 226.7 to a 1921 average of 143.3. Wages had lagged behind wholesale prices in the years 1916–19 inclusive. They had passed above wholesale prices in 1920. They dropped very moderately in 1921, when wholesale prices made a violent drop.

The decline in wages, however, was a very unequal one. In the hardest pressed industries they dropped very much more, and in their dropping facilitated industrial revival.

Because of Immigration Decline. The basic explanation of the failure of wages in the United States to decline with wholesale prices is to be found in a change that had taken place in our labor supply in the years following 1914. Prior to 1915 we had had an immense immigration, running over one million a year frequently and in two years running between 1.2 and 1.3 million. Of the immigrants that came in, moreover, a very high percentage were young men and women ready for work. This had imposed a drag on the rise of wages in the United States. Wages had risen with the growth of capital and with technological progress year by year. But wages had not risen nearly as rapidly as would have been the case had immigration been shut off and had we been dependent solely on our own internal population growth.

The coming of the war immediately shut off immigration from Europe, and legislation following the war sharply restricted immigration.

The effect of the cessation of immigration was particularly marked in the city of New York. Wages of maidservants, for example, had been $3.50 a week in 1913, with the maid's living provided by the employer. There was a steady stream of young German and Irish women coming into the city, as well as a good many Negro girls coming up from the South. Beginning very early in the war these wages began to mount, and the wages of maidservants reached $18 a week in 1918. After the slump in 1921 they remained at $14 to $15.

We could have had this rise of wages in the United States at any time before the war had we been willing to restrict immigration. The experience of the war itself led us to restrict immigration. We found to our surprise that we had admitted so many new Europeans that it had endangered the national unity. We found our country less homogeneous than seemed safe in wartime, and we restricted immigration.

The failure of wages to decline toward prewar levels, therefore, as commodity prices were declining toward prewar levels, was a legitimate supply-and-demand phenomenon. Men had become scarcer, and therefore dear in relation to the capital and natural resources of the country. A radical permanent rise in wages was therefore explained on economic grounds.

Artificially High Wages in Postwar England Create Chronic Unemployment in 1920s. It is noteworthy that the same phenomenon occurred in England without the same explanation. Wages rose with commodity prices during the war and postwar boom. When commodity prices slumped in England in 1920 and 1921, wages slumped very much less and remained high above prewar levels. In England, however, the explanation was not a change in the supply-and-demand situation affecting labor, but was rather the power of labor unions in maintaining artificially high wage rates. The result of this for England was chronic unemployment throughout the 1920s on a very heavy scale, while in the United States with the revival of 1921–23 we regained full employment at high wages which were economically justified.

Our Unit Bank System Compels Full Liquidation—Contrast with England. A further factor in the United States making for a much fuller and completer readjustment in 1920 than that which England had, was to be found in our system of independent unit banks as contrasted with the great British branch bank system. England had five great banks which dominated the picture, with branches all over the British Isles and over many parts of the world outside. We had 20,000 independent banks, every one of which was under obligation to meet its cash engagements at the clearinghouse every day. It was possible for us, with the aid of the Federal Reserve System, to make our credit readjustment in the crisis orderly, but we had to make it thorough. It was not possible for us to maintain stale and hopeless situations by means of bank credit. Each bank had to clean up in order to keep itself solvent. Certain of the great British banks, as late as 1925, had still uncollected loans to the cotton industry in Manchester, carried over from 1920, and other commitments of similar sort stale and frozen. The forbearance of the British banks had not saved these industries. It had, on the other hand, prevented their passing into stronger hands and into the hands of more alert and flexible management. It had prevented their freeing themselves through bankruptcy from impossible financial burdens. It had prevented their becoming effective again.

Many Worse Things Than Great Break in Prices. A collapse of commodity prices of one hundred points in a single year is not a pleasant thing. It is not a pleasant thing to see well-meaning but relatively ineffective men lose their capital and lose control of their companies and see their companies put into stronger hands through bankruptcy or informal reorganization. And it was certainly not a pleasant thing to see 4,754,000 workmen unemployed, as was the case in 1921. But there are many worse things.

Worse Was Far Heavier Unemployment, 1931–39. One worse thing was the much heavier volume of unemployment which we had in the United States from late 1931 to 1939, despite (or, as later chapters will show, *because of*) all the well-meaning efforts of the New Deal government to make employment by an outpouring of federal funds, by NRA, and by other unsound devices.

Japanese Stagnation, 1920–27. And a worse thing took place in Japan where, early in 1920, the great banks, the concentrated industries, and the government got together, destroyed the freedom of the markets, arrested the decline in commodity prices, and held the Japanese price level high above the receding world level for seven years. During these years Japan endured chronic industrial stagnation and at the end, in 1927, she had a banking crisis of such severity that many great branch bank systems went down, as well as many industries. It was a stupid policy. In the effort to avert losses on inventory representing one year's production, Japan lost seven years, only to incur greatly exaggerated losses at the end. The New Deal began in Japan in early 1920—a planned economy under government direction designed to prevent natural market forces from operating and, above all, designed to protect the general price level.

In contrast, in 1920–21 we took our losses, we readjusted our financial structure, we endured our depression, and in August 1921 we started up again. By the spring of 1923 we had reached new highs in industrial production and we had labor shortages in many lines.

9

The Rapid Revival—
August 1921 to March 1923

The rally in business production and employment that started in August 1921 was soundly based on a drastic cleaning up of credit weakness, a drastic reduction in the costs of production, and the free play of private enterprise. It was not based on governmental policy designed to make business good. The drop in the physical volume of production from the high of July 1920 to the low of 1921 was drastic and was indeed unprecedented in severity, so far as records went, down to that date. The depression was, however, much less severe than that of the 1930s. This was primarily because of the very rapidity of the break in prices and the general readjustment in costs. On the basis of the Federal Reserve Index of Production (which has as its base the average for the years 1923–25) the physical volume of production dropped from 89 in July 1920 to 65 in July 1921. Then the Index of Production began to rise. Moderate improvement began in August 1921. Through 1922 there was strong improvement and by March 1923 the Index of Production had risen to the radical new high of 103, and it rose further to 106 in April 1923.

Little Helped by Outside World. It is noteworthy also that, so far as the outside world was concerned, conditions during this period of strong recovery were very discouraging. Throughout the world there had been the gravest kind of crisis and very deep depression. The tide turned in the United States without outside help. The turn in the United States was followed by a turn in certain other parts of the world—namely, in those countries which had kept closest to the gold standard and which had maintained the soundest public finances—notably England, the Scandinavian countries, Switzerland, and the Netherlands. But prolonged difficulties continued in Germany, in France, in Italy, in Belgium, and in Japan, to say nothing of Austria, Poland, the Balkans, and Latin America.

Break in Building Cost Starts Building Upward in Early 1921. The first sign of recovery in the United States came early in 1921 in the building trade, several months before the general upturn in production began.

Building costs had risen to fantastic heights during the boom of 1919 and 1920. The Index of Construction, taking 1914 as a base, had been reduced to 64.9 in 1918, the second year of the war, had risen to 88.7 in 1919, but had dropped drastically to 48.5 in 1920. It rose to 91.8 in 1921, the rise beginning early in the year with the drop in building costs, and rose to very substantial volume in the latter part of the year. In 1922 it rose to 139.2. The Index of Construction and the Index of Production moved in opposite directions between 1920 and 1921. The volume of production dropped from 124.5 to 103.9 while the volume of construction was rising from 48.5 to 91.8. In 1922 the two indexes moved together again, construction reaching a new high with production approaching 1920 again. The table previously given (p. 39), showing the physical volume of production and construction for the years 1914–22 inclusive, is here repeated.

PHYSICAL VOLUME OF PRODUCTION AND CONSTRUCTION, 1914–22*

Year	Total volume of production	Total volume of construction
1914	100	100
1915	113.7	97.9
1916	120.6	111.3
1917	125.5	93.8
1918	124.5	64.9
1919	116.7	88.7
1920	124.5	48.5
1921	103.9	91.8
1922	121.6	139.2

* Frederick C. Mills, *Economic Tendencies in the United States* (New York, 1932), pp. 188, 191; bases changed from 1913 to 1914.

10

The Government's Contribution to the Revival, 1921–23

N*o Deficit Financing—Overbalanced Budgets Every Year*. From the standpoint of New Deal economics, the United States government in the period 1920–23 was extremely benighted. The idea that an unbalanced budget with vast pump-priming government expenditure is a necessary means of getting out of a depression received no consideration at all. It was not regarded as the function of the government to provide money to make business activity. It was rather the business of the United States Treasury to look after the solvency of the government, and the most important relief that the government felt that it could afford to business was to reduce as much as possible the amount of government expenditure, which had risen to great heights during the war; to reduce taxes—but not much; and to reduce public debt. Government expenditures ran as follows during these years:

UNITED STATES GOVERNMENT EXPENDITURES
(NOT INCLUDING PUBLIC DEBT RETIREMENT)
(In millions of dollars)

Fiscal year 1920 6,403
Fiscal year 1921 5,116
Fiscal year 1922 3,373
Fiscal year 1923 3,295

Taxes ran as follows during these years:

ORDINARY RECEIPTS OF THE
UNITED STATES GOVERNMENT
(In millions of dollars)

Fiscal year 1920 6,695
Fiscal year 1921 5,625
Fiscal year 1922 4,109
Fiscal year 1923 4,007

The public debt was rapidly reduced as the following figures show:

UNITED STATES GOVERNMENT DEBT
(In millions of dollars)
June 30
1920 24,298
1921 23,976
1922 22,964
1923 22,350

Rapid Reduction of Army, Navy, and Civil Service. Nor did the government increase public employment with a view to taking up idle labor. There was reduction in the army and navy in the course of these years, and there was a steady decline in the number of civilian employees of the federal government.

Sound Government Financial and Monetary Policy Generates Business Confidence. This policy on the part of the government generated, of course, a great confidence in the credit of the government, and the strength of the gold dollar was taken for granted. The credit of the government and confidence in the currency are basic foundations for general business confidence. The relief to business through reduced taxes was extremely helpful.

Great Spurt in New Technology, 1921–23. One major factor in the extraordinarily strong business revival of 1921–23 was a great spurt in the application of new technology to industry. During the war and the postwar boom, our industrial system had been overstrained by the heavy demands made upon it. Management, harassed by rush orders, did not have time to make far-reaching plans or to keep pace with the growth of technological knowledge. Our increased production during the war and the postwar boom was much more a matter of increasing the number of wage earners than of increasing the efficiency per man through new technology, through growing skill of labor, and through improved managerial policies.

In the depression of 1921 management had time once more to study new methods and to make long-run plans. Overtime work ceased, shop discipline improved, and men valued their jobs. A great body of new technological ideas was awaiting application. Many of these ideas had been developed as part of the technology of war in the fields of aircraft, artillery, naval construction, fortifications, and the chemistry of explosives. But the same ideas, with modifications, were to have fruitful application to peacetime pursuits. They were waiting to be used. In the years 1921–23 there was widespread application of the improved technology. The following table reveals the facts:

GROWTH OF MANUFACTURING PRODUCTION IN
THE UNITED STATES, 1914–23*

Index Numbers of Physical Volume of Production, Number
of Wage Earners, and per Capita Output

Year	Physical volume of production	Number of wage earners	Output per wage earner
1914	100.0	100.0	100.0
1919	127.7	124.5	102.6
1921	105.7	100.1	105.6
1923	156.3	130.3	120.0

* Frederick C. Mills, *Economic Tendencies in the United States* (New York, 1932), p. 192.

From 1914 to 1919 physical output per wage earner in manufacturing increased only 2.6 percent. From 1921 to 1923 output per wage earner increased 14.4 percent. If those who fear technological improvement were right, then this should have been accompanied by a falling off in the number of workers in manufacturing. It was, however, as shown by our table, accompanied by an increase of 30 percent in the number of wage earners. Rapidly improving technology did not make unemployment. Rather, it helped to generate an immense increase in employment. Production itself generates purchasing power, and therefore creates employment. Production in one place gives rise to demand for production in other places. Be it observed, moreover, that this rapid spurt in technological progress comes, not at the end of the great boom, 1921–29, but, rather, at the beginning of this great boom.

11

The Money Market, 1920–23— Renewed Bank Expansion

A very important factor in the revival, as in all revivals, was an easing of the money market and an expansion of bank credit. There was a very substantial liquidation of bank credit from the high figures of 1920 to the low figures of 1921, very impressive in dollar volume, though less impressive in percentage. The tide of bank credit turned, however, in the latter part of 1921 and a renewed expansion began. National bank figures are better than figures for member banks in the Federal Reserve System in the period 1914–23, because the number of national banks changed very little, while the number of member banks changed a good deal. The following tables make use of national bank figures, Federal Reserve bank figures, and reporting member bank figures.

Gold, Money in Circulation, and Rediscount Rates. The bank credit expansion, 1922–23, which reversed the process of liquidation, was due first to incoming gold, which amounted to about a billion dollars in the years 1921 and 1922; second, to an $800 million decline in money in circulation; and, third, to Federal Reserve policy. The Federal Reserve banks reduced their rediscount rates in 1921. Beginning in the first half of the year by successive stages of a half percent each, the New York Federal Reserve Bank reduced its rate from seven percent to four percent in the summer of 1922. During this same period rediscounts were steadily declining, though the steady reduction in the rate, which brought the Federal Reserve rate well below the market, undoubtedly retarded the decline in the volume of rediscounts. But member banks continued to get out of debt to the Federal Reserve banks, and rediscounts fell from the peak figure in the autumn of 1920 of $2.75 billion to $1 billion at the beginning of 1922.

The First Large Open Market Operation of the Federal Reserve Banks, 1922. A second contributing factor in Federal Reserve policy was open market purchases of United States government securities by the Federal Reserve banks. Beginning early in 1922 there was a sharp increase in the holdings of government securities by the Federal Reserve banks, the total rising from roughly $250 million to approximately $650 million.

The policy that lay behind these purchases initially was not a desire to make the money market easy, or a desire to facilitate bank expansion. These were unintended and unanticipated consequences. The motive, as explained privately by a member of the Federal Reserve Board early in 1922, was a much simpler one. The Federal Reserve System had grown enormously during the war and postwar boom. With its growth there had come a great volume of expense. The system needed $45 million a year to meet its expenses and to pay dividends on its stock. This meant a billion dollars of earning assets at 4.5 percent. When, in early 1922, rediscounts fell below a billion, the Federal Reserve banks began to buy government securities to uphold total earning assets. The authority for this statement, who was one of the very able men in the Federal Reserve System, was chuckling over the failure of some of his associates to realize that increased purchases of government securities by the Federal Reserve System would accelerate the process of paying off rediscounts. In buying government securities the Federal Reserve banks increased the reserve balances of the member banks, and the member banks used these increased reserves in reducing their debt to the Federal Reserve banks. Rediscounts dropped to around $400 million in the summer of 1922. But they did not thus use the whole of the increase in reserves, and the result of these government security purchases, taken in conjunction with the other factors mentioned above, was a relaxation in the money market, a lowering of interest rates generally, and a renewal of the expansion of bank credit.

At no time, however, did interest rates in the period, 1920–23, go really low, as shown by the following table on open market commercial paper rates in New York City.

OPEN MARKET COMMERCIAL PAPER RATES IN NEW YORK CITY*

	High	Low
1920	8	6
1921	7¾	5
1922	5	4
1923	5½	4½

* *Annual Report of Federal Reserve Board* (1927), p. 96

The lowest rate in the whole period for open market commercial paper was four percent, and this prevailed for only one month in the whole four years, 1920–23 inclusive. The Federal Reserve System gave the economic situation a dose of strychnine, but it was a relatively mild dose.

The *Chase Economic Bulletin* (July 20, 1921) contained an article called

OPERATIONS OF NATIONAL BANKS*
(In millions of dollars)

	Total resources	U.S. securities owned	Other securities owned	Total investments in securities	Loans and discounts	Total loans, discounts, and investments	Demand, time, and U.S. deposits
June 4, 1913	11,037	789	1,089	1,878	6,143	8,021	6,022
June 30, 1914	11,482	790	1,116	1,906	6,430	8,336	6,358
May 1, 1917	16,144	768	1,950	2,719	8,713	11,470	9,696
High point, 1919–20	22,711 Dec. 31, 1919	4,028 May 12, 1919	1,985 Dec. 31, 1919	5,877 May 12, 1919	12,416 Sept. 8, 1920	16,612 May 4, 1920	13,914 Dec. 31, 1919
Intermediate low point	19,014 Sept. 6, 1921	1,862 Sept. 6, 1921	1,917 June 30, 1920	3,835 Sept. 6, 1921	10,978 Sept. 6, 1921	14,813 Sept. 6, 1921	12,143 Sept. 6, 1921
Condition, December 29, 1922 ..	21,975	2,656	2,348	5,004	11,600	16,604	14,159

*Chase Economic Bulletin, March 27, 1923, p. 15.

OPERATIONS OF FEDERAL RESERVE BANKS AND REPORTING MEMBER BANKS
(In millions of dollars)

	Federal Reserve Banks		All Reporting Member Banks						
	Discounts	Total earning assets	Demand, time, and U.S. deposits	Total loans, discounts, and investments**	Total loans and discounts**	"All other" loans and discounts†	Total investments in securities	Investments in U.S. securities	Rediscounts and bills payable at Federal Reserve banks
March 30, 1917	20	168							
Approximate high point, 1919–20	2,827 Nov. 5, 1920	3,422 Oct. 15, 1920	14,465 June 18, 1920	17,284 Oct. 15, 1920	*	*	*	3,267 May 2, 1919	2,278 Nov. 5, 1920
Approximate intermediate low point	380 July 26, 1922	1,021 Aug. 9, 1922	13,002 July 27, 1921	14,526 Mar. 8, 1922	10,739 July 26, 1922	7,002 July 5, 1922	3,229 July 27, 1921	1,190 July 27, 1921	98 July 26, 1922
Condition, March 7, 1923	571	1,135	15,341	16,338	11,635	7,645	4,704	2,518	372

* Separate figures not available.
** Including rediscounts at Federal Reserve banks.
† "All other" loans and discounts are those not secured by United States obligations or by other bonds and stocks and are sometimes called "commercial" loans. These figures include rediscounts at Federal Reserve banks.

"The Gold and Rediscount Policy of the Federal Reserve Banks,"[1] which maintained that rediscount rates should always be held above the market, meaning by the "market" the rate which great city banks make to those prime borrowing customers who have accounts with several banks. The *Chase Economic Bulletin* of March 27, 1923, protested against the artificially generated expansion of bank credit as masking the underlying shortage of real capital which four years of war and four more years of disorganization after the war had brought about, and urged that higher interest rates be called for, both to increase the volume of savings and to make sure that the capital that was created would be used for the most important purposes. The tendency to substitute bank credit for real capital was looked upon as a very ominous tendency. The years 1924–29, as we shall later see, abundantly justified these apprehensions. The Federal Reserve System itself took alarm in late 1922, and reversed its policy in early 1923, the New York Federal Reserve Bank raising its rediscount rate from 4 percent to 4.5 percent, and the system selling substantial blocks of government securities.

In retrospect one may hold that this first dose of strychnine did little harm and some good, and may recognize it as one of the factors, although not the dominating factor, in the strong business revival of 1921 to 1923. Great harm came from the strychnine administered in 1924, and above all, from the renewal of the dose in 1927. There is no racetrack which has a code of ethics which permits doping the same horse three times.

---

[1] This article is reproduced as a chapter in A. Barton Hepburn's *History of Currency in the United States* (New York: Macmillan, 1924). It was reproduced in full also in the *Commercial & Financial Chronicle,* July 23, 1921, pp. 349–54.

12

Our Foreign Policy, 1919–24

The whole of the year 1923 was one of strong industrial activity in the United States. The Federal Reserve Index of Industrial Production,[1] based on physical volume shows 1923 standing high above 1922 and high above 1924. A sharply declining tendency showed itself in the early part of 1924, and the summer of 1924 revealed a real slump. We had reached the end of the time when we could make strong progress with the world outside slipping downward, and we had reached the end of the time when city industry alone could move forward with agriculture depressed by its bad export market.

Trade Balances, Tariffs, and Export Trade. From the end of the war it had been clear to economists and to bankers in the great financial centers that the United States, having changed from a prewar debtor position to a postwar creditor position, must maintain a liberal foreign trade policy or else suffer a great loss in export trade. Before the war we had sent out a surplus of exports over imports because we were in debt. Countries which before the war had an export surplus or a so-called favorable balance of trade were the United States, Brazil, British India, Haiti, and Guatemala—debtor countries, which like an individual debtor, could not afford to consume all that they produced and had to turn over a part of what they produced to their creditors. Countries which had the so-called unfavorable balance of trade, or import surplus, were Great Britain, France, Germany, Switzerland, the Netherlands—capitalist countries, creditor countries, which like an individual capitalist could afford to consume more than they produced with their own labor—and liked it. In prewar days Great Britain regularly sent out about $2 billion worth of exports and received about $3

---

[1] The curve for this index will be found in the Federal Reserve Chart Book issued November 9, 1939. I do not trust the new Federal Reserve Index of Production based on the 1935–39 average, for the reasons which have been presented by General Leonard Ayres in the monthly letter of the Cleveland Trust Company, September 15, 1940.

billion worth of imports—an import surplus of a billion dollars. This did not diminish the ability of the British people to buy their own products. The excess goods were sold in the British market, but the money was turned over in the form of interest and dividend payments to Britishers, increasing the national income by the same amount as the surplus goods which came in, and leaving their buying power for British goods undiminished. The import surplus represented a net addition to the welfare of the British Isles.

If, in the United States, we tried to prevent our foreign debtors from sending us goods with which to pay interest and amortization on their debts, by raising our tariffs to keep out their goods, then we necessarily ruined our export trade. They could pay their debts and continue to buy goods in our market only if they sent us a larger volume of goods than they had sent us in prewar days.

The Abortive Reeducation of the Republican Leaders. There was a pretty clear understanding of these points in 1920, both in financial circles and in Washington. The old Republican leaders understood it. Senator Boies Penrose of Pennsylvania understood it, and decided that it was necessary to have a reversal of Republican policy on the tariff.[2]

A report was made to the Republican National Convention in 1920 by an advisory committee on policies and platform (of which Ogden L. Mills was chairman of the Executive Committee, Samuel McCune Lindsay, staff director, and Jacob H. Hollander, associate staff director) which contained an important section on international trade and credits produced by a subcommittee, of which Frank A. Vanderlip was chairman. This report will be found in the *Republican Campaign Textbook* of 1920 (pp. 379–97), which discusses in a realistic way the shift of the United States from a debtor position to a creditor position, and the significance of that shift for our future trade balances. The able men of the Republican Party were really studying economics before the Republican National Convention met. It was clear that they knew that the Republican Party must reverse its position regarding tariffs if we were to continue to have a satisfactory export trade.

So well was this understood that there appeared in the Republican platform of 1920 a remarkable and unprecedented plank—the substance of which was that in view of "the uncertain and unsettled condition of international balances" the Republican Party could not say what it would do about the tariff a year hence—a cautious plank, a compromise designed to avoid unnecessary friction in the convention. The plank even included a reaffirmation of the Republican Party's belief in protective tariffs. Neither

---

[2] I learned this at the time from A. Barton Hepburn, and from the chairman of one of the important committees of the House of Representatives. Both these men told me that Republican policy on the tariff was definitely to be reversed, and I had the same information from others who knew what was going on.

the plank nor the committee report definitely drew the conclusion that the tariffs must not be raised above the rates of the Underwood Tariff of 1913—which rates, incidentally, included a great deal of protection. But both the committee report and the tariff plank were definitely designed to foreshadow a radical change in Republican attitude toward the tariff and were intended to serve notice that the tariffs were not to be raised.[3]

This plank traced especially to the work of four extraordinarily able and enlightened men: Ogden L. Mills, William Allen White, Professor Samuel McCune Lindsay of Columbia University, and Professor Jacob Hollander of Johns Hopkins University.[4]

Well-laid plans, however, are not always successful. The election of 1920 was a great landslide which brought into Congress a great many new and untried and inexperienced Republicans from the West and from the South. Penrose died and the old leadership lost its control. The election also brought into the White House a man little trained in economics, who looked at economic issues from the standpoint of political tradition and emotion, Warren G. Harding.

Following the election the four men named above, who were especially responsible for the tariff plank of the Republican platform in 1920, visited President Harding to urge upon him that the plank be respected and that the tariffs not be raised. One of the four remembered that President Harding said that he had always had an affection for the protective tariff as a political issue, and all four of them remembered that President Harding said, "But what would the Home Market Club of Boston say?"

The Tariffs of 1921 and 1922. And so the tariffs were raised, first by an agricultural tariff bill in 1921, which had relatively little significance because agriculture was an export industry, and, second, by the Fordney bill of 1922, which raised rates sharply on a wide range of manufactured goods, the kind of goods we ought to have been importing from Europe.

Even the agricultural tariff law made immediate trouble. At the Minnesota Bankers Convention of 1921 there was great complaint that Canadian wheat, which had formerly come to the Minneapolis mills to be ground, was being diverted to England, taking work away from the mills and transportation from the railroads which would have brought the grain to Minneapolis and would have taken the flour for export to the seaboard. And there was complaint too on the Montana border that cattlemen on the

---

[3] The full text of the plank follows: "International Trade and Tariff. The uncertain and unsettled conditions of international balances, the abnormal economic and trade situation of the world, and the impossibility of forecasting accurately even the near future preclude the formulation of a definite program to meet conditions a year hence. But the Republican Party reaffirms its belief in the protective principle and pledges itself to a revision of the tariff as soon as conditions shall make it necessary for the preservation of the home market for American labor, agriculture, and industry" (*Commercial & Financial Chronicle*, June 19, 1920, p. 2539).

[4] I have since talked with all four of these men about the plank.

Montana ranges were prevented by the tariff on Canadian cattle from bringing in the lean Canadian cattle to feed on the Montana ranges.

The Seeds of Death Planted. But the great harm came from the Fordney bill of 1922. This imposed a grave barrier against European industrial revival, and it imposed a deadly handicap on the export trade of the American farmer whose market was primarily in Europe—an export trade which amounted to sixty percent of the cotton produced, forty percent of the lard, more than twenty percent of the wheat, forty percent of the tobacco. The seeds of death were introduced into our industrial revival when this tariff bill was passed.

The high protective tariff of 1922 was one of three major mistakes in international policy which the United States contributed to the evil days that were to come. The two others were (a) our rejection of the League of Nations, and (b) our mishandling of the problem of the inter-Allied debts, the debt created by the approximately $10 billion which our government loaned to Allied governments during the war and in the post-Armistice period down to June 30, 1919.

Woodrow Wilson and the League of Nations. Woodrow Wilson had certain personal qualities which irritated and antagonized to an extraordinary degree those people who did not like him. But he was the greatest man, the most upright man, and the most far-seeing man who has held great public office anywhere in the world within the memory of men now living.[5]

Wilson doubtless erred in going in person to Paris. He doubtless erred in not taking with him important Republican leaders. He doubtless erred in taking too uncompromising a stand against amendments proposed to the League of Nations by honest opponents in the American Senate—among whom we should emphatically not include Henry Cabot Lodge. But Wilson's failure to accomplish his great purposes primarily arose from a different sort of weakness—he had a grave sickness, probably his first apoplectic stroke, in the midst of the peace negotiations in Paris. This was not publicly known at the time. A few people knew it. One man closely associated with President Wilson in Paris said in 1920 that in the early part of his stay there Wilson was alert, flexible, resourceful, eager for information, open-minded to suggestions. Then for a prolonged period nobody saw him. When he could be seen again he was aloof, remote, inflexible, uninterested in new ideas, dogmatic in his insistence on fixed purposes. This man was sure that Wilson had had his first stroke in that interval. Subsequent confirmation of a grave and disturbing sickness in Paris has come from two sources. Mrs. Wilson in her *My Memoirs*[6] gives a brief account of this sickness. The second confirmation comes in a series of

---

[5] This writer takes pride in the fact that he recognized this while Wilson was alive, and that he supported Woodrow Wilson in virtually every measure he proposed, with the exception of the Adamson bill of 1916, where Wilson made his one big concession to political expediency.

[6] (New York, 1938), pp. 348–49.

Saturday Evening Post articles[7] by former President Hoover. Had Woodrow Wilson had his full energies we should have entered the League of Nations.

The young student of economics, sociology, and history is easily impressed with the doctrine that history is made by impersonal social forces, irresistible in character. When one sees history being made from the inside it is impossible to avoid the conclusion that a vast deal depends upon the strengths and weaknesses of the leading participants. As this book proceeds, a good many such cases will be cited. The failure of the League of Nations was the failure of Woodrow Wilson's health, just as the passage of the tariff of 1922 traced primarily to Warren G. Harding's abysmal economic ignorance.

Ruinous Effect of Our Staying out of League. Our absence from the League of Nations left that organization with inadequate strength, and, above all, left it unduly weighted by France.

The peace treaties contained many dangerous and impossible provisions. They split the Austro-Hungarian Empire, which had been a great free trade area, into a large number of small succession states which, hating one another and fearing one another, erected high tariff barriers against one another. Instead of having one currency system, they had a large number of fluctuating currencies which each tried to protect, not merely by orthodox currency measures, but also by shifting restrictions on international payments and on the free movements of funds as well as commodities. Eastern Europe was Balkanized.

Austria, cut off from the great region of which she had been the governmental, financial, and trading center, found herself with an immense problem of readjustment. For many years she was incapable of solving the problem, and to a considerable extent lived on international charity. After ten years she appeared to have worked it out by a great reduction in the population of the city of Vienna, as city activities diminished, and by an increase in the proportion of her agricultural activities as her people moved from the valleys up the mountain sides to thinner land where meager crops could be obtained.

The heart of the problem left by the Treaty of Versailles centered about the relations between France and Germany, and the problem, above all, of reparations payments by Germany to France.

The problem of reparations was one which could be solved only if a very realistic economic policy were adopted. But French policy was primarily political. France still feared a stricken and beaten Germany. She was much more concerned about keeping Germany politically weak than she was about getting real reparations out of Germany. Real reparations from Germany could come only from a Germany which was economically strong.

---

[7] November 1, 8, 15, 1941.

It is not easy to assert that these French fears were foolish fears in the light of developments since 1936, or for that matter since early 1933. Similar fears were clearly shared by Denmark, which refused to take full advantage of the Treaty of Versailles. The treaty restored to Denmark Schleswig-Holstein, which Bismarck had wrested from her in 1864. Denmark, looking forward twenty years, sought to avoid German resentment by holding a plebiscite, leaving the people of Schleswig-Holstein themselves to decide whether they wished to stay with Germany or to return to Denmark, with the result that only the northern part returned to Denmark.

The two significant points from the standpoint of the American participation in the League of Nations are: (1) if we had been wholeheartedly in the League of Nations, France would have had much less fear regarding her future security, and (2) if we had been active and powerful in the League of Nations, we and the British, acting together, could have controlled League of Nations policy, and could have forced upon France a much more reasonable attitude toward the question of reparations and the question of Germany's industrial revival than England alone was able to do.

As will be seen later, the democratic Germany of the Weimar Constitution, the Germany of Ebert, of Wirth, of Stresemann, and of Bruening, was a Germany with which the world could have lived at peace, and was a Germany which could have endured, had outside pressure, and above all, French pressure, been less remorseless.

13

Germany, 1918–24

Germany a Hollow Shell at End of War. Germany at the end of the war was economically a hollow shell. Germany's war economic policy had been extraordinarily efficient in sucking out of the people all their resources and all their vitality to put guns and food into the hands of the soldiers at the front. She had not been invaded, but invaders could hardly have done a more efficient job of denuding her of resources than her own war government. Her government, moreover, had been financially a gambler, counting on winning the war, counting on bolstering the weakness of her internal finances with requisitions on a conquered France, and had overloaded the Reichsbank with government paper. Germany had, at the end of the war, a system of public finance and currency vulnerable in the extreme.

Unrealistic Reparations Demands of Versailles Treaty. To call upon Germany suddenly for great reparations payments in a situation of this sort was natural enough, perhaps inevitable, in the temper of the times, but it was certainly economically unrealistic. Whatever she paid under those conditions could only be at the expense of further economic demoralization, and lessened the ability to make systematic payments in the future. The Treaty of Versailles itself imposed reparations payments of a magnitude which not even an economically powerful Germany could have made. But the payments demanded of Germany in her weakened condition were wholly fantastic.

Heavy Initial Payments in Gold, Railroad Equipment, and Flocks and Herds. Heavy initial payments were made. Part of the gold of the Reichsbank was taken, the German merchant marine was surrendered. Payments were taken in the form of rolling stock of the railroads and flocks and herds—a not unnatural procedure on the part of people who had seen Germany systematically stealing rolling stock of railroads and flocks and herds from France and Belgium while the war was on. And it was not an unnatural procedure to take the merchant marine when the world had seen Germany, in defiance of international law, sinking merchant vessels, even neutral merchant vessels, without warning and without giving aid to the helpless seamen to save their lives.

Later Payments Made by Selling Paper Marks. But these things did not do the Allies much good, and they greatly impaired Germany's ability to make further reparations payments. Increasing demands were made for payments, and increasingly the only resource which Germany could find with which to make the payments was the sale of newly created marks in the speculative foreign exchange markets at whatever price they would bring.

The prewar gold mark had an exchange value of 23.8¢, but when postwar trade in the mark began in the summer of 1919, the mark was offered at 8¢. From then on, progressively, the mark went down.

German Income Tax System Helpless in Inflation—Contrast with France. The pressure of reparations payments did not constitute the only burden on the German mark. The German tax system, for one thing, admirable in a stable economy, was utterly helpless in a period of rapidly increasing currency depreciation. Germany relied primarily on the income tax, in which the taxes of a given year are based on the income of the preceding year. With rapid currency depreciation, prices rose rapidly and government expenditures rose rapidly while revenues based on last year's income could never catch up. France, as we shall see, with a much less scientific tax system, one in which the primary reliance was indirect taxes and the revenues from fiscal monopolies, had nonetheless a tax system much better adapted to meeting currency depreciation. French indirect taxes and French revenues from fiscal monopolies were based on prices currently prevailing, and as the franc went down and prices rose, these revenues automatically rose concurrently. As we shall later see, this was a very important factor in saving the French franc from the complete collapse that the German mark went through.

Weak and Shifting Governments Feed the People with Paper Marks. Germany, like France, had a succession of weak governments based on uncertain and shifting majorities in the Reichstag. The changes of ministry were less frequent in Germany than in France, but the position of the ministry was usually precarious. Weak democratic governments are very likely to yield in times of stress to popular clamor for increasing expenditures for relief and public works. Germany yielded to this pressure, borrowing paper marks from the Reichsbank for the people, and these marks, sold abroad in the foreign exchange markets, brought in year after year a great import surplus to Germany. The German people were kept alive at the expense of speculators in marks in foreign countries.

The German Inflation. The story of the German inflation has been told many times and it is unnecessary to go into detail with it here.

The government and the people lived on the credit of the Reichsbank while it lasted. The Reichsbank printed banknotes to supply the government with funds with which to employ and feed the prople. The law with respect to the banknotes issued was scrupulously observed, and the government never took any notes from the Reichsbank without turning over government bonds or other government securities to the Reichsbank in equal amount. As the notes increased in number and in size—1,000-mark notes replacing 10-mark notes, 1,000,000-mark notes replacing 1,000-mark notes, until finally trillion-mark notes were in common circulation (the trillion-mark note being valued at the end at one gold mark)—the notes continued to bear the legend "Verfaelschung gesetzlich verboten" ("Counterfeiting Forbidden by Law"). From the summer of 1919 to the time of the Dawes Plan in 1924, the history of the quotation for marks in the foreign exchange market in New York City is, briefly, as follows. They started in the summer of 1919 at approximately eight cents each. They reached, at the lowest, sixteen trillion marks to the dollar. They were finally stablilized at four trillion marks to the dollar.

Purchasers of the notes of the Reichsbank finally used them in not a few cases for wallpaper.

Inflation Produces Economic Demoralization. The effect of this unprecedented and incredible depreciation of paper money upon the economic life of a great industrial nation was utterly demoralizing. Thrift of course disappeared. Thrift became folly. Lloyd George told a story, which he placed in Austria, where a similar inflation took place—although a much more moderate one, because the Austrian crown was finally stabilized at only 14,000 to 1. The story was that of two brothers who shared equally in an inheritance. One was a steady, thrifty lad who, remembering the teaching of his father, saved his money, and put it in the bank. The other was a reckless blade who spent all his inheritance for bottles of wine. He drank up the wine and then he sold the empty bottles for more money than his thrifty brother had in the bank.

Speculators Grow Rich. It was a situation in which the business manager, the engineer, the producer had very little chance. Production was demoralized, speculation took its place. The most successful speculation was speculation on borrowed money. With the mark declining rapidly the wise thing to do was to go heavily into debt, purchase any kind of real values—real estate, commodities, foreign exchange—hold them for a time, then sell a small part of the purchases and pay off the debt. Huge concentrations of wealth were accomplished in precisely this way, the alert speculators borrowing money and buying up from their necessitous holders businesses, buildings, commodities, and every kind of real values.

But Are Often Ruined by Zigzag Course of Mark. The fly in the speculator's ointment came in the fact that the downward movement of the mark was not in a smooth curve but rather a very jagged curve. From time to time there would be convulsive recovery movements in the mark, commodity prices would drop violently, and the thinly margined speculator who had just borrowed a great deal of money would find himself bankrupt. Even Hugo Stinnes, the most notorious and the largest scale operator of this kind, who amassed a vast economic empire while the mark was declining, overplayed his hand, borrowed too heavily in the late stages of the depreciation, and was finally obliged to hand over to his creditors the greater part of his accumulation.

Economic Middle Class Wiped Out. The German economic middle class was pretty well wiped out in this process. One of the causes of the political weakness of the German democracy in later years was precisely this wiping out of the economic middle class.

Speculative Building. There was a good deal of feverish construction of a speculative character as the mark declined. Men could speculate in brick and mortar and men could speculate in labor with which to put brick and mortar together. Men engaging in building operations, however, could not plan intelligently to put up buildings that would be serviceable to the German economy, for with the constant violent fluctuation of values and prices there was no foundation for sound calculation.

Working Capital Disappears. Working capital largely disappeared in Germany during the course of this inflation, and the fixed capital which was created in the form of buildings, factories, and the like proved itself very inadequately adapted to the needs of a postwar Germany after the mark was stabilized and the nightmare was over. The standard of life of the people sank steadily.

The Fallacy That Progressive Exchange Depreciation Helps Exports. There was an important body of opinion which held that the depreciation of the German mark would stimulate German exports by giving Germany an advantage in competition in the international markets, and that this would stimulate production for export and make for general prosperity. But the figures all tell a different story. The following table gives representative figures for the years 1919–21 inclusive.

GERMAN FOREIGN TRADE*

	1,000,000 paper marks			1,000,000 gold marks**		
	Imports	Exports	Balances	Imports	Exports	Balances
Monthly average, 1913	. . . .	. . . .	. . . .	927	871	−56
Monthly average, July 1919– May 1920	4,984	2,924	−2,059	571	256	−315
Monthly average, May– December 1921	9,885	8,366	−1,518	373	304	−69

* *Journal of the American Bankers Association*, March 1922.
** Gold marks obtained by multiplying paper mark figures for each month by percentage of parity for that month of German mark in terms of American dollar.

The theory that exchange depreciation helped exports ran definitely contrary to the facts in all the major countries of postwar continental Europe. And the moment stabilization came to the currencies which were depreciated there was a radical improvement in the relation of exports to imports.

During the postwar years when their exchange rates were falling, French and Italian exports were hampered, not helped. Between 1919 and 1926 they amounted to only 74 percent of imports in the case of France, and 56 percent in the case of Italy. With the benefits of stable currency at work these figures rose for the 1927–31 period to 89 percent and 73 percent respectively. Figures are available in terms of quantities for Belgium and Germany. It appears that Belgian exports increased more than 30 percent in the three years following stabilization of the currency, while German exports increased no less than 160 percent.[1]

Amount of Reparations Payments to January 1923. The influence of pressure, primarily French pressure, upon Germany for reparations payments during this catastrophic period was very great. It was virtually impossible for Germany to get a breathing spell while the pressure continued, and quite impossible for the German government to get any foreign credits with which to gain time so that she might introduce financial reforms. In early 1923 the German government attempted to float a $50 million "gold loan." The Reparations Commission, after deliberating, vote that while Germany was free to issue such a loan, she would not be free to pay it back if, at the time of its maturity, she were in default on reparations account. Obviously no foreign lender could be interested in such a loan under such conditions. French insistence upon payment regardless of Germany's capacity to pay made the German situation pretty hopeless.

This is not, however, to excuse the German financial authorities for their failure to make use of very much more heroic measures.

The extent of the burden of payments by Germany from the Armistice down to January 1923 was very much in dispute at the time. Some German claims were fantastic, among them Rathenau's estimate that Germany had paid $11 billion. By January 1, 1923, Germany had surrendered in cash, in state properties in the ceded territories, in restitution of Allied property found in Germany, in Allied expenses in Germany, and in sequestrated German property in foreign lands, a sum estimated by the *New York Times* on April 15, 1923, at $3.85 billion.

German credits on reparations account as set forth by the Reparations Commission at the same time were very much smaller than these figures indicated. The significant point in connection with these figures, however,

---

[1] *Chase Economic Bulletin,* May 9, 1933, p. 6.

is not to be found in the benefit that the Allies got from them, which was comparatively small, but in the costs which they imposed on Germany.

France Moves into the Ruhr, January 11, 1923. With the German economic situation virtually hopeless, and with the German government clearly in default on reparations payments, the French government on January 11, 1923, exercised its undoubtedly legal rights under the treaty and moved into the German industrial Ruhr with an army of occupation to seize "productive guarantees" as a means of compelling German compliance with the impossible treaty requirements for reparations payments. France did this against the advice of her former Allies in the war, and the effect upon world opinion was very bad. Germany was further demoralized—France was in no way helped.

14

France, 1918–24

French Prewar and Wartime Deficits. We turn now to the parallel story of the financial developments in France during the period when Germany was sinking so rapidly. France entered the war with bad government finances. She had a national debt of 30 billion gold francs as against an estimated national wealth of 300 billion gold francs at the beginning of the war. France had had chronic deficits for many years before the war. There was governmental extravagance, and there was a great reluctance on the part of the people to submit to direct taxes. They did tolerate very heavy indirect taxes. When Caillaux undertook early in 1914 to introduce an income tax of 2 percent in the effort to balance the French budget, the outcry in France was so extreme that one would have supposed that the end of the world had come. During the war France did relatively little with taxation, and the public debt ran up from 30 billion to 147 billion francs before the war was over.

French Postwar Deficits. Then France began to have some real deficits. Adherents of the school of Keynes and Hansen would do well to study the history of French finance from 1918 to 1926. The one difference between the policies followed in France in this period and the policies advocated by the New Deal spenders for the United States is to be found in the fact that the French were ashamed of it and tried to conceal it and to find excuses for it, whereas the New Deal spenders would glorify it and call it "investment."

Exact facts regarding the French budget and the total of French expenditures were very difficult to obtain in the period following the war. Expenditures were concealed under a multitude of rubrics.[1]

---

[1] It was the present writer's unhappy duty at an international banking conference in Atlantic City late in 1919 to challenge the figures presented by French representatives, who asserted that the French budget was balanced, and to demonstrate that it was unbalanced by at least 13 billion francs. But the full figures were far from accessible at that time, and figures later available made it clear that the French government deficit in 1919 was not the paltry 13 billion which the present writer was then able to find, but rather was 46,735,000,000 francs.

The point was that French financial accounting dealt not only with "the budget," which could easily be balanced by making it equal the taxes, but also the "special budget recoverable" (from Germany), the "special budget" (not recoverable), the "annexed budgets," and the "special accounts." When all these were taken together the French figures ran approximately as follows:[2]

FRENCH GOVERNMENT POSTWAR DEFICITS
(In millions of francs)

	1919	1920	1921	1922	1923	1924
Expenditures	54,956	57,501	46,492	37,929	37,944	41,214
Revenues	8,221	15,469	18,511	19,014	21,307	27,083
Deficit	46,735	42,032	27,981	18,915	16,637	14,131

"Reparations" Actually Paid by French. France wanted reparations, and the term *reparations* had a very real meaning to the French people. Here were the devastated northern provinces, and they wanted them repaired. The Germans were obligated under the treaty to repair them. When German payments were insufficient for the purpose, the French government anticipated them, borrowing to set the work going to restore the devastation. When critics of French financial policy pointed out how inadequate the taxation was in relation to the vast expenditures, the answer was, "The Boche will pay"; and when year after year the German payments were disappointingly small, the declamation changed from the indicative to the imperative mood, and the answer was, "The Boche must pay."

Weak and Short-lived Ministries Afraid to Face Financial Facts. The French financial fabric was crumbling. Weak ministry succeeded weak ministry, each too much afraid of its own tenure of office to venture to tell the financial truth to the people, each holding onto office a few weeks longer, concealing the facts and waiting for the next ministry to tell the truth to the people. The franc slipped ominously in the foreign exchanges. A hectic inflation came in France. A financially collapsing Germany was blamed for the financial troubles of France, and the French Army moved in and occupied the Ruhr. This was on January 11, 1923. French economic evacuation of the Ruhr came November 15, 1923, and military evacuation July 1925.

Occupation of Ruhr Harmed Both Germany and France. The occupation of the Ruhr involved financial burdens rather than financial gains for France. It was demoralizing in the extreme to German industry and finance, both in the occupied and the unoccupied territory. Ordinary trade processes were dislocated. Military decisions were substituted for business contracts. The normal course of trade was interrupted. For example,

---

[2] *Chase Economic Bulletin,* June 21, 1926, p. 5.

shipments of coal from the Ruhr to East Prussia in cars which would have returned from East Prussia loaded with potatoes for Ruhr consumption—usual at the season when the occupation first began—were promptly stopped. France got very little coal and coke from the Ruhr compared with what she had been getting before the occupation. Unoccupied Germany likewise was unable to get coal in any quantity from the Ruhr and many of her industries were consequently in a precarious position. France experienced heavy losses and Germany's abilities to make reparations payments were gravely impaired.

In the holding of part of Germany by armies of occupation under the terms of the peace treaty, the Allies had sought "guaranties" that Germany would perform her obligations under the treaty. In the seizing of the Ruhr, France sought in addition a "productive guaranty." But the whole theory of guaranties and productive guaranties proved abortive. If Germany were to pay she must be put in a position of economic strength and not in a position of humiliating helplessness. Or at least so it seemed to us in that benighted time. We were not prepared in 1923 and 1924 to adopt the ideals and methods of Hitler, to occupy all of Germany, to turn the Germans into slaves, and to extract from an enslaved people by terroristic methods all their surplus over a bare subsistence. We turned to methods that were more humane, to methods designed to make it to the interest of Germany to pay what she could, and to methods designed to permit Germany and her conquerors to share in an expanding and productive economic life.

15

The Dawes Plan

The Reforms Needed. It was clear enough to informed students of economics and international finance what Europe and the United States needed to do to get things straightened out, long before the Ruhr crisis came. The elements in the problem were the following:

1. Reparations payments had been set far too high. They had to be reduced to magnitudes within the power of the German people to pay and to magnitudes that the German people recognized they could pay. It was necessary that they should be arrested entirely for a time, or almost entirely, and that a schedule should be established under which reparations payments could rise as Germany's capacity to pay increased.

2. The debts of Britain, France, Italy, and Belgium to the United States, and of France, Italy, and Belgium to Great Britain, were likewise of a magnitude that looked pretty hopeless in the early postwar years. Indeed, the debts of the Continental countries to the United States and Britain were obviously greater that could be paid in full, even if a long schedule of payments were arranged. The British, as we shall see in our chapter dealing with the intergovernmental debts, made a settlement with us in which they asked for and received very moderate concessions on June 19, 1923. For several years the other debts made very little of a problem for the foreign exchanges, as no payments were made and we contented ourselves with allowing interest to accrue. But it was obviously necessary, if these countries were to enjoy private credit, that the question of their debts to the United States government be adjusted in a sound way.

3. All the Continental belligerents, victors and vanquished, had unbalanced budgets, and were borrowing and spending far more than the tax revenues collected; and all of them had currencies which, lacking gold redemption and increasing steadily in volume, were fluctuating violently and depreciating rapidly. There was great need for the balancing of budgets and for the stabilization of currencies with gold.

4. As a means of facilitating the balancing of budgets and the stabilization of currencies, there was need of financial aid from the strong creditor countries. This should take the form of new loans, the proceeds of which were to be taken partly in gold, to build up the reserves of the banks of issue. These new loans would assist the financially stricken countries in reorganizing their finances, and above all, enable them to cease borrowing from the central banks of issue and ruining their currencies.

5. Finally, it was obviously necessary, if international credits were to be of any use or were ever to be repaid, that the movement of goods from country to country must be facilitated, that tariffs must be lowered, quotas or other trade barriers be removed, and that the men having bank balances in one country be free to dispose of them in the foreign exchange markets without encountering governmentally created difficulties.

Tying Foreign Loans to Internal Reforms. There was a great deal of discussion of these matters, much of which was summarized in the Conference on European Rehabilitation at the Institute of Politics at Williamstown, Massachusetts, in August 1922. This conference ran through about four weeks, and in the course of it there was a round-table discussion participated in by Paul D. Cravath, Paul Warburg, David Houston, former secretary of the Treasury, and this writer.

Much of the discussion hinged on the "vicious circle" that currencies could not be stabilized until budgets were balanced, but that budgets could not be balanced while currencies were depreciating. Europeans proclaimed their inability to make financial reforms unless the United States would make loans. Americans declared that the loans could not be made until the Europeans instituted the reforms. The answer was that we could straighten out this tangle by making one comprehensive settlement. Since budgets, currencies, reparations, foreign loans, and inter-Allied debts were all so intimately related it followed that we should tie them together in one comprehensive settlement.[1]

Warburg insisted that this was not politically feasible, that it was impossible to get things done simultaneously, that the best that could be hoped for was to bring them about piecemeal. However, it was possible to accomplish many of them simultaneously, if not for all countries at once, at least for each of the stricken countries one by one. In particular, when the question of foreign loans arose, the creditor was in a position to impose adequate requirements for internal reform upon the country which was receiving the credit, and investment bankers who acted as intermediaries in placing such loans with their own investors had an obligation to do this.

Austrian Loan Tied to Internal Reforms. The following year, 1923, it proved possible to do precisely this for Austria. The crown had depreciated

---

[1] This writer proposed a detailed scheme of this sort appropriate to the situation as it then stood, which will be found in the *Chase Economic Bulletin* of August 31, 1922.

to 14,000 to 1, and Austria was ready for anything that would get her out of the morass. Under the auspices of the League of Nations an international loan was arranged. The loan was issued in various currencies and placed in the markets of many different countries. The total was approximately $126 million (nominal value), of which $25 million (at a discount of 10 percent) was placed in the United States. London, Paris, Amsterdam, and even Italy took part. This loan was guaranteed by Great Britain, France, and Czechoslovakia to the extent of 24.5 percent each, by Italy to the extent of 20.5 percent, by Belgium 2 percent, Sweden 2 percent, Denmark 1 percent, and the Netherlands 1 percent. This guarantee applied to all of the loan except a small part which, instead of being placed with the public, took the form of advances by the Swiss and Spanish governments.[2] Austria agreed to rigorous conditions. She was to stabilize her currency on the gold basis. She was to submit to an adequate measure of foreign supervision of her finances.

Hungarian and Polish Loans. A similar rescue party was organized for Hungary. The creditors sent Jeremiah Smith of Boston to sit in a position of authority in Hungary, countersigning checks and passing on the use of the funds for which the loan was made while the reforms were being carried through. The sum[3] here was a good dealer smaller, about $50,650,000. It was enough. The same thing was done for Poland in 1927 when the Honorable Charles S. Dewey left the United States Treasury to perform a similar service. The amount of $72,000,000 sufficed for Poland.[4] Great sums were not required to stabilize a country when internal financial reforms were insisted upon in connection with the loan, and it was not difficult for the finance minister of an embarrassed country to persuade his people to submit to the necessary reforms when the outside help could thereby be obtained.

All three of these loans worked. All three of them stabilized the currencies. All three of them set the countries going in industrial activity again.

Dawes Plan Ties All Elements of Problem Together. The Dawes Plan for Germany in 1924 was based on the same principle. The Dawes Plan in principle undertook to tie all the elements together in one comprehensive

---

[2] *Commercial & Financial Chronicle*, June 16, 1923, pp. 2710–11.

[3] *Ibid.*, July 5, 1924, pp. 26–27. The terms of this loan were carried through till August 1932. The coupon was paid in full. Later there were irregular payments, and the loan was extended with a rate reduced from 7.5 percent to 4.5 percent, which was paid through August 1, 1941 (Moody's *Governments & Municipals* [1942], pp. 1927–28).

[4] *Commercial & Financial Chronicle*, October 22, 1927, pp. 2212–13. The Polish loan was pretty well serviced through 1935. The coupon was paid in full, except that dollars were substituted for gold dollars in 1933. The price range in 1935 was high 126½, low 99⅞. Some payments were continued until April 15, 1938. See Standard & Poor's *Corporation & Municipal Bond Guide*, April 7, 1943, p. 158; Moody's *Governments & Municipals* (1936), p. 2778.

settlement, and to create a framework under which Germany's economic life could revive, and under which it was to Germany's interest to pay as much as she could. By the end of 1923 Germany was desperate and was ready for anything. And France was convinced that from the standpoint of her own financial interests a radical change of policy was necessary.

A great international committee was created of so-called experts representing officially the governments of Great Britain, France, Italy, Belgium, and Germany, and representing unofficially the government of the United States. The American representatives of this committee were Gen. Charles G. Dawes, later Vice President of the United States, Owen D. Young, head of the General Electric Company, and Henry M. Robinson, president of the First National Bank of Los Angeles. More "expert" still were men like Col. Leonard P. Ayres and Professor E. W. Kemmerer, who assisted the nominal "experts." Expert also was Sir Josiah Stamp of England.

The committee, in its report, set its problem in very clean-cut terms: how can the German budget be balanced and German currency be stabilized while providing for adequate reparations payments? They proposed a plan to solve this problem, emphasizing that the entire plan was based on the assumption that the fiscal and economic unity of Germany would be restored, and that economic activity would not be hampered by political or military control.

Foreign Loan. A foreign loan of 800 million gold marks (roughly $200 million) was to be provided for the establishment of a new bank of issue for currency stabilization, and for the first year's reparations payments.

New Bank of Issue. A new bank of issue was to take over the assets and the liabilities of the Reichsbank, which included a substantial amount of gold. It was to get additional capital subscribed in Germany and abroad. It was to be privately owned and free of government control, though it was to be the fiscal agent and depository of the German government. It was to be administered by a German president and a German managing board and supervised in large matters affecting creditor nations by a board of seven Germans and seven foreigners, one of the foreigners being the bank commissioner.

Currency Stabilization. A gold reserve of 33.3 percent was to be maintained by the bank and the bank's notes were to be redeemed in gold. The report of the committee, however, stated that the committee believed that conditions would be unfavorable to immediate redemption at the inception of the bank.

American Participation in Loan Conditioned on Immediate Gold Payments by Bank. This last point in the committee's report represented a reluctant concession by the American members to the British, the French, and the Italians. The Italians and the French were sentimental about it. It was not fair that Germany should have the gold standard while they themselves did not have it. The British were not themselves ready to return immediately to the gold standard, and their idea was that Germany should go to the sterling standard, and that then they would take care both of sterling and of Germany.[5]

This aroused emphatic protests in the United States.[6] In point of fact, however, the new bank did immediately begin gold payments. There is adequate reason to believe that the Department of State informally made it clear that American participation in the proposed Dawes Plan loan to Germany would not be regarded favorably by the American government unless Germany went immediately to the gold standard. And American participation in the loan was, of course, essential to the success of the plan.

The plan involved an interesting allocation of sources of revenue for the payment in marks of reparations, and these included not only taxes but also first mortgages placed on the German railways and the German industries excepting agriculture.

Transfer of Payments out of Germany. The plan made a sharp distinction between payments by the Germans in marks, and the transfer of these marks into foreign currencies for payments to the creditor governments under reparations accounts. The Germans performed their obligations fully when they turned over marks in proper amount to a transfer committee, which was to consist of the agent general for reparations payments and five experts in foreign exchange and finance. It was then the business of the Transfer Committee, representing the creditor governments, to get the money out of Germany if they could.

Safeguards Under the Dawes Plan. Reparations funds in marks were first of all to be deposited by the Transfer Committee in the Reichsbank, and then they were to sell these marks as they could. But they were not to sell them in the foreign exchange market if they thereby endangered the stability of the mark in the foreign exchanges. The protection of the mark from depreciation and the protection of the exchange rates were the problem of the new Reichsbank, over which the Allies kept adequate supervision; the problem of the agent of the Allies, namely, the Transfer Committee; and the problem of the Allied governments, which framed their own commercial policy with reference to the admittance or the exclusion of German goods.

It was provided that not more than two billion gold marks should accumulate in the new Reichsbank to Transfer Committee account. The Transfer Committee might accumulate an additional three billion marks without transferring it, but was obliged to invest this sum in German

---

[5] I have not seen this publicly stated. My information regarding the attitude of the French, Italians, and British came from Col. Leonard P. Ayres, shortly after his return from the Dawes Plan Conference.

[6] *Chase Economic Bulletin,* April 28, 1924.

industries. The plan, moreover, provided that if after the accumulation reached five billion marks it was impossible to withdraw from Germany the full amount of Germany's annual payments, then Germany's payments in marks should be proportionately reduced. In addition the Transfer Committee had the power by a two-thirds vote to suspend accumulations in Germany before reaching the five-billion-mark limit, if its members should decide that such an accumulation was a menace to the economic situation in Germany or to the interests of the creditor nations.

Abandonment of Safeguards in Young Plan of 1929. These were significant safeguards. It was the abandonment of these safeguards, under the Young Plan of 1929 which succeeded the Dawes Plan, that was responsible for the collapse of Germany in 1931. Had the Dawes Plan been left alone, and properly administered, it would have accomplished its purpose.

Safeguards Gave Priority to Private Credits over Reparations. These safeguards, though they did not in terms give priority to private credits to Germany over the reparations payments, did in fact give priority to private credits. The private creditor would have no obligation to protect the German exchange rates. He would get his payments whether this put the mark below the lower gold point or not. Reparations payments could only be transferred if the exchange rate were not thereby endangered.

Without this priority for future private credits Germany could not have received the private credits which were later granted to her. The Dawes Plan explicitly stated that one of its purposes was to restore Germany's foreign credit.

The Schedule of Reparations Payments. For the first year, the fiscal year 1924–25, reparations payments were to be one billion marks. None of this was to come from the budget of the German government. Two hundred million of it was to come from interest on the German railway bonds and 800 million from the foreign loan. For subsequent years increasing amounts were to come from German sources. The total was to rise to 1,200 million marks in fiscal year 1926–27, 1,750 million marks in fiscal year 1927–28, and to reach the "standard years" payment of 2.5 billion marks in fiscal year 1928–29.

How Could Foreign Loan Supply Both Gold Reserve and Reparations? The question naturally arises as to how the loan of 800 million marks could simultaneously provide a gold reserve for the Reichsbank and be used in making payments on reparations account. The answer is not difficult. The German government, receiving the loan in gold, was to turn it over to the new Reichsbank, receiving in exchange a deposit credit against which it could draw for payments in marks inside Germany. These payments financed the "deliveries in kind" of goods, including coal and other commodities, which were to be turned over to the creditors under reparations. These creditor countries were to get their money through the sale of the goods. This put no burden on mark exchange. The plan called for substantial payments in kind and provided also an ingenious device whereby merchants in foreign countries and merchants in Germany might deal with one another, with the payments being made by the foreign merchants to their own governments, and the payments being made to the German exporters by the German government.

Schedule of Reparations Too High. The one great defect of the Dawes Plan was that the schedule of reparations payments was put too high, though, as indicated above, safeguards provided for the correction of this if it should later turn out to be true.

It is believed that in the conference which preceded the assembling of the nominal "experts" in Paris (the conferences among the real economic experts rather than the political experts) there had been reached an agreement by which the peak of payment should not exceed 1,800 million marks. With the assembling of the nominal "experts" a much larger sum was talked about by one of them. The French, unable to resist the temptation, jumped at this vast figure. The result was a compromise at 2,500 million marks, which was economically unrealistic, and which led to the unfortunate Young Plan of 1929, as a substitute for the Dawes Plan.

The Magic of Sound Money. The Dawes Committee knew very well that the plan could not work unless German industry and finance revived. But the committee had no doubt that industry and finance would revive if sound currency were established, if men once more had money in which they believed and in which they could safely make contracts, and if freedom of private initiative were restored. The fact is, as we shall later see, that the inauguration of the Dawes Plan brought to Germany an extraordinary industrial revival.

Part III

THE FIRST PHASE OF
THE NEW DEAL, 1924–32

16

Depression and Rally of 1924—The Beginning of the New Deal

There came a very sharp reaction in business in early 1924. The Federal Reserve Index of Industrial Production (1923–25 base), which had stood above 100 in the early part of the year, dropped rapidly to 85 by the middle of the summer. Security prices dipped only moderately, and there was no real loss of financial confidence because high hopes were entertained of the outcome of the work of the Dawes Committee. It was recognized in financial circles that the industrial difficulties were due in large degree to the foreign situation, and very specially to the unsatisfactory export trade for agricultural commodities.

There was a sharp dip in the prices of farm products, both an absolute drop and a drop in relation to the prices of other goods. Agriculture was under very great pressure. It needed a good export market at satisfactory prices for over twenty percent of its wheat, for fifty-five percent of its cotton, for forty percent of its tobacco and lard, and so on. With continental Europe slipping financially and, above all, with Germany utterly demoralized, this market was greatly impaired and gravely imperiled. With the high protective tariffs on manufactured goods, moreover, which prevented European manufactures from coming in in adequate volume to obtain the dollars needed for buying farm products, it was difficult for the farmers to see much hope.

Many of the leaders of agriculture, including important senators and congressmen from the farm states, were turning in their bewilderment to new and strange legislative devices. Preponderantly Republican, the agricultural West had accepted with some enthusiasm the tariff on farm products passed in 1921. But very speedily the West had learned that this did no good. The American wheat producer did, to be sure, keep the Canadian wheat grower out of Chicago, but he continued to meet him in Liverpool. The protective tariff did no good to a commodity where an export surplus existed. And agriculture was an export industry.

Even in the case of those agriculture activities like dairying, where exports and imports were in approximate balance,[1] the inability of agricultural producers in export lines to get a satisfactory export market made for reactionary tendencies. Unable to get good prices for wheat and hogs and cotton, a good many farmers who had produced wheat and hogs and corn and cotton were crowding into the dairy industry. All agriculture felt the pressure that came from weakened export trade.

Agriculture itself was so important in the total of our economic life that if it were depressed the rest of the industrial situation was pulled down. For the year 1919, agriculture, mining, and manufacturing may be compared as follows:

Net value of all agricultural products 40%
Net value of all mineral products 7%
Value added by all manufactures .... 53%[2]

The importance of agriculture was declining in American economic life, partly through the decline in agricultural prices as compared with other prices, and partly through the shift of population from country to city which was under way. But agriculture remained in 1924 a factor of such great importance that definitely reactionary agricultural tendencies operated to pull down the general situation.

That the high protective tariff on manufactured goods was in large measure responsible for this situation was recognized by farm leaders and their congressional representatives in the McNary-Haugen bill, which attracted a great deal of attention in early 1924—a bill designed as a counterweight to the tariff. This measure proposed an elaborate and complex machinery for giving the farmer a protected market on that part of his production which was consumed domestically. This was coupled with provisions for dumping abroad of the export surplus at whatever prices it might bring, and with high tariffs which would prevent the reimport of the surplus exported and sold at low prices abroad. The bill also contained provisions for taxing the farmers on the part sold at high prices at home to make good the losses incurred on the part sold abroad.[3]

Spokesmen for the farmers urged that everybody in the country was protected except the farmers. Manufacturers were protected by tariffs, laborers were protected by the immigration law and the Adamson bill, and the farmers "wanted theirs." Some of the advocates of the measure suggested that they would be perfectly willing to dispense with it if they

---

[1] See "Agriculture and Dairying in the World's Economic Equilibrium," *Chase Economic Bulletin*, October 4, 1923.

[2] See *ibid.*, August 24, 1925, Appendix B ("The Statistical Importance of Agriculture in American Economic Life").

[3] *Ibid.*, May 5, 1924.

could have the tariffs on manufactured goods reduced, so that our tariff legislation would not be weighting the balance against the farmer.

The McNary-Haugen bill is significant and interesting as constituting one of the first of the many ingenious devices for spoiling markets and perverting the price mechanism in the interest of special classes, which we have later come to know as the New Deal.

This particular New Deal measure was not adopted, but *the New Deal,* as a conscious and deliberate thing in governmental policy, *did begin in 1924* in an immense artificial manipulation of the money market, to which we shall give extended attention in what follows.

Three things combined to turn the tide in the summer of 1924, and, above all, to swing agricultural prices radically higher both absolutely and in relation to other prices. The marked improvement in the position of agriculture quickened industry in all lines and we started off on a period of "prosperity" which had no real interruption until the stock market crash in 1929. But, as we shall see, the seeds of death were in it from the beginning.

The three things which turned the tide were:

1. The acceptance of the Dawes Plan, which restored confidence among American financiers and American investors in the German situation and consequently in the general European situation, and made them willing to take German and other European bonds in large volume.

2. The purchase of approximately $500 million worth of government securities by the Federal Reserve banks. Part of this was used by the member banks in paying down rediscounts, which dropped very sharply in 1924. But the net outcome of the increase in Federal Reserve bank open market purchases of government securities, the decline in rediscounts, and the incoming gold (neglecting various minor factors) was to increase the reserves of the member banks of the Federal Reserve System from $1,900,000,000 on December 31, 1923, to $2,228,000,000 on December 31, 1924, an increase of over $300 million, or 17 percent, in a single year. The further result of this great increase in reserves was an expansion of member bank credit by over $4 billion, from $34,690,000,000 on March 31, 1924, to $38,946,000,000 on June 30, 1925, as measured by total assets or total liabilities—a multiple expansion based on excess reserves. The member banks of the Federal Reserve System had about 73 percent of the total banking assets of the country, and the total bank expansion in this period was consequently greater than $4 billion. The total deposits of the member banks increased from $28,270,000,000 on March 31, 1924, to $32,457,000,000 on June 30, 1925, an increase of over $4 billion, and the increase of deposits outside the system was again very substantial.

This additional bank credit was not needed by commerce and it went preponderantly into securities: in part into direct bond purchases by the banks and in part into stock and bond collateral loans. It went also into real estate mortgages purchased by banks and in part into installment finance paper.

This immense expansion of bank credit, added to the ordinary sources of capital, created the illusion of unlimited capital and made it easy for our markets to absorb gigantic quantities of foreign securities as well as a greatly increased volume of American security issues. The combination of the Dawes Plan, restoring confidence in the *quality* of European credit, and the cheap money policy of the Federal Reserve banks creating a vast *quantity* of available funds, enabled us to purchase in 1924 approximately $1 billion of foreign securities (refunding excluded). Our tariffs would not allow the Europeans to *earn* dollars here in adequate amounts to buy our farm products and to meet service on the past debts, so we proceeded to *lend* them the dollars they needed for these purposes! But we did not consider how they would ever repay the sums we were lending them if they could not sell goods here. We would take care of that by new loans next year! There was an immense quickening of European demand for American exports and, above all, for farms products at rapidly rising prices.

3. An accidental circumstance that lifted farm prices in the second half of 1924. There was a very poor Canadian wheat crop and our harvests were good. This, of course, was a factor that could be expected to iron itself out in the next year. But the policy of cheap money and excessive foreign loans was to continue long enough to keep American agriculture prosperous and to keep the country prosperous over five years, and to pile up an accumulation of uncollectible foreign debts which shook the country and the world to their foundations when the day of reckoning came.

Strong and Crissinger. Federal Reserve policy from early 1924 to late 1927 was dominated by an able but ill-equipped man, Benjamin Strong, governor of the Federal Reserve Bank of New York, assisted and supported by an untrained and inexperienced man in Washington, Daniel Richard Crissinger, governor of the Federal Reserve Board. Crissinger was a personal appointee of President Warren G. Harding.

The Federal Reserve Board had had a fine sense of responsibility from its inception down to the time of Crissinger's appointment. The Wilson appointees were in general high-minded and able men. The notion that the Federal Reserve Board should be an independent body, comparable with the Supreme Court of the United States in its independence and in its freedom from political considerations, was generally accepted. In W. P. G. Harding, who was governor of the Federal Reserve Board from August 10, 1916, to August 9, 1922, the system had the leadership of a man of great courage and high character. Governor Harding had come to the Federal Reserve Board from an Alabama bank, and had modestly recognized that the difference between the problems of central banking and the problems of Alabama banking were very great. He had consulted other members of the board, and especially the best informed economist on the board, as to what he ought to read to equip himself for the proper discharge of his duties. He had studied the theory of central banking conscientiously and thoroughly. Having done this he had asserted himself, and in his capacity of governor of the Federal Reserve Board he had become almost an autocrat, knowing what should be done and determined to do it properly. He enjoyed the confidence and respect of the financial community.

But Warren G. Harding, the President of the United States, wanted no such man as head of the Federal Reserve Board. Over the protest of the financial community and over the protest of the secretary of the Treasury, Warren Harding named Crissinger and displaced W. P. G. Harding. Crissinger had come from Warren Harding's home town and was Harding's personal friend, and had no other qualification for the office. Warren Harding is reported to have said, in reply to Secretary Mellon's protest, "This appointment is very dear to my heart." This appointment broke the heart and the courage of the Federal Reserve Board.

Leadership in the Federal Reserve System had never been clearly defined. One central bank with branches would have been far better than twelve Federal Reserve banks loosely linked together and loosely coordinated by the Federal Reserve Board. It was difficult to place legal or even moral responsibility upon any one individual or one bank or the board for policy decisions. With the dropping out of W. P. G. Harding and the coming in of Crissinger, leadership in the Federal Reserve System passed from the board to the governor of the New York Federal Reserve Bank, Benjamin Strong.

Crissinger had no grasp of Federal Reserve policy. His purposes were political. Those things were right which would help to reelect Warren G. Harding. Those things were wrong which would interfere with the reelection of Warren G. Harding. Sound Federal Reserve policy might be desirable, but not unless it were politically popular. It was easy for Governor Strong to dominate such a man and, through him, the board.

Governor Strong had no fundamental grasp of the problems of central banking. His statements in private discussion regarding his policies indicated that they were short-run policies and, at times, contradictory. But he had great personal charm. He had a dominating personality and he had a great deal of vivacity. Despite a tubercular weakness, he seemed physically vigorous and he seemed to have great social energy. His exact training was as a trust officer dealing with mortgage indentures. The head of one great New York bank said of him: "He has the best indenture mind in the city of New York." The head of another great New York bank, after listening to a long monologue from Strong regarding Bank of England policy—Strong had just returned from his first visit to the Bank of England, where he had been received with great courtesy and enthusiasm and where he had been told many things—said, "The governor has learned many interesting things, and some day he will put them together right." But he never did.

Strong dominated men when he could. All too frequently he could. But when he could not, he bore no malice and he kept pleasant personal relations with his critics.

Those who see history only from the outside easily convince themselves that impersonal social forces are overwhelming and that individual men in strategic places make little difference. But this is not true. The handling of Federal Reserve policy by Strong and Crissinger in the years 1924–27 led to ghastly consequences from which we have not yet recovered. Competent and courageous men occupying their positions would have avoided the mistakes which these men made.

17

Money, Bank Credit, and Capital

Capital is created when men produce machinery instead of hats and shoes and ice cream, when men build bridges and railroads instead of making phonograph records. Capital consists of producers' goods, of instruments to be used in further production, instead of commodities destined for immediate consumption. The growth of capital is a factor of first importance in the progress of civilization. Capital increases when the community produces more than it consumes. Capital decreases when the community consumes more than it produces.

The Five Main Sources of Capital. In the world of money and money transactions—the world of buying, selling, lending, and borrowing in terms of money—the formation of capital usually involves monetary transactions and generally involves monetary calculations. Even in such a world, however, there remains an important amount of capital creation without any intermediation of money.

1. *Direct Capitalization.* There are five main sources of capital. The first is direct capitalization, particularly important in agriculture today. This takes place when the farmer uses his spare time in building barns and fences and putting in subsoil drainage, in damming up gullies and making ponds. It takes place when the farmer lets his flocks and herds increase instead of selling off the whole of the annual increase. It takes place when the farmer turns his wheat land into orchard, and must wait eight years to get his return. A similar direct production of capital takes place often in a mechanic's shop when he makes or improves a tool or a workbench. It is especially important in European agriculture. Senator Luigi Einaudi, the distinguished Italian economist, in conversation has emphasized its importance. He remarked in 1937, for example, that he thought that the Italian peasant was creating enough new capital with his hands to offset the deficit in the national government's budget.

2. *Consumer Thrift.* The second main source of capital, and the one to which the older economists gave their chief attention, is consumer thrift.

The consumer has an income of $5,000. He and his family spend $4,500 in living. He saves $500. He may use this to buy machinery or tools or livestock to aid himself in his own work. He may, on the other hand, lend it to a neighbor who will use it in buying tools and equipment. Or he may put it in the savings bank and the savings bank may use it in buying the bond of a great industrial corporation which is erecting a new factory or which wishes more working capital to put into raw materials and work in process. In any of these cases, however, more capital is created and less consumers' goods are created as a result of the thrift of the consumer, than would have been the case if he and his family had spent the whole five thousand dollars in current living. Consumer thrift is, of course, of tremendous importance to the growth of capital.

3. *Business Thrift and Especially Corporate Thrift.* When a business house retains part of its profits to add to surplus, capital is created. The corporation which refrains from paying out all of its profits as dividends, retaining part to add to surplus, is creating capital. The importance of this and the extent of it was first forcibly brought to the attention of economists in David Friday's pioneer study, *Profits, Wages, and Prices* (New York, 1920). From 1909 to 1929 additions to corporate surplus ran as follows:

CORPORATE SAVINGS*
(In millions of dollars)

Year	Additions to corporate surplus
1909	1,296
1910	1,151
1911	690
1912	1,246
1913	1,400
1914	585
1915	2,117
1916	4,939
1917	4,732
1918	1,986
1919	4,330
1920	1,397
1921	−2,685
1922	1,676
1923	2,432
1924	1,463
1925	2,851
1926	2,223
1927	996
1928	2,388
1929	2,238

* From *America's Capacity to Consume* (Brookings Institution), p. 109.

4. *Taxation for Capital Purposes*. When government taxes inheritances at very high rates and uses the proceeds for current expenditures it is dissipating capital. When, however, government taxes income and uses the proceeds to pay down public debt it is creating new capital, returning capital to the investment market. In Boone County, Missouri, a generation ago, there was need for a new courthouse. The farmers of the county had had the unpleasant experience of paying off a bond issue, shortly after the Civil War, for a railroad that was never built, and in three elections they voted down the proposal to borrow money to build a courthouse. Then an able local editor, William Hirth, proposed a special tax levy for three years, which would raise the $100,000 needed while the work of building the courthouse was going on. The county would then own the courthouse free and clear of debt. The farmers liked this proposal and it was carried by a very large majority. The bankers paid the county interest on the money instead of the county's paying interest to bondholders on the money. This was taxation for capital purposes. It created new capital. During the period of the 1920s a great deal of capital was created by taxation. The federal government steadily collected more revenues than its ordinary expenses amounted to, steadily paid public debt and returned a great many billions of dollars to the capital market. Unfortunately, this tendency in federal finance was offset by a counter tendency in state and municipal finance.

First Four Sources of Capital Never Carried to Excess. These four sources of capital: direct capitalization, consumers' thrift, business thrift (and especially corporate thrift), and finally, taxation for capital purposes, are all wholesome, sound, and safe. They have never been overdone; no country has ever gone wrong in creating capital in these ways.[1] The great troubles of the 1920s grew out of a fifth source of capital, namely, new bank credit for capital purposes.

5. *New Bank Credit as Source of Capital*. Certain of the older economists would have denied that an expansion of bank credit could create capital. Bank credit expands when the customer gives the bank his note, which the bank takes in as an asset, and the bank in exchange gives a customer a deposit credit, a liability of the bank against which the customer may draw checks. In this transaction there is simply the interchange of two liabilities, the liability of the customer to the bank and the liability of the bank to the customer. The bank's balance sheet is increased on both sides by this transaction. Loans and discounts are increased on the asset side and deposits are increased on the liability side. How can the interchange of two liabilities create new capital? How can it serve as a substitute for direct capitalization, or for consumer thrift, or for business and corporate thrift,

---

[1] Keynes would not, of course, agree with this proposition. Keynes has, however, confused bank credit expansion with ordinary savings and has, moreover, by a very superficial dialectic misinterpreted the function of the interest rate in connection with savings. I make no concession to the Keynesian view. See chapter 60 herein, "Digression on Keynes."

or for taxation for capital purposes? How can it create a new machine instead of new hats and shoes?

Obviously, at the instant, there are no more hats or shoes or machines. There is simply more paper. And yet for the customer of the bank who wants machines the new bank credit is enough. He can use it to get the machines, and more machines will be produced than would otherwise have been produced, as a result of his demand based on the credit which the bank is giving him.

If at the time he orders a new machine, industry is fully employed, the new machine can be produced only by withdrawing labor and supplies from other employments, and his purchase of the machine will force upon the consumers a reduced consumption of hats or shoes or ice cream. There is involuntary "abstinence." If, on the other hand, there is a state of industrial slack with idle labor, the new machine can be added to the capital equipment of the country without any diminution in the flow of consumers' goods. In either case, however, new capital comes into existence which would not have existed if the bank had not extended credit.

Sound if Held Within Limits. It must be recognized that, held within limits, the expansion of bank credit is a wholesome and legitimate source of new capital. The nature of these limits involves the general theory of bank credit. To Adam Smith it would have seemed impossible that a bank should do much of this. The bank might properly lend to a merchant for quick turnover. The bank might lend to a manufacturer part of his working capital for the purchase of raw materials and the payment of the labor which worked up the raw materials in anticipation of a prompt sale. But the bank must lend to the manufacturer no part of his "forge" or "smelting house." The banker's liabilities are quick liabilities, and the banker must keep his assets quick also in order that he may meet his quick liabilities. The forge and the smelting house are not quick, are not liquid; they are fixed, and loans against them may safely be made only by those who can afford to wait a long time to get their money back—retired investors and the like.

Less rigid banking standards could recognize that a bank may put a substantial part of it resources into slow loans, provided it keeps a sufficient percent of cash and highly liquid paper to meet the variations in depositors' calls for cash. German banks have always gone much further in making capital loans to industries than banks in England or the United States. A regular practice of the German banks, both before and after World War I, was to make advances, usually in the form of overdrafts, to industries and to increase these with the growth of the industry year by year. Frequently, or even usually, in connection with such advances the bank would place its own officers on the board of directors of the borrowing industry. When the advance had reached a great enough magnitude, the bank would often have the industry give it bonds or even shares in cancellation of the advance; and then at a time when the stock market was rising and the affairs of the corporation looked favorable, the bank would make a public issue of the shares and the bonds.

British banks do not like to own shares and prefer that the long-time financing of an industry should be conducted through the capital market. Nonetheless, in the advances of the British banks there is usually a great deal of slow paper which in effect represents capital loans. American banks in the great cities try hard to adhere to the practice of having their borrowers "clean up once a year." But this is not always insisted upon in the case of the one-bank borrower, and even in the case of the borrower with several banks it is often accomplished only by an increase of loans at one bank as another bank is paid off. But American banks do expect, in any case, that the total borrowings of a concern shall have a seasonal peak, and that a substantial liquidation from this peak shall take place in total borrowings. Banks in smaller cities and country banks often do carry a substantial volume of paper for their customers, periodically renewed, which represents capital advances.[2]

Stock Market and Bank Credit for Capital Purposes. The main way, however, in which bank credit has gone into industrial equipment and other capital uses in the United States has been via the stock market, rather than by direct capital loans. The bank cannot safely lend a railroad funds for its roadbed or its terminals. But when the roadbed and the terminals are represented by $1,000 bonds or by $100 shares for which a broad and active market exists, then the banks may safely make collateral loans secured by such bonds and shares, knowing that it can get the money back promptly by calling upon the borrower to pay, and by selling his shares and bonds in the stock market if the borrower does not pay. The bank may even buy the bonds and own them itself, knowing that it can sell them promptly if it needs to. Through the stock market, therefore, bank credit has come to finance industry, as well as commerce, on a great scale.

There is no need whatever to be doctrinaire in objecting to the employment of bank credit for capital purposes, so long as the growth of this is kept proportionate to the growth of the industry of the country, so long as the prices and quality of the shares and bonds are closely scrutinized by the lending officials of the banks, and so long as adequate margins and proper diversification of collateral are maintained. But when in the period 1924–29 there came an extraordinary spurt of this kind of employment of bank funds, and when commercial loans began going down in the banks at the same time that the stock market loans and bank holdings of bonds were mounting rapidly, the careful observer grew alarmed. And when in addition there came a startling increase of several hundred percent in bank holdings of real estate mortgages, the thing seemed extremely ominous. Adam Smith's reasons against bank holding of mortgages were very nearly as valid in the 1922–33 period as they were in his day. The first lesson of a

---

[2] See my *Value of Money*, chaps. 23, 24.

young banker should be to learn the difference between a mortgage and a
bill of exchange.

Growth of Capital and Growth of Debt. With respect to the five sources of
capital it must be observed that when capital is created by direct capitalization, or by corporate and other business thrift, or by taxation for capital
purposes, the capital of the country increases without a corresponding
growth of debt. When capital is increased by consumer thrift, there need
not be a growth in debt. If the thrifty consumer invests his savings in
corporate shares, or if he uses them in his own business, there is no growth
of debt. If he puts them in the savings bank there is a growth of debt, in that
the savings bank now owes him money. If he lends to a neighbor there is an
increase of debt. But the growth of capital from consumer thrift moves
more rapidly than the related growth of debt. Direct capitalization and
corporate thrift involve no increase of debt at all. Governmental thrift
usually involves an actual decrease of debt.

When, however, new bank credit is employed to create new capital,
there is a dollar for dollar concomitant growth of capital and debt. Credit
and debt are merely different names for the same thing. There is no creditor
without a debtor and no debtor without a creditor. One of the obvious and
ominous aspects of rapid expansion of bank credit is the growth of debt—
the debt of the people to the banks and the debt of the banks to the people.
For this reason alone, if for no other, the employment of bank credit as a
substitute for the first four sources of capital should be used cautiously and
discreetly, and the growth of it should be held in proper relation to the
growth of the industrial activity of the country.[3]

*The Process of Bank Expansion, 1922–28, on the Basis of Excess Re-
serves.* When the cash reserves of the banks are not excessive, bank credit
does not easily expand. Banks will increase loans under these conditions to
customers, but they will usually sell investments as they increase loans and
they will increase the loans at rising rates of interest. A bank must always
be prepared to pay its depositors on demand. It must protect its cash. The
minimum ratio of reserves to deposits has long been fixed by law in the
United States, but even when there are no legal reserve requirements,

---

[3] The theory of the sources of capital here given was first presented by the present writer in an
address before the Indiana Bankers Convention on October 7, 1920, and was published in *The
Chase,* issued by the Chase National Bank of the city of New York in November 1920. The
central idea in the discussion of the role of bank credit in the formation of capital which the
present chapter contains will be found in the present writer's *Value of Money* (New York,
1917), pp. 484–85, fn. 2, and chap. 24. See particularly the discussion of Adam Smith on
pages 526–27. I believe that this constitutes the first recognition in American economic
literature of the role of bank credit as a substitute for voluntary abstinence, and of the role of
"forced savings" in the creation of capital. In the *Chase Economic Bulletin,* November 8,
1926, the theory is again elaborated and some additional points are presented, particularly the
point that if there are idle labor and a slack condition of industry, bank credit may create
capital without forcing abstinence upon the consumers.

banks know very well that they must protect their reserves in order to protect their solvency.

Multiple Expansion Impossible for a Single Bank. There is an old theory that when a bank receives an unaccustomed amount of cash above its reserve requirements, it may forthwith proceed to increase its loans and its deposits in some multiple ratio. An old New Jersey banker, repudiating this theory, once said that he had been trying for forty years to make one dollar do the work of four, but in the warfare of checks at the clearinghouse the other banks wouldn't let him. The practical banker knows that under ordinary circumstances an increase in loans promptly reflects itself in withdrawals of cash. Having an excess of $100,000 in reserves over his required reserves, the banker will ordinarily lend or invest $100,000, increasing his loans and investments by $100,000, and increasing his deposits by $100,000—the proceeds of the loan are ordinarily taken by the borrower in the form of a deposit credit. If the borrower promptly checks against his deposit balance to make payment to a depositor in another bank, the banker who has made the new loan will find his deposits reduced and his cash reserves reduced by $100,000 very speedily. His total assets and his total liabilities will be what they were before the loan was made, but the composition of his assets will be changed. His cash reserve will be reduced by $100,000 and his loans increased by $100,000.

This is the normal expectation of the banker, and represents the situation when the total volume of bank reserves is changing little and when, in the banking community generally, there is no excess of reserves over reserve requirements—some banks being a little over and others a little under the required reserves.

Takes Place When Banks in Aggregate Have Excess Reserves—The Process. But obviously the situation is different if on the same day many banks find themselves with excess reserves and all of them simultaneously try to lend out the excess. Assume a clearinghouse with three bank members, all approximately equal in size, and assume that each finds itself with $100,000 excess reserves, and that each is trying to put its money to profitable use, increasing its loans by $100,000 and its deposits by $100,000. Assume that the borrowers promptly use the proceeds of the loans in making payments, so that checks for $100,000 are drawn on bank A and deposited in bank B, checks for the same amount are drawn on bank B and deposited in bank C, and checks for $100,000 are drawn on bank C and deposited in bank A.

Next day at the clearinghouse each bank has to meet, as a consequence of its loan operations of the preceding day, checks drawn against it for $100,000. But, on the other hand, each bank has checks on one of the other banks to present for $100,000. They merely swap checks at the clearinghouse and none of them loses any cash. Deposits are up $100,000 in each bank; loans are up $100,000 in each bank; and reserves are still in excess in each bank. Next day they try again, each trying to get rid of its excess reserve, but again they merely swap checks at the clearinghouse and lose no cash.

The process will go on, on the assumptions laid down, until new bank credit is created in an amount such that the $100,000 original *excess reserve* in each bank is now needed as *required reserve* for the expanded deposits. There will be a multiple expansion based on the excess reserves. How great the multiple will be will depend upon the legal reserve requirement or the minimum reserve ratio that banking practices have dictated in the absence of legal reserve requirements. In New York City in the period of the 1920s the legal reserve requirement was 13 percent for demand deposits. On this basis the $100,000 excess reserve in each bank would permit new deposits of $769,230 to be created, growing out of new loans of the same amount. Then there would no longer be excess reserves, and the process would stop. For banks in reserve cities outside New York and Chicago, the rule was 10 percent for demand deposits, and for country banks 7 percent for demand deposits, while for all three classes of banks the legally required reserve for time deposits was 3 percent.

Limits on Bank Expansion—Largely Inoperative, 1922–28. The foregoing illustration is artificially simple. It ignores many complications, but it does illustrate the essential causation in the American money market in the period of the 1920s.

Among the complications ignored is the existence of outside markets which would pull away reserves, not merely from bank A, but from the whole system of banks A, B, and C. The expansion we will assume to take place in New York, but part of the proceeds of the expansion would be spent in Chicago or New Orleans or San Francisco. During the 1920s, however, the excess bank reserves were widely diffused over the country and the country as a whole expanded.

The illustration ignores the further fact that when increased loans are made for commercial purposes in connection with increasing commercial activities, there is usually an increased demand for hand-to-hand cash which pulls down banking reserves, checking the expansion. But the years 1924–29, inclusive, showed an amazing constancy in the volume of money in circulation, despite the immense growth in bank deposits that took place.

The illustration ignores the probability that bank expansion in the United States would cause foreign money markets to pull away gold from the United States, which would cut under the volume of bank reserves in the United States and check the expansion before it could go far. But from 1920 into 1927 the United States gained gold instead of losing it.

Excess Reserves Do Not Generate Expansion When Confidence Is Low. The illustration given above assumes, moreover, that the only factor governing the volume of loans that banks will make is the volume of reserves available. Now there have been times in the history of the country, notably in the 1870s and in the middle 1890s and in the 1930s, when reserves piled up without being used, either because the banks could not find satisfactory credits, or because good borrowers would not take loans even at low rates, or because many banks felt obliged to carry reserves high above the legal requirements in view of uncertainties and dangers. For the New York clearinghouse banks, the average reserves for the year stood in 1894 at 37.59 percent of deposits, though the legal requirement was only 25 percent. The figure stood at 45.2 percent in February 1894. The average for the whole of the United States was 26 percent in 1894, although the legal requirement was far below this. The same average for the year was 15 percent in 1906. Excess reserves rose to fantastic levels in the period of the 1930s, and interest rates literally dragged the ground without encouraging any great expansion of bank credit except as the government borrowed— noting the exception of a strong growth in commercial loans from early 1936 to the crash of 1937.

Federal Reserve Credits and Multiple Expansion—Rediscounts vs. Open Market Purchases. The proposition given above that, on the basis of *excess reserves,* a multiple expansion of bank credit can take place is very different from the proposition sometimes made that, on the basis of every dollar of *Federal Reserve bank credit,* a multiple expansion can take place. If Federal Reserve bank credit expands only in response to increased needs for money in circulation, or for the replenishment of member bank reserves in a period of active business, or in the normal seasonal crop moving time—and if the Federal Reserve bank expansion takes place only in response to rediscounting by the member banks, and if the member banks, as they normally do, pay off the rediscounts when the need is over—then the expansion and contraction of Federal Reserve bank credit need occasion no general expansion or contraction of commercial bank credit at all. The Federal Reserve banks in these cases will merely prevent tension and take in slack.

It is only when the Federal Reserve banks take the initiative, through their purchases of government securities, in creating Federal Reserve bank credit that surplus reserves of the member banks are created thereby, and that multiple expansion based on Federal Reserve credit takes place. This did happen on a colossal scale in the period of the 1920s, the two major episodes being in the years 1924 and 1927. Government security purchases by the Federal Reserve banks of several hundred million dollars in each of these years were promptly followed by multiple expansion of billions of dollars in general bank credit.

How Surplus Reserves and Bank Expansion Generate Time Deposits More than Demand Deposits. The great bank credit expansion in the 1920s took the form of time deposits to a greater extent than of demand deposits. Why was this? It would not have happened if, accompanying the immense bank expansion, there had been a corresponding increase in the demands of trade, and if the bank expansion had been called forth by trade needs instead of being pushed out by excess reserves. But there was no such growth in trade needs for money, and businessmen and most other people tend to be economical in the use of money. When banks pay interest on deposits and encourage deposits, people are glad to deposit unneeded pocket cash in the banks, and when banks pay more interest on time deposits than they pay on demand deposits, businessmen and others tend to put their excess funds into the form of time deposits rather than demand deposits. This expansion of time deposits, it may be observed, tended to reduce the reserve ratio required for a given volume of deposits and thus permitted the expansion to go much further than would otherwise have been the case.

Time Deposits and Savings. There were those who looked with great complacency upon our immense expansion of bank deposits in the 1920s on the theory that it took the form chiefly of time deposits and that time deposits represented savings. The view was largely fallacious. Time deposits expanded most rapidly when bank reserves were most excessive, and time deposits ceased to expand when the money market tightened. They showed none of the steady growth of ordinary savings deposits. Moreover, they outran ordinary savings deposits by an appalling percentage. The following table shows the comparative growth of savings deposits and time deposits in the commercial banks.

COMPARATIVE GROWTH OF SAVINGS DEPOSITS
AND TIME DEPOSITS
(In millions of dollars)

Date	Deposits of all mutual savings banks	Time deposits of national banks	Time deposits of reporting member banks in N. Y. district*	Time deposits of all reporting member banks*
June 30, 1922	5,780	4,112	666	3,380
June 30, 1923	6,289	4,755	901	4,000
June 30, 1924	6,693	5,260	972	4,418
June 30, 1925	7,147	5,925	1,174	5,172
June 30, 1926	7,578	6,314	1,263	5,650
June 30, 1927	8,077	7,316	1,472	6,212
January 1, 1928 ..	8,315**	7,808†	1,622	6,611
% increase over 1922	43.9	89.9	143.5	95.6

* *Figures for reporting member banks are for dates nearest June 30.*
** Estimated.
† December 31, 1927.

Time deposits in the great New York banks could be identified as consisting of temporarily idle money of large investors who had sold out in a rising stock market and were waiting to reinvest; as deposits of foreign banks subject to prompt recall; and as temporarily idle money of great industrial corporations. The great New York banks knew that they must keep just as liquid against these time deposits as against demand deposits. This was true in most of the major cities of the country, notable exceptions being Cleveland and Los Angeles, where the time deposits of the great banks represented in large degree true savings accounts.[4] Time deposits in country banks represented real savings far more than they did in city banks. But the most rapid growth of time deposits in this period was in the city banks, as is strikingly illustrated by the following table for the national banks:

NATIONAL BANK DEPOSITS
(In millions of dollars)

Date	Banks in central reserve cities		Banks in other reserve cities		Banks outside reserve cities	
	Net demand deposits	*Time deposits*	*Net demand deposits*	*Time deposits*	*Net demand deposits*	*Time deposits*
May 5, 1922	3,112	227	3,014	736	3,805	2,955
February 28, 1928 ...	3,394	636	4,210	2,398	4,574	4,959

Time deposits in the country banks increased only 68 percent, but in the central reserve cities increased 180 percent, and in the other reserve cities more than 225 percent. For approximately the same period time deposits in the New York Federal Reserve District increased 207 percent, in the Atlanta Federal Reserve District 65 percent, and in the Kansas City Reserve District 68 percent. Time deposits even in country banks were swollen by the temporarily idle funds of business corporations which went to them, attracted by the fact that country banks paid higher rates of interest on bank deposits than great city banks did. If the country banker were misled into thinking that he had here a true savings account, not subject to sudden withdrawal, which he could safely invest in slow local loans, including mortgages, he had a rude awakening. Repeatedly in the period of the 1920s the New York banks got frantic telegrams from country correspondent banks calling for help when one great automobile company suddenly withdrew its time deposit. These calls for help were honored, but usually with a spanking and with a warning not to do it again.

Even the deposits of the mutual savings banks were swollen by the rapid expansion of commercial bank credit which was taking place. This was particularly true in New York City, where the mutual savings banks would

---

[4] I have elaborated this argument and have given a great deal of detail for the behavior of time deposits in different parts of the country in "Bank Expansion Versus Savings," *Chase Economic Bulletin*, June 25, 1928, esp. pp. 12–16.

take deposits up to $7,500. There were many cases where investors, selling their securities at the rapidly rising prices of the period, put their funds into savings banks, placing $7,500 blocks in each of several such banks. These deposits did not represent new savings. They represented in part old savings displaced and in part capital gains based on expanded commercial bank credit. In 1928 and 1929 there was also a counterinfluence on savings bank deposits. Some savings bank depositors took funds out of the savings banks to put into stocks at rising prices.

In general, however, savings bank deposits moved steadily without showing great influence of contemporary expansion of commercial bank deposits. Time deposits of the commercial banks, however, moved by jerks. They moved rapidly when the Federal Reserve banks increased their open market purchases, and they expanded slowly or not at all when the Federal Reserve banks were selling government securities.

The year 1922 was a year of rapid expansion. The Federal Reserve banks increased their open market purchases, gold came in, and deposits moved rapidly. From January 4, 1922, to January 3, 1923, the time deposits of the reporting member banks increased from $3,011,000,000 to $3,748,000,000, or 24.5 percent. The year 1923 was one in which the Federal Reserve banks reversed their policy and offset the incoming gold by reducing their open market purchases and raising their rates of rediscount. The time deposits of the reporting member banks in this year rose from the $3,748,000,000 of January 3, 1923, to $4,104,000,000 by January 2, 1924, or 9.5 percent. The year 1924 was one of very great Federal Reserve bank expansion, great ease of money, and very rapid bank expansion. Time deposits moved up in this year from $4,104,000,000 on January 2 to $4,849,000,000 on January 7, 1925, or 18.2 percent.

The case is even more striking when we observe the behavior of time deposits in certain of the major cities. From April 12, 1922, to April 11, 1923, time deposits in New York City moved up from $353 million to $627 million, or 77.6 percent. In the following year, the period of restricted credit, the same time deposits moved up only from $627 million to $649 million, or 3.5 percent (by April 16, 1924). In the following year (to April 15, 1925), a period of great monetary ease, time deposits moved up to $816 million, or 25.7 percent, whereas in the next year (to April 14, 1926), there was an actual decrease of $2 million, the 1926 figure being $814 million.

A similar story can be told for Chicago. From April 5, 1922, to April 11, 1923, time deposits increased from $311 million to $372 million; but from April 11, 1923, to April 16, 1924, they increased only $1 million, to $373 million. This high variability in the growth of time deposits is very different from the steady growth which characterizes the figures of the savings banks.

Investors' Money vs. Bank Expansion. It was not easy to convince investment bankers and bond dealers in the period 1925–29 that it was commercial bank expansion which was generating the demand for the securities which they were selling. They insisted, and correctly, that real investors' money was coming in, and that a great many securities were being bought outright. They were impressed by the statistics showing the growth of stock and bond collateral loans in the banks, the growth of bank ownership of bonds, and the growth of bank deposits, but they still insisted that they were selling to investors. But here is a typical case where one could trace every step of the process. An old lady in Missouri held a mortgage which she had inherited from her father. A Missouri Joint Stock Land Bank floated a bond issue in New York, receiving cash for it, part of which came out of a syndicate loan which the underwriters placed with New York banks, and for which they got a deposit credit. The deposit was transferred to a great Missouri city, and from there to the smaller place where the old lady lived, and the mortgage which she held was refunded at a lower rate of interest by the Joint Stock Land Bank, and she was paid off. She first placed the money on deposit with the local bank, and then wrote a kinsman in a New York bank, sending a check which she asked to have placed in good bonds for her. Here was true investor's cash coming out of an interior town to New York to buy bonds, but it represented no new savings. The old lady's father had saved that money sixty years before. It was a displaced old investment. Newly created money sweeping out of New York had displaced her investment, and her investment funds came back to New York for reinvestment.

18

The Extent of Bank Expansion, 1922–28

Between June 30, 1922, and April 11, 1928, the deposits of the commercial banks of the United States increased by approximately $13.5 billion, while the loans and investments of the same banks increased by $14.5 billion. April 11, 1928, represents the culmination of this great expansion of bank credit, though it is far from representing the culmination of the consequences of this great expansion, as we shall see.[1]

DEPOSITS OF COMMERCIAL BANKS*

April 11, 1928 . . . .$44,234,000,000
June 30, 1922 30,690,000,000

Increase $13,544,000,000

LOANS, DISCOUNTS, AND INVESTMENTS OF COMMERCIAL BANKS

April 11, 1928 . . . .$47,607,000,000
June 30, 1922 33,095,000,000

Increase $14,512,000,000

* See *Chase Economic Bulletin,* June 4, 1928, p. 22 and Appendix A.

Expansion in 1922–28 Compared with Expansion Required to Win the War. This is obviously a great expansion. But great figures taken by themselves are not necessarily significant. Some sort of comparison is needed. How

---

[1] I choose the date April 11, 1928, on the basis of the behavior of the 101 weekly reporting member banks of the great cities. The total reserves of these banks with the Federal Reserve banks stood at $1,801,000,000 on that date, and did not get as high again for the rest of the year. The net demand deposits of these banks stood at $13,781,000,000 on April 11 and thereafter declined to $12,785,000,000 on August 22 and to $13,266,000,000 on December 26. The time deposits of these banks virtually ceased to expand for the rest of the year, the figure standing at $6,748,000,000 on April 11, and at $6,864,000,000 on December 26.

The figures for all member banks, which come only four times a year, do not enable us to

big is $13.5 billion as an increase in deposits? How big in $14.5 billion as an increase in loans and investments? A significant comparison is to be found in the expansion of credit by the same banks, needed during our participation in World War I. That expansion amounted to $5,835,000,000 in deposits and to $7,056,000,000 in loans and investments, as shown by the following table:[2]

DEPOSITS OF COMMERCIAL BANKS

December 31, 1918 . . . .$26,541,039,000
April 6, 1917 20,705,588,000

Increase . . . .$ 5,835,451,000

LOANS, DISCOUNTS, AND INVESTMENTS OF COMMERCIAL BANKS

December 31, 1918 . . . .$29,354,214,000
April 6, 1917 22,297,775,000

Increase . . . .$ 7,056,439,000

There was real need for bank expansion in winning the great war. We had to raise an army of four million men and send half of them to France. We had to transform our industries from a peacetime to a wartime basis. We had to finance the United States government, which had borrowed some $17 billion in the four liberty loans and some billions more on short maturities. We had to finance the shipments of munitions and supplies to our Allies in Europe, and to finance a great many shipments to them from other parts of the world. We had to do business on a price level high above the price level in the period between 1922 and 1928. There was need for the expansion of bank credit.

---

fix a precise date for the culmination of the move, but the following midyear figures will show that the expansion ceased for all member banks soon after it had ceased for the reporting member banks:

Total Deposits

June 30, 1924 . . . .$29,566,000,000
June 30, 1925 32,457,000,000
June 30, 1926 33,762,000,000
June 30, 1927 35,393,000,000
June 30, 1928 36,050,000,000
June 29, 1929 35,866,000,000

The total loans and investments of all member banks also ceased to grow rapidly. They had increased from $32,756,000,000 on June 30, 1927, to $35,061,000,000 on June 30, 1928, but had then risen only to $35,711,000,000 by June 29, 1929. The figures for all commercial banks likewise ceased to expand on the June to June basis in 1928. The total deposits of all commercial banks rose from $47,781,000,000 on June 30, 1927, to $49,215,000,000 on June 30, 1928, but then dropped slightly to $49,036,000,000 on June 29, 1929.

[2] *Chase Economic Bulletin,* November 8, 1926, p. 3.

We watched bank credit with fear and trembling as it expanded during World War I, because we knew then what we seem since to have forgotten, the dangers of overexpanded bank credit. We held it down all we could. But a great expansion was needed and we made it. It was enough. An expansion of $5.8 billion in deposits, with $7 billion in loans and investments, was enough.

Between the middle of 1922 and April 1928, without need, without justification, lightheartedly, irresponsibly, we expanded bank credit by more than twice as much, and in the years which followed we paid a terrible price for this.

Protests Against the 1922–28 Expansion. The process did not go on without criticism. The *Chase Economic Bulletin* challenged it again and again as it went on.[3] Again and again throughout the period the *Commercial & Financial Chronicle* of New York, in powerful editorials, attacked the Federal Reserve policy responsible for this great bank expansion, and gave warnings. And again and again as the process went on the late H. Parker Willis, professor of banking at Columbia University and formerly secretary of the Federal Reserve Board, sounded warnings. Inside the Federal Reserve System itself there were opposition and resistance. The Chicago Federal Reserve Bank held back, especially in 1927, and was compelled to lower its rediscount rate by a vote of the Federal Reserve Board. Governor Seay, of the Federal Reserve Bank of Richmond, protested. The influence of W. P. G. Harding, who after leaving the Federal Reserve Board became governor of the Boston Federal Reserve Bank, was strongly on the side of sound policy. Inside the New York Federal Reserve Bank Dr. W. Randolph Burgess, author of the excellent book *The Reserve Banks and the Money Market,* was definitely on the conservative side, although his influence in the bank was reduced by his comparative youth, and although he was doubtless inhibited by a great personal loyalty to and affection for his chief, Benjamin Strong.

But the system was adrift. It was hard to center responsibility, particularly after the Federal Reserve Board lost heart and courage when W. P. G. Harding was forced off the board by President Harding, and Crissinger took his place.

Federal Reserve Banks Used to Finance Stock Market Boom. The Federal Reserve Act would have worked well had traditional central bank policies been followed, namely, the holding of the rediscount rates above the market rates, and the use of open market operations primarily as an instrumentality for tightening the money market, not for relaxing it.

The Federal Reserve System was created to finance a crisis and to

---

[3] *Ibid.,* July 20, 1921; March 27, 1923; August 4, 1924; August 24, 1925; November 8, 1926; October 29, 1927; June 4, 1928; June 25, 1928; February 11, 1929; May 8, 1929; September 29, 1930; March 16, 1931.

finance seasonal needs for pocket cash. It was not created for the purpose of financing a boom, least of all for financing a stock market boom. But from early 1924 down to the spring of 1928 it was used to finance a boom and used to finance a stock market boom.

The Heart of the Money Market. The figures given above for the total of the deposits in the commercial banks of the country—over $44 billion on April 11, 1928—or for the loans and investments for the commercial banks, which stood above $47 billion on the same date, did not constitute the supply of loanable funds in the money market. The loans and investments represent money already supplied, money already loaned and invested. The deposits of the commercial banks do not constitute loanable funds for the banks. A depositor of the bank may loan his deposit balance to some other individual, but the bank cannot do so. A bank's deposits are its liabilities, not its assets. The bank's deposits are what the bank owes, not what the bank has. A bank can increase its loans or investments only when it is in a position to pay out cash or create a new deposit liability. And its ability to do either of these things depends upon its cash reserves, in relation to its existing deposit liabilities.

The reserves of the member banks of the Federal Reserve System on this same date, April 11, 1928, stood at $2,432,000,000, a figure very much smaller than the $44,000,000,000 of deposits or the $47,000,000,000 of loans and investments.[4]

But not even in this smaller figure of the reserves of the member banks have we reached the heart of the money market. Not nearly all of this $2,432,000,000 was available as a basis for bank expansion. Most of it was required to maintain the existing volume of bank credit. Most of it was legally required reserves. Sometimes all of the reserves are required, and sometimes all of the reserves are less than the requirements. It is only when reserves are excessive that bank expansion can move easily.

The real heart of the money market is in the marginal reserves, plus or minus, above or below the required reserves. During the 1920s this heart of the money market was contained within a maximum figure of $150 million: $100 million above the required reserves and $50 million below the required reserves. With excess reserves of $75 million to $100 million bank credit expanded rapidly. With a reserve deficiency of as much as $50 million the member banks would be under pressure, would hold back on expansion, would sell investments, would call loans at the stock market, and would rediscount at the Federal Reserve banks.

In the New York money market alone, it was the experience of the

---

[4] The member banks of the Federal Reserve System had over seventy-three percent of the bank resources of the country at this time. The remaining banks, of course, had their own reserves in part in the form of deposit balances with member banks, but I simplify the discussion by ignoring this.

middle 1920s that an increase or decrease of $20 million to $30 million in the reserve balances of the New York banks with the Federal Reserve Bank of New York could make a difference of 0.5 percent in the call loan rate.[5] The forces immediately involved in the short run adjustments of supply and demand in the money market, at a time when the banks are using their funds pretty fully, are concerned with marginal quantities—marginal quantities of Federal Reserve deposits, as distinguished from commercial bank deposits.

Federal Reserve Deposits "High-Powered" Dollars. Deposits with the Federal Reserve banks are "high-powered" dollars. To the ordinary individual a check drawn on the Federal Reserve bank looks like any other check. He deposits it with his own bank as he would deposit any other check. But to a member bank of the Federal Reserve System, a check on a Federal Reserve bank is a very different thing from a check on another bank in the clearinghouse. The great banks learned early to segregate checks on the Federal bank from other checks, so that they might be deposited at once with the Federal Reserve bank, instead of going to the Federal Reserve bank through the clearinghouse the next day. The point was simple—they got immediate credit in their reserve accounts by so doing, and immediately had additional loanable funds.

The reserve requirements of the commercial banks of the United States have long been fixed by law. This has not been generally true in other countries. In other countries the bankers have used their judgment and their experience in deciding how much reserve they would keep. A bank with a few large depositors, any of whom might withdraw large sums on short notice, would carry larger cash reserves than a bank with a large number of deposits of moderate size. A banker subject to heavy withdrawals at certain seasons of the year would build up his reserves in anticipation of these withdrawals. A banker, foreseeing a crisis, would try to increase his reserves before the crisis came. In general, reserve policy would be related: (a) to the variability of deposits and other demand liabilities, and (b) to the liquidity of assets other than reserves. Short-dated paper, spaced so that maturities come daily, and government bonds, instantly salable for cash, justify smaller cash reserves in a bank than would be the case if the bank's chief assets other than reserves were less liquid.

American bankers were, of course, not unaware of considerations of this sort. But accustomed for two generations to having their minimum reserves percentages fixed by law, they had no such grasp of the theory of bank reserves as the best foreign bankers had.

The American country banker, remote from a city correspondent or a Federal Reserve bank, would, indeed, carry a great deal of vault cash in

---

[5] W. Randolph Burgess, *The Reserve Banks and the Money Market* (New York, 1927), p. 163.

addition to his reserve balances in a city bank or with the Federal Reserve bank—cash reserves over and above his legal requirements. The abler city banks, seeing trouble in the future, in pre–Federal Reserve days did build up cash reserves above the legal requirements, in the form of cash in their own vaults. With the coming of the Federal Reserve System, however, the tendency was to carry only such reserves as the law required in the form of deposit balances with the Federal Reserve banks, and to look for the rest to "secondary reserves," and particularly to those assets other than cash which could be taken to the Federal Reserve banks for rediscount. The tendency was for the banker to use his cash to the full, maintaining the cash reserve required by law but no more.

When the reserve requirements were lowered by the wartime legislation of 1917, a dangerous situation was thus created, unless the Federal Reserve System watched closely to prevent the accumulation of even small excess reserves. On the basis of excess reserves in the form of credit balances with the Federal Reserve banks, member bank credit could expand in a multiple ratio, and with the very low reserve requirements the multiple was very high.

Decline in Reserve Ratios, 1921–28. When, moreover, the proportion of time deposits to demand deposits grew—and the preceding chapter has shown that this was the natural consequence of excessive bank expansion—then the reserve ratios went still lower, and the multiple still higher.

The following tables show how the increasing proportion of time deposits pulled down reserve percentages and pulled down required reserve percentages.

REPORTING MEMBER BANKS
(In millions of dollars)

Date	Net demand deposits	Time deposits	Actual reserve percentage
April 1, 1921	10,271	2,925	9.57
April 5, 1922	10,456	3,121	....
April 4, 1923	11,212	3,959	....
April 2, 1924	11,246	4,230	....
April 1, 1925	12,756	5,053	....
April 7, 1926	12,761	5,516	....
April 6, 1927	13,042	6,012	....
April 25, 1928	13,742	6,878	8.75

From April 1, 1921, to April 25, 1928, seven years, the increase in net demand deposits of the reporting member banks was $3,471,000,000, or roughly 33.8 percent, while the increase in their time deposits was $3,853,000,000, or 135.1 percent.

REPORTING MEMBER BANKS—
NEW YORK CITY
(In millions of dollars)

Date	Net demand deposits	Time deposits	Required reserve percentage
April 15, 1921	4,118	290	12.34
April 12, 1922	4,308	353	12.24
April 11, 1923	4,230	627	11.71
April 16, 1924	4,369	650	11.70
April 15, 1925	4,980	816	11.59
April 14, 1926	5,001	814	11.60
April 13, 1927	5,036	960	11.40
April 18, 1928	5,626	1,117	11.34

It is difficult to estimate the legal reserve requirements for all the commercial banks of the country. The table below gives the actual, rather than the required, reserve percentages. The member banks of the Federal Reserve System, though less than half in number of all the commercial banks of the country, held in the 1920s over seventy-three percent of the total deposits of all the commercial banks of the country. The nonmember commercial banks are linked closely with the Federal Reserve System through the fact that they carry the greater part of their reserves in the form of deposit balances with the member banks. Part of their reserves they carry in cash in their own vaults also. The following table, therefore, comparing the *deposits* of *all* the commercial banks with the *reserve balances* of the *member* banks, though misleading if it were interpreted as stating the total reserves of all the commercial banks, or the complete reserve percentage of all the commercial banks, still has real significance.

ALL STATE AND NATIONAL BANKS AND
TRUST COMPANIES
(In millions of dollars)

Date	Total deposits	Member bank reserve balances with the Federal Reserve banks	Actual percentage member bank reserve balances to all commercial bank deposits
June 30, 1922	30,690	1,865	6.08
June 30, 1923	32,726	1,868	5.71
June 30, 1924	35,326	2,016	5.71
June 30, 1925	38,539	2,199	5.71
June 30, 1926	40,126	2,229	5.56
June 30, 1927	41,587	2,342	5.63
April 11, 1928	44,234	2,432	5.50

19

The Causes of and the Responsibility for the Excess Reserves

Factors Feeding and Depleting Member Bank Reserves. It is possible to measure with a great deal of precision the factors involved in the increase or decrease of member bank reserves. "An Analysis of the Money Market"[1] presented a technique for doing this which some of the readers of this book will study. For example, an increase of money in circulation operates to reduce member bank reserves and to tighten the money market. This is regularly true in the autumn, when $300 or $400 million may go out, reaching a peak at Christmas time, followed in the two or three weeks thereafter by a heavy backflow of money to the banks, which enables them to build up their reserves again and eases the money market. An ordinary summer holiday, such as the Fourth of July, may mean an increase of $75 million in circulation, followed in two or three days by a return of the money to the banks. There are many other factors.

The present chapter, however, avoids technicalities as far as possible, and does not discuss those factors which show little variation or which show only a normal seasonal variation. It concentrates attention on the two main significant variables between the middle of 1922 and early 1928, which were: (1) the growth of our gold monetary stock, and (2) the volume and composition of Federal Reserve credit, primarily governed by Federal Reserve policy.

---

[1] *Chase Economic Bulletin,* June 4, 1928. At the time this study was made it was not possible to get all of the elements needed for the computation on the same dates. Most of them come from the consolidated balance sheet from the twelve Federal Reserve banks. Others, like the monetary gold stock of the country and the volume of money in circulation, were at that time obtainable only by accident on the dates of the weekly Federal Reserve statements, since they came in month-end statements from the Treasury. The figures for dates other than month-ends had to be estimated by indirect methods, not wholly satisfactory. Shortly following the study referred to, however, the Federal Reserve authorities, after some correspondence with the present writer, began to give us also money in circulation and monetary gold stock weekly, on the dates of the Federal Reserve statement.

Gold. The gold monetary stock of the country is controllable by five main factors: (a) gold imports, (b) gold exports, (c) gold production in the United States, (d) industrial consumption of gold in the United States, and (e) earmarkings and release from earmark of gold at the Federal Reserve banks, for foreign account. A foreign central bank, which has a deposit account with a Federal Reserve bank, might instruct the Federal Reserve bank to debit its account and earmark gold. The gold would then be the property of the foreign bank, and whether it were subsequently exported or not, it would be effectively withdrawn from the gold monetary stock of the United States. Conversely, a foreign bank with gold under earmark might instruct a Federal Reserve bank to release the gold from earmark and credit its deposit account, which meant that the gold would become the property of the Federal Reserve bank, part of its gold reserve, and part of the American gold monetary stock.

Gresham's Law and Gold Imports, 1920–24. From October 1920 to August 1924 we gained gold steadily from the outside world, our monetary gold stock rising from $2,581,000,000 to $4,234,000,000. The increase from the middle of 1922 to August 1924 was from $3,498,000,000 to $4,234,000,000, or $736,000,000. Part of this gold would have come in any case, because of the great pressure that Europe was under to pay urgent debts here, but after the great liquidation of 1920–21 the controlling factor was the operation of Gresham's law.

Gresham's law is an ancient principle, known apparently to some of the Greeks, but taking its name from Queen Elizabeth's financial adviser, Gresham, who is said to have explained it to the queen. It is the principle that bad money drives out good money, and that inferior money drives out better money. It operates particularly when paper money, formerly redeemable in gold, is no longer redeemed in gold, and consequently depreciates below its gold parity.

Virtually all the important countries of Europe, and most of the important countries of the world outside Europe, except the United States, had restricted gold payments or had ceased to make them. The paper currencies of the major countries outside the United States were depreciated, and fluctuating in value, in the whole period following the war down to late 1924. Under these circumstances additional gold would not go to the monetary reserves of those countries, and such gold as was free to move tended to leave those countries. A man would not take gold to the Bank of England to exchange it for a Bank of England note, because he would lose ten percent of its value thereby. He would not turn in gold to the Bank of France when he thereby lost more than half of its value. He would not use gold in paying debts in England or France. He would use the cheaper paper money instead. He would send his gold to the United States, where he could turn it in to the Federal Reserve bank in exchange for a currency which he could next day or next month or next year redeem in gold at the full face value.

Dangerous Concentration of Gold in United States. This made a dangerous situation. It meant that we were getting a great part of the newly mined gold of the world. It was a situation which could be expected to correct itself when two or three of the other main countries came back to the gold standard, and which did indeed in large measure correct itself when Germany came to the gold standard under the Dawes Plan in 1924, followed by the return of the Dutch guilder and the Swiss franc to par, and in the spring of 1925, by England's resumption of gold payments. When France came back to the gold standard in 1928 we lost gold heavily for a time.

It was widely recognized in the period following the war and throughout the 1920s that a considerable measure of redistribution of the world's gold was needed, and that the way to accomplish this was to restore the full gold standard in several major countries, so that they would compete with us and one another for the floating supply of gold, and so that at least the newly mined gold would go to those countries whose gold reserves were most in need of it and whose interest rates were consequently high enough to attract it.

Peak of Our Gold Holdings Reached in August 1924. The approximate peak of our gold monetary stock in the expansion period of the 1920s was reached in August 1924 at $4,234,000,000. There was a sharp drop in late 1924 and early 1925, due in considerable part to the shipment of gold to Germany following the Dawes Plan loan, and a gradual rise to a slightly higher peak of $4,323,000,000 in April 1927, followed by a steady decline to $3,822,000,000 in April 1928—which month, as we have previously seen, marked the peak of our 1922–28 bank expansion. *Incoming gold, in other words, ceased to be an important factor feeding member bank reserves after August 1924*.

Trustees of World's Gold. We were, and for a time we recognized that we were, trustees for the world's gold. We had no right to merge it so inextricably with our own financial system that we could not certainly and easily return it. It was in a high degree imprudent so to merge it with our own affairs that we could return it only by means of painful liquidation. Certainly it was unwise in the extreme to build upon it an unusual and illiquid kind of bank credit. It was unwise in the extreme to adopt a policy which would expand bank credit in capital uses, such as real estate mortgage loans, stock and bond collateral loans, bank investments in bonds, and the like. And yet we did these things.

Unsound Federal Reserve Policy. Had the Federal Reserve System followed orthodox central bank tradition, using no discretion at all but merely obeying the rules, we should have averted the disasters that followed. The orthodox tradition called for rediscount rates above the market rates and for strictly limited use of open market operations. The most important of these two rules related to open market operations.

Rediscount Rates Below Market Minor Factor. Federal Reserve rediscount rates were held below the market throughout this period, meaning by "the market" the prime customers' rate at great city banks.[2]

But the banks had learned a lesson in 1919 and 1920 about borrowing to relend at a profit. They had got much too deeply in debt to the Federal Reserve banks in the course of this, and they had been struggling since 1920 to get out of debt to the Federal Reserve banks. The tradition had grown that a bank should not borrow for the purpose of relending at a profit. The tradition was strong that great city banks did not like to be in debt at all to the Federal Reserve banks, and that the country banks, even though borrowing for their seasonal needs, wished to be completely out of debt to the Federal Reserve banks at least once a year.

When the total rediscounts were over $500 million, enough banks were under pressure, partly from this tradition and partly from shortage of paper for rediscount at the Federal Reserve banks, so that the money market was reasonably firm and bank expansion was retarded. Banks would rediscount to prevent a liquidation—they would discount heavily rather than force customers to liquidate. But they would not rediscount heavily, even at low rates, for the purpose of making new loans which their customers did not require or, above all, for the purpose of making investments.

Main Factor Open Market Purchases of Government Securities. The violation, therefore, of the established rule that rediscount rates should be above the market, though a contributing factor to the overexpansion of bank credit from June 1922 to April 11, 1928, was not the main element in Federal Reserve policy which was responsible. The main factor was their open market purchases of government securities.

Prewar Open Market Operations of Bank of England. The Bank of England had used open market purchases and sales of government securities in prewar days. But the transactions were small. The motive which commonly actuated the Bank of England in buying government securities seems to have been primarily profit, rather than the desire to make interest rates low. It was the *sales* of government securities, including Indian Council bills, which most impressed the London market—the purpose of such sales being to take up the floating supply of money and "make bank rate effective." The transactions were small. In one instance the sale of £1.1 million of Indian Council bills sufficed to make bank rate effective. Operations of £5 million were large operations. Often the Bank of England did not have enough securities to sell for the purpose and would go out and borrow money against gold collateral as a means of reducing the money supply. The operations were in general restrictive.

Wartime Open Market Operations in England and United States. At the

---

[2] See Hepburn and Anderson, "The Gold and Rediscount Policy of the Federal Reserve Banks," *ibid.*, July 20, 1921. Reproduced in full in *Commercial & Financial Chronicle*, July 23, 1921, pp. 349–54, and in Hepburn, *History of Currency in the United States* (1924).

outbreak of the war in 1914 a new discovery was made. The British government, needing money, first borrowed from the Bank of England, and the Bank of England also bought short-term Treasury bills in the open market. This had the double effect of giving the government the cash it immediately needed, and of putting additional deposit balances with the Bank of England into the hands of the Joint Stock Bank. As the government spent its balances with the Bank of England, the government checks were promptly transferred to customers of the Joint Stock Banks and thence to the Joint Stock Banks themselves. The Joint Stock Banks then deposited these checks in the Bank of England, building up their reserve balances there. This increased the volume of reserve money for the banking community, and made money rates go down, permitting an expansion of general bank credit—the banks buying Treasury bills and government war bonds and financing the community in buying government war bonds.

The London money market appears not to have understood the operation fully at the beginning of the war, and it is not certain that the government or the Bank of England did. The first recourse to the Bank of England was simply a quick way of getting money. But very speedily the trick was learned.

Each new British war loan was preceded by Bank of England buying of government securities, or by direct loans to the government. When the United States government entered the war, the Federal Reserve banks began to use similar tactics. Each of the four liberty loans was preceded by Federal Reserve purchases of United States government securities to ease off the money market. When the loan was over, the Federal Reserve banks promptly sold these government securities again.

Wartime Government Security Operations Small and for a Few Days Only. The magnitudes were not great. For each of the first three liberty loans they amounted to less than $100 million and were promptly reversed. With the fourth liberty loan of approximately $7 billion—a loan made at a time when the capital market had already been very thoroughly drained— the operation was larger. The holding of government securities stood at $96 million on October 18 and rose to $350 million on October 25, but promptly dropped again to $118 million on November 1. These relatively moderate operations were war emergency operations and were short-term operations. They temporarily greased the wheels while vast financial transactions needed for war were put through. But in general the Federal Reserve System financed the government in World War I, not by buying government securities, but by lending to member banks against government securities.

Peacetime Operations, 1922, 1924, and 1927, Gigantic, and for Many Months at a Time. The contrast between the almost microscopic open market operations of the Bank of England before the war and the very moderate, short open market operations of the Federal Reserve banks in connection with the liberty loans during the war, on the one hand, and the open market operations of the Federal Reserve banks in the period of 1922–28, on the other, is thus enormous. Where the Federal Reserve banks bought tens of millions for a few days, in connection with the first three liberty loans, they bought hundreds of millions and held them for many months in 1922, 1924, and 1927. And where the Bank of England had primarily used its open market operations for the purpose of tightening its money market in prewar days, the Federal Reserve System used them deliberately for the purpose of relaxing the money market and stimulating bank expansion in 1924 and 1927. At a time when unusual circumstances called for extra caution, they abandoned old standards and became daring innovators in the effort to play God.

Three Great Spurts in Bank Expansion Definitely Connected with Three Great Open Market Purchases. The process of the creation of excess reserves with the resultant great expansion of bank credit did not move slowly and gradually from early 1922 to early 1928. It was concentrated, rather, in three great moves. Each of these three great moves was inaugurated by heavy purchases of government securities by the Federal Reserve banks. The first of these has already been discussed. It came in 1922. It came because the Federal Reserve banks had very heavy expenses and did not wish their overhead to decline.

In 1924 the Federal Reserve banks bought government securities on a great scale for the deliberate purpose of expanding bank credit, and the process of bank expansion was resumed on a vast scale, with a carryover into 1925. In 1926 and early 1927 the bank expansion moved at a much slower rate.

Then again in the latter part of 1927 there came a third great move in the purchase of government securities, with a new great burst of expansion in bank credit.

The curve for member bank reserves rises very sharply from early 1924 to the year end. It moves very moderately from 1924 through 1926. It starts up again and reaches new highs in 1927. The main responsibility for excessive reserves and for multiple expansion of bank credit based on the excess reserves rests on the open market policy of the Federal Reserve System.

This chapter has ignored a great many factors in the money market in the period under discussion. It has concentrated on the two great essentials, gold and Federal Reserve bank open market policy. These are the two great variables. Responsibility rests with the Federal Reserve System.

Preceding chapters have discussed the open market purchases in 1922 and 1924. A later chapter will discuss more fully the culminating episode of 1927, which touched the match to the powder keg and set the uncontrollable forces working which blew us up late in 1929. But before discussing this it is best to give an account of the developments in the world outside the United States—particularly in Germany, France, and England—which explain the problems facing the Federal Reserve System in 1927, and to give an account of the developments in the American securities markets in the years 1924–26.

20

Germany, 1924–28

Dramatic Upswing, 1924–25. Following the inauguration of the Dawes Plan in 1924, there came a radical improvement in the whole German picture. The confidence of the Dawes Committee that private enterprise would work things out if only the budget could be balanced, the currency could be stabilized, and a political future assured under which the Germans could see that their reparations burdens were bearable, proved abundantly justified. The German government and the German people set to work with a tremendous determination to make the plan work. The upswing in industrial production was extraordinary. Foreign capital flowed into Germany, attracted by the high rates of interest which the Germans were eager to pay to replenish working capital which had been largely wiped out in the period of inflation.

Causes of Short-lived Drastic Crisis, Late 1925. In late 1925 there came a short-lived but drastic commercial crisis in Germany. The main causes were the following:

1. *Inflation Had Left Few Landmarks.* The chaotic conditions of the several years preceding the Dawes Plan left few dependable landmarks on the basis of which economic reckoning could proceed. Assumptions had to be made, guesses had to be made, and, necessarily, many were erroneous. German tax experts in days before the war could ordinarily make advance estimates of revenues with narrow margin of error. They could not in 1924. In a tranquil business situation every businessman will have tabulated experience, on the basis of which he can estimate his costs, markets, prices, and profits. No German industry was in this fortunate position in 1924. Many of the plans and calculations, therefore, made in 1924 were proved to be mistaken plans by the autumn of 1925. During the period when the mark was sinking rapidly in value, working capital largely disappeared. No small part of it was turned into fixed capital. It was better to build plants which might depreciate to fifty percent than to hold marks

that might go to zero. In 1924 Germany found herself with a vast deal of idle plant equipment. The future might or might not validate this investment in any given case. Some of it proved to be well adapted to the market demands which developed in late 1924 and 1925. Some of it was partially adapted, some of it could not be used. Some of it was used for purposes which later turned out to be unprofitable. There were grave uncertainties, too, as to the foreign markets; important miscalculations were made. Some foreign markets proved much better than expected, others proved disappointing. But in all cases the calculations and plans which had to be made in 1924 rested on very inadequate data.

2. *Inflation Had Wiped Out Working Capital.* Germany in 1924 was desperately short of working capital. Current stocks of goods were very low, and cash and credit with which a manufacturer might purchase raw materials, pay wages, and carry "work in process" were desperately short. A minor but painful feature of the crisis of 1925 was the elimination of a great many pitiful small businesses with hopelessly inadequate capital. German businessmen had come home to Germany from the German parts of Poland and from Alsace-Lorraine with very inadequate capital, but with a desire to continue as businessmen, rather than as workmen. These men established a multitude of petty businesses, frequently retail merchandising. Dr. Oskar Wassermann of the Deutsche Bank gave figures for the number of tobacco dealers. In 1907 there were in Germany 29,487 such dealers. In 1924 there were 412,000. Large numbers of these small people were eliminated as independent entrepreneurs in the crisis of 1925—later to become clerks or workmen in the employ of larger houses.

3. *Taxation Too Effective.* Perhaps the greatest factor of all in the interruption of the strong revival was the extraordinary effectiveness of the taxation inaugurated after the Dawes Plan was set up. The German people and the German government were determined that whatever else might not be done, they would balance their budget, and they inaugurated a system of taxation with ruthlessness and efficiency. The resulting revenues ran far beyond expectations and far beyond needs. The table on page 160 comparing actual revenues and budget estimates shows how greatly the tax experts underestimated the efficiency of their taxation.

4. *Government Banks vs. Private Banks.* It was unfortunate enough to take so much unneeded money away by taxation, but it was still worse that the government bodies put their excess tax money, not into the commercial banks where it could have been lent back to the businesses, but into government-controlled banking institutions. One-third or more of all bank deposits in Germany in 1925 were in public banks, chiefly deposits of public funds. These banks largely limited themselves to the purchase of prime bills of exchange, that is, "discounts," rather than the slow "advances" of the sort which German banks ordinarily made to their business

ACTUAL REVENUES AND BUDGET ESTIMATES*
(In millions of reichsmarks)

Financial year ended March 31, 1925	Budget estimates	Actual receipts	Surplus (+) Deficit (−)
Taxes on income, sales, transport, etc.:			
Income tax	1,344.0	2,213.3	+869.3
Corporation tax	144.0	313.9	+169.9
Tax on real and personal property ...	376.0	498.9	+122.9
Turnover tax:			
(a) Ordinary	1,260.0	1,798.5	+538.5
(b) Extraordinary (luxury)	180.0	119.3	− 60.7
Tax on bourse transactions	150.0	112.8	− 37.2
Transport tax	230.0	312.6	+ 82.6
Other recurring taxes	424.0	316.3	−107.7
Nonrecurring taxes	36.0	79.0	+ 43.0
Customs, and taxes on tobacco, beer, etc.:			
Customs	160.0	356.6	+196.6
Tobacco tax....................	360.0	513.7	+153.7
Beer tax	126.0	196.5	+ 70.5
Sugar tax	231.0	219.1	− 11.9
Spirits monopoly	140.0	141.4	+ 1.4
Nonassigned....................	82.7	123.0	+ 40.3
Miscellaneous	....	7.6	+ 7.6
	5,243.7	7,322.5	+2,078.8

* *Report of the Agent General for Reparations Payments,* November 30, 1925, pp. 32–33.

customers. The result was a relative excess of funds in the short-term money market and an appalling scarcity of funds available for the working capital of business.

5. *Foreign Loans to States and Municipalities.* The foreign flotations of German loans, particularly those placed in the United States, were to a very great extent loans to German states and municipalities, rather than to German businesses. There were important short credits given by foreign banks, especially American banks, to German banks, and to some extent short credits made by foreign and German banks "on joint account" to German businesses, with the German banks supervising the loan and sharing the risk, but with the American or other foreign banks providing most of the money.

In the autumn of 1925 one found in London and in Paris an inadequate understanding of the German situation. In the Netherlands the understanding was much clearer. In Sweden the German picture was well understood. Swedish banks urged the view that the German state and municipal loans which had been floated abroad, chiefly in the United States, were making trouble rather than doing good. The governing bodies already had too much money, as a result of the very heavy taxes. These loans gave them more. They were able to outbid business for labor and supplies, much of which they used in construction, which Germany could not afford with capital so acutely scarce. They thus raised the costs of general industry, the more so as officials, for political reasons, often wished to be generous to labor, and were not as sagacious and prudent as businessmen would be in their purchase of supplies. This was regarded as a special handicap to the export industries, which needed to expand if Germany were to carry through the Dawes Plan program.

The Swedish bankers urged that the United States should cease to make these state and municipal loans.

In Berlin one found an extraordinarily clear understanding by the German banks, Parker Gilbert (agent general for reparations payments), the Reichsbank, and the German Treasury of what was happening in Germany. The heads of several of the banks, Gilbert, and representatives of the Reichsbank and the Treasury all wished a cable sent to New York saying that although loans to the German industries were desirable and would do a great deal of good, loans to the states and municipalities should stop. The cable was sent. On the day that the cable from Berlin reached New York, Dr. Schacht, the head of the Reichsbank, personally appeared in New York to urge on the American banking community that there should be no more state and municipal loans made to Germany.[1]

Dr. Schacht made a tremendous effort then, and in the years that followed, to hold down Germany's borrowings from foreign countries.

But under the impact of the gigantic flood of bank money generated by the policy of the Federal Reserve System in 1924, money was superabundant in New York and the illusion of unlimited capital was growing. The market for high-yield foreign bonds in the United States seemed insatiable, and the American investment bankers were trying to supply the market. In late 1925 the agents of fourteen different American investment banking houses were in Germany soliciting loans from the German states and municipalities. It was impossible to control the competitive money market in New York, and it was difficult for the head of the Reichsbank to control the states and municipalities in Germany.

Rarely has an economic situation been more fully and clearly under-

---

[1] I am glad to be able to say that the securities affiliate of my own bank respected the advice of the German financial authorities, and ceased to initiate German state and municipal loans in the United States after November 1925, and participated in such issues only to the extent of $4 million thereafter. See the *Chase Economic Bulletin,* October 8, 1931, pp. 7–8. In the final reckoning the securities affiliate was reported as having sponsored a much greater volume of state and municipal loans to Germany, but this was due to the fact that, after 1929, mergers took place with institutions which had had greater activity in this matter.

stood by the men responsible for its management than was the German picture in late 1925.[2]

Hopefulness of Germany in the Midst of the Crisis. In the midst of this crisis, moreover, one found a hopefulness among the humble people. It seemed strange at a time when six percent of all the bills of exchange in the country had gone to protest, when unemployment was increasing every day, and when the newspapers were full of bankruptcy notices. German workmen showed with pride the new, shiny silver marks, which they trusted. They had a good currency again. They were suffering, yes. Times were hard, yes. But the inflation had been infinitely worse. Again and again workmen said, "No more war, no more inflation." And it was not only the workmen. In October 1925 an able French banker met for the first time the head of one of the great German banks at the latter's home. The two men had hardly exchanged greetings before the German said to the Frenchman, "Of course we both hate socialism, but we must nonetheless support the parties of the Left, for that means peace. We must put down the nationalists in both our countries." And the French banker cordially agreed.

Turn Upward to Full Employment in Spring 1926. The German tide turned upward again in spring 1926. Prices of securities of the German Bourse had an extraordinary rally, industry moved, employment grew full, and Germany had a period of nearly three years of strong, sustained industrial activity with excellent business profits.

Full Employment for Three Years at Extremely High Interest Rates. It must be said that this German business rally was on the basis of extremely high interest rates. There were occasionally times when the rates on call money, Taegliches Geld, were low. Thus on March 20, 1926, that rate dropped from 3 percent to 2 percent, after having averaged over 8.5 percent from March 1925 through December 1925; but thirty-day paper was still 7 percent in March 1926, the discount rate on prime bills of exchange still 5 percent, while bank "advances" remained between 11 percent and 14 percent.

These bank advances in Germany were in general much slower loans than ordinary customer's paper in the United States. They were the typical business loan made by German bank to German business. The lowest rate on these bank advances between 1924 and 1929 was 9 percent, and this was on three loans made by Goldschmidt of the Darmstaedter Und National-bank in 1927.

Cheap Money Not Essential for Full Employment. The theory that cheap

---

[2] In the midst of the crisis in late 1925, I received from German bankers and others, *as prophecy,* a picture which I was able to publish with very little alteration, as *history,* under the title "German Business and Finance Under the Dawes Plan," *Chase Economic Bulletin,* April 2, 1926.

money is essential for business revival and business activity received a pretty sharp test in this period, I think. The British, with much lower rates, and with rates held unduly low on the theory that cheap money was necessary for good business, went through a prolonged stagnation, with high unemployment. The Germans, more flexible, making the necessary readjustments in wages and other costs, endured both high interest rates and cruelly high taxation, but still did business and made money, with very full employment.

Cheap money plays no such dominating role as Keynes and Hawtrey and their followers would have us believe.

Throughout this period Germany continued to get a very great volume of foreign loans, much exceeding the total reparations she paid during the period. But never during the whole period from the inauguration of the Dawes Plan to her credit collapse in 1931 did she have enough liquid capital to make an easy working-capital situation for her industries.

21

France, 1925–26

*C*risis in Government Credit and Currency. Germany was rallying strongly in the spring of 1926. France was plunging lower and lower in a great crisis in currency and national credit. In a previous chapter we have seen the story of French postwar deficits. Government deficits had run approximately 47 billion francs in 1919, 42 billion francs in 1920, 28 billion francs in 1921, 19 billion francs in 1922, 17 billion francs in 1923, and 14 billion francs in 1924. It was harder and harder to borrow money to fill these gaps.

Bank of France Resists. In Germany, 1918–23, the gap had been filled simply by government borrowing from the Reichsbank. In France the Bank of France, partially independent, held back and resisted. The government got the greater part of its funds on short-term paper, the so-called bons de la défense nationale, largely taken by the private banks or by the people. The law, moreover, put a limit on the government borrowing from the Bank of France and on the issue of notes by the Bank of France, and while this limit was from time to time raised by act of the French Parliament, it was always a humiliating experience for the ministry to ask for an increase, and always a source of great concern to the French people when this was done.

Two figures were well understood by the working people, as well as by the merchants and financiers of France. They were the figures for "advances to the state" on the asset side of the balance sheet of the Bank of France, and the figure for banknote issue on the liability side of the balance sheet. One saw French hotel porters eagerly scanning the newspaper on the day when the balance sheet of the Bank of France was to be issued, and saying to one another, "The *bilan* is good today"—or bad, as the case might be. The Bank of France fought, and held back, and protected the French franc in so doing, though the franc fell far.

But Falsifies Its Balance Sheet at Year End, 1924–25. At the year end, 1924–25, the Bank of France falsified its balance sheet.[1] It had, in fact, in

[1] *Commercial & Financial Chronicle,* April 11, 1925.

making year-end advances to the government and others needing to meet year-end commitments, exceeded its legal note issue. The year-end statement showed the notes below the legal limit, but showed also an immense increase in a previously small item, *divers*, or miscellaneous, which did not deceive the informed reader of the balance sheet. Subsequently Baron Rothschild, a director of the Bank of France, forced a disclosure of this deception by threatening to make the facts public himself, and the Bank of France made the humiliating confession that it had exceeded its legal limit and that it had falsified its balance sheet. Confidence in France fell low and confidence throughout the world in French finance fell low. The franc continued its downward course.[2]

Even So, Bank's Resistance Helped. Nonetheless, despite this pitiful record, the bank did make an effort, and its effort did hold down the deficits and did retard the collapse of the franc. The effort did, moreover, leave the Bank of France in a strong position to protect the franc after the collapse and the readjustment.

Franc Drops to Two Cents, July 1926. Between May 1925 and late July 1926 the franc dropped rapidly from five cents to two cents in the foreign

---

[2] In late September 1925 I had occasion to discuss this episode with one of the chiefs of the Bank of France. He spoke with great frankness. Caillaux was then premier of France. Caillaux was undertaking financial reforms, but they were inadequate. One element involved the flotation of a gold loan with the promise that even if the franc should go lower, the loan would be paid in whatever sum of francs was necessary to give back the gold value stipulated in the bond. The public was skeptical and the loan was not going well. Drastic taxation was needed and drastic retrenchment in public expenditures, including pensions; and Caillaux did not have the courage for that.

The official of the Bank of France in substance said: "The bank hates and fears the government. The government lies to the bank. Last week my balance sheet looked terrible. The government had promised me revenues from the provinces and had not brought them to me. The government had continued to draw upon the bank. My notes were over the legal limit. I went to the other banks of Paris and persuaded them to take government securities from my portfolio and to give me back banknotes for one day. I was thus able to publish a correct balance sheet showing the notes under the legal limit. The next day I turned back the banknotes and took back the government securities. This week the revenues did come in and my balance sheet will be all right.

"But what can I do? If my father has stolen money, must I not make it good?" I said, "If the agent of my father has stolen money, do I have to make it good?" He said, "We cannot make that distinction in France. Le Gouvernement—c'est la France." I said, "Does that mean that you would falsify the balance sheet again?" He said, "What can I do? The Bank of France is paymaster for the government all over France. If I refuse to pay, a great crisis comes. Business stops. Merchants and laborers and everybody turn and rend the Bank of France. If I pay and publish, again a great crisis comes. What I shall do will be to pay and not publish and write a letter to the minister every day demanding that he regularize the position by legislation." I said "A British or American banker might feel that he had to yield to the government with respect to making payments, but still would not feel that he had the duty to sign a false balance sheet." He said, "It is so easy for a man standing on the bank of the river to give good advice to a man who is drowning in the middle of a stream." I then apologized and did not further press the point. But the best opinion I could get in Paris at that time was firm in the conviction that if the officials in the Bank of France had offered their resignations rather than falsify the balance sheet, the public would have sustained them, and the ministry, not the bank, would have fallen.

exchange market. Every day the housewife of Paris found that her bread and her herring and her wine were rising in price. A German housewife in the late autumn of 1925, speaking of the French housewife, said "Poor thing!" The German housewife had been there herself.

Public Demands Conservative Finance—Backs Poincaré. There came a great radical change of sentiment in France toward matters both political and financial, and by June 1926 the mob of Paris was swarming around the Palais Bourbon where the Deputies sat, threatening physical violence to the Deputies unless they should get behind the conservative old lawyer, Poincaré, who was promising to raise taxes, to cut expenses, to dismiss public employees, to cut pensions, and to save the franc.

Poincaré and Briand Unite to Save Franc. There came, too, a magnificent change in sentiment among the responsible men in public life in France. Briand had been Poincaré's leading opponent. Briand had many admirable qualities, but financial soundness was not one of them. He knew little about finance. He did know international relations. He had fought hard to bring about French and German conciliation. He had publicly defended the good faith of Germany in debate before the Chamber of Deputies. He had opposed the invasion of the Ruhr. Poincaré was the implacable foe of Germany. He distrusted Germany. Poincaré understood finance. He believed in economy. He believed in sound finance. The two men got together. Poincaré generously turned over to Briand the conduct of foreign affairs and the relation between France and Germany, backed him up in a policy with which he had personally little sympathy. Briand in turn gave generous, strong support to Poincaré's financial reforms, which he inadequately understood.

There was magic in it. July 1926 showed the bottom for the French franc. Poincaré made good in a magnificent way in his policy of cutting expenditures, cutting pensions, dismissing needless public functionaries, and raising taxes, and created a fiscal surplus.

Poincaré, moreover, knew his countrymen. He knew that his reforms would be subject to whittling down and modification and even drastic reversal by a succeeding ministry. He therefore did everything in his power to prevent this. Certain of his basic reforms, he enacted them into constitutional law. He took the two chambers of the Parliament, the Senate and the Chamber of Deputies, to Versailles, where he had them vote together on the basic framework of his reform legislation, which they could not subsequently constitutionally reverse sitting as separate houses in Paris.

The Franc in Dramatic Rally. The tide of confidence at home turned radically. In the long period when the franc was slipping an immense body of French capital left France and went into foreign values. French private holdings of dollars, sterling, Swiss francs, Dutch guilders, and securities of foreign countries had grown very large. This tide turned toward France again. Frenchmen were selling their foreign exchange and buying francs.

Foreigners also were buying francs as well as buying securities in the French Bourse. An immense tide of money turned toward France. With startling rapidity the French franc rose from two cents[3] to approximately four cents. The Bank of France and the government appear to have been caught unawares by the extent and strength of this movement.

The Preceding Collapse in Franc Made Poincaré's Task Technically Not Difficult. From the standpoint of technical finance, Poincaré's task in the summer of 1926 was not unduly difficult. The collapse in the franc had already brought it lower than the fundamentals of the situation justified.[4]

One factor which we have already mentioned in connection with the German debacle was the fact that France relied primarily on indirect taxation and the revenue of fiscal monopolies instead of income taxes based on last year's incomes. These revenues rose as the franc fell, as prices rose, and as the volume of transactions measured in francs rose.

Moreover, expenditures of the French government did not rise nearly as fast as the franc declined. Approximately fifty-three percent of the expenditures in 1926 were for service on the internal debt, including pensions, and were fixed in francs.

The Bank of France had a very low reserve ratio, taking the franc at par, as shown by the following figures for June 9, 1926:

Total reserves (gold in vault,
   3,684,000,000 francs, plus silver
   at bullion value plus foreign balances)* ..... 4,584,000,000 francs
Notes in circulation .... 53,353,000,000 francs
Reserve ratio 8.6%

* Estimated. The balance sheet of the bank did not disclose the amount of the Morgan loan remaining.

If, however, the franc were taken at 4¢, the reserve ratio similarly calculated would be 41.5 percent, and with the franc at 3¢ the reserve ratio would be 55.3 percent. At 3.5¢ per franc the reserve ratio would be 37.3 percent.

Four factors could be considered in figuring a reasonable new gold par for the franc: (1) the ratio of gold reserves to the Bank of France, (2) the relation of France's prices in paper money to the level of gold prices in the world outside, (3) current and recent exchange rates, and (4) most important, the relation of the public debt to the total national wealth of France. French wholesale prices in May 1926 were below the world level even if the franc were put at 4¢, while with the franc at 3.5¢ French wholesale prices would have been far below the world gold level. The test of current and recent exchange rates put the franc too low.

---

[3] The franc dropped to 1.94½¢ in the second half of July 1926 (*Commercial & Financial Chronicle*, July 24, 1926, p. 381). But this figure stood for a short time only. The average New York price for francs in the last five days of July was 2.42¢.

[4] See "Stabilizing the Franc," *Chase Economic Bulletin*, June 21, 1926.

NEW YORK PRICE OF FRANCS AND
WHOLESALE PRICES IN FRANCE*
(1913 = 100)

At end of:	French Wholesale Prices					Average of franc at New York last five days each month (in cents per franc)
	In French currency	In gold	Native French products (in French currency)	Imported products (in French currency)	Average of wholesale prices in gold in certain countries**	
(1925)						
January	525	147.2	. . . .	. . . .	160	5.41
February	526	140.6	. . . .	. . . .	159	5.16
March	524	143.6	. . . .	. . . .	158	5.29
April	523	141.5	. . . .	. . . .	153	5.22
May	531	138.4	. . . .	. . . .	153	5.03
June	554	131.5	. . . .	. . . .	154	4.58
July	569	139.7	. . . .	. . . .	155	4.74
August	569	138.3	. . . .	. . . .	154	4.69
September	567	139.0	. . . .	. . . .	152	4.73
October	584	126.8	. . . .	. . . .	151	4.19
November	618	123.6	. . . .	. . . .	150	3.86
December	646	124.2	. . . .	. . . .	150	3.71
(1926)						
January	647	125.7	. . . .	. . . .	148	3.75
February	649	123.1	. . . .	. . . .	146	3.66
March	645	115.3	. . . .	. . . .	143	3.45
April	664	113.9	. . . .	. . . .	143	3.31
May	702	118.2	. . . .	. . . .	143	3.25
June	754	112.5	682	883	144	2.88
July	854	107.1	733	1047	144	2.42
August	785	117.1	722	902	143	2.88
September	804	116.6	743	912	144	2.80
October	768	123.4	744	808	145	3.10
November	698	131.3	698	700	143	3.63
December	641	131.5	648	628	142	3.96

* *Chase Economic Bulletin,* February 18, 1927, p. 27.

** Countries included: United States, Sweden, Germany, Netherlands, and Switzerland for entire period; Great Britain added May 1925; Denmark added October 1926; Belgium added November 1926.

The test of the relation of the total national wealth to the total national debt showed that a return to parity was impossible. Taking the national wealth at 300 billion gold francs, old par, and the internal debt at 309 billion paper francs plus the external debt of 23 billion gold francs (assuming the expected reduction through the then pending debt settlements), the national debt would have clearly exceeded the national wealth at the old par. With the franc placed at 3.5¢, the debt would bear a ratio of 26 percent to the national wealth. If it were felt that France would carry a debt ratio of 29 percent to the national wealth, then the franc could have been placed at 4¢.

Having in mind the traditional French reluctance to pay taxes and the traditional French governmental tendency toward extravagance, 3.5¢ would have been a safer figure at which to stabilize the French franc than the nearly 4¢[5] finally chosen for the *de facto* stabilization in the winter 1926–27 and for the *de jure* stabilization in 1928.

It is convenient to interrupt the story of the French franc in the late autumn of 1926, because an understanding of the British position is

RETAIL FOOD PRICES AND COST OF
LIVING IN FRANCE*
(Prewar = 100)

	Retail food prices (in Paris)		Cost of living (in Paris)	
	(1925)	(1926)	(1925)	(1926)
January	408	480		
February	410	495		
March	415	497	386	451
April	409	503		
May	418	522		
June	422	544	390	485
July	421	574		
August	423	587		
September	431	590	401	539
October	433	624		
November	444	628		
December	463	599	421	545

* *Chase Economic Bulletin*, February 18, 1927, p. 27.

---

[5] *Ibid.*, June 21, 1926; February 18, 1927.

necessary before we can take up the next startling phase in the story of French finance. London and Paris are to become dangerously entangled with one another.

MONEY RATES IN PARIS—1926*

		Bank of France discount rate	Market rate commercial bills	Fortnightly loans at the official stock exchange	Fortnightly loans on curb securities	Bank advances to customers
Jan.	High	6	5	4	11	8
	Low		4⅛	3½	11	from Jan. 1
Feb.	High		5	5¼	11	
	Low		4	7	11	
Mar.	High		5⅛	4⅞	10½	
	Low		4¼	3⅜	10½	
Apr.	High		5	4¼	10¼	
	Low		4¼	3¼	10¼	
May	High		5⅜	5¼	10½	
	Low		4¼	5	10½	
June	High		5¾	7⅞	12	
	Low		4¾	7½	12	
July	High	7½	5⅞	7	14	9½
	Low	on July 31	4⅝	5⅞	14	from July 31
Aug.	High		7⅛	5	13	
	Low		6¾	4	13	
Sept.	High		6⅝ to 7⅛	11	14	
	Low		6½ to 7	7	14	
Oct.	High		6¾ to 7⅜	7½	10½	
	Low		6¼ to 6½	3¾	10½	
Nov.	High		6¼ to 6½	5¼	9	
	Low		5¾ to 6	2¼	9	
Dec.	High	6½	5¾ to 6	4		8½
	Low	on Dec. 16	5½ to 5¾	4		from Dec. 16

* *Chase Economic Bulletin,* February 18, 1927, p. 22.

22

Great Britain, 1925–27

Britain's Unemployment Remains High. The United States had enjoyed, as we have seen, a full industrial recovery between 1921 and 1923. Britain followed, but did not reach full recovery. There remained a heavy body of unemployment. There remained a heavy payment of doles to the unemployed as a burden on the British taxpayer. Britain demonstrated what the present writer believes to be a universal economic law, namely, that any country can have heavy unemployment if it is willing and able to pay for it.

Wages and Prices—United States and Britain. In the discussion of the American price and wage readjustment in 1920–21, we have seen that neither in the United States nor in Great Britain did wages drop nearly so much as wholesale prices dropped in the postwar readjustment. In the United States this was due to a supply-and-demand situation. We had an almost absolute cessation of immigration from Europe during the war, and we had by law restricted immigration in the years following the war. We had altered in a manner favorable to labor the relationship between labor on the one hand, and capital and natural resources on the other. Our high postwar wages were a normal and natural result of this supply-and-demand situation.

England, on the contrary, had had no such favorable change in her labor situation. When her wages failed to resume their prewar relationship to prices, it was primarily because of the strength of the trade unions, which forcibly held union wages above the level which supply and demand would have dictated, with the result that there was heavy chronic unemployment.

Britain's Return to Gold Standard at Par. Britain had straightened out her public finance and had balanced her budget. She had even made a reduction in public debt, and had resumed a great deal of her industrial activity. The pound, which had dropped from the par of $4.8668 to a low of $3.18 in February 1920, had made a strong recovery and stood in late 1924 and early 1925 at approximately ten percent below the gold parity. The British had been hesitant about restoring the pound to par and resuming gold payments. This, as we have seen, made an abnormal situation in which, under Gresham's law, we were receiving a very excessive amount of gold, much of which ought to have stayed in London.

The British had tried in 1924 to prevent the new German Reichsbank from going immediately on the gold standard. But informal pressure from the United States, in connection with American participation in the Dawes Plan loan, had forced Germany to go on a fixed gold basis at once. The British thereupon felt that their hand was forced, and both from pride and from business necessity they brought the pound back to par in April 1925.

Involved a Ten Percent Readjustment—Easy for a Flexible Economy. There has been a great deal of discussion since this time as to the wisdom of this move. There is a considerable body of opinion to the effect that the British put the pound too high, and that they would have done much better to stabilize at ninety percent of the old par, rather than coming all the way back.

Had Britain had anything like her normal flexibility she could have taken this ten percent easily in her stride. A readjustment of prices and costs of ten percent is not difficult and does not take long if a country is flexible.

We saw in the United States, between the summer of 1925 and the summer of 1927, a decline of ten percent in the general average of commodity prices, accompanied by good business, good profits, and the normal rate of growth of industry, with no complaint from anybody except Professor Cassel of Sweden, who thought that commodity price levels ought never to change.[1] The adjustment ought not to have been too difficult for England.

But England Had Lost Flexibility—Union Labor. But England had lost her economic flexibility to a startling degree. This loss of flexibility was not due solely to labor. Organized union labor was indeed inflexible. The British financial community in the autumn of 1925 was either fatalistic or sentimental about the question of reduction in money wages. The head of one great British bank said that one should regard it as axiomatic that there could be no reduction in money wages in England. The head of another great British bank, speaking with reference to the same point, said, "But, the poor beggars, they get so little!"

Rigidity in Industry—Price-Fixing Combines. But the development of rigidity seemed to be a British, rather than an exclusively British labor, characteristic. England in 1925 was shot through with price-fixing combines in her industries. The extent of this was emphasized by a statistical expert in one of the great British banks, and confirmation was readily at hand from many others. Sir Josiah Stamp, for example, told of one

---

[1] See *Chase Economic Bulletin*, May 1929.

combine of four establishments which involved price-fixing and quota agreements. Three of these establishments were well located and strong, and could have cut prices, increasing their volume and increasing their profits. The fourth was ill located and had inadequate equipment. It would have been ruined if the others had cut their prices. The prices were fixed at a point which enabled the weakest of the four to live. Under British law such an agreement was not illegal. It was, however, voidable, that is to say, it could not be enforced in the courts. England had no Sherman law. Sir Josiah, when asked why some of the other plants did not end the absurdity, said simply that it was not done. If the agreement were a legally enforceable agreement, some of the stronger ones would force the pace, break the agreement, cut the price, and let the injured weaker mill sue for damages. But since the agreement could not be legally enforced, it became a gentleman's agreement and of course could not be broken. It was a chivalrous attitude on the part of the stronger British concerns, but one very hard on the economic life of the country. England desperately needed a well-enforced Sherman law.

Clinging to Old Methods and Obsolete Plant and Equipment. There was, moreover, a sentimental clinging to inadequate methods and to physical plant and equipment which had long since outlived their usefulness. Charles M. Schwab, the American steelmaster, at about the same time made a survey of the British steel industry with a view to seeing whether a moderate capital investment and a certain degree of renovation might not turn it from an industry losing money to a profitable one. He concluded, however, that it would be better to scrap a great part of the existing plant and equipment and to build afresh, than to try to renovate what was there.

An American banking house had two interesting experiences which were not unique. One involved a German ironmaster, a customer of this American banking institution, who wished to see the actual operation of a British steel mill which also had banking relations with the American institution, and asked to be introduced to the British firm for this purpose. The American banking institution, carefully explaining to its British customer that the German was a competitor and that they well might not wish to show him what he wished to see, made the introduction. The British concern was more than glad to show the German everything. The German ironmaster was aghast at what he saw. With practically the same plant and equipment that the British mill had, he was getting three operations a day, while the British mill was getting only two operations a day. He told the British concern about it, and expressed his willingness to have them send a man over to see his own operations in Germany so that they might see how he got the three operations a day. The management of the British mill thanked him with great courtesy but was not interested. The management's way was to get two operations a day, and it would adhere to its accustomed procedure.

The second episode took place when British friends asked the American banking institution to interest itself in a British factory of good reputation and fine product, whose financial figures, however, were exceedingly unsatisfactory. It had been unable to pay its preferred dividend for some time. The owners wished, however, additional capital. The American banking institution studied the picture and did not like it. It "declined the opportunity." It was urged to continue its investigation and then went into the matter more fundamentally. It discovered a very large directorate, the members of which included boys of eighteen in college who were receiving £500 a year each—"guinea pigs," the British called them. By reducing the directorate and reducing directors' fees it would be possible to pay the preferred dividend, and it would then be possible to consider the permanent financing which had been requested. The American banking institution naively suggested that this be done. The negotiations abruptly ceased. The business institution was a family affair, and the family was to be taken care of whether the banks were willing to lend money or not.

Appalling Loss of Ablest Leaders Through Volunteer System in World War I. The period of the 1920s was a period in which British financial and industrial leadership had suffered a great deal. One able American observer, long resident in London, offered an interesting and probably highly significant explanation. He was concerned partly with the change in the financial district, "the City of London." But his explanation, he said, applied to the industries as well. England, in the first two and a half years of the war, had the terrible volunteer system under which her best and finest rushed first to the battlefield. And this included very many of the younger men and even men no longer young who would normally become, in a short time, the leaders in industry and finance. The result, he said, was that in the City of London in the middle 1920s you would find a few fine old veterans who remembered the ancient wisdom of London, and you would find their grandsons "miseducated by Keynes." And between the grandsons and the grandfathers was a barrier in ideas such that it was not easy for tradition and practical experience to pass. Meanwhile the sons, who ought to have been ruling the City of London, were dead in France. He may have exaggerated the picture, but there is surely something of pitiful truth in it. England lost an appalling percentage of her finest and best in that cruel war.

The British are not a philosophical people or a people whose practical education comes largely from books. British financial and industrial thinking, to a degree that is probably found in few other modern industrial countries, has been much more a matter of a living tradition passed on from father to son—plastic, modified by experience, but handed down much more by word of mouth than by books. A breach in the continuity of the living tradition would probably be more serious in England than in most other countries.

New Industries Growing in South with Nonunion Labor. The British picture in 1925 was not, however, all black with respect to these points. Both in British industry and in British labor there were flexible elements. The industries of the North and the coal mines might well be depressed, hampered by the rigidities of wages, hampered by price-fixing combines, hampered by antiquated methods. But in the South of England there was going on a new and promising development. New industries were springing up, nonunionized, paying lower wage rates *per hour* than the stagnant industries, but paying labor much more *per year,* because giving full employment. These industries were growing, expanding, making money, taking on new labor.

Four of "Big Five" Joint Stock Banks Liquid in 1925. The financial picture in London in the early autumn of 1925 was not a bad one. The head of one of the "Big Five" Joint Stock Banks said that his bank had gone as far as it dared go in extending credit. Its advances stood at fifty-six percent of its deposits. Ordinarily the British banks at that time looked on fifty percent as a deadline which suggested caution. ("Advances," as distinguished from "discounts," are slow loans to customers, often in the form of overdrafts. "Discounts" are usually highly liquid bills of exchange.) But only one of the five great banks had reached this position. Sir Felix Schuster, when asked about the matter next day, said. "I know who told you that. He's always overloaned!" Sir Felix added that his bank, the National Provincial, was in a very comfortable position, and that he would cheerfully go higher in his advances if the credits suited him. He added, "They do not." Similar information came from the heads of others of the Big Five, and from one or two of the smaller banks.

But All Grew Illiquid During General Strike of 1926. In 1926, however, the British banking position changed radically. The great strike came to England and industrial prostration was extreme. Britain, instead of exporting coal, was importing coal from the continent of Europe. And the British banks, instead of permitting a liquidation of credit—something that would have been inevitable in the United States, where we had twenty thousand independent unit banks—were able, by virtue of the high degree of concentration of the British banking system, to prevent liquidation. They extended credit on a great scale, and sterling went in large quantities to the continent of Europe in the purchase of coal and other goods which England ought to have been creating herself and ought to have been exporting herself. Instead of a readjustment of prices and costs in England and a breaking up of the rigidities, England by credit expansion held the fort and continued the rigidities. British banks increased (a) their slow assets, and (b) their quick liabilities in the form of deposits. Ownership of these deposits speedily came into foreign hands, especially on the continent of Europe.

Concentrated Branch Bank Systems Vulnerable to Governmental Pres-

sure. The British banks acted partly in a spirit of loyalty to the country, but primarily, against their better judgment, under pressure of the government and of public opinion.

A high degree of banking concentration is incompatible with the exercise of free banking judgment, and the substitution of government policy in credit matters for the free exercise of banking judgment is one of the most dangerous things that can come to a country. There are many objections to widespread branch banking. We should preserve competitive banking. Banks should be under pressure all the time to meet their engagements at the clearinghouse every day, so that the banker may be compelled to keep his bank liquid, to hold slow paper to a minimum, and to limit bank credit to proper bankable transactions. When, however, five hundred to a thousand banking offices are under the jurisdiction of a single central office, there is no such pressure on the individual offices; and if there can be concerted policy among a few great central offices, the competitive pressure is so greatly lessened that unsound policies can be carried very far.

London Times *on Bank Expansion and Illiquidity in England in 1927*. The London *Times* of August 8, 1927, said: "The British credit situation . . . remains as tight as a drum. The advances of the ten London clearing banks amount to £934,556,000, equal to 54.4 percent of the deposits; this is an increase of nearly £200,000,000 in five years; but unfortunately in the same period our reserves have not increased, as they have done in America."

In 1929 the ratio of advances to deposits had risen still further in the great banks, and stood for all of them around 55 to 56 percent. In 1925 only one of the great banks had so high a ratio of advances to deposits. Sir Felix Schuster, referring to this, said, "Yes, we are all in that position now. We have yielded against our better judgment to government pressure and to the sentiment of the City." When asked if it were possible to expand further, to take care of customers in a crisis, Sir Felix replied, "These are already panic figures."

23

The *De Facto* Stabilization
of the Franc, and the
Gold Exchange Standard

W e interrupted the story of French finance at the end of 1926 to give an account of significant developments in Great Britain in 1925 and 1926. We now return to the *de facto* stabilization of the French franc in December of 1926, when the French government and the Bank of France concluded that the franc had risen as far as they dared allow it to rise, and intervened to prevent a further rise. The franc by this time had risen from a low of 2¢ in late July 1926 to something over 4¢, and the stabilization was effected in the neighborhood of 4¢—approximately 20 percent of the prewar gold parity of 19.3¢.

But the stabilization was not effected by a definite resumption of the gold standard at a fixed par. Under the strict gold standard a paper currency is held in approximately fixed relation to gold by an automatic and very simple system: the monetary authority, in the case of francs the Bank of France, will pay out gold of fixed weight and fineness on demand as banknotes are presented for redemption, or as depositors request gold in exchange for their deposit balances. On the other hand, the bank will issue new banknotes freely or give new deposit credits in exchange for gold of the same fixed weight and fineness. A paper currency will never rise much above this parity, because if it rises enough to cover the moderate cost of shipping gold, gold will come in from abroad for presentation to the bank, and the supply of paper money will be increased. Nor will the paper money fall much below this parity, because if such a tendency starts, the holders of the paper will take it to the bank and get gold for it.

Lack of New Legal Par Prevents Bank of France from Receiving Gold in Paris. But in 1926 the Bank of France was not free under the laws which existed in France to make use of this simple procedure. The old prewar law still stood, under which gold presented to the Bank of France in Paris could be accepted only at the old parity, which was several hundred percent above the actual market value of the paper franc. No one would take gold to the bank on those terms, since he would thereby lose most of its value. The bank did not dare purchase gold freely in France at the actual market rate, because if the government should subsequently stabilize the franc at a higher parity, the bank would have a loss on all gold so purchased.

Could Buy and Sell Foreign Exchange and Gold Abroad, *Guaranteed Against Loss.* The government had, however, made provisions to indemnify the Bank of France for any losses which might occur on foreign exchange transactions in effecting stabilization, and the bank, when it intervened in the foreign exchange markets to hold down the franc, did so primarily by buying and selling foreign exchange. It could also deal in gold *abroad,* since this was regarded as a foreign exchange transaction, and to some extent the Bank of France purchased gold to be held in foreign countries for its account, increasing the supply of francs in the process and holding down the price of francs. But the overwhelming bulk of the operations in this stabilization process was in the purchase of foreign exchange. Occasionally, if the franc for a short time showed weakness, the Bank of France would reverse its operations, selling foreign exchange, but on balance the overwhelming bulk of its stabilization operations was purchases.

In Stabilizing Franc, Bought $1 Billion of Foreign Exchange in a Year. The foreign exchange holdings of the Bank of France moved upward with startling rapidity from a small sum in the summer of 1926 to a figure estimated at around a billion dollars in October 1927. Not all of this was shown in the balance sheet of the Bank of France. Part of it was supposed to be in the hands of governmental agents.

Chiefly Sterling. The Bank of France was thus creating new francs, not against gold in its own vault, but against deposits and short-term paper in foreign countries which were on the gold standard, and which could and would presumably pay gold. To an appalling extent, moreover, these foreign balances of the Bank of France were in the form of sterling. England had, as we have seen, engaged in a great expansion of bank credit in 1926, particularly during the prolonged strike, and a great deal of this sterling had gone to the Continent. When the tide turned in France and heavy speculation in the franc began, these Continental holdings of sterling were employed in the purchase of francs, and the Bank of France, to hold the franc down, had to buy sterling.

Startling Substitution of Gold Exchange for Gold Standard. This represented the substitution of the gold exchange standard for the gold standard on an unprecedented scale. France, it may be added, was not alone in this. A great many of the smaller central banks of Europe were doing the same thing. At the end of March 1927 the *Federal Reserve Bulletin* estimated that the liquid foreign assets of thirty central banks amounted to $1.6 billion, and by July 1927 the figure had risen to $1.9 billion.[1]

---

[1] *Federal Reserve Bulletin,* June 1927, p. 392.

Reichsbank Increases Gold and Reduces Foreign Balances. Most, but not all, of the continental European central banks increased their holdings during the year July 1926 to July 1927. Notable exceptions were the Reichsbank, which increased its gold at home and reduced its foreign balances sharply during the year, the Netherlands Bank, and the National Bank of Norway. The Bank of Italy tripled its foreign holdings from July 1926 to July 1927. The National Bank of Belgium figure rose from 30,000,000 francs in July 1926 to 2,220,000,000 francs in July 1927. Similar causes were at work for these banks. The great expansion of bank credit in the United States, with an immense volume of foreign loans, was putting dollars into the hands of Italians and Belgians and others who wished to convert them into their local currencies, and the central banks were buying them. They were also buying the overabundant sterling.

Dangers of Gold Exchange Standard—Extraordinary Ease of Bank Expansion. In the prewar days the gold exchange standard was recognized as a makeshift device, usually designed as a transitional step toward the full gold standard. It was a convenient device for small countries or poor countries. A poor country might well consider the interest it earned on foreign exchange holdings, and prefer not to hold all its reserves in non-interest-bearing gold. India had it. The Straits Settlement had it. The Philippines used it. The Austro-Hungarian Bank, prior to 1914, carried a substantial part of its reserve in the form of foreign bills and foreign balances, as did the National Bank of Belgium. But in general the great money markets carried their own gold. Redemption of paper money was generally made in gold throughout the gold standard world. The gold exchange standard was regarded as feasible only because it was unusual, and only because there was a great gold standard world on which to depend. Confined to minor countries, it constituted a safe enough device, but if the effort were made to universalize the gold exchange standard, it is obvious that insolvable problems would arise.

First, obviously, if no country is willing to hold gold and if every country upon receiving gold promptly redeposits it in some other country, the gold would find no home. There would, moreover, be a constant expansion of deposit balances as the gold moved from country to country. Second, if no country paid out gold in redeeming its paper money, but merely paid in checks on some other country, the holder of paper money could never get gold. The gold standard would everywhere cease to exist. And the gold exchange standard would itself break down, since it is predicated on the existence of gold standard countries and ultimate redemption in gold. Third, the process would lead to a violent break in money rates as surplus reserves piled up in every money market, making possible an unlimited expansion of bank credit as the banks all over the world tried to make use of their surplus reserves.

Bank of France Alert to Dangers. It was a dangerous situation, an alarming situation, and the Bank of France was in no way ignorant of the problems which its sudden immense increase in foreign exchange holdings involved. The policy in the Bank of France at the time was made by three extremely able men: Professor Charles Rist, of the University of Paris, who was more or less continually in its councils; Quesnay, later an official of the Bank for International Settlements, whose premature death official of the Bank for International Settlements, whose premature death saddened the international financial community; and Cariguel, a skillful trader in foreign exchange and a man with very much more than a foreign exchange trader's grasp of central banking problems. The Bank of France knew the danger.

Unable to use the procedure of the automatic gold standard, it nonetheless tried to check the flow of funds to Paris by acting on its own account in the way in which commercial forces would have acted had the *de jure* gold standard been established. Seeing that the use of the same gold as reserve in two money markets at the same time was generating an unsound expansion, the Bank of France sought to correct it by converting part of its foreign exchange holdings into gold—particularly by buying gold in London—and also began to transfer part of its holdings of foreign exchange from Europe to New York by selling sterling for dollars.

Had the Bank of France been free to buy gold in Paris in 1926, France would never have gained a billion dollars in foreign exchange. She would have gained instead perhaps $300 million of gold. The gold, coming to France from London, New York, and other gold centers, would have checked credit expansion at those centers, would have cut under the reserves of the Bank of England and the Federal Reserve System, would have forced a tightening of the money rates in New York and London and other financial centers, at the same time that it led to a decline in money rates in Paris. It may be observed that money rates did decline in Paris very sharply as the volume of francs increased through the foreign exchange purchases of the Bank of France, as shown by the following table:

OPEN MARKET DISCOUNT RATE—PARIS*

August 1926 .... 7.00
December 1926 .... 5.77
January 1927 .... 4.99
February 1927 .... 4.45
March 1927 .... 3.89
April 1927 .... 3.17
May 1927 .... 2.46
June 1927 .... 2.25
July 1927 .... 2.13
August 1927 .... 2.04

* *Federal Reserve Bulletin,* October 1927.

Bank of France Tries to Convert Sterling into Gold in London, and into Dollars. The Bank of France undertook to act as the foreign exchange dealers would have acted had the gold standard been in existence, in part by buying gold in London. It also began to transfer part of its exchange holdings from sterling to dollars.

Putting Burden on Sterling, and Draining Gold of Bank of England. These transactions put a heavy burden on sterling exchange, and made drains on the gold reserve of the Bank of England. The position of London became difficult. There was no question of London's ability to protect itself, but London was reluctant to employ the prewar expedient of raising bank rate and tightening the money market. London was under the spell of cheap money doctrine. France did take enough gold out of London in the early part of 1927, however, so that the London bill rate, which had stood at $3^{11}/_{16}$ percent on May 13, 1927, rose to 4⅜ percent (just under bank rate of 4½ percent) on June 3, 1927.

British, Reluctant to Raise Interest Rates, Protest. The British protested. There was a great deal of discussion of the matter in the London press during the first half of 1927. Montagu Norman, governor of the Bank of England, personally urged the Bank of France to do nothing of the sort, telling the bank that sterling was good for it, and that it could not have too much sterling. He tried to induce various Continental central banks to put pressure on the Bank of France to induce it not to take gold from London. One official of the Bank of France said privately during this period, "London is a free gold market, and that means that anybody is free to buy gold in London except the Bank of France." Another official said privately that it was possible for the Bank of France to sell some £3 million in a day in quiet ways, and through indirect channels, without attracting the attention of the Bank of England; but if more than that were sold, an immediate protest would come. It is very hard indeed for "money management" to do the thing that the full gold standard automatically does.

We have, then, the setting for the Governors Conference held in New York in the summer of 1927, in which conference four men participated: the governor of the Bank of England, Montagu Norman; the governor of the Federal Reserve Bank of New York, Benjamin Strong; the governor of the Reichsbank, Hjalmar Schacht; and Professor Charles Rist, deputy governor of the Bank of France. Before giving an account of this conference and its momentous consequences, however, it is best to give a resume of financial developments in the United States from spring 1924 to summer 1927.

24

The Consequences of the Cheap Money Policy in the United States Down to the Summer of 1927

An $11.5 Billion Unneeded Expansion of Bank Credit in Five Years. Bank credit expansion had moved far in the United States between June 30, 1922, and June 30, 1927. For the commercial banks of the United States, state and national banks, and trust companies, there had been an expansion between these dates—both in deposits on the liability side of the balance sheet, and in loans and investments on the asset side of the balance sheet—of not less than $11.5 billion. This expansion of bank credit was not needed by commerce, and commerce did not take it. Commercial loans were, in fact, decreasing after 1924. The figure for "all other loans and discounts" includes the commercial loans, but it also includes installment finance paper. Even so, the figure for "all other loans" was slightly smaller on June 30, 1927, than on the same date in 1921, 1923, and 1926 (all member banks).

Went into Real Estate Mortgages. Unneeded by commerce, the rapidly expanding bank credit went into capital uses and speculative uses. It went into real estate mortgage loans on a great scale. For the member banks of the Federal Reserve System, real estate mortgage loans stood at $460 million in 1918. This figure had risen to approximately $3 billion by the middle of 1927, an ominous increase in illiquid assets.

And Installment Finance Paper. There was, moreover, a great increase in installment finance paper, and by 1927 installment finance paper had become a source of a great deal of concern to the banking community. The terms and conditions were relaxing. Maturities were stretching from twelve to eighteen months, and finance companies were multiplying. It must be said that, in the final day of reckoning, installment finance paper made very little trouble; but this is because the bankers grew alarmed about it in 1926, and insisted on some radical reforms, which included the strengthening of the capital structure of the finance companies and the shortening of maturities. The bank credit men did a good job on this, and the major finance companies cooperated well.

And Security Loans and Bond Investments. The most startling increase, however, in the assets of the banks was in bank investments in bonds and in collateral loans against stocks and bonds.

ALL REPORTING MEMBER BANKS
(In billions of dollars)

End of June	Total demand, time and U.S. government deposits	Investments in securities		Loans against securities	Loans against securities plus investments in securities	All other loans and discounts
		U.S. government	Other			
1922	14.70	2.060	2.158	3.909	8.127	7.115
1923	15.40	2.555	1.968	4.157	8.680	7.748
1924	16.27	2.306	2.260	4.310	8.876	7.939
1925	18.13	2.611	2.655	5.289	10.555	8.085
1926	18.90	2.577	2.785	5.693	11.055	8.541
1927	19.72	2.591	3.067	6.220	11.878	8.628

Declining Liquidity of Banks. The changing character of bank assets had, as a necessary concomitant, a great decline in the percentage of paper eligible for rediscount with the Federal Reserve banks in the assets of the banks, as shown in the next table.

The figures in the table are for national banks only. Comparable figures for all the banks of the Federal Reserve System, for all these dates, are not available, but for the single date June 30, 1926, the Federal Reserve authorities made the following statement:

"Of the total loans and investments of all member banks on June 30, 1926, sixteen percent was eligible for rediscount at the reserve banks, and this proportion was eighteen percent for national banks and about twelve percent for nonnational member banks."[1]

The significance of these figures at the time seemed ominous. The great crisis of 1920–21 was primarily a crisis in commerce and industry, and in the course of the crisis customers who needed loans were able to supply the banks with paper which was available for rediscount at Federal Reserve banks. This circumstance made it far easier for the banks to extend additional accommodation and ease the strain of readjustment. The next crisis, however, seemed more likely to come in installment finance, in real estate, and, above all, in stocks and bonds. And none of these could supply paper eligible for rediscount at the Federal Reserve banks. It was, therefore, of first importance that the banks, in getting ready for major trouble,

---

[1] See *Thirteenth Annual Report of the Federal Reserve Board for the Year 1926* (Washington: Government Printing Office, 1927), p. 9.

NATIONAL BANKS—PAPER ELIGIBLE
FOR REDISCOUNT*
(Figures as of June 30)

		Percentage of eligible paper to total loans and discounts	*Percentage of eligible paper plus U.S. securities to total loans, discounts, and investments*
United States	1923	30.16	37.05
	1925	26.93	32.33
	1926	26.06	30.98
New York City	1923	25.49	38.62
	1925	21.03	31.97
	1926	19.71	30.32
Chicago	1923	36.47	40.50
	1925	30.11	33.50
	1926	27.33	31.38
Boston	1923	32.53	35.61
	1925	12.50	17.26
	1926	21.00	27.05
Reserves cities	1923	31.43	39.18
(excluding New	1925	26.55	33.53
York and Chicago)	1926	26.16	32.49
All reserve cities	1923	30.11	39.11
	1925	25.16	33.01
	1926	24.20	31.69
All country banks	1923	30.21	35.07
	1925	28.91	31.63
	1926	28.16	30.27
Country banks in	1923	31.07	31.59
New York State	1925	30.39	26.95
	1926	27.70	24.22

* *Chase Economic Bulletin,* April 8, 1927, p. 19.

should concern themselves with improving their liquidity, increasing as far as possible the percentage of paper which would be eligible at the Federal Reserve banks, and, also as far as possible, increasing their holdings of government securities which the Federal Reserve banks could lawfully lend against.

There had been a great deal of concern about this trend among thoughtful bankers. Breckinridge Jones, president of the Mississippi Valley Trust Company of St. Louis, and a member of the Federal Advisory Council, was particularly active in urging the matter both upon the Federal Reserve authorities and upon individual banks. The Boston bankers, too, had been alarmed at the sharp decline in their own percentage in 1925, as shown by the table above, and had already taken steps to improve their position, as shown by the figures for 1926.

Rapid Rise in Stock Prices. Along with the growing holdings of securities by banks and the growth in collateral loans against securities had come a great rise in the stock market. The monthly average of Standard & Poor's industrial common stocks index, which had stood at 44.4 in June 1921 and at 59.4 in June 1922, had risen to 103.4 by June 1927. Their railroad common stocks index, which stood at 156 in June 1921 and at 189.2 in June 1922, had risen to 316.2 by June 1927. The public utility common stocks index, standing at 66.6 in June 1921 and at 82 in June 1922, had risen to 135.1 by June 1927.

Stock prices were already high in the summer of 1927. There was an unhealthy tone. There was a growing belief that stocks, though high, were going much higher. There was an increasing readiness to use cheap money in stock speculation. The situation was still manageable. The intoxication was manifest, not so much in violent behavior as in slightly heightened color and increasing loquacity. The delirium was yet to come. It was waiting for another great dose of the intoxicant.

Great Increase in Security Issues. Moving concomitantly with the bank expansion and the rising stock prices was a great increase in new security issues. The following table is based on the annual securities summaries of the *Commercial & Financial Chronicle*.

PUBLIC ISSUES OF SECURITIES IN
UNITED STATES (REFUNDING EXCLUDED)
(In millions of dollars)

1922	4,304
1923	4,304
1924	5,593
1925	6,220
1926	6,344
1927	7,791
1928	8,114
1929	10,195

Growth of Foreign Security Issues. As part and parcel of this issue of new securities, and of strategic importance in connection with it, was the growth of foreign securities placed in the United States. This was significant (a) in getting out the exports of farm products, and (b) in building up the foreign holdings of deposits in American banks, which facilitated the growth of the gold exchange standard as distinguished from the gold standard discussed in an earlier chapter.

Our position in 1927 was thus an unwholesome and a precarious one. We were busy and active, we were making money, there was little unemployment. But we were going ahead despite a fundamental disequilibrium, namely, the weakness of the farmers and the producers of raw materials in the absence of satisfactory export trade. We were temporarily providing them with the export trade by increasing the volume of foreign loans, but we had tariffs so high that export trade would suffer immediately if the foreign loans ceased, and we were making the foreign loans primarily because we were expanding bank credit. The table below shows the relation between exports, imports, export balance, and foreign loans.

It is to be observed in connection with this financing of the export trade by means of foreign loans that an ever increasing volume of foreign loans was necessary if we were to maintain a given volume of exports and a given export balance. Each year that the foreign loans went on meant that an increasing part of next year's foreign loans must be used in paying interest on preceding loans, leaving a smaller percentage available for financing exports. The principle of compound interest was against this policy.

Spending Capital Gains. The continuance of the bank expansion for the purpose of making foreign loans was, moreover, bringing about ominously unhealthy conditions in our domestic life, as shown above. Our bank assets were growing illiquid. Speculation in real estate and securities was growing rapidly, and a very considerable part of the supposed income of the people which was sustaining our retail and other markets was coming, not from wages and salaries, rents and royalties, interest and dividends, but

AMERICAN EXPORTS, IMPORTS, AND FOREIGN LOANS
(000,000 omitted)

	Exports	Imports	Excess of exports	New foreign security issues
1922	3,832	3,113	719	630
1923	4,168	3,792	376	267
1924	4,591	3,610	981	1,047
1925	4,910	4,227	683	1,078
1926	4,808	4,431	377	1,145
1927	4,865	4,185	680	1,562
1928	5,128	4,091	1,037	1,319
1929	5,241	4,399	842	759
1930	3,843	3,061	782	1,010
1931	2,424	2,091	333	255
1932*	1,189	1,015	174	0

* First nine months.

from capital gains on stocks, bonds, and real estate, which men were treating as ordinary income and spending in increasing degree in luxurious consumption. The time for us to pull up was already overdue. The necessity for reducing our tariffs, so that Europe could send an adequate backflow of manufactured goods to us, was growing at an ominous rate. The dangers of the course we had been pursuing since 1922 were increasingly grave. We could prolong it for a time by further bank expansion and by further cheap money policies, but only at the cost of creating a desperately difficult situation at a later time.[2]

---

[2] I had emphasized this danger in the *Chase Economic Bulletin* of August 8, 1925, p. 16, where I forecast concerning the troubles of 1929. Increasingly thereafter I emphasized the danger.

25

The Conference of Governors
and the Intensification
of Cheap Money, 1927

We have now reviewed the main elements needed to understand the problems which faced the conference of central bank governors in New York in the summer of 1927. We have seen how England had become overexpanded, with a great increase in her quick foreign liabilities, particularly those held by the Bank of France. This was due especially to her policy of expanding bank credit in 1926 while the great strike was on, but due also to her general policy of trying to make money as cheap as possible despite the modest reserve position of the Bank of England. We have seen how the Bank of France had been obliged to buy sterling and other foreign exchange in the *de facto* stabilization of the franc, because of the hesitance of the French government to give a definitive new gold par to the franc. This made it impossible for the Bank of France to receive and pay out gold automatically at a fixed rate in Paris against the issuance or retirement of banknotes.

We have seen how the able authorities of the Bank of France had tried to meet this situation by converting their foreign exchange into gold, meeting, however, resistance and protests from the British monetary authorities. England had gone too far in the expansion of bank credit, and the time had already passed when she could have an easy liquidation and readjustment. Her credit, however, was still strong, and she could have eased off such a readjustment by placing long-term bonds in the American market to get the gold with which to meet the French requirements, and there was no question of her ability to stop the drain of gold from England by making rates of interest stiff enough.

Conference Called at Instance of Bank of England. But the Bank of England did not wish to pull up. Failing in his efforts to persuade the Bank of France to be content with sterling reserves, and in his efforts to get concerted pressure on the Bank of France from Continental central banks, Governor Norman turned for help to Governor Benjamin Strong of the New York Federal Reserve Bank. Governor Strong invited to New York for a secret conference the governor of the Reichsbank, Dr. Hjalmar Schacht; the governor of the Bank of France, who sent instead the able deputy governor, Charles Rist, professor of economics at the University of Paris; and Governor Norman of the Bank of England. These three, with Governor Strong, made the conference.

Conference Very Secret—Chairman of New York Federal Reserve Bank Excluded. The conference was, indeed, meant to be very secret. Gates W. McGarrah, chairman of the Board of Directors and Federal Reserve agent of the Federal Reserve Bank of New York, had asserted his right to be present at the conference; but Governor Strong refused, and McGarrah, instead of fighting, left the city. The whereabouts of the members of the conference was kept secret from the banking community of New York.[1]

Rist and Schacht Refuse to Join in Cheap Money Policy. Governors Strong and Norman tried hard to get the four countries to go along in a concerted policy of easier money. Professor Rist and Dr. Schacht held back. Schacht was alarmed at the extent to which the bank expansion had gone. He had manifested this in the preceding year by reducing his holdings of sterling and increasing his holdings of gold in the Reichsbank. He is reported to have said, "Don't give me a low rate. Give me a true rate, and then I shall know how to keep my house in order."

Rist and Schacht Go Home, Norman Remains. The Governors Conference broke up without agreement, and Schacht and Rist went home, promising nothing except to communicate their intentions with respect to the withdrawal of gold from Britain and the United States.

Strong, Norman, and Crissinger Force the Cheap Money Policy Through. Following the departure of Rist and Schacht, Norman and Strong forced through their program of cheap money in the United States. In Washington Governor Strong and Governor Norman met a rather supine Federal Re-

---

[1] I think that I may be the only man in the great New York chartered banks who had conversation with any of the participants of this conference. Deputy Governor Rist of the Bank of France invited me to come over to the Federal Reserve bank in New York to see him in his office there. Governor Strong saw me coming in and rushed into Deputy Governor Rist's office ahead of me and stayed a long time. Rist's secretary came to say that Governor Rist begged me to stay, he wished to see me. His secretary manifested indignation that Strong should intrude on the time set aside for me. I assured the secretary that I would stay indefinitely. (This was not my exact language.) At frequent intervals the secretary came out to see me, urging me to stay and apologizing for the delay. Finally, after fifty minutes or more, Rist's secretary brought me into Rist's office with Strong still there. Strong then yielded and I had a long talk with Rist.

In this conversation Rist was careful to make no disclosures as to what was going on in the conference. He wanted information and opinions from me. Our conversation was particularly concerned with the great growth of the gold exchange standard (as distinguished from the gold standard) that had taken place in the preceding year; and the accumulation of sterling and dollar exchange instead of gold reserves in the Bank of France, and in other European central banks. Rist asked searching questions regarding the banking situation in the United States, and regarding our security and commodity markets. From other sources I learned more about the conference.

serve Board. Governor Crissinger of the Federal Reserve Board was with them and supported them. The able Adolph Miller of the board fought, but was overridden by Strong and Norman.

President Coolidge's Attitude. Regarding the attitude of President Coolidge toward this particular episode, it has not been possible to get exact information. But Coolidge had stated in a speech late in the campaign of 1924, "It has been the policy of this administration to reduce discount rates." And it had been clearly the policy of the Coolidge administration to encourage rising stock market prices. We had seen for years the appalling spectacle of the President of the United States and the secretary of the Treasury, Andrew Mellon, giving out interviews to encourage the stock market whenever prices seemed to flag. For evidence on this point I would refer the reader to Ralph Robey's brilliant and justly indignant paper "The Capeadores of Wall Street," in the *Atlantic Monthly* of September 1928.[2]

Governors of Other Federal Reserve Banks Unfairly Treated. The governors of the eleven other Federal Reserve banks were called to Washington. They were not dealt with honestly. They were told that the proposed cheap money move was to "help the farmer." They were not told that the primary purpose of it was to make it unnecessary for England to honor her gold obligations to France, and to make it possible for England to continue an unwarranted degree of cheap money.

Governor Bailey of the Federal Reserve Bank of Kansas City was chosen as the man to inaugurate the policy. He was to take the first conspicuous step, that of lowering his rediscount rate. Governor Bailey was a good bank administrator. He handled the credits given to the member banks in his district with wisdom and discretion. He did not understand central bank policy. He had limited grasp of the basic forces governing the money market, and his grasp of international financial relations was vague. He trusted Governor Strong. Governor Strong had told him that the cheap money policy was for the purpose of helping the farmers, and Governor Bailey in announcing the reduction of his rediscount rate said it was for the purpose of helping the farmers. He said nothing about helping England, because he did not know that the purpose of the move was to help England. Governor Strong had not told him that.

Chronology of 1927 Cheap Money Policy. The chronological steps in the inauguration of the new 1927 policy were the following: (1) the buying rates on acceptances were lowered at the New York Federal Reserve Bank in late July and early August; (2) between July 27 and August 3 the Federal Reserve banks began a sharp increase in their purchases of government securities, the figure rising from $385 million on July 27 to $704 million on November 16, an increase of $320 million; (3) on July 29 the Kansas City

---

[2] See also the fuller story in William Allen White, *A Puritan in Babylon* (New York: Macmillan, 1938).

Federal Reserve Bank reduced its rate from 4 percent to 3.5 percent. The St. Louis, Boston, New York and Cleveland banks followed (August 4 to 6), and then the Dallas, Atlanta, and Richmond banks (August 12 to 16).

Chicago Federal Reserve Bank Coerced. The Chicago Federal Reserve Bank was suspicious and disapproved. The Chicago Federal Reserve Bank was in a better position to know what was really involved in the policy than the Federal Reserve banks of the more remote places. The governor of the Chicago Federal Reserve Bank had less confidence in Governor Strong than many of the other governors had. The Chicago bank refused to reduce its rate. But the Federal Reserve Board at Washington overrode the Chicago Federal Reserve Bank, and by action of the board, not of the bank, the Chicago rate was reduced on September 7.

Finally, the Federal Reserve banks at Philadelphia, San Francisco, and Minneapolis reduced their rates (September 8 to 13).

Impossible at Time to Get Official Explanation of Policy. It was impossible, at the time, to get definite official statements from the Federal Reserve authorities (other than Governor Bailey of Kansas City) regarding their policy and regarding their purposes. The most definite statement at the time was that of the governor of the Federal Reserve Bank of Philadelphia in a speech before the Philadelphia Association of Credit Men on September 21. The official text of this speech appears not to have been published, but the newspaper accounts represented the governor as indicating that the European situation, coupled with the desire for facilitating American exports, was the ground for the policy.

26

The Stock Market Boom, 1927–29

Summary of Stock Prices, 1922–27. Stock prices had responded sharply to the government security purchases of the Federal Reserve banks in 1922. The level had risen rapidly. With the reversal of Federal Reserve policy in 1923 we had a reactionary year in stock prices. The cheap money policy of 1924 was followed by a further very marked rise in stock prices which carried on through 1925. The spring of 1926 showed an important reaction, and by the end of the year prices were only moderately above the year end of 1925. The first half of 1927 showed a further rise to levels that were already definitely higher, and that suggested caution in conservative financial circles. With the renewal of the Federal Reserve cheap money policy late in the summer of 1927 a sharp acceleration of the upward movement of stock prices began. The following table tells this story.

STANDARD & POOR'S INDUSTRIALS (MONTHLY)—1922–27

January 1922	50.2
October 1922	64.6
June 1923	57.5
December 1923	60.7
June 1924	59.3
December 1924	70.4
December 1925	90.7
May 1926	83.6
December 1926	95.2
June 1927	103.4
December 1927	122.4

New Money Created by Federal Reserve Policy Goes into Stocks. The new credit created by the renewal of cheap money by the Federal Reserve System following the Governors Conference in 1927 went rapidly into security loans and bank investments in securities. There was a moderate seasonal increase in commercial loans during the autumn of 1927 which, however, was reversed at the year end, but the stock market continued to absorb the excess funds.

Intoxication Begins. At the beginning of the movement in the autumn, the stock market took the money somewhat languidly, tempted by the lower rates. But it took the money and it used it to put stocks rapidly higher. The rising prices themselves generated a psychological boom atmosphere.

Alarmed Reversal of Federal Reserve Policy. Alarmed, the Federal Reserve authorities reversed their policy in the winter of 1927–28. They sold government securities. They raised rediscount rates. The New York Federal Reserve Bank, which had reduced its rate to 3.5 percent in August 1927, raised it to 4 percent in February 1928, to 4.5 percent in May, and to 5 percent in July.

The government security holdings for the Federal Reserve System were rapidly reduced, dropping from $617 million at the year end, 1927, to $212 million at the end of June 1928.

Gold[1] also left the country in 1928, the gold monetary stock dropping from $4,379,000,000 at the end of December 1927, to $4,109,000,000 by June 1928.

The selling of government securities and the loss of gold cut into member bank reserves. The banks were forced to rediscount heavily with the Federal Reserve banks. Total rediscounts with the twelve Federal Reserve banks had stood at $423,000,000 on February 1, 1928. The figure rose rapidly to $1,089,000,000 on July 11, 1928.

The increase in rediscounts would not have been as great as it was if the rediscount rate at the Federal Reserve banks had been above the market. But even so the banks were reluctant to rediscount, and did, not rediscount enough to replenish their reserve balances completely. Member bank reserve balances stood at $2,405,000,000 on February 1, at $2,365,000,000 on July 11, and at $2,300,000,000 on July 25. With rediscounts above $500 million, enough banks were under pressure so that money rates stiffened, and with a decline of $100 million in member bank reserves, the money market was definitely under pressure. As we have seen before[2] bank expansion virtually ceased around April 11, 1928.

Interest Rates Rise Sharply. Interest rates rose sharply with the reversal of Federal Reserve bank policy.

The call rate on stock exchange loans had been under 4 percent in October and November 1927, and following year-end firmness had dropped under 4 percent again in January 1928. It rose to 5 percent in April, in June to more than 6 percent, in September to 7.5 percent, and in early

---

[1] This was partly connected with the *de jure* return of the Bank of France to the gold standard, which came in June 1928.

[2] See p. 144.

December to 8.5 percent—at the year end to over 10 percent. The rate for bankers' acceptances rose in 1928 from 3.25 percent at the beginning of the year to 4.5 percent in the second half of the year, while open market commercial paper, which had stood at 4 percent at the beginning of 1928, went to over 5.5 percent in the second half of the year.

But the Boom Went On. Here was a real restraining influence. The Federal Reserve authorities were using measures which, on the basis of their past experience, should have sufficed to stop the stock market boom, and did suffice to stop the expansion of bank credit. But the boom went on. There was a new factor in the situation. The public had taken the bit in its teeth. The rise in stock market prices and the lure of stock market profits had caught the public imagination. And the change in Federal Reserve policy, designed to restrict the supply of money, met with an overpowering increase in the demand for money. There was a momentary hesitance. The month of February 1928 was reactionary in the securities markets. And then, despite restraint, the boom was resumed. Brokers' loans had been taken languidly when interest rates were low in the autumn of 1927. But in 1928 and 1929 eager speculators, desiring brokers' loans, took them at rapidly rising rates of interest and in greatly increasing volume, bidding eagerly and greedily for them.

Roy Young, New Governor of Board. In the early spring of 1928 a visit to the office of the new governor of the Federal Reserve Board, the Honorable Roy A. Young, just after three o'clock one day, found him standing before the news ticker in his office, laughing. Stocks had had a sharp rise that day, and the news ticker reported the fact. Asked what he was laughing at, he said, "I am laughing at myself sitting here and trying to keep a hundred and twenty-five million people from doing what they want to do."

Governor Young is one of the ablest men ever to hold office in the Federal Reserve System, and one of the most upright. Before coming to the governorship of the Federal Board he had been governor of the Minneapolis Federal Reserve Bank. He had done an exceedingly fine job there. In the crisis of 1920–21 he had taken the best possible care of small country banks, member banks of his institution. He had saved many country banks by taking paper which, though technically eligible for rediscount, was far from being certainly good—asking at the same time of the eleven other Federal Reserve banks that the Minneapolis Federal Reserve Bank should hold more than its share of the government securities in the system, so that the income from the government securities might offset losses from possible bad loans to the small banks. But his judgment in making these loans had been extraordinarily good, and the losses were far fewer than he had prudently provided for. He had won the respect of his fellow governors in the system by letting them know this, and letting the share of the Minneapolis Federal Reserve Bank in the government security holdings be reduced. He "played fair" with everybody.

Governor Young, like the governors of the other interior Federal Reserve banks, had not been fully informed by Governor Benjamin Strong or Governor Crissinger as to the real purpose of the cheap money policy in 1927. It was not until after he became governor of the Federal Reserve Board on October 4, 1927, that he began really to understand the situation. But he learned fast. He moved with vigor toward restraining the unsound tendencies, and the Federal Reserve System would have moved with much greater vigor had he been able to dominate its policies. He came in, however, after the mischief had been done.

Benjamin Strong Drops Out. Governor Benjamin Strong of the New York Federal Reserve Bank dropped out of the picture, through illness, by the end of 1927. He remained governor till his death, October 16, 1928, but was too sick to accomplish anything. He was succeeded by George L. Harrison on November 22, 1928. Apologists for Governor Strong's policies have said repeatedly that if he had remained on the scene and been able to dominate the scene as he did in 1927, he would have stopped the boom early in 1928. They have said that he would have had rediscount rates go to six percent immediately, and would have taken such decisive measures that things would have been thrown into reverse. They have offered this as an excuse for his policy. If it were true that he would have done these things, this still would not have constituted a defense for the 1927 policy. It would merely constitute a recognition of the unsoundness of that policy.

We have given here a general and nontechnical account of Federal Reserve policy and the money market in the autumn of 1927 and in the first half[3] of 1928. The Federal Reserve authorities made a real effort in the first half of that year to hold down the expansion of bank credit and to hold down the growth of brokers' loans.

President Coolidge on Brokers' Loans. They had very little help from the President of the United States, Calvin Coolidge. He was asked by newspapermen in early January 1928 about brokers' loans. He promised to give them an answer next day. Associated Press advice from Washington, January 6, 1928, stated: "President Coolidge is of the opinion that the record breaking increase in brokers' loans held by Federal Reserve member banks is not large enough to cause any unfavorable comment."[4] Bankers in New York were shocked by what he said. The information was that in the twenty-four-hour interval he did not consult the Federal Reserve authorities, nor did he consult the Treasury with respect to the matter. One former newspaperman, whom he consulted, reported that he had told the President that he thought brokers' loans were all right, and took credit for

---

[3] I made at the time very exact clinical notes, tracing the stages of the disease and measuring the forces at work, which the reader who wishes the details may find in "An Analysis of the Money Market," *Chase Economic Bulletin*, June 4, 1928.

[4] *Commercial & Financial Chronicle*, January 7, 1928, p. 34.

the President's answer. Coolidge was still being one of the "Capeadores of Wall Street."[5]

New, Strange Counter Forces Offset Federal Reserve Restraints. When the Federal Reserve authorities tried to withdraw funds from the money market, the market found new and strange sources from which to draw funds. So much new money had been created in the period from 1922 to early 1928 that the problem of reabsorbing it and getting it under control was a very difficult one. When a bathtub in the upper part of the house has been overflowing for five minutes, it is not difficult to turn off the water and mop up. But when the bathtub has been overflowing for several years, the walls and the spaces between ceilings and floors have become full of water, and a great deal of work is required to get the house dry. Long after the faucet is turned off, water still comes pouring in from the walls and from the ceilings. It was so in 1928 and 1929. At a price, the speculator could get all the money that he wanted.

Brokers' Loans "for Account of Others." One major source from which additional money came was in the so-called brokers' loans "for account of others." New York banks had long been accustomed to making loans to the stock market for their own account and for the account of out-of-town banks, with occasional loans made for the account of other customers. These loans for "others" had never, prior to 1927, been large in volume. It would happen in the old days in time of monetary tension when the call rate got very high that a few foresighted men—Russell Sage was one—who had withdrawn from the stock market and who had their holdings in cash, would make loans to brokers against stock and bond collateral when the rate got to ten and twelve percent. This was ordinarily a useful service, which helped to relax a tight call loan market at a time of tension or crisis. It had never before been a baleful influence in the situation. In normal times not enough people would have surplus cash to do very much of this. But in 1928 and 1929 this factor rose to undreamed-of volume—not in a time of crisis, but in a boom.

Relax Money Market by Reducing Bank Deposits but Not Bank Reserves. The effect upon the money market of a bank's making a loan for a customer's account was definitely to relax the money market. A typical case, and a case which makes the point most clearly, would be the following. A New York bank, instructed by a customer to debit his account and lend a million dollars for his "account and risk" to the stock market, would turn over to the customer a broker's loan which the bank had already made, with the result that the bank's balance sheet would go down on both sides. Deposits would be down a million dollars and loans would be down a million dollars. The bank's cash reserves, however, would remain unchanged. And the ratio of the bank's reserves to the bank's remaining

---

[5] See Ralph Robey, "The Capeadores of Wall Street," *Atlantic Monthly,* September 1928.

deposits would thus be improved. The bank would be in a stronger position to make another loan. The tendency of this operation would be to ease the money market and to make interest rates lower than they would otherwise have been.

A more complex operation with the same result would be as follows. The bank would debit its customer's account a million dollars and would offer a million dollars at the money desk of the stock exchange, which a broker would borrow. The bank would give the broker a cashier's check and the bank would receive from the broker his note with acceptable diversified collateral. The note would be in the custody of the bank, but would not be entered in the bank's own loans. It would belong to the customer. The cashier's check would be a demand liability of the bank in the general category of deposits, so that the bank's figures would not yet be reduced on either side of the balance sheet. But the bank, knowing that next day it would have an additional million dollars to meet as the cashier's check for a million dollars came in against it at the clearinghouse, would itself call a loan which it had made for its own account to some other broker. When this other broker had paid off his loan and the bank had met its cashier's check at the clearinghouse, the bank's position would be the same as in the first illustration. Its deposits and loans would each be down a million dollars. New repercussions, however, would set in as the broker whose loan was called undertook to replace his money by borrowing somewhere else, but it is not profitable to follow this transaction in detail for present purposes.[6]

The evidence is clear that, taking the banking system of New York City as a whole, net demand deposits dropped as brokers' loans "for account of others" rose. Between May 2 and October 10, 1928, the following five closely related developments took place: (1) a decline in brokers' loans made by New York banks for their own account of $462 million; (2) an increase in loans for account of others of $642 million according to the figures reported by the member banks to the Federal Reserve banks, or of $846 million when the additional loans reported by the New York Stock Exchange are included; (3) a decline in net demand deposits for the member banks of the Federal Reserve System of $749 million of which $590 million was in New York City alone; (4) a decline in the legal reserves of the member banks of the Federal Reserve System of $129 million; and (5) a sharp tightening of interest rates, though not nearly so great a tightening as would have taken place with this decline in reserves had the net demand deposits not gone down. The reader will find the evidence on this point abundantly presented in "Brokers' Loans and Bank Credit."[7]

The Source of Brokers' Loans "for Account of Others." In no previous

---

[6] The various cases are analyzed in the *Chase Economic Bulletin,* October 31, 1928.

[7] *Ibid.*

period of our history had there been any great volume of outside funds available for lending in this way, but here in 1928 and 1929 we find the rising interest rates calling in incredible sums, which rose to over $5.5 billion at the peak of 1929.[8] Where did this money come from? What were its origin and source? The answer is to be found in the volume of bank credit which had previously been created and which, unneeded for ordinary purposes, had remained idle in bank deposits.

Business corporations, putting out new stocks at high prices, had accumulated funds far in excess of their needs and were holding them idle as deposits with their banks. The money had come to them from the stock market on a two or three percent stock yield basis, and when the stock market in turn was ready to pay seven, eight, and ten percent for their money, they loaned it back to the stock market. It came originally, not from investors' savings, but from bank expansion, as we have seen.

Foreigners, overborrowing in the United States, had accumulated vast sums of idle money, which they carried in bank deposits, as well as in other highly liquid forms. When the call loan rate went high enough, they put this money into call loans. See next table.

Well-to-do investors, who had sold securities at high prices and withdrawn from the market, had idle cash on a great scale which they expected to use again in buying securities when the prices once more suited them, but which, meanwhile, they were glad to lend at seven to ten percent to the stock market speculators on well-secured loans, carefully watched as to adequacy of margin and diversity of collateral by the skillful loan clerks of the great banks. The water poured out of the walls, pulled by the suction pump of rising interest rates.

New Bank Stock Issues Ease Money Market. Another very substantial factor in reducing the pressure on the bank reserves and making possible a greater expansion of credit than would otherwise have taken place was that the banks themselves, on a great scale, took advantage of the rising prices of stocks to issue new bank stocks at high prices. The effect of this on the banking system as a whole was a decline in deposits on the liability side of the bank's balance sheet, and a rise in capital and surplus on

---

[8] There are two sets of figures for brokers' loans: first, the figures reported by the New York City member banks *weekly* to the Federal Reserve Bank in New York; second, the figures reported *monthly* by the stock exchange itself. The figures reported by the stock exchange were much the larger figures. They included the figures of brokers' loans, reported to the Federal Reserve authorities, made by member banks or made through member banks. They included also loans made directly to stock exchange members by private banks, foreign banks, brokers, and others. At the peak, at the end of September 1929, the figures reported by the stock exchange were $8,549,000,000, whereas the peak figure reported by the member banks to the Federal Reserve Bank (that of October 2, 1929) was $6,804,000,000. The difference is $1,745,000,000, all of which is outside money. When to this we add that part of the loans made by weekly reporting New York member banks "for account of others," ($3,907,000,000 on October 2), we get a total of outside money of $5,652,000,000 at the peak. October 2 is close enough to the end of September to make this addition safe—though two days made an enormous difference late in October, as we shall see.

the liability side of the bank's balance sheet. There was a substitution of capital liabilities to stockholders for liabilities to depositors. Individual banks issuing new stock might get in additional cash, if their subscribers were not confined to their own depositors. But the banking system as a whole could not get any new cash from a new stock issue, except in the rare case where the new stock was paid for with hoarded currency. The issue of new bank stocks in 1928 and 1929 was very substantial in the aggregate. Between June 30, 1927, and December 31, 1929, the capital of the member banks of the Federal Reserve System increased from $2,274,000,000 to $2,757,000,000, while their surplus increased from $2,030,000,000 to $2,865,000,000. The aggregate increase in capital and surplus was $1,318,000,000, or 30.6 percent. Not all of this increase, of course, came from new stock issues. Part was profits turned back to surplus. But the greater part came from new bank stock issues. It will be observed in the figures that the increase in surplus in this process was greater than the increase in capital. The reason is very simple. A bank whose stock had a par of $100, but was selling in the market at $700, would offer its stockholders the right to subscribe for a new issue at $500. This was a valuable right. The stockholder might exercise the right or he might sell it. But in any case, the right was too valuable to remain unexercised. The bank would get $500 for the new share. In the subsequent adjustment of the bank's books, however, capital would be credited with $100 per share, and surplus would be credited with $400 per share. Surplus would increase in this case four times as much as capital. The sale of new bank stocks on this scale during this period held down the rise in demand deposits very substantially, held down the reserve requirements of the banks, and operated to lessen tension in the money market.

High Interest Rates Pull Money in Circulation into Bank Reserves. A third factor which operated to interfere with the Federal Reserve System's policy of restraint was a decline in money in circulation of $110 million (daily average) which took place in 1928 as compared with 1927. This made a corresponding addition to member bank reserves. The cause was the very high rates of interest, which meant that individual banks would find inducement to reduce their vault cash, and that merchants would carry slightly less till money. The figure for money in circulation included the vault cash of member banks, which, since the Federal Reserve System had come in, did not count as legal reserves for member banks of the Federal Reserve System.

Substitution of Acceptance Credits for Straight Loans Lessens Pressure. A fourth factor lessening tension in the 1928–29 money market was the substitution of acceptance credits for straight "line of credit" commercial loans, on a very substantial scale, by the banks.[9] When banks make straight loans to customers there is a corresponding increase in bank deposits, and

---

[9] See *Chase Economic Bulletin*, February 13, 1929.

STREET LOANS, DAILY REPORTING
BANKS, NEW YORK CITY
(In millions of dollars)

Date	Total	For own account	For correspondents*
June 25, 1924	1,478	869	609
June 24, 1925	2,237	1,063	1,175

BROKERS' LOANS, WEEKLY REPORTING
BANKS, NEW YORK CITY
(In millions of dollars)

Date	Total	For own account	For out-of-town banks*	For others
Jan. 6, 1926	3,141	1,338	1,239	564
Aug. 31, 1927	3,184	1,046	1,223	915
Dec. 28, 1927	3,718	1,374	1,338	1,006
Mar. 28, 1928	3,825	1,121	1,427	1,278
Aug. 29, 1928	4,235	793	1,535	1,907
Dec. 26, 1928	5,091	1,109	1,660	2,322
Mar. 20, 1929	5,793	1,091	1,768	2,934
Aug. 21, 1929	6,085	926	1,787	3,372
Oct. 9, 1929	6,713	973	1,799	3,941
Oct. 23, 1929	6,634	1,077	1,733	3,823
Oct. 30, 1929	5,538	2,069	1,005	2,464
Nov. 27, 1929	3,450	831	638	1,982
Dec. 31, 1929	3,424	1,167	709	1,548
June 4, 1930	4,101	1,911	995	1,195
Dec. 31, 1930	1,926	1,321	235	370
Dec. 30, 1931	591	544	41	6
July 27, 1932	331	306	17	8

* Figures before 1926 are for *daily reporting banks*. Those beginning with 1926 are for *weekly* reporting member banks. The difference between the two series on January 6, 1926, is moderate. The daily reporting member banks report $2,908,000,000 and the weekly reporting banks report $3,141,000,000, a difference of $233,000,000. See *Banking and Monetary Statistics,* Board of Governors, Federal Reserve System (1933), pp. 496–99. The figures for June 25, 1924, and for June 24, 1925, lump the loans made for out-of-town banks and for others in one figure under the general caption of "for correspondents." Figures beginning with 1926 separate "out-of-town banks" and "others."

in reserve requirements. But when a customer takes an acceptance credit from a bank, he gets merely the bank's assumption of responsibility for the debt when it is due, and the bank does not give him a deposit credit. The money his creditor gets is obtained through selling the bank acceptance in the open market.

Because Federal Reserve Banks Chief Market for Acceptances. In the well-established acceptance market of London, acceptances are bought by very many people, but especially by banks, or by discount houses which borrow from banks to carry the acceptances. In the American acceptance market, however, as it existed in 1928–29, the Federal Reserve System had itself become the primary market for acceptances. The Federal Reserve banks had made a "baby" of the acceptance market, had fostered it, and made acceptance rates artificially low in an effort to build it up, and therefore had succeeded in making a parasite of it. The market for acceptances was the Federal Reserve banks primarily, and certain foreign banks which bought acceptances, often with Federal Reserve bank guaranty.

Federal Reserve Acceptance Buying Breaks Rate on Brokers' Loans, Late 1928. The rise of the acceptance rate in 1928 forced the Federal Reserve banks either to abandon their baby or to buy far more acceptances than they wished to buy. They bought the acceptances, which meant increased Federal Reserve credit to the money market and additions to member bank reserves. Acceptance credits thus eased the money market, where straight bank loans would have tightened it. The New York Federal Reserve Bank made a protest about this. But their acceptance policy pulled down the acceptance rate from 4.63 percent in August 1928 to 4.50 percent for the rest of the year; and the call loan renewal rate, which had averaged 7.26 percent in September, dropped to 6.98 percent in October and to 6.67 percent in November.

Enormous Volume of New Securities—Domestic and Foreign. Through 1928 and 1929 to the October crash, the volume of new securities grew at an enormous pace, as shown by our table on page 185.

Foreign securities during this same period increased very rapidly in 1927 and remained high in 1928, but dropped off sharply in 1929, as shown by the following table:

FOREIGN SECURITIES PUBLICLY
PLACED IN THE UNITED STATES
(REFUNDING EXCLUDED)*
(In millions of dollars)

1922	631
1923	267
1924	997
1925	1,086
1926	1,145
1927	1,561
1928	1,319
1929	758

* *Chase Economic Bulletin,* March 14, 1930, p. 8

Notice the extraordinary bulge for the two years 1927 and 1928. But these calendar year figures do not tell the story adequately. In the twelve-month period from June 30, 1927, to June 30, 1928, we took approximately $1.8 billion worth of new securities. These are the *Commercial & Financial Chronicle's* figures for publicly placed issues. They do not include investments privately made, or funds placed by American businesses in their own plants abroad, or purchases made by Americans in European stock markets.

Fantastic Rise in Stock Prices, 1928–29. These new issues were in response to the rapidly rising prices of securities. The stock market rose by leaps and bounds, as shown by the following tables:

DOW-JONES INDUSTRIALS

Date	High	Low	Close
November 15, 1922	....	....	95.11
January 10, 1924	....	....	97.23
November 10, 1924	....	....	105.91
November 15, 1927	....	....	195.37
February 15, 1928	....	....	197.59
November 15, 1928	271.63	266.48	269.42
August 29, 1929	378.76	370.79	376.18

STANDARD & POOR'S
COMMON STOCKS (MONTHLY)
(Average of closing prices one day each week)

Date	Industrials	Rails	Public utilities
June 1921	44.4	156.0	66.6
June 1927	103.4	316.2	135.1
January 1928	124.1	332.4	151.3
December 1928	161.1	357.9	202.6
June 1929	172.5	384.1	272.2
September 1929	195.2	446.0	375.1

The reader will notice that as our own stock market rose progressively to fantastic heights in 1929, the volume of foreign issues fell off rapidly. We ceased to be interested in anything except stocks that would rise five or ten points in a week. We ceased to be interested in bonds.

Early in 1942 a Swiss banker in New York said that he could not understand his American friends. They had thought that he was very foolish in 1929 because he was not willing to borrow money at eight percent in order to buy stocks yielding two percent, and in early 1942 they thought he was very foolish because he wanted to borrow money at two percent to buy stocks yielding eight percent.

27

Mob Mind in 1928–29

One able Jewish investment banker said in the summer of 1928 that he did not understand what was going on. He said, "When I do not understand, I do nothing." He had withdrawn from the market. He had turned his holdings into cash, and he was waiting until he understood. After the crash in 1929, a speech was made before the New York State Chamber of Commerce to explain what had happened, which discussed, among other things, the phenomena of mob mind which had been so manifest in the year and a half that had preceded the crash.[1] The speaker made the generalization, familiar to social psychologists, that the more intense the craze, the higher the type of intellect that succumbs to it. The investment banker, seated near the speakers' table, nodded his head emphatically as he heard this generalization. Later he was asked about it. He said that he had reluctantly gone back into the market under the pressure of repeated advice from his associates and others, and that as stocks went higher and his friends and associates were borrowing money to increase their holdings, he too had borrowed money. He said that he had gone to London in the spring of 1929, had learned some things there that made him much concerned, and had cabled orders to New York to his associates to sell everything that he had bought. But they protested and told him that the move was not nearly over, and he had reversed his instructions and had stayed with the market. He said that he had come into the crash carrying stocks bought at high prices with $4 million of borrowed money. He was prepared to subscribe to the generalization that the wilder the craze, the higher the type of intellect that succumbs to it. He had a high I.Q., and he knew it.

When men of this type lost their heads, it was not strange that bootblacks did. It was not strange that charwomen bought one or two shares of

---

[1] *Chase Economic Bulletin,* November 22, 1929.

National City Bank stock. It was not strange that widows sold mortgages in order to get money with which to buy stocks.

Mob Mind in Manhattan Real Estate. It must be said, by the way, that the widow's mortgage itself was being undermined by the extravagances of the period from 1924 to 1929. Excessive money developed speculation in every field, and very specially in the field of real estate. The giant skyscrapers in midtown Manhattan which, viewed from Wall Street skyscrapers, look like a profile of the 1927–29 stock market averages, were, in large measure, set going, even when not completed, in 1927–29. Real estate mortgage bonds were issued at a tremendous pace. Real estate values soared and real estate mortgages of all kinds were so rapidly multiplied that in 1932–33 the widow might well have wondered whether she would not have done better to sell her mortgage in 1929, buying stocks with the money. Many stocks were still paying dividends, but in too many instances mortgages like hers had ceased to pay interest—including not a few mortgages guaranteed by mortgage guaranty companies which down to 1931 and 1932 had had high standing. Methods which they had found conservative and safe for forty years or more had not protected them or their clients when the whole fabric of real estate values had been undermined, and when they had given guaranties for a multiple of their capital.

28

The Effect on Europe of Tight Money in the United States in 1929

New York Speculation Participated in by World in 1929. By 1929 the extravagances of the New York stock market had become the central interest, not only for the whole country, but also for the whole world. In May 1929 a single Viennese bank was sending orders for $250,000 worth of New York stocks to be purchased for the account of its customers in one day, and this kind of thing had been going on for some time in Vienna. The same thing was happening in various other European cities in May and June, except that money was too tight in Germany and Hungary to permit it.

World's Investment Funds, Loan Funds, and Gold Turn to New York. The tide of investment funds turned definitely from Europe to the United States, whereas in the preceding years it had been from the United States to Europe. Our stock prices were mounting so rapidly that they were an irresistible magnet for a speculatively inclined world. Orders to buy New York stocks came from Asia and Africa. The high interest rates in New York, moreover, were a magnet for loose funds. Banks in Cairo and in Morocco, to say nothing of European banks, were sending funds to New York to be loaned on call at the high rates prevailing.

The tide of gold turned toward the United States again. Our gold monetary stock, which had dropped from $4,323,000,000 in April 1927 to $3,822,000,000 in June 1928, rose once more to $4,099,000,000 in October 1929.

Reversal of Flow of Funds Created Strain for European Debtor Countries. The rapid rise in interest rates in the United States in 1928–29 and the reversal of the flow of funds between Europe and the United States created a very definite strain in Europe. The lending countries of Europe ceased to be regular lenders to the borrowing countries of Europe, and in some cases withdrew funds previously loaned. The borrowing countries of Europe, which for several years had adjusted their economic life to a large inflow of foreign funds, found themselves suddenly pulled up short, with the necessity of paying rather than borrowing.

A borrowing country is an importing country. It brings in the proceeds of foreign loans primarily in the form of goods, and has a surplus of imports over exports. When a borrowing country begins to repay, the scene shifts. It must develop an excess of exports over imports. A transition of this sort, coming gradually, is easily accomplished and relatively painless. But when it must be made suddenly, it is almost inevitable that there should be a period of depression, during which labor and resources are released from producing goods for the domestic market to producing goods for export, and during which prices are reduced so that the country may more effectively compete in the export trade.

European Lenders Cease to Lend in Europe. The lending countries of Europe in the few years prior to 1929 had been England, the Netherlands, Sweden, and Switzerland, and following 1926, to some extent, France. By 1929 London had very little lending ability. Money had tightened sharply despite efforts made by Britain's financial leaders to keep rates as low as possible. Money had tightened in the Netherlands, and the Netherlands had been withdrawing funds from other countries, especially Germany. Sweden had ceased to be a ready lender.

Germany's Special Problem—Big Jump in Reparations Schedule. This sudden change came to Germany at a time when she was under the necessity of increasing her payments under the Dawes Plan from 1.75 billion marks per year to 2.5 billion marks, a sharp jump in the annuities schedule which might have occasioned difficulties even with a normal international money market. An acutely critical situation rose late in April and at the very beginning of May 1929. Negotiations had been under way for changing the Dawes Plan. The Young Plan conference was being held in Paris. The creditors under the Dawes Plan were ready to reduce the annuities schedules, but they were insisting on doing away with the safeguards which the Dawes Plan had provided and making the reduced schedules unconditionally payable. Dr. Hjalmar Schacht, representing Germany in this conference, was emphatically opposed to dispensing with the safeguards—and the event, of course, proved that he was right. It appeared that the negotiations would break down. A quiet but very substantial movement of funds out of Germany began, as Germans themselves, remembering the "inflation time," began to place their funds abroad for safety. Vigorous action by the Reichsbank and the German banks held this situation in hand, and New York and possibly some other foreign money markets lent temporary assistance. With the restoration of confidence which came with the success of the Paris negotiations and the adoption of the Young Plan, German funds went home, and the Reichsbank reserve ratio (which had approached, if it had not gone below, the statutory 40 percent) rose to 51.5 percent by June 22.

Dawes Plan and Young Plan. The Young Plan provided for a reduction of the Dawes Plan schedules from 2.5 billion marks to approximately 1.6 billion marks for the first years, with a rising scale of payments in the following years. But it was not to go into effect until September 1, 1929, so that for the year September 1, 1928, to September 1, 1929, Germany did, in fact, make the full payment of 2.5 billion marks.

It was necessary for Germany to reverse radically the whole course of her economic life. She had to reduce long-time construction for domestic purposes and increase production for export. Her people had to consume less and to export more. In part this was accomplished by a reduction in inventory in Germany with a more rapid turnover of goods. But the main change had to come through reduction in consumption, reduction in domestic construction, and the application of a greater proportion of Germany's economic energies to the export trade. Germany did, in fact, develop an export surplus around the middle of 1929, and in the two years that followed had a very large export surplus.

Hungary. Hungary was in a similar position. She had been borrowing. She had long-run plans. Germany's plans for development had been largely carried through. Hungary was still in the halfway stage. Her position was difficult.

England's Difficult Position. The position of London was particularly difficult. The British banks had gone to the limit in an effort to revive British trade by extending bank credit. Where ordinarily they had looked upon 50 percent of their deposits as a limit for their "advances," that is, customer's loans and overdrafts, and tried to keep the other 50 percent of their deposits in the form of bills or cash or short loans against highly liquid assets, they had allowed the percentage of advances to rise to over 56 percent. In addition, the drains upon the gold reserve of the Bank of England had reduced the reserve ratio from 55.8 percent on May 22 to 41.9 percent on July 10.

New issues in London had not gone well. Pressure on sterling continued. The Bank of England had got some momentary help from our cheap money policy in 1927, but long before the end of 1928 the bank was under pressure again, and in March 1929 it raised its rate from 4.5 to 5.5 percent. But the pressure on sterling continued. The Bank of France, with its enormous holdings of sterling exchange, remained anxious to get rid of its sterling. It had ceased to buy gold in London, and it did not sell sterling in such a way as to break the sterling rate below the gold export point, but whenever there was any strength in sterling there was French selling. Paris was quietly converting sterling into dollars whenever the sterling rate was strong enough to make this possible.

London was resorting to somewhat dubious devices to prevent the loss of gold. The London *Statist* of June 22, 1929, says:

> The persistent weakness of sterling exchange on New York has at last led to a substantial shipment of gold from this country to the USA. For some weeks

the sterling-dollar rate had hovered at or below the gold export point, yet little gold had left either the London open market or the Bank of England for shipment to New York. For some time it was customary for sterling exchange to make short-lived but effective recoveries whenever offerings of gold on the open market coincided with the departure of a fast boat from this country to New York, and thus, despite an average sterling-dollar rate which kept rather below the gold export point, the Bank of England continued to be able to supplement its gold reserve out of the weekly arrivals of new South African gold. As time went on, however, the weakness of sterling—or rather the strength of dollar[1]—became so marked that the cost of bringing about the required recoveries in the rate became presumably excessive.

London's manipulation of the sterling-dollar rate, just before the departure of a fast steamer for New York, was weak and dubious policy. It was a poor substitute for adequate money rates. It came two years before London abandoned the gold standard. It did not generate confidence in informed circles.

---

[1] It was, in fact, the weakness of sterling.

29

The "New Era," and the Precautions of the Commercial Banks in New York

The *New York Times* stock market average for twenty-five rails and twenty-five industrials reached a low of 58.35 on June 21, 1921, and the closing price for 1921 was 68.50. For 1923 the closing price was 84.15. With the great upswing created by the cheap money policy of 1924, this rose to 106.92 by year-end 1924, to 137.46 by year-end 1925, and to 139.53 by year-end 1926. The year-end figures of 1926 looked pretty high, but had many reasonable defenders who would point to substantial corporate profits for their justification. But 1927–28 and 1929 made these 1926 figures look conservative indeed. The stock market moved without impressive reactions to the fantastic high of 311 in September 1929.

Speculative Slogans and Theories. Every era of speculation brings forth a crop of theories designed to justify the speculation, and speculative slogans are easily seized upon. The term "new era" was the slogan for the 1927–29 period. We were in a new era in which old economic laws were suspended.[1]

Cassel and Fisher. We were troubled also in 1928–29 by the weird doctrine of Professor Gustav Cassel of Sweden (who had many American followers as well as wide vogue in Europe) that it was the business of central banks to maintain a fixed commodity price level, and that central banks must not concern themselves with the stock market and must not tighten credit to restrain stock market excesses because that would reduce

---

[1] I undertook to refute this doctrine in "Two New Eras Compared," *Chase Economic Bulletin,* February 11, 1929. In this study I compared two periods, the years 1921–28 and the years 1896–1903. Both these periods were characterized by very rapid bank expansion, by great growth in bank reserves, and by great growth in bank holdings of stock exchange paper and bonds. Both had rapidly rising security prices and rapidly growing new security issues. Both had fantastic stock exchange performances, and in both perspective was lost. But the first new era had been much more solidly based on expanding production and safely rising commodity prices, the latter resulting from a great increase in gold production, with gold well distributed throughout the world.

commodity prices. Professor Cassel even maintained that not enough credit was being supplied by the Federal Reserve System because there had been a decline in commodity prices between 1925 and 1927. Professor Cassel, moreover, maintained the remarkable doctrine that an increase in stock exchange loans does not raise rates of interest or withdraw money from other uses.[2]

We were told, moreover, by Professor Irving Fisher that we were on a "higher plateau" of stock exchange prices.[3] This was strongly reminiscent of Professor Fisher's defense of the commodity price level of 1919–20.

Industrial Consolidations for Stock Market Purposes. The new era of 1924–29, like the earlier new era of 1896–1903, was characterized by a great consolidation movement. The alleged "inevitable tendency toward monopoly" in American business has been largely confined to these two "new eras." It has not been due to technological or industrial reasons, but rather has been due to the ease with which new securities can be issued when money is excessive and stocks are rising—which makes it easy and profitable to organize holding companies and buy out competing concerns. There have been, in fact, only two great periods of consolidation in our history, the three-year period 1899–1902, and the five-year period 1924–29. Both were periods of cheap money and excited stock markets.[4] There were, in fact, a great many consolidations in the years 1924–29.

Bank Consolidations in an Era of Speculation. The movement ran far beyond industrial consolidations. Bank consolidation moved rapidly and branch banking was expanded with great rapidity, particularly in California. In certain states where branch banking was not permitted, or was permitted only within narrow limits, the consolidation movement took the form of bank holding companies, the stocks of which rose to fantastic levels and which pulled up bank stocks with them as they were exchanged for bank stocks. One of the most conspicuous and dangerous of these developments was in Detroit. Minneapolis was also a center, and the movement was found in other parts of the country. In New York City itself the development was chiefly in outright consolidations with an inter-

---

[2] I shall not interrupt the narrative here to discuss this theory, but content myself with referring to an address which I made before the Netherlands Commercial University at Rotterdam on May 7, 1929, which undertook to refute Professor Cassel's remarkable doctrines. See "Commodity Price Stabilization a False Goal of Central Bank Policy," *Chase Economic Bulletin,* vol. 9, no. 3.

[3] I cannot find when Professor Fisher first used this expression, "higher plateau." The last time he used it before the crash was on October 23, 1929, quoted by the *Commercial & Financial Chronicle,* October 26, 1929, pp. 2618–19. Even after the crash he retained his faith in it, saying that the "plateau of 1926–29 remains" (*The Stock Market Crash—And After* [New York, 1930], p. 267).

[4] The reader will find the evidence in *Big Business* (New York: Twentieth Century Fund, 1937), pp. 29–33.

change of stocks, and without the necessity for elaborate public security offerings.[5]

Bank consolidations, carefully considered, are often wholesome and beneficial, but the activities of promoters in throwing together a great many banks, as an incident to an excited stock market, were clearly unwholesome and dangerous.

Investment Trusts, 1928–29. Another development of the period was the rapid multiplication and rapid growth of investment trusts. The investment trust idea is good in itself, and investment trusts in England and Scotland had had a long and honorable history. Investment trust management in the United States following 1932 has been, on the whole, highly creditable. But the mushroom growth of institutions of this kind in a financial atmosphere such as obtained in 1928–29 was bound to bring a great deal of grief and humiliation. In the best of times the problem of investing funds prudently and wisely is difficult, and calls for exceptional experience, exceptional prudence, and exceptional brains. Investment trusts organized in 1928, and above all in 1929, if they used their stockholders' funds at all in investments other than government bonds, were foredoomed to incur heavy losses. Very many of the investment trusts organized during this period did make the best stock investments that could have been made, but the best were not good enough. In some conspicuous cases, however, their policies were not conservative, even by 1929 standards. The most conspicuous was doubtless the Goldman Sachs Trading Corporation which, with its two subsidiaries, Shenandoah and Blue Ridge, went through the sky like a blazing meteor for a time.[6]

We had the curious phenomenon that some of the investment trusts were buying shares of other investment trusts, as illustrating the difficulties of investment policy. This curious type of transaction became a definite pathology in certain cases in 1929, when the stocks of investment trust A rose because investment trust B was buying its shares, while the stock of the investment trust B rose because the investment trust A was buying its shares. This is an easy way to put stock prices up in an uncritical market, and it gives a brave semblance of success and prosperity for a limited time.

The most fortunate of the great investment trusts was probably the Lehman Corporation, which was organized so late in 1929 that its man-

---

[5] See my discussion of branch banking in France, in *Effects of the War on Money, Credit and Banking in France and the United States* (New York, 1919), chap. 2. See also "Bank Consolidations in an Era of Speculation," *Chase Economic Bulletin,* October 12, 1929, and "Branch Banking Throughout Federal Reserve Districts," *ibid.,* May 8, 1930. See also my testimony on Group, Chain, and Branch Banking before the House of Representatives' Committee on Banking and Currency, June 5, 1930, pp. 1853–1916.

[6] In the *Chase Economic Bulletin,* June 4, 1928, pp. 24–26, I called attention to the difficult problems of the investment trusts and gave a caution regarding them.

agement was definitely afraid of the stock market, and was able to come into the crash with its capital all in cash.

Investment Banks Lost Perspective. The speculators lost their heads. To too great an extent, the investment bankers did. American investment banking had had a long and honorable record. Investment banks had been for decades intermediaries between the railroads and the industrial corporations, on the one hand, and the investing public, on the other. They had underwritten billions of dollars' worth of securities, which had placed billions of dollars from the American investing public into sound and profitable uses in building up the railroads and industries of the country. They had been critical of the credits they extended. They had insisted upon sound policies on the part of the corporations for which they were obtaining investors' funds. They had been concerned about their reputations. They tried hard not to put out unsound issues, if only because they wished to be able to sell other issues in later years to the same investors. They had done their work well. But with the great flood of cheap money, and with insatiable demand for stocks and bonds, their perspective and their credit standard began to relax as early as 1925. And with the renewal of cheap money in 1927 perspective was badly lost and credit standards suffered a great deal.

Commercial Bankers in New York City Kept Perspective, in General. The commercial bankers in New York City, on the other hand, did not as commercial bankers lose their heads. Many country bankers, with excess funds even at crop-moving time, did load up with real estate mortgages and high-yield bonds. But the great banks tried to keep liquid. There was one conspicuous mushroom bank in New York City, the Bank of United States, which departed to an incredible degree from sound commercial bank practices, with the result that the bank later crashed and certain of its officials went to prison. But in general the commercial banks in New York were alert to the dangers and were afraid of the boom.

Charles E. Mitchell's Alleged Defiance of Federal Reserve Warning. There was one conspicuous exception among the heads of the great banks of New York in Charles E. Mitchell, head of the National City Bank. Mitchell was a conspicuous bull leader throughout the boom.

On March 26, 1929, the call loan rate had risen to twenty percent and threatened to go higher. Several of the New York City banks, including the National City Bank, had thereupon rediscounted at the Federal Reserve bank to get additional funds to lend on call in order to prevent a strangulation rate. None of the other banks said anything about it. But Mitchell gave out the following statement: "So far as this institution is concerned, we feel that we have an obligation which is paramount to any Federal Reserve warning, or anything else, to avert, so far as lies in our power, any dangerous crisis in the money market. . . ."[7] This was an unfortunate

---

[7] *Commercial & Financial Chronicle,* March 30, 1929, p. 2014.

utterance which made Mitchell a great deal of trouble later, particularly as it angered Senator Carter Glass of Virginia and led him to remorseless investigation of Mitchell's activities as a whole. It was, moreover, a misleading statement. There had been no defiance of the Federal Reserve authorities. On the contrary, the New York City banks acted in harmony with the Federal Reserve System. The facts were the following: the governor of the New York Federal Reserve Bank phoned the governor of the Federal Reserve Board to report to him what had happened. When the call loan rate went to twenty percent, several of the banks of the city called up the governor of the Federal Reserve bank to inquire if it were the wish of the Federal Reserve bank that they should rediscount—not to make a low call rate, but to prevent the rate from going to a very high figure—as the Federal Reserve bank had requested them to do at the preceding year end. The governor of the New York Federal Reserve Bank reported that he had told the New York bankers that they were closer to the money market than he was, and that if in their judgment it was the best thing to do, the Federal Reserve bank was at their service. Thereupon several of the New York banks did rediscount and did make additional loans on call to the stock exchange houses. The governor inquired if the Federal Reserve Board approved of what he had done. The governor of the Federal Reserve Board immediately called a meeting of the board and reported what the governor of the New York Federal Reserve Bank had told him. The board sat less than five minutes and approved what the New York Federal Reserve Bank had done. There was no defiance of the Federal Reserve authorities. But Mitchell's utterance was unfortunate as suggesting to the public that the great New York banks were behind the boom, when most of them were gravely concerned about it, and when most of them in the action they took that day were concerned merely with preventing a money market crisis.

It is proper to add that Mitchell's own bank, as a bank, did not, in its lending policy, follow his bullish enthusiasm. The vice presidents and managing staff of the bank took the same conservative measures that the other great New York banks were taking in getting ready for the stock market crash. And the National City Bank performed very well indeed when the stock market crash came.

Special New York Clearinghouse Committee, 1928. The great commercial banks of New York were in general troubled by the renewal of cheap money in 1927. By the summer of 1928, the clearinghouse was troubled. A committee of the clearinghouse was organized, some thirteen months before the grand smash, to provide for a system of weekly reports by every bank in the clearinghouse to the clearinghouse, showing in detail the extent of its liquidity and the extent of its illiquid assets. No more searching questionnaire was ever provided for bankers than those which the New York clearinghouse banks had answered every week, from the time this committee completed its work until the time when the great crash came. The questionnaire put every bank in the clearinghouse on notice, and it had a very real influence in bringing about housecleaning where housecleaning was needed.

Increased Margin Requirements and Reduced Loan Values—Diversification of Collateral. The banks too inaugurated the policy of increasingly rigorous requirements in connection with stock market loans. They were concerned particularly with the *quality* of the loans. Additional margins were required on loans, and, far more important, loan values were increasingly marked down. The commercial banks discounted a very substantial part of the fantastic prices of the stocks that had had the biggest speculative rises when it came to lending money against them. There was increasing rigor with respect to the diversification of collateral in every broker's loan, and increasing concern regarding the marketability of every security taken into brokers' loan envelopes. In the matter of customers' loans against securities, the banks were less rigorous. But there was a great deal of discussion of cases where strong customers had large loans against particular types of securities, and increasing pressure was put on such customers either to reduce their loans or to diversify their collateral.

We distinguish brokers' loans and customer's loans against securities, but it is proper to make a further distinction between "strict brokers' loans" and loans to broker customers. Strict brokers' loans, those made through the money brokers at the "money desk" of the stock exchange, were the loans where the standards were most rigorous. Sometimes brokers who had long been good customers of a bank borrowed part of their money as customers rather than as brokers, and the full rigors were not applied always to loans of this kind. The great bulk of the broker's loans, however, were strict brokers' loans.

Stock Exchange Houses Follow Commercial Bank Practices in Rigid Loan Standards. The stock exchange brokerage houses, likewise— whatever might be their individual positions with respect to the stock market, and whatever might be their expectations with respect to the market prices—nonetheless, as brokers, behaved with increasing conservatism as the market went higher. Partly because of pressure from the banks and partly because of the instinctive conservatism of financial men, they too required higher and higher margins from their customers, and they too took stocks held by their customers into their loan envelopes at increasing discounts from the prevailing high prices. For the brokers as well as for the banks loan values were far below market values. When the crash came both the commercial banks and the stock exchange brokers were ready for it.

30

The Stock Market Crash
of 1929

The stock market prices of September 1929 and, for that matter, long before September had reached levels so fantastic that a disastrous break was merely a question of time. Any one of a multitude of circumstances could have started the break, and the break, once clearly started, was certain to go very far.

Break Not Caused by Increasing Money Market Pressure. The break did not come, as had often been the case in our past stock market history, from a sudden great rise in the call loan rate. Financial pressure on the stock exchange was relaxing, rather than increasing, when the crash came on October 24.

To be sure, the New York Federal Reserve Bank had raised its discount rate from five to six percent on August 9, 1929. But this was symbolic merely, as it represented a compromise. The other side, and the really important side, of this compromise was that the Federal Reserve buying rate for prime bankers' acceptances was reduced on the same day from 5¼ to 5⅛ percent. As the open market rate for acceptances was 5⅛ percent at this time, this pulled down the Federal Reserve rate to the level of the market and opened up the Federal Reserve banks to acceptances at the pleasure of the market. Following this there was an increase in acceptances held by the Federal Reserve banks from $72 million on July 31 to $275 million on September 30, which meant a relief to member bank reserves sufficient to ease the money market. The call loan rate dropped from 9.6 percent on August 10 to 6.2 percent on October 12. Stock exchange time loans eased from 8.88 percent on August 10 to 7.75 percent on October 19.

Federal Reserve Policy Indecisive. The New York Federal Reserve Bank had for a long time been trying to get the consent of the Federal Reserve Board to an increase of its rediscount rate from five to six percent. One heard credible reports in the summer of 1929 of animated and even angry telephone conversations between Gates McGarrah, chairman of the board and Federal Reserve agent of the New York Federal Reserve Bank, and the secretary of the Treasury, Andrew Mellon, who was a member of the Federal Reserve Board, and who was opposing the increase in the rate upon which McGarrah was insisting. The Federal Reserve authorities from early 1928 on pursued an inconclusive policy based on three partially conflicting motives: (a) the desire to restrain the use of credit for stock market speculation; (b) the desire not to tighten money in foreign countries and not to pull in more gold from abroad; and (c) the desire not to let money grow tight in business uses at home. The conflict among these policies meant that the efforts at restraint were handicapped and inconclusive, and that the wild speculation ran on for a year and nine months after the restraining efforts began.

Hatry Failure in London. It is probable, though not certain, that the first real blow to the market came from foreign selling induced by a radical change in sentiment in London and in Europe, in view of the Hatry failure[1] in London, and the long overdue increase in the Bank of England's discount rate, from 5.5 to 6.5 percent on September 26. Hatry had put out forged securities in London on a vast scale, which had deceived even the great banks, and the disclosure when it came was shocking.

Massachusetts Public Utilities Decision. There came a Massachusetts public utility commission decision regarding the split-up of public utility shares, which probably induced further hesitation and suggested that pencil and paper might properly be of assistance in the evaluation of securities in this field. Various other causes might be assigned.

But Break Long Overdue. But there is no point to assigning any particular cause for the break's coming at the particular time it did. It was overdue, and long overdue. A great collapse was certain the moment that doubt and reflection broke the spell of mob contagion, while the fantastic structure of prices was doomed the moment any considerale number of people began to use pencil and paper.

Short Selling Returns. Short selling came into the picture once more. The "bears" had been so unmercifully licked in the period of late 1927 to September 1929, that there was no adequate short interest in the market in midsummer 1929. Short selling is one of the most wholesome factors in the broad and active stock market. The bear, selling stocks short when they go too high, tends to hold them down, and that same bear, in order to take his profits, must buy stocks when they break. Short covering is thus one of the most helpful influences in a bad market break. Stocks would go a great deal lower than they do if the short were not there buying to take his profits. One great difference between stock market speculation and real estate speculation is to be found in the fact that no one dares to sell a piece of real estate

---

[1] The London Stock Exchange suspended dealings in Hatry's stocks on September 20. When Hatry came to trial, December 16, his liabilities were placed at $67.5 million (*Commercial & Financial Chronicle,* September 21, 1929, p. 1820; December 21, 1929, p. 3891).

short, since he must deliver that piece of real estate and no other in closing his transaction; whereas if he sells General Motors or United States Steel stocks short, he may make deliveries with any of a good many millions of shares, and he can always get them at a price. The end of a the real estate boom and crash is, partly for this reason, a prolonged period of stagnation, while the end of the stock market boom and crash is simply lower prices with activity still going on. Some of the ablest operators in Wall Street began to get active on the bear side in September 1929. One of them said in September, "I am selling motors short for an investment."

On October 23, 1929, it became clear that the great break was at hand, when one learned that one of the most powerful underwriting syndicates in the country, which was sponsoring an additional issue of a highly rated common stock, had been unable to hold the price of the stock against a short-selling attack.

Avalanche of Selling Begins, October 24, 1929—Floor Prices Far Below Tape Prices. In the morning of October 24 the avalanche began. The stock ticker showed drastic declines in prices, but word came from the floor of the stock exchange that the ticker was half an hour behind, and that prices on the floor were far lower than ticker prices. Word came too that fine stocks were being offered in large volume "at the market," which meant at whatever price could be obtained, but were encountering no bids. The stock ticker is a marvelous instrumentality. On ordinary days the customer of a brokerage house can give his order, have it phoned to the floor of the exchange, have it executed, and see his purchase or his sale appear on the ticker in two or three minutes from the time he has given the order, in the case of an active stock. The ticker could carry two or three million shares a day with great ease. Four or five million had been repeatedly carried, with some strain, but no real embarrassment.

Ticker Swamped by 12,895,000 Shares. On October 23, 1929, 6,369,000 shares had been sold and reported, with the ticker running several minutes behind frequently during the day, and still busy for half an hour or more after the market closed. But on October 24 the recorded share sales ran to 12,895,000, and the ticker was swamped.

Many "Green" Brokers. The problem of executing orders was complicated by the fact that there were a great many "green" brokers on the floor. The New York Stock Exchange, when the price of its seats went up to fantastic levels, had authorized a "seat dividend" of forty percent, which made it possible for the holders of old seats to sell fractional shares which new brokers, approved by the stock exchange committee, could purchase, thereby obtaining membership. These new men were all veterans before the great smash was over, but on the first day they were bewildered. There was one incident when one of the new brokers received an order to sell one thousand shares of a high-priced, well-rated railroad stock "at the market," which he undertook to do—offering it down first a point at a time, and then finally five points at a time in an effort to find a buyer—but there were no bids. Finally, one of the older brokers grabbed his arm and said to him, "This is a disgrace to the New York Stock Exchange. Give *me* that order!" The older broker thereupon phoned to his office that this fine stock was being offered with no takers, called for some supporting orders, and delayed the execution of the order. Speedily the supporting orders came and the stock was sold fifteen points above the lowest price at which the young broker had offered it. Men who put in buying orders in the midst of this demoralization were well repaid (provided they sold again by the end of the following day!), as shown by the following figures for the Dow-Jones industrial averages: October 24, high, 312.76, low, 272.32, close, 299.47; October 25, high, 306.02, low, 295.59, close, 301.22.

A situation of this sort had not been unanticipated by the banks or by the brokers. We have already discussed the higher margin requirements and the reduced loan values which had been applied with increasing rigor as the wild boom went on, and have referred to the rigorous examination with respect to liquidity which the clearinghouse had inaugurated for the clearinghouse banks in 1928.

Noon Conference of Leading Bankers, October 24. Most of the heads of the great banks and banking houses had been aware that grave trouble was impending, had had informal conferences with one another regarding it, and had discussed tentative plans for dealing with it if it should come. The chief financial leaders met in the banking house of J. P. Morgan & Company at 23 Wall Street at twelve o'clock on October 24, in the midst of the panic. They were Albert H. Wiggin, head of the Chase National Bank, Charles E. Mitchell, head of the National City Bank, William C. Potter, head of the Guaranty Trust Company, Seward Prosser, head of the Bankers Trust Company, and Thomas W. Lamont, a senior partner of the Morgan firm.

Panic Quiets—Supporting Orders. With the announcement of the meeting of these men, the panic began to quiet. Supporting orders from many quarters came into the market. After the conference Lamont spoke to the reporters, saying that no plan of concerted action to support the market had been agreed upon. Despite this statement Wall Street was convinced that the bankers had agreed to bring support to the market. Whether or not such an agreement was reached, it was reliably reported in brokerage circles later in the day that large orders emanating from these banking houses had been executed on the floor of the exchange shortly after the conference ended.[2] The bankers reconvened at 4:30 P.M. on October 24.

Bankers' Pool, October 25. The next day, October 25, announcement was made that this group, with the addition of George F. Baker, head of the First National Bank, had organized[3] a $200 million banking pool to be used

---

[2] *New York Times,* October 25, 1929.
[3] *New York Evening Post,* October 25, 1929.

in the market, not for the purpose (as they carefully explained in their statement) of putting the market up or of holding prices, but for the purpose of making the market orderly. Lamont used the picturesque analogy of air pockets in the market, and the need for supporting bids to fill in air pockets when they occurred for particular stocks. The pool undertook to do in a few minutes what the great market all over the country itself would have done if the ticker had been abreast of the transactions, namely, to buy stocks at a price. This pool is believed to have bought on breaks and to have sold on rallies as the market declined, and it was finally closed out[4] after the trouble was over without having incurred losses.

The great banks, of course, could not directly participate in such a pool, as they were not authorized to buy stocks, but their security affiliates could; and of course J. P. Morgan & Company, being private bankers and primarily investment bankers, could.

Break Resumed October 26—Ends November 13. The rally was short-lived. It lasted through October 25, when the Dow-Jones industrials closed at 301.22. October 28 showed a further violent break, opening at 295.18 and closing at 260.64 with the ticker again badly embarrassed with its load of 9,213,000 shares. October 29, 1929, showed a wide-open "selling climax." That day 16,410,000 shares were sold and the ticker was no guide to trading. But by this time the brokerage houses and the "buy and sell" departments of the banks, which executed customers' orders, had learned how to get reports directly from the floor. The Dow-Jones industrials dropped to a low of 212.33 on October 29. On that day "short covering" showed itself in great volume, and a great many experienced speculators bought stocks with pretty full confidence that a real rally must follow. The close on October 29 was at 230.07. The high of October 30 was at 260.93, and the high of October 31 was at 281.54. Renewed weakness came in the course of the day on October 31. The market continued downward. It closed on November 6 at 232.13 and on November 12 at 209.74. Bottom was reached on November 13, when the Dow-Jones industrials closed at 198.69, a figure only slightly above the low for the day, which was 195.35.

Extent of Break—Industrials 52.9 Percent. Another set of figures showing the magnitude of this break is that of the *New York Times* stock index. The average price of fifty active stocks, half rails and half industrials, fell from a high point of 311.90 on September 19 to 164.43 on November 13, a break of 47.3 percent. The twenty-five industrial stocks dropped a good deal more, their high having been 469.49 on September 19 and their low 220.95 on November 13, a drop of 52.9 percent. Most of this decline came between October 23 and November 13.

Panic in Brokers' Loans "for Account of Others." We came through this great smash with the credit position of both the banks and the stock

---

[4] On February 24, 1930 *(Commercial & Financial Chronicle,* March 1, 1930, p. 1372).

exchange unshaken. There was a panic of another kind which showed itself on October 24 and which continued through the resulting violent break down through November 13, when the bottom of the market was reached. It was a panic on the part of the outside lenders to the stock market, a panic in brokers' loans "for the account of others." All the great city banks were receiving frightened calls from their customers who had used them as agents for making these loans, instructing them to call the loans. The banks had known that this was coming, and in general were braced for it. One repeatedly heard loan officers saying to such customers over the telephone, "All right, old man, your loan is called, and the money is at this moment credited to your deposit account." What the bank was doing, in fact, was taking over the loan from the customer and paying him for it, and subsequently deciding whether to call it from the broker, conferring with the broker to find out if it would be convenient for him to pay it. On October 24 it frequently was not convenient! Out-of-town banks also were ordering their loans called on a tremendous scale, and on a tremendous scale the banks of New York City took them over. They stood in the breach. Policy was not uniform among the great banks on this point. One great trust company was arguing with its customers, urging them not to call their loans or to call only a certain percentage in such a crisis, assuring them that the loans were properly margined and that further margin would be obtained, and trying to persuade these frightened lenders to bear their part of the burden. The better policy, however, was that which most of the banks followed, namely, to let the frightened lender out at once, to call the loan where the broker was able to pay it easily, but to take over the loan if it were going to make unnecessary hardship if the broker were required to pay immediately. Usually the broker would voluntarily reduce his loans as his customers sold their stocks and paid off their loans to him.

New York Banks Courageously Expand Credit. But there was an unaccustomed time lag due to the immense volume of transactions. It was physically impossible to clear such a vast volume of transactions in the usual time. A stock sold one day was ordinarily paid for the next day. But the brokers could not get their clearance sheets complete in time to do this. The brokerage houses worked until midnight, and still the records were incomplete. Moreover, there were physical difficulties in making the vast volume of stock deliveries. Stocks were not paid for till delivered, and loans could not be repaid easily till stocks were paid for. It was necessary that there should be forbearance in the matter of calling loans, and it was necessary that there should be a great expansion of bank credit to cover the extended clearance interval.

The total decline of brokers' loans, as shown by the figures reported from the New York Stock Exchange at the month end, was gigantic. At the end of September 1929 the stock exchange reported total borrowings of $8,549,000,000. By the end of October this figure had dropped to $6,109,000,000, virtually all of the decline having come after October 23.

By the end of November the figure was down to $4,017,000,000. The stock exchange paid. But in the week of October 23–30, the New York banks had to expand loans.

The figures which follow are for brokers' loans reported by the weekly reporting member banks of New York City—figures which stood far below those reported by the stock exchange, since the stock exchange got a great deal of its money, not from or through member banks, but directly from private banks, foreign banks, and others.

BROKERS' LOANS—FEDERAL RESERVE FIGURES

Date	Total	For own account	For out-of-town banks	For others
August 21, 1929	6,085	926	1,787	3,372
October 9, 1929	6,713	973	1,799	3,941
October 23, 1929	6,634	1,077	1,733	3,823
October 30, 1929	5,538	2,069	1,005	2,464
November 27, 1929	3,450	831	638	1,982
December 31, 1929	3,424	1,167	709	1,548

The reader will observe for the week October 23–30 a decline of nearly $1.4 billion in the loans for account of "others," and of over $700 million in loans for out-of-town banks. In the same week the New York banks virtually doubled loans for their own account to the brokers, the increase being approximately $1 billion.

Most of the credit expansion of the New York banks that week was to brokers, but part was to customers who were buying securities on the break, and part was the usual seasonal expansion of loans to country banks for crop moving. The total loan expansion by the New York City banks, members of the Federal Reserve System, for the week October 23–30 was $1,292,000,000. Credit was given freely to everybody who had proper collateral, giving men time to turn around and giving the brokers time to make their delayed clearances.[5]

Federal Reserve Banks Expand Credit Adequately. The Federal Reserve banks, and above all, the New York Federal Reserve Bank, also acted with promptness and decision in meeting this terrific shock adequately. It has been necessary many times in this book to criticize Federal Reserve policy. But one must give wholehearted commendation to its policy in this panic week. For the Federal Reserve System there was an expansion of credit of $312,000,000; and an expansion in total bills and securities from $1,337,000,000 to $1,649,000,000, an increase of 23.3 percent. About

---

[5] I take particular pride in the fact, which I was privileged to announce in a speech before the Milwaukee Bond Club on November 13, 1929, that of this increase in loans in New York City, $373 million, or 28.9 percent, was provided by my own bank, the Chase National Bank of the city of New York (see *Commercial & Financial Chronicle*, November 16, 1929, p. 3104). The Chase was not then the largest bank in the city. It became the largest bank only after its merger with the Equitable Trust in the following year.

half of this represented bills discounted, and the other half represented government securities and bills purchased. This book has often criticized the Federal Reserve banks for buying government securities when the effect was to create an excess of funds beyond the needs of trade. But one must approve thoroughly the purchases of $150 million of government securities which the Federal Reserve authorities carried through in the panic week of October 23–30.

The Federal Reserve Bank of New York did not reduce its discount rate during the panic week from the 6 percent figure at which it had been placed on August 9 to 1929, though it did reduce it to 5 percent November 1 while the panic was still on, and to 4½ percent on November 15 as the tide was turning. In the first week of the panic, however, on October 25, it reduced its buying rate on acceptances from 5⅛ to 5 percent. On November 1 it reduced the rate to 4¾ percent, on November 15 to 4¼ percent, and on November 21 to 4 percent.

The expansion of bank credit for the United States in this panic week was virtually all in the city of New York. Outside New York the expansion of reporting member banks was only $156 million—$65 million in the Chicago Federal Reserve District, $39 million in the Cleveland district, $22 million in the Philadelphia district, and $13 million in the Boston district. There was no change in Atlanta, and there was a decline of $8 million in Richmond. All the other districts showed slight gains.

Rapid Liquidation of Emergency Credit. There was rapid liquidation of this emergency credit. Federal Reserve bank credit declined $119 million between October 30 and November 20, and New York City member bank loans on securities, which had expanded $1.2 billion from October 23 to October 30, declined $1.1 billion from October 30 to November 20.

Another form of credit relief to the market in this great break was a prompt revocation of unusual margin requirements, and of loan values below the market. The New York banks did this promptly in 1929. In 1937 the Federal Reserve authorities, in whose hands the Congress had placed margin requirements in the reform legislation of the early 1930s, moved to reduce margin requirements much too late and much too little in the great break of that year, as we shall later see.

Strict Brokers' Loans Were Good. The banks had no problem regarding margins on the strict brokers' loans made at the "money desk" of the stock exchange in the regular way. Sometimes there were problems connected with slower loans made to brokers in their capacity of customers. At about seven o'clock one evening, on a day when stocks had had a particularly bad break, a visit was made to the loan department of a New York bank to see how margin calls were being met. Loan clerks had been watching the ticker through the day on every stock that was in the collateral to secured loans, and margin calls had gone out to every broker whose margins were impaired. The head of the department said that all such calls had been met except two or three, and that he was sure that additional collateral in those cases would come during the evening. Then he broke into a spontaneous panegyric on the immense fabric of good faith that held in Wall Street. He was not a sentimentalist. He was a very tough and hardheaded man. He had to be to hold that job.

Bottom of 1929 Market, November 13. The bottom of the market came on November 13. There was more gloom in Chicago and Milwaukee that day than in New York. Brokers in Chicago at the luncheon hour were saying to the waitresses as they looked over the menus, "That order is priced at 95¢. I think it's too high. Put in my bid at 90¢. I think I'll get it." And the waitresses understood the joke and brought the order, but charged 95¢ on the check. The same thing was happening in the stock market. You could no longer put in bids below the market with confidence that they would be executed. It was a grand selling climax. Stocks had already hit bottom. Short sellers were covering, and investors were buying. There were cushions and springs at the bottom. Incidentally, the volume that day, though very great, was manageable. It was 7,761,000 shares, greater than the volume of the two preceding days by a couple of million, but nothing like the 13,000,000 of October 21 or the 16,400,000 of October 29. The break had run its course.

Symbolized by Two Gestures: Secretary Mellon and Rockefeller. Some sort of gesture was needed to symbolize this, and two such gestures were provided. Without them the market would have risen anyhow, but they improved the atmosphere. One was an announcement by Andrew Mellon, secretary of the Treasury, that he would recommend a reduction of income taxes payable the following year. The other was an announcement that someone had placed an order for a million shares of Standard Oil of New Jersey at $50 a share. This was supposed to have been placed by John D. Rockefeller or his son. As a result of this announcement, the stock, which had closed at 50¾ on November 13, opened at 59 on November 14, and closed at 58½. It is interesting to note in this connection that in the preceding wild boom Standard Oil of New Jersey did not go above 83. It was reported at the time that one of the most reckless leaders of speculative pools had tried to put Standard Oil of New Jersey up. He had bought the stock all one day in the effort to break through 83. But the resistance was insurmountable. When deliveries came the following day, a great deal of the stock that was delivered was said to have been in the name of John D. Rockefeller. The pool leader thereupon quit, so far as that stock was concerned.

The market turned up. The Dow-Jones industrials, which had closed at 198.69 on November 13, had a low of 205.61 on November 14, and closed at 217.28; closed at 227.56 on November 18; at 245.72 on November 22; and at 258.44 on December 11.

31

The New Deal in 1929–30

Change of Tariff and Federal Reserve Policies Clearly Called For. The stock market crash demonstrated that fundamentally wrong policies had been pursued. It was surely time for a slowing down and a change of policy. The evidence was particularly clear (a) that the policy of cheap money and rapid expansion of credit was a fallacious one, and (b) that high tariffs interfering with the movement of goods and preventing our European debtors from paying their debts with goods was a fallacious policy. But to have recognized these things would have meant humiliation for the political party in power.

Would Have Involved Severe Readjustment. If we had taken our medicine in 1929 and early 1930, we should have had a severe depression. There were a good many unsound points in the credit structure, and they would have had to be liquidated or readjusted. The credit structure of business was generally extremely strong. Almost any business that could make a reasonable showing of earning power, and not a few that could make only a *prima facie* showing, had been able to issue stocks in the enthusiastic stock market that had preceded the crash. Businesses had refunded a good many bond issues with the proceeds of stock issues, had reduced their debts to the bank with money obtained from the stock market, and had increased their holdings of cash. The financial structure of business was exceedingly strong.

But there were weak points in the banking system where there were excessive holdings of illiquid bonds, or where there were large loans to customers on collateral inadequately diversified, liquidation of which would break the market. There were weak points in the real estate mortgage situation based on very exaggerated real estate prices. Many smaller banks later fell into grave difficulties because they had bought such mortgages in too great volume and too uncritically when they had excess funds and didn't know how to use them. A great deal of water had to be squeezed out of the sponge.

There were dangerous weak spots in the international credit picture. But if we had lowered our tariffs so that the weak foreign debtors could pay with goods, most of these could have been kept solvent. The country and the world were probably strong enough, despite the folly of the years preceding, to have gone through an orderly liquidation and readjustment, with a normal revival, if we had recognized our mistakes in policy in late 1929 and proceeded forthwith to change them.

But Administration Turned to Governmental Economic Planning. But the administration at Washington was dead set against any such readjustment. It turned instead to frantic governmental economic planning. Governmental economic planning is back seat driving by a man who doesn't know how to drive and who, except in wartime, doesn't know where he wants to go. It is, moreover, back seat driving by a man who makes a very heavy charge for his services at the expense of the chauffeur's wages, and who increases these heavy charges month after month. As the chauffeur's wages prove inadequate to support the governmental back seat driver, a mortgage is placed on the car, and inroads are made on the gas and oil of the automobile. Damaged fenders are left untouched. The automobile begins to miss its periodic overhauling. Cylinders accumulate carbon and don't all work. The machine slows down, and the chauffeur grows jittery.

We had had a great deal of this back seat driving for several years preceding the stock market crash, as Secretary Mellon and President Coolidge gave out utterances which whipped up the stock market and encouraged the speculators, while the Federal Reserve System supplied the chauffeur with high-powered gasoline.

Hoover Tells Business to Hold Up Wages and Prices. Even while the stock market crash was going on, President Hoover called together in Washington[1] the leaders in business, in railroads, and others, to urge upon them the policies of not cutting prices, not cutting wages, increasing capital outlay, and the like. This was the personal conduct of business by the back seat driver which is the essence of the New Deal and of governmental economic planning. Municipalities and states were also called upon to increase their borrowing for public works. The poor old St. Louis and San Francisco railroad, impressed with its duty to keep purchasing power high, thereupon proceeded to declare its preferred dividend a full year in advance—with unsatisfactory consequences.

International Staples Break in Price. Almost immediately following the stock market crash, there was an ominous downward movement in the prices of many raw materials and basic foods—the great staples of international trade. Bradstreet's index of commodity prices, which is heavily weighted with raw materials, moved downward nearly 5 percent in the

---

[1] *Commercial & Financial Chronicle,* November 16, 1929, p. 3108; November 23, 1929, pp. 3261–64; November 30, 1929, pp. 3415–19.

month of December alone. By early January 1930 jute prices in New York were at 6.25¢ a pound as against 7.4¢ a year before. Foreign wool prices were about 30 percent under the prices of the preceding year. Coffee was selling at about one-half the price of the year before, with demoralization in Brazil and trouble in Colombia and Salvador and a number of other countries. Rubber was 14.7¢ a pound as against 18¢ at the same time in 1928. Business conditions in Malaya and other chief rubber producing sections were reported as much depressed. Silk, after a sharp decline in November and December 1929, was selling at the lowest price since World War I, being quoted in New York at $4.65 per pound, as against $5.20 the year before. Silver had declined drastically, selling in January at 43⅞¢ per fine ounce as against 57¼¢ the year before. Cotton was off 3¢ a pound from the preceding year. Wheat prices were declining. This concerted general decline in basic international staples, affecting most material- and food-producing regions all over the world, was ominous. Such a movement may usually be taken as a forecast of a very severe reaction and depression.

Hoover Farm Board and Wheat Prices. Much more significant, however, than the relatively moderate decline in wheat prices, was the fact that these prices declined in the face of strenuous efforts by the government to hold them up. The Hoover New Deal had put the government into the wheat business. The Farm Board had begun to function in the late autumn of 1929. The Farm Board came into the game late. In the two or three preceding years many parts of the world had been trying to uphold the price of wheat by artificial measures. Canada had been conspicuous in this matter, speculating with her wheat pool, holding instead of selling. Hungary and Poland had been playing the game. The figures on page 227[2] show the approximate carryover of wheat on August 1 for the six-year period ending in 1929.

The world's wheat carryover had doubled in the three years ending in 1929, before our own Farm Board entered the picture. Wheat prices had broken badly between May and August 1928, and there was a further sharp break in May and June 1929 under the growing pressure of this load.[3] But the federal Farm Board (organized July 15, 1929) stepped into the breach, with the result that the United States took over an undue share of the cumulative load which the world had been carrying. It promptly advised farmers not to send wheat forward too rapidly.[4] On October 26 the Farm Board stated that it would loan to qualified wheat cooperatives approximately $150 million, funds which the cooperatives would not have needed

---

[2] *Wheat Studies,* Food Research Institute of Stanford University, December 1929, p. 62.
[3] *Ibid.,* p. 68.
[4] *Ibid.,* January 1930, p. 121.

for orderly marketing, but which they did need for holding.[5] North America held wheat in the autumn and winter of 1929–30. The Argentine sold.[6] We held our wheat too high, and we lost our share of the export trade of the world, though the export trade of the world as a whole in wheat fell off drastically,[7] and although prices of wheat here and abroad continued to decline. President Hoover, early in March 1930, asked the Congress for an additional $100 million, making a total of $250 million, to enable the Farm Board to continue its policy—which, though concentrated on wheat, involved cotton and some other farm products as well.[8]

WHEAT CARRYOVER, AUGUST 1, 1924–29
(In millions of bushels)

	1924	1925	1926	1927	1928	1929
United States	165	135	111	138	142	262
Canada	41	26	35	48	78	104
Canadian in U.S.	3	3	4	5	14	23
Argentina	66	56	61	65	90	120
Australia	38	36	30	34	43	45
Afloat for Europe	42	33	39	46	45	38
United Kindom ports	10	9	4	8	10	6
Totals	365	298	284	344	422	598

It is probable that there was more planting of wheat in the United States than would have occurred had the Farm Board not entered the picture, which meant an intensified problem for the following crop year.

Those who condemn the New Deal for its agricultural follies in 1933 and succeeding years, and above all, for loans to farmers which held back cotton which would otherwise have gone into the export trade, should not credit Roosevelt's New Deal with originality on this point.

Cheap Money Renewed, Early 1930. Early 1930 saw also a renewal of artificially cheap money. Talking with a small group of leading Federal Reserve officials in the last week of December 1929, one came away with the conviction that Federal Reserve policies, if left free from political interference, would be conservative, and that the disposition was to let the money market "sweat it out" and reach monetary ease by the wholesome process of liquidation. The opinion was expressed by a particularly well-informed Federal Reserve official that easy money was not in sight on the basis of any natural forces, and a good deal of time must pass before easy money could be looked for.

---

[5] *Ibid.*, p. 135.
[6] *Ibid. Commercial & Financial Chronicle,* March 15, 1930, pp. 1706, 1750–51.
[7] *Wheat Studies,* May 1930, p. 289.
[8] *Commercial & Financial Chronicle,* March 15, 1930, p. 1706.

But very early in 1930, easy money came through a policy change.[9] The rediscount rate of the New York Federal Reserve Bank dropped a half percent at a time, from 4.5 percent on February 6, 1930, to 2 percent by the following year end. The Federal Reserve banks' buying rate for ninety-day acceptances, which was 4 percent at the beginning of 1930, dropped rapidly to 3 percent by March 19, to 2 percent by the middle of the year, and to 1.75 percent in December. The call money rate, which ranged from 4.5 percent to 6 percent in January 1930, dropped to 2 percent by the end of the following July, and remained at approximately that level till the year-end week beginning December 28. Going with this, and a primary causal factor in it, was a renewal of government security purchases by the Federal Reserve banks on a great scale.

In 1929 the figure for government securities owned by the Federal Reserve banks stood at $136 million on October 23, rising to $533 million on December 18, and standing at $511 million on December 31. Dropping off to $477 million on January 29, the figure rose again to $602 million on August 27, 1930.

The sum of $600 million was approximately twenty-five percent of the total legal reserves of all the member banks of the Federal Reserve System in 1930. Federal Reserve bank operation in government securities, on a scale much smaller than this, could turn the money market upside down, could make a scarcity of capital look like a superfluity of capital, and could generate incredible abnormalities in the monetary picture. We renewed in 1930 many of the illusions which the stock market crash of 1929 should have dispelled.

Stocks Rise Again, but Business Steadily Declines. New corporate security issues, which had fallen off very sharply in the final quarter of 1929, rose again rapidly in the first two quarters of 1930, the figure for new capital for the second quarter of 1930 exceeding any preceding quarter,[10] even in 1929. Foreign security issues, publicly placed in the United States, which had dropped from $1,319,000,000 in 1928 to $758,000,000 in 1929, rose again in 1930 to approximately $1,000,000,000. These foreign securities issues included another great block of German government bonds, the Young Plan bonds. There came, too, in the first half of 1930 another strong upward move in the stock market—another specific response to the injection of dope—reaching a new high level in April, only to fall back again in May and June, with later a violent break culminating in December 1930.

---

[9] Governor Roy A. Young left the Federal Reserve Board on August 27, 1930, to become governor of the Federal Reserve Bank of Boston, and Eugene Meyer, Jr. became governor of the Federal Reserve Board. For the full story of this, see *Commercial & Financial Chronicle*, August 1930, p. 1355; September 6, 1930, p. 1507; September 13, 1930, p. 1654.

[10] See *Federal Reserve Charts on Bank Credit, Money Rates and Business*, February 1941, p. 32.

An examination of the curve for production shows a strong upward movement following the open market purchases of government securities by the Federal Reserve banks in 1924, as well as a strong upward movement in the stock market, and the same thing is true in 1927. In 1930, however, although the stock market and the issue of new securities responded to the renewal of cheap money, the curve for production makes no response at all. It moves downward steadily through the whole year 1930, dropping from a level of 105 at the beginning of the year to 84 at the end.[11] The jaded economic organism could no longer respond to financial stimulus.

Crowning Folly of Tariff of 1930. But there came another folly of governmental intervention in 1930 transcending all the rest in its significance and in its baleful consequences. In a world staggering under a load of international debt which could be carried only if countries under pressure could produce goods and export them to their creditors, we, the great creditor nation of the world, with tariffs already far too high, raised our tariffs again. The Hawley-Smoot Tariff Act of June 1930 was the crowning financial folly of the whole period from 1920 to 1933.

Before our passage of the tariff bill, there had still been hope. Some of the weaker countries of Europe, under extreme pressure to protect their currencies, had raised their tariffs—reducing imports but also at the same time reducing their exports—getting a little temporary relief from the pressure on their exchange rates, but at the same time increasing domestic unemployment for those in the export industries. But there was not a great deal of this, and the influence of the more powerful countries upon the weaker countries in the direction of protecting what freedom of trade there was, was strong. Moreover, it was possible for financial advisers in the great banks in the financial centers to offer cogent arguments to the governments of the weaker countries which helped to hold them back. But once we raised our tariffs, an irresistible movement all over the world to raise tariffs and to erect other trade barriers, including quotas, began. Protectionism ran wild over the world. Markets were cut off. Trade lines were narrowed. Unemployment in the export industries all over the world grew with great rapidity, and the prices of export commodities, notably farm commodities in the United States, dropped with ominous rapidity. Farm prices in the United States dropped sharply through the whole of 1930, but the most rapid rate of decline came following the passage of the tariff bill.

Industrial Stocks Break Twenty Points on Tariff News. The dangers of this measure were so well understood in financial circles that, up to the very last, the New York financial district retained hope that President Hoover

---

[11] *Ibid.*, November 1939, p. 34.

would veto the tariff bill. But late on Sunday, June 15, it was announced that he would sign the bill. This was headline news Monday morning. The stock market broke twelve points in the *New York Times* averages that day, and the industrials broke nearly twenty points. The market, not the President, was right.

Young Plan German Bonds and Tariff. It was the regular practice in the financial district of New York for investment houses contemplating the issue of new foreign loans to make inquiry of the State Department as to whether the State Department objected to particular loans. The State Department assumed no responsibility for the loans to which it made no objections, but it did occasionally interpose objections, which were always respected. Under the laws as they stood in the period prior to 1933, there was no legal authority for the federal government to take authoritative action to prevent a foreign bond issue in the United States, but this authority was not needed. There was, on the one hand, respect for the wishes of the State Department, and there was, on the other hand, the knowledge that an expression of disapproval by the State Department could spoil the market and ruin an issue. In some cases State Department disapproval was expressed when a foreign government had not yet taken steps to fund its debt to the United States government. In one notable case, that of the Dawes Plan loan of 1924, it is believed that there was an informal intervention by Secretary Hughes to make sure that Germany would go on the gold standard before he would give the "all clear" on the placement of this loan in the United States.

This procedure was followed for the Young Plan German loan of 1930, as disclosed in a two-volume publication of the State Department issued on July 21, 1945, of which an account is given in the *New York Times* of Sunday, July 22: "Details of the department's treatment of the loan proposal were handled by the late Joseph P. Cotton, undersecretary of state. The approval through the nonobjection formula was given by the then secretary of state, Henry L. Stimson, to J. P. Morgan & Company."

The Young Plan loan, or the German government international loan of 1930, with a coupon rate of 5.5 percent, was offered in the United States in the amount of $98,250,000 on Thursday morning, June 12. If this loan were to be good, Germany must be in a position to obtain dollars with which to make it good, and to obtain these dollars, she must be able to sell goods in adequate volume in foreign countries, including the United States. Three days later, on the afternoon of June 15, the President of the United States let it be known that he would sign the tariff bill, the effect of which was to interpose a grave barrier in the way of Germany's obtaining the dollars with which to pay debt service on the Young Plan bonds and, for that matter, on all her other numerous outstanding bonds in the United States and elsewhere in the world. The right hand surely did not know what the left hand was doing.

Late 1930—Hitler Gains; Bank of United States Crashes

The second half of 1930 saw the shadows deepening. Interest rates continued to decline under the influence of Federal Reserve policy. The open market commercial paper rate dropped to three percent in the third quarter, and below three percent in the fourth quarter. The rate on bankers' acceptances went under two percent in the third quarter and declined further at the year end, while the New York Federal Reserve Bank discount rate dropped to two percent as the year end came. But the cheap money magic was over. Declining interest rates were a feeble candle in the midst of growing gloom.

Quality of Credit Questioned—Foreign Bonds and Mortgages. The real forces which governed business and markets were of a different character. Exports and imports were declining. The curve of industrial production moved steadily downward. The level of commodity prices moved rapidly downward. Questions were being raised regarding the *quality* of credit, and particularly, regarding foreign bonds and real estate mortgage bonds. Real estate values were being questioned, and the market for second mortgages and third mortgages (documents which multiply in a real estate boom) became demoralized in the extreme.

Hitler Danger Recognized. The foreign bond picture, badly shaken by the Smoot-Hawley Tariff Act, was further shaken by the German election held Sunday, September 14, 1930. Down to this time Hitler's name had not been well known in the United States and, where it had been known, it had been looked upon as merely a bad joke. There had been a good deal more apprehension in Germany itself than elsewhere. But even in Germany, the disposition had been generally to look upon him as a troublesome irritant rather than a serious danger.

In this election, however, he showed real strength. In the campaign which preceded the election, there was a real scare in Germany. Hitler made a strong appeal to many discontented elements, including young men of good family who had been kept out of the civil service by the dominant Social Democratic Party, and who had no opportunities for military careers because the German army was held down to 100,000 by the Treaty of Versailles. He appealed to the growing body of unemployed in Germany, and he appealed to national sentiment as a whole in his denunciation of reparations and in his denunciation of the Young Plan of 1930, which revised the Dawes Plan and under which a new German international bond issue had just been floated. In the election, he showed real strength. He gained 107 seats in the new Reichstag as compared with 12 seats held in the previous Reichstag. In the total popular vote, there were 35,000,000 ballots cast, of which 8,572,016 were for the Social Democrats; 6,401,210 were for the Hitlerites (the National Socialists, or Nazis, as they were beginning to be called); 4,587,708 were for the communists; and the rest were distributed among the Catholic Centrists and other older parties. Hitler's party thus stood second in size among the parties, no one of which had a majority. That he got so few votes brought relief to German opinion, but that he got so many created grave concern in the financial world outside Germany. There were definitely bad reactions both in stocks and in bonds as a result of this election.

Bank of United States. By the year end, markets were dominated by an acute domestic development. The Standard Statistics Average of 420 stocks, which had stood at a little over 70 in the first quarter of 1924, rising to 225 at the peak of 1929 (monthly figures), had dropped to 150 at the low of 1929, and in the first half of 1930 had risen again to 170. The reaction in May and June was sharp and brought the level back to around 150 again. August and September showed a measure of resistance. By the end of the third quarter a drastic decline was again under way, helped very definitely by the Hitler election, but speeded up and intensified by the trouble with the Bank of United States, which occasioned grave concern during the last quarter of 1930.

The Bank of United States was a bank which ought never to have existed, and which certainly ought never to have had the name which it had. One leading banker of New York went personally to Albany to protest against the giving of such a name to that bank or to any other bank, and was told that there was a political debt to pay. In the period 1924 to 1929, with excess reserves and rapid bank expansion, it was easy for plungers and speculators to grow rapidly. There was a heavy discount on sound banking, and a high premium on reckless plunging. One watched it with apprehension, afraid not merely that bankers would lose their judgment but also that in many cases moral standards would crack. We must pay high tribute to the banking profession of the United States with respect to this latter point. In very few cases did moral standards crack. In many cases judgment went bad, and in more cases traditional practices, sound and tested, proved bad practices in such an abnormal money market. But the great majority of

American bankers kept their integrity and tried to adhere to established and approved banking practices. But it was an era in which the bold speculator and promoter could gain ground rapidly at the expense of the conservative banker, and it was a period in which departures from convention and apppoved banking practices would seem to be brilliant strokes of genius— while the new era lasted.

The Bank of United States grew very rapidly down to 1929. The name itself meant, as it was designed to mean, to many of the ignorant people of Europe, that this was the national bank, the state bank, the official bank of the United States. Deposits came to it from a great many of those people and from a great many of the ignorant and the poor on the East Side of New York. And a great deal of business was brought to it, too, by men engaging in speculative activities who could get the desired kind of accommodation from this bank which the other banks of New York would not give. Loans against mortgages were generally looked at askance by great New York banks. The first principle of commercial banking is to know "the difference between a bill of exchange and a mortgage." Second mortgages and third mortgages were notoriously improper documents in a bank's portfolio or as a collateral to its loans. But the Bank of United States went in heavily for these. It had an affiliate also—the Bankus Corporation. This was engaged in many yet more questionable transactions, including manipulation of the stock of the bank and loans against the stock of the bank. In addition to the utterly unsound banking practices, there were definitely criminal acts for which the head of the bank subsequently went to prison— not unaccompanied.

When the first mortgages grew shaky, when second and third mortgages had no market, and when the bank's stock was crashing, the Bank of United States and its affiliate, the Bankus Corporation, were in grave peril. Depositors grew very uneasy and they made heavy withdrawals of funds.

Unsuccessful Efforts to Save It. The great New York clearinghouse banks, the Federal Reserve bank, and the state superintendent of banking, Joseph A. Broderick (who had no part in giving the name to the bank and whose job was primarily salvage), made strenuous efforts to save the situation. The great clearinghouse banks were prepared, in the interest of the good name of banking in New York, to stand part of the losses. On Monday, November 24, 1930, it was announced that there would be a merger of the Bank of United States with the Manufacturers Trust Company, the Public National Bank & Trust Company, and the Interstate Trust Company, with J. Herbert Case, Federal Reserve agent and chairman of the Board of Directors of the Federal Reserve Bank of New York, as head of the merger.

This looked like an admirable solution of the problem. The financial community breathed a great sigh of relief when it appeared that J. Herbert Case thought that this situation could be solved in this way. It appeared that the aggregate capital funds of all these banks would suffice to absorb the losses and still leave a strong institution. But the agreement was a contingent agreement, and the other banks were to have time to look with great care at the assets of the Bank of United States. As they looked at these assets, the merger clearly became impossible. The officials of the other banks and J. Herbert Case could not assume the responsibility for such a mess. The problem remained. The clearinghouse worked hard upon it.

A conference, lasting beyond midnight, of leading New York bankers sat with Broderick, state superintendent of banks, on the night of December 10 and the early morning of December 11. A plan was worked out by which a wholly new management, under the presidency of the head of one of the small but sound banks of the city, was to take over the Bank of United States with the guaranty of the great clearinghouse banks against loss. But after this able young president and his associates, accustomed to clean, sound banking, looked at the assets of the Bank of United States, looked at the second and third mortgages, looked at the tangled and involved transactions they would have to deal with, they declined. They did not know how to do that kind of banking. No other New York bank knew how to do that kind of banking. On Thursday morning, December 11, 1930, the Bank of United States was closed.

To ease the shock and to relieve the plight of the depositors of the bank, the other banks of the city agreed to make loans against deposit accounts in the Bank of United States up to fifty percent of their face value.

With the announcement of the closing of the Bank of the United States, the stock market plunged still lower. Money remained extraordinarily cheap in this stock market crisis. Call loan renewal dates ranged from 2 to 2.3 percent between December 13 and December 27. But cheap money could not help the stock market in a situation like this. It reached a wide-open selling climax on Wednesday, December 17. Then, as is usual after a selling climax, it rallied, and the rally carried over through the early months of 1931.

33

The Tragic Year—1931

Climax of Unsound Tendencies. The year 1931 brought to a climax all the unsound tendencies which we have described in preceding chapters. The carelessly created and very excessive fabric of international debt was tested, and debtor countries found themselves with too great an excess of quick liabilities over their quick assets. The strangling effects of the old trade barriers, our own tariffs of 1921 and 1922, and the numerous tariffs erected around the small states of Eastern and Southern Europe, were greatly intensified by our tariff of 1930 and the rapidly growing trade barriers throughout the world which followed. Countries under pressure to pay had increasing obstacles thrown in their way as they sought to pay by shipping out goods.

Failure of Cooperation: London, Paris, New York. Finally, new adverse factors of an unprecedented sort entered the picture. In all past crises, we had been able to count on the effective cooperation of New York, London, and Paris. These great centers had always aided one another when necessary—at a stiff rate of interest—in crises. Certainly it was taken for granted that they would not interfere with one another in their efforts to aid critical situations in weaker countries. This cooperation failed in 1931, except that New York and Paris did help London when the pressure on England came.

Failure of Cooperation in Wall Street, and Between Government and Finance. We had, moreover, in all previous crises been able to count upon effective cooperation within the financial district of New York itself. In 1931 this failed. Previous crises, moreover, had shown excellent teamwork as between government and finance. Washington and Wall Street in past crises had worked well together, and if Washington felt that there was housecleaning to do, the housecleaning was deferred until the acute crisis was over. The later part of 1931, however, saw a new and ominous political factor in the United States. The Congress which assembled on December 4, 1931, was an angry Congress, grimly determined to investigate and to punish the banking community, which it blamed for the disaster.

Belated Realization of Fiscal Deficit Brings Stock Market Break in Late April 1931. The year 1931 started out with some improvement in financial sentiment. The stock market, after its selling climax of December 17, 1930, had staged a rally which carried on with great vigor till February 24, 1931. The market sagged after that, but did not have a violent downward movement until the last eight days of April 1931. Then came a development which ought not to have caught the market by surprise, but which did, namely, the announcement by the Bureau of Internal Revenue of a startling decline in the March 15 tax revenues of the United States government, and of a heavy government deficit. With the appearance on the news ticker of the figures showing the deficit, selling began, and the next few days showed convulsive downward movements. The Dow-Jones industrials dropped from a high of 164.06 on April 21 to a low of 141.78 on April 29.

The revenues of the United States government for the calendar year 1930 from individual and corporate income taxes were based, of course, upon the extraordinary earnings of 1929, and despite the heavy losses in the crash of 1929 these were very large. For the fiscal year ending June 30, 1930, revenues stood above the fiscal year ending June 30, 1929, by $140,000,000; but the fiscal year ending June 30, 1931, showed a drop of $860,000,000. Public debt retirement had continued in 1930, the gross debt standing at $16,185,000,000 on June 30, 1930, as against $16,931,000,000 on June 30, 1929. By June 30, 1931, the public debt had risen again to $16,801,000,000, and it moved upward for the rest of the year. The Treasury itself apparently had been living in an unreal world. Despite the steady decline in business which 1930 showed, with the inevitable decline in future revenues which this must mean, it took the actual figures of March 15 tax collections in 1931 to bring home the fiscal realities.

Parenthetically it may be observed that this has important implications with respect to the general policy of putting income taxes on a pay-as-you-go basis. If the Treasury had been harder pressed in 1930 that it was, we might have had a general clarification of the financial situation sooner, with less disastrous consequences.

Boden-Kredit-Anstalt in Austria Insolvent. But the main troubles of 1931 came to a head in Europe and centered in the position of a bank which had been weak and, for that matter, hopelessly involved in the first half of 1929, namely, the Boden-Kredit-Anstalt, with headquarters in Vienna and with branches throughout the succession states of the old Austro-Hungarian Empire.[1]

---

[1] I had learned of the weakness of this institution in Vienna in late May or early June 1929 from good nonbanking sources. The one case in which a banker has deliberately lied to me regarding credit information came then. I went to an important official of another Vienna bank, who owed me the truth with respect to such matters, and received from him the

On October 7, 1929, the weakness of the Boden-Kredit-Anstalt was publicly recognized in a merger of that institution with the older, much stronger Oesterreichische-Credit-Anstalt, a merger which had been announced late the Sunday night preceding. New capital was provided by an international syndicate which included J. P. Morgan & Company, the English house of Schroeder, and the Belgian Solvay group. The syndicate was headed by Rothschild of Vienna. The Austrian government guaranteed certain of the investments of the Boden-Kredit-Anstalt, and the supposition was that this weak spot had been sufficiently strengthened.

Inadequately Refinanced in Merger with Credit-Anstalt. In fact, however, the big merged institution was still insolvent. The job had been done inadequately. But even those who thought that inadequate capital had been provided were convinced that the Austrian government and the Austrian National Bank would see the institution through. The Austrian situation remained quiet through 1930. Indeed, in the week ending July 19, 1930, the Austrian government floated a loan totaling approximately $62 million face value, to which subscriptions were made in Italy, Austria, Switzerland, Great Britain, Holland, and the United States, with the Bank of International Settlements as trustee for the loan.

Austro-German Customs Union, March 1931. This weakened Austrian bank might well have been carried through, however, with gradual improvement, with the credit of the Austrian government and of the Austrian National Bank behind it, but for a very adverse political development. Hard pressed for foreign commerce, with trade barriers and tariffs mounting in the world, and with its natural markets in Hungary, Czechoslovakia, and the Balkans increasingly narrowed by such barriers, Austria turned to Germany. On March 21, 1931, the announcement was made that Germany and Austria had agreed to come into a customs union together, a *Zollverein* under which Austrian goods would have free access to the German market and German goods would have free access to Austrian markets, with the same tariff structure as against other countries for both of them. This move on the part of both Germany and Austria was primarily an economic move. Bruening was chancellor of Germany, and his purposes were peaceful purposes. Doubtless he looked upon the measure as one which would strengthen his political position in Germany and make it easier for him to carry through. But the economic advantages both to Germany and Austria were real. Each had more elbow room. Each could immediately give employment to people who would otherwise be idle, in producing goods for the other country to consume.[2]

---

unqualified assurance that the Boden-Kredit-Anstalt was perfectly safe and sound. I remained skeptical and reported all the information I had obtained to my own bank in New York, together with the expression of my own reserve.

[2] The general question of bilateral versus multilateral trade agreements is not involved here. I agree fully with Secretary Hull's position on this point. The *Zollverein,* or Customs Union, went far beyond a bilateral trade agreement.

Frightens and Angers France. The reaction in France to this German-Austrian move was very adverse. To France, it was a violation of the Treaty of Versailles. To France, it was a political move—not a *Zollverein* but an *Anschluss,* namely, an annexation. Austria was being annexed by Germany. Germany was extending her political boundaries. Germany was strengthening herself in a political and in a military way, gaining new soldiers and new resources for war.

France was the strongest financial power in Europe at that time. We have seen, with the financial reforms of France in 1926 under Poincaré, how the tide had turned in France. Capital, which had been flowing out of France, had returned, and France had become a magnet for the world's gold. The Bank of France had enormous gold holdings and, in addition, enormous holdings in foreign exchange. London was heavily in debt to France on short account. The United States was heavily in debt to France on short account.

France had immense financial power. That in this situation France should have turned from economic cooperation to political fears was an ominous thing.

Run on Credit-Anstalt, May 12, 1931. On May 12, 1931, there came an unexpected run on the Oesterreichische-Credit-Anstalt, and rumors of impending great disaster in continental Europe poured in on the great banks of New York.[3]

It was believed in New York and London that French bankers, instead of aiding the Austrian situation, were pulling funds out of Austria and, in particular, pulling funds out of the Credit-Anstalt—that the run, in fact, had begun through French withdrawals of funds from Vienna. The effort was made, nonetheless, to bring about a consortium of American, British, and French banks which would save the Austrian situation. Adequate, prompt lending of a small sum as a joint act of these three great money markets would have stopped the run. An amount of $25 million would probably have sufficed; $50 million would certainly have sufficed. New York and London alone could have done it, had there been unity. The Bank of England was eager to do it, but division appeared. In New York a number of the great banks were quite ready and anxious to take part in a

---

[3] I myself remained hopeful that cooperation among Paris, London, and New York could easily enough correct this relatively small focus of international disorder, until late in May when I was visited in my office by the head of one of the great banks of Paris. In all previous conversations with this man I had found him a calm, dispassionate, well-informed financier with breadth of international vision and a disposition to work well with the bankers of other countries in holding things steady. I had found him critical of narrow nationalistic policies, and had found him disposed to look upon banking transactions between France and Germany as business and financial transactions rather than as political transactions. On this occasion, however, I found myself talking with a frightened French patriot, in whose mind political fears for the future of France transcended all other considerations. It was, he held, not a *Zollverein,* but an *Anschluss.* French bankers could not be expected to join in a rescue party for Austria when they would thereby merely strengthen the great military enemy of France.

credit to Austria if all would go along. But as several important banks held back, all held back. Finally the Bank of England acted alone, but inadequately and unsuccessfully.

Inadequate Help from Bank for International Settlements. The Austrian government did what it could. It advanced funds to the Credit-Anstalt. Rothschild of Vienna made another effort, but where $25 million was needed, provided only $3.3 million. On May 14, 1931, the Bank for International Settlements offered aid in the form of 100 million schilling credit ($14 million), of which 40 million schilling was underwritten by eleven central banks: the Federal Reserve Bank of New York, the central banks of France, England, Belgium, Germany, Italy, Switzerland, the Netherlands, Czechoslovakia, Poland, and Greece. This made a great show of international cooperation, with the Bank of France taking part, but the effect was bad when eleven central banks were providing among them only $5.6 million. Creditors grew more frightened, rather than less. If the thing were to be done at all, it should have been done adequately. The first principle of bank loans in a crisis is that if a borrower needs $100,000 to save him, you give him $100,000 or you give him nothing at all. You don't give him $20,000.

Austria Collapses. The Austrian government on May 29, 1931, was authorized by the Parliament to guarantee the liabilities of the Credit-Anstalt up to $150 million, but the fabric of confidence was shaken by the delay, by the attitude of France, and by the divisions in New York. Panics are not dealt with effectively through delay, through public discussion, and through fighting for position. A loan of $25 million made promptly at the first sign of the panic would probably have stopped it. There came a time when $100 million would not stop it. By the time the Austrian government on May 29 voted the guarantee of $150 million the credit of the Austrian government was so shaken that no one cared about the pledge. When, on June 6, 1931, the Bank for International Settlements arranged to give a second 100 million schilling credit to Austria, the Austrian financial disaster was very little helped thereby.

Germany's Growing Difficulties, 1929–31. Austria[4] collapsed, and the run on Germany came. June 1, 1931, showed important withdrawals of foreign balances from Germany. Germany had been under increasing pressure since the middle of 1928, when the effects of tight money in New York began to manifest themselves in Europe. We have discussed this in an earlier chapter. Germany had been getting foreign loans in great volume from 1924 into 1928. But interest rates remained very high in Germany despite the foreign loans, and she remained a magnet for available international funds by virtue of her high rates, even after the New York money market stiffened and led to tightening elsewhere. It was harder to get

---

[4] On September 3, 1931, Germany and Austria gave up the *Zollverein,* yielding to French demands.

long-term money, but short-term banking funds continued to go to Germany. The table below shows in milliards of reichsmark the changes in Germany's international debtor and creditor relationships from the end of the year 1926 to July 1931.

It will be observed that Germany gained only 300 million marks, or $75 million, in long-term investments between 1928 and 1929. But her short debt, largely in the form of loans by foreign banks to German banks, or of foreign bank loans to German industries on the guaranty of German banks, increased by 2.7 billion marks, or $675 million.

This was offset to the extent of 1 billion marks or $250 million by

ESTIMATED MOVEMENTS IN GERMANY'S INTERNATIONAL CAPITAL POSITION*
(In milliards of reichsmarks)

Situation at end of	1926	1927	1928	1929	1930	July 1931
Foreign investments in Germany:						
Short	4.1	6.6	9.0	11.7	10.3	8.0
Long	4.1	5.4	7.0	7.3	9.2	9.0
Other investments** ...	3.5	4.5	5.5	6.0	6.0	6.0
Total	11.7	16.5	21.5	25.0	25.5	23.0
German investments abroad:						
Short	3.6	3.9	4.5	5.5	5.3	3.5
Long	4.5	4.5	4.5	4.5	4.4	5.0
Total	8.1	8.4	9.0	10.0	9.7	8.5

* This table is an abridgement of a table which appears in the *Chase Economic Bulletin*, October 8, 1931, p. 19, drawn from the Annexes of the Report of the Basel Committee, the first Standstill Committee, which was drafted by Sir Walter T. Layton. An account of this committee is given in the text *infra*. The figure of 8 billion marks for the short-term foreign debt of Germany in July 1931, reached by the Basel Committee, was subsequently added to by a very substantial amount through an investigation made under the authority of the German government. Sitting with the second Standstill Committee in Berlin in the winter of 1931–32, the present writer, secretary of the committee, conducted an investigation of the basis for the additional figures. His conclusion, as set forth in the report of the second Standstill Committee, issued in Berlin on January 23, 1932, and published in full in the *Commercial & Financial Chronicle*, January 30, 1932, p. 764, was that the methods made use of were incorrect and that figures of the Basel Committee in its report of August 1931 were essentially right. Making this investigation, the author had the benefit of full disclosure by the authorities of the Reichsbank and the aid of able German economists. See *Report of the Foreign Creditors' Standstill Committee* (Berlin), January 23, 1932, pp. 9, 10.

** Includes foreign purchases of German shares and obligations in marks, foreign purchases of real estate in Germany, foreign factories constructed in Germany, and other miscellaneous items.

German short-term investments abroad, much of which took the form of deposits or short-term, high-grade paper in foreign money markets, so that the net growth of her short debt from the end of 1928 to 1929 was $425 million. The net short debt of Germany at the end of 1929 was $1,550,000,000. This was not an impossible short-term debt for a great country to owe to foreign countries, but it did create a precarious position in the event of a concerted move by foreign countries to withdraw their funds.

Germany had also an increase in the schedule of reparations payments under the Dawes Plan from 1.75 billion marks ($437,500,000) in the fiscal year 1927–28, to 2.5 billion marks ($625 million) in the fiscal year 1928–29, which very greatly increased the pressure.

Germany met the pressure by a reversal of her foreign trade position, turning from an importing to an exporting country around the middle of 1929, and had a heavy excess of exports over imports in the period that followed. Had her creditors shown forbearance and had the world's market remained reasonably open to her goods, she could in time have readjusted her position without collapse.

Forbearance was shown through 1929 and 1930, though withdrawals of funds occurred. The Germans themselves put some short-term money out of Germany, as the table above shows. Between the end of 1928 and the end of 1929 they increased their short-term holdings abroad by 1 billion marks or $250 million, though this was very much more than offset by increased foreign short-term credits to Germany.

In 1930, however, Germany was paying down her foreign short-term obligations at a good rate. The figure dropped from 11.7 billion marks ($2,925,000,000) to 10.3 billion marks ($2,575,000,000) at the end of 1930, while there was a modest return of short-term German funds held abroad of some 200 million marks ($50 million) in that year.

Germany Vulnerable When Run Came, June 1, 1931. But these payments lessened Germany's liquidity, and when the foreign run on Germany began around the first of June 1931, she was very vulnerable. The assets of the German banks, though generally good, were slow. The volume of internationally valid cash was limited. Between the end of 1930 and the end of July 1931 Germany paid an additional 2.3 billion marks ($575 million) to her foreign creditors, reducing at the same time her holdings of foreign cash from 5.3 billion marks ($1,325,000,000) to 3.5 billion marks ($875 million). Most of this took place between the first of June and the end of July 1931. In the course of it, pressure was extreme. There was a cruel pressure by German banks upon their own debtor customers. There were many bankruptcies, a terrific growth of unemployment, and a banking crisis of the first magnitude.

Unsuccessful Efforts at International "Rescue Party." In the beginning of the run on Germany, again the effort at international banking cooperation was made. Again $100 million, promptly provided by concerted action of British, American, and French banks, publicly announced and instantly made available, could have stopped the crisis. A month later $500 million would have been insufficient. Again there was failure of adequate and prompt cooperation. Again the political fears of France prevailed over her economic interests. Again there was division among the great New York banks as to the proper policies to pursue. Even when most of the banks of New York reached an agreement that they would not withdraw more funds from Germany for the moment, certain other banks held apart from the agreement and continued to pull funds out.

Then $100 million was provided under the auspices of the Bank for International Settlements, by the Federal Reserve Bank of New York, the Bank of England, the Bank of France, and certain other central banks, in the form of credit to the Reichsbank itself, to give it additional gold reserve. The Germans always felt that there were strings on this money, and that they could not properly make use of it. Certainly German bankers in the winter of 1931–32 were not counting upon it as an available resource. The Reichsbank subsequently repaid it out of its gold and foreign exchange reserves. The same amount of money, provided as a commercial transaction by French, British, and American money markets as a whole, would have been far more convincing.

Hoover's Moratorium Proposal, June 20. In the midst of the disorder, on June 20, the country and the world were electrified by an announcement from President Hoover. The Congress was not in session, but the President had been conferring with leaders of the Congress, and by telegram and telephone with a majority of the members of both Houses. He was in a position to assure the country and the world that the Congress would endorse the proposal that he was making, and in this statement he was backed up by leading Democrats, as well as leading Republicans—among the Democrats being Senators Joseph T. Robinson, Carter Glass, and Pat Harrison; and among the Republicans, Senators James E. Watson, William Borah, and Reed Smoot. President Hoover's proposal was that there should be a year's moratorium, both on the debts of European governments to the United States government, and on Germany's debts on reparations account, the first being conditioned upon the second. The proposal was made on behalf of the United States to the governments of England, France, and other creditors to Germany on reparations account.

France Delays Too Long—Germany Collapses. The effect was electric. The markets rallied. The foreign run on Germany was arrested. Hope returned. But again France held back too long. Most of Germany's creditors very promptly accepted the proposal. France felt that if she gave up reparations for one year she was giving them up forever. It is, moreover, in the French character and the French tradition that immediate acceptance of a contract proposed by another party is out of the question. There must always be discussion and bargaining. There must always be some show of gaining concessions. France delayed, and France delayed too long. It was not until July 6, 1931, sixteen days after the proposal was made, that France accepted the Hoover moratorium. Meanwhile the panic had been renewed. The pressure on the German banks had increased. The German people, as well as foreign creditors, were engaged in the run on the German banks, and finally, on July 15, 1931, the inability of the German banks to weather the strain was publicly confessed. Restrictions were made on withdrawals of deposits, and all the great banks but one assumed joint responsibility for one another's liabilities.

The one great bank left out was the Darmstädter und Nationalbank, sometimes known as the Danatbank, headed by Jakob Goldschmidt.

The German government, however, sent cables immediately to the banks in New York which had advanced credits to the Danatbank, giving its guarantee to those credits.

Communiqué of Seven Governments, Including United States, July 23. The government of the United States and other governments made a second effort to meet the German situation. A conference was held in London of seven governments, namely, Belgium, France, Germany, Great Britain, Italy, Japan, and the United States, and these seven governments in a communiqué of July 23, 1931, said:

[*Promises Governmental Cooperation to Restore Confidence.*] In order to ensure maintenance of the financial stability of Germany, which is essential in the interests of the whole world, the governments represented at the conference are ready to cooperate so far as lies within their power, to restore confidence.

The governments . . . recommend . . . for relieving the immediate situation:

First, that the central bank credit of $100 million recently granted to the Reichsbank under the auspices of the Bank for International Settlements, be renewed at maturity for a period of three months.

[*Asks Banks to Leave Funds in Germany.*] Second, that concerted measures should be taken by the financial institutions in the different countries with a view to maintaining the volume of credits they have already extended to Germany.

[*Calls for International Committee.*] The conference recommended that the Bank for International Settlements should be invited to set up without delay a committee of representatives nominated by the governors of the central banks interested to inquire into the immediate further credit needs of Germany and to study the possibilities of converting a portion of the short-term credits into long-term credits. . . .

The conference considers that, if these measures are carried through, they will form a basis for more permanent action to follow.

Express Confidence in German Credit. The communiqué also stated: "The recent excessive withdrawals of capital from Germany have created an acute financial crisis. These withdrawals have been caused by *a lack of confidence,* which is *not justified by the economic and budgetary situation of the country"* (italics mine).

It will be noted that there is indefiniteness in this communiqué, because it does not state whom the "representatives" nominated by the governors of the central banks should represent. The government of the United States had no relation with the Bank for International Settlements. The Federal Reserve Bank of New York held no stock in the Bank for International Settlements. Such stock as was held in that bank in New York was held by commercial banks. The government of the United States had taken no official part either in the Dawes Plan or in the Young Plan, and the Bank for International Settlements was an outgrowth of the Young Plan of 1930.

The Basel Committee—First Standstill Agreement. But the Bank for International Settlements and the central banks immediately concerned, including the Federal Reserve Bank of New York, interpreted the invitation as meaning that representatives of the banking creditors of Germany should be appointed. Such a committee was promptly appointed, sat in Basel in August 1931, with representatives of the German government and of the German banks, and promptly reached an agreement by which a standstill, or Stillhaltung, was created, to last for six months, during which foreign banks would withdraw only very small amounts from Germany, and during which it was hoped the governments would make good their promise to "cooperate so far as lies within their power to restore confidence." This agreement was generally accepted by Germany's bank creditors throughout the world, and very especially in the United States, England, France, Holland, and Switzerland.

The committee was an extraordinarily able one, consisting of the following members:

> Albert H. Wiggin (chairman), USA
> Alberto Beneduce, Italy
> Dr. R. G. Bindschedler, Switzerland
> E. Francqui, Belgium
> P. Hofstede de Groot, Netherlands
> Walter T. Layton, Great Britain
> C. Melchior, Germany
> E. Moreau, France
> O. Rydbeck, Sweden
> T. Tanaka, Japan

Its report, drafted by Sir Walton Layton, is an extraordinarily able document of first-rate historical significance.

Bankers Did Their Part, Governments Did Not. The plan made by the committee was, of course, a standstill, a temporary measure. It could be effective only if the governments kept their promise made in the communiqué above. The governments did not keep their promise. The bankers did their part and the governments did not do their part.

Hoover-Laval Meeting. October 1931 saw another development looking toward the permanent rectification of the reparations and inter-Allied debt problem—a cautious move by two of the seven governments which had promised the world in their London communiqué of June 23, 1931, that they were "ready to cooperate so far as lies within their power to restore confidence" and had called upon the banks of the countries to continue their credits to Germany. In October 1931 Pierre Laval, premier of France, visited President Hoover in the United States and the two of them issued a joint statement which contained the following cautious but significant paragraph:

> In so far as intergovernmental obligations are concerned, we recognize that prior to the expiration of the Hoover year of postponement some agreement regarding them may be necessary covering the period of business depression, as to the terms and conditions of which the two governments make all reservations. The initiative in this matter should be taken at an early date by the European powers principally concerned within the framework of the agreements existing prior to July 1, 1931.

In this statement President Hoover says in substance to Premier Laval, "Now, Laval, you go home and fix it up with Germany within the Hoover year of postponement, and then come back to me and I will talk business with you."

It is probable that if Laval on his return to Europe had immediately taken action, some real solution might have been worked out. The second Standstill Committee in Berlin, in December 1931 and January 1932, was hoping against hope that prompt action could be taken, that the promises of the governments would be made good, and that, in particular, France could be induced to act so that the air might be cleared regarding reparations and inter-Allied debts, and so that the credits which had been given to Germany could be straightened out in an orderly way. If the governments had acted that winter, Hitler would never have come into power, and we should have saved the democratic regime in Germany.

But governments move slowly and politicians look to the next election. It was not until the Lausanne Conference, June 16–July 10, 1932, that France and Germany and other European governments, creditors of Germany on reparations, worked out an adjustment with Germany which practically abolished reparations, contingent on our making big concessions on inter-Allied debts. By that time President Hoover found himself with a political campaign on his hands, and he did not talk business with the European governments "within the Hoover year of postponement." The political atmosphere had changed. Public sentiment in the United States had grown bitter with respect to our European debtors, and nothing was done.

34

1931 Continued—England's Abandonment of the Gold Standard

First Austria, then Germany, then England—each in turn was tested and each in turn yielded. Austria and Germany each made a strenuous fight. Both had to contend with the political fears of France and with a divided attitude on the part of the outside world. England, although supported by ready cooperation on the part of New York and Paris, and by great forbearance in Amsterdam and other minor financial centers, made no fight at all.

Summary of Background. Previous chapters have shown the growing weakness of the British economic and financial structure. We have seen the growing rigidities in the internal economic structure. We have seen trade union policy holding British wage rates well above the supply-and-demand level, with resultant chronic unemployment, buttressed by doles. We have seen price-fixing combines and quota agreements among British industries which ought to have been competing. A structure of this sort is extremely vulnerable to alterations in world trade conditions. Moderate recessions in world prices, not met by internal readjustment, cut heavily into such a country's export trade.

We have seen, too, how Britain, yielding to cheap money theories and yielding to the doctrine that increasing credit would make prosperity, had progressively expanded bank credit in a volume not justified by her gold reserves and to an extent that had greatly impaired the liquidity of her banking position. We have seen how this expansion of credit—increasing loans and advances on the part of the British banks matched by increasing deposits in British banks—had led to an excessive flow of sterling balances into foreign hands, in particular into the hands of the Bank of France and the Paris money market. This situation had become dangerous by the spring of 1927. It had grown ominous in the years that followed. London was vulnerable.

Run on England Begins, July 13, 1931. With the collapse in Austria and in Germany, there came a disposition to question the credit of other countries.

Men and institutions outside England, who had an excess of pound sterling on their hands, readily grew worried. Was sterling as good as gold? They undertook to find out.

The effects of the German crisis were felt heavily in the London Stock Exchange on July 13, 1931, and there were adverse movements in sterling exchange. The Bank of England's statement for the week ending July 15 reveals losses in gold holdings—the first in thirteen weeks. On Wednesday, July 15, the foreign exchanges suffered their most severe dislocation since the war. London, as the principal European depository of Europe's liquid funds, was drawn upon heavily, with the result that sterling exchange fell 2¼¢ at one time to a price at which New York and other centers could profitably draw gold from the Bank of England. The *New York Times* in its account of developments in London that day said: "In preparation for the expected demands, the Bank of England boxed $100 million of gold ready for shipment abroad as a measure for maintaining the price of sterling." On Wednesday, July 22, withdrawals from the Bank of England were very large. The bank had lost $125 million in gold in nine days. Bank rate was raised from 2.5 to 3.5 percent.

Bank Rate at 2.5 Percent. It must be observed that for the Bank of England to have come into a situation of this sort with its rate at 2.5 percent was in itself an evidence of financial shell shock. An alert, competent management would have had bank rate high above 3.5 percent early in the year, and would, indeed, never have allowed the rate to go as low as 3.5 percent with the overextended position of England. The next week showed further huge gold exports from London to the Continent, and on Thursday, July 30, the Bank of England again raised its discount rate from the low figure of 3.5 percent to the very modest figure of 4.5 percent.

$250 Million from Federal Reserve Banks and Bank of France. Meanwhile, the Bank of England turned for help to the Bank of France and the Federal Reserve banks. On August 1, it was announced that the Bank of France and the Federal Reserve banks would each lend $125 million. Gold was going out of England. They replenished it by borrowing. There was no disposition to let the outflowing gold operate to tighten the money market and to bring into operation counteracting forces which would check the outflow of gold.

There was a great deal of discussion in England about balancing the budget and cutting the dole. Prime Minister Ramsay MacDonald and his Labor ministry resigned August 24 because the Labor Party was opposed to cutting the dole. MacDonald then promptly organized a national government containing leading members of the Conservative and Liberal parties. Certain Labor leaders also joined this cabinet, but were repudiated by the Labor Party, which refused, as a party, to join the coalition. This coalition cabinet was expected to save the gold standard.

$400 Million More Loaned England by United States and France. On

August 28 an additional credit of $400 million was given to London, divided between France and the United States, and provided this time, not by the Bank of France or the Federal Reserve banks, but by a consortium of commercial banks and private bankers. The expectation was that this would surely be enough if Britain made the necessary readjustments. But Britain did not fight. As gold went out, it was not allowed to make any real reduction in the reserve funds of the British money market.

But England Did Not Fight—Money Market Kept Easy. The Bank of England bought government securities in the open market, providing reserve funds for the British banks which tended to offset the depletion of their reserves as gold went out.[1]

Netherlands Bank and Bank of England. The Bank of France cooperated loyally during this period. The holdings of the Bank of France in sterling were so enormous that any serious break in sterling would strip the bank of all of its capital and very much more. The Netherlands Bank, which had great holdings of sterling, did not withdraw its funds from London. On Friday, September 18, Doctor Vissering, head of the Netherlands Bank, phoned Governor Montagu Norman[2] of the Bank of England to inquire if it were safe for him to continue to hold sterling, and received unqualified assurance that England would remain on the gold standard. He held his sterling.

Impending collapse of sterling was definitely signaled to New York on Saturday, September 19, as the Bank of France, concluding that the matter was hopeless and wishing to save as much as possible, gave orders to each of six New York banks by cable to sell a million pounds sterling, a total of six million pounds. These orders, coming to New York near the end of the short Saturday trading day, broke the price of sterling exchange in New York by over two cents.

Announcement on Sunday, September 20, of Suspension of Gold Payment Next Day—New York's Policy. On Sunday, September 20, the announce-

---

[1] Government securities of the Bank of England stood at £30,401,000 on June 24, 1931, and bankers' balances on the books of the Bank of England (corresponding to member bank reserves in our Federal Reserve bank balance sheet) stood at £61,644,000 on the same day. On September 2, 1931, government securities stood at £53,736,000 while bankers' deposits stood at £60,351,000. The Bank of England had given credit to the money market by buying government securities of over £23 million ($115 million), and bankers' deposits had declined only a little over a million pounds. Virtually all this increase in government security holdings came between July 15 and July 29. For the week ending September 23 (England abandoned the gold standard on September 21) the government security holdings stood at £60,176,000, and the bankers' deposits stood at £64,915,000.

[2] I learned of this conversation shortly after it occurred. The only published reference to it which I have seen is the following: "In the days preceding September 21, statements were made in high places that were not conducive to proper knowledge of the market, as the Bank of Holland learned to its sorrow, when it failed to withdraw its deposit from England during the run, after telephone communication with bank officials" (Walter A. Morton, *British Finance, 1930–1940* [University of Wisconsin Press, 1943], p. 46).

ment was made that England would abandon the gold standard, and Sunday conferences were hurriedly called in New York with respect to bank policy next day, first among the officers of individual banks and then, late in the evening, by the heads of the great banks meeting together.[3]

New York Meets Shock Calmly. The decisions made by the heads of the banks in New York as they got together that night were courageous decisions. The banks would oppose any closing of the stock exchange. The banks would carry on as usual. New York met the shock on September 21 calmly.

One compromise was made with the fears of those who wanted to close the stock exchange. On September 21, short selling was forbidden by the stock exchange authorities. This rule was rescinded September 23. But on October 5 restrictions on short selling were renewed, and these restrictions were tightened[4] on November 23, and on January 22, 1932. Partly as a result of this the downward movements in stock prices which followed, down to the summer of 1932, were more extreme, and the rallies were far feebler than would otherwise have been the case. The short seller is a very irritating person at the beginning of a decline, but an extremely comforting person as the decline goes on. He must buy again in order to take his profits, and when he buys, rallies come. He provides a cushion at the bottom.

England Leaves Gold Standard with Bank Rate at 4.5 Percent. England went off the gold standard with bank rate at 4.5 percent.[5] To a British banker in 1913, this would have been an incredible thing. In a much less grave crisis bank rate would have gone to ten percent long before anything like so much gold had left the country. The Bank of England would have supplied needed credit to the London market, but at a stiff rate, and on discounts. The Bank of England would not have bought government securities to ease off the market.

Abandonment of Gold Unnecessary. The collapse of the gold standard in

---

[3] I do not know, of course, what took place in the councils of other banks, but I know that in the conference of the officers of my own bank there was a great deal of calm confidence. We could meet the shock. Our resources were adequate. We would lend as usual next day. We would oppose the proposed closing of the New York Stock Exchange. We would carry on. In the midst of this conference, there came a call from a banker in another city who had been subject to a run, and whom we had been helping. He reported that he had been having very little sleep for three nights, but that he had succeeded in raising $7 million of new capital among the capitalists and industries of his community. His bank was safe. He would pay off next day a loan we had made him of $5 million, and he wished to inquire if that loan could be obtained again in the event that he needed it. This was heartening news in the midst of the British disaster. The banker of the other city, of course, received the assurance that the loan that he was to pay the next day could be reinstated if he needed it.

[4] I give the details of control of short selling by the stock exchange and the SEC in connection with the stock market crash of 1937, below.

[5] Strangely enough, bank rate went to six percent *after* the disaster.

England was absolutely unnecessary. It was the product of prolonged violation of gold standard rules, and, even at the end, it could have been averted by the return to orthodox gold standard methods.

Even in the summer of 1931 the position could have been saved. Had bank rate gone to eight percent when the Bank of England obtained its first credit of $250 million from the Federal Reserve banks and the Bank of France, or to nine percent when the second credit of $400 million was obtained from the French and American money markets, England would not have gone off the gold standard.[6]

How Tight Money Policy Would Have Saved Gold Standard. A tight money policy in England during the run would have led to the following developments: (1) many foreigners indebted in London would have borrowed elsewhere to pay off their debts; (2) British people having funds abroad and debts in London would have been compelled by their London bankers to bring home their funds to pay their debts; (3) British people who had debts in London and the ability to borrow abroad would have been under heavy pressure to do so; (4) the prices of securities in London would have fallen drastically, making attractive bargains for informed outsiders; (5) British people holding foreign securities and having debts in London would have sold their securities abroad to pay their debts at home; (6) many foreigners and foreign banks, watching the good fight which London was making, would have taken a "sporting chance" and would have put funds in London, attracted by a 9 percent rate, whereas a 4.5 percent rate was uninteresting as offering no compensation for risk; (7) very speedily the pressure on import credits in England would have slowed down imports, while the credit pressure on British producers of goods would have forced them to reduce prices, wages, and other costs, so that outsiders could buy British exports.

Possible Explanations of England's Course. Why did not the Bank of England adopt the traditional policy? One possible reason was the strength of labor unions, which resisted any reduction in money wages. Another possibility was that the internal banking picture in England had grown so illiquid that great banking institutions would have been pulled down by heavy money market pressure, and that a good many weak industries would have been forced into bankruptcy, including some large ones which had long been financially weak. A third possibility was the fear of the drop in security prices which would have helped to turn the tide in London's favor, but this break in security prices the London stock market got in any case.

---

[6] See *Chase Economic Bulletin,* November 20, 1931, where this opinion is expressed and elaborated. The opinion gave offense to certain friends in England, which, of course, I regret. But after talking with many informed people in England since—not a few of whom shared my opinion—I have found no reason to change it.

One cannot be sure of the facts with respect to the basis of England's decision, and with respect to the reasons for the Bank of England's policy of buying government securities to prevent pressure on the market as the gold went out. There is good reason to believe that British labor leaders did inform the British government that they would consent to a reduction in British wages if it were necessary to save the gold standard.

There is good reason to believe that the positions of the "Big Five," the great Joint Stock Banks—Lloyds, Midland, Barclays, Westminster, and National Provincial—were strong enough so that they could unquestionably have withstood the shock and that, in general, the clearinghouse banks could have withstood the shock and the pressure.

It has been said that the crux of the matter lay in the position of two[7] great acceptance houses which had given a large volume of acceptance credits to Germany, whose liabilities for acceptance on German account constituted a multiple of their capital, and that it was feared that an extreme money pressure would pull those houses down. This would surely have been an inadequate reason. In the first place, the disaster to England of the collapse of these houses would have been nothing like so great as the disaster of abandonment of the gold standard and the breaking of faith with the world. In the second place, even in a greater crisis it would have been possible for concerted action to have saved these houses. Acceptance houses had proved a weak spot at the time of the outbreak of World War I, and they had been rehabilitated without disaster to the general situation. It could have been done again.

The opinion has been expressed that, once the scare was on, nothing could have stopped it. But if this had been the opinion of the British financial authorities, they would hardly have felt justified in borrowing $650 million from New York and Paris to throw into the maelstrom.

The most reasonable interpretation of their failure to raise bank rate and tighten the money market at the time when the run first began was partly financial shell shock, partly a reliance upon the great prestige of England and the pound sterling, partly that the long surrender to the cheap money policy had induced a kind of paralysis with respect to the use of the old methods, and partly a belief that the foreign credits combined with the prestige of the pound would suffice.

Prestige of the Pound. The pound sterling and England had immense prestige, even when the trouble came. The prestige was not completely destroyed by the abandonment of the gold standard. Following the abandonment of the gold standard and the break in sterling, there came a great buying of sterling from the Far East, from India, and from other parts of the world. The pound at the new low levels looked cheap to many experienced

---

[7] Morton, *op. cit.*, p. 33, says three acceptance houses.

foreign exchange traders. England threw away an immense asset, but not all of it. Even with the abandonment of the gold standard, it took years more of unsound financial policy to bring her to the pitiful picture that the pound exhibited at the outbreak of World War II in 1939.

Had England used orthodox measures in the summer of 1931, these measures, combined with her still great financial prestige, would have sufficed.

The Myth That England Gained by Dropping Gold Standard. A myth has arisen in the intervening years that England gained greatly by the abandonment of gold and that there came an immediate stimulus to British industry and trade. The figures do not reveal it. There was a kind of psychological relief. The worst had happened. The strain was over. The

WHOLESALE PRICES IN ENGLAND
(1913 = 100)

Foods		*Industrial products*	
1931		**1931**	
Jan.	113	Jan.	104
Feb.	112	Feb.	103
Mar.	111	Mar.	103
Apr.	113	Apr.	102
May	113	May	100
June	113	June	98
July	110	July	98
Aug.	108	Aug.	95
Sept.	108	Sept.	95
Oct.	113	Oct.	100
Nov.	115	Nov.	102
Dec.	113	Dec.	102
1932		**1932**	
Jan.	114	Jan.	101
Feb.	114	Feb.	101
Mar.	116	Mar.	99
Apr.	115	Apr.	96
May	114	May	94
June	112	June	91
July	108	July	92
Aug.	107	Aug.	95
Sept.	107	Sept.	99
Oct.	106	Oct.	98
Nov.	107	Nov.	98
Dec.	108	Dec.	97

surrender had been made. The humiliation had been gone through with. Men could pause and take stock and see the extent of the damage. England still stood. There was, moreover, a cessation in the downward trend of the British industrial figures. But the year that followed showed no real improvement in the British industrial position. Despite the sharp drop in the value of the currency, wholesale prices made a very modest response. The table on page 252 shows British wholesale prices on the 1913 base for the years 1931 and 1932, by months.

It will be seen that there was a modest jump in wholesale prices between September and October 1931, but that the wholesale prices of British industrial products began to go down again with January 1932, and by August 1932 they had fallen to the level of August and September 1931. The prices of foods also showed a modest rise, but again by August 1932 had gone below the levels of August and September 1931.

If the abandonment of the gold standard had magic in it for British industry, the figures do not reveal the fact. The following table gives a comprehensive picture of British economic life for the years 1931 and 1932. The general index shows a loss of one point in 1932 as compared with 1931. Taken as a whole it cannot be said to reveal any improvement at all.

VOLUME OF PRODUCTION
UNITED KINGDOM*

	Gen- eral index	Min- ing	Indus- tries, manu- fac- tures	Iron, steel prod.	Other metals	Engi- neer- ing, ship- build- ing	Tex- tiles	Chem- ical prod.	Leath- er foot wear	Food stuffs	Gas and elect.
1930	100	100	100	100	100	100	100	100	100	100	100
1931	91	89	91	74	84	81	97	96	98	99	103
1932	90	85	92	75	81	76	107	99	95	93	106

* *Statistical Yearbook of the League of Nations, 1938–39*, p. 195.

Effect Disastrous for World as a Whole. The one thing that is sure is that the effect of England's abandonment of the gold standard upon the economic picture of the world as a whole was disastrous in the extreme. The ten months that followed for the rest of the world were months of the deepest gloom.

Immense Damage to World Confidence in Promises. Fear gripped the world regarding the value of every currency. There is no worse fear than this, from the standpoint of economic functioning.

First of all, and obviously, there was a great shock as it developed that the Bank of France had lost seven times its capital through its holdings of sterling, through trusting the Bank of England, and the perhaps even more shocking discovery that the Netherlands Bank, trusting the word of the Bank of England, had lost all of its capital in the decline in sterling. The officials of the Bank of France could hardly be blamed by the French government. They had been in closest cooperation with the government, and they had warned the government again and again, in the period when their sterling holdings were being accumulated, that the policy involved was dangerous, and that a *de jure* stabilization of the franc, which would permit them to receive gold at a fixed rate in Paris, would prevent it. The Bank of France made a pathetic effort to revalue certain of its assets, including even the furniture of the bank, in the effort to wipe out some of the loss on its balance sheet. But the real relief came when the French government gave the Bank of France non-interest-bearing government securities which, for bookkeeping purposes, restored the capital of the bank as a bookkeeping item.

The Netherlands Bank was severely blamed by the Netherlands government. It meant personal shipwreck for Doctor Vissering, who was a fine person and an able and upright man. The Netherlands government made good half the capital of the Netherlands Bank by turning over government securities to it, but with a severe warning against a repetition of the occurrence. Governments could no longer trust governments in financial matters, and the confidence of central banks in one another was gravely shaken. An immense world asset was destroyed when the Bank of England and the British government broke faith with the world. Years later, after we in the United States had also broken faith with the world, the head of the national bank of one of the Scandinavian countries said, "I have lost money in sterling. I have lost money in dollars. I have never lost money by holding gold."

Gold's Greatest Competitor. The value of gold rose all over the world following England's abandonment of the gold standard, because of the immense weakening which this involved for gold's greatest competitor. Gold's greatest competitor is the confidence men have in the paper promises of governments and central banks to pay gold.

United States Hard Hit. The figures on page 255 for industrial production and security prices show how hard we were hit in the United States in the months following August 1931, the months coinciding with and following England's abandonment of the gold standard.

The table on page 256 makes it very clear that the abandonment of the gold standard in England was followed by a violent decline in exports, both in the United States and in Europe, as measured in gold.

INDUSTRIAL PRODUCTION AND SECURITY PRICES IN THE UNITED STATES

| | Production | | Prices of Common Stocks | |
| | Federal Reserve Board (seasonally adjusted) | New York Times (seasonally adjusted) estimated | New York Times average of 50 industrials and rails | |
1931	1923–25 = 100	normal = 100	High	Low
April	88	86.4	155.82	133.15
May	87	85.1	143.54	119.33
June	83	82.6	144.78	112.25
July	82	83.1	142.82	122.53
August.......	78	78.9	129.34	119.65
September ...	76	76.3	123.60	88.27
October	73	72.6	100.11	79.07
November....	73	72.2	104.95	78.82
December	74	72.1	83.46	67.61
1932				
January	72	70.1	80.88	65.36
February	69	68.1	80.56	64.70
March	67	66.7	79.57	64.40
April	63	63.2	65.30	48.79
May	60	60.9	52.13	38.64
June	59	60.4	44.15	35.48
July	58	59.7	47.75	33.98
August.......	60	61.3	68.71	44.97
September ...	66	65.2	72.38	57.27
October	67	65.4	65.57	51.63
November....	65	64.7	62.12	51.70
December	66	64.8	58.83	51.38

EXPORTS OF FIVE COUNTRIES IN
DOLLARS, 1929–32
(Sterling figures* reduced to dollars at current rates
of exchange—000 omitted)

	1929	1930	1931	1932
United States—				
January	480,384	404,309	245,727	146,785
February	434,531	342,884	220,666	150,997
March	481,716	363,131	231,077	156,000
England—				
January	325,472	283,532	182,805	106,783
February	270,894	252,688	154,721	103,680
March	285,289	262,528	165,407	113,522
Germany—				
January	246,537	245,822	172,457	126,246
February	219,144	228,910	174,601	128,152
March	221,526	248,204	195,800	125,531
France—				
January	145,118	145,589	100,901	70,795
February	161,426	157,506	108,074	69,306
March	163,856	155,154	120,579	67,424
Holland—				
January	61,181	88,428	47,265	28,122
February	49,693	80,694	44,016	30,311
March	70,387	90,934	46,819	29,185

* Even as measured in sterling, British exports declined. Comparing the first nine months of 1931 with the first nine months of 1932, we find a decline of 7 percent in British exports measured in sterling. There is also a decline of 19 percent in the case of Sweden, measured in her domestic currency. Sweden followed England in abandoning the gold standard.

35

The Year 1931 Continued—
The First Foreign Run
on the Gold of the
United States

F irst Austria, then Germany, then England went under. The Germans did not surrender the nominal gold parity of the mark. Rather, the government blocked payments and took control of foreign exchange transactions, limiting drastically the volume of mark exchange that could be offered on the markets. The British, leaving the exchanges free, frankly abandoned the gold standard, and the pound dropped drastically on the foreign exchange markets. Foreign holders of mark balances with German banks found, for the most part, that they could use them only inside Germany, and faced an increasing number of restrictions upon the ways in which they could employ them. Holders of sterling balances with British banks were free to draw checks and sell them for what they would bring, but found that they had heavy losses as they did this.

A great fear ran over the world regarding foreign balances in all countries and regarding the value of all currencies. If sterling was not good, was anything good? Was the Swedish crown good? Was the Dutch guilder good? Were Swiss francs good? Were French francs good? Was the dollar good? Switzerland and the Netherlands had handled themselves well and their liabilities in foreign hands were not excessive. They stood, as did Belgium and France. France was so strong in gold and in foreign balances that no serious question rose regarding the ability of the French financial authorities to protect their currency in the foreign exchanges.

Sweden Abandons Gold Reluctantly. Sweden proved a weak spot, because of her losses in sterling. On September 27 Sweden (accompanied by Norway) also abandoned the gold standard. The Swedish crown followed the pound sterling downward.

There have been some misapprehensions regarding this. It has been supposed by some that this was a matter of deliberate policy on Sweden's part, and there has even been a beautiful myth developed that the Swedes by very skillful manipulation have worked out the first scientific system of

money in the history of the world, thereby keeping the commodity price
level stabilized.[1]

After Failing to Get Loan in New York. The fact is that the Swedes were
most reluctant to abandon the gold standard, and that they sent a delegation
to New York to negotiate a loan or a bank credit with which to defend the
gold standard. They had heavy losses on sterling when England abandoned
gold, and their position was greatly weakened thereby, but if they could
borrow dollars they would hold the fort. This delegation from Sweden,
chiefly bankers, representing the government and the central bank, met a
friendly reception in New York, but did not get the needed money. Most of
the New York banks were ready to go along in joint action, had all the big
banks joined. But the New York banks had large holdings in foreign
countries, and especially had large holdings in Germany. There was apprehension by this time in New York that American depositors might
question the action of American banks if they extended their commitments
in foreign countries. If all acted in concert this danger would be overcome,
but it was impossible to get concerted action. One of the largest of the New
York institutions refused to join, and the others reluctantly advised the
Swedish bankers that New York could not help. It was an unduly timid
course for New York to have taken. It was only after the failure of this effort
to get a loan or bank credit that Sweden yielded.

Foreign Run on America's Gold Immediately Follows England's Collapse.
With dramatic suddenness there came a foreign run on the gold of the
United States. The run began immediately when England abandoned the
gold standard. The figure for our monetary gold stock[2] on September 16,
1931, stood at $5,015,000,000. The next available figure is that of Sep-
tember 23, two days after the abandonment of the gold standard by
England. By that date the figure had dropped to $4,897,000,000, showing
a loss of $118,000,000 of gold, practically all of which took place in two
days. The drop was steady thereafter down to October 28, on which date
the figure stood at $4,287,000,000, meaning a loss of gold of
$728,000,000 from September 16. The next two weeks showed improve-
ment. The figure for November 7 rises to $4,311,000,000, and the figure
for November 11 to $4,346,000,000.

---

[1] Dr. Rufus Tucker and Prof. B. H. Beckhart have effectively demolished this myth. Tucker's
discussion appears in *Barron's*, June 13, 1933. For Beckhart's discussion, see *New York
Herald Tribune*, November 26, 1933, and editorial "Sweden's Managed Currency" in same
paper, April 2, 1934. There was an approximate stability in the general average of commodity
prices, but this concealed two developments, both of which were adverse to Sweden: (1) a
decline in the price of Swedish domestic products; (2) a rise in the price of imported foreign
products. That these two factors happened to offset one another was an accident.

[2] I am using here the figures which we worked with at the time, and not the revised figures of
the Federal Reserve *Banking and Monetary Statistics* (1943), which have arbitrarily cut off
$287 million from our gold monetary stock, and from money in circulation, primarily on the
ground that private holdings of gold coin had become *illegal* in 1934. But they then revised
earlier figures by the subtraction of the same $287 million. See p. 522 of that volume.

The American Gold Tradition Held. The country and the Federal Reserve banks met the shock with calm incredulity. We were very strong in gold. We had a record of paying gold. Our whole financial tradition rested on the principle that we would pay gold. Grover Cleveland in the middle 1890s had defended our currency with gold payments under very much more adverse conditions. On February 12, 1895, the net gold in the Treasury dropped to $41,300,000, but he continued to pay gold. That was what the gold was for. President Cleveland called upon the bankers of the United States to get him more gold. They did it. Henry W. Cannon, former president of the Chase National Bank, and a director of that institution, once told of sitting up all night with other bankers in New York as they cabled London, negotiating a gold loan for Cleveland, and of the exultation with which, weary and bleary-eyed, they were able to turn over to the newspapers early in the morning the news that a ship in New York harbor with a cargo of gold destined for London would be unloaded, and the gold returned to the United States Treasury, and that a ship was being loaded with gold in London to be sent to New York. This was Cleveland's low point. His courage in paying gold when his gold stock grew low, his determination to maintain the gold standard, brought to his rescue the gold resources of American banks and of London, and the gold in the United States Treasury never fell to so low a point again. He had $108 million in gold in the Treasury at the end of the year.[3]

We had met a sudden call for our gold at the outbreak of World War I, as we have seen in an earlier chapter. Unable to ship gold to London because of German cruisers on the sea, we had made arrangements with the Bank of England that the gold might be received in Ottawa. And we had exported gold and pulled down the price of the pound sterling to a figure within the gold points and restored the dollar to its normal position in the foreign exchanges.

That the outside world should question either our ability to pay gold or our determination to pay gold aroused incredulity. We paid, of course. There was no question about it.

No Domestic Gold Hoarding. During this foreign run on our gold, domestic hoarding of gold in the United States was absolutely negligible. There was a great deal of gold hoarding among the people of Europe, especially in France. France was not subject to a foreign run; rather, France was pulling gold out of the United States. It is proper to add that the Bank of France itself behaved very well, in the opinion of the Federal Reserve authorities at the time.

Our own people did not hoard gold. In one Federal Reserve district the total hoarding of gold was $5,000. In another, one of the largest, it was less

[3] Cleveland really stood a four-year run on the Treasury's gold reserve, which ended only when we had defeated the "Free Silver" movement in the election of 1896. For the figures, see *Chase Economic Bulletin,* November 20, 1931, p. 7.

than $100,000. The total for all Federal Reserve districts was less than $20 million, and of this, $6 million was accounted for by two known transactions which involved, not domestic hoarding, but hoarding by domestic agencies of foreign concerns.

Our people were in many cases doubtful about the goodness of individual banks, but they had no doubt whatever of the soundness of our gold standard and the good faith of the government and the Federal Reserve banks with respect to redeeming paper money in gold.

Federal Reserve Money Market Policy. The Federal Reserve banks and the member banks had a further problem to meet while the foreign run on our gold was going on. Between July 31 and December 31, 1931, there was an increase in money in circulation in the United States of $810 million. The impact, both of the drain on our gold and of the increased money in circulation, fell in first instance upon the reserves of the member banks of the Federal Reserve System. And it was necessary either to replenish these reserves or to have an immense liquidation of bank credit.

The reserves were in part replenished by rediscounting with the Federal Reserve banks, but not all the banks had assets of the kind which the Federal Reserve banks could take, in sufficient amount. The Federal Reserve banks could rediscount commercial paper, and the Federal Reserve banks could lend against government securities. They could not lend against real estate mortgages or installment finance paper or loans secured by stocks and bonds. Rediscounts rose from $169 million (a very low figure) for the daily average of July, to $774 million as the daily average for December, a figure high enough to make real money market pressure. This figure rose to $848 million in February 1932.

Acceptance Policy. The Federal Reserve banks could also aid in replenishing member bank reserves by open market purchases of acceptances. They did buy acceptances in large amounts during the actual foreign run on our gold, the figure rising from $79 million in July 1931 to $768 million in the week of October 24. They accomplished this by holding their buying rate for acceptances somewhat below the market rate as interest rates rose in the course of the run. They then raised the official buying rate on October 24, and their acceptances holdings fell off rapidly, dropping to $36 million by the end of March 1932. This was partially ameliorated by Federal Reserve bank purchases of acceptances for foreign correspondents, which rose from $99,000,000 at the end of October 1931 to $335 million by the end of March 1932.[4]

The buying of acceptances helped greatly in the meeting of the foreign run on our gold, but the decline in acceptance holdings of the Federal Reserve banks after the week of October 24 intensified the pressure on

---

[4] I have rarely found myself in agreement with Dr. Lauchlin Currie, but I concur in his criticism of Federal Reserve bank acceptance policy with respect to this episode.

member bank reserves which the continuing increase in money in circulation involved.

Federal Reserve Banks Had Previously Exhausted Ability to Buy Government Securities. It was unfortunate that the Federal Reserve System was unable to make use of the device of buying government securities in moderating the shock to the money market of the first foreign run on our gold. We have pointed out earlier how helpful it was that the Federal Reserve banks did increase their holdings of government securities by slightly over $150 million in the stock market panic week, October 23–30, 1929. But the Federal Reserve banks could not do this in late 1931 because they had previously exhausted this resource in making the artificially cheap money and renewed bank expansion of 1930–31, as we shall see.

The Bank of England has been criticized in a previous chapter for the buying of government securities in July, August, and September 1931 to offset the withdrawal of gold, and to prevent the withdrawal of gold from tightening the British money market. The difference between the British position in meeting this foreign run and that of the Federal Reserve System in meeting our foreign run was a very simple one. We had enough gold. We could pay the foreigners all that they were able to take. The Bank of England did not have enough gold, and its only recourse, if it were going to defend the gold standard, was to submit to a radical tightening of its money market, and indeed, to take the first step in such a tightening by raising bank rate to a panic level. But the Federal Reserve System had gold enough so that it would have been well justified in expanding the purchases of government securities to ease off the strain, had it not previously exhausted its ability to do so.

Government Security Purchases and "Free Gold." The inability of the Federal Reserve System to increase government security purchases in the midst of the foreign run on our gold, and in the midst of domestic runs on our banks in that winter of 1931–32, was due to a technical point, which must be understood if we are to grasp the significance of the Glass-Steagall bill of early 1932, which eased the situation.

The term "free gold" has a technical meaning. For the purpose of redeeming Federal Reserve notes, or for the purpose of honoring checks against deposits with the Federal Reserve banks, all the gold in the Federal Reserve System is free gold. That is what the gold was for. For the purpose of permitting credit expansion by discounting for member banks or by buying acceptances of member banks, all the gold of the Federal Reserve System was free gold. The legal reserve requirements were forty percent gold reserve against Federal Reserve notes, and thirty-five percent gold and lawful money (including greenbacks and silver dollars) against deposits; and the gold reserves of the Federal Reserve banks stood high above these legal reserve ratios at the worst point of the foreign run on our gold. If the legal reserve ratio had been reached, the system would have just begun to fight, and would still have had the power and the duty to pay out gold in redeeming notes or in honoring checks against deposits, though it would have been subjected to a progressive tax as the reserves went lower and would have been under obligation to raise the discount rates as the reserves went lower.

But the term "free gold" does not relate to the ability of the Federal Reserve System to meet its demand liabilities in gold. It relates rather to the ability of the system to make an artificial ease in money by buying government securities. The technical point is as follows. The Federal Reserve System was designed to be a commercial paper system. When the Federal Reserve Act was passed in 1913, the total of the federal government debt outstanding was approximately one billion dollars, and about three-quarters of this was pledged to secure national banknotes. A good deal of the rest was tied up in trust funds. The floating supply was very small. The Federal Reserve System was given the power to buy government securities as an incidental matter, but its main work was intended to be rediscounting paper from member banks to meet seasonal needs for additional currency and to meet crisis needs. Federal Reserve notes were to be issued against the rediscounting of commercial paper and were to be retired as these discounts were paid off. Federal Reserve notes were to be elastic, expanding and contracting in volume with the needs of trade.

Moreover, Federal Reserve notes were not created by the Federal Reserve banks, though practically they were intended to be banknotes. In legal theory they were obligations of the government of the United States issued not *by* but *through* the Federal Reserve banks. They were issued *to* the Federal Reserve banks *by* the government, and then by the Federal Reserve banks to the member banks, and through the latter to the people. But when the government issued Federal Reserve notes to the Federal Reserve banks it had to receive collateral in exchange for them. This collateral could consist, in the first instance, of sixty percent commercial paper and forty percent gold. Later, in 1917, the law was changed so that it might consist of 100 percent gold, without commercial paper. But in any case gold or commercial paper had to be given by the Federal Reserve banks to the Federal Reserve agent representing the government when notes were issued. The term "commercial paper" for this purpose included not only commercial paper in the strict sense (including acceptances bought), but also bills of the member banks secured by government obligations. It did not, however, include the government obligations themselves.

As long as the Federal Reserve System had plenty of rediscounts and acceptances, the problem of issuing Federal Reserve notes was a simple one. Notes could expand as rediscounts expanded. The only gold requirement was the forty percent legal reserve requirement.

In the crisis of 1920–21 there was a very great expansion of Federal Reserve notes, but there was a simultaneous great expansion of discounts with the Federal Reserve banks, and the Federal Reserve banks always had plenty of collateral to give the Federal Reserve agent without unnecessarily locking up gold.

A different situation arose, however, when the Federal Reserve banks had been putting out their credit, not through rediscounts, but through the purchase of government securities. As they put out their credit in this form, several things happened. First, immediately, there was an increase in member bank reserves. Second, the major part of this increase was used by member banks in paying off rediscounts, though part of it remained in the hands of the member banks as a basis for additional bank expansion. Third, as rediscounts declined in the Federal Reserve System, the Federal Reserve banks were obliged to substitute gold for commercial paper as collateral against Federal Reserve notes with the Federal Reserve agent.

With the renewal of government security purchases in 1930, the time came on August 27, 1930, when Federal Reserve notes were secured by 104.9 percent in gold.[5] Gold actually segregated to secure Federal Reserve notes stood at $1,575,000,000 on that date, as against Federal Reserve notes in actual circulation of $1,337,000,000. The gold required by law to be held behind Federal Reserve notes on that date was $1,402,000,000, which is 104.9 percent of the Federal Reserve notes in actual circulation. This excess above 100 percent is to be explained by the fact that, in order to be able to issue Federal Reserve notes freely and quickly, the Federal Reserve banks themselves maintained "counter cash" in Federal Reserve notes over and above the notes in actual circulation.

A reversal of the Federal Reserve policy would, of course, free this gold very rapidly. If the Federal Reserve banks chose to sell government securities and to force the member banks to rediscount thereby, they could substitute rediscounts for gold in the collateral with the Federal Reserve agents, and thereby free the gold held as collateral. But this meant tightening the money market and raising interest rates.

Reckless Buying of Government Securities in 1930 Made for Money Market Tension in Winter of 1931–32. It was this consideration which made not a few responsible men in the Federal Reserve System apprehensive of the renewal of artificially cheap money which came in 1930. Late in December 1929 one found the conviction among them that monetary ease would have to wait for a substantial liquidation of the volume of bank credit outstanding, secured by stocks and bonds. We were strong enough at that time to have gone through an orderly liquidation. But early in 1930 Federal Reserve policy quickly veered in the other direction, and the purchase of government securities was resumed. The Federal Reserve System was gambling, using dangerous devices to stave off an unpleasant liquidation, and hoping for a return of the prosperity which was "just around the

---

[5] "The 'Free Gold' of the Federal Reserve System and the Cheap Money Policy," *Chase Economic Bulletin,* September 29, 1930.

corner." They succeeded in making cheap money. They succeeded in bringing about a further expansion of bank credit against securities (see table below).

But the Federal Reserve System also succeeded in bringing the banking system of the United States into an extremely vulnerable position, tragically revealed when the foreign run on our gold came in late 1931, and when depositors, fearful of individual banks, were taking cash out of these banks and hoarding it. Had the Federal Reserve banks been able, in the autumn and winter of 1931–32, to buy the $290 million of government securities which they had previously bought between November 13, 1929, and August 20, 1930, they could have eased the strain a great deal.

REPORTING MEMBER BANK
CREDIT OUTSTANDING
(In millions of dollars)

Date	Total deposits	Total loans and invest-ments	Invest-ments in securities	Loans on securi-ties	All other loans	Loans on securities plus investments to total loans and investments
Aug. 28, 1929	19,787	22,405	5,456	7,521	9,429	57.92%
Oct. 23, 1929	20,328	22,895	5,395	7,920	9,580	58.157%
Aug. 27, 1930	21,091	23,122	6,329	8,377	8,416	63.6%

The Great Liquidation of Bank Credit, 1931–32. As it was, we met the foreign run, but we went through a terrific liquidation of bank credit. Between June 30, 1931, and December 31, 1931, the deposits of the member banks of the Federal Reserve System dropped $5,522,000,000, while the loans and investments dropped $3,347,000,000. The process of liquidation went further in the months that followed. The table on page 265 shows the history of the member banks of the Federal Reserve System with respect to this point.

Many Interior Banks Unable to Lend to Good Customers. A new factor came into our economic situation at this time. There had been no shortage of bank reserves in 1930 or the first half of 1931. There had been excess reserves, and interest rates had been very low. There had been no inability on the part of the banks generally to supply good customers with adequate loans. There had rather been a reaching out by the banks for good loans. There had been progressive questioning of individual credits, and there had been a progressive realization of the unsatisfactory quality of a good deal of the credit, but there had been no limitation on quantity of credit to anybody who was good. We had had, incidentally, a complete demonstra-

DEPOSITS, LOANS, AND INVESTMENTS OF
MEMBER BANKS OF THE FEDERAL
RESERVE SYSTEM
(In millions of dollars)

	Weekly reporting member banks		All member banks		
	Deposits (time, demand, and U.S.)	*Total loans and investments*		*Total deposits*	*Total loans and investments*
1927					
Feb. 16	18,908	19,538	Mar. 23	33,756	31,949
July 6	19,700	20,584	June 30	35,398	32,756
1928					
Feb. 29	20,344	21,328	Feb. 28	35,375	33,688
July 3	20,601	22,314	June 30	36,060	35,061
1929					
Feb. 27	20,302	22,338	Mar. 27	36,799	35,393
			Oct. 4	36,694	35,914
1930					
Feb. 26	19,822	22,003	Mar. 27	35,836	35,056
June 25	21,051	23,140	June 30	38,139	35,656
Sept. 24	21,213	23,297	Sept. 24	36,364	35,472
Oct. 29	21,540	23,495			
1931					
Feb. 25	20,969	22,647	Mar. 25	36,000	34,729
June 24	20,764	22,343	June 30	36,268	33,922
July 29	20,807	22,296			
Sept. 30	20,378	22,107	Sept. 29	33,480	33,073
Dec. 30	18,127	20,532	Dec. 31	30,746	30,575
1932					
Mar. 30	17,073	19,354			
Apr. 27	17,006	19,033			
May 4	17,272	19,277			
May 25	17,102	18,994			
June 29	16,807	18,754	June 30	27,836	28,001
July 27	16,411	18,334			
Aug. 31	16,796	18,539	Sept. 30	28,417	28,045
Oct. 19	17,672	19,121	Dec. 31	28,690	27,469

tion of inability of abundant and superabundant money and credit to offset deterioration in the quality of credit, and to reverse a decisive down trend in business.

But now there came a new factor. In the autumn of 1931 and the winter of 1932 we had real money pressure. Great banks in New York continued through the whole of this period to lend adequately to all good customers, but there were important parts of the country where this was not done. There were important parts of the country where good merchants had their loans reduced or even cut off because the banks themselves were short of money. There came, too, an attitude of fear on the part of the banks. In many cases, banks able to make loans were afraid to do so through fear that their depositors might suddenly make runs upon them.

Reverse Side of Low Reserve Ratios—Multiple Contraction of Bank Credit. One factor of special significance in connection with the severity of this liquidation was the excessively low legal reserve requirements set in the Federal Reserve wartime legislation of 1917. We have previously discussed this. The legal reserves for demand deposits were set at thirteen percent for the central reserve cities, ten percent for the other reserve cities, and at seven percent for the country banks, while the reserve requirement for time deposits everywhere was three percent. This, as we have seen, made *multiple expansion* of bank credit on the basis of increasing reserves move with startling rapidity. On the other hand, decreases in reserves meant *multiple contraction* of bank credit to a startling degree when the pressure came. We had created a highly vulnerable situation. The first foreign run on our gold touched off the testing of our unsound internal credit situation. We easily met the foreign run on our gold. The standard of value was safe. But the fabric of domestic credit was also tested, and much of it was precarious.

The Federal Reserve banks were designed to take only the cream of the paper held by the other banks. This was sound central bank policy and our laws with respect to it were well devised. For the rest, when small banks needed an additional credit and did not have the kind of paper that the Federal Reserve banks required, the usual practice was to go to the correspondent banks in the great cities, and these correspondent banks tided them over. Indeed, country banks very often borrowed from city correspondents in preference to borrowing from Federal Reserve banks, even when they had collateral which suited the Federal Reserve banks.

The National Credit Corporation. But the pressure of liquidation called for further remedies. President Hoover called upon the strong banks of the country to create a special fund for the rescue of weaker banks. The great banks responded, receiving the assurance of the President that when Congress assembled he would ask the Congress to create an emergency government corporation which could take over the load. The great banks were to create a temporary emergency corporation to fill in the gap. On

October 8 a plan was adopted for the creation of the National Credit Corporation by an organization appointed by the governor of the Federal Reserve Bank of New York. This corporation received $500 million of funds subscribed by the participating banks. It was to lend to banks under pressure, upon the basis of sound assets which were not legal for rediscount at the Federal Reserve banks. There was further a provision for the issue of debentures to obtain additional funds. The National Credit Corporation functioned, aiding the situation greatly, and ceased to function when the Reconstruction Finance Corporation, created by the Congress on the recommendation of President Hoover, took over the work. It performed a vitally needed service in a critical time.

The Year 1932

Slaughter in Security Prices, September 1931–July 1932. The period from September 1931 to midsummer 1932 was one of deep gloom. Securities of all kinds tumbled. The stock market moved down drastically. Standard & Poor's common stocks index (1935–39 = 100), which had stood at the average price of 103.7 for the month of July 1931 dropped to 61 as the average for December, and to 35.9 as the average for June 1932. On monthly averages there were no rallies in this long decline, which was the greatest in percentage for the whole period of decline following September 1929. February 1932 shows a rally inside the month. Thus, the *New York Times* average of 50 stocks, 25 rails, and 25 industrials rallied from 65.62 on February 10 to 80.56 on February 19, 1932, but then started again on an almost uninterrupted decline to a low of 33.98 in July 1932—a break of over 58 percent in five months.

Even more startling was the break in the price of bonds in the winter of 1931–32. Even United States government bonds yielded moderately. Moody's corporate "Aaa" bonds moved downward sharply, the declining prices being reflected in a rise in yield from 4.40 percent in August 1931 to 5.32 percent in December 1931. The slaughter in less highly rated bonds was appalling. Moody's corporate "Baa" bonds, which had a yield of 7.47 percent in August 1931, were yielding 10.42 percent in December, and by May 1932 this yield had risen to 11.63 percent. Fear ran over the market regarding all bonds not absolutely secure. There were bonds in the "Baa" list, undoubtedly good by credit standards, "money good," which were selling in the low 60s and in the 50s. The average yield for railroad bonds, which had been 6.01 percent in August 1931, had risen to 9.30 percent by May 1932.

Drop in Production. Industrial production dropped with startling rapidity, the Federal Reserve index (1923–25 = 100) dropping from 80 in the late summer of 1931 to below 60 in the summer of 1932. In late July 1932 the tide began to turn, and the autumn of 1932 showed a decided rally with respect to all these matters.

Good Record of Strict Brokers' Loans. The strict brokers' loans made a magnificent performance. The total of brokers' loans in New York had stood at $8.5 billion at the peak of 1929, and were paid down to something like $300 million by midsummer 1932. I think it is correct to say that there were almost no losses on strict brokers' loans, that is, those made in the regular way against diversified, readily marketable collateral and with regular margins. These loans, scrutinized every day, with margin calls whenever margin deficiencies appeared, with strict scrutiny of collateral as substitutions of collateral were made, and with great care that diversification be at all times adequate, made an extraordinarily fine record.

Severe Losses on Other Security Loans. But the banks had losses in loans to brokers made to the brokers in their capacity of customers of the bank, and the banks had heavy losses on security loans to others customers. This was particularly true of loans made against large blocks of one type of security, and was particularly true of loans made by one bank against the stock of another bank. Losses were frequently severe in cases where officers of interior banks, holding stocks of their own banks for which the market was narrow, had negotiated loans against these stocks with their city correspondents.

And on Real Estate Loans. Very heavy losses came in connection with real estate mortgage loans. The major banks in New York City held comparatively few of these. The one New York City bank which had gone in most heavily for this kind of paper, the Bank of United States, had, as we have seen, blown up at the end of 1930. But the country districts and in the smaller cities there had been altogether too many mortgage loans made by banks, and in one great city, Detroit, the pressure was very heavy, due in part to this cause. The ultimate salvage on this kind of loan proved better than anticipated, but for banks under pressure to get cash to meet depositors' withdrawals in 1932 and early 1933, such paper had very limited availability.

There had been an immense issue of real estate mortgage bonds, and real estate mortgages, and a great excess of new building. With the decline of earnings in city real estate, and the break in real estate prices, the foundation of these mortgages was undermined, while, with the virtual collapse of agricultural prices, farm mortgages presented a sorry picture.

The Tragedy of Agriculture—Industrial Unbalance. Basic, of course, in the agricultural situation was the collapse of the export markets, due first to our high tariffs; second, to the immense volume of foreign indebtedness, including the intergovernmental debts; and third, to the rapidly growing trade restrictions, including tariffs, quotas, foreign exchange controls, and other devices which the debtor countries of Europe, normally our customers for agricultural goods, were rapidly erecting.

Agricultural commodity prices, which had stood well above 100 in 1927–29, dropped to 50 by February 1932, and went as low as 47 by the summer of 1932. The general level of commodity prices had a much less extreme swing. Averaging around 97 in 1927 to 1929, it had dropped to 68 by early 1932, and to a low of 64 in the summer of 1932. Farm commodity prices had been better than the average of commodity prices in the years 1927, 1928, and 1929, but dropped far below the average in 1931 and 1932. While the heavy volume of foreign loans was being made in the 1920s, farm prices were being maintained and our farm exports went to Europe in good volume. With the cessation of those foreign loans, our tariffs got in their strangling effect, and with the raising of the tariff in 1930, farm prices almost immediately dropped below the general average of prices, and sank to unprecedented depths. With the immense decline in agricultural prices, the domestic market for manufactured goods was badly weakened, and unemployment grew rapidly in the cities because the farmers could not buy the products of the city workers. We had grave industrial unbalance.

The Glass-Steagall Act. In the first two months of 1932 there were further withdrawals of gold by foreign countries, and our gold monetary stock declined by $106,500,000. Our banks were under increasing pressure.

A remedy was found in the Glass-Steagall bill, introduced on February 11, 1932, rapidly put through the Congress, and signed by the President on February 27. This act authorized the substitution of government securities for commercial paper as collateral for Federal Reserve notes for a period of one year. This was contrary to the original theory of the Federal Reserve Act. It was an emergency measure somewhat analogous to the "Suspension of Peel's Act" employed by the Bank of England, with the sanction of the government, in great crises in Great Britain after 1844. It would have been wholly unnecessary if Federal Reserve policy in the preceding period had been sound policy. As an emergency measure, however, it was itself sound.

When word reached New York that Senator Glass was willing to have this done and would sponsor it, the effect was very great. Senator Glass had immense prestige in the financial community. It was recognized that he had been opposed to the follies in the preceding period. It was recognized that he would not sanction anything which he did not believe to be sound. The fact that he did sanction this measure meant to the broker and banker in Wall Street that the extreme pressure could be removed. The Dow-Jones average of industrial stocks rose 14 points from a close of 71.80 on February 10, when Senator Glass's position was announced, to a close of 85.82 on February 13.

The Reconstruction Finance Corporation. We have already referred to two other relief measures which came in the critical winter of 1931–32. The first was the National Credit Corporation organized by the banks at the request of President Hoover, whereby $500 million was made available for the relief of banks which had good paper, but paper ineligible for rediscount at the Federal Reserve banks. When this corporation was organized the President promised that he would ask the Congress as soon as it assembled to create a government corporation to take over the rescue work. The National Credit Corporation was an interim organization. President Hoover made good his promise, and the Congress acquiesced.

The Reconstruction Finance Corporation was created by act of Congress signed by the President on January 22, 1932. It was provided by the Congress with capital of $500 million and empowered to issue its debentures to the amount of $1.5 billion. With the Reconstruction Finance Corporation we had put ourselves in position to give banks with assets which were good but slow, opportunity to mobilize their slow assets to meet quick liabilities. With the Glass-Steagall Act we had put it into the power of the Federal Reserve banks to buy government securities so as to relieve money market pressure.

We knew that it was in the power of the foreigners to make further heavy gold withdrawals, but we had put ourselves in a position to stand these heavy gold withdrawals and still maintain a comfortable domestic money market.

The Federal Reserve banks immediately began a program of government bond buying.

The Second Foreign Run on Our Gold Met Without Shock. The second great foreign run on our gold came in the spring of 1932. Our gold monetary stock dropped over $450 million between the end of March 1932 and June 1932. We met this withdrawal without any shock at all. One of the fears which had made the gloom in the winter of 1931–32 was the fear of further foreign withdrawals of gold, with the resultant further acute tightening of our money markets. But we met this second foreign withdrawal with a steady decline in our interest rates. The renewal rate on call money at the stock exchange held around 2.5 percent as the gold was going out. The Federal Reserve rediscount rate in New York, holding at 3 percent while the run was on, dropped to 2.5 percent when it was over. Open market commercial paper, standing at 3.75 percent at the beginning of 1932, had dropped to 3 percent by the middle of the summer. The rate for customers' loans in the great city banks declined moderately even while the run was on.

The Glass-Steagall Act, permitting Federal Reserve banks to resume their purchases of government securities, stopped the contraction. Member bank reserves rose again from $1,878,000,000 on February 24, 1932, to $2,192,000,000 by May 18, 1932. Money market pressure was decisively relieved.

Quality of Credit vs. Money Market Ease. But quantity of money and credit are less important than quality of money and credit. There remained deep wounds, and the curve for the stock market, after a short-lived rally on Senator Glass's endorsement of the Glass-Steagall bill, moved down decisively in the greatest percentage break of the whole decline, that from February 1932 to July 1932, and to levels that were appallingly low. The curve for industrial production, moreover, continued to move down with scarcely an upward ripple into decisively lower territory in the summer of 1932.

Runs on Banks—Chicago. Weaknesses in the structure of individual banks, or supposed weaknesses, continued to create runs on banks. Grave fears and disorders arose in connection with the Chicago banking situation in particular. Money in circulation which had stood at the end of August 1931 at $4,765,000,000, rose to $5,193,000,000 by the end of May 1932 and jumped further in the single month of June to $5,408,000,000, representing primarily money hoarded by people afraid of banks. Unemployment grew to unprecedented levels. It was a gloomy and distressing period.

37

The Upturn in the Summer of 1932—Five Favorable Developments

Five favorable things came together in June and July 1932 to reverse the long down trend in industry, in farm prices, in stock prices, and in business and financial confidence.

1. *The Second Foreign Run on Our Gold Successfully Met.* The first of these was the successful meeting of the second foreign run on our gold.[1]

When the foreigners had taken all the gold they could take, and the run was over, our Federal Reserve banks had $959 million of gold in excess of the legal requirements. If we had got down to the legal requirements, we still had just begun to fight; we had an abundance of gold for maintaining the gold standard—that was what the gold was for. If we went below the legal requirements, we would have to raise our interest rates, but we could still pay gold. If any of the foreign countries felt that they wanted more gold, let them come and get it. But the Federal Reserve authorities had full information as to foreign balances subject to withdrawal—information provided them by every bank and every brokerage house that had any foreign customers—and they knew very well that the foreigners could not take substantially more. The Federal Reserve banks aided by the Glass-Steagall Act had done an admirable job in meeting this second foreign run.

2. *Defeat of the Soldiers' Bonus Paper Money Bill.* The second favorable development was the Senate vote on the soldiers' bonus bill. This bill was designed, not primarily to give more money to the veterans of World War I, but to make an inflationary increase in the paper money of the country, and it was prepared by its sponsors as a soldiers' bonus bill in order to get soldier support for the monetary purpose. It provided for the issue of over

---

[1] This writer had the satisfaction of announcing the end of this run in an address to the correspondents of the foreign newspapers in New York City on June 17, 1932. The writer felt pretty cocky that day!

$2 billion of new paper money to be used in paying the soldiers. It was regarded as a blow at the gold standard and as a blow at sound money. Its defeat was imperative if we were to maintain the integrity of our dollar and financial confidence. In a mood of irresponsibility the House of Representatives passed the bill, "passing the buck" to the Senate. The senators met the responsibility. By a vote of 62 to 18 on June 17, 1932, they defeated the bill decisively.

3. *The Lausanne Agreement.* The third favorable development was the Lausanne Conference. We have seen that the Hoover-Laval agreement of October 26, 1931, had contemplated that the European debtors to the United States, who were also creditors to Germany under reparations, should straighten things out with Germany during the "Hoover year of postponement" and then come back to the United States to discuss their debt position with us.

At Lausanne they had agreed to abolish reparation payments by Germany, but had made a separate agreement that final ratification of this agreement was to wait until adjustments could be made regarding inter-Allied debts with the United States. This was in full harmony with the Hoover-Laval agreement of October 1931, but when it came it received adverse comment from Hoover.[2] Nonetheless, it was looked upon as a highly favorable development, paving the way for a real settlement of the appalling problem of intergovernmental debts.

4. *Chicago Banking Situation Cleared Up.* The fourth favorable development was the clearing up of the Chicago banking situation. There had developed in the spring and early summer of 1932 an extraordinary pressure on Chicago banks. There were a good many failures of smaller independent unit banks in the outlying regions of Chicago, banks in many cases overloaded with real estate mortgage loans. Most of the great banks were adequately strong. Runs on the First National Bank, for example, were grotesque in the light of subsequent developments. But one bank, the Central Republic Bank & Trust Company, an institution of which Gen. Charles G. Dawes had been the head, was very vulnerable. General Dawes had withdrawn from the management of this bank when he was elected Vice President of the United States in 1924. Finishing his term as Vice President, he had been made head of the newly created Reconstruction Finance Corporation, designed to rescue banks over the country. Suddenly he learned of the dangerous position of his old bank in Chicago. He resigned as president of the Reconstruction Finance Corporation and went to Chicago to meet what he regarded as his most urgent responsibility, that of conducting a desperate rearguard action to save his old friends and associates, and, at all events, to save his depositors, if he could not save his

---

[2] *Commercial & Financial Chronicle,* July 16, 1932, p. 392.

stockholders, from disaster. The general was no longer young and he met a cruel shock gallantly.

After he had left the Reconstruction Finance Corporation, he found it necessary to appeal to the Reconstruction Finance Corporation for help—a perfectly proper thing, in accordance both with the letter and the spirit of the law creating the Reconstruction Finance Corporation. The Reconstruction Finance Corporation made a loan which made it possible to reorganize the institution, to establish a new, entirely clean bank, fully liquid, that took over all the deposit liabilities of the original institution. The general had saved his depositors, including a large number of country correspondent banks. The Reconstruction Finance Corporation was assisted in this by loans from New York banks and by loans from other Chicago banks.

Most Chicago banks were under very heavy pressure. Deposits were withdrawn from some of the greatest of them. Two other Chicago institutions, on the other hand, were beneficiaries of the situation in that the public had high confidence in them and placed in them deposits withdrawn from the other banks. For a time carloads of currency were being shipped to Chicago to meet this situation. But in July the Chicago trouble ended. The small banks that were going to fail had failed. The great banks stood, and the Chicago situation cleared up.

5. *Both Political Parties Adopt Conservative Platforms.* Finally, the fifth favorable development came in the political conventions of the two great parties, both of which met in Chicago.[3] There had been fears of radical developments and unsound financial proposals in the platforms of these parties. Advocates of such proposals appeared before the platform committees of both parties, but both parties adopted conservative platforms. Fears regarding the Democratic platform, in particular, proved groundless. The two greatest statesmen of either party, Cordell Hull and Carter Glass, came to Chicago for the single purpose of seeing to it that the Democratic Party had a sound platform. Their prestige was great, and they dominated the Platform Committee. The platform called for drastic economies in governmental expenditure, it called for a "competitive tariff for revenue," striking at the very root of the evil which had precipitated the disaster, and it called for "a sound currency to be maintained at all hazards." Both parties in their conventions showed real concern for the financial situation and manifested a sense of responsibility for it.

These five favorable developments in combination, and the relief from money market pressure which the Glass-Steagall Act had made possible, made a radical change in the financial and economic atmosphere.

---

[3] President Hoover was renominated by the Republican National Convention on June 16. Governor Roosevelt was nominated by the Democratic Convention on July 1. Both of these conventions met in the shadow of the Chicago banking troubles, and both exhibited restraint and a sense of responsibility regarding these troubles.

Stocks Rally Briskly in July 1932. Late May, June, and early July had been times of great gloom in the stock market. Prices of the best stocks had dropped to absurdly low levels. Fine dividend-paying stocks were yielding ten percent. Investors seemed to have no confidence. There was virtually no short interest in the market (whose covering operations could have put it up), in view of the rules (adopted in late 1931 and early 1932)[4] restricting short sales. The volume of trading had fallen very low. The total shares sold on the stock exchange in a single day moved for only a few million dollars. The time came when purchases of an additional few million dollars a day could turn the scale decisively, and suddenly, in July, we got these purchases.

From June to September the averages rose (Standard & Poor's corporation common stocks) from 35.9 to 61.5, a rise of 71 percent—the rise, incidentally, validating a great body of security loans which had been "under water."

Farm Prices and Industrial Production Rally. Farm commodity prices, in the same period, moved up very sharply, though not enough to straighten out the farm situation. The curve of industrial production moved up rapidly, the rise beginning very shortly after the rise in securities and continuing into the autumn. It was a modest but a very heartening rise, from about 58 (1923–25 = 100) on the Federal Reserve Industrial Production chart to about 67. The tide turned.

---

[4] For details, see the discussion, *infra*, of the causes of the stock market weakness in 1937.

38

The Impact of Politics
on the 1932 Revival

The summer of 1932 was the turning point for the world as a whole. It was the turning point for Great Britain, for Canada, and for most of continental Europe, and for much of Latin America. It proved not to be for the United States. We were to have one more heavy shock. The reasons for this were primarily political.

Publication of Reconstruction Finance Corporation Loans. Men in both parties were to blame. The Democratic Party grew suspicious of the Reconstruction Finance Corporation. There was sharp criticism of the loan made to General Dawes' bank—unjustified criticism. The thought grew that the Reconstruction Finance Corporation was making loans on a political basis and for political purposes, a wholly unjustifiable belief. It was trying to save banks and to protect depositors. It was making loans where loans were needed, and it was making them with intelligence and discrimination.[1]

That a bank should be unable to get adequate accommodation in regular course from the Federal Reserve banks because it lacked a sufficient volume of eligible paper was an evidence of weakness, of course, but not of fatal weakness; that a country bank should be unable to get adequate accommodation from its city correspondent in regular course was an evidence of weakness, but not necessarily of fatal weakness. The Reconstruction Finance Corporation was designed to meet precisely this situation. It was not wasting money on hopelessly insolvent banks. It was lending to banks which, given time, could work things out and emerge solvent.

But public knowledge that a bank had borrowed from the Reconstruction Finance Corporation would arouse concern in the minds of depositors, and the Reconstruction Finance Corporation was not publishing the names of

---

[1] I was in a position to know a good deal in connection with not a few of these loans.

its borrowers. It was dealing intelligently with the credit situation as the great city banks did, and as the Federal Reserve banks did, making the loans and saying nothing about them. With the suspicion, however, of its purposes, and the suspicion that it was being made a political instrumentality, the Democratic leaders of the House of Representatives, which was under Democratic control, required that the Reconstruction Finance Corporation make reports to the clerk of the House of Representatives of new loans made by the corporation. Speedily these reports were given to the press. This was first done on August 22, 1932.

Democratic bitterness regarding supposed political use of the Reconstruction Finance Corporation was intensified by a campaign speech made by President Hoover on November 2, in which he told the voters of three states, California, Washington, and Oregon, how many loans, and in what amounts, the RFC had made in those states.[2] Walter Lippmann, in his syndicated article, promptly excoriated President Hoover for this speech.

Subsequently, on January 6, 1933, the demand was made that loans made by the RFC in its first five months should also be reported. This involved 5,084 loans. Against the protest of the Reconstruction Finance Corporation, the clerk of the House of Representatives, acting under instruction from the Speaker, made these reports available to the public, including the press.[3]

The fears that publication would immediately start runs on the banks which had borrowed from the Reconstruction Finance Corporation were not immediately realized in a wholesale way in August and September, but as further adverse developments came, they were realized. Institutions needing help from the Reconstruction Finance Corporation became afraid to go to it for help. The publication of these loans came in time to mean runs on the institutions whose names were published. One savings and loan association in New Jersey, a strong, well-managed company, came to a great New York bank for help in meeting unusual withdrawals. The New York bank made the suggestion, "Why don't you get under the umbrella?"—meaning the Reconstruction Finance Corporation. The answer was, "The umbrella leaks!" The New York bank recognized the propriety of the observation, and itself took care of the New Jersey savings and loan association.

The worst of the trouble with the publication of the Reconstruction Finance Corporation loans did not come until after the election, and, indeed, until January and February 1933.

---

[2] *Commercial & Financial Chronicle,* November 5, 1932, pp. 3085–86.

[3] *Ibid.,* August 27, 1932, p. 1422. New funds and new responsibilities had been given the Reconstruction Finance Corporation under the Emergency Relief and Construction Act of July 21, 1932 (*ibid.,* October 8, 1932, p. 2430; January 7, 1933, p. 80; and January 14, 1933, p. 271).

President Hoover's Incorrect Statement Regarding the Federal Reserve Banks and the Gold Standard. The second political development of an extremely unfortunate character was the statement of President Hoover in his campaign speech in Des Moines on October 4, 1932, that the Federal Reserve banks had been within two weeks of going off the gold standard earlier in the year. The statement was, in the first place, untrue. In the second place, if it had been true, the President of the United States was the last man to have made it. The father of the house does not make public announcement of a scandal in his family. But the statement was untrue. It was promptly challenged, October 7, by Senator Carter Glass; October 10, by former Senator James A. Reed; and October 11, by Senator Cordell Hull.[4] Senator Reed bluntly charged President Hoover with being "willing to spread false rumors about the Federal Reserve banks in the effort to win an election." The President's statement was demonstrated to be untrue by Senator Carter Glass in his devastating reply on November 1 in the campaign.[5]

The President's statement regarding the gold standard renewed foreign fears regarding our position. The foreigners were not in a place to hurt us much. Gold had come in from abroad during the late summer and autumn, and some gold could be withdrawn, but not enough to do us serious damage. But the statement also aroused in the minds of the American public fears which had not previously existed.

The Failure of Cooperation Between Roosevelt and Hoover. A third political factor which served to pull down the delicate fabric of reviving financial confidence was the failure of cooperation between President Hoover and President-elect Roosevelt in the interval between the election November 8, 1932, and the inauguration of March 4, 1933. Cooperation between the two in so critical a state of the country's affairs was absolutely essential. Both men knew it, and both men made efforts in that direction. The first overture looking toward cooperation probably came from the side

---

[4] *Ibid.,* October 15, 1932, pp. 2588–91.

[5] It was demonstrated to be untrue by the present writer in his address before the Forum in Investment Banking delivered at the New York Stock Exchange on November 10, 1932, two days after the election. The author presented figures which showed that the lowest point of the gold holdings of the Federal Reserve System in 1932, namely, on July 15, after the second foreign run had been completed and after the domestic gold hoardings (never large) had spent their force, our Federal Reserve banks had forty percent of gold against Federal Reserve notes and thirty-five percent of gold and lawful money (almost wholly gold) against deposits, and over and above these approximately $1 billion in gold.

See *Chase Economic Bulletin,* November 10, 1932. I may say for the record that I was prepared to deliver this speech a few days after President Hoover's statement was made. The foreign exchanges had been disturbed by President Hoover's speech. I did not desire to make a political speech in the campaign, but I did wish to correct, as far as I could, the harm which President Hoover had done by this statement. The foreign exchange market corrected itself, however, and I therefore withheld my statement until after the election.

of Governor Roosevelt. A message was sent by Colonel House, in Governor Roosevelt's name, informing President Hoover that Governor Roosevelt would welcome an invitation to discuss with President Hoover the impending December 15 payments of British and French debts to the United States.[6]

When President Hoover's telegram (dated November 12) came to Governor Roosevelt, however, it did not seem to be a telegram which paved the way for cooperation. It was a very lengthy telegram given to the public as well as to President-elect Roosevelt.[7] It reviewed the debt question at

---

[6] Within two days after the election, Col. E. M. House, who was very close to the President-elect, sent for me. Colonel House and I had cooperated in the effort to elect Governor Roosevelt President, and had cooperated in the effort to keep his campaign utterances sound, and to offset the influence of the new group of "Brain Trusters," whom neither of us at the time regarded as particularly dangerous or particularly important. We subsequently learned better. We had made an effort early in the campaign to eliminate the intergovernmental debts as a campaign issue by proposing to Governor Roosevelt that he should write to President Hoover urging him to make a prompt settlement of the inter-Allied debts without awaiting the results of the election, and promising President Hoover his support in the effort to get accepted by Congress the settlement which President Hoover might negotiate. In this effort we had been unsuccessful.

The colonel, when I saw him just after the election, said to me in substance: "When Lincoln thought that he was going to be beaten by McClellan in 1864, he wrote a letter in which he stated his intention of turning the government over immediately to McClellan if McClellan should be elected, so that there should be no delay at this critical time in the adoption of whatever policy the new President saw fit to introduce. I know that President Wilson had the same purpose in 1916. It was his intention, in the event of Hughes' election in that critical time, immediately to make Hughes secretary of state and to follow that appointment by his own resignation and by the resignation of Vice President Marshall—a course in which Vice President Marshall was prepared to acquiesce. Governor Roosevelt has no intention of making such a suggestion to President Hoover."

Colonel House added: "Both the British and French ambassadors have been to see Governor Roosevelt and me, since the election, to tell us that making the December 15 payment on the intergovernmental debts to the United States would have grave consequences both for Europe and for America."

The colonel asked my opinion as to whether that view were correct, and I assured him that it was, telling him for one thing that the magnitude of the payments, in comparison with the volume of European exports to the United States for the whole of the calendar year to date, was such that the payments could only be made in gold, and that delay in this payment and readjustment of the whole debt relationship were absolutely essential.

The colonel then said that Governor Roosevelt would welcome an invitation from President Hoover to a conference regarding the intergovernmental debts before the Congress assembled, and before the President made up his mind as to what should be done about the December payments. "Can you get that message to President Hoover?"

I said that I was the last man to take a message to President Hoover, particularly in view of the fact that I was almost immediately to make a speech refuting the President's misstatement about our gold position in the spring. We decided, however, upon an appropriate channel for conveying the message, and I have every reason to believe that the message was conveyed. Shortly thereafter the word came back that President Hoover, who was then either in California, where he had gone to vote, or returning from California, would send the invitation. It looked as if the stage were set for cooperation between the incoming and outgoing Presidents.

[7] The text of the telegram will be found in *Commercial & Financial Chronicle*, November 19, 1932, p. 2447.

length. It stated the position which the President had taken. It stated the position which the Congress had taken—a very uncompromising position. It included an invitation to Governor Roosevelt to confer with President Hoover about the matter.

Had the telegram been a brief telegram which included no discussion of policy, and which merely asked Governor Roosevelt to share in the formulation of a policy, it is possible that the two men might have got together and that constructive results might have come from their conference. Taking the telegram as it stood, it seemed to put Governor Roosevelt "on the spot." If he had gone, advising President Hoover to recommend that the position already taken by President Hoover and the Congress should be reversed and the debt payments of December 15 should not be required, he might easily have found himself in a politically embarrassing situation.

It was doubtless the intention of Governor Roosevelt to cooperate when the suggestion was made that he be invited to the conference. It was doubtless the intention of President Hoover to cooperate when he sent the invitation. But the form of the invitation went far to preclude cooperation between the men, both of whom were so largely motivated by political considerations.

They did meet, however, on November 22—Governor Roosevelt accompanied by Professor Raymond Moley, and President Hoover accompanied by the secretary of the Treasury, Ogden L. Mills. No constructive results were achieved.

Subsequent efforts of President Hoover to enlist the cooperation of President-elect Roosevelt were still less successful. The President-elect shortly went to Warm Springs, Georgia. The press in this period does not contain a great deal of information as to what happened there. It was supposed that he took with him a group of New Deal advisers. It is certain that in January and February the congressional leaders of the Democratic Party were in the dark as to the President-elect's wishes and purposes. They were angry and troubled. There was growing concern in their minds as to the kind of advice he was getting, and as to the people he was getting advice from.[8]

Rumors Regarding Roosevelt's Gold Policy, Undenied, Start Domestic Gold Hoarding. Rumors that the President-elect was going to take the country off the gold standard began late in December and grew in January and in February. Efforts to persuade the President-elect to deny these rumors were unsuccessful. A new factor came into the banking situation—domestic hoarding was resumed on the part of men who were distrustful, not of the banks in which they kept their deposits, but of the

---

[8] I learned this in conversations with several of the Democratic leaders in January and February. One of the members of the Brain Trust told me in January or early February 1933 that he was one of four men who were running the government of the United States in the incapacity of President Hoover and the absence of President-elect Roosevelt. I discounted his statement, but could not entirely disregard it.

currency. Deposits were withdrawn from strong banks by men who knew that the banks would be able to pay out dollars, but who doubted that the dollars would be redeemable in gold. Depositors were asking the banks to pay them their deposits in gold, and depositors were withdrawing paper money from the banks and going to the Federal Reserve banks to get gold which they put in bank safe deposit vaults, or which they put in less secure places in their own homes. For the first time in the whole of this trouble we had domestic hoarding of gold on a great scale.

Congressional Bank Investigation—Senator Glass and Charles E. Mitchell. A fourth political factor of an ominous character began to manifest itself with the assembling of Congress on December 4, 1932, and grew in intensity. The Congress was very angry at the banks. The Congress blamed the banks for the troubles in which the country found itself. This factor had shown itself with the assembling of Congress on December 4, 1931, but a year later it was greatly intensified.

Senator Glass in particular was outraged at the behavior of Charles E. Mitchell, head of the National City Bank. The senator had been outraged at the unfortunate statement of Mitchell on March 26, 1929, that his institution had an obligation paramount to any Federal Reserve warning to avert any dangerous crisis in the money market. An account of this is given in an earlier chapter. Mitchell, far from having defied the Federal Reserve System, had worked in harmony with it in this particular episode. But Senator Glass had been angered and outraged by the statement, and subsequently had watched the actions of Mitchell closely. He had been angered by the manipulation of National City Bank stock in late 1929, and the subsequent losses to purchasers of that stock, and was determined to bring Mitchell to book. The Senate investigating committee had Mitchell and certain of his associates before it for a number of days. The disclosures were startling, and Mitchell shortly resigned from the bank, the statement being made in the press that his withdrawal was in accordance with the judgment of President-elect Roosevelt, as conveyed through Woodin, who was to be the new secretary of the Treasury.[9]

These disclosures ought to have been made. But the timing of the investigation was exceedingly unfortunate. Banks all over the country were discredited and banking troubles intensified by the investigation in a very critical and tense time. Let it be made a matter of record here, however, that the National City Bank itself held strong through these troubles; that it continued to pay, to make loans to customers, and to help the general situation in an impressive way. The officers and staff of that great institution held up their heads and did their work despite the humiliation of their chief.

---

[9] *Commercial & Financial Chronicle,* February 25, 1933, pp. 1290–93; March 4, 1933, pp. 1467, 1487–88; March 11, 1933, p. 1652.

One cannot blame Senator Glass or his angry associates for what they did in this investigation. The historian can say only that part of the ensuing bank troubles was due to the timing of the investigation. If the investigation could have been deferred to, say, the time of the investigation of the Chase National Bank in late 1933, after the banking crisis was over, the disclosures would have been equally effective for purposes of legislation, and the harm to the country could have been avoided.

Government Largely Paralyzed from November 1932 to March 4, 1933. The situation was difficult at best, with the government largely paralyzed so far as effective action was concerned. Congressional committees could investigate, but the government could do little else. The Congress was a lame duck Congress. A very large number of the sitting members of Congress in both houses were slated for retirement on March 4. There was anguish and despair among the personnel of the government departments, as virtually everybody whose tenure was not absolutely protected by civil service rules knew that he would have to find a new job shortly after March 4 in the midst of a great depression. Responsible public officials, notably Ogden L. Mills, secretary of the Treasury, were doing their best. President Hoover did all that he could. But policy could not be defined unless the newly elected President would cooperate, and cooperation after November 1932, despite sincere and earnest efforts of President Hoover to secure it, was virtually nil. In November the newly elected President had conferred with President Hoover inconclusively regarding the settlement of inter-Allied debts, and subsequently in Warm Springs, Georgia, had, on January 29, 1933, received the British ambassador in an interview arranged by the State Department, with the approval of President Hoover. A joint communiqué of Roosevelt and the ambassador, Sir Ronald Lindsay, described their conference regarding the British debt as "very satisfactory," but later developments made it appear that this was an overly optimistic statement.[10]

Dangerous schemes were afloat in the Congress, especially schemes for the devaluation of the dollar, and other "inflationary" money measures. There were steady and responsible men in the Congress who succeeded in holding such measures down. One able New York congressman had organized a congressional group which met at frequent intervals with the distinguished economist, Professor E. W. Kemmerer, who outlined the principles and history of money to them, providing them with ammunition with which to ward off the wild schemes.

Hearings Before Senate Finance Committee. The Senate Finance Committee provided a forum for the discussion of crisis remedies, and had long hearings which attracted a great deal of attention in the country. Various points of view were presented and many distinguished men appeared

---

[10] *Ibid.*, February 4, 1933, p. 737.

before the committee. To the sorrow of Senator Reed Smoot, who presided over these hearings, the demand was made by many important witnesses for radically lower tariffs—Winthrop W. Aldrich, of the Chase National Bank, and Henry J. Haskell, of the *Kansas City Star,* being particularly effective in presenting this demand. These hearings were primarily for the purpose of getting all the light that could be had upon the situation, but a very important incidental purpose appears to have been to defer action of a fundamental sort until the new administration should make its purposes known.

39

The Banking Holiday

Banking troubles had quieted down after the clearing up of the Chicago situation in the summer of 1932. Money circulation had ceased to rise after the summer of 1932 and had even gone down a little, returning to the banks, improving their condition. Gold had come back to the country and the gold monetary stock had risen from $3,622,000,000 on June 15, 1932, to $4,269,000,000 on January 25, 1933.[1] Member bank reserves had risen from $1,878,000,000 on February 24, 1932, to $2,574,000,000 on January 11, 1933. Rediscounts by member banks with the Federal Reserve banks, which had stood at $846,000,000 on February 17, 1932, had declined steadily to $248,000,000 by January 11, 1933. Bank failures had declined sharply, both in number and in volume of deposits, for the months July to November 1932, though the figures began to rise again in December 1932.

Renewed Runs on Banks, January 1933. But the pressure of all the adverse factors which the preceding chapter has discussed suddenly precipitated a new, violent, and convulsive assault upon the banks. There was the new factor of fear regarding the gold standard in the United States, both abroad and among the American people, growing out of the controversy in the campaign and growing out of fears regarding the new administration's intentions. Gold monetary stock began to decline as foreigners withdrew their gold. Money in circulation rose rapidly as the people took their money out of the banks to put it into gold, and member bank reserve balances began to decline rapidly. There came a renewed pressure, and with it a highly important weak spot yielded.

The Detroit Banking Collapse—The Spread of Bank Moratoria. Detroit had had an extraordinary growth in the boom of the 1920s with the rapid

---

[1] I am using here the revised figures given in *Banking and Monetary Statistics,* Board of Governors of the Federal Reserve System, which are $278 million less than the figures with which we worked at the time.

development of the automobile industry. Real estate values had mounted rapidly, and credit against real estate had increased greatly. Too much of this credit had got into the banks themselves. Moreover, there had been a particularly aggressive "group bank" movement centering in Detroit and moving out into Michigan. The stock of the holding company of this group had gone to fantastic levels and had had altogether too much bank credit put behind it.

The Detroit banking situation was vulnerable. In the absence of the renewed general pressure it could have been nursed along and straightened out, with great losses to bank stockholders, but without losses to depositors. Indeed, in the final reckoning which came years later, enough of the assets of these banks were made good to pay off depositors pretty fully.[2] If there had been no forced liquidation in the Great Depression, the thing would have been manageable. Heroic efforts were made to save the Michigan situation. Great loans were made by New York banks to Detroit banks. Local Detroit industrialists made efforts to provide new capital for the banks under greatest pressure. But there came a collapse in the Michigan banking situation, and the governor of the state proclaimed a moratorium.

Following this, moratoria were proclaimed in state after state. Had the moratoria been complete, had the banks been relieved for a period of making all payments, as happened in 1907 in the banking holidays proclaimed by certain of the governors, there would have been time to straighten things out in most cases. But the moratoria were partial moratoria. In the typical case they applied to ninety-five percent of the deposits, but depositors were allowed to withdraw five percent of their deposits in cash. Superficially this seemed a reasonable thing to do, but practically it meant that the country bank which had a seven percent reserve requirement was obliged to pay out five-sevenths of its legal reserve in cash, and this in all too many cases meant that it had little or no cash left.

Procedure in 1907 Far Better than in 1933. We had handled things much better in the panic of 1907. The banks then had a tradition regarding the matter. We had restricted *cash* payments by the banks, but had maintained a 100 percent mobility of *deposits* so far as checks were concerned. A depositor could not go to his bank and get all the cash he wanted, but he could draw a check on his bank and pay a debt with it. And the recipient of the check could deposit that check in his own bank and have it honored through the clearinghouse, and could draw checks against the deposit thus created to make his own payments. Absolutely necessary cash was provided by the banks.

Over the country generally in 1907 the clearinghouses had provided

---

[2] I have been told by an able New York banker who watched the Detroit situation closely throughout, that the depositors of the closed Detroit banks were finally paid off in full, but I have not seen official figures with respect to the matter.

emergency substitutes for cash in the form of clearinghouse checks, printed or engraved to look something like paper money, though usually on white paper—payable, not in cash, but "through the clearinghouse," endorsed by all the banks of the clearinghouse. This paper was accepted for local currency. Such currency was not readily accepted far from home. In a typical Missouri town of 35,000 people in 1907 these clearinghouse checks or certificates were readily obtainable at the banks and were readily accepted by the local merchants. If, however, one needed to make a railroad trip, these certificates were not acceptable by the railroad for railroad tickets, nor were they readily acceptable by merchants or others in a nearby city. The local banker understood this, and provided enough actual money for the purpose of making these trips. In this community, also, there was a great increase in the drawing of small checks, even as small as 25¢, in making local payments.

Among the banks in this small city, and very generally throughout the country, clearinghouse *loan certificates*, "good only between the banks," were provided. These are to be distinguished from the clearinghouse checks described above. They did not circulate among the people. They were certificates, again endorsed by all the banks, which a bank, short of cash for meeting deficits at the clearinghouse, could borrow from the clearinghouse against good collateral, which other banks in the clearinghouse would accept in the settling of clearinghouse balances.

In New York City in 1907 the banks did not issue clearinghouse checks to circulate among the people. It was feared that New York currency would be "too good" and would circulate too far from home. They paid out cash for necessary purposes, but restricted cash payments. They provided, for payments inside the clearinghouse, clearinghouse *loan certificates* "good between the banks," which they issued to individual banks, at six percent interest. In New York, however, important industrial companies issued printed checks for payroll purposes, usually in $5 denominations, which the merchants would accept. Thus the Standard Oil Company printed checks drawn on the National City Bank which it used for payroll purposes, and these had a very considerable circulation as actual currency with these two good names upon it. These checks were good through the clearinghouse. They would be received by any bank for deposit, and checks could be drawn against the deposits thus created. The deposit was kept mobile.

In New York in 1907 there came a discount on checks, as compared with cash, which ran as high as four percent. But the checks made payments, and the business of the country went on. The banks in New York differed in their policy with respect to making loans and to sending money out of town to country banks and country bank correspondents. Some of them were unduly timid in this matter. Some went very far in the effort to meet the needs of correspondents. But the lines held. Deposits were kept mobile.

Finally, in 1907, the importation of $100,000,000 in gold from Europe eased the pressure on cash. Cash payments were resumed, the emergency currency quickly disappeared, and the money panic was over.

The contrast between the procedure in meeting a money panic in 1907 and in 1933 is thus a startling one. In 1907, with restricted cash payments and with emergency substitutes for cash, deposits were kept 100 percent mobile and business went on. In 1933, with the banks relieved of paying all but five percent of their deposits, but obliged to pay that five percent in cash, cash reserves were quickly pulled to very low levels. Deposits were ninety-five percent unavailable for any use, and banking ceased to serve business in the states where these rules applied.

Calendar of Bank Holidays. The movement to restrict or suspend the banks moved with startling rapidity, as shown by the following schedule:

1933
February 14—Michigan
23—Indiana
25—Maryland
27—Arkansas
28—Ohio

March 1—Alabama, Kentucky, Nevada, and Tennessee
2—Arizona, California, Louisiana, Mississippi, Oklahoma, and Oregon
3—Georgia, Idaho, New Mexico, Texas, Utah, Washington, and Wisconsin
4—Colorado, Connecticut, Delaware, Florida, Illinois, Iowa, Kansas, Maine, Massachusetts, Minnesota, Missouri, Montana, Nebraska, New Hampshire, New Jersey, New York, North Carolina, North Dakota, Pennsylvania, Rhode Island, South Dakota, Vermont, Virginia, West Virginia, and Wyoming[3]

New York City Banks Reluctantly Yield to Governor's Request Late on March 3. Late at night on March 3 the New York City banks reluctantly yielded to the request of the governor that they join the Federal Reserve Bank of New York in petitioning the governor for a banking holiday in New York State. New York City banks did not need to do this. They were strong in the last week. They had paid out great sums to depositors and they had made great loans, and they were prepared to go further. Cash was even returning to them from the interior, as closed banks did not need it. A great deal of cash, for example, was coming back from Michigan which New York had previously sent there. But it appeared that there were upstate

---

[3] I am indebted for the summary to Frederick A. Bradford, *Money and Banking* (New York: Longmans, Green, 1939), p. 376.

banks in New York which could not stand further pressure, and the banks of the city of New York reluctantly met the governor's request.

The new Roosevelt administration came in with almost every bank in the country closed.

New York City Procedure in 1933 Before March 3. The banks and the governors did not handle the situation well. With the coming of the Federal Reserve System, they had generally assumed that no money panic could ever come again. The great banks of New York, which in the earlier days had felt an immense responsibility for the money market, had abdicated their control of the money market to the Federal Reserve System. The New York clearinghouse, which had once been the center of financial responsibility in the country, had long since ceased to feel this responsibility. In the old days the clearinghouse authorities of every major city had known that there would be money market pressure in the autumn. In 1873, in 1884, in 1893, and in 1907 they had devised a procedure for dealing with it if it became too acute. We had an emergency machinery understood not only by the New York clearinghouse, but also by veteran bankers all over the country. There was a ruling by the attorney general of the United States, issued in 1893, which held that emergency currency "good through the clearinghouse" was not subject to the ten percent tax applied to state banknotes, since cash could not be collected on it in a suit at common law.

Memories Are Short. But men's memories are short. Men come into positions of great responsibility fairly late in life, and the interval between 1907 and 1933 was too great an interval. There was no man left of the heads of great New York banks in the panic of 1907 who was still in that position in 1933. And the same thing was generally true over the country.

In the New York clearinghouse there was a decision to provide a clearinghouse note or certificate which should circulate as cash among the people, contrary to the precedent of 1907. A clearinghouse committee sat and passed on collateral. The committee seemed to move with undue deliberation and it was a very strict committee. It was proposed that obligations of the city of New York, for example, should be taken in at only eighty percent of their face value, though whether this was finally decided, is uncertain. Finally, notes were engraved and ready to be issued. One saw a few in the hands of bankers, but probably none was actually issued to the people.

National banks which had unused note issue power considered how rapidly they could get new currency by issuing new national banknotes. One great bank discovered that its plates could print only a few million in a week and that a new plate could not be got quickly.[4]

---

[4] There was, however, an increase in national banknotes, little noticed at the time, from $691 million in February 1932 to $922 million in May 1933; $102 million of this came between December 1932 and May 1933.

Very late in the deliberations of the New York clearinghouse one fine old veteran came back from his winter place in Florida and talked with vigor and definiteness to the heads of the clearinghouse banks, explained the procedures of 1907 to them, and had them ready for action along the lines of 1907. But it was already too late. Too much of the country had ninety-five percent of its deposits already tied up. Senator Glass remarked at the time that the bankers ought to have had their scrip out some weeks before.[5]

Washington Excludes Banks and Federal Reserve Banks from Its Councils. With the coming in of the new administration with virtually every bank in the country closed, control of the banking situation passed both from the banks and from the Federal Reserve banks to Washington. It was exceedingly difficult, moreover, for the New York clearinghouse or banks to find out what was happening in Washington. Information regarding particular points would come in by telephone from Chicago or Boston or St. Louis. Officers of the Federal Reserve Bank of New York even made inquiries of officers of other New York banks as to what was happening in Washington. The new administration was deliberately shutting out the banking community from its councils as it dealt with an extraordinarily difficult banking situation.

---

[5] I remember this well, but cannot find a newspaper account of his statement now.

40

The Intergovernmental Debts

The legacy of World War I in the form of vast reparations debts and vast inter-Allied debts proved to be one of the major causes of the failure to restore a sound economic equilibrium in the 1920s, and one of the major causes of the breakdown of international credit in 1931 and 1932. The reparations problem we have discussed in our chapters dealing with Germany. References have been made from time to time to the inter-Allied debts.

Our European Allies, chiefly Great Britain, France, Italy, and Belgium, owed us approximately $10 billion for advances made by our government between April 1917 and June 30, 1919. Interest on these advances was to be at five percent. The terms of the contract, however, provided that at any time the government of the United States might call upon the borrowers to fund these debts in marketable bonds bearing interest at a rate now lower than the highest rate paid by our government on bonds issued to the American people during the war, which proved to be the 4.25 percent rate of the fourth liberty loan. The sum grew by the accrual of interest at five percent.

In addition there was a debt of something over $400 million due from the French government to the American government for war supplies which we sold to France at the end of the war. The French government always made a distinction between this debt and the rest of the debt. The debt for the war stores was known as the "commercial debt," and the other, much greater, debt was known as the "political debt." In addition there was a debt from Germany to the American government to cover the expenses of the American army of occupation.

There were also debts of great magnitude from France and other Continental Allies to the British Treasury. And there were other reparation debts. Bulgaria, for example, had one, and Hungary did. In 1926 the Bulgarian National Bank tried, through an Italian bank intermediary, to borrow in New York a sum which, on examination, proved to be approximately the amount of the reparations for that year, and also approximately the amount by which its gold and foreign exchange reserve had declined in the preceding twelve months. When this was pointed out to the Italian bank (which had proposed to share the risk in a "joint account" arrangement), that bank lost interest in the loan! But the items which made the most trouble were the reparations due from Germany to France, Britain, Belgium, and Italy, and the debts due from Britain, France, Italy, and Belgium to the United States.

Our government from time to time in 1921 and 1922 reminded the governments of our European Allies of the existence of these debts, but only Great Britain felt itself in a position to do anything about the matter. There was a great deal of discussion of the equities in the matter. On the part of the French, it was urged that we ought to take account of the fact that Germany was not paying reparations. Our government took the position that there was no connection between French receipt of reparations and the French obligation to pay the United States government. The latter was a matter of contract which contained no provision regarding reparations and which had no provisions covering contingencies.

Our Debt Funding Commission Created, February 1922. On February 9, 1922, we created a Debt Funding Commission, headed by the secretary of the Treasury, Andrew Mellon. Another member was the secretary of state, Charles Evans Hughes. A third was the chairman of the Senate Finance Committee, Senator Reed Smoot. Other able members included the secretary of commerce, Herbert Hoover, and Congressmen Theodore E. Burton and Charles R. Crisp. It was a distinguished commission. The Debt Funding Commission was not empowered to reduce, modify, or cancel any of the debt, and the only conclusive bargains which it could work out with Europe would be on the basis of interest at 4.25 percent and maturity at the end of twenty-five years. The first impression was that the commission would be able to do nothing. But the commission properly conceived as its function to explore every possibility and to entertain every possible proposal. It could not settle anything itself, but it could recommend a settlement to the Congress of the United States.

Reginald McKenna's Speech, October 1922. In October 1922 the Right Honorable Reginald McKenna, chairman of the London Joint City and Midland Bank, Limited, spoke before the American Bankers' Association at its annual meeting in New York. His speech was supposed to represent the official views of the British government. McKenna took the position that heavy payments of intergovernmental debts made through exports of goods were not to be expected in peacetime, and that the extent to which payments could be made depended upon the volume of available liquid international securities held by the debtor countries. Great Britain, he maintained, had internationally valid foreign securities in adequate volume, and consequently could and would surely pay. He did not believe, however, that our Continental Allies could pay very much because they had used up virtually all their liquid securities. Britain was saying, "We can pay and we will pay, but don't expect much from the Continent; be generous in your dealing with the Continent."

The British Too Proud to Ask Adequate Concessions—The British Settlement. The British were superb in this. They were proud. They asked little consideration. When they came to deal with our Debt Funding Commission, they asked two concessions. The first was that the interest rate be scaled down to 3.5 percent, because that was what Britain's historical credit standing entitled her to. And they asked, second, that in consideration of their heavy losses during the war they be given a 3 percent rate for the first ten years. A schedule of payments was worked out and the British began to pay.

Britain could have had much greater concessions from us at that time if she had asked for them. She was proud. She was magnificently proud. We did what she asked.

There is one mitigating factor with respect to the British debt which makes this settlement somewhat less severe than it appears to be on its face. André Tardieu, who handled the French borrowing in Washington during the war, stated privately in early October 1925 that of every $3 which he borrowed for France from the United States, he promptly turned over $1 to Brtain in meeting French obligations to Britain. In other words, Britain got from France good American dollars during the war and early postwar period instead of the very dubious sterling obligations of France. The French debt to the United States was thus larger than would otherwise have been the case. The British debt to the United States was smaller, and the French debt to Britain was smaller.[1]

Even so, Britain ought to have had much more generous terms, as was clearly demonstrated by later events.

The arrangement above described with Britain was reported by the Debt Funding Commission to the Congress, which ratified it.

Belgian and Italian Settlements, 1925. Settlements with Belgium, Italy, and France came much more slowly. In 1925 our Debt Funding Commission made settlements with Belgium and Italy on terms very much more generous. The Italian payment was to start at $5 million a year and was gradually to work up to $80 million a year. Rome was jubilant.[2]

The French Settlement. Caillaux, in the midst of a great crisis in the

---

[1] I was subsequently able to get confirmation of this from two men, one British and the other American, who had had part in these transactions, though the American was at pains to make it clear that the dollars advanced to France were used not in paying old French debts to Britain, but in paying for current goods and services sent by Britain to France—which, however, would otherwise not have been paid for at the time, but would have been added to the French debt to Britain.

[2] I was in Rome when the settlement was announced. I talked with an official of the Treasury—the Chief was, of course, in Washington—and he expressed great satisfaction. Five million dollars a year Italy could pay. I asked him how Italy would pay the $80 million which was to come many years later. He said, "Thank God, I shall then be dead!"

franc, had also been in Washington with a commission which included Senator Bérenger and Senator Dausset, but he had made no settlement. It was reported that in the course of the transaction with the American Debt Funding Commission Senator Reed Smoot had said to Caillaux, "You are a trader." Caillaux, whose English was not perfect, misunderstood the senator. He thought he was being called a traitor. He had been called a traitor before, for having discussed peace terms with Germans in Switzerland while the war was on, and had had a narrow escape. He was said to have grown very vehement in his indignation until Senator Smoot's meaning was with difficulty explained to him. But he was in no position to sign a settlement. His own government finances in France were rapidly disintegrating and the franc was in a very precarious position.[3]

Senator Dausset, of Caillaux's delegation, came back from Washington to Paris aghast at the reception the French had received from the American Debt Funding Commission. He spoke of Secretary Mellon as being very hard and very unyielding. Senator Bérenger, on the other hand, spoke of Secretary Mellon with great respect and said that he had found him alert, flexible, fair, ready to explore every possibility, quick with a formula to meet the needs of the French situation, and that he felt it ought to be possible to work out readily enough a solution of the French debts as soon as French finances could be put in order.

Tardieu said that while he was getting money for France from the United States Treasury, he repeatedly said to the American authorities that he did not see how France could ever pay, and that he was repeatedly told not to worry about it, but to take the money and fight the war.

Chapter 21 contains the story of the French crisis of 1926 when the franc dropped to two cents in the foreign exchange market in July 1926, the financial and monetary reforms introduced by Poincaré in that year, and the *de facto* stabilization of the franc in the neighborhood of four cents late in 1926. A tentative agreement on the French debt was reached in April 1926 in the Mellon-Bérenger agreement, but it was not finally ratified by the French until 1928, and the actual gold stabilization of the franc remained unsettled, waiting for the settlement of the intergovernmental debt problem.

The French delay in ratifying the Mellon-Bérenger agreement put into sharp relief the French discussion of the "commercial debt" and the "political debt." The commercial debt they felt they must pay. If the French Parliament were unwilling to ratify the agreement, they must still pay the commercial debt and leave the political debt floating for later discussion. They carried in gold and foreign exchange a sum equal to the

---

[3] André Tardieu, in the conversation referred to above, said to me, "It is success. Caillaux has been to Washington and he has signed nothing. He has been to London and he has signed nothing. It is success!"

"commercial debt" ready for this use. They did not feel prepared to stabilize their currency definitely against gold until they knew that this great sum of approximately $400 million in gold and gold exchange could safely be added to the reserves of the Bank of France as part of the basis for stabilization.

The details of the schedules of payments of these long-dead intergovernmental debts of the first war are of no interest here.

The general theory of these settlements was that we should get our principal back, and that the concessions should be made in the interest charged. The payments were to run through several decades. The British settlement alone provided for anything like full repayment, including both interest and principal. It was to run at approximately $161,000,000 a year from 1923 to 1932 inclusive, after which, with the increased rate of interest, the annual payments were to run up to $183,900,000 in 1933 and to $184,420,000 in 1937.

France, which owed almost as much as England did, was given a very much lighter schedule of payments. It was to start a $30,000,000 in 1926, all of which was to be credited to principal. Interest payments were not to begin until 1931, and then the schedule was to run up from $40,000,000 a year in 1931 to $100,000,000 a year in 1937. The Italian payments in the earlier years were to be very light: $5,000,000 from 1926 to 1930 inclusive, all of which was to be credited to principal. Then very modest interest payments were to begin, but the total of interest and principal by 1937 was to be $16,627,000. The big payments by Italy were to come later.

The schedule of payments was carried to the Hoover moratorium in the summer of 1931. Other chapters give an account of the Hoover moratorium, the Hoover-Laval agreement of late 1931, the failure to build upon this agreement in 1932, the desperate efforts of Britain and France to avoid default by working out a new settlement following the election of 1932, the failure of President Hoover and President-elect Roosevelt to cooperate in dealing with this matter, Britain's payment in gold and France's default (December 15, 1932), the token payments of silver under the Thomas Amendment made by Britain and certain other countries in 1933, and the final complete default on the debts, by all the countries except Finland.

Britain Remains Anxious to Effect New Settlement After Default in 1933. Britain did not cease her efforts to accomplish a settlement after Roosevelt became President. Governor Eugene Black of the Federal Reserve Board said once that Sir Ronald Lindsay, the British ambassador, had spent two hours with him and with Oliphant of the Treasury, trying very hard to reach an adjustment. Governor Black said that his instructions were not to make an agreement and not to refuse to make an agreement. He said it had been a humiliating two hours. He added that when the session was over and newspapermen came to him and Oliphant to ask what had happened, he had said to them, "Gentlemen, I cannot tell you. You see, Sir Ronald spoke only English. You had better ask Oliphant." Governor Black added that Oliphant's rejoinder was most profane.

As late as 1937 unimpeachable sources in London indicated that the British still wished to settle this debt, and were prepared to undertake to make annual payments of £10 million a year ($50 million at the current rate of exchange), if that were acceptable to the United States government. Alternatively, they were prepared to send us $1 billion in gold if we would let that clear the slate.

Some Lessons. The lesson is clear that we want no hangovers after World War II of intergovernmental debts that are going to put a continuing burden on the foreign exchanges through the coming decades, and that are going to be a continuing burden on the budgets of our Allies through the coming decades.

Had we made more reasonable schedules of debt payments in the years 1922–28, and had we had a low tariff policy so that Europe could have paid us with goods, we could have collected. We could probably have collected even the schedules agreed upon if we had had a low tariff policy.

The time came by 1927 when the burden of debt service on the debts of Europe to private creditors in the United States was much larger than the burden of intergovernmental debt payments. But there was a great difference between private debts which grew out of income-creating investments due from merchants and industries to foreign creditors, and the debts of governments, which represented the dead horse of a war and which had to be paid out of fiscal surpluses—surpluses which did not exist in time of depression. There was, too, a great difference between debts believed to be just by individual firms and corporations which had voluntarily contracted them, and the intergovernmental debts created in the midst of desperate war needs, and believed by the peoples of the debtor countries not to be just. There was a difference, too, between debts created by warring governments to private creditors in Allied countries; and debts of these same warring countries to Allied governments. Both the peoples and the governments of the debtor countries respected their debts to private lenders, whereas they felt that they were entitled to consideration and readjustment in their financial relations with the governmental Allies.

A further point must be added as to the atmosphere in which most of these debt settlements were made. The period of the 1920s was a period of immense bank credit expansion, as we have seen, a period in which the scarcity of real capital in the world was masked for several years by the creation of excessive bank deposits and bank loans and investments. Our Debt Funding Commission and the governments of our European debtors were both misled by this atmosphere. As a result, the schedules were placed much higher than would otherwise have been the case.

PART IV

THE NEW DEAL IN
MATURITY, 1933–39

41

"My Father Also Chastised You with Whips, but I Will Chastise You with Scorpions"

When Solomon died Rehoboam ruled in his stead. Solomon had laid heavy burdens upon the people, and the people petitioned Rehoboam for a lighter yoke. The young king consulted with the old men, who advised him to lighten the burdens, but "the young men that grew up with him" (his "brain trust") gave him the advice which he followed; and he said to the people, "My father made your yoke heavy and I will add to your yoke: my father also chastised you with whips, but I will chastise you with scorpions."[1]

In preceding chapters we have seen the trend in governmental policy toward New Deal measures. The high protective tariff is the mother of the New Deal, though the tariffs of 1921 and 1922 grew, not out of New Deal purposes and ideals, but out of a blind adherence to an outworn political tradition. But they created an economic disequilibrium which invited the first conscious step in the New Deal, namely, the cheap money policy of the Federal Reserve System in 1924, which was designed to offset the strangling effects of the tariff on our export trade by making possible a vast volume of foreign loans.

We have seen the personal leadership of the bull stock market by President Coolidge and Secretary of the Treasury Mellon. We have seen the Farm Board legislation designed to give artificial support to farm prices. We have seen the President of the United States, after the stock exchange crash of 1929, calling the business community into conference and urging them not to reduce wages, not to reduce prices, and also urging them and the states and municipalities to engage in heavy capital expenditure for the prupose of keeping the business boom going. We have seen the renewal of artificially cheap money by the Federal Reserve System in 1930, with the revival of foreign lending in 1930 on a vast scale, and we have seen the

---

[1] I Kings 12:11.

policy, violently contradictory to this, of the further raising of the tariffs in 1930, which choked off the export trade and turned the world toward autarky.

Liberal Foreign Trade Policy Versus Internal Planning. A liberal foreign trade policy is contradictory to governmental economic planning, and the movement toward governmental economic planning grows rapidly when foreign trade is cut off. This was recognized a long time ago. One of the original economic planners was the German philosopher Fichte, a follower of Kant and a precursor of Hegel, who in his book *The Closed Commercial State* maintains the following propositions:

> The state must adjust in proper proportions the three chief classes of producers—(1) farmers, miners and the like, (2) artisans, and (3) merchants, limiting each to a fixed number of individuals; must ensure to each individual a proportionate share of all the raw and manufactured products of the country; must for this purpose fix and maintain the relative value and money price of all these commodities; and finally, as absolutely indispensable to the foregoing ends, must render impossible direct trade between citizens and the foreign world. So far as commerce with other peoples may be deemed desirable, it must be carried on by the state itself.[2]

The Advice of Professional Economists, Early January 1933—Restore Foreign Trade and Protect Gold Standard. What was called for in early 1933 was an undoing of the unsound things that we had been doing. The opinion of professional economists was pretty clear on the subject. Early in January 1933 a group of representative economists sent a letter to President-elect Roosevelt, at the same time giving it to the press, where it was widely printed:

> The following statement is in the judgment of the undersigned economists a minimum program for economic recovery:
> The urgent immediate problem is the foreign trade situation. Lacking an adequate export market, agricultural products and raw materials bring ruinously low prices, and there is an immense unbalance between them and manufactured goods. As a result even the relatively scant output of the factories is marketed with difficulty.
> There should be prompt reciprocal lowering of tariffs and prompt settlement of inter-Allied debts. Our own tariffs should be lowered to such an extent as will admit enough additional imports of diversified finished manufactures to take out our own agricultural and raw material exports without the necessity of foreign loans.
> We are convinced that such lowering of tariffs on finished manufactured goods will not decrease employment in manufacturing. On the contrary, by

---

[2] W. A. Dunning, *Political Theories from Rousseau to Spencer* (New York: Macmillan, 1920), pp. 142–43.

stimulating price improvement in agricultural commodities and purchasing power in agricultural communities, and by stimulating recovery in Europe as well, it will produce a very great increase in manufacturing activity and employment in the United States.

The settlement of inter-Allied debts should be on a negotiated basis which will probably not be satisfactory to public opinion in any country, but which, promptly accomplished, will be immensely beneficial to all countries.

The gold standard of present weight and fineness should be unflinchingly maintained. We should also encourage and facilitate the prompt restoration of the gold standard abroad—which settlement of inter-Allied debts and tariff reductions will do. With adequate movement of goods across international borders, the gold of the United States and of the world is more than adequate for all credit needs. If, however, trade restrictions throw an undue burden on gold in making international payments, then debtor countries have difficulties in maintaining the gold standard and confidence is so low in creditor countries that they cannot make effective use of their own gold in expanding credit.

Credit rests on the movement of goods as well as on the gold supply. Agitation for currency experiments would impair confidence and retard recovery.

Those signing the letter were:

Frank A. Fetter, Princeton University
Benjamin H. Hibbard, University of Wisconsin
Davis R. Dewey, Massachusetts Institute of Technology
E. W. Kemmerer, Princeton University
Ernest M. Patterson, University of Pennsylvania
Abraham Berglund, University of Virginia
Francis Tyson, University of Pittsburgh
George Heberton Evans, Jr., Johns Hopkins University
M. B. Hammond, Ohio State University
George E. Barnett, Johns Hopkins University
B. M. Anderson, Jr., Chase National Bank
E. L. Bogart, University of Illinois
Bernhard Ostrolenk, College of City of New York
Morris A. Copeland, University of Michigan
F. A. Deibler, Northwestern University
J. F. Ebersole, Harvard University
Claudius Murchison, University of North Carolina
Willard E. Atkins, New York University
Joseph H. Willits, University of Pennsylvania
Broadus Mitchell, Johns Hopkins University[3]

The Democratic platform of 1932, largely written by Senator Carter Glass and Cordell Hull, had taken a similar position, so far as tariffs and

---

[3] *Commercial & Financial Chronicle,* January 7, 1933, p. 71.

currency were concerned. This platform had protested, moreover, against the growth of bureaucracy and had promised rigorous economy in governmental expenditures.

Vital Need for Lower Tariffs, Restoring Export Trade. Prompt action in the restoration of foreign trade would have straightened out rapidly most of our domestic difficulties. Prompt lowering of the tariffs against the imports of manufactures would have led to a radical revival, an almost explosive revival of domestic trade in the United States.

There was no reason to fear even temporarily adverse effects from a drastic downward revision of the tariff on manufactured goods in the winter of 1932–33. Our industries were out of equilibrium largely because of the high tariff. Lowering the tariff would have gone far to restore the equilibrium. Our export industries, above all agriculture, were appallingly depressed, and their depression had reacted in an extreme way on all industry. The first effect of reducing the tariffs, well before any goods could be loaded on ships on the other side to come to the United States, would have been a great upswing in the prices of farm products and raw materials in the United States. It would have been manifest that European buyers of our farm products and raw materials had earning power once more and consequently they would have had credit for purchases.

Even before the first cargo of manufactured goods came from the other side, we should have had a better domestic market in which to receive it. Cables work faster than ships, and speculators work faster than merchants. Moreover, prices of foods and raw materials move faster than prices of manufactured goods.

Europe could not have sent a heavy volume of manufactures to us immediately in the spring of 1933. Europe had been under cruel pressure to liquidate for the preceding three years or more. Stocks of raw materials and stocks of imported foods were very low in Europe. Stocks of finished manufactures were low in Europe. She would have needed to import a great deal of raw materials before she could have sent out a great volume of manufactures.

In the winter of 1932–33, this question was put to Jesse Livermore, one of the most active and alert speculators of the country: "If you woke up tomorrow and found the tariffs down so that Europe, including Germany, could send us manufactured goods, and you wanted to make some money out of that, what would you do?" He said, "Well, I might buy some German bonds." And then suddenly he said, "No. I'd buy commodities." "Which commodities would you buy?" "I'd buy the ones they have to have and the ones that they would be buying in that situation. I'd buy copper. I'd buy lard. I'd buy cotton. I'd buy wheat."

Financing a Round Trip. At about the same time a different question was put to the head of the foreign department of a great bank, a bank which had large credits in Germany frozen by the standstill agreement. The question was, "If our tariffs on manufactured goods were reduced so that Germany could easily send manufactured goods to the United States, would Germany have additional credit with you for the purchase of raw materials and necessary foods?" He answered, "Of course she would. I am always ready to finance a round trip. I don't intend to finance a one-way passage any more."

Low Tariffs Would Have Meant Radical Rise in Farm Products and Raw Materials. With an adequate reduction of our tariffs, Europe would have had credit for buying foods and raw materials in our markets. A moderate increase in demand for foods and raw materials in a time of acute depression means a radical upswing in food and raw material prices. A moderate increase in activities in the manufacturing centers means very large changes in raw material prices, especially at a time when they are greatly depressed. The further away goods are from the consumer, the more radical are the swings, up and down, in their prices. With a radical rise in the prices of farm products and raw materials, our own manufacturers would immediately have found an expanding domestic market, and, sharing that domestic market with foreign competition, they would have sold far more goods and would have made far more profits than was possible when they had a dwindling market all to themselves.

The full restoration of foreign trade called, moreover, for a clarification of the inter-Allied debt situation and called for sound gold money that international commerce could trust.

Plans for International Conference on Tariffs, Debts, and Currency Stabilization. These things were well understood in informed circles. An international conference had been planned to deal with them. The agenda for this conference had been prepared under the Hoover administration, and President Roosevelt in the very beginning of his administration manifested great interest in the plans for the conference. He was visited by various distinguished foreign representatives, among them the prime minister of England, Ramsay MacDonald, and a high official of the Italian government, Signor Guido Jung. Communiqués were given out following certain of these visits. Of particular interest were the joint statements of President Roosevelt and Prime Minister MacDonald of England, issued late in April,[4] and the joint statement of the President and Guido Jung, Italy's finance minister, issued early in May.[5] Both statements recognized the necessity of a moderation of tariffs and other trade restrictions. With respect to gold MacDonald did not commit himself. The statement regarding money in the Roosevelt-MacDonald document is the following: "We must when circumstances permit reestablish an international monetary standard which will operate successfully without depressing prices and

[4] The full text is in *Commercial & Financial Chronicle*, April 29, 1933, p. 2875.
[5] For full text, see *ibid.*, May 13, 1933, p. 3259.

avoid the repetition of the mistakes which have produced such disastrous results in the past. In this connection the question of silver, which is of such importance in trade with the Orient, was discussed and proposals were tentatively suggested for the improvement of its status." The statement in the Jung-Roosevelt document, however, is explicit: "We are in agreement that a fixed measure of exchange values must be reestablished in the world and we believe that this measure must be gold."

The difference between these two communiqués is significant. Mac-Donald was not prepared to take England back to the gold standard. Continental Europe was strongly for the gold standard. Apart from England's reluctance to go back immediately to gold, the scene was set for the restoration of international trade, and for the restoration of sound foreign exchange relations.

But the "Young Men" Wanted Neither Foreign Trade nor Gold. But the "young men" who advised the President did not want either foreign trade or gold. They wanted internal regimentation. It takes economic imagination and economic understanding to look beyond the particular industry or particular trade in dealing with the tariff problem, and the "young men" lacked economic understanding, though it cannot be denied that they had a good deal of imagination regarding economic matters.

They wanted direct action. They wanted to deal with the symptoms of the economic disorder. They wanted the government, not merely as backseat driver, but actually in the driver's seat. They were not content with having the government clear away from the highway the barriers which the government had itself erected.

Some direct action by the federal government dealing with the most acute symptoms of the crisis was also needed. Bankruptcy laws were moderated even before the new administration came in. In addition there was need for emergency measures to bring relief in the farm mortgage situation.[6]

---

[6] This writer at the time urged a plan which would make use of local banking knowledge in refunding farm mortgages, with a federal government guaranty, in such a way as to keep good farmers and the land together. Farm prices had fallen to such fantastically low levels that the ablest farmers were embarrassed.

In May 1932 I had studied the farm mortgage situation firsthand in Boone County, Missouri, where in many cases I not only knew the farmers, but also had known their fathers before them. I had found the banks and other local creditors showing great forbearance to embarrassed farmers. In one case, for example, a good farmer had come in, proposing to deed his farm to the two banks to which he owed money, to save them the expense of foreclosure. He was unable to pay interest. The bankers told him that of course he could not pay interest with farm prices as they were, but that he could run the farm so much better than anybody else they knew that he should go back and run the farm. There would be no interest in 1932, and the next year the interest would be half of what the contract called for. The farmer walked out with his head high. In another case, where a farmer was incompetent, the creditors had reluctantly taken the farm over, but had told the farmer and his wife to stay in the house, and had given the farmer employment on the place.

Such discrimination was much more difficult for the great life insurance companies

In addition there was necessity that additional federal funds be granted to the hardest pressed states and municipalities for the direct relief of the unemployed. But these measures should have been temporary things, and the need for them would have quickly disappeared with the revival of business which the restoration of economic equilibrium would bring about. The prompt restoration of a two-sided foreign trade would have been the major factor in restoring this equilibrium.

Internal Regimentation Triumphs over Foreign Trade. The New Deal is far too complex to be described in any simple terms, but the conflict between a liberal foreign trade policy and the policy of internal regimentation is one of the clues to much that follows. Internal regimentation policy triumphed completely in 1933, as we shall see. But the President came back to the other policy in 1934, and is entitled to credit for doing a good deal in behalf of the foreign trade policy of Secretary Hull.

---

operating from a distance, and the writer had made a point of talking with the heads of certain life insurance companies in New York upon his return, urging closer cooperation with local bankers in dealing with defaulted loans.

In personal conversations in my office in New York with bankers from rural regions, and in correspondence with country bankers in many parts of the country, I accumulated a great deal of information as to the actual farm mortgage situation and rural bank situation. It was distressing in the extreme, and in many cases the banks themselves were under such pressure that they could not show forbearance. There was need for relief from the immediate pressure of farm indebtedness.

42

The Reopening of the Banks

Reopening Well Handled by Administration. On the whole, the reopening of the banks was well handled by the administration. The proclamation closing all banks for a few days, which the President issued on the morning of Monday, March 6, two days after the inauguration, declared a four-day holiday from Monday, March 6, to Thursday, March 9, inclusive. It was designed to give time to study the situation. Authority for the issuance of the proclamation was claimed under a wartime statute of 1917. Unlike the proclamations of certain of the governors, which had left the banks open but limited the withdrawal of deposits to five percent, this proclaimed a complete bank holiday for all banks in the country. People could neither put money into banks nor take money out of banks. It gave time for the people to cool off, and during the cooling-off period, which was extended by a proclamation of March 9 "until further proclamations," the people did have time to worry a good deal about the inadequately protected cash which they had in their homes.

Meanwhile the President called a special session of Congress, which promptly assembled, and on the same day, March 9, the Congress in a few hours passed an act "to provide relief in the existing national emergency in banking, and for other purposes." This act had been prepared by the President's advisers and was put through with hardly any debate. The act validated what the President had already done, and gave wide authority for the further executive acts to be taken. Congress abdicated control of the situation to the President.

On March 12, 1933, at 10 P.M., the President delivered over the radio an address to the people, calling upon them to bring their money back to the banks, and assuring them that the banks which reopened would be good. He announced the plan of reopening the banks, not all on the same day, but on successive days. On Monday, March 13, the banks in the twelve Federal Reserve cities would be reopened. On Tuesday the banks in other cities where there were recognized clearinghouses would be opened. On

Wednesday and succeeding days banks in smaller places all through the country were to be reopened. Unsound banks were not to be allowed to reopen. There was to be cooperation of the comptroller of the currency, Federal Reserve banks, and the state banking authorities in deciding which banks should reopen. The President's statement did a great deal to reassure the country as to the banking situation. The program was carried out. The banks reopened.

Hoarded Cash Pours into Banks. Immediately upon the reopening of the banks an immense volume of hoarded currency poured in upon them. The panic was over. The *Federal Reserve Bulletin* of April 1933 (p. 209) states that between March 4 and April 5, $1,225,000,000 of money returned to the Reserve banks and the Federal Reserve ratio advanced from 45.1 percent to 59.7 percent. The *Federal Reserve Bulletin* of May 1933 (p. 265) states that between March 4 and May 10 the total volume of currency returned was $1,595,000,000. It adds that only about $250,000,000 of the currency paid out to the public between February 1 and March 4 was still outstanding.

Mortality Among Banks in 1933. The mortality in banks in the year 1933 is exhibited by the following figures:

ALL COMMERCIAL BANKS—NUMBER, LOANS, INVESTMENTS, AND DEPOSITS
(In millions of dollars)

Date	Number of banks	Loans and Investments			Deposits		
		Total	Loans	Investments	Total	Interbank	Other
Dec. 29, 1932	17,802	35,083	20,081	15,002	35,957	4,134	31,823
June 30, 1933	13,949	30,357	16,349	14,008	31,911	3,443	28,468
Dec. 31, 1933	14,440	30,789	16,246	14,543	32,637	3,537	29,100

It will be observed that the percentage drop in the number of banks was much greater than the percentage drop in deposits. A great many small banks outside the Federal Reserve System ceased to exist. The number of banks was further reduced by consolidations, many of which represented the taking over of weak institutions by strong ones. The increase in the number of banks on December 31 as compared with June 30 does not represent the starting of new banks, but rather the belated reopening of banks regarding which there had been question.

The estimated losses borne by depositors from the bank failures in 1933 amounted to $540,000,000, out of a total $3,597,000,000 deposited in the banks which were suspended either permanently or for part of the year.[1]

---

[1] *Banking and Monetary Statistics,* Board of Governors of the Federal Reserve System (1943), p. 283.

43

The Mortality Among
Small Banks

The number of commercial banks in the United States stood at 29,087 on June 30, 1920. The figure stood at 15,353 on June 30, 1934. A great many of these banks had been closed or had failed, however, between June 30, 1920, and July 1, 1929, during which period about 5,000 banks, nearly all of them in agricultural communities, closed their doors and tied up deposits totaling $1.5 billion. The average deposits per bank thus tied up was very small, being only $300,000. Over 40 percent of these failed banks were situated in towns and villages having a population of less than 500 persons; over 60 percent were in towns of 1,000 or less; 80 percent were in towns of 2,500 people or less; and 92 percent were in places having less than 10,000. Of the remaining 8 percent of the failures, a high percentage was in very small banks in larger places. Sixty-three percent of the failures were among banks having $25,000 capital or less, and 88 percent among banks having less than $100,000 capital. There were no failures during this period of banks having a capital of $2 million or more, and there were only four failures of banks having over $1 million capital.

Many of these banks failed as the aftermath of the collapse of the agricultural boom in 1920 and the adverse conditions in agricultural communities which continued for a long time. Another great cause was real estate speculation after 1920 in certain important sections of the country, notably Florida.

During this same period all of New England had only 26 failures, New York had 12, and New Jersey had none at all.

Hard Roads and Automobiles—County Seat vs. Village. But a further factor of major importance, which weakened small banks in many small places, was the coming of hard roads and automobiles, which largely destroyed the usefulness of the small village, doing away with the local merchant, the local mill, and the local church, as well as the local banker, as the people did their business and sought their social life in the county seat and other nearby larger cities. Industrial consolidations, moreover, while leaving local factories in small places, very often took away the banking business which the local factory gave to the local banker. The growth of chain stores had a similar effect. When the troubles of 1930–33 came, they found a great many very small banks already under such pressure that they could not survive. An illustration would be one county in Missouri where four adequately capitalized banks, with deposits ranging from $750,000 to $3,000,000, in the county seat, stood firm through the troubles of 1933, but where most of the banks in local villages went under—one, for example failing with deposits of $48,000. In a smaller town in the same county, a railway center, a well-managed national bank with deposits of $200,000 went safely through the 1933 trouble without assistance.

But many of the local banks away from the county seat showed extraordinary vitality and stood firm. There is one in a village whose population had been 203 people in 1930 and which had 176 people in 1940. The bank is about 30 miles from the railroad in every direction and the automobile roads are not very good. The soil in the country roundabout is thin except for an occasional creek bottom. It is in the foothills of the Ozards. This bank had, in 1928, capital of $10,000, surplus of $3,000, and undivided profits of $624. It had deposits of $70,000 and loans of $35,000. Its 1933 figures showed a reduction of deposits to $35,000. It had paid out half its deposits. Its loans were down to $20,000. But its capital stood intact at $10,000, its surplus had increased to $5,000, and its undivided profits had risen to over $1,200. In 1938 its figures showed deposits of $85,000, loans of $40,000, capital of $10,000, and surplus and undivided profits of $10,000. It would be hard to find a big bank in the United States which made anything like so good a record in this period.

A very high percentage indeed in the decline of the number of banks between 1920 and 1934 represented the disappearance of the microscopic banks, banks that had once performed a useful service, but which in a changed world were no longer needed. Many of these small banks, indeed, were never needed. Some parts of the country were badly overbanked. This was especially true in rural Iowa.

44

Branch Banking Versus
Unit Banking

In view of the mortality among small banks in the decade of the 1920s, legislation was proposed in early 1930 calling for branch banking throughout Federal Reserve districts. The present writer opposed this plan in the *Chase Economic Bulletin* of May 8, 1920, and was subsequently called before the House Committee on Banking and Currency, which was considering the legislation. One question under consideration was whether branch banking would move money to the local community from the head office, or away from the local community to the head office. The answer to the committee was that this varied. In France, before World War I, the branch banks had been largely bond houses, selling bonds which originated in Paris to local depositors, and making very few local loans, except for the discount of bills of exchange. In Canada, on the other hand, there had been complaint from the eastern provinces that too much money had been taken away from the cities of the East to lend to the agricultural provinces of the West. There was no general rule.

The view was maintained that a system of unit banking gave, on the whole, a better adaptation of banking facilities to local needs than the branch bank system did.

MR. ANDERSON: How are you going to adapt the number of offices, the number of paying tellers' windows, and so forth, the facilities, to the needs of the community?

When the thing is done locally it is at least locally studied and decisions made locally. Sometimes they overdo it. They have overdone it in North Dakota and they have overdone it in Iowa and a great many rural communities in this country; too many little banks where fewer and bigger banks would have been more useful and would have survived. But I think we have done it better in this country, judging it from an American angle, than many foreign countries have done it.

In Holland there was, in 1919–20, competition between two great banking institutions that filled the villages with branches, unprofitable branches. They had to pull up, close them out, in a good many cases.

Here is the picture in England. In the business part of London you go about the streets; there is a bank office on every corner, almost. You go into a branch. You are often the only man there, the only customer there. You go in to cash a check under a letter of credit and the officer of the bank has lots of time to talk to you. He is glad to see you. He is a little bored. I do not mean that this is true of all of them, but of a lot of them. I think they have too many there. I think it is not profitable. I think it involves needless overhead.

What about it in the provinces? I will give you some illustrations in the provinces.

For your records, Mr. Chairman, I will give you an unsatisfactory document as to form, but fairly satisfactory as to the information. Having to prepare this in great haste, I simply had sheets torn out of the *British Bankers Almanac and Year Book* (published by Thomas Skinner & Co., London), giving the locations of the banks throughout Great Britain and Ireland. Then I had some clerks get me the populations of the cities and towns as far as possible. They worked rapidly and their population figures may not be exactly right in some places. The population figures are written on the margin and in pencil.

I have not gone through it all myself, but here are some samples. Abbots Langley, a town of 3,400 people. Here are the complete banking accommodations of Abbots Langley: Barclays Bank (Ltd.), open on Thursday; Lloyds Bank (Ltd.), open on Thursday. These are the banking accommodations of this town of 3,400 people.

MR. STRONG: Open one day in the week?

MR. ANDERSON: One day in the week; yes, sir.

MR. STRONG: If anybody wants to do any business with the bank on any other day, he finds on the door, "We have gone fishing."

MR. ANDERSON: They have not gone fishing.

MR. STRONG: But there are no other accommodations.

MR. ANDERSON: They have gone to another town. There is a crew of bankers. They work six days in the week; sometimes in one town, sometimes in another town.

MR. STRONG: They go around from one town to the other?

MR. ANDERSON: Yes, sir.

MR. STRONG: If a man wants banking accommodations, he waits until they get back?

MR. ANDERSON: Yes.

MR. STRONG: Fine!

MR. ANDERSON: Amondsbury; this is in Gloucester. Twenty-two hundred people. The National Provincial Bank is open on Friday.

Abertillery, 22,000 people. That is what the figures on my margin show and I raise a question as to whether that figure is right, because it looks incredible. I should like to have your committee, if you are interested in this, have an independent check made of these population figures. They were hastily got by clerks, working under time pressure. [A later checking with Hammond's *World Atlas* shows the population of Abertillery to be 38,805. It is in Monmouthshire, England, near the border of Wales.]

MR. SIEBERLING: I would like to have you give us the proximity to larger towns where they can get banking facilities all the time.

MR. ANDERSON: I regret I cannot.

MR. SIEBERLING: You can see that is important.

MR. ANDERSON: It is, and if I had had time, I would do it. . . . Barclays, Lloyds, Midland, and National Provincial, open on Monday.

MR. STRONG: In a town of 22,000?

MR. ANDERSON: I say, the thing is so startling, I want you to make an independent check of the population figures there. . . .

Here is an Irish town, Carrick Fergus, 4,208 people; Tuesdays and fair days, the Belfast Banking Co. . . .

Before I leave that, let me say another thing. Here are some very little places that have something. Here is Allonby, 450; the Midland Bank (Ltd.), Tuesday, October to June, and Tuesday and Thursday, July to September.

There are some very small ones that have something that probably would not have anything if it were not for the branch banking system. I think we may learn something from that.

I think that branch banking perhaps centered about a county seat, with little offices in small places that could not afford independent banks, is worth studying. . . .

I do not want to see good bankers disappear from the smaller communities. I think that it is a good thing to have strong, trained, independent bankers, interested in the local community, stay in the local community. As I have traveled about meeting bankers in this country, meeting bankers in Europe— there are extraordinarily able bankers in the financial centers of Europe, but you go into the branches away from the head office, and you do not find bankers of the caliber that you find in cities of the same size in the United States, where they are independent men handling their problems and masters of their own banks.

I believe that the country would lose a very important influence making for good business, for initiative, for business eduation, not right away but in the course of time, if we change from the general system of unit banking to the general system of branch banking away from the city of your head office. . . .

The causes of these failures I do not find in things that have any particular concern with the question of branch banking on the one hand or unit banking on the other.

The first and foremost cause was the great boom of agricultural prices and land values before 1920, the collapse of agricultural prices and land values following 1920, and the adverse conditions in agriculture that have since continued.

The second great cause is real estate speculation in the period since 1920 in certain important sections of the country, notably Florida and some adjacent states. . . .

What about branch banking during that same period and exposed to these same causes? You had in Georgia, and running into Florida, as I remember, a chain, which went down, which would have gone down if it had been a group, which would have gone down if it had been a branch banking system.

In Canada, the Home Bank, and the Merchants Bank with 400 branches, went under from these same causes.

In Denmark, a great bank with branches widespread, went under.

The Banque Industrielle de Chine in China collapsed with its notes out, bringing disaster all over that great country.

The Banca di Sconto in Italy, with a great head office and big branches in the big cities, with little branches in the smaller cities, all went down together at one time. That is a fearful thing. . . .[1]

Nothing in the experiences of the years since 1930 when this testimony was given has seemed to call for modification of the position then taken. Widespread branch banking in a country that is used to it works well, under normal conditions. Our American unit banking system, except for the microscopic banks, has worked well under normal conditions. Neither system can go unharmed through great world wars, or through governmental and central bank abuse of credit. A radical change in this country from the unit banking system to which we have been accustomed, to nationwide branch banking, or branch banking throughout Federal Reserves districts, could easily make us very grave problems of readjustment. Where an American state wishes to have branch banking systems within its own borders, it has the right to do so, but there should be no federal legislation which would force the hands of the state in the matter. Where an American state has a well-developed system of branch banking it should not be advised to reverse its policy, though even there the survival of strong unit banks is eminently desirable.

---

[1] U. S., Congress, House, Committee on Banking and Currency, *Hearings on Branch, Chain and Group Banking*, June 5, 1930, pp. 1864–71.

45

Roosevelt's Abandonment
of the Gold Standard

We can only commend the administration's reopening of the banks. But the banking holiday was made the excuse for a radical change in monetary policy. In the hastily adopted act of Congress of March 9, blanket authority was given the President to do pretty much as he saw fit regarding money and banking, including authority for the seizing of the gold and gold certificates in the hands of the people.

The Seizure of the People's Gold. Very speedily (April 5) this authority was invoked and it became unlawful to own or hold gold coins, gold bullion, or gold certificates. Control of gold exports and foreign exchange transactions were also provided for in the bill, and it ceased to be lawful to export gold in making payments abroad except under license from the Treasury. Provision was made in the proclamation dealing with this matter to allow jewelers, dentists, and others having industrial use for gold, to obtain gold to meet their reasonable needs. The crisis was made the excuse for the abandonment of the gold standard.

For a time the pretense was maintained that these measures were temporary, and the hope persisted that we would resume the gold standard in its full integrity. The dollar dipped in the foreign exchanges as against the gold standard countries, but rallied, and the dollar stood practically at mint parity with the French gold franc until the middle of April.

The Thomas Amendment. Then came developments of a startling sort which revealed the real purposes of the administration. A show of "inflationist" sentiment in the United States Senate in connection with a bimetallic proposal led the President to take the position that he wanted control of "inflation," and, with the support of the administration, Senator Thomas of Oklahoma on April 20 sponsored a monetary amendment to the pending agricultural bill which gave the President vast powers regarding money:

1. He could direct the secretary of the Treasury to enter into agreements with the Federal Reserve banks and the Federal Reserve Board, whereby

the Federal Reserve banks would buy obligations of the United States in the open market to the extent of $3 billion regardless of reserve deficiencies which might be created thereby.

2. He could direct the secretary of the Treasury to issue $3 billion of greenbacks, United States notes. These notes were to be issued in paying maturing federal obligations and for purchasing United States bonds. These notes were to be retired, but only at the rate of four percent per annum.

3. He could establish bimetallism at any ratio he found necessary.

4. He could reduce the weight of the gold dollar by any amount up to fifty percent.

5. He could accept silver at a price of 50¢ per ounce up to $200 million from foreign governments in payment of debts to the United States.

These powers were discretionary rather than mandatory. The President did not have to do any of these things, and the hope persisted that he might have asked for the powers so that he would have weapons in his hands to force an agreement regarding money from foreign governments at the coming London Conference. The thought was that he might have wanted the powers so that he could check the threat of competitive currency debasement in the world, by being in a position to engage in that competition in a big way if foreign governments, particularly England, were not willing to stabilize on gold. But the dollar broke in the foreign exchange as this amendment became part of the pending agricultural bill. The amendment was adopted by the committee on April 20, though the bill itself did not become law until May 12.

The measure struck in virtually every known way at the integrity of the currency, providing both for quantitative increase and for qualitative deterioration.

Senator Glass and President Roosevelt—"It's Dishonor!" Senator Glass said, as he talked in his office on the day that this amendment was first announced: "It's dishonor, sir. This great government, strong in gold, is breaking its promises to pay gold to widows and orphans to whom it has sold government bonds with a pledge to pay gold coin of the present standard of value. It is breaking its promise to redeem its paper money in gold coin of the present standard of value. It's dishonor, sir." To the grand old senator, morality was something written in the heavens, eternal and unchangeable. But the pragmatic philosopher, to whom morality is human-social discipline, growing out of the needs and experiences of human social life, was no less shocked than the senator. There is no need in human life so great as that men should trust one another and should trust their government, should believe in promises, and should keep promises in order that future promises may be believed in and in order that confident cooperation may be possible. Good faith—personal, national, and international—is the first prerequisite of decent living, of the steady going on of industry, of governmental financial strength, and of international peace.

The President's course in connection with the gold standard and in connection with the Thomas Amendment, represented an act of absolute bad faith. He had not dared to make any suggestion of anything but adherence to the gold standard in the campaign. Both political parties had stood for the gold standard in the campaign. The President had given "100 percent" endorsement to Senator Glass's magnificent speech in the campaign replying to President Hoover's gold standard statement—and Glass, in that speech, had pledged the Democratic Party to protect the gold standard. The government, after the defeat of the Free Silver movement in 1896, had twice pledged the faith of the government to the maintenance of the gold standard, once in legislation in 1900 adopted by a Republican majority, and once in 1913 in the Federal Reserve Act adopted by a Democratic majority. The government had written the word *gold* not only on the Federal Reserve notes, but also on all its bonds and on every interest coupon attached to them. The government was bound by its solemn promises, and the President was personally bound by his campaign utterances and by the platform of his party. It was dishonor.[1]

Dishonor Creates Hot Money. We knew nothing of "hot money" on a large scale in the decades that preceded World War I, when great governments protected the gold standing of their currency as a matter of course because it was the honorable and expected thing to do. But since the bad faith of the two greatest governments in the world, Great Britain in 1931 and the United States in 1933, we have had a world full of hot money, jumping about nervously from place to place, seeing no safety anywhere, but going from places that seemed unsafe to places that seemed less unsafe. We have had a world in which men have been afraid to make long-run plans. We have had a world in which conscientious and scrupulous trustees have been turning from "gilt-edged bonds" toward common stocks, not because the common stocks were safe, but because they were less unsafe

---

[1] Two years later I had the satisfaction of telling Senator Thomas precisely what I thought of his policy, across the committee table of the Senate Committee on Agriculture, as he was quizzing me in the effort to get me to agree that his monetary policy had been a good one. I said to him: "What has happened, I think, is that the devaluation of the gold dollar has been such a shock all over the world that you have turned men's thoughts to gold. Formerly gold has had great competitors, the promise of a government, the promise of a central bank, and you could use that promise as a substitute for gold. The devaluation of the gold dollar has shaken that faith. The Bank of France will hardly trust its reserves in sterling again. It lost eight times its capital from trusting sterling and the promise of the Bank of England.

"The Netherlands Bank will hardly trust sterling again. It lost its capital from trusting sterling.

"And they will hardly trust the American dollar for a long time. You have destroyed the great competitor of gold, credit; and you have raised the value of gold for decades in the world as a whole as a result" (U.S., Congress, Senate, Committee on Agriculture and Forestry, *Hearings on the Causes of the Loss of Export Trade and the Means of Recovery* [Washington: Government Printing Office, 1935], p. 284).

than government obligations, and we have had them doing this with the approval of scrupulous and upright judges who have taken cognizance of the bad faith of the government.

President Roosevelt and Senator Gore. President Roosevelt did not escape sharp rebuke from distinguished men in his own party who opposed this bad faith. As part and parcel of his policy of debasing the gold dollar, he had introduced into Congress a joint resolution (signed by the President on June 5, 1933) abrogating the gold clause in existing governmental and private obligations. The resolution not only forbade private debtors to keep their gold obligations, but also freed the government itself from its solemn promise. Before the introduction of this resolution, the President conferred with a group of senators regarding it. Among them was Senator Thomas P. Gore, the great blind senator from Oklahoma. When the President asked Senator Gore for his opinion regarding the matter, the senator replied, "Why, that's just plain stealing, isn't it, Mr. President?" Senator Gore, moreover, in debate on the Senate floor, said, in substance, this: "Henry VIII approached total depravity, as nearly as the imperfections of human nature would allow. But the vilest thing that Henry ever did was to debase the coin of the realm!"[2]

Senator Gore, who, though blind since the age of twelve, made himself a great scholar and who mastered the literature of money as few professional economists have, exhibited throughout his career courage and independence and tenacious adherence to principle almost unmatched in our history. He defied two Presidents of his own party when he believed that they were wrong. He lost his seat in the Senate as a result of defying Woodrow Wilson, but he came back. After his defiance of President Roosevelt in the conference above referred to, he was a marked man. Roosevelt succeeded in beating him for renomination to the Senate in 1936. He could have made his peace and would have been reelected, had he yielded on any one of several issues[3] in the period between 1933 and 1936, but he would not yield. The country's greatest need today is more men like Senator Gore in high places.

There was bad faith by the British government, and there was bad faith by the United States government in abandoning the gold standard. The British at least had the excuse of being under heavy pressure and of being short of gold. It has been shown that the excuse was not a valid one. But we had no pretext of an excuse. We went off the gold standard with $3 billion of gold in the Federal Reserve banks, and we passed the Thomas Amendment at a time when gold was still pouring into the Federal Reserve banks from the people.

---

[2] I am unable at the present time to locate this in the *Congressional Record*. I think it was said in the course of the very brief debate on the Thomas Amendment in 1933, but it may have been in the debate on the Gold Reserve Act of 1934.

[3] This information comes to me not from Senator Gore himself, but from several of his colleagues in the Senate and from one Democratic leader in the House of Representatives.

There was divergent opinion in Washington at the time as to whether the Thomas Amendment represented President Roosevelt's deliberate choice or whether his hand was more or less forced. One view was that if the President had stood against it, it would have been easy enough to defeat the inflationist sentiment in Congress. Another view was that this sentiment was altogether too strong. An intermediate view was that while the President could have resisted successfully and would have been sustained by at least one House of Congress, it would have meant an open break between the President and Congress. In retrospect, it is pretty clear that Congress was so subservient to the President at that time that the President could have taken any course that he chose, and that it would have been entirely possible for him to have carried out the Democratic platform with respect to money, tariffs, and everything else.

46

The Banking Act of 1933—
Extreme Reform Bill,
Not New Deal Measure

The Glass banking bill, adopted June 16, 1933, was a reform measure designed to prevent the abuses that had developed, particularly in the relation of the banks to the securities market, in the wild period, 1924–29. One sympathized with some of the provisions of the bill. But it went a great deal too far in dealing with symptoms, and it failed entirely to strike at the basic evil, which was the unsound Federal Reserve policy for the period 1924–28, which blew up the appalling bubble of stock market speculation and reckless security issues. It was not, however, in essence a New Deal measure. It was a measure directed toward conservative finance rather than toward monetary manipulation and inflation.

Separation of Commercial and Investment Banking—Investment Affiliates. One important provision of the act was that designed to effect a complete separation of commercial and investment banking. The first draft of the act undertook to accomplish this in a one-sided way, by requiring the commercial banks to divorce themselves from their investment affiliates within one year. Steps had already been taken in this direction by the National City Bank and by the Chase National Bank. The chairman of the Chase National Bank proposed that the separation of commercial and investment banking be made complete, by forbidding investment bankers to receive deposits, and by forbidding partners or officers of investment banks to sit on the boards of commercial banks. This suggestion was welcomed by Senator Glass, and adopted in the Banking Act of 1933.

The conspicuous abuses of the period 1927–29 had made legislation of this sort politically necessary. From the economic point of view, the abolition of the investment affiliates of the great banks was unfortunate, and legislation regulating their activities would have been better. The investment affiliates of the great banks had had, in general, good records down to 1927. In one conspicuous case the rule had been that the invest-ment affiliate, whose capital was entirely separate from the capital of the bank, would risk its money, but would not risk its reputation or the bank's reputation. It did engage in underwriting. It did deal in securities with wholesalers and retailers of securities. But it did not put its name or the bank's name upon an issue, and it did not sell securities to the public. These investment affiliates brought a needed element of competition, and a very substantial additional amount of capital, into the investment banking field.

Great Harm Came in Retailing by Investment Affiliates. The great harm came when they began to put their names upon issues and, above all, when they established retail selling organizations with enterprising, high-pressure salesmen selling securities to individuals in the name of a great bank. This changed their character in many respects. One change was this: as long as the investment affiliate had no retail sales organization, it could have an inexpensive organization. It could afford to wait until satisfactory underwriting opportunities appeared. When, however, it had a large body of salesmen out in the field, they had to be supplied with securities to sell. The pressure on the head office to provide securities was immense. If first-rate securities were not available, the temptation was great to provide them with something to sell anyway. This was a factor of real importance in the deterioration of the quality of new securities offered to the public in the period of 1924–29. I think that if the investment affiliates had had no retail organizations they would be in existence and doing useful work today. The Glass Act forced upon the investment banking field a great liquidation at a time when investment banking, chastened by the bitter experiences of the preceding years, would otherwise have been doing a great deal of useful and constructive work.

Bank Underwriting of Bonds. The Glass Act also limited very strictly the underwriting of bonds by commercial banks. It went much too far in this. There are times when participation by the banks in bond issues is highly important, highly necessary. A case in point is the refunding issue of $230 million of the Great Northern and Northern Pacific railroads in 1921, which would have been a failure with disastrous consequences to the country if the great banks had not participated in the underwriting syndicate. The Glass Act forbade the participation by commercial banks in underwriting bonds of any kind except federal, state, and municipal bonds, and the bonds of government corporations. This went too far. Commercial banks should be allowed to underwrite any bonds which they are allowed to buy, and when bond issues meet the specifications of the comptroller of the currency for bonds appropriate for purchase by a bank, they may very well be underwritten by a bank. Commercial banks, of course, ought not to underwrite stock issues, but this they were not doing in any case, and were not allowed to do under legislation previously existing.

Loans to Bank Officers. The Glass Banking Act forbade loans by banks to their own officers. In this it went too far. Banks should not make loans to their senior officers, but it is very well that the junior officer of a bank should borrow from his own bank and borrow only from his own bank, or at all events, borrow from another bank only with the knowledge and approval of his own bank, so that the bank may be fully informed as to what he is doing. It is very important that a bank should be free to help its younger men in emergencies.

It is unnecessary to give here a detailed account of the many provisions of this act. It included a provision for deposit insurance. It dealt with branch banking and group banking. It gave the Federal Reserve Board carefully limited power to remove officers of member banks, after a hearing. It abolished interest on demand deposits, and gave the Federal Reserve Board power to regulate interest on time and savings deposits.

Interest on Deposits. With respect to the provisions of the act forbidding the payment of interest on demand deposits, the present writer had the opportunity of an interchange of views with Senators McAdoo and Glass two years later in the Senate Committee Hearings on the Banking Act[1] of 1935.

---

[1] U.S., Congress, Senate, subcommittee of the Committee on Banking and Currency, Hearings on S. 1715 and H.R. 7617, May 16, 1935, pp. 490–92.

SENATOR McADOO: Do you think we did a wise thing in prohibiting the payment of interest on demand deposits?

MR. ANDERSON: I am glad you raised that point, Senator. I believe we are going to have to change the law just as soon as we approach a normal money market. I think at all events interbank interest—interest on deposits of one bank with another—ought to be allowed. Here is a great lot of excess reserves in one Federal Reserve district which can be used in another section if it is needed. They ought to be able to get it by paying for it.

SENATOR McADOO: I was speaking more, of course, of demand deposits. Do you think we did a wise thing in prohibiting the payment of interest on demand deposits?

MR. ANDERSON: I think the only place where a definite abuse existed that needed public regulation was time deposits in smaller places. I think they paid rates much too high, and there should have been public regulation of that; but I think that the practice in New York as to interest on demand deposits and interest on time deposits under clearinghouse regulations was quite wholesome. Some bankers did not like it. Some of them welcome your abolition of interest. But I am looking at it as an economist. I want a good flow of funds, and interest is the way to move them.

SENATOR McADOO: Suppose, for instance, we had said that we would permit the payment of interest on demand deposits on interbank transactions; would you still say that we should also permit the payment of interest on customers' demand deposits?

MR. ANDERSON: My view would be "yes." . . .

SENATOR McADOO: In the city of Los Angeles, a city of 1,250,000 people, with quite a large number of banks, the abuse got to be very great, so bankers have informed me. One bank would offer a large depositor a very much higher rate of interest than was justified, and at the first sign of trouble this large depositor got uneasy and withdrew his whole deposit at once, which was a very bad thing for the bank, or it might have been, whereas, in the ordinary course of business, where interest was not paid on demand deposits, and deposits might be more widely distributed, less injury might follow from a large number of small withdrawals.

MR. ANDERSON: You could have a rule that the rate in each city should be the same so that the banks in a particular city are not competing, by varying the rate, against one another. The main thing that I have in mind to be accomplished is that if Los Angeles is needing money which Chicago has, it should be possible to bring that money to Los Angeles at a higher rate.

SENATOR McADOO: It was experimental, of course, to prohibit the payment of interest on customers' demand deposits. If it has not worked well or if it is inadvisable, the question in my mind is whether or not it might not be restored with the provision for the regulation of the

Senator Glass's point regarding country banks sending their money to the great centers to get two percent instead of lending it out at home is one which he had in mind at the time when he was drafting the Federal Reserve Act. He wanted to stop the practice of country banks' sending their money to New York City, which New York City banks would often lend on call to the stock market. He wanted the money left in the local communities. But the senator did not adequately reckon with the seasonal needs of the country banks in his evaluation of this phenomenon. The typical country bank has an excess of cash after crops have been moved and sold in the late autumn or early winter, but is going to need all that cash in lending to the farmers as crops are being made in the following spring and summer, and it is going to need a great deal more, borrowed from city correspondents or from the Federal Reserve banks, at the peak of the crop-moving season. If it lends it out at home in January, February, and March, it will not be able to take care of its customers' needs in the later months of the year. The best thing it can do from a standpoint of taking good care of the community needs is to keep the funds liquid by sending them to the financial centers as deposits with correspondent banks, or for the purchase of commercial paper or acceptances, or for call loans to the stock market. One especially important reason for making deposits with correspondent banks is that the country bank thereby acquires a "borrowing equity" from the city correspondent and thereby earns the right to have the city correspondent serve it in selecting sound commercial paper, sound acceptances, or in making and supervising stock market loans instantly available on need, and in performing a multitude of other services.

It is significant that both of Senator Glass's efforts to stop the practice of country banks' sending their surplus funds to the great cities failed. The Federal Reserve System and the requirement that banks keep their legal reserves with the Federal Reserve banks did not stop the practice on the part of country banks (even though members of the Federal Reserve System) of keeping large deposit balances with city correspondents during the season

---

rate of interest by the Federal Reserve bank of the district or by government authority, just as we permit the regulation of the rate of interest now on time deposits.

MR. ANDERSON: I would so recommend, Senator.

SENATOR GLASS: As a matter of fact, there were various reaons why we did that. In the first place, country banks had what they call standard rates of discount. It is almost impossible ever to get them to depart from that standard rate of discount. They would rather bundle up their surplus funds and send them to the money centers at a nominal rate of two percent than to give the merchants of the town or the industries of the town, or the locality the benefit of an abundance of money and an abundance of credit. . . .

SENATOR MCADOO: And also for another reason, that where we were requiring the banks to pay a premium to insure any part of their deposits, to relieve them of this payment of interest on demand deposits we gave them an additional means by which they could pay premiums upon insurance.

MR. ANDERSON: With these very low interest rates now prevailing the banks are moving very rapidly to protect themselves anyhow. We have abolished interest on time deposits in New York because we cannot afford to pay it. We don't want money that we have to pay for.

when they have surplus cash. Nor has the abolition of interest on demand deposits stopped the practice. The country bank needs the city correspondent. The sound country bank does not lend out all its funds at home all the year round.

Securities Act of 1933. Another piece of legislation adopted in the spring of 1933 was the Securities Act (signed May 27), designed to compel truth in securities. The purpose was admirable. There had been altogether too many recklessly drawn and irresponsible security prospectuses, concluding usually with the statement that "the information herein contained is obtained from sources believed to be reliable but not guaranteed by us." It was right to require full disclosure of all relevant facts and to impose full responsibility for the truth of the prospectus upon those who issued it, including both the underwriting bankers and the issuing corporation. But the terms of the legislation were so drastic, and the responsibilities imposed were so great, that they paralyzed the issue of new securities. We shall discuss this matter more fully in connection with the stock market episode of 1937.

Contradictory Policies

We have seen the contradiction in the New Deal between the policy of liberal foreign trade and foreign exchange stabilization on the one hand, and the policy of internal regimentation on the other. There are further contradictions. There is a contradiction between the policy of inflation and internal currency depreciation, and the policy of foreign exchange stabilization. And there is a contradiction between the policy of inflation and the policy of internal regimentation. There is a contradiction also between the policy of the Thomas Amendment inflation measure on the one hand, and the policy of the Glass Act and the Securities Act, which look toward extreme conservatism in finance, on the other.

For inflationary measures to be effective there must be markets in which money can be used, and prices must be free to respond to the use of money. If, however, as we build up a flood of money, we simultaneously erect dams to prevent the use of money, as was done by the Securities Act and as was done by the policy of self-contained isolation which needed to retain high tariffs and even to increase tariffs if it were to be effective—the inflationary measures, which presupposed open markets, were neutralized. Both the agricultural act of the spring of 1933 and the National Industrial Recovery Act of 1933 looked toward internal regimentation, and both contained provisions for restrictions on imports. These were necessary to protect the higher agricultural prices and the higher industrial prices aimed at by these measures.

If our economic life had been a closely meshed mechanism, it would have been shattered to pieces by the various contradictory measures of the spring of 1933. Fortunately, however, our economic life is not a closely meshed mechanism, but rather a loosely articulated organism with a very tough hide and with an immense vitality. It could respond to the contradictory, painful stimuli by shrinking at both ends, by twisting and turning, and by enduring pain. It was not killed.

The National Industrial
Recovery Act

Certain Trade Associations Enthusiastic at First. Adam Smith remarked ago that there was rarely a meeting of businessmen without some conspiracy against the public. In its origin the National Industrial Recovery Act may have been such a conspiracy. Businessmen wanted to restrict competition. Businessmen and their trade associations wanted to get rid of the Sherman law. They wanted to restrict production (euphemistically called "adjusting supply to demand") so that they could raise prices and fix prices by concerted action. Whether the idea originated with trade associations or whether it originated with certain of the New Dealers is not certain, but it is certain that the New Dealers responded enthusiastically to the idea and there was enthusiasm for the idea in certain business circles.

The business circles most enthusiastic about the idea were those most eager to preserve the high tariffs. They wanted a controlled market all to themselves, and the linkage of the two ideas of high protective tariffs and controlled markets made a strong appeal. They could not see that "adjusting supply to demand," at the lowest state of demand of our greatest depression, would have precluded general industrial revival. It was beyond the imagination of a particular group of businessmen in a particular trade, who looked only at the supply-and-demand situation in their own trade, to see how greatly the demand for their product would increase if only other industries could expand.

But Enthusiasm Wanes When Labor Leaders Enter Picture. The enthusiasm of the businessmen, however, was dampened sharply when a new factor entered the picture. Labor leaders were quick to see their opportunity. To the proposal for restricted production and minimum prices, they added the proposal of the thirty-hour week for labor and minimum wages, and in the final form of the bill the demands of the labor leaders met more generous recognition than did the demands of the businessmen for monopoly.

Hull Goes to London Without Tariff Powers. The progress of the move toward what later became our NRA raised increasing doubts as to the policy of international cooperation to be worked out in the scheduled London International Economic Conference, and, above all, put increasing obstacles in the way of Secretary Hull's request for a reciprocal tariff act which would give him tariff powers when he went to London to negotiate. He finally went to London without these powers.

NRA Imposes Import Restrictions to Protect Artificial Prices— Exemptions from Antitrust Act. The passage of the National Industrial Recovery Act was not completed until after the London Conference assembled on June 12. The National Industrial Recovery Act was introduced on May 17, 1933, and was signed by the President on June 16, 1933. As Hull went to London to urge the reduction of tariffs throughout the world, the Congress in the National Industrial Recovery Act authorized additional restrictions on imports. Among the purposes of the act was definitely the raising of the prices of manufactured commodities in the United States. The act further gave exemptions from the antitrust laws of the United States to combinations in restraint of trade under codes drawn in conformity with the act.

Monopolistic Codes—Prices, Wages, and Hours. Even before the passage of the act, Gen. Hugh Johnson, who was to have charge of the administration of the act, had conferred with leaders in various industries urging them to have codes prepared for immediate submission. With the passage of the act there came a frantic code movement. Industries of all kinds were called upon to prepare codes. These codes were concerned with shorter hours, with minimum wages, with increased employment, and with price fixing, usually disguised as prohibitions of sales "below costs." It was obvious that an immense increase in industrial costs was in prospect.

"Purchasing Power" Means Payrolls. A naive economic theory was developed as the guiding principle of NRA. The object of the administration of NRA was to "increase purchasing power." Purchasing power meant payrolls. The point was to keep payrolls advancing faster than the production of goods. If this could be done, steady progress could be maintained, according to this theory.

Obviously payrolls of industrial labor constitute only a part of the purchasing power of the country. Obviously, too, if payrolls were increased only at the expense of profits and the income of shareholders, there was no increase in aggregate purchasing power.[1] More fundamental still was the complete ignoring of the mainspring in industrial decisions, namely, the prospects of profits or losses. Under a system of free enterprise

---

[1] The Keynesian will object, of course, that laborers are spenders, while shareholders and corporations "oversave." I deal with this view below, in chapter 59, "The Undistributed Profits Tax of 1936," and in chapter 60, "Digression on Keynes."

this is absolutely basic. When businessmen see prospects of growing profits, they expand their activities. They borrow more capital. They hire more labor. When profits are cut and when losses emerge, they contract their operations. This is fundamental in the theory of business cycles. It is the sound theory. It is the explicit major premise of Wesley Mitchell's great book *Business Cycles*, published in 1913. The idea that the purchasing power of labor is the mainspring of business activity seems to be incredibly naive.

"Purchasing Power" vs. Profits as Dynamo. We were to see in August 1933 a dramatic testing of the validity of these two contrasting theories, with the complete demolition (insofar as facts can demolish a theory) of the theory that increasing purchasing power of labor at the expense of business profits can make increasing business activity.

The obvious disharmony between internal regimentation of the NRA and AAA type on the one hand, and a liberal foreign trade policy based on low tariffs and sound currencies with fixed exchange rates on the other, could not fail to be evident. And the disharmony between exchange stabilization agreements and a policy of price raising based on depreciating currency was obviously great. The President's enthusiasm for the London Conference rapidly diminished.

49

The London Economic Conference, 1933

The world economic conference convened in London on June 12. Simultaneously, discussions among the Bank of England, the Bank of France, and the Federal Reserve System were taking place, looking toward a temporary, tentative exchange stabilization agreement. Rumors that an exchange stabilization agreement had been or shortly would be arrived at appeared in the press and the speculative markets reacted adversely. On June 15 the dollar advanced sharply in the foreign exchange markets, and securities and some important commodity prices reacted. President Roosevelt speedily made it clear that he would not accept the tentative agreement. The conference came to a standstill pending the arrival of Raymond Moley, whom the President sent to London as his special emissary, and who presumably knew the President's views.

Agreement on Money After Moley Comes. After Professor Moley's arrival in London immediate exchange stabilization was given up, but discussion continued in the conference, and finally a joint declaration on monetary policy was discussed and generally approved:

> (a) The signatory governments were to agree that restoration of stability in the international monetary field as quickly as possible is in the interests of all concerned, and that gold should be reestablished as the international measure of exchange value, each nongold country to be free to determine the time and parity at which it could undertake to stabilize on a gold basis.
>
> (b) Gold standard countries signing the declaration were to reassert their determination to maintain the free working of the gold standard at existing gold parities.
>
> (c) Nongold countries signing the declaration were to take note of the above and recognize its importance, their ultimate object being to restore the gold standard.
>
> (d) Nongold signatory countries were to undertake to limit exchange speculation so far as possible in cooperation with other signatory countries.

(e) Each signatory country was to agree to ask its central bank to cooperate with the central banks of the other signatory governments in limiting speculation in exchanges, and, when the time came, in reestablishing the general international gold standard.

(f) The declaration was declared open to signature by other governments.[1]

But Dynamited by Roosevelt. The declaration received the approval of the American delegation as well as Professor Moley. The text of the declaration was submitted to President Roosevelt for approval on June 30. A few days later came a great shock when the President addressed a message to the London Conference rejecting these propositions. The message contained the following passages:

> The world will not long be lulled by the specious fallacy of achieving a temporary and probably an artificial stability in foreign exchange on the part of a few large countries only.
>
> The sound internal economic system of a nation is a greater factor in its well-being than the price of its currency in changing terms of the currencies of other nations.
>
> It is for this reason that reduced cost of government, adequate government income, and ability to service government debts are so all-important to ultimate stability. So, too, old fetishes of so-called international bankers are being replaced by efforts to plan national currencies with the objective of giving to those currencies a continuing purchasing power which does not greatly vary in terms of the commodities and need of modern civilization. Let me be frank in saying that the United States seeks the kind of dollar which a generation hence will have the same purchasing and debt-paying power as the dollar value we hope to attain in the near future. That objective means more to the good of the other nations than a fixed ratio for a month or two in terms of the pound or franc.[2]

Writing about this episode many years later, Professor Raymond Moley said: "In 1933, an international conference was held in which all the great issues were undecided before the meeting began. When things started, delegates wandered around in a fog, trying to learn by remote control what Roosevelt was currently thinking. The whole conference fell to pieces."[3]

The London Conference came to a futile end. Practically its only accomplishment was a relatively innocuous agreement regarding silver. Senator Key Pittman of Nevada, the leader of the silver forces in the United States, was the one victor in the London Conference, and even his triumph did not go very far.

---

[1] Frederick A. Bradford, *Money and Banking* (New York: Longmans, Green, 1939), p. 79.

[2] *Ibid.*, p. 80.

[3] *Los Angeles Times,* April 7, 1945.

Hull After Failure of London Conference. Secretary Hull returned from the conference grim and silent, and had an interview with the President. Following this interview, Professor Moley withdrew from the State Department. Hull's position was one which only a very great and selfless man could have tolerated. His purposes were defeated. He could make no move toward lower tariffs in the near future. His tariff powers were denied him. Moreover, under NRA further restrictions on imports were provided for, and under the Agricultural Adjustment Act compensatory taxes on agricultural imports were provided for, to offset the processing taxes.[4] All that Hull could do was to stay in Washington and keep the flag up. He chose to stay, and earned thereby the gratitude of the country. Hull outlived the NRA and his policies survived. Hull outlived the presidential power to alter the gold content of the dollar. Hull got his tariff powers in 1934, and moved steadily, if slowly, toward reducing tariffs by reciprocal agreements, agreements which gave the benefit of any tariff reduction to all nations with which either signatory had "most favored nation" clauses in their commercial treaties. Hull fought bilateralism and economic isolation. And Hull saw an ever-widening acceptance of the principle of economic cooperation under liberal trade policies, not only among informed students, but also in American legislation. It is to the credit of President Roosevelt that, beginning with 1934, he aided and supported Cordell Hull's policies.

---

[4] National Industrial Recovery Act, 1933, sec. 3 (E); Agricultural Adjustment Act, 1933, sec. 15 (E).

50

The Strong Business Rally, March–July 1933
—Turns Downward with NRA

With the reopening of the banks in the middle of March 1933 there came an extraordinary rally in American business. The worst had happened. Production had dropped to unprecedentedly low levels. Banks which had reopened were believed to be sound. The people were putting their money back into the banks. Inventories had fallen to absurdly low levels, and this was especially true of goods on merchants' shelves. Hand-to-mouth buying on a great scale had prevailed. Great department stores in New York City had been ordering sheets and towels in lots of a half a dozen. The panic was over, and something like normal orderly buying on the part of retailers began, which meant a vast increase in the volume of buying.

Expansion of plant and equipment was hardly in order at the moment, because there was so much unused plant and equipment, but ordinary maintenance of plant and equipment meant a great increase in buying as compared with that which had prevailed. A powerful upward movement began. The Federal Reserve Index of Production[1] was just under 60 in March 1933 and ran up to 100 by July 1933.

The explanation of this rally was, first of all, the inevitable upswing from extreme panic and depression. It started, as the weekly indices of production show, immediately with the reopening of the banks.

Speculative excitement following the introduction of the Thomas Amendment on April 20, with its provisions authorizing currency debasement, $3 billion of greenbacks, $3 billion of purchases of government securities by the Federal Reserve banks, and even bimetallism, though

---

[1] The Federal Reserve Index of Production here referred to is the old series with the 1923–25 base. I do not use the new index which first appeared just before the election in 1940. I share the distrust which Gen. Leonard P. Ayres and others have expressed regarding the new Federal Reserve Index of Production.

reflecting itself chiefly in the speculative markets, also tended to intensify the upward movement in business. Money magic was a new thing in America, and it had its influence for a little while.

NEW YORK TIMES WEEKLY INDEX OF
BUSINESS ACTIVITY
(Seasonally adjusted)

March 11	64.0
March 18	63.7
March 25	66.8
April 1	68.0
April 8	69.1
April 15	69.8
April 22	71.1
April 29	73.7
May 6	74.7
May 13	76.3
May 20	77.9
May 27	79.5
June 3	82.9
June 10	84.4
June 17	87.0
June 24	89.1
July 1	92.5
July 8	93.1
July 15	93.4

It must be observed, however, that there is nothing in the foregoing figures of the weekly index of business activity that can be easily identified as showing the influence of this "inflation" factor.

In the latter phases of this upswing a new factor appeared. It came with the passage of the National Industrial Recovery Act on June 16, and in some cases even before the passage of this act. Businessmen suddenly realized that with the application of the NRA codes, and with the application of the processing taxes which the Agricultural Adjustment Act provided, there would come a great increase in the costs of production.

They speeded up production to get as much done as possible before these increased costs began to operate. This undoubtedly brought the production curve to a higher point that it would otherwise have reached so soon.

NRA and the processing taxes came in July and August, and the production curve turned sharply downward, the Federal Reserve index dropping from 100 in July to 72 in November 1933.

We had then the first of two dramatic and conclusive tests of the theory that raising wage rates and shortening hours to increase factory employment and factory payrolls, and to increase the buying power of factory labor, would increase business activity. The second test was to come in 1937–38, to be discussed below.

From March 1933 to July 1933 there was an increase in factory employment of twenty-three percent, and an increase of factory payrolls of thirty-five percent. NRA came. Hours were shortened. Wages were raised arbitrarily. With what result? There was, between July and December 1933, a further increase in factory employment of three percent, and a further increase in factory payrolls of six percent. NRA made this addition to the buying power of factory labor. Did this increase production and business activity? The answer is startlingly clear. From July 1933 to December 1933 industrial production dropped twenty-five percent.

The rise in activity from March to July 1933 meant a sharp *decline* of twenty-six percent in labor costs per unit of output. Overhead cost was there anyway. Hiring additional laborers and adding to payrolls did not mean that the cost per unit of output was correspondingly increased, because overhead was spread thinner. It was still profitable to put on additional laborers. But with the arbitrary imposition of shorter hours and higher rates, the situation was radically reversed between July and December. The combination of the drop in industrial production and increased payrolls meant a fifty-four percent *increase* in labor cost per unit of output between July 1933 and December 1933 (see table on page 334).

In August and September 1933 the combined effect of the NRA increases in costs and of the processing taxes upon the situation was a very dramatic one, and a very discouraging one, as a banker, talking with his customers, could see it at that time. Here are some cases. One large industrial organization, producing consumer goods, had had a 300 percent increase in its volume between March and July. Its profits were large, and it absorbed without any difficulty the increased costs of NRA and the processing taxes, both of which affected it, and went on with a large volume of activity. At the opposite end was a large organization, producing capital goods and equipment, which had been running a deficit of $3 million a year. It was not affected by the processing taxes, but was affected by NRA rules as to wages and hours. This industry had its $3 million deficit increased to a $6 million deficit. In between were a great many cases of businesses which reported that, for the first time in two or three years, they had had profits between March and July 1933, but that, with the coming of NRA and, in some cases, the processing taxes, they found these profits largely wiped out or turned into deficits.

NRA Antirevival Measure. NRA was not a revival measure. It was an antirevival measure. The theory that shortening hours and raising wages would increase business activity was conclusively exploded in this six-month period of actual test.

Through the whole of the NRA period industrial production did not rise

NRA AND BUSINESS INDICES*
(Percentage increases or decreases)

	Preceding establishment of NRA (March to July 1933)	Following establishment of NRA (July to December 1933
Industrial production (a) (adjusted)	+69	−25
Factory employment (a) (adjusted)	+23	+3
Factory payrolls (a)	+35	+6
Wholesale prices (b)......................	+15	+3
Cost of living (d)........................	+5	+3
Food.................................	+16	−
Clothing	+4	+21
Stocks of manufactured goods (c)	+7	+6
Labor costs per unit of output	−26	+54
Department store sales (a) (adjusted)	+23	−1
Department store stocks (a) (adjusted)	+11	+8

    (a) Federal Reserve Board, 1923–25 base.
    (b) U. S. Bureau of Labor statistics.
    (c) U. S. Department of Commerce.
    (d) National Industrial Conference Board.

* This table is from Arthur Robert Burns, "The First Phase of the National Industrial Recovery Act, 1933," *Political Science Quarterly* (June 1934). In cases where later figures have appeared to replace preliminary figures, revision has been made. The cost of living figures published by the National Industrial Conference Board have been used in the above table. The figures for "labor costs per unit of output" are estimates by Professor Burns.

as high as it had been in July 1933, before NRA came in. Following the disappearance of NRA, after the Supreme Court decision in May 1935, there came the first real recovery. We passed the July 1933 peak in the autumn of 1935, and then, with rapidly growing volume of production and with decreasing unemployment, had approximately two years of growing business activity—though at the best, in 1937, we had 6,372,000, or 12 percent of the total labor force, unemployed.

Fearful Burden of Reports Placed on Business—Shifting Rulings Replace Settled Law. One of the most appalling things about NRA was the sudden multiplication of new rules with which businesses must comply, rules not resting on settled law but on arbitrary decisions of administrative bodies, subject to change almost without notice. The business community was suddenly called upon to rush to Washington to participate in the making of codes, codes which represented bargains among different elements of the industries, bargains with labor, and bargains with an extraordinarily incapable set of government officials and employees, many of whom were extremely radical, and few of whom knew anything about business.

The business community was suddenly called upon to prepare replies to a great mass of questionnaires, which often called for information that could not readily be obtained from the books of the businesses as ordinarily kept, and which involved immense labor on the part of the accounting offices and gravely burdened the attention of the chiefs of business, as categories had to be interpreted and the laws and the rules had to be interpreted.

All this was complicated for the financial community by the new laws and regulations connected with the Banking Act of 1933 and the new security legislation. The definition of "affiliates" under the Banking Act of 1933 was such as to impose upon financial institutions, and especially upon the banks and the security affiliates of the banks, responsibility for reporting on the financial affairs of a great many institutions that they did not in fact control and to whose detailed figures they had no legal access. One fine veteran, a very upright man, faced this problem, labored with it for several days and finally threw up his hands in despair. He died that night. Many men turned suddenly old under the heavy pressure.

Lawyers Replace Engineers and Salesmen. It is not easy to keep a powerful business move going when the head of the business must give more time to his lawyers than he can give to his engineers or to his salesmen. Under NRA, especially in the early stages, the main time and the main energies of the business leaders went into conferences with their lawyers.

NRA Hardest on Small Businesses. Hard as NRA was on the great businesses of the country, it was harder still on the small businesses and on businesses in smaller places. Businesses with limited working capital simply could not stand the sudden increase in costs. Fortunately the enforcement of NRA was lax where small businesses in small places were involved.[1]

But over the country there was a great mortality in small businesses, and this was particularly true in regions where capital was scarce and labor relatively abundant. An effort was made under NRA to meet unequal

---

[1] I was in the New England village of Provincetown, at the tip of Cape Cod, on the day that the experiment began. The New Englanders were skeptical; the Portuguese were willing to try it; and the artists and the authors were enthusiastic. Not very much happened. The bank did not need to make any change in its practices. It already had all the clerks that it needed and they were already working less than forty hours a week. A branch of a great national chain store system took on an additional clerk. The Railway Express Agency had one man who worked nine hours, and was obliged to hire another man for two or three hours a day. The most serious problem came in connection with the local cold storage plant to which the fishermen brought their fish. It had two engineers, each of whom worked twelve hours a day, though the work was light and the primary requirement was that an engineer should be in attendance. It was required to have three engineers at eight hours a day. The manager said very simply to the NRA official, "I can't do that. I have a heavy loan at the bank and my deposit balance at the bank is very low. If you enforce this rule, I shall have to close the plant." Nothing was done about this and the plant continued with two engineers at twelve hours each.

conditions in different parts of the country by allowing differentials as between regions, but these differentials did not begin to meet the problem.

And on the South. NRA created a great deal of unemployment in the South. Despite the differentials, the greatest percentage increase in wages, the greatest shortening of hours, and the greatest percentage increase in labor costs under NRA were in the South. In the lumber trade, for example, very little increase was made in western wages, while a very great increase was made in southern wages, even though they remained well below those of the West. This illustration, by the way, strikingly reveals how absurd the contention is that cost of production in a given industry is wholly a question of wage rates. In the case of lumber, far more depends upon the quality of the stumpage, its accessibility to transportation, the degree of mechanization in the methods of getting out the timber, the quality of labor, and a wide variety of other factors. An interesting book by Charles Frederick Roos, who was formerly director of research of the NRA, gives significant figures in connection with this point and says: "In view of these data, it is not surprising that lumber business was diverted from the South to the Pacific Northwest."[2]

Forces 500,000 Negroes out of Work. Roos estimates that, by reason of the minimum-wage provisions of the codes, about 500,000 Negro workers were on relief in 1934.[3]

Roos adds that a minimum wage definitely causes the displacement of the young, inexperienced worker and the old worker.[4] He adds that the NRA favored the highly mechanized units of industry,[5] that insuperable difficulties arose in fixing fair differentials, not only as between sections but also as between large and small places,[6] that small firms survived, frequently, by disregarding the provisions of the code,[7] and that, had the codes been rigorously enforced, employment at the expiration of the NRA might have been considerably less than it was.

NRA Struck Especially at Capital Goods Industries. He adds that rising wage rates and increasing prices delayed recovery, especially in residential building and replacement machinery,[8] and, in general, it is his view that the NRA struck especially at the capital goods industries.[9]

---

[2] Charles Roos, *NRA Economic Planning* (Bloomington, Ind.: Principia Press, 1937), p. 166.
[3] *Ibid.*, p. 173.
[4] *Ibid.*, p. 193.
[5] *Ibid.*, p. 416.
[6] *Ibid.*, p. 162.
[7] *Ibid.*, p. 143.
[8] *Ibid.*, p. 150.
[9] *Ibid.*, p. 124.

AAA Versus NRA. Under the Agricultural Adjustment Act, we had the remarkable spectacle in the summer of 1933 of a radical reversal of all previous practices in agriculture, with the farmers being paid by the government to plow under their crops and to reduce production, and with a variety of measures for artificially raising agricultural prices.

Between the agricultural program and the NRA program there was an absurd inconsistency. The agricultural program was designed to lift agricultural prices not merely absolutely, but also in relation to the price of manufactured goods. The agricultural program was designed to give farm products the same purchasing power in relation to manufactured goods that they had in the base period 1909–14. But NRA was designed to raise the price of manufactured goods.

There was in the spring and early summer of 1933 a radical rise in the price of agricultural goods, amounting to nearly fifty percent, with a sharp reaction after July. There was a sharp rise of other prices, smaller in percentage, but not followed by reaction in the latter half of the year. The general average of all prices declined from its high of the year by December. By December 1933 the gap between agricultural prices and other prices was very nearly as great as it had been in early April. The effort of the Agricultural Adjustment Administration to achieve prewar parity was defeated in 1933 by NRA.

Nervous Speculative Markets. The AAA program, moreover, added to the complications of business. New rules and new procedures were announced with great frequency, creating violent speculative disturbances and creating new business uncertainties.

The stock market and the speculative markets in commodities had violent upswings between March and July, and both had violent downswings in July. Speculation is a product of uncertainty, and the same uncertainties which made heavy speculative markets in July and August made inhibitions and confusion for business planning and for business activities. The autumn of 1933 was a pretty blue period for the business community, for the speculative markets, and for the economic planners in Washington who saw their plans go wrong.

51

More Money Magic—The Gold-Buying Program

But the planners in Washington were far from having exhausted their repertory. There were many things yet to be tried. If one did not work, perhaps another would. One is reminded of the account of the deathbed of King Charles II, where a group of physicians were trying every possible method of reviving the unhappy king, including the use of sneezing powder of hellebore root.[1]

Professor Warren. The administration turned in late October 1933 to a new form of money magic. The new doctor who prescribed this magic was George F. Warren, professor of agricultural economics at Cornell University. Professor Warren was recognized by professional economists as having made some important contributions to the study of agriculture. He was not recognized as an authority on the subject of money, though he had written about money, and many economists shuddered at the selection of Professor Warren as monetary adviser.

The new program called for the control of commodity prices by varying the gold content of the dollar. The general average of commodity prices was to be raised by lowering the gold content of the dollar until it reached a satisfactory point, and then stabilized by further alterations in the gold content of the dollar—the gold content being raised if necessary to hold the price level down, and the gold content being reduced if necessary to hold it up.[2]

> *On the Practical Impossibility of a Commodity Dollar.* Human beings who have to use money simply will not stand still while the government or the bank of issue is putting through the manipulations. They will, on the contrary,

---

[1] Howard W. Haggard, *Devils, Drugs and Doctors* (New York: Harper, 1929), p. 334.

[2] I discussed this program in *Chase Economic Bulletin,* December 13, 1933, in the course of the discussion giving an account of what had actually happened in the relation of the gold content to prices. What follows with respect to this point is taken from that *Bulletin.*

inevitably, in order to protect their own interests, do things which will defeat the purpose of the government or the bank of issue.

Price Stabilization by Varying the Gold Content of the Dollar. There are three main types of proposal for regulating the price level by currency or credit manipulation. The most definite and exact is that of Professor Irving Fisher, who has proposed to have the government or the Federal Reserve banks redeem paper money in a varying amount of gold, the amount increasing as prices rise, with a view to pulling them down, and the amount decreasing as prices fall, with a view to raising them again.

At the opposite extreme is Professor Cassel's plan. Professor Cassel, leaving the gold standard in operation, would undertake to stabilize prices by regulating the volume of credit. If prices are falling, he would have the Federal Reserve authorities increase credit, and if prices are rising, he would have them decrease credit, expecting by this procedure to hold the general average of commodity prices stable.

In between is the plan of J. M. Keynes. He would seek to manipulate the quantity of money and credit, with a view to keeping prices stable, but he would also make use of gold in the process by having the central bank fix temporary buying and selling prices for gold, varying these two prices from time to time. The great difference between Fisher's plan and Keynes' plan with respect to the use of gold is as follows: Fisher would have an automatic rule; Keynes, on the other hand, would leave discretion to the managing authorities, both as to the time and as to the amount of the change in the gold behind the currency. Both Fisher and Keynes would, in general, make changes in the same direction.

Professor George F. Warren, the well-known agricultural economist of Cornell University, whose doctrines are supposed to have had large influence in the making of our recent policy, has himself offered no independent plan. His views seem to lean most strongly toward those of Professor Fisher, though there is evidence that he has been influenced by other writers as well.

Varying the Gold Content Defeats Its Own Purpose. We assume the plan in operation. We must consider how human beings would react to it before we can predict its effect. Let us suppose that the rule is definitely established that the Federal Reserve banks or the Treasury will reduce by one percent a month the amount of gold bullion paid out in redeeming paper dollars in a period of falling prices, and that, conversely, the redeeming authority will increase by one percent a month the amount of gold paid out in redeeming paper dollars in a period of rising prices. How will men react?

We take first the case of falling prices. We shall assume that prices have fallen two percent or three percent and that the tendency is still downward, so that we can confidently expect that for the next two or three months the redeeming authority will progressively lighten the gold content. Will not foreigners withdraw their money from our markets, turning their cash in American banks into gold in order to avoid the loss of two percent or three percent which they can clearly anticipate? Will not speculators rush to turn in their dollars for gold, anticipating that at a later time they can turn back the same gold to the redeeming authority and get more dollars for it? Will not everyone who has foreign payments to make hasten to purchase foreign exchange, thereby increasing the foreign drain upon our gold? And will not all of these transactions operate to reduce the money supply of the country— since it is by turning in paper money that the gold is obtained from the central authority? And will not all these operations withdraw money from bank reserves, tightening the money market, raising rates of interest on short loans, reducing the credit available for the carrying of commodities and securities? But is tightening the money market the correct procedure when one wishes to raise prices?

Take the reverse case. Assume that prices are rising, that they have risen by two percent or three percent in a short time, and that the tendency is still strongly upward. Under these conditions men can look forward with confidence to a progressive increase for the next two or three months of one percent a month in the amount of gold to be paid for paper money by the redeeming authority, as a means of raising the value of money and pulling down commodity prices. Will not, in this case, reverse reactions take place? Will not men hasten to bring gold to the redeeming authority and take out more paper money in the expectation that two or three months later they can get more gold for that paper money? Will not foreign funds come into the country and gold come in from abroad to be exchanged for paper money? Will not speculators bring gold to the Treasury or the Federal Reserve banks and take our paper money in exchange, and will not all these operations tend to increase the money supply of the country and the volume of bank reserves, reducing interest rates, making money easy, making it easier to borrow to carry securities and to carry commodities? But will these conditions operate to lower prices?

Varying Gold Content Spoils Credit Control. The plan of regulating prices by varying the gold content cannot be successfully combined with the plan of controlling prices by increasing or decreasing credit, as Keynes proposes to do. The point is that when you manipulate the gold content, you surrender control of your money market to the play of speculators in gold and foreign exchange and to the transfer of capital funds from one money market to another. This has been shown above in the demonstration that the money supply would be shortened, bank reserves would be depleted, and interest rates would rise when it was anticipated that the gold content of the dollar was to be lowered, while the reverse movements would take place if it was anticipated that the gold content was to be increased. At the times when your policy of controlling prices by increasing or decreasing credit called for expansion, credit would contract, and, at the times when your policy called for contracting credit, credit would relax.

Space does not permit me to discuss here the general question of control of commodity prices by means of expansion and contraction of credit. I content myself by referring to an earlier number of the *Chase Economic Bulletin,* published in 1929, called "Commodity Price Stabilization a False Goal of Central Bank Policy," and to a *Bulletin* on the Goldsborough bill, published in 1932, in which the statistical evidence is brought down to a later date. My contention, elaborated in these studies, is that commodity price stabilization by means of credit manipulation is both a practical and a theoretical impossibility.

The point I wish to make at present is that these two plans of stabilization by credit manipulation and stabilization by varying gold content are contradictory plans and cannot successfully be combined in the same scheme, because speculation in gold and transfers of funds between one country and another will spoil the power to control credit.

Varying Gold Content Spoils Automatic Corrective Through Exports. If a country on the gold standard finds its prices falling in relation to prices in the outside world, an automatic corrective comes—the country becomes a good market in which to buy and a bad market in which to sell. Its exports increase and its imports diminish. The tendency is for gold to flow into it. These forces all tend to check the price decline. A country operating under the Fisher-Keynes plan, however, would find these forces reversed. Foreign activity, as shown above, would be concentrated on taking out gold, rather than sending in gold to take out goods.

Can Governments Outwit Speculators? There are some who would make rejoinder to considerations of this sort that there is a very simple way of meeting all these difficulties. Why should a government pay out gold at all if speculators are going to play against the government, drawing out gold and returning it as their interests dictate? Why should we permit foreigners to take out gold or send in gold at their pleasure rather than at ours? We will cut through it all by paying out no gold, and have irredeemable paper money. Or we will let it be known that if speculators and foreigners do not behave, we shall from time to time suspend gold payment, resuming it after the speculators and foreigners have learned their lesson, or we will keep them uncertain as to what we are going to do, so that they won't know what to do. It may be observed, however, that it is precisely on uncertainty that speculation thrives.

But the main point here, of course, is that measures of this sort throw away the whole project of commodity price stabilization by varying the gold content of the dollar. If commodity prices are to be regulated by gold manipulation, then gold must be manipulated and the rules must be adhered to, including redemption of paper money in gold. The subject here under discussion is the possibility of regulating commodity prices and stabilizing commodity prices by varying the gold content of the dollar, and the verdict is that it is a practical as well as a theoretical and technical impossibility.

Price Raising by Reducing Gold Content. There has been an immense disappointment on the part of those who expected a great rise in commodity prices to follow the sharp reduction in the value of the dollar as measured against gold, or as measured in the foreign exchange market of gold standard countries. The mathematical theory of the thing would have called for a rise of nearly 66 percent in commodity prices in the United States to accompany the nearly 40 percent decline in the gold value of the dollar.

But the student of money and banking had few illusions about it in advance. It was clear that the shock to confidence throughout the world that would follow the cutting of the gold content of the American dollar would be so great that it would destroy credit on a great scale, and make men hesitant and timid for a prolonged period, and that a 50 percent cut in the gold value of the dollar, far from leading to a 100 percent rise in commodity prices, would lead rather to a great fall in prices as measured against gold and a very disappointingly small increase in prices as measured in the reduced dollar.

After all, the great bulk of the business of the world is done on credit. Moreover, in times when men distrust the future of paper money, gold itself rises in value as measured not only against paper money but also against goods, because men turn to gold as the one sure thing that will survive the wreck of currencies and the changing policies of governments, and seek to protect themselves by hiding away their wealth instead of using it courageously in production as they would do in a world of reasonable financial certainties.

Prices in this country following our abandonment of the gold standard and our progressive debasement of the dollar have not moved in the manner indicated by the devaluationist theory. On November 25 the dollar showed a decline, in terms of French francs, amounting to 36.6 percent. From the January–February level, wholesale commodity prices, according to the United States Department of Labor, showed an increase of 17 percent up to November 25 instead of the increase of 57.7 percent which, according to the devaluationist theory, should have accompanied a reduction of 36.6 percent in the gold value of the dollar.

Practically all of the increase in prices which had been experienced since February took place before the end of July, during which time general productive activity in the country was experiencing spectacular improvement. Since July productive activity has declined. Between the dates of July 29 and November 25 the gold value of the dollar showed a decline of 14.3 percent. Wholesale commodity prices during the same period, according to the Department of Labor, increased 2.6 percent, whereas an increase proportionate to the decline in the dollar would have been 16.7 percent.

Again, if the period of most aggressive activity in depressing the dollar, that since October 22, is taken into account it is to be observed that between the dates of October 21 and November 25 the value of the dollar, as measured in gold francs, declined 10.7 percent. Wholesale commodity prices, according to the Department of Labor, increased only $9/10$ percent, whereas the mathematical theory would require an increase of 12 percent.

Gold prices, that is, the prices of commodities measured in gold dollars rather than in paper dollars, have gone down drastically since February. The decline from the January–February average to November 25 was 25.9 percent. From July 29 to November 25 it was 12.1 percent, and from October 21 to November 25 the decline was 10 percent.

Failure of Gold-buying Plan Recognized by January 1934. The actual procedure in reducing the gold content of the dollar was the purchase of gold, chiefly in London, by the Reconstruction Finance Corporation through the sale of dollars in the London market. Legal warrant for this procedure was dubious enough, so that in Section 13 of the Gold Reserve

SUMMARY OF WHOLESALE COMMODITY
PRICE MOVEMENTS IN THE
UNITED STATES SINCE
JANUARY–FEBRUARY 1933

	Value of the dollar as measured in gold francs	Wholesale commodity prices in terms of paper (Bureau of Labor statistics index— 1926 = 100)	Index of whole-sale commodity prices as meas-ured in gold rather than in paper
January–February	100	60.7	60.7
November 25	63.4	71.0	45.0
Percent of change	− 36.6	+ 17.0	− 25.9
Percent of increase called for by devaluationist theory	....	57.7	....
July 29	74.0	69.2	51.2
November 25	63.4	71.0	45.0
Percent of change	− 10.7	+ .9	− 10.0
Percent of increase called for by devaluationist theory	....	12.0	....

Act of 1934 it was felt necessary to obtain congressional sanction for it, *nunc pro tunc*. Day after day as the Reconstruction Finance Corporation sold dollars and bought gold, the price of gold against dollars rose, and the price of the dollar fell in the foreign exchange markets against gold standard currencies.

There were stories of an eager group of New Dealers standing each morning by the news ticker, to watch the anticipated percentage jump in commodity prices with each percentage rise in the price of gold. Their disappointment and bewilderment were said to have been very great. Commodities barely moved. The markets were bewildered, bowed to the storm, and waited until some clarification should come.

Meanwhile the dollar itself fought hard. It took a tremendous volume of selling of dollars and a tremendous volume of gold buying to beat it down. As the process went on in January 1934, anxiety grew lest our continued purchases of gold should pull down the gold bloc, France, the Netherlands, Belgium, Switzerland, and some other countries. The only possibility of success of a program for manipulating the dollar by foreign exchange and gold transactions was regarded as depending on the existence of outside gold standard markets against which we could play. Our program was threatening to break the gold standard in these outside countries. Our financial power was great and its reckless employment was disturbing to the world.

The policy was a complete failure as regards regulating and controlling commodity prices, as we have seen above. In the Gold Reserve Act introduced in early January 1934, and in the executive rulings following

344 •   *The New Deal in Maturity, 1933–39*

the passage of that act, this policy of varying the gold content of the dollar was abandoned.

By January the failure was too complete and too obvious, and the policy changed. We turned to a debased gold dollar, but to one with fixed gold content.

52

The Gold Reserve Act
of 1934

*M*easure Forced Through with Little Discussion. The Gold Reserve Act became law on January 30, 1934. It was passed through both Houses of Congress with a minimum of discussion. The hearings before the House Committee on Banking and Currency were exceedingly brief. Those before the Senate Committee on Banking and Currency lasted from January 19 to January 23 only. There was no time for witnesses called by the committee to make adequate study of the bill or to plan carefully prepared statements.

Moreover, there was a very deliberate effort made by administration senators on the committee to prevent the introduction of testimony adverse to the measure, by constant interruptions with irrelevant questions, and by interruption of partially completed answers to these questions by more irrelevant questions.[1]

Gold of Federal Reserve Banks Seized—"Gold Certificates." The measure was a shocking one. It deliberately took away from the Federal Reserve banks the legal title to all their gold and vested the title in the United States Treasury. The act provided that in exchange for this gold the Federal Reserve banks were to be given "gold certificates," but what a gold certificate meant was exceedingly vague and indefinite. No gold was to be specifically segregated against the gold certificates and no specific value in gold was to be assigned to the gold certificates. Following a protest on this point before the Senate committee, the witness was taken aside by

---

[1] The present writer would have been quite unable to present his case had not Senator Glass sat down beside him and made a protest.

SENATOR GLASS: I suggest the witness be allowed to answer one question before he is asked another.

SENATOR BANKHEAD: I have not been able to get him to answer one yet.

SENATOR GLASS: You do not give him a chance.

U.S., Congress, Senate, Committee on Banking and Currency, *Hearings on Gold Reserve Act of 1934,* 73d Cong., 2d sess., p. 122.

one of the administration senators, who grinned and said, "Doctor, you don't understand about these gold certificates. These are not certificates that you can get gold. These are certificates that gold has been taken away from you."

Gold Content Placed at Between Fifty Percent and Sixty Percent of Old Par, at President's Discretion. The measure amended the Thomas Amendment to the Agricultural Act of May 12, 1933, by directing the President to reduce the weight of the gold dollar by not less than forty percent and not more than fifty percent, and gave the President the power to revalue the gold dollar within the specified limits from time to time.

The cutting of the gold content of the dollar by forty percent meant that, by what some called an act of magic, but what was really an act of theft, a great "gold profit" was created.

Placed at 59.06 Percent of Old Par, January 31, 1934. The President promptly on January 31, 1934, the day after the passage of the bill, fixed the weight of the gold dollar at $15^5/_{21}$ grains of gold, nine-tenths fine. This was a reduction of 40.94 percent in the gold content of the dollar, the new dollar containing 59.06 percent of the old standard, which had been 25.8 grains, nine-tenths fine. The price of gold was thus fixed at $35.00 per ounce instead of the old figure of $20.67 per ounce. As a result of this change in the gold content of the dollar, there was an overnight increase in the number of gold dollars in the hands of the Treasury and the Federal Reserve banks. The monetary gold stock stood on January 31, 1934, at $4,033,000,000, all of which was either in the Treasury or Federal Reserve banks.[2] On February 1, 1934, this was increased by $2,985,000,000, of which $2,806,000,000 was the "increment" resulting from the reduction in the weight of the gold dollar, and the remainder was gold which had been purchased by the Treasury but not previously added to the figures for gold monetary stock. This $2,806,000,000 was the so-called gold profit. What was to be done with the gold profit?

A $2 Billion Stabilization Fund Created out of "Gold Profit." The Gold Reserve Act provided that $2 billion of this should be segregated in a Stabilization Fund to be used in foreign exchange transactions and in dealing in gold in foreign exchange under the control of the Treasury. The Stabilization Fund also had power to deal in government securities.

One of the points made by the opponents in testimony regarding the bill was that no part of the gold profit could be used without a further increase in member bank reserves, and in the surplus reserves of the member banks,

---

[2] I have elsewhere called attention to the fact that the Federal Reserve volume *Banking and Monetary Statistics* (pp. 537–38), from which I am taking the figures in the text above, arbitrarily abolished from the gold monetary stock of the country, and from the figures for money in circulation, the sum of $287 million on January 30, 1934, primarily on the ground that if this gold were in the country, it was held illegally. They also revised earlier figures for gold stock, by making the same subtraction—which I am sure is excessive.

which had already grown to an ominous figure. The Treasury evidently felt the force of this consideration, because in the course of a few months it used the major part of the surplus left after the Stabilization Fund had been created in retiring the government bonds which secured national banknotes, with the resultant retirement of the national banknotes, thus removing from the money supply of the country an amount equal to the gold (or "gold certificates") thus employed. Moreover, only $200 million of the Stabilization Fund of $2 billion of gold was put into use, prior to the Bretton Woods legislation of 1945, which established liens upon it.

Divides Control of Money Market Between Treasury and Federal Reserve. One consequence of the Stabilization Fund in the hands of the Treasury was to split the control of the money market between the Federal Reserve System and the Treasury. It was now in the power of the Treasury by the use of its Stabilization Fund to offset action by the Federal Reserve System designed to take up excess reserves or to tighten the money market.

Gold Content on "Twenty-four-Hour" Basis. Not even the passage of the bill and the President's proclamation fixing the gold content of the dollar at 59.06 percent of the old parity brought the dollar immediately to the new parity. The dollar fought hard in the foreign exchanges. It was necessary, in order to bring it down, to continue heavy buying of gold and heavy selling of dollars in European markets. There was continued fear that before the process was complete the gold standard countries would be shaken from their moorings. When at last the process was complete and the dollar reached its new parity, reports came from Washington that the administration had breathed a great sigh of relief, and had no disposition to play with the manipulation of the gold content of the dollar any further. The only official announcement on the subject was a statement from the Treasury that the gold content of the dollar was on a twenty-four-hour basis. But in fact no change was made in the figure set in the President's proclamation of January 31, 1934, until his power to make a change was taken away from him by the Congress, or rather by the inaction of Congress, in the summer of 1943.

Opponents Put Three-Year Time Limit on President's Power to Devalue Further. Opponents of the measure could accomplish little with respect to its main provisions. They were, however, successful in putting a time limit upon the President's power to alter the gold content of the dollar within the fifty percent to sixty percent range, and in putting a time limit upon the life of the Stabilization Fund. The act limited these powers to two years, though they could be extended for one year further by proclamation of the President. In 1937 the renewal was accomplished for two more years without great difficulty. In 1939 the fight was close, and on a vote in the Senate the extension of the powers was denied. But the President, through a deal with the silver senators, was able to reverse this and have the powers extended for two more years, to 1941. In 1941, through a surprising reversal of attitude by Senator Carter Glass, who took the position that the President ought to have all the powers he asked for in the war situation, the power was again renewed.

No Further Change Made and Power Finally Expired in 1943. But in 1943 the Congress refused to renew the President's power with respect to the gold content of the dollar, and it thereupon expired, leaving the gold content of the dollar at 59.06 percent of the old parity, as a matter of law.

At the same time the Congress, in renewing the power of the secretary of the Treasury over the exchange Stabilization Fund, imposed limitations upon these powers, designed to prevent the use of the fund in an international foreign exchange stabilization institution along the lines of the Keynes-Morgenthau proposals of 1943.

"Buying Price" and "Selling Price" of Gold. The Congress had at last reasserted its authority over the gold content of the dollar. But there remained ambiguities and uncertainties growing out of the Gold Reserve Act of 1934. This act really contained three provisions regarding the relation of gold to the dollar. In addition to the provision regarding the gold content of the dollar, Section 8 of the act authorizes the secretary of the Treasury to *purchase* gold in any amounts at home or abroad at such rates and upon such terms and conditions as he may deem most advantageous to the public interest, "any provision of law relating to the maintenance of parity . . . to the contrary notwithstanding."

Section 9 of the act provides that "he may sell gold in any amounts, at home or abroad, in such manner and at such rates and upon such terms and conditions as he may deem most advantageous to the public interest, and the proceeds of any gold so sold shall be covered into the general fund of the Treasury."

These two provisions have no relation to the provisions of Section 12, which covers the gold content of the dollar, nor have they any relation to one another. There remains a dangerous ambiguity in our law regarding the gold content until this matter is rectified. It is apparently possible under the law, as it still stands, for the Treasury to have a buying price of gold different from its selling price, and to have both buying price and selling price of gold different from the gold content of the dollar.

The Gold Reserve Act of 1934 amended all preceding Federal Reserve legislation by substituting the words "gold certificates" for the word "gold" in provisions relating to the reserve against Federal Reserve notes and against deposits, and relating to the collateral for Federal Reserve notes.

Not yet is the story complete of the extraordinary currency legislation of the New Deal. There remains the ghastly and iniquitous silver legislation of 1934, and the scandals which followed it. But it is convenient to defer discussion of this until we have considered the new spending program of the administration.

53

The Spending Program

The spending program began in December 1933 and was officially announced on January 4, 1934. It was one more gigantic dose from the medicine man's pharmacopoeia. The administration had begun with the pledge of a reduction of twenty-five percent in the expenditures of the government. The Democratic platform had promised it, and the President promised it in his campaign speeches. The President had apparently been in earnest about it as his administration began. He had persuaded the Honorable Lewis W. Douglas, congressman from Arizona, one of the very able and upright men of the country, to assume the position of budget director with the view to carrying out the pledge. Douglas had worked strenuously and effectively, cutting out a great many government extravagances and reducing department budgets, and in the course of this resisted an immense political pressure. Expenditures were high in view of the new farm legislation, the agricultural mortgage legislation, the activities of the Reconstruction Finance Corporation, and other special expenditures, but these were looked upon as emergency things which would drop into the background with recovery. A balanced budget was aimed at in the not distant future. Taxes were raised sharply. The new agricultural program, which was to provide a great deal of money for the farmers, was still intended to be "self-supporting" in that the processing taxes on agricultural products were supposed to provide the money that the farmers got. It must be said, however, that the Agricultural Adjustment Act itself provided an extra $100 million and the Bankhead Amendment to the National Industrial Recovery Act provided an additional $100 million, both to be obtained from borrowing. But, compared with the rest of the New Deal years, 1933 was not a year of heavy spending. The total governmental expenditures for the first eleven months of 1933 were $4,518,000,000.

Begins December 1933. Expenditures were $505 million for November 1933. They moved up suddenly to $703 million in December and to $956 million in January 1934.

Keynes Had Seen President. John Maynard Keynes had seen the President. Keynes and his followers had at one time believed that monetary manipulations alone could make prosperity, but Keynes had apparently already reached the conclusion that this was inadequate. In his book, *The General Theory of Employment, Interest, and Money* (p. 164), Keynes indicates that he has reached the conclusion that monetary manipulations need to be supplemented by government control of investment, and he had apparently reached this conclusion very definitely by 1933. The President accepted the doctrine. It is possible, of course, to attribute too much influence to Keynes in this connection, and one cannot pretend to know precisely what forces moved the President to this decision.

President Promises Deficit of Seven Billion by June 30, 1934. On January 4, 1934, the President announced the great spending program in his budget message. The President indicated that there would be a federal deficit for the fiscal year 1934 (that is to say, by July 1 of 1934) of over $7 billion. We must credit the President with every sincerity in this forecast of a $7 billion deficit. We must credit him with trying by every possible method to achieve it. The late unlamented CWA, the leaf-raking and snow-shoveling program, was part of this expenditure. A multitude of other things were involved in it. The government loan organizations were pressed to lend more money. The all-important thing was to get money, borrowed money, out of the Treasury, to make prosperity.

But, Despite Honest Effort, Achieves Deficit of Only $4 Billion. But with all his good intentions, the President could not spend money that fast. The loan organizations were, after all, manned by men who had financial training and who felt a responsibility for the government's money. They could not make loans which were nothing but gifts. They had the same ingrained reluctance to give away money that the mules on the farms had exhibited in the preceding summer to trample down rows of corn or rows of cotton. It was against nature. The President's achievement was great, however. He did achieve a $4 billion deficit[1] by June 30, 1934, the end of the fiscal year.

Results of Program. An evaluation of this spending program and its effect upon business is not difficult. The curve of industrial production had dropped on the Federal Reserve Index (old series) from 100 in July to 72 in November 1933. If we attribute all of the business history of the ensuing ten months to the government's spending program, the record is very disappointing. Business rallied from the 72 index number of November 1933 to 86 in May 1934. Then the curve turned sharply downward and by September 1934 it had dropped to 71, one point below the level at which it started in November 1933. In September, moreover, there came a grave

---

[1] This includes outlays by the government corporations.

disturbance in the government bond market and a grave concern regarding the government's credit.

The Silent Panic in Government Bonds, September 1934. The published figures of government bond quotations on the New York Stock Exchange are startling enough. The 3¾'s of 1946–56, which had closed at $106^{1}/_{32}$ on September 4, dropped to $103^{21}/_{32}$ on September 12; the 3⅜'s of 1943–47, which had closed at $103^{20}/_{32}$ on August 25, dropped to $100^{10}/_{32}$ on September 12; the 3's of 1951–55, selling at $100^{5}/_{32}$ on September 4, had a low of $98^{11}/_{32}$ on September 12, and closed at $97^{27}/_{32}$ on September 17; the 4¼'s of 1947–52, closing at $112^{3}/_{32}$ on September 1, closed at $110^{30}/_{32}$ on September 5, at $109^{8}/_{32}$ on September 12, and at $108^{24}/_{32}$ on September 19. The average yield on United States government bonds, as computed by the Treasury, which had stood at 2.85 percent as the average for July 1934, rose to 3.20 percent as the average for September 1934. The three- to five-year Treasury notes performed much worse than the long-term government bonds. They had had a yield in July of only 1.5 percent, but this rose sharply in the September panic to nearly 2.5 percent.

But these figures are the publicly recorded figures based on quotations on the New York Stock Exchange. The bulk of government bond transactions is in the over-the-counter market, a market in which the bond departments of the banks play a very important role. Here there was quiet panic. Government bonds in large blocks in the worst of the panic period, September 4 to September 12, were often very difficult to sell and would sometimes break a point between sales. Telephone communications between interior banks and their New York correspondents, with the interior banks frightened and the New York banks none too happy—in which orders were given to sell large blocks "at the market"—not infrequently found the New York bank suggesting to the interior bank that the price be limited and that time be given to work off the order.[2]

The episode passed. The government bond market cleared up. The supposition was that the Stabilization Fund stepped in and manipulated the market, using the Federal Reserve banks as agents, and doing things which the securities exchange legislation of 1934 had forbidden to private financial institutions. But the government was not obliged to make a report to the Securities and Exchange Commission, and one can only state what the financial community believed at the time, rather than what was publicly

---

[2] Many country bankers came to my office in the course of the panic week in September 1934 to say something like this: "I have always looked upon my government bonds as a source of strength, and my depositors, seeing government bonds in my balance sheet, when I published, have always looked upon them as an element of strength. When I publish next time and show large holdings of government bonds, will they look upon this as an element of strength or as an element of weakness?" I listened to this for about three days, and then I had had enough. I went down to Washington. I talked with several members of the cabinet about it. I found the gravest concern among them.

known. A responsible Federal Reserve official stated privately in 1946 that only the Federal Reserve banks acted, and only with their own funds, and that the amounts involved could be obtained from their published records. It appears, however, that his memory is in fault. One finds no increase in the government bond holdings of the Federal Reserve banks for the month of September 1934. Indeed, there was a decline as compared with the month of August. Nor is there any appreciable change in the total government security holdings of the Federal Reserve banks in the period, August, September,[3] and October 1934.

Those who look upon government spending as a sure magic for bringing about business revival should study very carefully this period, November 1933 to September 1934. This episode in our very recent history should surely shake confidence (on the part of those who have it) in pump-priming through government deficits as a certain means of bringing about large results or lasting results. The first ten months brought business back to a point below where it started, and damaged the credit of the government. It was very costly, and the results at the end of ten months were less than zero.

Contrasted with Economy Program, 1921–23. It is worthwhile to contrast the spending, pump-priming policy of the government in 1933–34 with the old-fashioned economy program of the government in 1921–23, in a preceding chapter. In 1921 the government did not know about the new wisdom of Keynes. Its financial job was to protect its own solvency, to protect the currency, to reduce public expenditure as rapidly as possible from the wartime levels, and to cut taxes. Business recovery, of course, the government desired, but business recovery was for the people to bring about and not for the government to engineer. Employment was something for the people to find, not something for the government to give. The government, as a matter of course, protected the currency in its full integrity. The gold standard was unshaken. The government steadily reduced public expenditures (not including public debt retirement) from $6,403,000,000 in fiscal year 1920, to $3,295,000,000 for fiscal year 1923.

The government cut taxes, also, but not so much. Taxes in the fiscal year 1920 were $6,695,000,000 and for 1923 $4,007,000,000. The government reduced public debt in the crisis year, the fiscal year ending June 30, 1921, by $300 million. And from June 30, 1920, to June 30, 1923, it reduced public debt by approximately $2 billion.

The government steadily reduced federal employees and federal payrolls. Army and navy were, of course, reduced, and there was also a steady decline in the number of civilian employees of the government.

In August 1921 the tide turned from acute depression, and we had a labor shortage in the spring of 1923.

---

[3] See *Banking and Monetary Statistics*, pp. 343, 388.

54

The Silver Legislation
of 1934

For a long time we have had a group of senators from silver-producing states who have been alert to take advantage of every opportunity to increase the demand for silver and the price of silver in the interests of the silver mining industry. They constituted a very important element in the silver movement at the time of the Bland-Allison Act of 1878, of the Sherman silver bill of 1890, and, of course, in the Free Silver movement of 1896. Senator Teller of Colorado withdrew from the Republican Convention in 1896 after the gold standard plank was adopted, and the silver Republicans played an important role in the campaign of 1896. The silver forces in the Senate were strong enough, even after the defeat of the Free Silver movement in 1896, to prevent affirmative gold standard legislation until 1900.

Flare-up of Silver Senators in 1918. In the years that followed, they were relatively quiescent, but the movement was not dead. In 1918 it came vigorously to life when the Pittman Act was passed—which act allowed us, to be sure, to sell the silver in the United States Treasury securing the silver certificates (with a retirement of the silver certificates) to meet the urgent need for silver in India and other parts of Asia; but (here was the triumph of the silver forces) which also required us to repurchase an equivalent amount of silver at $1 an ounce when the price of silver in the world's market should go low enough to permit this. We had a great opportunity to purify our currency by eliminating silver, except as subsidiary coin. But the silver senators were strong enough to prevent this.

Silver Interests See Their Great Opportunity in 1933. Always in times of depression inflationist political forces grow active, and always the silver senators have been alert to take advantage of such a situation. In the severe depression of 1931–33, the silver interests saw their great opportunity. Senator Key Pittman of Nevada was their leader. Senator Elmer Thomas of Oklahoma, not a silver state, was the leader of the inflationists. Senator Thomas was in favor of inflation by any means whatever—greenbacks, bimetallism, silver, open market purchases of government securities by the Federal Reserve banks, debasement of the gold dollar, anything. President Roosevelt, also, was interested in every kind of monetary experiment. The farm forces in Congress, led by Senator Thomas, were sympathetic, and the stage was set. There was, moreover, a kind of sadism in the attitude of the administration and the inflationist forces. Banking opinion was strongly against silver legislation and strongly against the big inflationist movement. The bankers were in disgrace, and it was fun to humiliate and distress them further.

Senator Key Pittman's Triumph in London Conference. Senator Pittman was a member of the American delegation to the International Economic Conference at London. He had the one triumph of that conference. He succeeded in the negotiation of an agreement among the sixty-six participating nations to the effect that these governments would abandon the policy of issuing silver coins with a fineness below .800, and would substitute silver coins for low-value paper currency when conditions should permit. Moreover, the United States entered into a supplemental agreement between the chief users and chief producers of silver, under which India was to limit her sale of her silver to 35 million ounces a year, and under which the major producing countries agreed to absorb and keep off the market for a period of four years silver in the amount of 35 million ounces. The share to be absorbed by the United Stated was 24,421,410 ounces.

Silver in Thomas Amendment. We have seen that the Thomas Amendment to the Agricultural Adjustment Act of May 1933 contained silver provisions, including the provision that foreign countries debtor to the United States might pay their debts in silver, and a provision under which President Roosevelt on December 21, 1933, authorized the mints to accept domestically produced silver for coinage into silver dollars. Under this order of the President, the government retained half of the silver presented for coinage as "seigniorage," but in effect the silver producers received for their silver legal tender money at 64.5¢ per ounce, which was high above the world market.[1]

Silver Purchase Act of 1934. But the silver interests were far from satisfied. This was their great opportunity. Further silver legislation was presented, and on June 19 the President signed the Silver Purchase Act of 1934.

This act directed and authorized the secretary of the Treasury to buy silver at home and abroad until one of two objectives should be reached: (a) until the government's stock of silver should reach 25 percent of the total monetary stock of gold and silver; or (b) until the price of silver should reach $1.29 per ounce. The act also authorized and directed

---

[1] Bradford, *Money and Banking,* p. 98.

the secretary of the Treasury to issue silver certificates, the face value of the certificates to be not less than the cost of all the silver bought under the act. Silver certificates were made legal tender, and were redeemable on demand in silver dollars. The act also authorized the President to "nationalize silver," that is to say, to compel all holders of silver in the country to sell their silver to the government at a price set by the government.

The one redeeming feature in this appalling legislation was certain discretion given to the secretary of the Treasury, which meant, practically, that he could pull up if he got too much frightened.

The Silver Scandal of 1934. We had in connection with this one of the most scandalous episodes in the history of the country—speculation in silver on the basis of inside information by governmental "insiders" and their friends and political associates. Exposure was made in one case only, apparently, that of a clergyman who was alleged to have made a "nice" profit for his church by silver speculation.

Acting under the power to nationalize silver, the President on August 9, 1934, issued an order requiring the delivery to the Treasury, within a ninety-day period, of all silver in the United States at a price of 50.01¢ per fine ounce, a price high above the market on that date. The order did not apply to silver coins or manufactured silver articles or newly mined domestic silver, but rather to the stock of silver held by speculators in the country. The order was highly profitable to the bull speculators in silver.

Silver Legislation Weakens Public Credit. The silver legislation contributed to the gloom of 1934, and the action of the President especially contributed to the weakening of the public credit which culminated in the panic in government bonds in September 1934. The dollar weakened in the foreign exchange markets, and some gold was exported before the exchanges recovered.

Causes Major Crisis in China. The Treasury promptly began to buy silver in accordance with the provisions of this act. One of the theories behind the act had been that raising the price of silver would help China and improve our Far Eastern market. What happened was that our aggressive purchases of silver pulled silver out of China, reduced the silver reserves of the Chinese banks, tightened the money market, and let to a major crisis in China. The Chinese government appealed to the American government to cease these silver purchases, but without result. China first established a customs tax on exports of silver, but this proved ineffective, and in November 1935 China finally abandoned the silver standard. We were playing recklessly with the welfare of foreign countries as an incident to the iniquitous triumph of a special interest in the United States, as well as playing recklessly with the stability of our own currency.

Volume of Silver Purchases—Rising Price of Silver. Silver purchases were made on a great scale. The government silver stock at the close of 1934 reached 1,003,000,000 ounces. Meanwhile gold had continued to come into the country and we were still far from the 25 percent goal. Our gold holdings at the end of the year amounted to $8,238,000,000. Consequently the administration was faced with the necessity of acquiring an additional 1,122,000,000 ounces of silver[2] to comply with the provisions of the law.

Purchases of silver continued in 1935. The world price rose. It reached 64.5¢ in April 1935. On April 10 the President raised the Treasury's buying of domestic silver to 71.11¢ per ounce. The market price continued to rise, pushed up by speculative purchases.

Injures Mexico. A New York bank was visited at about this time by officials of the National Bank of Mexico, who were gravely apprehensive that the continued rise in silver would make Mexico's silver coin worth more as bullion than as coin. They wondered also if anything could be done to stop our government from further buying, as they dreaded the money market disorder that would come from the melting down of Mexican coins for export as bullion. Nothing, however, could be done.

The Treasury and the speculators went on forcing up the price of silver. The Treasury price went to 77.57¢ per ounce on April 23, 1935. Speculative forces pushed the price still higher to 80¢, but the Treasury by this time had had enough. It refused to raise its price further and it ceased aggressive purchases of foreign silver. The world price of silver dropped to around 45¢ by the end of the year, and continued close to that figure during 1936. But the Treasury[3] continued to buy silver from the domestic producers at the 77.57¢ figure set on April 23, 1935.

New Silver Certificates Add $1.3 Billion to Excess Reserves. Silver certificates issued against the silver purchased by the Treasury appeared on a great scale. In December 1942 the total of silver certificates outstanding was $1,751,000,000, representing an increase of roughly $1,300,000,000 from early 1933. The additional silver certificates constituted net additions to the reserves of the member banks of the country, and were responsible for $1,300,000,000 of the excess reserves of the member banks, which we shall later discuss.

---

[2] *Ibid.*, p. 101.
[3] *Ibid.*

55

Government Confusion, Government Hostility, and Private Enterprise

The impact of these multitudinous measures—industrial, agricultural, financial, monetary, and other—upon a bewildered industrial and financial community was extraordinarily heavy. We must add the effect of continuing disquieting utterances by the President. The President had castigated the bankers in his inaugural speech. He had made a slurring comparison of British and American bankers in a speech in the summer of 1934. When government bonds broke badly in September 1934, conversations were held with various members of the cabinet and others in Washington, as well as with Colonel House in New York. One cabinet member said that, regardless of the merits of the individual reforms which the President had been pushing, the pace was obviously too fast, more was being done than could be digested. But he added that more was coming, including a Social Security Act which would impose heavy tax burdens upon business corporations. He and others of the President's advisers were trying to hold him down, and were trying to get him to make reassuring statements to offset the bad effects of things which he had said regarding bankers and finance. But his hopes were not high.

At this same time the effort was made to find in Washington if there were any man who understood it all, if there were any man charged with responsibility for seeing all the different parts of the New Deal in their interrelations, if there were any man who knew all the new bureaus that had been created and could see the government as a whole. One could find no such man. One could find no man who claimed this knowledge or who knew anybody else who had it. We were turning loose forces of incalculable magnitude so rapidly that the men who were in official position could know only the parts for which they themselves had administrative responsibility.

That private enterprise could survive and rally in the midst of so great a disorder is an amazing demonstration of the vitality of private enterprise. It did revive. From the extreme gloom of September 1934 there came a rally in the autumn.

Through manipulation by the Treasury of the Federal Reserve banks, government bonds rose in price. The yield on three- to five-year Treasury notes, which had risen from 1.5 percent to nearly 2.5 percent, dropped again to 1.75 percent by the end of the year.[1]

The price of industrial stocks moved up very moderately in the autumn. The Federal Reserve Index of Production (1923–25 = 100), which had dropped to 71 in September 1934, moved up to 90 by January 1935. Levels were still very low, but the vitality of private enterprise under extremely adverse conditions was manifest.

---

[1] *Federal Reserve Charts*, November 9, 1939, p. 21.

56

Supreme Court Decision
on Gold Clauses,
February 1935

To the end of 1934 there had been no resistance of an effective kind to the President's policies. His domination over the Congress seemed complete. The Supreme Court had no important cases before it which would test his powers. In early 1935 there came a test. Four cases came before the Supreme Court involving the constitutionality of the legislation of June 5, 1933, which abrogated the gold clauses in public and private contracts. It became evident that the government in defending this abrogation of the gold clauses was to have hard sledding. The Supreme Court began its hearings on January 8, 1935. Some of the justices manifested a very critical attitude toward the presentation of the government's case by the government's counsel. The decision was delayed and was finally rendered on February 18. There was a good deal of disquiet in the financial community pending the settlement of this case. Financial markets and the foreign exchange markets were disturbed. There was a great deal of disquiet, too, in administration circles.

Uphold Abrogation in Private Contracts, Five to Four. The decision was finally made by a 5 to 4 vote upholding the abrogation of the gold clauses in private contracts, on the ground that to uphold the gold clauses would allow private contracts to interfere with the government's constitutional power to regulate the value of money.

But Not in Government Obligations—Unanimously. With respect to the government's own obligation under the gold clauses, all nine of the justices concurred in holding that the legislation of June 5, 1933, was unconstitutional. The gold clauses in the government's own contracts were still binding on the conscience of the government.

Where Loss Could Be Shown. The Court, however, refused to allow damages on the ground that "the plaintiff has not shown or attempted to show that in relation to buying power, he has sustained any loss whatsoever." This reference to "buying power" was a departure from all precedent, but it left open to future litigants the possibility of collecting from the government where they could show loss. In particular, it left to foreign holders of the United States government bonds with gold clauses, who lived in gold standard countries, a very clear case. They could certainly demonstrate a loss. The President called upon the Congress to forestall this by closing the Court of Claims to suits of this sort, but the Congress, shamed and shocked by the rebuke of the Supreme Court, declined to do this immediately, and instead accepted an amendment offered by Senator McAdoo which left such litigants the right for a period of six months to bring suit in the Court of Claims. This legislation was approved on August 27, 1935. No successful suits were brought during this interval.[1]

Evaluation of Chief Justice Hughes' Attitude. The decision of the Supreme Court in the gold cases represented a statesmanlike attitude on the part of the Court, concerned more with the preservation of constitutional government than with the rights of a particular litigant. On precedents the Court should have upheld the gold clauses, but there was, after all, the provision of the Constitution giving the Congress the right to coin money and to regulate the value thereof, and of foreign coins. The Court had yet to consider a great deal of legislation where the Congress had acted without any explicit constitutional sanction at all, and where the Congress had clearly acted in violation of the Constitution. It had to deal with a President impatient of constitutional restraints, who might well undertake to override the courts, and who in fact did in 1937 attempt precisely that thing. Chief Justice Hughes was taking a long view when he cast the deciding vote in favor of abrogating the gold clauses in early 1935. The Court must fight, the Court must defend the Constitution as far as it could, but the Court must also consider congressional opinion and public opinion. In bowing before the storm at one point, it strengthened its case for a fight at other points.

Before considering the action of the Supreme Court, however, with respect to NRA and with respect to the processing taxes under the AAA, it is best first to discuss the first successful congressional opposition to the New Deal financial program. This came in the Banking Act of 1935.

---

[1] Ericksson, *The Supreme Court and the New Deal* (Rosemead, Calif., 1940), pp. 95–96.

57

First Successful Resistance to New Deal—Banking Act of 1935

The Banking Act of 1935 as introduced into the House of Representatives was a bill dangerous in the extreme.

We do not here discuss Title I or Title III of the act—Title I being concerned primarily with the Federal Deposit Insurance Corporation and providing for the insurance of bank deposits up to $5,000, Title III being concerned with a variety of technical amendments to the Banking Act.

Title II Attacks Liquidity of Bank Assets. The heart of the danger was in Title II, which was designed to amend the Federal Reserve Act in such a way as to give legal sanction to dangerous, unsound theories of money and credit. It was designed to give the government power to regulate the *quantity* of bank deposits with a view to regulating the level of prices and the volume of employment, instead of regulating the *quality* of bank assets with a view to keeping bank credit sound. It contained provisions for bank loans on real estate mortgages running for twenty years, and up to seventy-five percent of the value of the real estate. It authorized the Federal Reserve banks to lend on "any sound asset," instead of limiting them, as the original statute had done, to commercial paper of ninety days or less maturity and to paper secured by United States government bonds. It tended to take away all distinctions regarding liquidity in bank assets. It substituted a legal-conventional liquidity for natural liquidity. If the Federal Reserve banks would take anything a banker had, then a shortsighted banker would have much less incentive to concern himself about the liquidity of his assets. It proposed, moreover, to put open market operations under the control of the Federal Reserve Board, a governmental body, instead of leaving them in the hands of the Federal Reserve banks.

The preparation of the measure had been dominated by the Honorable Marriner S. Eccles, governor of the Federal Reserve Board, who was an ardent advocate of the theory that the regulation of the quantity of money could make or unmake business prosperity and could control commodity prices. Eccles, an exceedingly able man, was an extreme Keynesian in his general doctrines.

Senator Glass Fights—Turns Bad Bill into Harmless Bill. The banking community was frightened but felt hopeless. The administration was all-powerful, and Governor Eccles was powerful in the administration. Senator Carter Glass was aghast at the tenor of the bill. He was not chairman of the Senate Committee on Banking and Currency, but was the ranking member, and was by all odds the member with the greatest prestige. The chairman of the committee, Senator Duncan Fletcher of Florida, was in favor of the bill, and a majority of the members of the committee favored the bill. Senator Glass succeeded, however, in having a subcommittee appointed of which he was made chairman, and prepared to hold exhaustive hearings which would give opportunity for expert opinion in the country to be presented regarding the measure.

Senator Glass was no longer young. The task was a hard one. His subcommittee sat from April 19, 1935, to June 3, 1935. It was at first difficult to get the bankers to fight. They were afraid. The senator said very simply, "If the bankers will fight, I'll help them. I can't do the job alone."[1]

Senator Glass started his task with a hostile full committee and with a hostile subcommittee. By sheer force of logic and the presentation of evidence, he gradually won his subcommittee over.[2] The subcommittee unanimously recommended to the full committee amendments that almost completely changed the character of Title II. He won the full committee. He turned a dangerously bad bill into a relatively innocuous bill, and a bill which even had some good features. Over powerful administration opposition, he won the Senate to his version of the bill. Over powerful administration opposition he dominated the conference committee which settled the differences between the House version and the Senate version, and finally

---

[1] This writer had a part in this fight. Behind the bill was a book called *The Supply and Control of Money in the United States,* by Lauchlin Currie, who had been made technical adviser of the Federal Reserve Board and whose book embodied the economic theories that lay behind Title II of the bill. In an address before the New York Chapter of the American Statistical Association on April 26, 1935, I undertook a comprehensive refutation of this book. There were 100,000 copies of this address issued at the time by the Chase National Bank, but the supply has long since been exhausted. It was published virtually in full in *The Annalist* (issued by the *New York Times*), May 3, 1935, and it appears in full in Senate Committee on Banking and Currency, *Hearings on S.1715 and H.R.7617,* April 19 to June 3, 1935, pp. 439–56. Dr. Currie had written a very vulnerable book. It was important solely because it was the basis of a major legislative proposal. Dr. Currie had been very active before the committees of Congress in supporting the original version of the banking bill of 1935.

[2] I was called to testify before the subcommittee on May 16, 1935. I had the satisfaction of feeling that two of the senators, members of the subcommittee, who had been uncertain as to their position with respect to the matter, and who had been asking preceding witnesses searching questions in the effort to get important points cleared up, definitely turned that day against the administration draft of Title II. They were Senators McAdoo and Couzens.

both House and Senate adopted the Glass version of the bill. It was a tremendously heartening thing.

Triumph of Senator Glass and of Facts and Logic. It represented, first of all, the power of logic and facts and evidence, which had not been allowed to have much play in connection with the preceding New Deal measures. It represented, in the second place, the triumph of personality. Senator Glass had immense prestige in the Senate. His colleagues had great affection for him, and the greatest respect for him, and they knew that he understood banking as none of the rest of them did. It was almost the first evidence, moreover, of congressional willingness to oppose the President on any matter.

The main lines of sound banking practice were protected. Law did not interfere with the banking tradition that emphasized liquidity in bank assets. The real estate loan provisions were sharply restricted, though they remained too lax.

Law Tries to Make Board of Governors Independent. There was a reconstitution of the Federal Reserve System, but the effort was made to give it greater independence, rather than make it more dependent upon the administration. The secretary of the Treasury and the comptroller of the currency were eliminated from the Federal Reserve Board. The terms of members of the Federal Reserve Board were lengthened to fourteen years and members were made ineligible for reappointment. The salaries were placed at $15,000. It was hoped that men with this salary, with fourteen years tenure and with ineligibility to reappointment, might prove themselves to be courageous and independent.

There was humiliation for the executives of the Federal Reserve banks in that the title "governor" was taken away from them and reserved for members of the Federal Reserve Board. Formerly only one member of the Federal Reserve Board had the title "governor," while the head of each of the twelve Federal Reserve banks was called governor. With this change every member of the Federal Reserve Board became a governor and the heads of the Federal Reserve banks became merely presidents. The Federal Reserve Board became the "Board of Governors of the Federal Reserve System."

Open Market Committee. The original draft of the act had sought to concentrate control of open market operations in the hands of the Federal Reserve Board. The act as finally passed created an open market committee in which the board had a majority of one, but in which, also, "representatives" (in practice, certain of the presidents) of the Federal Reserve banks should be members. As one banker put it at the time, "We may hope that there will be at least one honest and courageous man on the board."

"Any Sound Asset." The act made a concession to the idea of rediscounts based on "any sound asset," though it changed the language to "secured to the satisfaction of the Federal Reserve bank." It provided, however, that

discounts of this character should be subject to a penalty rate as compared with discounts of regularly eligible paper, the rate on such loans to be at least one-half percent above the discount rate on eligible paper. There was further a limitation to four months' maturity for such loans.

It is a confession of weakness for a bank to have to resort to loans "secured to the satisfaction of the Federal Reserve Bank," and there is a stigma attached to paying the penalty rate. The one-half percent differential is not enough, but it is at least something. There remained a real incentive for the member bank to keep its assets liquid and to keep an adequate supply of eligible paper.

Limits Power of Board over Member Bank Reserve Requirements. Where Title II in its original form would have given the Federal Reserve authorities unlimited authority over reserve requirements of member banks (a power they already had under the Thomas Amendment to the Agricultural Act of 1933), Senator Glass succeeded in getting a real limitation upon this power. Reserve requirements could not be reduced below the 1917 statutory levels, which, for demand deposits, were thirteen percent in the central reserve cities, ten percent in the reserve cities, and seven percent for country banks, and which for time deposits were three percent for all classes of banks. These figures remained statutory minima. The Banking Act of 1935 allowed the Federal Reserve authorities to double these reserve requirements and to vary them within the statutory limits. This meant, for the New York and Chicago banks, a range of thirteen to twenty-six percent, for reserve city banks, a range of ten to twenty percent, and for country banks, a range of seven to fourteen percent on demand deposits; while all classes of banks had a range of three to six percent on time deposits. We shall later have occasion to discuss the use made of this power by the Federal Reserve authorities.

58

Taxation Under the New Deal—The Redistribution of Wealth

Taxes in 1934 in Upper Brackets Highest in World—Redistribution of Wealth. The New Deal tax policy from the beginning has been more concerned with the redistribution of wealth than with raising revenue. When the Congress, in the period of the interregnum between the election of 1932 and the inauguration on March 4, 1933, was pledging a balanced budget and when something like an agreement had been reached that a sales tax would be employed in the effort to reach a balanced budget, President-elect Roosevelt intervened with a protest[1] which led to the abandonment of the sales tax proposal. Revenue legislation in 1933 raised income tax rates very sharply in the higher brackets and imposed a five percent withholding tax on corporate dividends, a tax subsequently abandoned. In 1934 there were further drastic increases, both in income tax rates, particularly in the higher brackets, and in federal estate taxes, bringing them to levels unmatched in the rest of the world.

Huey Long Frightens Roosevelt in 1935. Then suddenly in 1935, in the midst of the summer heat, President Roosevelt demanded of the Congress immediate action on a new and incredibly drastic tax proposal. Senator Huey Long of Louisiana had "stolen the show." He had made an immense propaganda over the radio for a "Share the Wealth" program. It seemed that there was danger that Senator Long rather than the President might become the leader of the radical New Deal movement.

President Demands Unconstitutional Tax Rider on Senate Bill. The President demanded that great increases in taxes be added as a rider to a pending Senate bill, and put through with great speed, despite the constitutional provision that tax bills must originate in the House of Representatives, and despite the obvious need for careful study if sound tax legislation were to be adopted. An immense protest went up over the country. Walter

---

[1] *New York Times,* December 28, 1932.

Lippmann, in particular, did valiant service in demanding more time for the study of such a proposal. Denial was made for the President that he had demanded that this change be made as a rider to a Senate bill. Senator Pat Harrison, chairman of the Senate Finance Committee, protected the President by taking responsibility for the action, but nobody believed Senator Harrison's statement. Everybody knew that Senator Harrison was far too sound and sensible a man to have originated such an idea himself, and there was general expression of respect rather than condemnation for the senator as he assumed the role of "goat" for the administration.

But Public Protest Forced Constitutional Procedure—The Revenue Bill of 1935. A more regular procedure was adopted, and the proposal[2] was embodied in a House of Representatives bill, H.R. 8974.

This measure proposed in the first place a drastic increase in the federal personal income tax rates. The following table shows these proposed rates, and also shows how high the rates had already gone in the 1934 tax legislation.

EXISTING AND PROPOSED
PERSONAL INCOME TAX RATES*

Income magnitude	Existing rates, federal and New York State combined	Proposed federal and existing New York rates combined
$ 20,000	13.5	13.5
30,000	18.4	18.4
100,000	37.7	41.3
200,000	51.0	55.2
300,000	56.7	62.5
1,000,000	65.3	76.1
5,000,000	69.9	83.8

* *Chase Economic Bulletin,* August 6, 1935, p. 10.

Federal Inheritance Tax to Be Added to Federal Estate Tax. A second major proposal in the bill was the addition of a federal inheritance tax to the existing federal and state estate and inheritance taxes.

An estate tax is one levied on the estate as a whole without reference to the size of the individual shares in the estate. An inheritance tax is a tax imposed upon the distributive shares to each of the separate heirs. The following table shows how high these taxes had already gone in the upper brackets before the new federal proposal, shows the proposed additional

[2] The House Committee on Ways and Means toned down the original Roosevelt proposals a little, particularly in the matter of graduating corporate income tax rates.

federal inheritance tax, and shows the total rate if the pending tax bill were to be enacted. For simplicity in calculation, the assumption is made that there is only one direct heir.

EXISTING AND PROPOSED RATES
OF DEATH DUTIES*

Net estate (before exemption)	Federal estate tax (1934 rates) (%)	New York State transfer tax rate (%)	Total tax rate before proposed federal inheritance tax	Tax rate, proposed federal inheritance tax	Total rate if proposed bill enacted
$ 20,000	....	0.75	0.75	....	0.75
50,000	....	0.90	0.90	....	0.90
100,000	1.50	0.95	2.45	5.338	7.66
200,000	5.20	1.225	6.425	13.099	18.68
400,000	8.70	2.362	11.063	20.64	29.42
1,000,000	13.59	4.245	17.835	29.24	41.86
4,000,000	23.62	8.786	32.404	41.85	60.69
10,000,000	33.20	13.354	46.555	49.77	73.16
20,000,000	38.59	16.672	55.271	57.19	80.85
50,000,000	41.84	18.669	60.508	66.77	86.88

* *Chase Economic Bulletin,* August 6, 1935, p. 9. Only one direct heir.

These rates, before the proposed increases, far outran any rates to be found then in any other part of the world. The top British rate on death duties, which were the highest in the world, was fifty percent, with an additional one percent inheritance tax or succession duty on direct heirs— the succession duty ran up to ten percent for bequests to strangers in England. The next highest rate in foreign countries was in Saskatchewan, where the figures ran from about thirteen percent on estates of $1 million to twenty-four percent on estates of $50 million.

Increased Rates Could Add Little to Revenue. There was resistance of a sort to the drastic proposals. The Treasury estimates of the additional yield from the new legislation showed that it could not make any real contribution to federal revenues. We had already reached the point of diminishing returns. It was a measure aimed at the redistribution of wealth.

Federal Inheritance Tax Rejected, but Estate and Income Taxes Radically Raised. The proposal to add a federal inheritance tax to the existing federal estate tax was defeated, but the federal estate tax was increased. The proposed increases in federal income taxes were accepted pretty much as they were made. The following tables show taxes after the 1935 legislation was completed.

TAX RATES IN 1936*

Estate Taxes			Income Taxes**		
Net estate (before exemption)	Total federal and New York estate taxes	% Tax to estate	Net income	Total federal and New York State income taxes	% Tax to net income
$ 50,000	$ 500	1.000	$ 2,000	$ ...	0.000
100,000	5,000	5.000	4,000	98	2.450
200,000	20,900	10.450	8,000	508	6.350
300,000	40,300	13.433	12,000	1,148	9.567
400,000	61,100	15.275	16,000	1,918	11.988
1,000,000	220,100	22.010	20,000	2,783	13.915
2,000,000	569,300	28.465	40,000	8,773	21.933
3,000,000	982,500	32.750	80,000	27,263	34.080
4,000,000	1,459,700	36.493	100,000	40,063	40.063
9,000,000	4,517,300	50.192	200,000	110,938	55.469
10,000,000	5,204,300	52.043	240,000	140,488	58.537
20,000,000	12,303,300	61.517	280,000	170,638	60.942
30,000,000	19,602,500	65.342	320,000	201,388	62.934
40,000,000	26,902,500	67.256	400,000	263,788	65.947
50,000,000	34,202,500	68.405	600,000	425,688	70.948
75,000,000	52,702,100	70.269	1,000,000	758,638	75.864
150,000,000	108,202,100	72.135	2,000,000	1,608,613	80.431
			4,000,000	3,328,588	83.215

* Prepared by tax department of Chase National Bank, and reproduced in *Chase Economic Bulletin,* May 12, 1936, p. 11.

** *Income taxes.* Exemption—Married man with no dependents. Earned income credit of $300.

Dividend income—Where dividends from domestic corporations are included in net income, reduce amount of tax by four percent of dividend income.

Rates Paralyzed Initiative of Rich Men. It will be seen from the tables above that the top rate on income taxes went practically as high as the President's proposal, but that the rate on death duties, which would have been 86.88 percent on an estate of $50 million if the President's proposal had been adopted, was made only 68.405 percent. But these rates were high enough to paralyze initiative on the part of men of large fortunes.

The Case of a Man with $30 Million. Reasonably typical is the case of one rich man who, at the age of 25, had inherited an estate of about $12 million—some thirty years before these 1935 taxes came. He had nursed his $12 million into an estate of about $30 million during those thirty years. He had done it by a kind of activity particularly helpful and useful to the country, the financing of new inventions and new explorations, the purchase of shares in new and promising businesses. He had taken a great many risks, knowing that many of them would turn out badly, but counting on a few of them to turn out well enough so that the profits on the successful ones would offset the much more numerous losses on the unsuccessful ones.

New ventures are usually not financed through the sale of securities to the public. In buoyant stock markets, when speculative excitement runs high, exceptions occur, as the recent Kaiser-Frazer automobile venture shows. In this case however, the new venture was led by men who had previously had business success, who were conspicuous, and who were supposed to be rich. But the general rule is that before public issues can be made successful, the enterprise must have established itself, must have an earning history, must give evidence of stability.

The mortality among new ventures is high, and this is particularly true when the new venture means, not merely the starting of a new firm, but also a real innovation. It sometimes happens that such ventures can be financed by men of small means but great enthusiasm, who convince other people that the project is workable and thus accumulate the necessary funds for making a start. But in American economic history such new ventures have often been financed by men of fortunes sufficiently large so that they could scatter their risks. The small capitalist cannot afford to put everything he has into one of these ventures. The hazard is too great. The large capitalist can scatter his risks.

In the case of the individual above referred to, a vigorous man fifty-five years old, the effects of the new taxes were paralyzing. More than three-fourths of any profits which he might have from a new venture would be taken away from him by income taxes. Any losses which he might incur from a new venture would be his own. But further, if he should die, his estate would have to pay the federal government and to the state of New York (but chiefly to the federal government) $19,602,500, or 65.342 percent of the estate. How could an estate pay this tax if it were spread out in new ventures, in assets for which no ready market existed, in assets which could not be liquidated without great loss? It was a painful thing to watch him turn his energies from creative production to consultation with tax lawyers as to how he could save as much as possible for his heirs. It was a painful thing to watch a vigorous man of fifty-five turning from creative activities to preparation for death.

He fought hard against the advice of his business advisers and the advice of his lawyers. He still wanted to take part in enterprise. But their arguments were overwhelming, and he had to yield, with the thought of his family in his mind. He carried some $10 million in cash to have it ready to pay the first installment in death duties. He withdrew as far as possible from illiquid investments, and turned to investments of a high degree of liquidity, including municipal tax-exempt securities—not one of which he had owned before.

He had a beautiful country estate which had cost a quarter of a million dollars. This would have been a dreadful thing to die with, under the new tax laws. Nobody could afford to own it with the tax laws as they were, and it was absolutely unmarketable. But at appraised value as part of the estate it would have been subject to a sixty-five percent tax. He tried to give it away to the Boy Scouts and to the YMCA, but neither of them could afford to take it. He finally succeeded in giving it to the county.

One may well raise the question as to just what good it did to the people of the United States to put this typical man in this position.

The spirit of enterprise in this particular individual was not killed by four years of this kind of tax problem. In 1938 when Senator Pat Harrison finally succeeded in substituting a capital gains tax of fifteen percent for the income tax on profits from capital assets held over eighteen months, he was jubilant. He broke away from his lawyers and his conservative financial advisers, and he undertook a new venture. He still knew that he must keep highly liquid in order to protect his estate at the time of his death, but part of his liquid capital he was going to use in doing things.

The Importance to the Country of Entrepreneurs—The Profit Motive. The man with a $2 million estate, or with an $80,000 income, was greatly inhibited, as the foregoing table shows. It is difficult to exaggerate the importance to the country of the motives and attitudes of the men who have the management of and proprietary interest in the industries of the country. Leadership of economic activity rests with a body of dynamic men— enterprisers, risk takers, men fertile in new ideas and quick in the appreciation and evaluation of new ideas.

The profit motive and the desire for the accumulation of wealth are very powerful with these men. These are not their only motives. They desire also the approbation of their fellow men. They desire triumph in competition. They desire power. They find an immense satisfaction in achievement and in efficient work. They have the "instinct of workmanship." But these motives are found also among men who choose other careers than the business career, and the distinguishing motive of the businessman, as compared with the man in certain of the less lucrative professions, is a much greater relative intensification of the profit motive.

The scholar may express his personality in a book which he hopes will live. The creative businessman expresses his personality in the development of a business which he hopes will live. And in order that the business may be created and may grow and live and may continue to express his personality, he must be able to acquire and to conserve economic resources. It is not necessarily profit for its own sake, but, in part at least, profit and wealth as instruments for carrying through his creative purposes.

The Continuity of Family Plans. In conspicuous cases, well advertised in the headlines, sons of rich men have had escapades which suggest that they may not be the best successors of their fathers in the conduct of great businesses. But the man who reaches his conclusions, not on the basis of the headlines, but rather on the basis of the study of the credit files of a great bank dealing with many business houses (including banks), reaches the conclusion, that it is usually fortunate when a son trained by an able father succeeds that father as the owner of a business. Such sons do not have prominent places in the sensational headlines and do not get into the statistics based on such headlines. Such sons are not always chosen by their fathers as the active heads of the businesses. Sons-in-law, other kinsmen, or capable and trusted lieutenants of the fathers may be chosen in that capacity. But the sons, as owners, tend to keep the continuity of organization and policy.

Family ties have weakened in the United States in the last generation, and family tradition and family pride are not so important with us as they once were. But the family is still a tremendously vital institution, with a vitally important social function, and is particularly significant from the standpoint of keeping the continuity of ideals, plans, purposes, and organization in our economic system. We should not ruthlessly destroy this family function.

The Limits of Desirable Death Duties. We should not be hostile to inheritance taxes and estate taxes as such. Rather, we should favor reasonable taxes of this kind, though recognizing that, to the extent that they are a tax on capital, the proceeds of the tax ought to be used by the state for capital purposes, including the reduction of public debt, rather than dissipated in operating expenditures. There is good ground for the belief that vast fortunes involve undesirable political and social potentialities, and that public policy should be directed: (a) toward making sure that such fortunes cannot be accumulated in antisocial ways, and (b) toward holding down the growth and the transmission of vast fortunes to the extent that this can be done without checking the accumulation of capital and the spirit of enterprise. The practical question is how far we can go without damaging the community in these matters.

How far does concern for his children and his grandchildren and his great-grandchildren constitute a stimulus which keeps a rich man of forty, fifty, fifty-five, or sixty active in business, when he might instead retire and enjoy himself in spending money? There can be little question, I think, that concern for his children is a motive of vast importance, and that concern for his grandchildren already born is a motive of vast importance. Concern for his great-grandchildren is more remote. It is there, but he would often be disposed to let them take their chances. Inheritance taxes, without slowing down the activities of the creative businessman, could be pushed far enough so that if a great fortune is to reach grandchildren and great-grandchildren, each generation must add very substantially to it by productive activity.

Estate and inheritance taxes graduated up to fifty percent in the case of a great fortune, with administrative procedure such that the problem of liquidation is a manageable one, might not spoil the incentives of the founder of the fortune, though fifty percent is dangerously high.

59

The Undistributed
Profits Tax of 1936

But the New Deal was not content with striking at the accumulation of capital by well-to-do men, or with forcing the dissipation of the capital already accumulated in great fortunes through estate taxes that could not possibly be paid out of income and that must be paid by the liquidation of capital assets. In 1936 it struck a heavy blow at the accumulation of capital out of corporate profits by proposing a confiscatory tax on profits retained for use in the business.

The proposal was designed, for one thing, to force the distribution of corporate profits by dividends, so that a greatly increased volume of dividends might become subject to income taxes. The corporation itself was to be relieved from corporate income taxes and from the corporate tax on capital stock. The proposal involved, also, taxing dividends received by stockholders at the "normal" rate from which they were then exempt.

Corporate Savings, *Not* Income, *Taxed—Terrific Rates Proposed.* Corporations would be taxed, not on their *incomes*, but on their *savings*. If a corporation paid out all its profits in dividends, it paid no tax at all. To the extent that it saved, however, it would have to pay a terrific tax, as shown by the tables on page 373.

The tax rates indicated in the bill were those of the second column in our table, but the significant rate is that shown in the third column, namely, the tax as a percentage of corporate *savings,* which is derived from the comparison of the first and second columns. For corporations with incomes of less than $10,000 a year, the tax on savings ran from 10 to 42.14 percent, while for corporations with incomes of more than $10,000 a year, the tax ran from 40 to 73.91 percent.

The Business Community Fights—Their Arguments. The business community made a magnificent fight against this bill and the congressional committees listened to them, in the hearings before both the House committee on Ways and Means and the Senate Finance Committee.

Retaining Profits Major Cause of Country's Growth. Case after case was presented showing the history of small businesses which, employing three or four laborers, had in relatively short periods of time (fifteen or twenty years) grown into very substantial businesses employing several hundreds of laborers, by withholding dividends from stockholders, putting profits back into the business, and expanding. The classical case, of course, was that of the Ford automobile company, which grew to be the biggest business in the country by precisely this process.

THE PROPOSED TAX ON CORPORATE SAVINGS FROM ADJUSTED NET INCOMES OF $10,000 OR LESS*

Percentage of adjusted net income undistributed (%)	The tax as a percentage of adjusted net income (%)	The tax as a percentage of corporate savings (%)
1	.10	10.00
5	.50	10.00
10	1.00	10.00
15	2.25	15.00
20	3.50	17.50
30	7.50	25.00
40	13.00	32.50
50	18.50	37.00
60	24.00	40.00
70	29.50	42.14

* See *Chase Economic Bulletin*, May 12, 1936, p. 16.

THE PROPOSED TAX ON CORPORATE SAVINGS FROM ADJUSTED NET INCOMES OF MORE THAN $10,000*

Percentage of adjusted net income undistributed (%)	The tax as a percentage of adjusted net income (%)	The tax as a percentage of corporate savings (%)
1	.4	40.00
5	2.0	40.00
10	4.0	40.00
15	6.5	43.33
20	9.0	45.00
30	15.0	50.00
40	25.0	62.50
50	35.0	70.00
57.5	42.5	73.91

* See *Chase Economic Bulletin*, May 12, 1936, p. 16.

The New Deal in Maturity, 1933–39

The argument was pressed that this was one of the greatest contributions to the country's growth. The agrument was pressed that there was need for development of new industries giving increased employment to offset the dwindling of old industries.

Tax Would Create Monopolies. The second major point, a corollary, was that the penalty tax on undistributed profits would operate to create and entrench monopolies through preventing the rise of vigorous competitors.

It was pointed out that there were great corporations with vast surpluses already created which would escape federal taxation entirely or almost entirely, because they were then paying out practically all of their current incomes as dividends, whereas small and growing businesses with inadequate surpluses would be heavily taxed.

Savings in Good Times Offset Losses in Bad Times. Stress was laid on the immense variation in the need for large surpluses in business, depending on the regularity or irregularity of their annual profits. Those with less stable incomes must save for the rainy day or be ruined when the years of losses came.

The immense variation in incomes of virtually all businesses with the cycle of prosperity, crisis, and depression was stressed, and the need to save in the periods of prosperity in order to be safe in periods of depression was emphasized.

Capital losses in the preceding period of depression had weakened many corporations, and the need to rebuild their capital was urged.

Many Businesses Under Contract to Retain Profits. It was pointed out that many businesses were under contract to refrain from paying out dividends in whole or in part, under sinking fund provisions or under other contracts with creditors, or were required to build up reserves by state laws. Some concession had been made to this in the House bill, which recognized contracts made in writing prior to March 3, 1936, as justifying the retention of profits without the payment of the progressive rate, though even the profits retained were to be subject to the very high rate of 22.5 percent.

Bank "Lines of Credit" and Dividends. This concession took no account, however, of the very common case where bank lines of credit were subject to the understanding that dividends be withheld in whole or in part. Bank lines of credit were not usually written contracts but verbal understandings.

Bank credit men were aghast. There is a constant issue between bank credit men and many borrowing corporations over dividend policy. In many cases bank loans can be made safe if dividends are withheld which would be entirely unsafe if all profits were paid out. The new tax would have presented an almost insuperable obstacle to the conservative corporation director and the bank credit official in the case of the underfinanced corporation. They would be met by the argument that no tax at all is paid if all profits are paid out in dividends, while the government would take from forty percent to over seventy-three percent of every dollar saved; and the further argument would be made that competitors were reducing costs by paying out dividends and thus escaping taxes.

The Law Hits Heavy Industries. The argument was made, too, that reduced savings by corporations meant reduction demand directed toward the heavy industries. Business corporations constitute the main market for capital equipment. The securities market was supplying them with very little capital for such purposes. If they could not save their profits, they could not buy any new capital equipment.

Business Receiving Little Capital from Securities Market. The following table will show how low the volume of new capital issues had fallen in the United States, both as compared with earlier times and as compared with foreign countries. The securities legislation of 1933 and 1934, and the interpretations given this legislation by the Securities and Exchange Commission, had largely paralyzed new issues in the United States.

INDICES OF NEW DOMESTIC CORPORATE CAPITAL ISSUES IN DIFFERENT COUNTRIES*

	United States- (1923 = 100)	United Kingdom (1923 = 100)	Germany (1924 = 100)	Japan (1923 = 100)	Switzer- land (1923 = 100)	Italy (1923 = 100)	Nether- lands (1923 = 100)
1923.........	100	100	...	100	100	100	100
1924.........	114.9	132.1	100	67.7	245.1	152.2	352.7
1925.........	136.7	195.5	286.6	88.2	228.5	225.9	296.6
1926.........	142.5	208.4	606.7	111.9	159.2	142.6	295.0
1927.........	176.7	260.5	635.5	102.8	169.1	79.4	229.6
1928.........	202.8	324.2	638.3	98.3	204.7	135.5	707.7
1929.........	303.6	235.9	382.2	70.3	523.2	182.8	505.5
1930.........	170.1	188.4	526.2	30.8	458.8	154.8	321.7
1931.........	58.9	63.0	340.1	37.6	560.8	108.8	67.7
1932.........	12.3	124.0	82.5	29.7	212.9	91.6	47.6
1933.........	6.1	140.7	92.0	76.6	275.2	84.0	18.9
1934.........	6.8	157.9	121.4	90.0	182.7	89.1	79.2
1935.........	15.3	239.6		96.1			
1936 (1st q.) .	15.8						

* *Chase Economic Bulletin,* May 12, 1936, p. 13.

The argument was urged, too, that a tax on corporate savings of this magnitude would force a great many small corporations to disincorporate and to revert to partnership or individual ownership.

Basis of Law the Fallacy of Oversavings. Behind this proposal was the general fallacy of "oversavings." There was the belief that the troubles of 1929 had grown out of corporate savings in the preceding years. The Treasury at first denied that it entertained this theory. An official spokesman for the Treasury said before the House Committee on Ways and

Means, "This is not a reform bill. This is a tax bill." But the same Treasury spokesman also said, "The greatest depression in the history of the country followed the accumulation of the greatest corporate surpluses in the history of the country."[1] Finally, before the Senate committee the Treasury admitted, through an official spokesman, that it inclined toward the theory in question: "We also have some ground for suspecting that the accumulation of these very corporate surpluses assisted materially in causing the depression."[2]

If this statement is taken to mean that the greatest accumulation of corporate surpluses in the history of the country preceded the 1929–33 depression, it simply is not true. The table on page 377 shows that it is not true. The greatest accumulation of corporate surpluses came with the boom which preceded the crisis and depression of 1920–21. We have seen, moreover, that the 1920–21 crisis and depression were made very much less disastrous by virtue of the great accumulation of corporate surpluses that had preceded them. We had a quick comeback from that depression.

Additions to corporate surpluses from 1916 to 1919, inclusive, amounted to $14,865,000,000, whereas the comparable four years preceding the crisis of 1929, namely, 1925 to 1928, inclusive, show increases in corporate surpluses of only $8,807,000,000.

There is no doubt that the theory that corporate savings preceding 1929 caused the crisis, was responsible for this legislative proposal. The President himself, in his speech of acceptance before the Chicago convention in 1932, had given voice to this theory.[3] It was one phase of the old indictment of the capitalist system which—originating with Sismondi and Rodbertus[4]—had passed on with successive modifications through Karl Marx to John A. Hobson, and from him to J. M. Keynes—the belief that excessive savings are responsible for crises and depressions.

Applied When Corporate Savings Were Negative. It must be said that if this theory had any validity at all, the New Deal chose a very bad time in which to apply it. The table following shows that beginning with 1930 there had been an uninterrupted series of years where corporate surpluses were depleted instead of being added to, years of gigantic corporate deficits instead of additions to corporate surpluses. Certainly additions to

---

[1] U.S., Congress, House, Committee on Ways and Means, *Hearings,* pp. 654, 640.

[2] See "Eating the Seed Corn," *Chase Economic Bulletin,* May 12, 1936, p. 5.

[3] I heard Governor Roosevelt make this speech over the radio. Most of the time he spoke fluently and without strain. When he came to this part of his speech, there was an evident tenseness. It was apparent that he was reading his manuscript closely. It was a newly learned lesson which he hadn't yet learned very well. I thought then that it was merely a little decoration which one of the Keynesians in the Brain Trust had persuaded him to put in, and which he himself did not understand well enough to take seriously. By 1936, however, it was evident that he had learned the lesson only too well.

[4] See W. A. Scott, *The Development of Economics,* pp. 256–58, 282.

corporate surpluses were not retarding prosperity in 1936, nor could they have been doing so since 1929.

NET DIVIDEND PAYMENTS AND RETAINED
NET INCOME OF ALL ACTIVE
CORPORATIONS IN THE UNITED STATES*
(In millions of dollars)

	Net income after taxes (a)	Net dividend payments (a)		Retained net income	
		Amount	% of net income	Amount	% of net income
1909	$2,599	$1,567	60.3	$1,032	39.7
1910	2,906	1,828	62.9	1,078	37.1
1911	2,531	1,866	73.7	665	26.3
1912	3,425	1,950	56.9	1,475	43.1
1913	3,347	2,167	64.7	1,180	35.3
1914	2,371	2,028	85.5	343	14.5
1915	4,083	2,055	50.3	2,028	49.7
1916	7,408	2,500	33.7	4,908	66.3
1917	7,342	3,025	41.2	4,317	58.8
1918	4,553	2,620	57.5	1,933	42.5
1919	6,307	2,600	41.2	3,707	58.8
1920	4,343	2,900	66.8	1,443	33.2
1921	24	2,639	(b)	(d)−2,606	(c)
1922	4,380	2,634	60.1	1,746	39.9
1923	5,827	3,299	56.6	2,528	43.4
1924	4,998	3,424	68.5	1,574	31.5
1925	6,971	4,014	57.6	2,957	42.4
1926	6,774	4,439	65.5	2,335	34.5
1927	5,880	4,765	81.0	1,115	19.0
1928	7,566	5,166	68.3	2,400	31.7
1929	8,084	5,927	73.3	2,157	26.7
1930	1,366	5,613	(b)	(d)−4,247	(c)
1931	(d)−3,145	4,182	(c)	(d)−7,327	(c)
1932	(d)−5,375	2,626	(c)	(d)−8,001	(c)
1933	(d)−2,379	2,101	(c)	(d)−4,480	(c)
1934	157	2,642	(b)	(d)−2,485	(c)
1935	1,674	2,927	(b)	(d)−1,253	(c)
1936	3,903	4,702	(b)	(d)−799	(c)
1937	3,872	4,832	(b)	(d)−960	(c)
1938	1,480	3,222	(b)	(d)−1,742	(c)
1939	4,040	3,841	95.1	199	4.9
1940	4,778	4,067	85.1	711	14.9
1941-p	7,209	4,464	61.9	2,745	38.1

SOURCES: 1909–37 from Temporary National Economic Committee, Monograph No. 12, entitled "Profits, Productive Activities and New Investment," Table VI, based largely upon Treasury Department "Statistics of Income"; 1938–41 from "Statistics of Income."

(a) Excluding intercorporate dividends; (b) over 100 percent; (c) no percentage computed because of net deficit; (d) deficit; (p) preliminary.

* This table is taken from the excellent monthly letter of the National City Bank of New York, September 1943, p. 104.

The New Deal in Maturity, 1933–39

Prevailing economic doctrine has been and is that the accumulation of capital is of first importance for economic progress and for the interests of labor. When capital and natural resources are abundant and men are scarce, the worker is important and his wages are high. When, on the other hand, as in China, population is very dense, natural resources relatively scarce, and capital very scarce and timid, it is cheaper to hire men for draft purposes than to feed an animal for draft purposes. Retarding the rate of capital accumulation or, worse still, diminishing the total of the capital of the country, are policies definitely hostile to the interests of the masses of men.

Confusion of Bank Expansion and Savings, 1922–29. This has long been accepted economic doctrine, according with history and experience. In the course of the Great Depression that followed 1929, however, there came to be a considerable body of opinion which held that the great crisis was caused by an excessive accumulation of capital between 1922 and 1929.

The fact is that what took place in the years 1922–29 was an excessive expansion of bank credit, based on inflowing gold and the cheap money policy of the Federal Reserve banks. This bank credit, unneeded for normal banking uses, flowed into capital uses and speculative uses, creating appalling distortions in the general financial picture. In earlier chapters this has been discussed at length.

Part of this doctrine of oversavings related to the savings of corporations. It was complained that they had withheld dividends from their stockholders, piling up corporate surpluses. At this point, however, the complaint broke down into two contradictory lines. One complaint was that they used these withheld profits to build unneeded plant and equipment, which unduly increased the productive power of the country, leading to further unneeded production of goods, which finally broke the markets and brought on the crisis.

The second complaint regarding them, however, was that they did not use these surpluses to build additional plant and equipment, but held them in the form of cash which they lent to the stock market at ten percent in the form of brokers' loans "for account of others" in 1928 and 1929, and that their failure to employ these funds in additional plant and equipment led to a falling off in demand for goods from the heavy industries, which brought reaction and depression.

Now, the facts are far from receiving correct interpretation in either of these views. The facts are that corporate savings of ordinary business profits declined in the latter part of the period under discussion. In 1929, for example, according to the Brookings Institution figures, only a billion dollars was added to corporate surpluses out of ordinary business profits. Altogether $2,238,000,000 was added to business surpluses, but more than half of this grew out of realized capital gains,[5] due to the corporations

---

[5] *America's Capacity to Consume* (Brookings Institution), p. 152 n. "g."

selling previously acquired securities at the fantastic prices of 1929. And the further fact is that the greater part of the abnormal cash reserves which corporations had, came, not from savings, even of capital gains, but rather from the new stock issues which corporations were able to put out in the wild stock market at very high prices. They thus accumulated funds far in excess of their needs, which they held as cash, because they did not know what else to do with them, and which they lent at ten percent to the stock market when the stock market was willing to pay ten percent.

And the further fact is that the capital gains and the wild stock market and the excess cash in the hands of corporations were all the product of the vast and unneeded expansion of bank credit which took place between June 30 of 1922 and early April 1928. The same expansion of bank credit put liquid reserves not only into the hands of business corporations, but also into the hands of many others, who took part in lending to the stock market at ten percent in the form of brokers' loans for the account of others.

To attribute this complicated financial mess to the old, sound, traditional policy of American business corporations putting aside a part of their profits for expansion or to build up working capital or to provide against the rainy day, is a grotesque misunderstanding of the pathology that took place.

The Fallacy of Excess Capacity. With respect to the other version of the complaint, that the piling up of corporate surpluses between 1922 and 1929 led to excessive plant and equipment, the evidence is that there did not take place,[6] during this period, the creation of a greater percentage of unused capacity than we had previously had. Always there is unused capacity. Our economic organism is loosely articulated. There are great variations from time to time in the demands made upon the different branches of industry. If we did not have excess capacity all along the line, we should not have enough at particular times, and the failure to have enough at strategic points can easily mean the slowing down of the whole industrial machine—witness the shortage of railway facilities in 1919–20.

The Heart of the Doctrine of Oversavings. Two writers have independently given us the same "dilemma" of savings. Harold G. Moulton in his *Formation of Capital,*[7] offers the "dilemma" that savings by the individual, withholding funds from the purchase of consumers' goods in order to divert them to producers' goods, means such a falling off in the demand for consumers' goods as to lead to business reaction, which in turn reduces the demand for producers' goods, and so makes the savings pointless. J. M. Keynes, in his *General Theory of Employment, Interest, and Money,* presents the same argument.[8]

This looks like a dilemma when one examines it only from the front. But

---

[6] *Ibid.*

[7] P. 168, and *passim.*

[8] I deal with Lord Keynes's fallacies more fully in chapter 60, "Digression on Keynes."

when one looks at it from the side, it is quite clear that it is not a dilemma, but merely a chimera in dilemma's clothing. The difficulty arises from the fact that both these writers are assuming an *uncaused* increase in savings. Savings may be increased from many causes. If there comes a great fear regarding the economic future—as in 1914 at the outbreak of World War I—men may curtail their expenditures and may not invest the savings. But this is not the typical cause of an increase in savings, and indeed could not be the cause of a general increase in savings, because too many men would be under pressure to use capital assets in maintaining consumption in such a situation. A more typical cause would be the following. Let us suppose, for example, that there is a new invention which promises great profits, but which cannot be exploited without new capital, and let us suppose that the inventor, to get new capital, offers a high enough rate of interest to induce other individuals to curtail their current consumption and turn over to him the funds that he needs. Assume that, assured of these funds, he immediately gives orders for the new capital equipment he needs, creating an additional demand for producers' goods, which leads the producers of the equipment to hire more labor and to buy more materials. Is there anything in this likely to lead to business reaction?

It will be observed here that it is not necessary to introduce bank credit into this illustration. The hypothesis can be altered so as to eliminate all credit. We could assume that the savings of the inventor and his friends take the form of proprietors' capital in the new enterprise, and that they pay cash for the new machinery day by day as it is being produced out of funds which they save day by day by reducing their current consumption.

The general point can be further illustrated by assuming the discovery of new oil fields, with everybody in the region saving all that he possibly can to buy drilling equipment, or to buy stock of oil companies, with all available labor in the community diverted from the production of current goods and services to developing the oil fields, and with men bidding high rates of interest to get any loans that are available. Does such a situation lead to business reaction and stagnation?

The Undistributed Profits Tax Bill as Passed. The President's power over the Congress in 1936 was great, but the opposition to this appalling proposal, led by Senator Harry Byrd of Virginia, fought hard. They could not defeat the bill but they could hold it down.

Instead of a top rate of 73.91 percent for the tax on undistributed profits[9] proposed in the original bill, they held the top rate for this tax down to 27 percent on undistributed net income amounting to 60 percent or over of the adjusted net income. The rate was 12 percent on undistributed net income which ran between 10 percent and 20 percent of the adjusted net income,

---

[9] As shown in our table at the bottom of page 373.

and was 7 percent for undistributed net income of 10 percent or less, as contrasted with the 40 percent tax for undistributed net income of 10 percent or less proposed in the original bill.[10]

Evil Effects Immediately Manifest. It was a triumph for sanity, but a very inadequate triumph. The effect of the undistributed profits tax was great and immediate. There was a great increase in corporate dividends in 1936 and 1937. Many of the evils forecast in the presentation of the objections to the bill before the congressional committee promptly manifested themselves. There are many corporations which, even in 1946, have reason to regret that they were forced by this law to pay dividends as large as those which they paid in 1936 and 1937. The flood of dividends at the year end, both in 1936 and 1937, was particularly heavy, and this was true even after the crisis of 1937–38 had begun and the outlook for business profits was very gloomy.

The table on page 377, for net dividend payments and for retained net income for all active corporations in the United States, shows that dividend payments, which had been $2,642,000,000 in 1934 and $2,927,000,000 in 1935, spurted to $4,702,000,000 in 1936 and to $4,832,000,000 in 1937, dropping again in 1938 to $3,222,000,000.

Moreover, fears that business corporations would reduce their purchase of new equipment out of profits were promptly realized. Case after case of this sort was observed in the latter part of 1936. The measure was eminently successful in diverting corporate profits from the purchase of producers' goods to income for consumers. It was eminently successful in holding down the capital accumulation of the country.

Repeal of Undistributed Profits Tax Early 1938. But the evils were so manifest that the Congress finally broke away from the President in early 1938. Under the leadership of Senator Pat Harrison, chairman of the Senate Finance Committee, the Congress repealed the undistributed profits tax, and simultaneously gave the taxpayer the option of taking capital gains on assets held more than eighteen months out of the category of the income tax and paying a special capital gains tax upon them of 15 percent. This made it possible for men with large incomes to engage in long-run ventures and retain 85 percent of the profits which such long-run ventures might bring, instead of having to pay rates of 40 percent, 50 percent, and even 83 percent upon them.

A full explanation of this vigorous assertion of congressional independence must await our discussion of the crisis of 1937, but it was a very thorough assertion of independence. The President did not dare to veto the bill. Instead he held it for ten days and then let it become a law without his signature.

---

[10] *Commercial & Financial Chronicle,* July 4, 1936, sec. 2, p. 3.

Roosevelt and Pat Harrison. The President announced his decision on this point in a pathetic speech to a group of schoolchildren, who did not know what it was all about, making sharp criticism of the action of the Congress. Following this speech of the President's, Senator Pat Harrison made a reply before the Senate. The Senate was in full attendance and members of the House crowded all available space to hear the senator. Senator Harrison met the President's arguments with vigor and clarity. He expressed his regret that the President had not seen fit to veto the bill, because in that case he had no doubt as to what the action of the Congress would have been. He implied that he was quite sure that the Congress would have overridden the veto.

No member of the Senate, not even the President's closest adherents, replied to Senator Harrison. Congressional approval of the speech was emphatic. The Congress had watched the theories of Sismondi and Rodbertus, Marx, John A. Hobson, and Keynes, as applied to American corporations, in action, and the Congress had repudiated these theories.[11]

---

[11] It is due Dr. Harold G. Moulton, whose statement of the doctrine of oversavings I have referred to above, to state that he was an opponent of the undistributed profits tax bill, and a very effective one.

60

Digression on Keynes

I. *A Refutation of Keynes' Attack on the Doctrine That Aggregate Supply Creates Aggregate Demand.* The central theoretical issue involved in the problem of postwar economic readjustment, and in the problem of full employment in the postwar period, is the issue between the equilibrium doctrine and the purchasing power doctrine.

Those who advocate vast governmental expenditures and deficit financing after the war as the only means of getting full employment, separate production and purchasing power sharply. Purchasing power must be kept above production if production is to expand, in their view. If purchasing power falls off, production will fall off.

The prevailing view among economists, on the other hand, has long been that purchasing power grows out of production. The great producing countries are the great consuming countries. The twentieth-century world consumes vastly more than the eighteenth-century world because it produces vastly more. Supply of wheat gives rise to demand for automobiles, silks, shoes, cotton goods, and other things that the wheat producer wants. Supply of shoes gives rise to demand for wheat, for silks, for automobiles and for other things that the shoe producer wants. Supply and demand in the aggregate are thus not merely equal, but they are identical, since every commodity may be looked upon either as supply of its own kind or as demand for other things. But this doctrine is subject to the great qualification that the proportions must be right; that there must be equilibrium.

On the equilibrium theory occasional periods of readjustment are inevitable and are useful. An active boom almost inevitably generates disequilibria. The story in the present volume of the boom of 1919–20 and the crisis of 1920–21 gives a classical illustration. The period of readjustment may be relatively short and need not be severe, but a period of shakedown, a period in which overexpanded industries are contracted and opportunities made for underdeveloped industries to expand, a period in which prices and costs come into equilibrium, a period in which weak spots in the credit situation are cleaned up, a period in which excessive debts are liquidated—such periods we must have from time to time. The effort to prevent adjustment and liquidation by the pouring out of artificial purchasing power is, from the standpoint of the equilibrium doctrine, an utterly futile and wasteful and dangerous performance. Once a reequilibration is accomplished, moreover, the equilibrium doctrine would regard pouring out new artificial purchasing power as wholly unnecessary and further as dangerous, since it would tend to create new disequilibria.

The late Lord Keynes was the leading advocate of the purchasing power doctrine, and the leading opponent of the doctrine that supply creates its own demand. The present chapter is concerned with Keynes' attack on the doctrine that supply creates its own demand.

Keynes was a dangerously unsound thinker.[1] His influence in the Roosevelt administration was very great. His influence upon most of the economists in the employ of the government is incredibly great. There has arisen a volume of theoretical literature regarding Keynes almost equal to that which has arisen around Karl Marx.[2] His followers are satisfied that he has destroyed the long-accepted economic doctrine that aggregate supply and aggregate demand grow together. It seems necessary to analyze Keynes' argument with respect to this point.

Keynes Ignores the Essential Point in the Doctrine He Attacks. Keynes presents his argument in his *The General Theory of Employment, Interest, and Money,* published in 1936. But he nowhere in the book takes account of the law of equilibrium among the industries, which has always been recognized as an essential part of the doctrine that supply creates its own demand. He takes as his target a seemingly crude statement from J. S. Mill's *Principles of Political Economy* (bk. 3, chap. 14, par. 2), which follows:

> What constitutes the means of payment for commodities is simply commodities. Each person's means of paying for the productions of other people consist of those which he himself possesses. All sellers are inevitably, and by the meaning of the word, buyers. Could we suddenly double the productive powers of the country, we should double the supply of commodities in every market; but we should, by the same stroke, double the purchasing power. Everybody would bring a double demand as well as supply: everybody would be able to buy twice as much, because every one would have twice as much to offer in exchange.

---

[1] Lord Keynes was a man of genius. He had great abilities and great personal charm.

[2] I have not read much of this elaborate literature. Keynes himself I have studied with care. I think it probable that other critics have anticipated many of the points I make here, and I would gladly give them credit if I knew.

Now this passage by itself does not present the essentials of the doctrine. If we doubled the productive power of the country, we should not double the supply of commodities in every market, and if we did, we should not clear the markets of the double supply in every market. If we doubled the supply in the salt market, for example, we should have an appalling glut of salt. The great increases would come in the items where demand is elastic. We should change very radically the proportions in which we produced commodities.

But it is unfair to Mill to take this brief passage out of its context and present it as if it represented the heart of the doctrine. If Keynes had quoted only the three sentences immediately following, he would have introduced us to the conception of balance and proportion and equilibrium which is the heart of the doctrine—a notion which Keynes nowhere considers in this book. Mill's next few lines, immediately following the passage torn from its context, quoted above, are as follows:

> It is probable, indeed, that there would now be a superfluity of certain things. Although the community would willingly double its aggregate consumption, it may already have as much as it desires of some commodities, and it may prefer to do more than double its consumption of others, or to exercise its increased purchasing power on some new thing. If so, the supply will adapt itself accordingly, and the values of things will continue to conform to their cost of production.

Keynes, furthermore, ignores entirely the rich, fine work done by such writers as J. B. Clark and the Austrian school, who elaborated the laws of proportionality and equilibrium.

The doctrine that supply creates its own demand, as presented by John Stuart Mill, assumes a proper equilibrium among the different kinds of production, assumes proper terms of exchange (that is, price relationships) among different kinds of products, assumes proper relations between prices and costs. And the doctrine expects competition and free markets to be the instrumentality by means of which these proportions and price relations will be brought about. The modern version of the doctrine[3] would make explicit certain additional factors. There must be a proper balance in the international balance sheet. If foreign debts are excessive in relation to the volume of foreign trade, grave disorders can come. Moreover, the money and capital markets must be in a state of balance. When there is an excess of bank credit used as a substitute for savings, when bank credit goes in undue amounts into capital uses and speculative uses, impairing the liquidity of bank assets, or when the total volume of money and credit is

---

[3] See *Chase Economic Bulletin,* June 12, 1931.

expanded far beyond the growth of production and trade, disequilibria arise, and, above all, the *quality* of credit is impaired. Confidence may be suddenly shaken and a countermovement may set in.

With respect to all these points, automatic market forces tend to restore equilibrium in the absence of overwhelming governmental interference.

Keynes has nothing to say in his attack upon the doctrine that supply creates its own demand, in the volume referred to, with respect to these matters.

Indeed, far from considering the intricacies of the interrelations of markets, prices and different kinds of production, Keynes prefers to look at things in block. He says:

> In dealing with the theory of employment I propose, therefore, to make use of only two fundamental units of quantity, namely, quantities of money value and quantities of employment. The first of these is strictly homogeneous, and the second can be made so. For, in so far as different grades and kinds of labor and salaried assistance enjoy a more or less fixed relative remuneration, the quantity of employment can be sufficiently defined for our purpose by taking an hour's employment of ordinary labor as our unit *and weighting an hour's employment of special labor in proportion to its remuneration; i.e., an hour of special labor remunerated at double ordinary rates will count as two units. . . .*[4] [Italics mine.]
>
> It is my belief that much unnecessary preplexity can be avoided if we limit ourselves strictly to the two units, money and labor, when we are dealing with the behavior of the economic system as a whole.[5]

Procedure of this kind is empty and tells us nothing about economic life. How empty it is becomes apparent when we observe that these two supposedly independent units of quantity, namely, "quantities of money value" and "quantities of employment," are both merely quantities of money value. If ten laborers working for $2 a day are dismissed and two laborers working for $10 a day are taken on, there is no change in the volume of employment, by Keynes' method of reckoning, as is obvious from the italicized portion of the quotation above. His "quantity of employment" is not a quantity of employment. It is a quantity of money received by laborers who are employed.[6]

Throughout Keynes' analysis he is working with aggregate, block concepts. He has an aggregate supply function and an aggregate demand function.[7] But nowhere is there any discussion of the interrelationships of

---

[4] *The General Theory of Employment, Interest, and Money*, p. 41.

[5] *Ibid.*, p. 43.

[6] See my criticism of the analogous procedure by Irving Fisher in his "Equation of Exchange," in my *Value of Money* (New York, 1917 and 1936), pp. 158–62.

[7] *Ibid.*, p. 29.

the elements in these vast aggregates, or of elements in one aggregate with elements in another. Nowhere is there a recognition that different elements in the aggregate supply give rise to demand for other elements in the aggregate supply. In Keynes' discussion, purchasing power and production are sharply sundered.

The Function of Prices. It is part of the equilibrium doctrine that prices tend to equate supply and demand in various markets: commodities, labor, capital, and so on. If prices go down in particular markets this constitutes a signal for producers to produce less, and a signal for consumers to consume more. In the markets, on the other hand, where prices are rising we have a signal for producers to produce more, for consumers to consume less, and a signal for men in fields where prices are less satisfactory to shift their labor and, to the extent that this is possible, to shift their capital to the more productive field. Free prices, telling the truth about supply and demand, thus constitute the great equilibrating factor.

The Function of the Rate of Interest. Among these prices is the rate of interest. The traditional doctrine is that the rate of interest equates supply and demand in the capital market and equates saving and investment. Interest is looked upon as reward for saving and as inducement to saving. The old doctrine which looked upon consumer's thrift as the primary source of capital is inadequate. It must be broadened to include producer's thrift, and especially corporate thrift, and direct capitalization, as when the farmer uses his spare time in building fences and putting other improvements on his farm, or when the farmer lets his flocks and herds increase instead of selling off the whole of the annual increase, and so forth. It must include governmental thrift, as when government taxes to pay down public debt or when government taxes for capital purposes instead of borrowing—historically very important! The doctrine needs a major qualification, moreover, with respect to the use of bank credit for capital purposes.[8]

Keynes' Attack on the Interest Rate as Equilibrator. It is with respect to the interest rate as the equilibrating factor that Keynes has made his most vigorous assault upon prevailing views. Where economists generally have held that saving and avoiding unnecessary debt and paying off debt where possible are good things, Keynes holds that they are bad things. He disparages depreciation reserves for business corporations. He disparages amortization of public debt by municipalities. He disparages additions to corporate surpluses out of earnings. His philosophy is responsible for the ill-fated undistributed profits tax which we adopted in 1936 and which we

---

[8] *Ibid.*, pp. 484–89; chap. 24. Also my address before the Indiana Bankers Association, in *The Chase* (house organ of Chase National Bank), November 1920; the *Chase Economic Bulletin*, November 1926 and May 1936. See also my article "The Future of Interest Rates," *Commercial & Financial Chronicle*, August 26, 1943.

abandoned with a great sigh of relief, over the President's plaintive protest, in 1938.

In *General Theory* Keynes gives two reasons for his rejection of prevailing ideas with respect to interest and savings, and the equilibrating function of the rate of interest. The first, found on pages 110 and 111, is:

> The influence of changes in the rate of interest on the amount actually saved is of paramount importance, but is *in the opposite direction* to that usually supposed. For even if the attraction of the larger future income to be earned from a higher rate of interest has the effect of diminishing the propensity to consume, nevertheless we can be certain that a rise in the rate of interest will have the effect of reducing the amount actually saved. For aggregate saving is governed by aggregate investment; a rise in the rate of interest (*unless it is offset by a corresponding change in the demand schedule for investment*) [italics mine] will diminish investment; hence a rise in the rate of interest must have the effect of reducing incomes to a level at which saving is decreased in the same measure as investment. Since incomes will decrease by a greater absolute amount than investment, it is, indeed, true that, when the rate of interest rises, the rate of consumption will decrease. But this does not mean that there will be a wider margin for saving. On the contrary, saving and spending will both decrease.

This is an extraordinarily superficial argument.[9] The whole case is given away by the parenthetical passage, "(unless it is offset by a corresponding change in the demand schedule for investment)." The usual *cause* of an increase in the rate of interest is a *rise* in the demand schedule for investment. Interest usually rises because of an increased demand for capital on the part of those who wish to increase their investments, of business which wish to expand, of speculators for the rise, of homebuilders, and so on. Usually, when the interest rate rises, it rises because investment is increasing, and the increased savings which rising interest rates induce are promptly invested. Indeed, investment often *precedes* saving[10] in such a situation, through an expansion of bank credit, also induced by the rising rate of interest.

Keynes is assuming an *uncaused* rise in the rate of interest, and he has

---

[9] Harold G. Moulton, whose book *The Formation of Capital* was published at about the same time that Keynes' book appeared, independently presents essentially the same argument, which Moulton calls "The Dilemma of Savings." I have discussed Moulton's view in "Eating the Seed Corn," *Chase Economic Bulletin,* May 12, 1936, and in my discussion of the undistributed profits tax in the present volume.

[10] The Keynesian reader will observe that I am using the word *savings* in the ordinary sense, and not in Keynes' peculiar sense. I am under no obligation to use Keynes' terminology, since Keynes himself, as shown in the first sentence of the passage quoted above, is discussing the usual view of the relation of the rate of interest to savings. To the extent that there is any shift in the meaning of terms in the course of the argument, it is done by Keynes and not by me. I use the word *savings* in the ordinary sense throughout.

very little difficulty in disposing of this. But economic phenomena do not occur without *causes*.

Keynes' second argument against the prevailing doctrine is found in chapter 14, "The Classical Theory of the Rate of Interest." Here (with a diagram on page 180) he complains that the static theory of interest has not taken account of the possibility of changes in the level of income, or the possibility that the level of income is actually a function of the rate of investment.

Now it may be observed that Keynes is here introducing dynamic considerations into a static analysis. By this device one may equally destroy the law of supply and demand, the law of cost of production, the capitalization theory, or any other of the standard working tools of the static analysis. Thus the static law of supply and demand is that a decrease in price will lead to an increase in the amount demanded. But with a sudden, violent general fall in prices the tendency is for buyers to hold off and wait until they see where prices are going to settle.

The static economist has known all this almost from the beginning. He has been aware that he was making abstractions. He has protected himself in general by the well-known phrase *ceteris paribus* (other things equal), and the general level of income has been among those other things assumed to be unchanged. Moreover, the static economist has concerned himself with delicate marginal adjustments, and with infinitesimal variations in the region of the margin, a device which Keynes is very glad to borrow from static economics in his conception of the "marginal propensity to consume" and in his initial conception of the "marginal efficiency of capital."

The Multiplier. Rejecting the function of the interest rate as the equilibrator of saving and investment, Keynes is so impressed with the danger of thrift that he finally convinces himself in one of his major doctrines that *no part* of an increase in income which is not consumed is invested; *that all of the unconsumed increase in income is hoarded.* This major doctrine is the much praised Keynesian "investment multiplier theory."[11] If any investment is made it gives a certain amount of employment, but that is not the end of the story. Investment tends to multiply itself in subsequent stages of spending. The recipients of the proceeds of the investment spend at least part of it, and the recipients of their spending spend part of what they get, and so on. How many times does the original investment multiply itself? Keynes gives a definite mathematical answer in which his investment multiplier rests solely on what he calls "the marginal propensity to consume." The multiplier figure rests on the assumption that the subsequent spending consists entirely of purchases for consumption. None of the unconsumed increase in income is invested. If any of the recipients of the proceeds of the investment should add to their expenditures for consump-

---

[11] *General Theory,* pp. 113–19.

tion any investment at all, the mathematics of the Keynes multiplier would be upset, and the multiplier would be increased. It is a source of satisfaction to find this view in agreement with that of Professor James W. Angell on this point.[12]

The multiplier concept is an unfruitful notion. In times when the business cycle is moving upward, particularly in the early stages of revival, increased expenditure, whether for investment or consumption, tends to multiply itself manyfold, as Wesley Mitchell has shown.[13]

In times of business reaction there may be very little multiplication. The soldiers' bonus payments by the government under Hoover made no difference in the business picture. On the other hand, the soldiers' bonus payments under Roosevelt in 1936, at a time when the business curve was moving upward sharply, appear to have intensified the movement.

The Relation of Savings to Investment. The preoccupation with the varying relationship of saving to investment is superficial. Investment tends to equal saving in a reasonably good business situation, when bank credit is not expanding. In a strong upward move, when bank credit is readily obtainable, investment tends to exceed saving because men borrow at the banks and because expanding bank credit facilitates the issue of new securities. In a crisis and in the liquidation that follows a crisis, saving exceeds investment. Men and businesses are saving to pay down debts and especially to repay bank loans—a necessary preliminary to a subsequent revival of business. But the *reasons* for these changes in the relation of saving to investment are the all-important things. The relation of saving to investment is itself a very superficial thing. The *reasons* lie in the factors which govern the prospects of profits, including the price and cost equilibrium, the industrial equilibrium, and the *quality* of credit.

Keynes strives desperately to rule out bank credit as a factor in the relation of savings to investment. At one point he does it very simply indeed: "We have, indeed, to adjust for the creation and discharge of debts (including changes in the quantity of credit or money); but since for the community as a whole the increase or decrease of the aggregate creditor position is always exactly equal to the increase or decrease of the aggregate debtor position, this complication also cancels out when we are dealing with aggregate investment."[14]

But bank credit is not so easily canceled out as a factor in the volume of money available for investment. The borrower at the bank is, of course, both debtor to and creditor of the bank when he gets his loan. But his debt is an obligation which is *not* money, and his credit is a demand deposit, which

---

[12] James W. Angell, *Investment and Business Cycles* (New York, 1941), pp. 190–91.

[13] *Business Cycles* (University of California Press, 1913), pp. 453–54.

[14] *General Theory,* p. 75.

is money. When he uses this money for investment, he is making an investment in addition to the investment which comes from savings.

On pages 81 to 85 of the same book, Keynes engages in a very confused further argument on this point.

> It is supposed that a depositor and his bank can somehow contrive between them to perform an operation by which savings can disappear into the banking system so that they are lost to investment, or, contrariwise, that the banking system can make it possible for investment to occur, to which no saving corresponds. But no one can save without acquiring an asset, whether it be cash or a debt or capital goods; and no one can acquire an asset which he did not previously possess, unless *either* an asset of equal value is newly produced *or* someone else parts with an asset of that value which he previously had. In the first alternative there is a corresponding new investment: in the second alternative someone else must be dissaving an equal sum. For his loss of wealth must be due to his consumption exceeding his income.

But the assumption that a man who parts with an asset for cash is losing wealth, and that this must be due to his consumption exceeding his income, is purely gratuitous. The man who sells an asset for cash may hold his cash or he may reinvest it in something else. It is not "dissaving" unless he spends it for current consumption, and he does not have to do that unless he wants to. Indeed on the next page (p. 83) the man who holds the additional money corresponding to the new bank credit is said to be *saving*. "Moreover the savings which result from this decision are just as genuine as any other savings. No one can be compelled to own the additional money corresponding to the new bank credit, unless he deliberately prefers to hold more money rather than some other form of wealth."

Keynes' confusion here could be interpreted as due to his effort to carry out a puckish joke on the Keynesians. He had got them excited in his earlier writings about the relation between savings and investment. Then, in his *General Theory,* he propounds the doctrine that savings are always equal to investment.[15] This makes the theology harder for the devout follower to understand, and calls, moreover, for a miracle by which the disturbing factor of bank credit may be abolished. This miracle Keynes attempts in the pages cited above, with indifferent success.

One must here protest against the dangerous identification of bank expansion with savings, which is part of the Keynesian doctrine. This fallacy is discussed at length in the chapters dealing with the expansion of bank credit in the 1920s and the discussion of the doctrine of oversaving in connection with the undistributed profits tax. This doctrine is particularly dangerous today, when we find our vast increase in money and bank deposits growing out of war finance described as "savings," just because

---

[15] *Ibid.,* pp. 61–65.

somebody happens to hold them at a given moment of time. On this doctrine, the greater the inflation, the greater the savings! The alleged excess of savings over investment in the period 1924–29 was merely a failure to invest *all* of the rapidly expanding bank credit. All of the real savings of this period were invested, and far too much new bank credit in addition.

The Wage Rate as Equilibrator of the Supply and Demand of Labor. Keynes also tries to destroy the accepted doctrine regarding the rate of wages as the equilibrating factor between the supply and demand of labor. He attempts at various places to suggest that a reduction in money wages "may be" ineffective in increasing the demand for labor (e.g., p. 13), but he nowhere, so far as I can find, positively states this. He does suggest (p. 264) that a fall in wages would mean a fall in prices, and that this could lead to embarrassment and insolvency to entrepreneurs who are heavily indebted, and to an increase in the real burden of the national debt. On this point it is sufficient to say that the fall in wages in a depression usually follows, and does not precede, the fall in prices, and that it is usually more moderate than the fall in prices. It does not need to be so great as the fall in prices in order to bring about a reequilibration, since wages are only part of cost of production, and since the efficiency of labor increases in such a situation.

Keynes accuses other economists of reasoning regarding the demand schedule for labor on the basis of a single industry, and then, without substantial modification, making a simple extension of the argument to industry as a whole (pp. 258–59). But this is merely additional evidence that he has ignored John Bates Clark's *Distribution of Wealth,* and the theory of costs of the Austrian school, for whom the law of costs, including wages, is merely the law of the leveling of values among the different industries. Moreover, the studies of Paul Douglas, dealing with the elasticity of the demand for labor as a whole, constitute a sufficient answer to Keynes on this point. Douglas holds that the demand for labor is highly elastic; so much so that a one percent decline in wages can mean a three or four percent increase in employment, when wages are held above the marginal product of labor.[16]

But the practical issue does not usually relate to wages as a whole. The wages of nonunion labor, and especially agricultural labor, usually recede promptly and sometimes to extremes, in a depression. The issue usually relates to union wage scales held so high in particular industries that employment falls off very heavily in these industries, and that the industries constitute bottlenecks.[17]

---

[16] Paul H. Douglas, *The Theory of Wages* (New York, 1934), pp. 113–58, 501–2.

[17] See figures showing wide disparities of wage reductions as among different groups, in 1931, in *Chase Economic Bulletin,* vol. 11, no. 3.

But Keynes does not come to the theoretical conclusion that a reduction in money wages could not bring about an increase in employment. He rather reaches the practical conclusion that this is not the best way to do it. Instead, he would prefer in a closed economy, that is, one without foreign trade, to make such readjustments as are necessary by manipulations of money, and for an open economy, that is, one with large foreign trade, to accomplish it by letting the foreign exchanges fluctuate (p. 270).

The fact seems to be that Keynes entertains a settled prejudice against any reduction in money wages. He is opposed to flexibility downward in wage scales. He has, however, no such prejudice against flexibility upward. On the contrary, in the Keynes plan for an international clearing union of April 8, 1943, Keynes proposes, as a means of maintaining stability in foreign exchange rates, that a member state in the clearing union whose credit balance is increasing unduly, shall encourage an increase in money rates of earnings (meaning wages).[18] This would increase the cost of its goods in foreign trade, and consequently reduce its exports, and consequently hold down its credit balance. But Keynes makes no corresponding demand on the country whose *debit* in the clearing union is increasing unduly that it should encourage a *decrease* in money rates of earnings.

II. *Keynes' Constructive Theory.* The foregoing discussion of Keynes' doctrines has been primarily concerned with refuting his attack upon the long-established view that, given equilibrium, aggregate supply creates aggregate demand, that consumption keeps pace with production, and that the power to consume grows out of production. Now, however, it is planned to go further and to demonstrate that Keynes' constructive substitute for prevailing economic doctrine is essentially fallacious. Keynes builds his positive doctrine around three central notions: (1) the propensity to consume, (2) the schedule of the marginal efficiency of capital, and (3) the rate of interest. These three Keynes regards as independent variables. These three independent variables govern the dependent variables, namely, the volume of employment, and national income measured in "wage units."[19]

There are two main criticisms of this scheme, either of which would invalidate it. (1) Keynes does not adhere to fixed meanings for his terms in the case of the rate of interest or in the case of the marginal efficiency of capital. (2) The three independent variables are not independent of one another, either in fact or on Keynes' own showing.

Keynes' Terms Lack Fixed Meanings. Let us consider first Keynes' failure to adhere to fixed meanings for his terms.

Keynes at times uses the rate of interest to mean a rate of discount,

---

[18] *Chase Economic Bulletin,* vol. 11, no. 3, *op. cit.,* 9 (b).

[19] *General Theory,* p. 245.

measuring the premium on present goods over future goods. This is implied in his initial definition of the marginal efficiency of capital, to which later reference is made on page 135 of his book. It is, moreover, made explicit by Keynes on page 93, where he says that, as an approximation, we can identify the rate of time-discounting, that is, the ratio of exchange between present goods and future goods, with the rate of interest. Later, however, Keynes gives us a radically different theory of interest. He makes the rate of interest depend on liquidity preference and the quantity of money. And he holds that interest is not paid for the purpose of inducing men *to save* but for the purpose of inducing men *not to hoard*. He holds that if money is made sufficiently abundant so that it can satiate liquidity preference, it will pull down, not merely the short time rate of interest or the short time money rates, but also the whole complex of interest rates, long and short.[20] The whole complex of interest rates (with a given liquidity preference scale) can be governed, and is governed, in his system, by the abundance or scarcity of money. Interest becomes a phenomenon of money *par excellence*. Strangely enough, however, we find Keynes playing with the notion of commodity rates of interest, or "own rates of interest," the rate between future wheat and present wheat, and designating this rate as the "wheat rate of interest." Every commodity can have its own rate of interest in terms of itself, and Keynes says that there is no reason why the wheat rate of interest should be equal to the copper rate of interest, because the relation between the spot and future contracts, as quoted in the markets, is notoriously different for different commodities.[21] The reader will find whatever he pleases in Keynes about the rates of interest, though his formal theory is the doctrine that the quantity of money, taken in conjunction with liquidity preference, governs the rate of interest.

But Keynes does not adhere long to his own theory of interest. In the same volume, twenty-nine pages later, he has abandoned it. After saying (pp. 167–68) that the supply of money in relation to liquidity preference will govern the whole complex of interest rates, long and short, he criticizes (p. 197) the Federal Reserve banks for their open market policy, 1933–34, on the ground that they purchased only short-term securities, the effect of which "may, of course, be mainly confined to the very short-term rate of interest and have little reaction on the much more important long-term rates of interest." And he calls upon the central banks to regulate all rates of interest by having fixed rates at which they will buy obligations of differing maturities, long and short.[22]

---

[20] *Ibid.*, p. 167 n.2.
[21] *Ibid.*, pp. 223–24.
[22] *Ibid.*, pp. 205–6.

There is no consistency in Keynes' use of the term *rate of interest* in this volume.

The conception of the "marginal efficiency of capital" has an even more extraordinary history in this volume. His initial definition of this phrase (pp. 135–36) appears in the following passage:

> Over against the prospective yield of the investment we have the *supply price* of the capital asset, meaning by this, not the market price at which an asset of the type in question can be purchased in the market, but the price which would just induce a manufacturer newly to produce an additional unit of such assets, *i.e.,* what is sometimes called its *replacement cost.* The relation between the prospective yield of one more unit of that type of capital and the cost of producing that unit, furnishes us with the *marginal efficiency of capital* of that type. More precisely *I define the marginal efficiency of capital as being equal to that rate of discount which would make the present value of the series of annuities given by the returns expected from the capital asset during its life just equal to its supply price.* [Italics in this sentence are mine.] This gives us the marginal efficiencies of particular types of capital assets. The greatest of these marginal efficiencies can then be regarded as the marginal efficiency of capital in general.
>
> The reader should note that the marginal efficiency of capital is here defined in terms of the *expectation* of yield and of the *current* supply price of the capital asset. It depends on the rate of return expected to be obtainable on money if it were invested in a *newly* produced asset; not on the historical result of what an investment has yielded on its original cost if we look back on its record after its life is over. . . .
>
> For each type of capital we can build up a schedule, showing by how much investment in it will have to increase within the period, in order that its marginal efficiency should fall to any given figure. We can then aggregate these schedules for all the different types of capital, so as to provide a schedule relating the rate of aggregate investment to the corresponding marginal efficiency of capital in general which that rate of investment will establish. We shall call this the investment demand schedule; or, alternatively, the schedule of the marginal efficiency of capital.

Keynes seems here to be talking about the calculation which an entrepreneur would make in deciding whether or not to buy a machine or other productive capital instrument. This impression is intensified when he states that the definition which he has given is fairly close to what Marshall intended to mean by the term, Marshall's phrase being the "marginal net efficiency" of a factor of production, or alternatively the "marginal utility of capital," and by the passage which he quotes from Marshall's *Principles*, from which the following is taken:

> "There may be machinery which the trade would have refused to dispense with if the *rate of interest* had been 20 percent per annum. If the rate had been

10 percent, more would have been used; if it had been 6 percent, still more; if 4 percent, still more; and finally, the rate being 3 percent, they use more still. When they have this amount, the *marginal utility of the machinery, i.e.,* the utility of that machinery which it is only just worth their while to employ, is measured by 3 percent.[23] [Italics mine.]

We seem, in the initial definition, to have the marginal efficiency of capital tied up with specific instruments of production, and the "expectation" regarding the future to be tied up with the anticipated returns from these specific instruments of production. These are familiar notions of static economics. But Keynes, before he has finished this chapter, gives us a warning against static economics, and indicates that the notion of the marginal efficiency of capital is going to be a dynamic concept, much more so even than the rate of interest, which is a *current* phenomenon.

In what follows in his volume, the marginal efficiency of capital becomes dynamic by ceasing to be a fixed notion. It goes through more metamorphoses than even Ovid knew about! In chapter 12 of the book, "The State of Long-Term Expectation," the expectation factor becomes everything and the efficiency of specific capital goods is forgotten, except for one footnote later to be quoted. This chapter develops a fantastic economic theory based on the somewhat less fantastic behavior of the New York stock market in 1928 and 1929. Expectation comes to mean expectations regarding expectations, and expectations regarding the reactions of different buyers and sellers of securities who are anticipating future expectations. It would seem that this, at best, could explain the selling prices of securities representing industries with a great variety of physical capital assets, rather than the marginal efficiency of specific capital goods. Keynes, however, does not hesitate to identify the two. He says in a footnote on page 151 of that chapter, "A high quotation for existing equities involves an increase in the marginal efficiency of the corresponding type of capital. . . ."

At times the marginal efficiency of capital means simply expectation regarding business profits, which may be due to entrepreneurial efficiency or to labor efficiency, quite as much as to the efficiency of capital instruments, or which may be due to maladjustments in the proportions of the industries, or between prices and costs, or to a war or war scare. On page 149 he makes "the state of confidence" one of the major factors governing the marginal efficiency of capital, and here he is clearly making the marginal efficiency of capital mean business profits rather than the specific return to a specific instrument of production. On page 315, talking about the business cycle, he suggests that "a more typical, and often the predom-

---

[23] *Ibid.,* pp. 139–40.

inant, explanation of the crisis, is, not primarily a rise in the rate of interest, but a sudden collapse in the marginal efficiency of capital." Here, clearly, marginal efficiency of capital means anticipations regarding business profits rather than any specific return to specific capital instruments.

Keynes' doctrine that the schedule of the marginal efficiency of capital is today, and presumably for the future, much lower than it was in the nineteenth century (pp. 307–9) seems to rest primarily on the view that employers were strong enough in the nineteenth century to prevent wages from rising much faster than the efficiency of labor, whereas they are not strong enough to do this today or presumably in the future. Here the "marginal efficiency of capital" would seem to depend on the relation between wages and the marginal efficiency of labor.

Finally, on page 207, the marginal efficiency of capital, "(especially of stocks of liquid goods)," comes to mean the speculative money profits which a man can anticipate from holding goods in a wild inflation, under the expectation of an ever greater fall in the value of money.

The maker of a new system of economics may be expected to adhere more closely than Keynes does to the meanings of his terms if he is to be taken seriously. Lumping all the causes of changes in anticipations regarding business profits under the one term *marginal efficiency of capital* does not represent progress in the economic analysis of cause and effect.

Keynes' "Independent Variables" Not Independent. We come now to the second main criticism of Keynes' constructive system. As shown above, he takes as his three independent variables (1) the propensity to consume, (2) the schedule of the marginal efficiency of capital, and (3) the rate of interest. Now, these supposedly independent variables are in fact dependent on one another, and are even dependent on Keynes' own showing.

The schedule of *the marginal efficiency of capital* is said, on page 136, to be the equivalent of *the investment demand schedule.* But on page 106 we have been told that every weakening in the propensity to consume, regarded as a permanent habit, must weaken the demand for capital. On Keynes' own showing, the schedule of the marginal efficiency of capital is, in part, dependent on the propensity to consume.

The propensity to consume is, in part, dependent upon the rate of interest. From the standpoint of the old analysis, the rate of interest, the propensity to consume, and the propensity to save are all three *interdependent* variables. The rate of interest is, indeed, the equilibrating factor which brings savings and consumption into balance. Human nature being more concerned with present consumption than with future consumption,[24] there is need for an inducement to make men save. The future looks

---

[24] Keynes does not believe this, but offers no evidence against it.

smaller than the present. The pressure to consume today is great. Human wants of specific kinds are often satiable, but human wants in general are not. As old wants are satisfied, new wants spring up. The pressure to consume is insistent. Men must be induced to save for the future by a reward, and that reward is interest.

When savings are large and capital increases, the rate of interest goes down. When interest is high because accumulated capital is scarce, men are forced to make savings that they would not otherwise make, or are induced to make savings that they would not otherwise make. The farmer who can borrow at four percent to buy additional capital goods for his farm, will have a higher propensity to consume than the farmer who must pay ten percent. If he can borrow at four percent, he will let his wife have a new dress and his family buy a new automobile. If he must pay ten percent, the new dress and the new automobile are not bought and new savings go into fertilizer, harrows, and combines. The propensity to consume is definitely dependent on the rate of interest.

The interdependence of the rate of interest, savings, and the propensity to consume, Keynes escapes formally, in part, by giving us the new theory of interest stated above. He makes the rate of interest dependent, not on the necessity of paying interest to induce men *to save,* but rather on the necessity to induce them *not to hoard* what they save. Interest rates are governed (given the scale of liquidity preference) by the quantity of money. We have seen above that he adheres to this theory for twenty-nine pages.

But even this emancipation of the rate of interest from time preference does not emancipate the propensity to consume from interest rates. If interest rates are high, whether from scarcity of money or from scarcity of real savings, men will be forced or induced to save more than would otherwise be the case, and the propensity to consume will be lower. The independence of the interest rate would still leave the propensity to consume dependent upon interest rates.

It has been shown above that, on Keynes' own showing, his schedule of marginal efficiency of capital, as initially defined, is dependent upon the propensity to consume. In the later meanings of the marginal efficiency of capital, however, it becomes dependent upon both the other variables. When marginal efficiency of capital comes to mean speculative profits in the stock market, or general business profits, it is clear that changes in the rate of interest, or in the propensity to consume, can radically alter the schedule of the marginal efficiency of capital. Keynes' three great independent variables are not independent.

III. *Static Economic Theory and the Business Cycle.* One reason why Keynes has found inadequate resistance among the younger economists to his casual throwing aside of the sound and subtle work of the great masters of static economic theory is that increasingly in the last two or three decades economists have been interested in the laws of the business cycle, in the ups and downs of business, and too many of them have felt that they could get very little help in the study of the business cycle from the generalizations of static economics.

The economic theorist has indeed devoted himself much too exclusively to the laws of completed equilibrium, to theory concerned with what prices and costs, and the proportions of the productive forces, would be if markets were fluid and if industry were in perfect balance. Students of the business cycle, on the other hand, have been concerned much too exclusively with the sequence and flow of events, losing sight of the goal in watching the motions of the runners.

It must be apparent, however, that in ignoring the static conceptions, the business forecaster is throwing away a most valuable aid. Static theory does describe underlying economic forces. If it tells nothing about the *rate* at which they will move, it does at least indicate the *directions* in which they move. It indicates their relative power and it indicates their relations *inter se*. The student of change who knows the goal toward which his forces are tending is certainly much better informed than the man who does not know what the goal is, but merely knows that change is taking place and that some things change first and others later.

Wesley C. Mitchell's *Business Cycles* could not have been written by a man who was not deeply learned in static theory and the equilibrium notion. Mitchell objects to the expression "the static state," but his interpretation of the busines cycle constantly employs equilibrium notions. The later stages of prosperity generate abnormalities, stresses, and strains. Costs rise faster than prices. There are inequalities in the rise of costs and prices. Other abnormalities occur, such as shortages of particular kinds of raw materials, with excess industrial equipment in some lines and inadequate equipment in others. A crisis comes and corrects these abnormalities, restoring equilibrium—not a previous equilibrium, but a new equilibrium—roughly and approximately. Then revival comes.

Mitchell's analysis makes business profits and the prospect of business profits the dynamo in the ups and downs of business. When the outlook for profits is good, business expands. When profits are cut, business contracts. The analysis runs in highly realistic terms, taking account of labor costs, rentals, and raw material costs as well as interest charges, taking account of rigidities and fluidities, of rigid prices and flexible prices.

There is no more startling instance of deterioration in a great science than the recent trends, largely influenced by Keynes, to turn away from an analysis that takes account of *all* the changing factors in economic life, and to concentrate attention almost exclusively upon monetary and budgetary phenomena, in explaining the business cycle and in formulating public policy with respect to prosperity and employment.

This writer's testimony,[25] after a quarter of a century devoted very largely to the study of markets and the ups and downs of business, would be to the effect that the equilibrium notion is the most useful tool of thought to be found. When economic forces are working toward balance, we may trust the situation. When they are obviously working toward unbalance, we should grow increasingly concerned. From theoretical concepts of the Keynesian type we receive no help at all.

---

[25] See also the chapters in the present volume dealing with the crisis of 1920–21 and the period of the 1920s. Interpretations of economic and financial history given in this volume center about the equilibrium principle.

61

Gold, Excess Reserves,
and Money Rates,
1934–41

G *rowth of Gold Stock from $4 Billion to $23 Billion, 1933–41.* Our gold monetary stock stood at $4 billion (old gold dollars, 23.22 grains of fine gold) at the beginning of 1934. The devaluation by presidential proclamation which followed immediately after the passage of the Gold Reserve Act of January 1934 meant an immediate markup in dollars of our gold monetary stock of approximately 69 percent, to nearly $7 billion. In the years that followed, gold moved steadily from the outside world to the United States and our gold monetary stock (new gold dollars, 13.7 grains of fine gold) reached the astounding figure of $22.8 billion by October 1941.

Gresham's Law. Two major influences brought this gold to us. The first was the working of Gresham's law. Under Gresham's law gold leaves countries which have fluctuating, irredeemable paper money and goes to countries which are on the gold standard. If no country is on the full gold standard, gold will still go to countries where some semblance of a fixed rate is kept, in preference to countries where there is no fixed rate or where the fluctuations are expected to be greater.

The *de facto* stabilization of the dollar in terms of gold at 59.06 percent of the old par strengthened the confidence of the American people in their own currency, a confidence which manifested itself in the revival of the bond market, and in a great increase in the purchase of annuities from life insurance companies. It also led to a resumption of gold movements to the United States from outside.

Fear of Hitler. The second great factor sending gold to us from Europe was a growing fear of Hitler. This fear was felt especially by the Jewish population of virtually all European countries throughout the period 1934–41. But it became very acute for Europe as a whole as Hitler's strength, and the weakness of England and France, were so dramatically revealed at Munich in September 1938. Our gold monetary stock stood at $13,136,000,000 at the end of August 1938. Thereafter it rose at a startling rate as nearly $10 billion more came in between Munich and October 1941. The single month June 1940 shows gold imports of $1,163,000,000, reflecting Hitler's actual invasion of the Netherlands, Belgium, and France.

Effect on Member Bank Reserves. The effect of this great markup in our monetary gold stock upon member bank reserve balances was very impressive. The original markup of the gold stock under the President's proclamation made no difference in member bank balances. The so-called gold profit was not immediately put into play. Two billion dollars of it were put into a Stabilization Fund in the hands of the United States Treasury, of which the Treasury transferred $200 million to "Special Account No. 1" in April 1934.[1] The major part of the rest was used in retiring bonds which secured national banknotes, and consequently in retiring the national banknotes—transactions which neutralized one another so far as the volume of member bank reserves was concerned.

But the new gold coming in from abroad went immediately into member bank reserves, creating $35 of member bank reserves for every ounce of gold imported. The imported gold would be sold to the Federal Reserve banks for Treasury account. The importer, whether a bank or a broker, would receive checks drawn on the Federal Reserve banks, which would speedily be deposited by a commercial bank in the Federal Reserve banks, adding to member bank reserves. Member bank reserve balances stood at $2,851,000,000 on January 24, 1934, and rose to $14,400,000,000 in January 1941.

The Startling Growth of Excess *Reserves.* Excess reserves[2] of the member banks of the Federal Reserve System were never very great in the years prior to 1932. The banks worked their reserves closely in the periods when confidence was high, 1914 to 1919 inclusive and 1922 to 1929 inclusive. And on the other hand, bank reserves were pulled low in 1921 and in 1931. Even in 1924 and 1927, years in which the Federal Reserve banks were increasing reserves rapidly by purchases of government securities, excess reserves for the dates available were not large because commercial bank expansion was moving so rapidly on the basis of increased reserves, and expanding deposits took up the slack. The only available figures for excess reserves in excess of $100 million prior to 1932, are June 29, 1918, when the figure was $215 million, June 30, 1919 ($133 million), and September 29, 1930 ($130 million). It is probable that the years 1924

---

[1] For partial revelations of this well-concealed account, see *Banking and Monetary Statistics* (Washington, 1943), p. 526.

[2] Monthly figures for excess reserves apparently are available since January 1929 (*ibid.,* pp. 370 *et seq.*). Weekly figures apparently become available only in September 1931 (*ibid.,* pp. 386 *et seq.*). Occasional figures, from one to three times a year, are, however, available beginning with December 31, 1914 (*ibid.,* pp. 395–96).

and 1927 would both show certain dates when the figure again exceeded $100 million, but this does not appear in any of the four dates given for either of these years. There were a good many times when reserve deficiency, instead of excess reserves, was shown in the years 1914 to 1931 inclusive. But in 1932, with the very heavy purchases of government securities made possible by the Glass-Steagall Act, excess reserves increased rapidly, rising from $27 million on February 24, 1932, to $554 million on December 28. With the passage of the Thomas Amendment in May 1933, which authorized the Treasury to make a contract with the Federal Reserve banks to buy $3 billion of government securities, the Federal Reserve System (though the contract was never formally made) once more began heavy purchases of government securities; and by January 1934, when the Gold Reserve Act was passed, it had increased its government securities from $1,837,000,000 to $2,432,000,000. Excess reserves stood at $938 million on January 24, 1934, a figure already very difficult to manage.

Peak of Excess Reserves $7 Billion, January 1941. In the period from early 1934 to January 15, 1941, excess reserves rose to approximately $7 billion (actually $6,896,000,000). This was the peak, and under the influence of our governmental war borrowings from the banks, later to be described, the excess reserves began to run down, and following March 12, 1941, ran down rapidly.

The primary cause of this great growth in reserves and excess reserves was the incoming gold, every ounce of which now made $35.00 instead of $20.67. An additional important factor was the issue of silver certificates exceeding $1.25 billion which followed the silver purchases of the federal government under the silver legislation of May 1934 (of which an account is given in an earlier chapter). Excess reserves would have risen to even higher levels, of course, had there not been (1) a $3 billion growth in money in circulation in the years 1934–40, (2) a great growth in demand deposits in the banks, due chiefly to member bank purchases of government securities, and (3) increases in the reserve requirements of the member banks by action of the Federal Reserve authorities in 1936 and 1937.

Excess Reserves Cause Very Low Interest Rates. The effect of the increasing member bank reserves upon money rates and the yield on United States government bonds was very striking. The following table tells the story.

When the excess reserves reached $2,779,000,000 in August 1935, interest rates had broken to fantastic levels. A very significant fact shown by the following table is that most of this beating down of interest rates had been accomplished by July 1934, at which time excess reserves stood at $1,873,000,000. On that date open market commercial paper had a range of .75 to 1 percent, and prime bankers' acceptances were discounted at .125 to .25 percent. Treasury bills, three to six months, were yielding only .08 percent and the yield on government bonds was 2.85 percent. In other

The New Deal in Maturity, 1933–39

MEMBER BANK RESERVES AND MONEY RATES*

Date	Member bank reserves	Excess reserves (estimated by Federal Reserve Board)	Prevailing rates on prime commercial paper (4–6 mos.)	Prevailing rates on prime bankers' acceptances (90 days)	Average yield on U. S. Treasury notes & certificates (3–6 mos.)	Average yield on U. S. Treasury bills (e) (3–6 mos.)	Yield on U. S. government bonds (b)
	Millions of dollars		Monthly average percent per annum				
1929—Sept.	2,335 (a)	34 (a)	6¼	5⅛	4.58	—	3.68
1930—Jan.	2,349 (a)	45 (a)	4¾–5	3⅞–4	3.39	—	3.43
July	2,417 (a)	74 (a)	3–3½	1⅞	1.83	—	3.23
1931—July	2,407 (a)	124 (a)	2	⅞	.41	.49	3.11
Dec. 2	2,073	25	3¾–4	3	2.41	3.25	3.92
1932—Feb. 24	1,878	27	3¾–4	2¾–2⅞	2.42	2.66	4.11
May 4	2,147	289	2¾–3½	⅞–1⅛	.31	.43	3.71
Dec. 28	2,482	554	1¼–1¾	⅜	.04	.09	3.31
1933—Mar. 8	1,776	129	1½–4½	1⅛–3⅝	1.34	2.29	3.44
Apr. 12	2,096	388	2–3¼	½–1¼	.45	.57	3.43
Sept.	2,596 (c)	774 (c)	1¼–1½	¼	.04	.10	3.20
Nov.	2,573	727	1¼	¼–½	.22	.42	3.46
1934—Jan.	2,652	745	1¼–1½	½	.25	.67	3.50
Mar.	3,439	1,432	1–1¼	¼–½	.01	.08	3.21
July	4,020	1,873	¾–1	⅛–¼	(d)	.08	2.85
Sept.	3,970	1,768	¾–1	⅛–¼	(d)	.27	3.20
1935—Jan.	4,542	2,203	¾–1	⅛	(f)	.14	2.83
May	4,827	2,322	¾	⅛	—	.10	2.61
July	5,100	2,513	¾	⅛	—	.07	2.59
Aug.	5,346 (c)	2,749 (c)	¾	⅛	—	—	2.66

(a) Monthly averages.
(b) Average yield computed by Treasury.
(c) From September 1933 to August 1935 inclusive, these figures are for the last Wednesday in the month.
(d) Negative yield (figures from Annual Report of Federal Reserve Board).
(e) Figures from July 1931 to May 1934 are for 3-month bills; those from July 1934 to January 1935 are for 6-month bills; March, May, and July 1935 are for 133-day bills.
(f) Series not continued by Federal Reserve Board.
* This table is taken from my address before the Investment Bankers' Association of America, October 30, 1935, "The Control of the Excess Reserves of the Member Banks of the Federal Reserve System." It will be found in the year book of the association. The yields on United States government bonds are slightly different for certain dates from those which appear in *Banking and Monetary Statistics* (Washington, 1943). The table was carefully made on the basis of data available at that time, and I have not altered it.

words, when excess reserves grew as large as $1,873,000,000, subsequent additions to excess reserves made very little difference. The money market was completely flooded and money rates could go very little lower.

Call loans to the stock market were pegged at 1 percent and would have gone much lower in the absence of the pegging. Prime customers' loans at the great city banks were pegged at 1.5 percent, with occasional undercutting by banks in St. Louis and Chicago.

The immense increase in the excess reserves which followed the last date of the table, August 1935—an increase from $2.75 billion to nearly $7 billion at the beginning of 1941—made very little difference indeed in interest rates, except that the yield of long government bonds had moved down from 2.74 to 2.23 percent by August 1940.[3]

Board of Governors Raises Reserve Requirements, 1936–37. The growing volume of excess reserves was a matter of grave concern to most informed students of money and banking, and the Federal Reserve authorities were greatly troubled about it.[4]

The Federal Reserve banks could, of course, have cut into the excess reserves by selling government securities, of which they had in 1935 and 1936 $2,431,000,000. But they had no desire to do this because it would cut their earnings and it was, moreover, a procedure politically in bad odor. Raising their discount rates would have made no difference, since total bills discounted in 1935 were only $7 million and in 1936 only $6 million. But they had the device (authorized by the Congress under the Thomas Amendment of 1933 and, under limitations, in the Banking Act of 1935) of raising reserve requirements, which would reduce excess reserves. This, being a New Deal device, was politically much easier. It had the further great merit that it would reduce the expansion potential of such excess reserves as remained.

The effect of raising reserve requirements as a restraining measure would be different from the effect of selling government securities or even of raising discount rates. Raising reserve requirements would immediately hit every member bank, whereas the selling of government securities would have its immediate effect upon those banks which had excess reserves and were prepared to buy government securities. There was always the possibility that, even though reserves in the aggregate were

---

[3] The yield of 2.74 percent for August 1935 on long government bonds is higher than that given in my preceding table, where it stands at 2.66 percent. I am using now the figures of *Banking and Monetary Statistics* (Washington, 1943). I do not carry government bond yields further here, as there is some uncertainty as to the comparability of Federal Reserve figures on this point before and after August 1940. See this volume, p. 474, and the not entirely clear statement in the text on p. 429.

[4] In an address before the Investment Banker's Association of America on October 30, 1935, I took the position that the Federal Reserve authorities should use their power to raise member bank reserve requirements. I emphasized the dangerously high potential of credit expansion on the basis of the existing low reserve requirements and large excess reserves. I made the generalization that excess reserves beyond a billion and a half made very little difference in money rates—an opinion which was strikingly confirmed in the summer of 1943 when, in the midst of the government's immense borrowing program, excess reserves dropped to approximately a billion and a half without making a real difference in money rates or in the ability of the banks to absorb government securities. I pointed out that, on the basis of the foregoing table, the increase in excess reserves from $27 million to $289 million between February 4, 1932, and May 4, 1932, had made vastly more difference in rates and yields than the whole of the $2 billion added to excess reserves between early 1934 and October 1935.

excessive, still a good many individual banks might not have excess reserves, and a move which struck at all the banks might catch a good many of them unprepared. Of course, the Federal Reserve authorities were in a position to have exact information regarding the position of individual member banks and could know to what extent individual banks might be put under pressure by such a measure.

The Board of Governors of the Federal Reserve System moved. On August 16, 1936, they raised reserve requirements by 50 percent, and announced that there would be two more increases of 25 percent each on March 1 and May 1, 1937, so that the reserve requirements of the country would be doubled by May 1, 1937. This program was carried through. Reserves for demand deposits in New York and Chicago were raised to 26 percent, for the other reserve cities requirements were raised to 20 percent, and for country banks to 14 percent, while reserve requirements against time deposits were everywhere made 6 percent—all these figures being double the requirements that had previously existed. These measures reduced excess reserves to something like a billion dollars.

But excess reserves continued to grow. In April 1938 the Federal Reserve authorities canceled the last 25 percent increase in reserve requirements, but in November 1941 restored it. Subsequently, in 1942, reserve requirements on demand deposits for New York and Chicago banks were reduced to the 20 percent level of the other reserve cities.

62

Gold Remains
Standard of Value

France, Switzerland, and the Netherlands Abandon Gold Standard. The story of gold in the period from 1933 down to the time of Munich is a very interesting and dramatic one. By early 1937 the gold standard in its old form had ceased to exist. There remained no important country in the world where paper currencies would be automatically and regularly redeemed either in gold coin or in gold bars. First France and then Switzerland and the Netherlands had abandoned the gold standard. France, extraordinarily strong in 1930, had gone back to her chronic deficits. Her finances were weakening, and in late 1936 the Bank of France informed the Federal Reserve authorities and the Bank of England that it would have to suspend gold payments.

The Tripartite Monetary Agreement. A tripartite agreement involving England, France, and the United States came into existence, with the Stabilization Fund of the United States and the Equalization Account of England cooperating with the Bank of France in preventing violent disorder in the foreign exchange market when France suspended gold payments. After the abandonment of the gold standard by France, Switzerland and the Netherlands followed with suspension of gold payments and more moderate depreciation of their currencies. The European gold bloc ceased to exist.

Exchange Stability Based on Gold Payments. Nevertheless, gold remained the standard of value, the ultimate regulator of the values of paper currencies. What stability there was in the foreign exchanges in the period that followed grew out of gold, and the indirect relations of the currencies to gold. There remained a great free gold market in London, and operations by our Stabilization Fund and the stabilization funds or central banks of other countries in this free gold market held gold and paper money more or less closely together. Our own dollar had been held approximately within the gold points since early 1934 by the continued issue of dollars against gold at a fixed rate, and by the release of gold for export whenever the dollar reached the lower gold point in the foreign exchange or foreign gold market. Between May 1, 1935, and early 1937 sterling did not vary over 2⅔ percent in its relation to gold. Following the collapse of the gold bloc and the readjustments immediately ensuing, the major Continental currencies were held in very close relation to gold. Between October 17, 1936, and January 9, 1937, for example, French francs varied less than 1 percent in their relation to gold, Swiss francs ¹/₇ percent, Dutch guilders 1½ percent and Italian lire ⅛ percent.

Because No Government Would Trust Another's Paper Money. Gold remained the standard of value because neither individuals nor governments would trust anything else. None of the stabilization funds of the various countries had any desire to accumulate the paper currencies of other countries. The Bank of France wanted no sterling because the Bank of France remembered only too well that in 1931 it had lost eight times its capital through its sterling holdings when England abandoned the gold standard. The Netherlands bank had had a similar experience. Our Stabilization Fund had no enthusiasm for holdings of sterling. The stabilization funds dealing with one another apparently settled their differences in gold very promptly, and frequently every night.

The great advantage of the tripartite agreement was, not in fixing exchange rates and holding them, but in moderating fluctuations. One major advantage of the agreement, as distinguished from separate action by the British Equalization Fund and the American Stabilization Fund, was that the men operating the American Stabilization Fund did not have to get up so early in the morning, and the men operating the British Equalization Fund did not have to stay up so late at night, as would otherwise have been the case. With five hours' difference in time between New York and London, this was a very real advantage. Of course, had there been the orthodox gold standard in both countries, nobody would have had to lose any sleep at all.

Increase in Gold Production—Ounces and Dollars. A further reason for our great gain in gold was a startling increase of world production of gold measured in ounces following 1930. Declining prices and wages made it profitable to reopen closed mines and develop new gold mines. When, following England's abandonment of the gold standard in 1931 and our debasement of the gold dollar, there came, measured in pounds or dollars, a greatly increased price of gold with no corresponding increase in the cost of mining gold, gold production was further greatly stimulated. Measured in fine ounces, the increase was nearly 50 percent between 1930 and 1935 and was almost 100 percent between 1930 and 1940. The increase in gold production, measured in dollars, is even more startling beginning with 1934, since after January of that year each fine ounce of gold would make $35.00 intead of $20.67 as in preceding years.

WORLD PRODUCTION OF GOLD*

Calendar year	Fine ounces	Value in dollars**
1890	5,749,306	$ 118,848,700
1900	12,315,135	254,576,300
1910	22,022,180	455,239,100
1920	16,146,830	333,784,924
1930	20,903,736	432,118,638
1931	22,284,290	460,650,527
1932	24,098,676	498,163,970
1933	25,400,295	525,070,547
1934	27,372,374	958,033,090
1935	29,999,245	1,049,973,580
1936	32,930,554	1,152,569,390
1937	35,118,298	1,229,140,430
1938	37,703,334	1,319,616,690
1939	39,534,430	1,383,705,050
1940	41,067,101	1,437,348,535
1941	40,332,204	1,411,627,140

* These figures are from the Annual Reports of the director of the mint, 1936 (pp. 108–9), and 1942 (p. 104). The *Federal Reserve Bulletin,* February 1946, gives figures after 1941 for several countries but attempts no world summary after 1941.

** At $20.67 per fine ounce prior to 1934; at $35.00 per fine ounce 1934 and thereafter.

The world production of gold, in old gold dollars, in 1930 was $432,000,000. By 1936 it reached $1,152,000,000 (new gold dollars). Here was a world problem of first magnitude. The absorption of this gold in the ordinary way, letting it have its usual effects upon the money markets, meant eventually a rapid growth in the excess reserves of the banks of the countries which absorbed it, meant inevitably a great and progressive credit expansion, and meant inevitably a great rise in commodity prices measured in terms of gold.

This, to be sure, was what had been aimed at when the devaluation took place in early 1934 and when the gold buying policy had begun in 1933, but the expected thing on the part of the men who did it was that there would be an immediate and automatic response in higher prices. This had failed, but the danger of an unmanageable explosion with the steady piling up of money market resources remained.

63

The British Equalization Account, the American Stabilization Fund, and the American Sterilization Fund

Under the gold standard, imports of gold ease the money market of the importing country. Gold goes from the importing commercial banks to the central bank or (in our case) the Federal Reserve banks, and the commercial banks get additional reserves in exchange for the gold. Gold leaving a country reduces the reserves of the commercial banks. They are obliged to pull down their reserve balances with the central bank in getting the gold for export. This tightens the money market.

British Equalization Account—Created out of Government Debt. With abandonment of the gold standard in England this automatic working of gold imports and exports ceased. When sterling dropped low after the abandonment of the gold standard considerable amounts of gold and foreign exchange came to England to purchase sterling. India, in particular, sent a good deal of gold to England. By July 1932 the Bank of England was said to have had substantial holdings of gold and foreign exchange gained in this way. Apparently they were put into a special account, as examination of the figures of the bank for gold in the issue department, cash reserves and other assets of the banking department, and bankers' balances and other elements in the bank's liabilities, shows no clear evidence of it, though there was an increase in bankers' balances between October 28, 1931, and June 29, 1932, from £63.5 million to £86.6 million, or £23.1 million.

Beginning with July 1, 1932, the British Equalization Account came into existence. It was created primarily out of government securities, government debt. It took over the foreign exchange holdings of the Bank of England, giving to the bank government securities (presumably Treasury bills) in exchange.[1] Its secrets were well kept and statements regarding it

---

[1] London *Economist,* May 13, 1933. The Bank of England's balance sheet, during the next few months after June 29, 1932, does not reveal this transaction.

are based primarily upon the opinions of informed men in London and in New York.

One purpose of the creation of the Equalization Account was to let the government rather than the bank assume the risks of fluctuating gold prices and fluctuating foreign exchange prices. Another purpose was to *moderate fluctuations* in the foreign exchange markets—not to *stabilize the pound*.

Created primarily out of government securities, it could function effectively only insofar as gold movements toward England gave it enough gold to offset gold movements out of England at a later time.

Perverse Effect of Gold Movements on British Money Market. Under the functioning of the British Equalization Account, British gold imports and exports had a *perverse* effect upon the money market. When gold came in, the Equalization Account, in order to purchase the gold, had to borrow sterling, which it would normally do by selling British government securities to the commercial banks.[2] This would increase the investments and the deposits of the British banks, operating to tighten the money market. When the Equalization Account was losing gold, exchanging gold for sterling, it would use the sterling thus obtained to repurchase government securities from the commercial banks. This reduced the investments and deposits of the commercial banks and eased off the British money market. So far as the working of the Equalization Account was concerned, the more gold England lost, the lower her money rates went. Of course the Bank of England could take separate action to offset this, and doubtless sometimes did, but there was nothing automatic about it.

American Stabilization Fund—Created out of Gold—Early 1934. Now the American Stabilization Fund, on the contrary, was created solely out of gold. It consisted initially, as we have seen, of $2 billion in gold taken out of the so-called gold profit which arose from reducing the gold content of the American dollar to 59.06 percent of the old parity. The British Equalization Account functioned most effectively in accumulating incoming gold and keeping it from having the ordinary effect on the money market. It was, in effect, when England was receiving gold, a "sterilization fund." But our Stabilization Fund, consisting of gold, had nothing with which to buy gold except gold itself.

Gold Movements Had Normal Effects on Our Money Market. Incoming gold in the United States, in general, did not go into our exchange Stabilization Fund,[3] but rather, via the Federal Reserve banks, into that part of the gold in the Treasury which stands behind the gold certificates.

---

[2] The *Economist* article of May 13, 1933, says that the Account "probably" borrowed from the Bank of England, but later information tends to justify the statement here made.

[3] See *Banking and Monetary Statistics* for the gold in the active account of the exchange Stabilization Fund. The inactive account remained unchanged, at $1.8 billion, from early 1934 to July 1946. See Treasury daily statements, p. 1.

The Federal Reserve banks bought incoming gold for the Treasury, paying for it with Federal Reserve checks, which almost immediately created new reserves for the member banks, beating down money rates. We restored the automatism of the gold standard, so far as the relation of the money market to gold was concerned.

When our Stabilization Fund of $2 billion was created by the Gold Reserve Act of 1934, it was supposed to be something like the British Equalization Account, though in fact it differed radically from it. The Senate committee dealing with the bill obviously knew nothing about the actual workings of the British Account. The chairman of the committee said, "We were told that there were only three men in all England who knew what they did."[4] There is no reason to suppose that our Treasury at that time knew more about the workings of the British Equalization Account than the Senate committee did. It was said privately at the time that one reason for creating our exchange Stabilization Fund was to put the gold in a special account so that Congress could not appropriate it for anything else, but the probability is that the Treasury was simply trying to follow a British model.

Our Sterilization Fund More Nearly Based on British Model—December 1936. Our Treasury, having failed in 1934 to create a Stabilization Fund on the model of the British Equalization Account, and having become aware of that fact, tried again.

In December 1936 alarmed at the continued inflow of foreign gold, our Treasury adopted the policy of "sterilizing" this gold by borrowing money from the commercial banks with which to buy it, much as the British Equalization Account did, instead of allowing the incoming gold to increase the money supply and to "pay for itself." The gold thus purchased did not add to the credit base. If our bank reserves had not been excessive, the operations would have tended, as was the case in England, to tighten the money market as the gold came in. But with our great volume of excess reserves it had no effect on the money market other than to increase the already excessive volume of commercial bank deposits.

In January 1937 it seemed probable[5] that the sterilization policy was only a temporary palliative. This proved to be the case. In April 1938, when the fund had grown to $1,392,000,000, it was suddenly abandoned. Gold certificates in a corresponding amount were placed in the Federal Reserve banks, and the government got a corresponding deposit with the Federal Reserve banks, which promptly began to go into member bank reserves as the government spent the money. We discuss this episode in connection with the crisis and depression of 1937–38.

---

[4] U.S., Congress, Senate, Committee on Banking and Currency, *Hearings on the Gold Reserve Act of 1934,* S. 2366, p. 132.

[5] "Gold, Stabilization Funds, and Prices," *Chase Economic Bulletin,* January 26, 1937.

British Opinion Regarding Great Increase in Gold Production in 1937. In May 1937 the proposal was made, in consultation with bankers in London, that we and Britain should simultaneously raise the gold content of the pound and the dollar, and anchor the currencies at this higher valuation. The danger to money market stability and to the long-run future of an annual production of gold of $1,200 million was stressed. The total "bankers' balances" of the British banks with the Bank of England amounted to about £90 million at that time—say $450 million. If Britain were to receive, in the regular way, one-third of the world's gold production and let it have its ordinary effect on the money market, it would very nearly double bankers' balances in a single year, nearly treble them in two years, and so on. The proposal met with a sympathetic response in influential quarters.

An empire conference was being held in London at the time of the coronation, May 1937. The South Africans, who were very influential, had come prepared to demand a continued high price of gold in terms of sterling.[6] But as the price of gold was increasingly discussed, the South Africans were said to have come to the view that a lower price of gold (that is, a higher gold content of the pound) would suit them very well, if only they could be sure that the pound would be definitely stabilized in terms of gold. England was strong in gold at this time, and the pound, partly under the influence of tourists' expenditures in London in the coronation month, was rising against both dollars and gold (March, $4.88; May, $4.94; August, $4.98). Our own gold position was so strong that it would have made very little difference to us if we had lowered the price of gold to a point which would have used up the "gold profit."

But the war clouds gathered in 1938. Gold suddenly began to leave Europe on a greatly intensified scale, and there was speedily no disposition anywhere in Europe to do anything about lowering the price of gold. Everybody began to expect a further rise in the price of gold (that is, a further depreciation of European paper moneys).

---

[6] This information came from Australians and other participants in the conference at the time.

64

The Tyranny of Gold

G old needs no endorsement. It can be tested with scales and with acids. The recipient of gold does not have to trust the government stamp upon it, if he does not trust the government that stamped it. No act of faith is called for when gold is used in payments, and no compulsion is required.

Men everywhere, governments everywhere, and central banks everywhere are glad to get it. When paper is offered instead of gold, it will be accepted on faith if the government or the bank which has issued the paper has proved itself worthy of confidence by a satisfactory record of redeeming the paper in gold on demand.

Irredeemable Paper and Gresham's Law. Complaints are always made about gold and the behavior of gold when there is irredeemable paper money. Under Gresham's law, gold is hoarded, or leaves the country. It ceases to circulate, leaving the dishonored promissory note in possession of the field. Gold will stay only in countries which submit to its discipline. Gold is an unimaginative taskmaster. It demands that men and governments and central banks be honest. It demands that they keep their promises on demand or at maturity. It demands that they keep their demand liabilities safely within the limits of their quick assets. It demands that they create no debts without seeing clearly how these debts can be paid. If a country will do these things, gold will stay with it and will come to it from other countries which are not meeting the requirements. But when a country creates debt lightheartedly, when a central bank makes rates of discount low and buys government securities to feed its money market, and permits an expansion of credit that goes into slow and illiquid assets, then gold grows nervous. Mobile capital funds of all kinds grow nervous. There comes a flight of capital out of the country. Foreigners withdraw their funds from it, and its own citizens send their liquid funds away for safety.

Irredeemable Paper as Discounted Promissory Note. When suspension of gold payments comes, speculators in the foreign exchange market treat paper currency most disrespectfully. They sell it short. They buy it only at a discount. The amount of discount in a free gold market or in a free foreign exchange market will be governed primarily by speculative expectation as to whether and when resumption of gold payments are coming, as to whether and when the government and the central bank will reverse its unsound policy and work back toward orthodoxy. Gold is blamed, speculators are blamed, capital movements are blamed, "hot money" is blamed.

In the seventeen years between January 1, 1862, and January 1, 1879, our greenback period, we had a classical illustration of the behavior of irredeemable paper money with a free gold market and with a free foreign exchange market. The episode has been elaborately worked out by Wesley C. Mitchell in his *History of the Greenbacks*. The standing of the irredeemable paper in the gold market and in the foreign exchange market was influenced by every circumstance that would affect the probability of its redemption, and the probable time of its redemption. The cessation of printing greenbacks, and the adoption of a strong tax and funded loan policy, made for strong improvement in the standing of the greenbacks. Most influential of all was the success or failure of the Northern armies in the war. The Battle of Chickamauga made the greenbacks drop four percent. Gettysburg, Vicksburg, and Port Hudson pulled down the price of gold from $145 in greenbacks for $100 in gold to $122 in twenty days. Grant's successful campaign against Richmond and Lee's surrender led to a very dramatic rise in the value of the greenbacks (or, reversely, to a very dramatic fall in the price of gold as measured in greenbacks).

In June 1864 the Congress undertook to punish the speculators by closing the gold market and forbidding futures in gold. The results were disastrous. In isolated markets the greenbacks fell to approximately 35¢ in gold, and Congress, two weeks later, without debate, repealed the measure.

The country submitted to the tyranny of gold. It was old-fashioned and it was honest. It had promised to redeem its paper money in gold, and it settled down to get its house in order so that it could do so. In 1876 a definite program promising gold redemption on January 1, 1879, was adopted by the Congress, and shortly thereafter John Sherman, one of the ablest financiers in the history of the country, as secretary of the Treasury, began to take definite steps to redeem the greenbacks on that date. Once the country was convinced that Sherman meant to do it, the greenbacks, like a discounted promissory note approaching maturity, moved up month by month to the redemption date, with the discount disappearing entirely in late 1878. On January 1, 1879, we resumed gold payments. In 1879 the Treasury gained gold instead of losing it. Incidentally, commodity prices rose in 1879 and continued to rise for some time thereafter. Credit was restored. The country was jubilant.

Paper Money as Legal Tender. Here you have the main story of irredeemable paper money in a free country with free markets. Paper money is not merely a promissory note, of course. It is also legal tender. The government, moreover, as tax collector will receive it, and finally there are various elements of patriotic support from a loyal people for the paper.

Paper Money as a "Thing in Itself." There also arises, in a time of monetary disorder, the doctrine that "a dollar's a dollar" or "a pound's a pound" and that the dishonored paper money is somehow or other a "thing in itself." Our "Greenbackers," in the period of our currency disorder, anticipated very many of the doctrines which one found current in London in the period between 1931 and 1939 regarding the pound. One has never heard this mystical theory more profoundly or more poetically expressed than by a Polish statesman, who in 1922 protested against the retirement of a single Polish banknote on the ground that every banknote was "imbued with the soul of the Polish people."[1]

Prestige of Pound and Loyalty of the City. The prestige of a great government and a long-established government can go far in upholding the value of its paper money even if rational foundations for the value of paper money have waned. In regions where governments do not last long, this factor is rather feeble. A recent writer points out that in Iraq, and in general in the Near East, where few existing governments have lasted more than twenty years, there is a very strong preference for hard money over irredeemable paper. But the pound sterling, in the years 1931 to 1939, made a brave show on the basis of this kind of prestige. The people of Britain seem to have accepted it almost without question, though doubtless many of the more sagacious of them put anchor to windward when they could without giving too much offense to associates in the City. But the City, the financial district of London, itself was very loyal to the pound. There was no great flight of British capital from England, though there may have been heavy British investment in gold in the London gold market. But the whole world had long used sterling. As sterling went low the outside world bought it, and we even had the extraordinary spectacle of Scandinavian countries, Baltic countries, and the British dominions on a sterling basis

---

[1] See the chapter "Dodo-Bones" in my book, *The Value of Money* (New York: Macmillan, 1917; and Richard R. Smith, 1936). See also in the same volume the discussion of Knapp's *Staatliche Theorie des Geldes*, pp. 433–35 n. I refer to Knapp here because Lord Keynes accepts Knapp's doctrine (*A Treatise on Money* [New York, 1930], vol. 1, p. 4), and because this is the only discussion by Lord Keynes that I have been able to find which even purports to explain the forces which make value for irredeemable paper. There is really very little about the *value* of money in Knapp's book. It is a juridical rather than an economic study. Knapp is a keen logician and a fine hairsplitter, and is good at turning a clever phrase against his opponents. When his thesis, that whatever the state declares to be money is money, is met with the objection that state paper money, if irredeemable, is bad money, he still holds his ground: "da es ja Geld sein muss, um Schlimmes Geld zu sein" ("because it must indeed be money in order to be bad money"). I am content to leave the matter with this statement of Knapp's.

putting their central bank reserves into sterling in part, and letting their own currencies fluctuate with the pound against gold. A "Sterling Area" was created, and London thought she had made a new discovery.

The Untranquil Sterling Area. But all was not tranquil in the Sterling Area. The London *Economist* of September 2, 1939 (p. 452), sums the matter up very well in the following passage:

> For some years past the British Exchange Equalization Account had found to its cost that the adherence of certain foreign countries to the sterling bloc had been a factor of instability and not of strength. Many sterling bloc countries have panicked into and then out of sterling with the abandon of the most highly strung speculator. Some of the hottest of London's hot money has consisted of the sterling reserves of the sterling bloc, and their partial disappearance will not be altogether a loss.

Sterling unanchored to gold was subject to constant fevers and chills, which the Exchange Equalization Account could moderate but could not eliminate.

Hot Money. The "hot money" referred to by the *Economist* passage above was essentially a product of the unsound monetary policy.

In the period from 1931 on there was a great deal of hot money, nervous money, jumping about from place to place seeking safety. The origin of this money was in the excessive bank expansion of the 1920s. Bank balances had risen tremendously under the cheap money policy of the 1920s. Sterling had been overexpanded. The British banks had made loans which created new sterling deposits far in excess of what was justified by the gold reserve position of the Bank of England, and foreigners had got hold of these sterling balances because England had spent them abroad or had loaned them abroad.

When the foreigner tried to cash in these excessive British liabilities for gold in 1931, England quit paying gold and went off the gold standard. But the balances remained on the books of the British banks, and the balances even grew as gold came to England from India and other places to buy sterling when sterling went low. The excessive *amount* is due primarily to the excessive expansion of credit in the 1920s. The *nervousness* of the funds is due to the deterioration in *quality* of this excessive credit, and to the abandonment of gold.

How to Avoid Hot Money. A country which is afraid of hot money, money which may suddenly jump to another country, has a very simple way of avoiding this danger. It does not need to control capital movements. It protects itself from this danger by having a sound currency, firmly anchored to gold at a fixed rate, by keeping control of its money market so that its demand liabilities do not grow excessive in relation to its gold, by keeping a balanced budget—by making a financial environment in which money cools off and wants to stay.

England a Sieve for Gold, 1931–39. Between 1931 and the outbreak of the war in 1939 England became a sieve for gold. Gold came in. Gold went out. The automatic gold standard controls were gone, and British money market policy did very little to control the movements either way. The fetish of cheap money as the great essential, more important than the safety of the currency, more important than the prestige of the pound, more important than stability in foreign exchange rates, dominated the picture.

65

Governmental Coercion and the Value of Money

It was prevailing doctrine among economists down to World War I that governments could not coerce their peoples into accepting at face value a dishonored paper money. But World War I brought an immense revival and intensification of governmental power. And in the years 1915–18 a good many new techniques of price fixing and control of foreign exchange operations were introduced which tended to prevent transactions which would recognize the depreciation of irredeemable paper money.

After the war, during the currency disorders of 1919–24, a good many ineffective efforts were made by various countries to use coercion to replace waning faith. The head of the Bank of Athens said about 1923 that in Greece they had tried to stop all export of currency and securities from Greece. They had succeeded pretty well, inside Greece, in controlling foreign exchange transactions, and they had got a good control of the mails and of the telegraph, but couriers, carrying currency and carrying securities, found it easy enough to slip through mountain passes, and the depreciation of the drachma went on in the outside foreign exchange markets.

Even where coercion might succeed in forcing a dishonored paper currency to be accepted at home, it continued to be true that nothing could prevent it from depreciating in the foreign exchange markets.

Currency Policy in Russia. We saw develop under the Bolshevik regime in Russia an authority over the lives of the people unmatched until Hitler surpassed it, but Russia's control of its currency never reached a point that would justify abandoning the older beliefs with respect to the power of the state over currency. The first Bolshevik policy, based on ideas of pure communism, was to ruin and discredit the currency in the naive belief that direct action, direct control of production and consumption would make money unnecessary. Rubles were printed recklessly for the deliberate purpose of ruining them.

By 1921, however, Lenin had reached the conclusion that pure communism would not work, and the "New Economic Policy" announced by Lenin in his famous speech of October 17, 1921, frankly acknowledged a partial return to capitalism. The reestablishment of capitalism in Russia involved the redevelopment of a money held as closely as possible at a parity with gold. In the years that followed Russia had repeated slumps in the value of its currency, but always resisted them, and finally turned decisively toward heavy gold production, recognizing the need of gold both for international use and as an element of strength in the domestic currency situation.

Russia never succeeded in eliminating the black market in foreign exchange inside Russia. An official of the state Bank of Russia in 1927 or 1928 was told of a report made by an American traveling in Russia of the shooting of certain of the "comrades" in Moscow who had been caught speculating in foreign exchange. The official of the state bank replied that the bank had changed its method of handling the problem. The bank had found it more effective to send its own agents to the black bourse to buy and sell, and thus to regulate the exchange rates on the black bourse. He added that he was paying high rates of interest on deposits to Russian depositors, and was giving them assurances that he would not report their earnings to the tax collector. As late as 1938 there were reports from certain travelers of the existence of a black market in foreign exchange in Russia.

It was not usually possible to sell checks drawn on Russian banks in the foreign exchange markets, because usually transfer of funds on the books of Russian banks by outsiders would be forbidden. There was one case in the late 1930s of an author who had some funds in a Russian bank as the result of royalties, and who found that the only way to make any use of these funds was to go to Russia and spend a few months living there, under which conditions the funds would be available. The power of the Russian state over the lives of its people was very great, but Russia could never get entirely free from the "tyranny of gold," and Russia could never make its paper money a thing in itself, created by the state and held fixed by the state's fiat.

The Tyranny of Hitler and the Tyranny of Gold. Hitler could. Hitler inherited a people, intelligent and docile, accustomed to bookkeeping and trained for generations in the tradition of state authority and respect for state authority such as no other modern country has ever exhibited. Fichte, Hegel, Bismarck, and a multitude of other less significant figures, including the *Schulemeister,* had drilled into the German people an attitude which made it possible for the German state under Hitler really to substitute the tyranny of Hitler for the tyranny of gold.

It did not come all at once. The efforts of the Bruening government and of the Reichsbank in the first year of the Standstill (1931) to control foreign exchange transactions, and to prevent the transfer of funds out of Germany, were only partially successful. There was discussion in the second Standstill Committee (Berlin, 1931–32) in which French bankers were complaining that they knew of such transactions because the funds were coming to their own banks. A representative of the Reichsbank said, "If you will give me the names, I will put them in prison. " But the French bankers were, of course, under the banker's obligation to protect the privacy of accounts which came to them lawfully under French law.

But as Hitler came in, the lines tightened. The exchange controls became very effective, while price fixing, covering a very wide range of commodities, became extraordinarily effective. Price fixing was accompanied by strict commodity control. The German farmer kept books which showed not merely what he had sold, but also all that he had produced, and all that he had *consumed* of his production in his own home.

Tricks were at first devised along lines like these. The farmer and the butcher would make a deal whereby the pigs were sold at the fixed price, but whereby the farmer's little dog was sold to the butcher at an absurdly high price. If the little dog happened to come home, well, that was just what the little dog would do, and the butcher didn't care. But very speedily the German government clamped down on transactions like this. Severe penalties were imposed and the fixed price was made effective.

There was control over the books of every corporation. If funds accumulated, the corporation was directed to put substantial sums into government securities. In cases where bookkeeping was difficult to enforce—as with the tips of a waitress in a restaurant—the tax gatherer would come around each day to have an accounting with the waitress and to make his collections. Hitler had an enormous and very effective army of officials, and a very powerful and utterly ruthless secret police in the Gestapo. Hitler had succeeded in shattering family loyalties, breaking the ties between parents and children, and parents did not know but that their own sons and daughters might be members of Hitler's Gestapo.

Control over foreign exchange transactions in Germany and outside was tremendously effective. Men feared to buy dollars with marks in Germany or to hold dollars. If they had dollars, it was their duty to turn them over to the state, and they did so. On a German ship carrying passengers between New York and Bremerhaven, a special kind of ship money was employed which could not be spent off the ship, and ordinary German marks could not be used on the ship. The steward was absolutely afraid to take a tip in the regular marks. If he got a tip in dollars or in sterling, he could take that, but he must at once report to the purser and have it converted into ship's money. When he left the ship, the ship's money would be exchanged for him into regular marks, but it was made impossible for him to bring regular marks obtained outside Germany into Germany.

Between 1937 and 1938 the control over Reichsbank notes which got outside Germany was tightened decisively. Travelers leaving Germany made every effort to carry no paper marks over the border. It was dangerous to do so. In 1937, leaving Germany, an American banker found that he had taken with him, in the pocket of a suit he was not wearing, a ten-mark note. He turned it in at a bank in Paris and the bank took it at par of exchange. But when a similar thing happened in 1938, he found he had a useless piece of paper on his hands. Interested in testing the matter, he offered it at several banks, including one in Holland and two in Paris. In every case he was told that the note was "too good." There was no way in which the bank could get it back into Berlin to be used.

German paper marks practically ceased to be dealt in outside Germany.

Deposits in German banks held in the outside world began to be very strictly controlled with the Standstill of 1931, and the controls grew stricter as time went on. They were blocked. You could not automatically transfer them. But arrangements were made whereby, for various purposes, they could be sold, in definitely limited amounts. "Travel marks" very quickly were created, which were sold at a discount from the official rate. The Swiss plan, adopted by agreement with the German banks at the second Standstill in Berlin in the winter of 1931–32, provided another type of mark. Mark deposits and mark credits held by foreigners could be used, under certain conditions, under the supervision of the Reichsbank, for investment in German securities or in German real estate. These marks also sold at a discount. The rates of discount were far from being free supply-and-demand rates. Always the government could intervene to limit the volume of such transactions.

There were "benevolent marks"—funds sent by people outside Germany, under special controls, as gifts to people in Germany—with the payments supervised by the state, subject to income tax collected at the time. There was a very large number of different kinds of marks. Only the specialist in a great New York bank would know the details, and he would have to keep in daily touch with the German authorities in order to be sure of them.

The authoritative control of markets, both foreign and domestic, including the intimate searching into the bookkeeping and the pockets of the people, reached a degree of perfection which nobody would have dreamed possible on the basis of the previous history of money.

The Reichsbank's gold reserve dwindled until it was microscopic. The published gold reserve of the Reichsbank in late September 1939, after the outbreak of the war, was 77 million reichsmarks as against, roughly, 11 billion reichsmarks of outstanding notes—a microscopic gold reserve. The Reichsbank had more gold than that. It could have had, perhaps, as much as 700 million reichsmarks in undeclared reserves, but it still had an utterly inadequate gold reserve on the basis of all banking experience. During the war Germany went on holding her prices, holding her public finance, and holding her currency. The point is simply that she had found a way to dispense with gold. You need gold when free men are to be *induced* to take your currency at a fixed rate. You do not need gold if slaves can be coerced into taking your currency.

The British Empire Versus the German Reich in Monetary Coercion. The British Empire tried no coercion down to the outbreak of the war in 1939. Sterling then collapsed violently. It had no vitality. Its prestige was largely gone. Britain turned toward German methods. Sterling in general was blocked. An "official sterling" at a fixed rate, for a limited number of transactions especially approved, was created. Commodity prices were fixed in England. A ban was put upon the reimporting into England of Bank of England notes, except as their history could be ascertained.

But the pound sterling ceased to be valid even within the limits of the British Empire. Very speedily the blocked balances included the balances of Canada, Australia, Eire, Malaya, New Zealand, and, above all, India. Men in these countries, holding pound sterling balances in British banks, had to be prevented from using them by the same process of blocking that applied to Scandinavian countries, or other countries. Imperial power was not strong enough to make a pound valid throughout the empire.

Is it realism to suppose that the whole world can hang together, under the International Monetary Fund, in the support of fixed foreign exchange rates, when the British Empire could not hang together in support of sterling *within the British Empire?*

Austria's Return to a Free Exchange in 1934. Is it possible for a country with blocked exchange to return to a free exchange? We saw Germany, following the Standstill of 1931, with the exchange control that accompanied the Standstill, move steadily toward a tighter and tighter control of foreign exchange, with an increased blocking of balances owned by foreigners, and with the development of many different kinds of marks, some of which could be used for one purpose and some for another, but with ever tighter controls. We saw Italian exchange increasingly controlled in the period of the 1930s. Is it possible to get out of this cycle once you get into it? We have an answer in the experience of Austria. Austria also went into "standstill," with blocked foreign balances and strict exchange controls in 1931, and Austria returned to a free exchange in 1934. The difference was not that Austria was financially stronger than Germany. The difference was that Austria preferred freedom of exchange and commerce and worked toward it. Italy's problem was complicated by the Ethiopian War. Austria had no such problem. Germany's problem was complicated by a government which loved control, which deliberately sought *autarky,* and which in the latter years of the 1930s was deliberately planning war and seeking self-sufficiency for war. Austria, financially and industrially weaker, but turning toward orthodox financial and monetary policy, achieved a free exchange[1] and maintained it from 1934 until she was absorbed by Germany in 1938.

---

[1] The fullest account of this episode that I know is contained in an article by Dr. Oskar Morgenstern in *Revista Di Storia Economica* (published in Italy, and edited by the distinguished economist Luigi Einaudi), December 1937. I have been able to get some further details from banks and other sources. Apparently there was a good deal of composition of the old debt, and a gradual repayment of much of it. New transactions became free. Dr. Morgenstern says that in 1937 there remained some "residues of surveillance on the part of the bank of issue, due to the fact that all institutions have a tendency to perpetuate themselves, and that the bank of issue is interested in watching capital movements."

The Business Rally of
1935–37 and the Major
Crisis of 1937

The Federal Reserve Index of Industrial Production (old series 1923–25 = 100) rose from approximately 60 in March 1933 to 100 in July 1933; then with the coming of NRA and the processing taxes, dropped to 72 in November 1933. Partly under the impetus of the President's spending program, it rose to 86 in May 1934, dropping again, however, to 71 in September 1934. There came a moderate rally to 90 at the beginning of 1935, and then a sagging in the spring to about 86 again.

These were all very subnormal figures, taking into account the growth which we ought to have had following 1923–25. Unemployment ran very high, standing well above ten million at all points down to the summer of 1935.

Congress Gives Roosevelt Blank Check for $4.88 Billion, April 1935. President Roosevelt tried his spending magic again. He demanded and received from Congress a blank check of $4.88 billion as a work relief measure. There were some formal but large ineffective limitations on the possible uses of the funds. One limitation that was absolutely definite was a provision that no part of the money should be spent for munitions, war ships, and so on. The President signed the bill on April 8, 1935.

What should he do with the money!

Out of Which Roosevelt Allocates $13.6 Billion! Later, soon after he had retired from office, Comptroller General McCarl said privately that out of the $4.88 billion, President Roosevelt promptly made allocations totaling $13.6 billion. All of these allocations, of course, came to the comptroller general's office, as it was his duty, under the law of the land, to pass upon the legality of all expenditures. The comptroller said that he went to President Roosevelt and told him that any one of the items in this vast $13.6 billion was apparently legal, but that the total was too great. The total could be only $4.88 billion. Did the President wish to revise the list, or did the President wish the comptroller general to approve the items in the order in which they had come to him up to the total of $4.88 billion? McCarl said that the President felt that he, McCarl, was most unreasonable. He added, however, that this was not the point on which he and the President had definitely split. That came when he was obliged to inform the President that his proposal to plant a wide belt of trees, stretching from the Canadian border to the Mexican border, would not be legal under the terms of the agricultural appropriation act.

Comptroller General McCarl on Guard—Business Curve Sags. Until his retirement from office Comptroller McCarl was a thorn in the side of President Roosevelt. He was absolutely independent. The law had made him independent. He was inflexible in the performance of his duties and the law had prescribed his duties. After his retirement the President was very slow in appointing his successor.

The legislation giving President Roosevelt this blank check was passed by the House of Representatives in late January. It was debated in the Senate and finally became a law April 8. The business curve continued to sag while this legislation was in process, and after its passage.

The Supreme Court Declares NRA Unconstitutional. American business was working under fearful handicaps, as we have seen in preceding chapters. NRA, in particular, was a nightmare, with the constant shifting of rulings by bureaucrats—rulings that were supposed to have the force of law, under a general grant of power by the Congress in the National Industrial Recovery Act. There was no legal certainty anywhere. The businessman, contemplating any move, had to consult his lawyers before he could safely give instructions to his engineers, his production manager, or his sales manager.

On May 27, 1935, came the sweeping, unanimous decision of the United States Supreme Court outlawing NRA, in the famous *Schechter* case. Questions of the demarcation of interstate commerce and intrastate commerce were involved in this case, but the central point in the court's decision, as emphasized in the concurring opinion by Justice Cardozo, joined by Justice Stone, was the denunciation of Section 3 of the National Industrial Recovery Act dealing with code making and the fixing of hours and wages as "delegation running riot." Whatever powers Congress might have, the Congress could not delegate its powers without qualifications and restrictions and without clear definition of congressional policy, and yet in the National Industrial Recovery Act it had done just this. The act was unconstitutional, null and void. The bureaucrats had no power under the act. NRA was finished.

Supreme Court Gives People and Congress Time to React. This Supreme Court decision is a great landmark in our history. If the Court had been as cowardly as the Congress, we should have lost our constitutional liberties. The Court could not, of course, indefinitely save them for us, but it could and did give time for the people to take second thought, and for the Congress to reassert its independence. By the time the Court was finally reconstituted through the retirement of old judges and new appointments by President Roosevelt, the Congress was already in revolt on many points, and the public was backing it up. Today we look to the Congress, rather than to the Supreme Court, for the defense of the Constitution.

Dramatic Effect of Decision on Business and Markets. The effect of the NRA decision upon the business and financial community was extraordinarily great. The effect in the stock market was almost immediate. A great rally in stocks began which carried them by the autumn to levels unreached since early 1931, and which carried them by 1937 to levels that had not been reached since 1930.

The effect on business, as shown by the Federal Reserve Index of Industrial Production (base 1923–25), follows the stock market rise with a lag of two or three months. By August 1935 a strong move was under way which pulled the index up to 104 in December, a new high since 1930. There was a moderate dip in early 1936, then the curve moved up with vigor to above 120, and it remained above 115 until after the stock market break in August 1937.

Business felt itself free again after the Supreme Court decision and a great many activities, which business had lacked the courage to undertake while NRA was in force, were undertaken. Production of durable goods in particular showed its first sustained upward move after the Surpreme Court decision. Capital expenditures began to be made, and the gap between the production of durable and nondurable goods in the Federal Reserve curves,[1] which was very wide at the time of the Supreme Court decision, practically disappeared in the third quarter of 1937.

Effect of Soldiers' Bonus and Blank Check. The spending policy of the government had been quite ineffective in turning the Great Depression into a sustained rally when applied at the end of 1933. But when a natural rally came following the Supreme Court decision, the government spending accentuated it. The payment of the soldiers' bonus in the Hoover administration[2] in the spring of 1931 had perhaps made a minor upward ripple in the trend of the business curve, which was then strongly downward. The soldiers' bonus payment in June 1936, when the trend was already strongly upward, made a real difference in accentuating the trend.

The soldiers' bonus payments in the Hoover administration were made in the spring of 1931. The cash payments of the soldiers' bonus in the Roosevelt administration were concentrated heavily in June 1936. Total "adjusted service certificate fund" expenditures for fiscal year 1936 were $1,773,000,000, and most of this came in June 1936. Additional pay-

---

[1] Federal Reserve *Charts on Bank Credit, Money Rates and Business,* November 9, 1939, pp. 36–37.

[2] The soldiers' bonus bill of 1931, vetoed by President Hoover on February 26, was promptly passed over his veto by overwhelming majorities in House and Senate. The soldiers' bonus bill of 1936, vetoed by President Roosevelt, was again promptly passed over the veto by overwhelming majorities in both House and Senate.

ments, however, under the Adjusted Compensation Act of 1936, were made in June 1937. Of this, $56,000,000 was in cash, $500,158,000 consisted of bonds paid into the United States Life Insurance Fund.[3] Doubtless too, once the business move was on, the government expenditures for relief and recovery accelerated it. President Roosevelt's blank check of $4,880,000,000 was not without effect—after the Supreme Court decision on NRA.

1935–37 Rally Far Below Normal Expectation. We had a strong rally, but at no point in the rally did we approach the normal expectations which the growth of the country would ordinarily have justified, and at no point did we reach anything approximating full employment. The best year was 1937, when the annual average figure for unemployment dropped to 6¼ million. There remained altogether too many governmental interferences with business. Governmental financial policy continued to undermine long-run confidence. The course of taxation, described in preceding chapters, continued to paralyze a great deal of venture capital, the undistributed profits tax cut capital expenditures heavily, as did the securities legislation, and unsatisfactory conditions in the outside world and in our foreign trade relations and our trade policy continued to retard recovery.

Secretary Hull was making a valiant, steady effort to reduce trade barriers throughout the world, but the adverse forces, both foreign and domestic, with which he had to contend were very strong.

Election of 1936. Political developments in the United States in 1936 and 1937 were not of a sort that tended to increase business and financial confidence. The Republican Party, in its convention in 1936, had a reactionary and excessively timid Resolutions Committee which the Republican nominee for the presidency had not been able to control. Old ghosts walked, and certain reactionary Republican leaders, who had been retired from public office, made themselves very powerful in this platform committee. Governor Landon's personal representative on the committee, William Allen White, fought hard for four days to get a sound platform. In the course of this fight four requests which he made on one day, in Governor Landon's name, were turned down. The plank on money failed to call for a return to the gold standard. The plank on the tariff was reactionary in the extreme, although containing one passage which had been inserted in deference to the wishes of Governor Landon, to the effect that the Republican Party would adjust tariffs with a view to increasing foreign trade—the economic meaning of which was that it would lower protective tariffs. Governer Landon sent a telegram to the convention, *before his nomination*, commenting on the platform, in which he expressed his own belief in gold, and in which he told the delegates that they should

[3] See *Statistical Abstract of the United States* (1937), pp. 162, 164, 165.

not nominate him if they disapproved of his position. It was a courageous and statesmanlike telegram.

In the campaign which followed the Republican candidate made a number of very effective speeches, but he made one unfortunate speech at Minneapolis, dealing with the tariff, which was interpreted by the country as taking an ultrahigh protective tariff view, and which alienated a great body of conservative Democrats who would otherwise have supported him, including the powerful and influential *Baltimore Sun*. Subsequently, in a speech at Albuquerque late in the campaign, he corrected this unfortunate Minneapolis speech, and placed the emphasis upon the particular part of the Republican tariff plank above referred to, namely, that the tariff should be adjusted with a view to increasing foreign trade. The Minneapolis speech attracted wide attention. The Albuquerque speech attracted little attention. Whatever chance the Republicans had had to win in 1936 was destroyed at Minneapolis.

Governor Landon—a man of fine quality and high purposes—made a gallant fight, culminating in a speech that revealed great dignity and elevation of thought at Madison Square Garden in New York at the end of the campaign.

He probably faced hopeless odds in any case. President Roosevelt still had immense personal popularity and still had the confidence of the country. Suggestions that the President planned to undermine the Supreme Court were received with incredulity. The rising tide of business activity, moreover, was in his favor. And finally, the immense outpouring of federal funds to farmers, to WPA workers, to college students, and to other elements of the population, constituted a "slush fund" so vast that more than one informed and judicious man, including Democratic members of the Senate from northern states who had actively supported President Roosevelt both for the renomination and for election, privately characterized the election of 1936 as a "bought election." One may recognize that many doubtful electoral votes were bought (as in Kansas itself), and still hesitate to endorse this view of a bought election—having in mind the warm support the President got in 1936 from a great many conservative people who certainly were not bought, who approved the President's general purposes, even though questioning his methods, who refused to believe the accusation that he was contemplating an attack upon the Supreme Court, and who turned violently against him when, early in 1937, he did attack the Supreme Court.

The Wagner Act. The Wagner Act, passed July 5, 1935, did not immediately lead to great changes in labor relations. But following the election of 1936 there came an immense activity in unionization and in wage raising, with a great deal of labor disturbance—the conspicuous leader of the movement being the CIO headed by John L. Lewis. Ugly developments came, centering especially around Detroit.

The Court-Packing Fight. Early in 1937 the President made his demand on the Congress for a bill that would enable him to pack the Supreme Court with new appointees additional to the existing judges. The country was shocked. Here was a naked bid for dictatorship by a President who felt that he already had the Congress in the hollow of his hand, and who wished to force this subservient Congress to put the courts in the same position, so that the will and purposes of one man, freed from the checks and balances of the Constitution, might dominate the making of the laws, the interpretation of the laws, and the execution of the laws.

The country was shocked and the country rallied to the defense of its institutions. Party antagonism disappeared in this great fight, and differences among radicals and liberals and conservatives did not prevent effective cooperation. The Republican Party, very weak in both houses of Congress, refrained from making the matter a party issue lest they should thereby make it possible for the administration to make it a party issue. Instead, the Republicans gladly accepted Democratic leadership in the fight against the President's proposal. The leader in the fight was a brilliant and able left-wing Democrat, Senator Burton K. Wheeler of Montana, who had given enthusiastic support to most of the President's New Deal measures, but who was nonetheless aghast at the proposal to pack the Court and to subordinate the judiciary to the executive. There has probably never been a situation, short of war itself, in which so many men of diverse views, interests and opinions, turned with one purpose to the defense of the country.

The President sustained a sweeping defeat. The Court was saved. But the old judges began to drop out, and in a comparatively short time after the President's defeat he was able to reconstitute the Court by the lawful process of making new appointments, so that it would sustain a great deal of legislation which had previously been regarded as unconstitutional.

The Violent Stock Market Crash and Business Crisis, 1937. The stock market, which had reached a high of 195.59[4] in early 1937, weakened with the attack on the Supreme Court, and then, as the evidence grew that the attack would be beaten off, rallied to 190.38 on August 14. Then, out of a clear sky, there came a violent break in the stock market, which moved, almost without interruption, to a low of 97.46 on March 31, 1938. Following the stock market break, with a lag of about four weeks, as shown by the *New York Times* seasonally adjusted business index, there began a decisive downward move in industrial production. The Federal Reserve index shows a break from a level above 115 in August 1937 to 76 in May 1938.

The break in the stock market was one of the most violent in our whole history. The decline in the curve for industrial production, 1937–38, was the most violent decline in an eight- or nine-month period that our history

---

[4] Dow-Jones industrials.

records. The break amounted to 34.5 percent. The break between the summer of 1920 and the low in the second quarter of 1921 was definitely more moderate, amounting to only 28 percent, and this was the most violent sudden break which our history had shown down to that time. The extreme down swing between the peak of 1929 and the low of 1932 in volume of business was greater, but at no stage of that decline was anything like so rapid a downward movement revealed.[5]

---

[5] The reader may examine the curve for industrial production covering the years 1919 to 1939 in Federal Reserve *Charts on Bank Credit, Money Rates and Business,* November 9, 1939, pp. 34, 35.

67

The Causes of the Crisis
of 1937

What caused the major crisis of 1937? Why did the stock market yield so suddenly and so violently? And why did the volume of business and industrial production decline so rapidly?

The Erroneous Explanation Based on Money Market and Federal Finance. One explanation has been offered from the standpoint of those who believe that artificially cheap money and expanding bank credit and government deficit spending are needed to make prosperity, a view which is wholly invalid. This view blames the crisis on three factors. (1) The Federal Reserve authorities doubled the reserve requirements of the member banks in 1936 and 1937 by stages, beginning in 1936 and ending in early 1937, as we have seen in a preceding chapter. This reduced excess reserves from around $3 billion to $927 million as the average for May 1937. (2) The secretary of the Treasury, in the winter of 1936–37, adopted the policy of "sterilizing" the incoming gold, so far as effect on our money market was concerned, by not issuing new gold certificates against it, but instead by borrowing money from the commercial banks with which to buy it, so that for a time incoming gold ceased to add to member bank reserves. (3) It was alleged that the government's deficit was radically reduced, and that it disappeared when social-security taxes and disbursements were taken into account. The theory was that government "investment" (that is, government deficit spending), which, it was assumed, was needed to offset deficiencies in private investment, failed to do its duty, with an inevitable crash in the business structure.

It is easy to demonstrate that this view is a mare's nest. The financial phenomena of the period, taken altogether, were definitely favorable to increasing business activity.

Increased Reserve Requirements Accompanied by Great Increase in Commercial Loans. First, it may be observed with respect to the volume of excess reserves that reducing the excess reserves could not reduce the volume of business unless real differences were made thereby in interest rates, and unless restrictions were imposed thereby upon the use of money and credit. Now the evidence is overwhelming that nothing of this sort occurred. The rate on open market commercial paper, four to six months, moved up from .75 to 1 percent. Rates on customers' loans by banks continued to sag. The average in 19 cities stood at 2.70 percent in July 1936 and sagged to 2.55 percent in August 1937.[1] The rate on Treasury bills moved up from a little over $^1/_{10}$ percent in December 1936, to $^6/_{10}$ percent in April 1937, dropping again to less than $^3/_{10}$ percent in July and August 1937. All these rates remained absurdly low. The call rate on stock exchange loans remained unchanged, pegged at 1 percent. The yield on long-term United States government bonds moved up from 2.65 percent in July 1936 to 2.80 percent in April 1937, dropping again to 2.72 percent in August 1937. The yield on tax-exempt Treasury notes, three to five years, moved up from a 1936 average of 1.11 percent to a 1937 average of 1.40 percent. Absolutely no restriction was placed on any transaction by interest changes of this kind.

On the contrary, coincident with the increase in the reserve requirements two highly encouraging developments in banking and in investment banking took place.

(1) Commercial loans of the banks increased dramatically, beginning in the third quarter of 1935 and moving through 1937. The increase in this period was over $2 billion for the member banks of the Federal Reserve System alone—from $4,834,000,000 on June 29, 1935, to $6,996,000,000 on December 31, 1937—a striking commentary upon the theory which Lauchlin Currie had advanced in his book, *The Supply and Control of Money in the United States,* in 1934, that commercial loans in American banking "belong to a past era" (p. 152).

(2) Coincident with the increase in reserve requirements of the member banks was a great increase in new issues of securities. The issue of new securities had been at an appallingly low level through the years 1932, 1933, 1934, and 1935, and the first quarter of 1936, the average volume for this period being well below 15 percent of the volume of new securities issued in the year 1923. The first quarter of 1936 showed new securities at 15.8 percent of the first quarter of 1923. This figure began to rise in the second quarter of 1936 and moved steadily through the second quarter of 1937 to a level of approximately 50 percent of the new securities issued in 1923. New security issues in strong volume continued in 1937 until the stock market crash.

Bank Deposits and Brokers' Loans Rise. We have seen in the preceding chapter how little effect upon money rates excess reserves had after the first billion. The foregoing figures for the rapid growth of commercial loans and

---

[1] *Banking and Monetary Statistics* (1943), p. 464.

the rapid growth of new security issues are enough to prove that increases of fractions of one percent in interest rates, from levels absurdly low to levels still absurdly low, made no difference at all in the willingness of the markets to use money, so long as they had any confidence that its use would bring a return.

It is true that there was a decline in member bank holdings of government securities in this period, amounting to $900 million between June 30, 1936, and June 30, 1937. But this is a wholesome and natural phenomenon in a time of reviving business, and a recurrent phenomenon in times of reviving business. And the decline of less than a billion in government securities in the assets of member banks was very much more than offset by the rise of $2 billion in commercial loans in its effect on aggregate bank credit. The *deposits* of these banks rose nearly $800 million between June 1936 and June 1937.

There was, further, a rise in 1936 and 1937 in the volume of money borrowed by brokers from banks and in the volume of money lent by brokers to customers. Money borrowed by brokers from banks increased from approximately $800 million in early 1936 to approximately $1,250 million at the peak of 1937, while brokers' credit to customers increased in the same period from about $1,200 million to nearly $1,600 million between the low of 1936 and the high of 1937.[2]

Governmental Deficit Continues. The third proposition, that the government's deficit, taking into account the social-security taxes, virtually disappeared, and that this was the cause of the business crisis, simply will not stand a careful examination of the figures, taken month by month. The table following shows the government's expenditures, revenues (including customs and social-security taxes) and deficits (or surpluses) month by month for the whole of 1937 and the first quarter of 1938.

It will be observed that there are occasional small surpluses coming at a time when great surpluses ought always to come, in the tax months March, June, September, and December. In 1937 there was no such surplus in June, but rather a deficit of $427 million. June expenditures, however, included $500 million *of bonds* placed into the United States government Life Insurance Fund, under the soldiers' bonus legislation of 1936, so that there was an actual "cash surplus" for June, of $73 million—a trifling surplus for an income tax month.[3] The surplus even in September 1937 was small, only $114. Government deficit financing was doing its full duty (if it has a duty) in 1937, and it was in the ninth month of 1937 that the disastrous business crash began.

Even on "Cash Income and Outgo" Basis. A refinement of this theory has

---

[2] Federal Reserve *Charts on Bank Credit, Money Rates and Business,* September 3, 1941, p. 31.

[3] See *Statistical Abstract of the United States* (1937), pp. 162, 164.

SUMMARY OF TREASURY RECEIPTS
AND EXPENDITURES*
(000,000 omitted)

	Revenues		Expenditures	
	Social-security taxes	Total receipts	(Excl. debt retirement)	Deficit
1937				
January	3	284	539	300
February	10	275	547	317
March	50	1,012	766	201 Surplus
April	78	363	695	377
May	59	335	514	224
June	53	868	1,254	427
July	53	409	638	271
August	60	453	517	104
September	50	788	633	114 Surplus
October	52	333	565	273
November	60	327	453	167
December	138	866	635	188 Surplus
1938				
January	57	335	492	198
February	110	349	474	166
March	3	959	705	211 Surplus
April	34	273	631	369

* *Banking and Monetary Statistics* (1943), p. 514.

developed since the Treasury began, in 1939, to give us figures for the "cash income" and "cash outgo" of the Treasury. These figures are different from the budgetary figures of receipts, expenditures, and deficit (or surplus) which appear in our table above, in that they take account of expenditures and receipts by the trust funds and by the government corporations. They are summarized in chart form, by quarters, in the Federal Reserve *Charts on Bank Credit, Money Rates and Business,* of February 11, 1941 (p. 18). The chart shows an excess of cash outgo over cash income for the first two quarters of 1937, the excess for the second quarter being large; but it shows a small excess of cash income over cash outgo for the third quarter of 1937. The argument seems to be now that this excess of cash income over cash outgo for the third quarter of 1937 precipitated the stock market break and the business crisis of 1937.

An examination, however, of the actual figures of the Treasury[4] reveals

---

[4] *Bulletin of the Treasury,* July 1939, p. 14.

two things: (1) the excess of cash income over cash outgo in the third quarter of 1937 was only $58 million, an extraordinarily small sum of money, even on this theory, to have upset a great economy which was pressing forward, with bank credit expanding and with new corporate security issues at the peak for many years; (2) the whole of the excess of cash income over cash outgo for the third quarter of 1937 came in September, the income tax month, where it appears as $203 million, instead of the $114 million surplus given in our table for the budget figures, above. The months of July and August 1937 show an excess of cash outgo, July's excess being $120 million and the excess of August being $25 million.

Now the stock market break started in August, before the September excess of cash income over cash outgo appeared, and it moved far in August. The Dow-Jones industrials stood at 190.38 on August 14, and at 175.09 on August 27.

The business break, as shown by the weekly business index of the *New York Times,* starts about four weeks after the stock market break began, but, unfortunately for this theory, it begins on September 11, before the big income tax payments came and while the Treasury was still undoubtedly having an excess of cash outgo over cash income. The business break, of course, actually began before September 11, since even weekly figures represent history rather than the contemporary fact on a given date. Moreover, the business break continues increasing momentum in October and November, during which months the Treasury had an excess of cash outgo over cash income, the figure for October being $193 million and the figure for November being $90 million.

This refinement does not help the doctrine very much.

"Sterilization Fund" Did Not Reduce Excessive Bank Reserves. The contention that the secretary of the Treasury's sterilization policy took money away from the reserves of the banks or took money away from industry and trade or the securities market is simply absurd. The sterilization took no money away. It merely prevented incoming gold from *adding* to the money supply, a supply already very excessive.

The raising of the reserve requirements of the member banks did not deny any credit to anyone who could otherwise have got credit. It stopped no transaction which would otherwise have been made. It did not in any way interfere with the rising tide of business, with the rising tide of commercial loans, with rising bank deposits, with the issuing of securities, or with the rising prices of securities.

It is very important that we clear up misunderstandings regarding these points, lest excessive timidity regarding future money market control be generated by them.

Wages, Prices, and Profits. What then, were the explanations of the stock market crash and the business crisis? With respect to business, there is one outstanding fact. Business expands when profits are improving.

Business contracts when profits decline or when there is a serious threat to profits. Now, profits are what is left of gross income after costs are subtracted, and the labor factor in costs is overwhelmingly important. In the years 1936 and 1937 labor income was running well over 70 percent of the total national income, whereas profit income did not exceed 15.3 percent.[5]

A 10 percent increase in aggregate labor income at the expense of aggregate profit income would thus mean cutting profit income approximately in half, which would lead to violent business reaction.

In individual establishments the amount of cost directly attributable to labor varies very greatly, and the percentage would normally be a good deal lower than 70 percent. The point is that many industries are working on prefabricated materials. They have already paid for labor when they bought the materials, and this labor element does not reveal itself in their direct labor costs.

Immense Union Activity Under Wagner Act Follows 1936 Election. There had not been a great deal of trade union activity, taking advantage of the opportunities made by the Wagner Act, until after the election of 1936. Then there came an immense activity headed by the CIO under John L. Lewis, although the AFL and other labor organizations were not inactive. The focus of this was the automobile industry centering in Detroit. Here, there were immense strikes, including sitdown strikes, where laborers occupied the plants, refusing to vacate them, at the same time refusing to work—a clear violation of the law. But legal remedies were difficult to obtain from the state of Michigan at that time. Under these circumstances the automobile industries yielded. Unionization was rapidly accomplished and wages were rapidly raised. But all over the country, in lesser degree, similar movements were under way, and wages of manufacturing laborers generally were rapidly rising.

Rapid Rise in Wages Compared with Prices, 1937. A high official of the United States government in the autumn of 1937 had in his office a chart which he had prepared comparing Japan, Great Britain, France, and the United States with respect to the relationships among prices, wages, and the cost of living. The chart seemed significant and the present writer subsequently had it reproduced and continued through 1937 and into 1939 (see following page). The official's comment upon this chart was that, whereas in Great Britain and Japan there had been no very great variation in the relationship of these three series since 1929, in France there had been an appalling distortion in a startling rise of wages above wholesale prices and above cost of living, due to the Blum New Deal, with the resultant collapse in French industrial activity. He then called attention to the sharp rise in

---

[5] See my chapter "The Road Back to Full Employment" in *Financing American Prosperity, a Symposium of Economists* (New York: Twentieth Century Fund, 1945), pp. 17–22.

wages, running high above the cost of living and wholesale prices, beginning in 1936 and running into 1937 in the United States, and he said, "That looks too much like France."

This a Main Factor in Crisis. A main factor on the industrial side in bringing the revival of 1935–37 to a close was this startling increase in wages arising not from scarcity of labor, because unemployment remained at 6.25 million for the year 1937, but from a tremendous burst of activity by trade unions under the Wagner Act—a rise in wages unmatched by a corresponding rise in the productivity of labor.

There was also a very powerful financial cause of the business crisis, which we shall discuss in the next chapter.

PRICES, WAGES AND THE COST OF LIVING

1929 = 100   United States, France, Great Britain and Japan

KEY: Cost of Living ·············· Wages – – – – Wholesale Prices – · – · –

UNITED STATES

1927 1928 1929 1930 1931 1932 1933 1934 1935 1936 1937 1938 1939 1940

FRANCE

GREAT BRITAIN

JAPAN

68

The Stock Market Crash of 1937—A Major Cause of Business Crisis

A major factor partly precipitating and certainly intensifying the collapse in industrial activity in the autumn of 1937 and the winter and early spring of 1938, was the sudden break in the stock market and the revelation of an extraordinary weakness in the internal stock market situation. A recapitulation of stock market history following the Supreme Court decision on May 27, 1935, and continuing through 1938 will be useful here. The following table for the Dow-Jones industrials will tell the story.

DOW-JONES INDUSTRIALS, 1935–38

1935	High		Low
June 24	121.30	June 1	108.64
July 31	127.04	July 3	117.80
Nov. 20	149.42	Nov. 4	139.99
1936			
April 6	163.07	April 30	141.53
Oct. 19	178.44	Oct. 1	167.54
1937			
Mar. 10	195.59	Mar. 22	179.28
June 5	175.66	June 17	163.31
Aug. 14	190.38	Aug. 27	175.09
Sept. 1	176.11	Sept. 24	146.22
Oct. 1	155.11	Oct. 19	115.84
Nov. 1	137.01	Nov. 23	112.54
1938			
Mar. 1	131.03	Mar. 31	97.46
Oct. 24	155.38	Oct. 1	141.56
Nov. 10	158.90	Nov. 28	145.21

It will be observed here that the market began an almost immediate advance following the Supreme Court decision on NRA, May 27, 1935, moving up from a low of 108.64 on June 1, 1935, to a high of 121.30 on June 24, and advancing with very little interruption to a high of 195.59 on March 10, 1937.

Stock Market and Supreme Court Fight. The market yielded with the attack on the Supreme Court, reaching a low of 163.31 on June 17, 1937, from which point it moved upward to a high of 190.38 on August 14, the rally coinciding with favorable developments in the Supreme Court fight, and the high of August 14 being almost as high as the top figure of the year on March 10.

Startling Break After August 14, 1937. Then with startling rapidity the market weakened, dropping from 190.38 on August 14 to 175.09 on August 27, to 146.22 on September 24, to 115.84 on October 19, to 112.54 on November 23, and finally to 97.46 on March 31, 1938, which was the low for the downward move.

With Business Still Good. The break came with the weekly business figures still good, and the weekly business figures continued good in the early stages of the break. The business community in general was incredulous when the stock market break began, though the leaders of the automobile industry had been very apprehensive well before the break. They had stood the main impact of the rising labor costs which unionization involved. They had done extraordinary things in making managerial adjustments to offset these costs, but they felt that they had reached the end of their rope in this matter, and that profits were certain to go down drastically. The business community as a whole, however, was still hopeful. They had orders on their books. They felt that they could still make adjustments to offset a part at least of the rising wages, and they saw no valid reason for the violent break in stocks when it first came. The table on page 441 shows the *New York Times* weekly index of business for August, September, and October.

The break traced neither to a heavy volume of selling nor to foreign selling. Over the period August 4 to September 29, foreigners bought more than they sold. Foreign buying and selling, moreover, were at no time large in volume during the break. There was no extraordinarily disturbing news, for the most part, except the appointment of Justice Hugo Black to the first vacancy in the Supreme Court after the President's defeat on the Court-packing bill. This startled the business and financial community a great deal, and disclosure that Justice Black had belonged to the Ku Klux Klan, which speedily followed, shocked and frightened the country.

The declining prospects of profits due to the developments in the labor and wage situation, referred to above, taken in conjunction with the very high level to which the stock market had risen, could well have been expected to lead to stock market reaction and to business reaction. But the violence and the severity of the stock market break were due to internal factors in the stock market, and to impaired efficiency in the stock market, due to governmental policy.

WEEKLY SERIES, *NEW YORK TIMES*, 1937,
COMBINED BUSINESS INDEX
(Seasonally adjusted)

August 7 .... 108.2
August 14 .... 111.2 (stock market, 190.38)
August 21 .... 109.9
August 28 .... 109.4 (August 27, stock market, 175.09)
September 4 .... 109.3
September 11 .... 106.6
September 18 .... 104.9
September 25 .... 104.6
October 2 .... 103.5
October 9 .... 101.3
October 16 .... 100.2
October 23 .... 97.9

Governmental Policy Impairs Efficiency of Stock Market—A "Thin Market." The market had grown extraordinarily "thin"; that is to say, the stock market, which, in the past, had been capable of absorbing an immense volume of selling with moderate recessions in price, had been brought to a state in which very moderate selling brought very large changes in price.

Officials of the stock exchange itself had realized this before the break came. Mr. Gay, the president of the New York Stock Exchange, in his annual report for the year ending May 1937, dated August 11, and released to the press on August 18, had given a warning on this point. A small volume of selling would make sharp breaks in price, a small volume of buying would make sharp rises in prices—the market had grown very thin. The table on page 442 shows the progressive thinness of the market.[1]

High Income Taxes. The causes for this change and for the acute thinness of the stock market are to be found in various governmental policies. One was extraordinary rates of taxes and especially the tax on capital gains, which was at that time part of the general income tax. We have seen in a preceding chapter the levels to which income taxes had run in the upper brackets. These rates, applied to profits made in the stock market, meant that men of substantial means simply could not engage in many stock market transactions. If they were successful, the government took most of the profits. If they had losses, they took them themselves. They bought and sold only when they had a very powerful reason for doing so, such as the conviction that a particular security was no longer a good investment.

---

[1] See address by Winthrop W. Aldrich, chairman of the Chase National Bank, "The Stock Market from the Viewpoint of a Commercial Banker," before the Rochester Chamber of Commerce, October 14, 1937. This writer acknowledges indebtedness to this carefully prepared and thoroughly verified study for a number of the main propositions which follow in the explanation of the thinness of the stock market in 1937.

SHARE SALES ON DAYS OF DECLINING PRICES, RELATED TO
NET CHANGES IN
CLOSING PRICES OF THE INCLUDED STOCKS

Group of 30 common stocks	Thousands of Shares Sold	
	Per 1% price decline	Per $1 price decline
12 days, 1930–31	13.1	23.1
July 21, 1933	8.9	23.4
12 days, 1936–37	4.7	6.7
May 13, 1937	3.6	5.4
September 7, 1937	2.1	3.4
September 10, 1937	2.6	4.2

Moreover, if a man of substantial fortune sold a security in which he had a profit, he was very likely to sell at the same time a security in which he had a loss—a double selling which added very substantially to the burdens of a thin market. The extraordinarily high income taxes, moreover, largely eliminated the *current savings* of men of substantial means, savings which had formerly gone into the stock market to a greater degree than other savings.

Elimination of Informed Traders—"Insiders' " Trading. The elimination of men of substantial means from the stock market, moreover, tended to eliminate informed trading in the stock market. In the past, on bad days in the market, we could expect that men with knowledge, buying power and courage would be on the lookout for bargains and would buy them. Even when the trend was definitely downward, such men would come in on days of sharp breaks, cushioning the market, selling out again on the automatic rally, moderating the movements and increasing the breadth of the market.

The securities and exchange legislation and the rulings of the Securities and Exchange Commission under this legislation had added a great many additional burdens. In the past, insiders of a corporation informed as to its affairs—officers, directors or large shareholders—seeing the stock of the corporation beaten down in the market, would step in and buy, expecting to be able to sell again at a profit when the movement was arrested and the market had steadied itself. This was informed buying, and in general was very useful to the market and to the small investors in the corporation's stock. The Securities and Exchange Act of 1934, Section 16b, operated to prevent this. It provided that if officers, directors, or large stockholders of a corporation should buy their stocks and sell them again within six months, or should sell their stocks and buy them again within six months and make a profit thereby, they would be liable to suit by any other stockholder of the corporation to recover the profit for the corporation itself.

The Congress in this legislation had a commendable purpose. That purpose was stated in Section 16b: "For the purpose of preventing the unfair use of information which may have been obtained by such beneficial owner, director, or officer by reason of his relationship to the issuer. . . ." However, the Congress recognized that not all such buying and selling by insiders was of an unfair character, and in the same section it provided for exemptions to be given by the Securities and Exchange Commission, in the following language: "This subsection shall not be construed to cover . . . any transaction or transactions which the commission by rules and regulations may exempt as not comprehended within the purpose of this subsection."

The Securities and Exchange Commission had not given the exemptions contemplated by Congress, giving freedom of action to insiders where this does not involve unfair use of inside information. At the time of the stock market break in 1937, three years had passed without these exemptions being given. In 1944, ten years after the passage of the act, no such ruling had been given, though the Congress had clearly contemplated that such rulings should be given.[2]

Now this is a very unfortunate situation and one for which the Securities and Exchange Commission is to be sharply condemned. It is right that the insider should be forbidden to take unfair advantage of inside information to the detriment of less informed shareholders, or of the public. It is wrong that the insider should be forbidden to act in the stock market on the basis of inside information when such action is to the interest of the corporation and of the other shareholders, and of the public.

It is perfectly possible to distinguish in objective terms between fair and unfair buying and selling by insiders. The typical case where an insider is trading against the interest of the corporation and the other shareholders would be where the chief executive, knowing before anybody else knows that the dividend is to be cut or omitted, because he is himself making the decision, proceeds to sell his stock with a resultant break in price, and buys it back later after the bad news is out; or where, knowing before others know it of some favorable development affecting the corporation, he buys the stock to sell it out at a higher price when the good news is generally known. On the other hand, the case where his action is clearly in the interest of the corporation would be where a break has occurred, not initiated by him, and where he steps in and steadies the market; or where a rise has occurred, not initiated by him, and where he sells the stock because he thinks it is going too high. In the first case, he prevents other shareholders from suffering losses if they are obliged to sell in a weak market, and in the latter case, he prevents uninformed buyers from paying too much for the stock of his corporation.

---

[2] *SEC General Rules and Regulations*, February 15, 1944, pp. 1601–07. I believe that no such ruling has been subsequently given.

A rule differentiating fair and unfair use of inside information in perfectly objective terms should be easy to formulate, and the Securities and Exchange Commission should long since have done it. It could exempt transactions by insiders which *follow* a break or rise of a certain percent, say five or seven percent, which takes place within a stated period of time, say two days, the first transaction by the insider being at a price five or seven percent below the highest price of the preceding two days in the case of a purchase on a break, or, in the case of a sale on a rise, five or seven percent above the lowest price of the preceding two days. This would be an absolutely definite rule. It would eliminate the *initiation* of price changes by insider action. It would limit insider action to *resisting* price changes initiated by others. It would bring back the informed, protective trading of insiders concerned with the good of the corporation and concerned with the market for the corporation's securities.[3]

Inquisitorial Practices of SEC. A further very important factor reducing trading by men of substantial fortune and by informed men, was the frequent inquisitorial visits of agents of the Securities and Exchange Commission to brokerage houses when large transactions appeared on the ticker. These agents would demand full information not only as to the name of the customer for whom the transaction was put through, but also the details of all other transactions by that customer for a period preceding, and in some cases would then go to the customer himself. In any case, the broker would feel obliged to inform the customer of the visit. In one case in 1937, an agent of the commission visited the executor of a large estate to inquire why he had sold a quarter of a million dollars' worth of securities in a single morning. The agent was informed that the executor was selling to get cash with which to pay the United States Treasury the estate tax! A great many men simply withdrew from the market rather than have the details of their transactions thus inquired into by the government. However innocent their purposes, however legitimate their transactions, men do not welcome governmental inquiry into them. The effect upon the stock market was very bad. In more recent years there has been a shift in the occasion of these inquisitorial visits. They come less frequently upon the appearance of a large number of shares in a particular transaction on the ticker tape, and they come more frequently when transactions appear at a substantial change in price.

As late as February 23, 1947, the *New York Times* reports an elaborate investigation made by the Securities and Exchange Commission of the stock market break of September 3, 1946, involving such voluminous detail that the report, based on data in the commission's hands by October 7, 1946, had not yet been completed.

---

[3] This proposal was made by Aldrich, *op. cit.*

In addition to the data obtained from member firms of the stock exchange, the commission's investigators also interviewed 100 of the largest buyers and sellers of stocks on that day in a nationwide canvass. Besides these individuals, a *random selection* of 450 buyers and sellers, together with a miscellaneous number of firms throughout the country, was asked to give information on the subject. . . .

The investigation was ordered on September 23, when the SEC said it would attempt to learn the cause of the market's decline on September 3 by reconstructing all roundlot transactions on the stock exchange on that date. . . . At the time, it was stated that if any irregularities in the sale of stock or if any pool operations were uncovered, the SEC was prepared to take swift actions against such manipulators.[4]

We have here apparently a pure fishing investigation, digging into the private affairs of a large number of people at random without even the pretext that the particular individuals investigated had acted in a suspicious manner, but merely on the chance that somewhere something suspicious might turn up. A federal grand jury would be much more respectful of the rights of people to privacy in their personal transactions!

Action of this kind by the SEC continues to deter men from taking part in the stock market, and is no small part of the explanation of the thinness of the market which makes possible wide breaks on a single day—which in turn start the SEC on a new investigation!

Specialists and Floor Traders. At the instance of the Securities and Exchange Commission, the stock exchange itself had adopted complicated rules sharply restricting the activities of specialists and floor traders. These rules created a great deal of uncertainty as to what specialists and floor traders might do. It was often necessary at critical times, when quick action by specialists and floor traders was needed, for specialists to confer with members of the stock exchange committee instead of taking the prompt action called for.

The Securities and Exchange Commission had even made a ruling putting the burden of proof upon the specialist, requiring affirmative proof that the specialist's action was beneficial. It is not easy for a man to act quickly with such a burden of proof against him. There was an immense area of uncertainty, paralyzing action.

The Margin Requirements. A further factor narrowing the market and intensifying the difficulties of the 1937 break was the high and inflexible margin requirement. The Congress, desiring to regulate the use of credit in the stock market, had given the Federal Reserve authorities control over margin requirements—a control that had previously been in the hands of the banks and the brokers. The Federal Reserve authorities had raised margin requirements to a very high level. As they calculated margins, it

---

[4] *New York Times*, February 23, 1947, p. 2F; italics mine.

was called a margin of 55 percent. As the brokers calculated, it was a margin of 122 percent. If a man bought $10,000 worth of stock, the rule required that he pay in cash $5,500 and that he borrow only $4,500. His margin was 55 percent of the cost of the stock, but it was 122 percent of the $4,500 loan. In ordinary times, bankers and brokers had usually considered that 20 to 25 percent of the loan was a satisfactory margin from the standpoint of the safety of the loan, assuming that the loan was well diversified, though they always reserved the right to raise the margin if special circumstances called for it. Very much higher margins had been required by bankers and brokers in the wild stock market of 1929.

This sharp increase in margin requirements from 20 to 25 percent of the loan to 122 percent of the loan meant that anyone purchasing securities on margin must employ very much larger sums of capital than formerly. His capacity to act was greatly reduced. It further meant that his account was frozen the moment the market receded. Even with a very high margin from the standpoint of the loan, he could not buy any more stocks on moderate declines, nor could he withdraw any cash from his account. This last factor intensified the break very decidedly in September 1937 because many individuals had to use their large margins with the brokers for the purpose of paying the September 15 income tax, and this made it necessary for them to sell a great many shares of stocks in order to bring the margins up above the 122 percent so that cash could be withdrawn for income tax purposes.

In 1929, in the stock market break, the bankers and brokers who had raised margin requirements and placed "loan values" far below market values while the boom was on, promptly reduced margin requirements in the midst of the crash as a means of easing the credit situation, always keeping them high enough, however, to protect the loans. The Federal Reserve authorities should have done the same thing when the 1937 break began, but they did nothing until after the break had gone very far, and until after the chairman of the Chase National Bank had made the demand that they lower the margin requirements, and the chairman of the Rules Committee of the House of Representatives had reinforced this demand. Governmental regulation of the stock market in 1937 by the Securities and Exchange Commission and by the Federal Reserve authorities was not a brilliant performance.

The margin requirements for customers were very high, but the margin requirements were made still higher for specialists and floor traders on the floor of the stock exchange. In May 1937 the rule was promulgated that floor traders and other stock exchange partners must have a margin of 122 percent on their maximum obligations during the course of the day, whereas customers need not put up additional margin until their net position was ascertained at the end of the day. It was estimated at the time that with margin requirements at 122 percent, the ability of the floor traders and specialists to carry stocks was reduced by approximately 70 percent from what it had been under the old 20 percent rule, and that this was still further reduced by the rule promulgated in May.

Restrictions on Short Selling—Stock Exchange Rules, 1931–May 1935. A further factor involved in the thinness of the market was the restrictions on short selling. These had been operative from late 1931 through the stock market smash of 1937, and continue operative today—originally as a matter of New York Stock Exchange voluntary action, and since 1935 as a matter of SEC recommendation or action. We have noted, in discussing the decision to keep the stock exchange open on September 21, 1931, when England abandoned the gold standard, that a rule forbidding short selling was adopted by the president and the governing committee of the New York Stock Exchange, due to the emergency. On September 23 this rule was rescinded. But on October 5, 1931, the Business Conduct Committee of the stock exchange ruled that before executing any sell orders on the floor, members should ascertain and notify floor members whether such orders were long or short, and that members would be held responsible under Section 4, Article 17, of the stock exchange's constitution which covers the bringing about of a condition of demoralization in prices. At that time a practice grew up of giving preference to orders to sell for long account. On November 23, 1931, the Business Conduct Committee, in conjunction with other committees, decided that no stock could be "stopped"[5] for short account below the last sale, and on January 22, 1932, the Business Conduct Committee ruled that identification of orders applied to bonds as well as stocks. So far we have restrictions voluntarily created by the stock exchange itself on short selling.

SEC Rules on Short Selling Begin May 1935. On May 27, 1935, however, a recommendation by the SEC led to a stock exchange rule that no member of the exchange should use any facility of the exchange to effect on the exchange a short sale in the unit of trading below the last regular sale price. Exemption was provided for "odd-lot" dealers and for equalization of prices on other exchanges. This rule went into effect on June 3, 1935, and remained in effect until 1938. It was under this rule, growing out of a recommendation of the SEC which the stock exchange felt obliged to accept, that the great smash of 1937–38 occurred on the stock exchange.

In 1938, on February 10, the SEC began to make direct regulations which took the place of rules by the Governing Committee of the stock exchange. The rule of the SEC as it appears in *General Rules and Regulations . . . as Amended to and Including February 15, 1944,* "Rule X-104A-1 Short Sales," reads in part as follows:

---

[5] A "stop," or "stop loss order," is an order to sell if a given price, lower than the prevailing price, is reached, or to buy if a given price, higher than the prevailing price, is reached. Such orders become orders "at the market," that is, at any price obtainable, if the designated price is reached.

(a) No person shall, for his own account or for the account of any other person, effect on a national securities exchange a short sale of any security (1) below the price at which the last sale thereof, regular way, was effected on such exchange, or (2) at such price unless such price is above the next preceding different price at which a sale of such security, regular way, was effected on such exchange.[6]

This rule is stricter than the rule which prevailed in 1937, although a little less strict than the rule first promulgated by the Securities and Exchange Commission, effective February 8, 1938. That rule forbade "short sale of any securities at or below the price at which the last sale thereof, regular way, was effected." The difference between the rule quoted above, which was in effect in 1944, and the rule promulgated in February 1938 seems to be that under the 1938 rule, short sales could be made only at rising prices, whereas, under the rule in effect in 1944, short sales could be continued at an unchanged price, provided that the last *different* price had been lower.

The rule in effect in 1937 eliminated an effective short interest, which would bring about rallies in a declining market. It was a rule that prevented the short sellers from initiating a downward move in the market. Short sellers could operate only on a rising market. This was a very nice rule for the bulls, superficially viewed, but it did not help if the purpose was to create a steady market for investors.

The short seller is extremely useful when prices are breaking. He must cover (that is, buy) then to take his profits. It is perfectly legitimate that the short seller should be active in the early stages of a break, and, indeed, desirable that he should be, in order that there may be an adequate short interest in the market to cushion the bottom, in order that the magnitude of the break may be lessened by short covering, and in order that there may be frequent strong rallies in the course of the break.

Now, all of this legislation and all of these rulings were benevolently designed to protect investors and to prevent wild excesses in the stock market. They were designed to prevent a repetition of such events as the stock market rise of 1924–29, and the stock market crash of 1929. But the Dow-Jones industrials rose from 108.64 on June 1, 1935, to 190.38 on August 14, 1937, and then dropped to 97.46 by March 31, 1938. This is not a brilliant record for a governmentally controlled, daily inspected, constantly managed stock market, designed to give protection to investors and designed to eliminate wide fluctuations in security prices.

---

[6] The exact date of the promulgation of this rule is not stated in the document.

69

A Verdict on the SEC

SEC Versus Congress on Marketability. The concept of the stock market as a broad and active market in which men who need to sell can find buyers and men who wish to buy can find sellers, in which the spread between the bid price and asked price is narrow, a market in which securities can be marketable, encountered definite hostility upon the part of the Securities and Exchange Commission. The commission questions the value and importance of liquidity in the securities market in pages 98 to 102 of its *Report on Segregation,* of June 20, 1936. In this the commission runs definitely counter to the intention of Congress, which in the Banking Act of 1935 (legislation more recent than the securities and exchange legislation of 1934) reasserts its long-standing emphasis on *marketability* as an essential attribute of investment securities. Section 308 of the Banking Act of 1935 says, "As used in this section, the term 'investment securities' shall mean marketable obligations." This is in harmony with long-established banking law, and long-established practice of the comptroller of the currency in dealing with national banks. The bank examiners, in examining a bank's bond portfolio, have been constantly concerned with marketability as measured by frequency of quotations and by number of transactions, and they have always been concerned with marketability in examining the stock exchange collateral behind bank loans. The Securities and Exchange Commission allowed its own theories, rather than the law of Congress, to guide its policy in dealing with the stock market.

SEC Does Much More Harm than Good. The Securities and Exchange Commission has done very much more harm than good. The Securities Act of 1933 was itself incredibly drastic and imposed such limitations on the issue of new securities as virtually to stop them. It is to the credit of the Securities and Exchange Commission, as constituted at that date, that it aided investment bankers in getting from the Congress certain modifications of the extreme restrictions of the original act. But the legislation, as administered by the Securities and Exchange Commission, has radically limited the issue of new securities as well as contributed to the stock market situation just reviewed.

"Truth-in-Securities" Legislation Needed. The Securities Act of 1933, designed by the Congress to compel "truth in securities" and full disclosure of all material facts in connection with new security issues, had a very laudable purpose. We had had an orgy of new security issues between 1925 and the latter part of 1929, many of which ought not to have been issued, and many of which could not have been sold if full disclosure had been made regarding them.

Before mid-1924 our investment bankers on the whole had shown a great deal of concern for their reputations and a real sense of responsibility toward investors. There were occasional lapses, notably in the period 1897–1903, which was like the 1924–29 period in that there was a great excess of money and credit available, and a very eager public with too much cash in its hands and anxious to speculate in stocks. But with the appalling excess of money and credit created by the cheap money policies of the Federal Reserve banks, particularly after the renewal of cheap money in the autumn of 1927, credit standards broke badly, financial judgment went haywire, and great abuses came.

The impressive fact is that so many men kept sane and remained responsible, rather than the fact that a good many failed to keep sane and failed to meet responsibilities. There is no worse intoxicant than prolonged cheap money and excess credit. But control of this lay with a governmental institution, the Federal Reserve System, rather than with private finance.

But Actual Legislation and Administration Paralyzing. Nonetheless, the legislation compelling truth in securities was called for, and there was sympathy (which this writer shared) among men informed regarding financial matters, with the purposes of the Securities Act of 1933. On the other hand, as such men read the bill, there was general recognition that it was so drastic that it would stop normal functioning as well as prevent abuses. The business of issuing new securities became very pure but very sterile.

Taking the year 1923 as a standard—one should not make the comparison with the wild years 1925–29—we find no year in the period 1933–45 in which new corporate security issues amounted to as much as 50 percent of the issues of 1923. In 1934 new security issues were less than 7 percent of the 1923 levels, while in 1935 they were 15 percent. In the more prosperous years of 1936 and 1937 new corporate issues were higher, and even then they were only 46 percent of those in 1923,while in 1938 and 1939 they fell to 33 and 14 percent, respectively, of the 1923 levels.

Hampering and Expensive Legal Details—Not Needed for Truth in Securities. The British law requiring truth in securities is ordinarily satisfied by a prospectus of four pages or less. The prospectuses issued under the British law are brief, clear, readable documents. A whole year's series, as reproduced in an annual publication in the London *Times,* shows none more than six pages in length, and most four pages or under. But these are adequate. The failure to include a material fact in one of them sent Lord Kylsant to prison.

In contrast, the prospectuses issued under our Securities and Exchange Commission are impossibly long things. Fifty, sixty, and seventy pages are very common. The shortest found was twenty-three pages, in large collection in a substantial financial house.

It is widely believed that nobody reads the prospectuses except the people who prepare them, but one house at least has a man whose main job it is to read the prospectuses, and to initial them as legal proof that he has read them. The purpose of this, however, is apparently to make a legal record. The other members of the firm do not use the prospectuses when they are discussing securities with customers, but instead use the workable documents prepared by security analysts. No one seems to know an investor who has read a prospectus through before buying a security. Perhaps the case exists, but it is very rare.

The legal requirement that a prospectus must accompany every sale of a given security during the first year of life of the security is an absurd and utterly useless requirement. Its effect is to make work and expense, and that is all. A financial house selling securities makes a careful record that it has sent the prospectus with the securities, and it makes a request of the customer that he acknowledge receipt of the prospectus. In the course of the next few weeks a check is made to see if he has replied, acknowledging receipt of the prospectus. If not, he is again requested to do so. If no receipt then comes, the house, wishing to be absolutely safe on the legal side, will send him a registered letter, marked "Addressee only," in which it is stated that a copy of the prospectus has been sent to the customer, and that if no reply has been received from him within ten days, it is assumed that he has received the prospectus. This involves a great deal of work and cost which has absolutely no economic justification, but which the house regards as necessary for its legal protection.

Long and uninteresting as are the prospectuses, the registration documents are, of course, very much longer and more voluminous. The really worthwhile information contained in registration documents and prospectuses could be condensed into a very much smaller space and a very much smaller number of documents. The cost of registration could be greatly reduced without sacrificing anything of the reasonable objective that full disclosure of all relevant facts be made.

Arms-Length Bargaining. There is full justification for the protests of the investment bankers against the efforts of the Securities and Exchange Commission to require competitive bidding through sealed bids or in other ways, on new public utilities security issues. It is apparently only in this field that the Securities and Exchange Commission has a semblance of legal authority to suggest such a requirement, as it bases its claim to this authority on an "arms-length bargaining" provision of the Public Utilities Holding Company Act of 1935, rather than on the Securities Act of 1933 or the Securities Exchange Act of 1934.

There should be arms-length bargaining between borrower and lender and between issuer and underwriter, but there is no reason at all why this should preclude enduring relations between banker and customer, whether in the commercial banking field or in the investment banking field. You have arms-length bargaining so long as the parties to the bargain are each considering primarily the interests that they represent, whether they are doing business with one another for the first time or whether they have been enjoying mutually satisfactory business relations for forty years. Business houses do not change their commercial bank relationships lightly, though constantly solicited to do so in the highly competitive commercial banking field. Each prefers to deal with the institution that knows its business, knows its needs, and feels responsibility for it in times of pressure and crisis. Similarly, in the underwriting field the investment banker who knows his customer's business and who feels responsibility for him when maturities come in bad money markets, gives him a far more useful service than he could get if he were shopping around all the time.

There should be a competitive investment market in which corporations are free to shift their investment bankers if dissatsified with their services or with their charges. The strong corporate issuer with its financial affairs in good order and with prestige such that the public is readily interested in its securities, ought to find a market situation highly competitive, in the sense that there are a number of strong banking groups ready to do the business, if it wishes to turn from the institution with which it has been accustomed to doing business.

On the other hand, the weak borrower or the weak issuer, or the issuer or borrower who has been engaging in venturesome financial practices, does well not to find a highly competitive situation. Both investment banks and commercial banks do well, in the interests of the credit situation, to hold to financial standards; and when a weak borrower seeks to escape the financial discipline of its existing financial connections, it is well if it finds that other banks, informed of the credit issues involved, suggest that it stay with its existing banking connections and conform to the requirements of sound practice laid down. Competition there ought to be among both commercial banks and investment banks, but the competition ought not to be in credit standards.

Further, a requirement which would rest the whole basis of investment bank competition on the question of the price and yield of a particular new security misses some of the greatest essentials of investment banking service. A second-rate group with limited financial power and limited distributing power might outbid a strong investment group with greater prestige, greater financial power, and greater distributing power. A corporation accepting this higher bid might well find at a later time that its securities had been badly placed, were selling at unreasonably low prices, and that its ability to put out further securities had been seriously prejudiced.

Distrust of SEC. There is pretty general confidence in the financial community in the traditions and purposes of not a few of the governmental regulatory bodies. It is particularly true that the national banks trust the good judgment and sense of fair play of the office of the comptroller of the currency, which has been examining national banks and giving advice regarding national bank policy since the Civil War. Individual banks at different times have their issues with the comptroller of the currency, and there was a period around 1916 when the banking community felt that the comptroller was arbitrary and unfair. But by and large, the comptroller's office knows what normal functioning is, and it is disposed to encourage it; and the comptroller's office and the national banks have gone through a good many crises together with helpful cooperation.

There is a good deal of feeling of confidence between the Federal Reserve banks and the member banks, and the regulatory activities of the Federal Reserve banks are felt by the banking community to be fair. While many have been troubled regarding the money market policies both of the Federal Reserve banks and of the Board of Governors of the Federal Reserve System, there is a strong feeling that the individual bank can get a square deal both from the Federal Reserve banks and from the Board of Governors.

One does not find this confidence with respect to the purposes and policies of the Securities and Exchange Commission. We have here an institution which is not sympathetic with the normal functioning of the securities market, which does not believe in the desirability of, or the need for, liquidity and marketability and active functioning, which doubts the desirability of a great deal of private financing, which inclines to the view that the government should in greater or less degree take over financial functions, and which is itself greedy for power to interfere in minute details of financial transactions. It seems to delight in multiplying technicalities which cost money and make work both for itself and for the financial institutions of the country. It has been utterly indefensible in dealing with the matter of proxies, and it has imposed inexcusable trouble and expense upon many corporations in connection with this matter. It has gone far out of its way in interfering in the relations and terms of contracts between investment bankers and issuers.

The Securities and Exchange Commission aroused a great deal of apprehension by its part in the so-called monopoly investigation of the Temporary National Economic Committee, the so-called TNEC, where it developed a one-sided presentation designed to show that there is little need for private investment, with the conclusion that a great deal of government investment is called for. They carefully excluded witnesses whose testimony would not have been agreeable to them, and picked witnesses whose testimony would contribute to their one-sided case. This is particularly true of the testimony on the theory of capital, which is not representative of prevailing views among authoritative economists. The TNEC was largely dominated by the representatives of the Securities and Exchange Commission. There were able congressional members of the commission, including the chairman, who tried hard to have fair hearings, but the hearings were not fair.

SEC Greedy for Power. The Securities and Exchange Commission has seemed greedy for more power. The bringing of the life insurance companies into the TNEC investigation aroused fear in many minds that the Securities and Exchange Commission was looking for another field to regulate.

The Securities and Exchange Commission prepared a bill which was introduced in 1940 into the Senate and House of Representatives, designed for the regulation of investment trusts, which involved a sweeping delegation of ill-defined powers to the Securities and Exchange Commission, even giving them authority over the courts of the United States in certain connections, and giving them authority to substitute their regulations for existing laws of Congress, subject only to vague limitations. This bill aroused the resentment of the Senate Committee on Banking and Currency, and the Securities and Exchange Commission met its first congressional rebuff at this point. Able men in the investment trust field went before the Senate committee and presented with great clarity and frankness the facts regarding their business, and protested with great effectiveness against the bill sponsored by the Securities and Exchange Commission. The upshot was that the Senate committee invited the representatives of the investment trusts to suggest legislation, and that the Securities and Exchange Commission rather meekly requested that it be allowed to participate in the preparation of these legislative suggestions. The investment trust law as finally passed by the Congress was a very different bill indeed from that which the SEC had originally proposed.

A striking instance, attracting wide public attention, of greed for power on the part of the Securities and Exchange Commission came in 1943. The thinness of transactions on the floor of the stock exchange itself had led to the development of a new practice, that of offering through brokerage or investment houses, off the stock exchange, at the closing price, large blocks of stocks which security houses over the country could offer to their customers. The practice has become well established and has doubtless alleviated in some measure the thinness of the market in good times, though how efficacious it would be in a rapidly declining market has not been adequately tested. Under this established practice, in 1943 a wealthy individual, through his investment banker, publicly announced that he was offering off the stock exchange $25 million worth of stocks. At the same time it was announced that his purpose in making the sale was to get cash with which to buy government war bonds. The offering was suddenly withdrawn. The Securities and Exchange Commission, however, denied that it had interfered. It had merely had inquiry made of the attorneys of the wealthy individual as to whether they had considered "the possibility of registering the proposed distribution with the commission."[1]

Radical Changes in Method Called For—Settled Law vs. Bureaucratic Regulation. The Congress was right in demanding truth in securities, and in forbidding stock market manipulation. But a radical change in the whole approach to this problem is called for. There is no more reason in the security and security exchange field than in any other field of private enterprise for constant government interference in the details of transactions. The security business is in general a clean and sound business. The men in the field are in general high-minded, upright, and able men. The normal functioning of the security business, including the stock market, is clean and sound. Indeed, the standard of integrity in this field is among the highest in all fields. Every day transactions involving many tens of millions of dollars, and often hundreds of millions of dollars, are made by word of mouth over the telephone. Transactions between the brokers on the floor of the exchanges are made by a word or even a nod of the head, each man making a memorandum of his own part in the transaction, but neither man giving the other a written document. Disputes regarding these transactions are very rare, and when they occur the assumption is that they stem from an honest misunderstanding and they are quickly adjusted. A very high order of integrity is necessary to make such a system work.

Occasionally, however, criminal acts occur, as in every field where human beings deal with one another. For these occasional criminal acts, there is need for criminal law and punishment. But there is no more need for the kind of supervision of multitudinous details in which the Securities and Exchange Commission engages there than in any other field. What we should do, in the interest of normal functioning, is to set the business free in a framework of definite law, and do away with the detailed regulation.

This should involve the following: (1) The Securities and Exchange Commission should be abolished. (2) The function of the Securities and Exchange Commission, of receiving and filing sworn registration statements and prospectuses, should be put in the hands of a purely ministerial body in some such place as the Department of Commerce. You want a legal record of the statements of fact made by men who are putting out new

---

[1] *New York Times,* October 28, 1943. There was nothing in the law that required this registration. Subsequently, indeed, the transaction was put through without registration. But the question put to the attorneys interrupted the transaction for some months. The Securities and Exchange Commission was clearly reaching out far beyond its jurisdiction as laid down by Congress, in an effort to get more power.

securities, so that they may be punished if they make false statements or if they omit essential information regarding the issues they put out. (3) There should be created in the Department of Justice a security and exchange division, whose business it should be to prosecute by criminal law in the courts of the United States men who make false registration statements or who put out false prospectuses, and men who otherwise violate the federal laws governing securities and security exchanges. One may oppose a governmental agency interfering with the details of the transactions in securities, but still strongly favor criminal laws that will prevent abuses and want them enforced. (4) The existing rules and regulations of the Securities and Exchange Commission, together with the security and exchange legislation, should be thoroughly reviewed, with a view to eliminating most of the detail, and with a view to saving that part which is needed and valuable for the protection of investors and for the prevention of fraud and misrepresentation. In this connection, the congressional committees should call before them the able men in investment banks and brokerage houses, who watch the Securities and Exchange Commission and who know the details, and get from them recommendations as to what parts of the law and the rulings should be preserved in the form of statute law. The congressional committees will find reluctance on the part of many of these men to testify, because of fear of reprisal by the SEC.

Finally, (5) the law itself with respect to prospectuses and registration statements should be greatly simplified. Altogether too much detail is called for. The procedure is altogether too expensive. There is no reason for a registration statement. A prospectus should suffice, and the prospectus should be short enough so that men will read it. But it is important that the prospectus should be a responsible document on the basis of which men may be put in prison if they falsify, and on the basis of which the purchasers of securities will have legal evidence for bringing suit in the event that they have been tricked or cheated.

70

The Severe Depression, 1937–38, and the Mild Rally, 1938–39

The winter of 1937–38 was a period of gloom and apprehension both for the country and for the administration and its supporters in Washington. Efforts were made by close advisers of the President to persuade him to moderate his bitterness toward American business and finance.

Secretary of Treasury Makes Conservative Speech, November 1937. The secretary of the Treasury was permitted to make an address before the New York Academy of Political Science on November 11, 1937, in which he promised a determined move toward a balanced budget and stated that deficit spending was no longer needed. He said that the trust funds of the Treasury could be expected to take public debt out of private hands, and argued that it would be unwise to reduce the public debt in private hands too fast, indicating that $1 billion to $1,300 million a year would be enough![1] The distinguished audience made it very plain that it did not take the secretary of the Treasury very seriously.

Thomas Lamont and John L. Lewis Visit President. Adolf A. Berle, one of the original Brain Trust, arranged an interview with the President for a strangely assorted pair, Thomas Lamont, of J. P. Morgan & Company, and John L. Lewis, of the CIO. Lewis was really concerned about the depression because he wanted work for the members of his unions. Unemployment rose from 12 percent in 1937 to 18.8 percent in 1938. Interesting stories as to what took place at this interview were current for a time, but it has not been possible to confirm any of them. The impression was that the President did not listen very much, and if policies were in any way modified by the conference, there was no objective evidence of it.

President Repudiates Secretary of Treasury, April 1938. The speech of the secretary of the Treasury, made in late 1937, was repudiated by the administration when it was announced in the middle of April 1938 that the Federal

[1] *Commercial & Financial Chronicle*, November 13, 1937, pp. 3133–35.

Reserve action in raising reserve requirements would be partially rescinded, that the Sterilization Fund of the Treasury was to be abandoned,
and that further pump-priming expenditures were to be employed. A
balanced budget and, above all, public debt reduction were thrown out of
the window. On April 16, 1938, reserve requirements were lowered from
200 to 175 percent of the minimum requirements. At approximately the
same time the Sterilization Fund was put into active use, as the Treasury
turned over gold certificates to the Federal Reserve banks and received
deposit credits with the Federal Reserve banks in exchange.

Repudiates Agreement with Democratic Leaders. The Democratic leaders of the House and Senate advised the President that he should content
himself with getting appropriation bills passed by the Congress, abandon,
for the time at least, the effort to get the wage and hour bill adopted by the
Congress, and let the Congress and the people rest. The President agreed to
this program. But the next day, April 26, without consulting them again,
the President made it known that he would demand the passage of the wage
and hour bill in the current session. This was revealed at a press conference, after the President had called Chairman John J. O'Connor, of the
Rules Committee, to the White House, to discuss the situation. The
Democratic leaders were angry. The Rules Committee for a time refused to
yield. On April 29, the House Rules Committee by a vote of 8 to 6, voted to
bury the bill in committee for the remainder of the session.[2]

The Wages and Hours Act—Last New Deal Law. The President, however,
forced through the Wages and Hours Act and signed it on June 25, 1938. It
was the last important New Deal legislation before the war. It was a very
dangerous piece of legislation, and, coming on top of all the other measures which had made complications for business, it had very ominous
possibilities. It provided that hours should be limited to 44 hours a week for
the first year, 42 hours a week for the second year, and 40 hours a week after
two years. Work in excess of those hours should be paid for at not less than
1½ times the regular wage rate. Minimum wages were set at 25¢ an hour for
the first year, 30¢ an hour for the following six years, and 40¢ after seven
years. Provisions were made for industry committees to speed up the
application of the increases in minimum wages.

It was thought by many that, in the first year, the provision would not
affect many industries outside the South, though the framers of the law
apparently forgot about Puerto Rico, and very grave disturbances came in
that island, where capital is scarce and population dense. Immense unemployment resulted there through the sheer inability of important industries
to pay the 25¢ an hour. Wages are high when men are scarce and capital and

---

[2] *Ibid.*, April 30, 1938, p. 2778.

natural resources abundant, and wages are low when men are abundant and capital and resources are scarce. In Puerto Rico population increases without restraint, and constantly presses on subsistence. Puerto Rico is a verification of Malthus' law.

The coming of the war, with its immense increase in wages, made these minima relatively harmless, even in the South. The provisions regarding hours, however, as we shall later see, tied our hands very badly when it came to fighting a war.

The trough of stock market prices was reached in March 1938 and the trough of business depression, as measured by the Federal Reserve Index of Industrial Production, was reached in May. There came a substantial rally in the Index of Industrial Production (1923–25 = 100) from 76 in May 1938 to 105 in December of that year, followed by a drop to 92 in April and May 1939, with a rally to 103 in August, just before the outbreak of the war. Unemployment averaged over 9 million, or 16.7 percent of the working force, for 1939. The Dow-Jones industrial averages in the stock market, which had dropped to a low of 97.46 on March 31, 1938, rose to 158.90 on November 10 of that year, the rise being accentuated in the latter part of the year by improving Republican prospects in the autumn congressional elections and by the sweeping Republican gains in the election.

71

The Turn in the
Political Tide, 1938

The Wages and Hours Act was President Roosevelt's last successful effort to override a reluctant Congress. Congressional opposition was growing and public opposition was growing. This came out strikingly in the President's failure in his effort to "purge" the Senate of the Democrats who had opposed him in the Supreme Court fight and in other matters. His one successful effort to purge was in the New York City primary, where he succeeded in defeating for renomination Chairman John J. O'Connor, of the House Rules Committee. But in his efforts to purge the Senate, he received blow after blow in the face from the voters of the Democratic Party itself. The most conspicuous cases were those of Senator Millard E. Tydings, of Maryland, Senator Walter F. George, of Georgia, and the picturesque Senator Ellison D. Smith, of South Carolina. These men stood and fought, and the people of their states resented the presidential invasion of the states.

Low Tide for Republicans in Election of 1936. Republican gains in the election of 1938 represented a definite turn in the political tide. The Republicans had had a dramatic victory in 1928. In 1930, as our table below shows, there was a tie in the Senate, but the Republicans retained the committee chairmanships—Senator Reed Smoot, for instance, remaining chairman of the Senate Finance Committee. The Republicans lost, however, the House of Representatives by a very narrow vote and the Speakership went to the Democrats. In 1932 Senate and House became overwhelmingly Democratic. In 1934 the Democratic tide swept still higher, and after the election in 1936, the Democratic majority was so overwhelming in the Senate, where there were just 16 Republicans left, that there were not enough Republican senators adequately to man the committees. In the House of Representatives there were only 88 Republicans out of the membership of 435. In 1938, however, the Republicans gained 7 senators, while in the House of Representatives their vote rose from 88 to 169.

Roosevelt Holds Control of Democratic Congress. Democratic Party discipline held pretty well from 1932 to 1936, though we have noted exceptions in the cases of Senator Glass and Senator Gore, and there were a good many others of the old-school Democrats who believed in states' rights, limited functions of the federal government, economy in government and sound money, and white supremacy in the South. They were extremely restive under the party discipline. Senator Ellison D. Smith of South Carolina had made a dramatic protest at the Democratic National Convention in 1936 in Philadelphia, against the bringing in of the Negroes into the Democratic Party. The South was unhappy but it stayed with the party. Senator Smith, who was chairman of the Senate Committee on Agriculture, had also manifested a great deal of impatience with the New Deal agricultural policies.[1] But, on the whole, party discipline had held.

Till Supreme Court Fight, 1937—Informal Bipartisan Coalition. It broke, however, with the President's effort to pack the Supreme Court in 1937, and in 1937–38 there was a growing informal coalition between conservative Democrats and Republicans. With the Republican congressional gains in 1938, this informal coalition grew strong enough to make it pretty clear that the New Deal was finished insofar as it depended upon further congressional support. The opposition was not strong enough to undo what had been done over presidential veto, but it was strong enough to prevent further New Deal legislation.

The composition of House and Senate following the elections stood as shown on the following page.

Election of 1940. Beginning with 1938 there seems to be clear evidence of an ebbing tide for the Democratic Party and, above all, for the New Deal, whenever the prople could vote primarily on domestic issues. The election of 1940 showed a Republican loss of seven seats in the House of Representatives, but a Republican gain of five senators. This was a presidential year, and foreign problems dominated the picture. President Roosevelt won primarily because people were afraid to "change horses in the middle of the stream." His opponent, Wendell L. Willkie, made a surprisingly ineffective and amateurish campaign. He damaged his voice at the very beginning. He largely cut himself off from the organization of the Republican National Committee, and from the stream of information and campaign materials which they had prepared to send him. He early lost a big part of his radio audience by repetitions in new speeches of what had already been said in others. And finally, he took the heart out of a good many of his followers by a surrender to labor leaders on the wage and hour law and on the Wagner Act—which brought him few if any labor union votes. Before the campaign was over there was a sham fight on domestic issues, and President Roosevelt won very easily on the foreign issues.

Sweeping Victory for Anti–New Deal Coalition in 1942. In 1942, with

---

[1] See U.S., Congress, Senate, Committee on Agriculture and Forestry, *Hearings on Causes of the Loss of Export Trade and the Means of Recovery,* January 30–February 7, 1935.

domestic issues again to the fore, the Republican congressional gains were very impressive. The Republicans gained 10 seats in the Senate and 46 seats in the House of Representatives, so that the standing of the parties in the Senate was 38 Republicans to 57 Democrats, while in the House it was 208 Republicans, 222 Democrats. This made possible an informal but very effective bipartisan conservative majority on domestic issues in both House and Senate. In 1944 the war once more dominated the scene and once more President Roosevelt's Republican opponent, the brilliant Thomas E. Dewey, in his West Coast speeches, surrendered to the New Deal in domestic issues. Roosevelt won his fourth term as President. Even so, the Democrats lost one seat in the Senate, and the Republican losses in the House of Representatives (their membership dropped from 208 to 190) left them far stronger in the House of Representatives than they had been following the election of 1938. An effective bipartisan coalition of conservatives in Congress remained, which, while supporting the President loyally in matters concerned with the war, nonetheless resisted him successfully with respect to many matters of domestic policy.

COMPOSITION OF CONGRESS AFTER ELECTIONS—1930–44
Senate

Congress	Year elected	Total	Rep.	Dem.	Farmer-Labor	Prog.	Ind.	Vacant
72d	1930	96	47	47	1			1
73d	1932	96	35	60	1			
74th	1934	96	25	69	1	1		
75th	1936	96	16	75	2	1	1	1
76th	1938	96	23	69	2	1	1	
77th	1940	96	28	66		1	1	
78th	1942	96	38	57		1		
79th	1944	96	38	56		1		1

House of Representatives

Congress	Year elected	Total	Rep.	Dem.	Farmer-Labor	Prog.	Ind.	Amer. Labor	Vacant
72d	1930	435	214	218	1				2
73d	1932	435	117	310	5				3
74th	1934	435	102	322	3	7			1
75th	1936	435	88	333	5	8			1
76th	1938	435	169	261	1	2		1	1
77th	1940	435	162	268	1	3		1	
78th	1942	435	208	222	1	2		1	1
79th	1944	435	190	242		1		1	1

72

International Political Relations
in the Decade of the Thirties

The economic crash of 1929–32 was accompanied, as we have seen, by a breakdown of international credit and by a great intensification of economic nationalism, which, of course, made the breakdown of international credit more complete. If goods could not move in international trade, and if the whole burden of paying debts had to fall on gold, then there was not enough gold available for the purpose, and international debts could not be paid.

The Breakdown of International Political Cooperation. With this came a great disintegration of international political relations, and a general failure of international political cooperation. The agreements and the treaties and the organizations, notably the League of Nations, which had been designed to make a peaceful world, proved feeble and undependable reliances. And the predatory governments, which had been held in check in the decade of the 1920s, increasingly found that they had free hands. The first manifestation of this was in 1930 when Secretary Stimson's protests against the occupation of Manchuria (called Manchukuo by the Japanese) met little response from Britain or from the League of Nations.

Germany and Italy Helpful Until Hitler Came In. Germany remained, so long as the democratic government lasted, a peaceful country whose government made every effort at conciliation. Mussolini, moreover, was a very good citizen of Europe from about 1930 down to the time of his Ethiopian venture.

In the winter of 1931–32, representatives of the bankers of thirteen nations were sitting in Berlin extending the Standstill Agreement which they had made at the request of seven governments, namely, Belgium, France, Germany, Great Britain, Italy, Japan, and the United States. The Italian government gave instructions to the Italian representatives on that committee to cooperate in every way to bring about a workable settlement, and in particular to cooperate with the British and American bankers in resisting the unreasonable political attitude of the French banking delegation. The French representatives, meanwhile, under instructions from their government, were constantly making political difficulties. The American banking group received no help at all from the American government. The German government cooperated with great loyalty.

Negative Attitude of France. The seven governments in their communiqué of July 23, 1931, in which they asked the bankers to make the Standstill Agreement, had promised "to cooperate, so far as lies within their power, to restore confidence," but the promise was an empty promise so far as most of the governments were concerned, while on the part of France there was a negative attitude. In an earlier chapter we have seen the French turning from economic cooperation to political fears early in 1931 at the time of the German-Austrian Customs Union Agreement, and using their great financial power to tear down Austria and Germany instead of helping to save them.

If we could have got from France in the winter of 1931–32 the concessions regarding reparations which she made at Lausanne in the summer of 1932, we could have saved the democratic government of Germany, and Hitler would not have come in.

Mussolini and Hitler, 1934. After Hitler came in, Mussolini cooperated for a time with the peace-loving countries of the world, notably when he moved the Italian army to the borders of Austria at the Brenner Pass in July 1934 in a successful warning to Hitler to stay out of Austria. It was not until after the Ethiopian episode began at the very end of 1934 and in early 1935 that Mussolini turned from cooperation with France and England to a closer and closer relation with Hitler.

In the beginning, the relations between Hitler and Mussolini were somewhat comical. Hitler had taken Mussolini as his model, and Hitler meant to repeat in Germany the steps which Mussolini had taken in reaching supreme power in Italy. He was reported at one time as having been very much humiliated and outraged because President Hindenburg would not allow him to do what the king of Italy had allowed Mussolini to do at a similar phase of Mussolini's career. Mussolini for his part is reported to have had a great contempt and dislike for Hitler, and on the occasion of Hitler's first visit to Italy, June 14 and 15, 1934, is said to have remarked to one of his associates, after he had listened to a two-hour oration from Hitler, "His face is an insult to the universe."

Ethiopia—British and French Weakness. After the ineffective resistance of Britain, France, and the League of Nations to Mussolini's Ethiopian plans—resistance which came after Mussolini had already matured his plans, and had reason to believe that Britain and France would not interfere with them—Mussolini turned against the League, Britain, and France, partly in anger and partly in contempt.

The British had indeed allowed their naval strength to fall very low by the time of the Ethiopian episode. They had inadequate supplies of munitions on their naval vessels. They were not ready to fight. France, torn by political dissension and a growing pacifism, had allowed her military alliances, designed to keep Germany from aggression, to grow very weak. The first decisive symptom of this appeared on January 26, 1934, when Germany made a ten-year nonaggression pact with Poland. There were credible reports at the time that the Polish government, before signing this treaty with Germany, asked definite assurances of the French government of adequate military support from France in the event that Poland failed to sign it, and that Poland did not receive these assurances.

Economic Nationalism: Ottawa, 1932, and London, 1933. On the part of the British Empire, the most significant move made in 1932, breaching international unity and cooperation, was the Ottawa Imperial Economic Conference of August, under which trade preferences were given within the British Empire to the detriment of outside countries. This had been preceded in February 1932 by protective tariff acts in England, with the abandonment of England's historical policy of free trade.

Our own government, as we have seen, turned decisively away from international cooperation in 1933, when President Roosevelt wrecked the London Conference.

Baldwin, Mussolini, Ethiopia, and the League of Nations, 1935–36. On June 7, 1935, Stanley Baldwin became prime minister of Great Britain and Sir Samuel Hoare foreign secretary. Immediately thereafter, on June 18, 1935, the British made an Anglo-German naval agreement under which Germany was to have not more than thirty-five percent of British naval tonnage. This gave up important provisions of the Versailles treaty, and was very much resented in France. Tentative resistance by Britain to Italy on the Ethiopian matter continued through 1935. Anthony Eden visited Rome on June 23 and 24, 1935, offering Mussolini concessions which were refused as inadequate. Italian-Ethiopian arbitration negotiations at The Hague (June 25 to July 9) produced nothing. The League of Nations Council on June 25 set September 4 as the date when it would itself begin to investigate the situation.

On October 3 Italian forces began the invasion of Ethiopia. On October 7 the League of Nations Council called Italy the aggressor. On November 18 the League of Nations voted the application of economic sanctions against Italy. On May 5, 1936, the Italian forces occupied Addis Ababa and the resistance of Ethiopia ceased. On May 19, 1936, the Italian government formally proclaimed the annexation of all Ethiopia. On June 4, 1936, the League council voted to discontinue sanctions. There was a complete collapse of international opposition to Italy's defiance of the League.

Baldwin and Edward VIII. England meanwhile had preoccupations. Stanley Baldwin apparently forgot that he had the duty of rearming England, and that England had undergone an immense humiliation in her dealings with Italy. He was busy with the problem of Edward VIII.

Edward became king January 20, 1936. He was a very troublesome king. It was not merely that he wished to marry a woman regarded by the British Empire as an unsuitable queen. He also undertook to interfere in minor ways in affairs of state. He failed to give the English people the ceremonies which they expected from the king. One distinguished British statesman said privately that he had told the king, "The British people are paying you to give them a good show, and you are not giving them a good show." The king of England has no power. He is a figurehead. He must sign the documents his ministers present. He must go through laborious ceremonies. He must be a figurehead and a front.

From January 20, 1936, to his abdication on December 10, 1936, Edward was the central concern of the British government, and especially of Stanley Baldwin. Meanwhile, Britain did not rearm, though on April 30, 1936, plans for constructing thirty-eight warships were announced.

Hitler Reoccupies the Rhineland Without Opposition, 1936. Meanwhile, Britain and France allowed Hitler, pursuing his systematic plans for undoing the Treaty of Versailles, to reoccupy the Rhineland with military force in March 1936. At the same time the German government denounced the Locarno Pact of 1925.

Rome-Berlin-Tokyo, 1936. On October 27, 1936, moreover, the Berlin-Rome Axis was formed. In November 1936 Hitler denounced the clauses of the Versailles treaty providing for international control of Germany's rivers, and announced also the conclusion of the German-Japanese Pact.

Hitler Begins Mass Production of Military Planes, 1936. On January 2, 1937, an Anglo-Italian Mediterranean Agreement was signed, but it led to nothing. The situation became speedily worse with the development of the Spanish Civil War and with the open flouting of nonintervention agreements by the Italian government. Meanwhile, in 1936, Germany had begun the mass production of military aircraft. The British were experimenting with aircraft, were dissatisfied with the models, and continued for the next two years (down to the time of Munich) to improve the models rather than to produce aircraft.

Spanish Civil War. The Spanish Civil War broke out on July 18, 1936. One speaks with diffidence of the political forces in Spain, but it seems fantastic to describe the conflict as one between communism and fascism. There had, indeed, been a powerful anarchist movement in Barcelona even before World War I, but the democratic government which had thrown out Alfonso and which was in control of the country at the time of the outbreak of the Spanish Civil War in 1936 was neither communist nor anarchist. It was, rather, democracy of the French Revolution type, and the issues of the Spanish Civil War were much more the issues of the French Revolution than they were issues of the twentieth century. General Franco represented a counteraction of nobles and an eighteenth-century church and religious peasants against the anticlerical democracy of the cities. But it pleased Germany and Italy to look upon Franco as a fascist and Franco was very glad to have their aid. And it pleased Russia to look upon the Loyalists in Madrid as communists, and they were very glad to have Russia's aid. They were glad, also, to get such aid as the Blum government in France was willing to give.

In November 1936 Germany and Italy recognized the government of Franco. Great Britain and France tried to pursue a policy of nonintervention, putting a ban on supplies to the legitimate government and attempting to bring about an international policy of nonintervention. This culminated in the Italian-British Mediterranean Pact, already referred to, of January 2, 1937, but led to nothing.

Democracy Dangerously Pacifist—England, France, and United States, 1936–37. Democracy is pacifist, dangerously pacifist, in a world where there are powerful, aggressive, and ruthless autocracies. Young men in the British universities in 1936 were passing resolutions that they would not fight for king and country. Pacifism was rampant among young men in American universities. Pacifism was so widespread among the French people that there was doubt in the minds of the government as to whether the army would march if called upon to go into the Rhineland to drive Hitler out. The governments of England, France, and the United States preferred to close their eyes to the dangers threatening from the Berlin-Rome-Tokyo Axis created in 1936. In the United States in May 1937 we passed the Neutrality Act, enlarging the statutes of August 1935 and February 1936, so that our law provided that when the President proclaimed a state of war outside the United States, the export of arms to belligerents was prohibited. Certain other materials designated by the President could be taken by belligerents only on a "cash and carry" basis, and all other exports to belligerents must be paid for with cash, even though they could be carried in American bottoms. No American loans were permitted to warring powers, and American citizens were forbidden to travel on ships of belligerent registry. This was a deliberate surrender of our neutral rights, and of the "freedom of the seas," for which we had fought in 1812, and for which we had gone to war in 1917 under Woodrow Wilson. We vainly thought we could insulate ourselves from the troubles of Europe and Asia by expedients like these.

Our legislation put a premium upon the construction of plants for building munitions, naval vessels, aircraft, and so on, in every foreign country. If foreign countries could not count on purchasing munitions abroad when war came, then they must either make themselves into arsenals or go under. Germany, Japan, and Italy did move rapidly in making themselves into arsenals, but the democracies did not.

Secretary Hull Alert to the Danger. Not all of us were blind. Secretary of State Cordell Hull knew early, almost as soon as the Berlin-Rome-Tokyo Axis was formed, that anything which he said to the German, Japanese, or

Italian ambassador was known to the two other governments immediately. The secretary of state was gravely concerned long before the country was aroused from its fantastic dream. President Roosevelt came to share these fears. He ought, of course, to have vetoed the neutrality legislation. He did ask for modification of the Neutrality Act in June 1939 but Congress failed to act.

Russia. Russia's course in the international picture in the 1930s, viewed in retrospect, shows probably more consistency of purpose than was apparent at the time. To the outside world Russia was a dark country, keeping her secrets well, and arousing continual apprehension, partly by her secretiveness, and partly by her propaganda for communism in other countries through the Third International. English opinion vacillated between fear of Germany and fear of communism.

Early Bolshevik Policy Uses Up Russia's Physical Capital. The early efforts of the Bolsheviki in managing Russian economic life were farcically tragic. They deliberately ruined the money of the country and they precipitated an economic collapse in 1921. Then Lenin turned to the New Economic Policy with the effort to give Russia a good money to operate with again, and with a large place for private trading. Revival came, but by late 1926 and early 1927 it became apparent that Russia was using up the capital which she had inherited from the czarist regime without replacing it.[1]

Lenin died in January 1924. The two or three years that followed represented a struggle between Stalin and Trotsky for control, ending with Stalin's decisive victory in December 1927.

Russia's Five-Year Plan, 1928. Stalin was much more interested in developing Russia internally than he was in spreading communism throughout the world. In October 1928 Stalin announced the First Five-Year Plan. Russia needed capital, in the sense of physical instruments of production, of plants and equipment, dams and turbines, of products of the heavy industries. Russian industry was producing less than was needed for the consumption of the people. The five-year plan curtailed production of consumers' goods still more, diverting Russia's industry from producing hats and shoes to producing machines. The people suffered, but the physical capital was created. Agriculture was turned toward collective agriculture and state farms, with the elimination and "liquidation" of the kulaks, the peasant farmers who had some capital of their own. The cost was high, the waste was great, the human suffering was immense; but Russia built up her capital equipment. The First Five-Year Plan of 1928 was followed by other vast plans, carried out with greater efficiency.

Russia Turns Toward Western Powers, 1932. Russia had seemingly cared little, in the period of the 1920s, about outside public opinion, but in 1932

---

[1] *Chase Economic Bulletin,* May 6, 1922, and June 21, 1927, pp. 11–17.

she had become alarmed about the activity of Japan on her eastern borders and she turned toward consultation with the Western powers. In July 1932 she made nonaggression pacts with Estonia, Latvia, and Finland. She took part, also, in the Disarmament Conference, February–July 1932, and she made a nonaggression pact with France in November of that year.

In November 1933 the government of the United States gave recognition to the Soviet government of Russia, and the Russians promised to abstain from propaganda in the United States. In September 1934 Russia joined the League of Nations, which previously had been very much hated in Russia.

Russia and Hitler. While the rest of the world vacillated over the international significance of Hitler's coming to power, Russia had no illusions, and she immediately began to direct both her political and economic activities toward preparation for a war with Germany which she feared was inevitable. The Russians had read *Mein Kampf* and took very seriously Hitler's threats of expansion to the East and his hostility to communism. Trade relations with Germany continued and even expanded, but Moscow armed.

Russian Alliances: France and Czechoslovakia, 1935. In June 1934 Moscow made agreements with Czechoslovakia and with Rumania. On May 2, 1935, Russia and France made an alliance, and on May 16 Russia made an alliance with Czechoslovakia which obliged Russia to come to the assistance of Czechoslovakia, provided France decided to act. This agreement created great anger in Germany.

At the meeting of the Third International, in July–August 1935, it was decided that Soviet Russia, in view of the growing tension between the democratic and fascist states, should throw its weight on the side of the democracies against the common enemy. At the outbreak of the Spanish Civil War, in July 1936, the Russian government at once took the side of the Madrid government.

Russian Purge of 1937. Moving toward the democratic governments against the common enemy, Russia nonetheless used measures which shocked and outraged the democratic governments. The purges of January 1937 were very shocking. On June 12 Marshal Tukhachevski and several other generals of the highest rank were executed after a secret court-martial. They were accused of conspiracy with the Germans and Japanese. There followed further purges, in the course of which Trotskyites and others objectionable to Stalin were liquidated. The outside world was shocked, and the opinion prevailed for a time that Russia was undermining her own military organization and military strength by killing her high-ranking generals.

Divided Opinion in England—Germany vs. Communism. There were important elements in Britain which looked upon Germany as a safeguard against bolshevism. There was, moreover, in England a good deal of sympathy with certain phases of Hitler's so-called social reforms, notably the "youth movement." The head of a college of one of the great English universities was enthusiastic about what Hitler was doing for the youth of Germany as late as May 1937. The head of the college had just returned from an extended trip to Germany. He had been taken around. He had been shown the scenes. He had seen the physical health and enthusiasm of the young people in the youth movement. He did not know the sinister character of the German youth movement. He had swallowed whole what the Nazis had told him. He thought that Hitler was a great man.

There was too in 1936, when Hitler went into the Rhineland, no inconsiderable sentiment both in England and France that, after all, you could not keep Germany down forever, that a nation had a right to its own territory, and had a right to move its army wherever it pleased within its own territory. Democracies are dangerously pacifist.

Progressive Disintegration in France. Meanwhile, there had been a progressive disintegration in France. The appalling parliamentary system of France meant short-lived ministries. Scandals arose. In December 1933 the Stavisky affair shocked France and in February 1934 there were serious riots in Paris and other cities resulting from it, and a general strike. Foreign Minister Barthou made a grand tour of European capitals, April–June 1934, in the hope of building up a strong alliance against Nazi Germany, but on October 9 he was assassinated at Marseilles, along with King Alexander of Yugoslavia. France did, however, conclude an alliance in May 1935 with Soviet Russia, as we have seen.

Meanwhile, financial difficulties multiplied. The inveterate French habit of fiscal deficits, which Poincaré had brought to an end in 1926, was resumed. There was immense discord among the French people. Bitterness between the extreme reactionaries and the extreme radicals was probably more intense in France than in almost any other country. Moderate men in France could form ministries, but without dependable majorities behind them.

The Blum "New Deal." The various radical groups in parliament united to form the so-called Popular Front in November 1935. In May 1936 parliamentary elections gave the Popular Front a majority and the first Popular Front ministry was formed on June 5, 1936, under Leon Blum. Then came appalling disorders. There was a great wave of sitdown strikes. On June 12 the forty-hour week was established. The Bank of France was nationalized. There was a suppression of fascist groups (June 30). There was a nationalization of the munitions industry (July 17). Compulsory arbitration of labor disputes was provided for, and workmen were to be given vacations with pay.

The forty-hour week brought a catastrophic rise in production costs in France. It led in one case to a 30 percent increase in personnel in a building. In a second case, where profits were already too low, it led to a 22.5 percent increase in total costs, and in a third case, a factory, it led to a 60 percent increase in labor costs, which meant a 30 percent increase in total costs. A violent business reaction came.

The financial difficulties of the government grew, the franc weakened in the foreign exchanges, and on October 2, 1936, a bill devaluing the franc but not definitely fixing its gold content was passed. In March 1937 Blum was obliged to announce a "breathing spell" in the French New Deal, and from then on government policy moved toward undoing and relaxing the rigor of the sudden drastic legislation. But the damage was done. France was decisively weakened. Military aircraft production, which had been nationalized by the Blum legislation, fell virtually to zero, and it was reported that the French government had established aircraft plants in Switzerland in order to get away from the restraints of the French labor laws. The French franc, which had been so strong from the autumn of 1926 through 1934, had lost its prestige, and the flight of capital from France had been resumed.

Hull Keeps Up Tariff Reduction Efforts. Hope remained that even Germany and Italy might be brought back into the concert of nations and into the current of world trade and world finance. Secretary Hull believed, correctly, that if nations could work for their raw materials, producing goods and sending them out to get foreign products they needed in the free markets of the world, they would not need to fight for them, and that by turning Germany and Italy toward the free exchange of goods with the world again, and toward the interchange of products in fair multilateral trade, much could be accomplished.

Neville Chamberlain and the City of London. Hull's most serious obstacle in bringing about reciprocal trade agreements in Europe in early 1937 was England rather than Italy or even, for that matter, Germany. Neville Chamberlain was chancellor of the Exchequer in early 1937, and on May 28, 1937, became prime minister. Chamberlain was the inadequate son of a strong father. His father, Joseph Chamberlain, had led the fight in 1906 for protective tariffs in England and had been defeated. Neville Chamberlain sought to continue his father's tradition. It was possible, however, to arouse the City of London, namely, the financial district, to put vigorous pressure on Chamberlain in the direction of freer trade, and in November 1938 Hull was able to bring about a trade agreement involving Great Britain, Canada, and the United States. In early 1937, however, England's delay on this point was a factor in keeping both Italy and Germany from making the necessary moves toward reentering the world trade picture.

Hitler's Decision to Make No Compromise Probably Came in June 1937. In retrospect, it seems probable that Hitler's decision to resist all efforts at conciliation and to move definitely toward domination, by bluff if possible, by war if necessary, came in June 1937. England still looked very strong then. Her prestige was great and she herself had little apprehension of the German danger. Dr. Schacht in Germany, who was both head of the Reichsbank and minister of economics, was extremely anxious to turn Germany from her isolationist economic course, and from controlled exchanges, back to the current of world trade. He was extremely anxious also to have Germany at peace with the world instead of multiplying antagonisms. He had worked for a good many weeks to secure from the British government an invitation to Baron Constantin von Neurath, the German foreign minister, to visit London to bring about an understanding with England regarding various matters, including the Spanish Civil War, and to pave the way for better economic relations. The British were not anxious to extend the invitation, but it was extended and accepted. Schacht's hopes were high.

On June 21, 1937, Hitler suddenly canceled Neurath's visit to London.[2] The excuse given was that other powers would not act against Loyalist Spain over the alleged submarine attack on the cruiser *Leipzig*.

Why did Hitler cancel this visit? The probable explanation is that Hitler had suddenly concluded that neither Russia nor France need any longer be feared. It was on June 12 that the Russians had executed Marshal Tukhachevski and the seven other generals of the highest rank. There had been, moreover, in late May and early June renewed weakness of the French franc in the foreign exchange market. Hitler was no longer afraid. His cancellation of the visit of von Neurath on June 21 seems, in retrospect, to have been the decisive turning point.

Hitler's judgment was good. He met no effective resistance from then on until the war itself came.

Schacht's influence in German affairs waned. In November 1937 Walther Funk replaced Schacht as minister of economics, though Schacht remained president of the Reichsbank. By early 1939 he was out of the Reichsbank also, though Hitler had refused to release him from the cabinet, where he remained a minister without portfolio.

The German Annexation of Austria. In March 1938 Hitler invaded and annexed Austria with the acquiescence of Italy, and with no show of resistance by any other power. Mussolini had visited Hitler in Berlin in September 1937, and in May 1938 Hitler had visited Mussolini in Rome.

Munich, September 1938. In May 1938 the first Czechoslovakian crisis came. In September 1938 came the great Czechoslovakian crisis. Chamberlain and Édouard Daladier, the premier of France, visited Hitler and Mussolini in Munich to surrender meekly. Roosevelt made appeals to Hitler and Mussolini. War was averted. Chamberlain brought home Hit-

---

[2] I talked at length with Schacht in Berlin on that day. He was very downhearted. When I saw Schacht again in Berlin a few weeks after Munich, in October 1938, he told me that he had not seen Hitler for thirteen months.

ler's signed agreement that England and Germany would not fight. A great gloom fell over the world.[3]

European Opinion After Munich. The question was asked in several European capitals shortly after Munich, "Is it a peace or is it a truce?" In London the explanation was that Britain was not ready in the air but was determined speedily to be ready, and there would be peace because England would be strong enough to assure peace. One cynic, however, said, "It is a peace because when Hitler makes a new demand it will be yielded to, and when he makes yet another demand, it will be yielded to." A high official in Paris said, "It is a truce. In 1936 governmental opinion was ahead of public opinion. We should have struck then, of course, but the people were not ready. This time public opinion was in advance of governmental opinion. The people are ashamed of what the governments have done. Next time public opinion will force the governments to stand their ground."

There was little appreciation on the Continent of the immense military power of Hitler, even after Munich. Swiss and Dutch opinion both held that England had been unduly afraid of Hitler's aircraft. One distinguished Dutch statesman said that the Spanish Civil War had proved that cities could not be conquered by aircraft, that it took an army and artillery to capture cities. He felt that England had yielded unnecessarily. He was sure that Holland could be defended in the event of a German attack. On a great map of Holland he showed where he could cut his dikes, if necessary, to flood the country to stop the German army. France felt quite serene behind the Maginot Line, though there were French workingmen who said that France could not afford a forty-hour week when the Germans were working sixty hours. There appeared to be more concern and more courage among the humbler people, both in France and in England, than in high places, after Munich.

Russian Reaction to Munich. Russia's role in 1938 was not a conspicuous one. Russia was not included in the Munich Conference. Distrust had arisen again. It was said in London that when the Russians were asked, before Munich, what they would do if Czechoslovakia were attacked and England and France moved to her aid, the Russians had said, "We will do our bit."

But when they were asked for specific information as to how many divisions, how much aircraft, and so on, they would have available, they were uncommunicative. The British excused leaving Russia out of the

---

[3] Going to Europe on an English liner shortly after Munich, I was sitting in the smoking room with a high official of the British government. The head steward, who knew him, came up and said, "Two weeks ago I thought we were strong, sir." And the British official said sadly, "So did I."

picture on this ground. The Russians deeply resented being left out. Benes of Czechoslovakia said at the time that the Russians had been entirely loyal. The Russian-Czechoslovakian agreement was predicated on action by France. The great bitterness of the Czechs was directed toward France, though they were very bitter toward Britain also.

The Munich crisis of September 1938 gave Hitler three million Germans of the Sudeten region of Czechoslovakia. On March 15, 1939, Germany occupied Bohemia and Moravia. In March 1939 Hitler made demands on Poland with special reference to Danzig. The firmness of the Poles and the alarm of Britain and France made the Germans hold back. German demands on Poland continued.

Litvinov Dropped, May 3, 1939. On May 3 Maxim Litvinov was dismissed from the Russian Ministry of Foreign Affairs after eighteen years of service. Litvinov had tried hard to bring Russia into the concert of the democratic powers. At Geneva and the League of Nations he fought valiantly for vigorous League action toward suppressing aggression. As Russia came again to distrust the Western powers, Litvinov came into disfavor. He was too much an internationalist and too little a Russian in the minds of men who knew only Russia, and he was replaced by Molotov, who was said not to have traveled in foreign countries. Distrusting the democratic Western powers, Russia turned to playing her own game.

German-Russian Nonaggression Pact, August 1939. On August 20 and 21, 1939, a trade pact was concluded between Russia and Germany and an announcement was made of a forthcoming nonaggression pact, concluded August 23. Stalin's later explanation of this was that he knew war between Russia and Germany was inevitable and that he wished to purchase time.

War Begins, September 1, 1939. With this elimination of Russia from all alliances with France and England, Hitler felt free and all-powerful. War between Germany and Poland began on September 1 without formal declaration, and on September 3 England and France declared war on Germany.

73

The Effect of Government Economic Planning upon Employment and the Utilization of Our National Productive Powers

In a preceding chapter we have seen the sudden collapse of the partial recovery of 1935–37 and the sudden, extraordinarily severe and precipitous break both in the volume of business and in stock market prices running through autumn 1937 into spring 1938. At its best, the recovery, 1935–37, did not bring levels of industrial production as high as those of 1929, seven years before. The Federal Reserve Index of Industrial Production (1923–25 = 100) reached a high of 125 in 1929, while its peak in the 1935–37 revival (reached in late 1936) was 121. This had never happened before in our history. Always in our past, following a major boom and crisis, we had reached new highs before another serious setback came.

The Record of Employment and Unemployment. The following table is borrowed from the authoritative studies of the National Industrial Conference Board.[1] It covers the years 1900 to 1939.

TOTAL UNEMPLOYMENT IN THE LABOR FORCE
(In thousands)

	Total labor force	Employment	Unemployment	Unemployment at percent of labor force
Annual Average				
1900	29,025	27,378	1,647	5.7
1901	29,959	28,238	1,721	5.7
1902	30,905	30,405	500	1.6
1903	31,842	30,319	1,523	4.8
1904	32,605	31,175	1,430	4.4
1905	33,653	33,032	621	1.8
1906	34,647	34,790	−143*	...

[1] *Conference Board Economic Record*, March 20, 1940.

TOTAL UNEMPLOYMENT IN THE
LABOR FORCE—Cont.

	Total labor force	Employment	Unemploy- ment	Unemployment at percent of labor force
Annual Average				
1907	35,631	34,875	756	2.1
1908	36,580	34,284	2,296	6.3
1909	37,454	36,735	719	1.9
1910	38,133	37,580	553	1.5
1911	38,668	37,097	1,571	4.1
1912	39,089	38,169	920	2.4
1913	39,500	38,482	1,018	2.6
1914	39,789	37,575	2,214	5.6
1915	40,083	37,728	2,355	5.9
1916	40,314	40,127	187	0.5
1917	40,752	42,685	−1,933*	. . .
1918	41,088	44,187	−3,099*	. . .
1919	41,159	42,029	−870*	. . .
1920	41,897	41,339	558	1.3
1921	42,445	37,691	4,754	11.2
1922	42,966	40,049	2,917	6.8
1923	43,760	43,011	749	1.7
1924	44,549	42,515	2,034	4.6
1925	45,009	44,192	817	1.8
1926	45,962	45,498	464	1.0
1927	46,939	45,319	1,620	3.5
1928	47,914	46,057	1,857	3.9
1929	48,354	47,925	429	0.9
1930	49,025	45,216	3,809	7.8
1931	49,664	41,551	8,113	16.3
1932	50,182	37,704	12,478	24.9
1933	50,830	38,086	12,744	25.1
1934	51,402	41,002	10,400	20.2
1935	51,879	42,357	9,522	18.4
1936	52,382	44,783	7,599	14.5
1937	53,011	46,639	6,372	12.0
1938	53,699	43,600	10,099	18.8
1939	54,393	45,314	9,080	16.7

* Such negative unemployment arises statistically from the fact that persons are drawn into the labor force during periods of increased labor demand who are not reckoned as members of the labor force.

In the period covered by this table before World War I, the worst percentage of unemployment was in the year 1908, following the panic of 1907. Unemployment in that year averaged 6.3 percent of the labor force.

There were 2,296,000 workers unemployed in that year. In 1906, the year before the panic, there was actual negative unemployment, meaning that persons were drawn into the labor force who did not ordinarily belong there, because of increased labor demand. In 1910 unemployment was reckoned a little over 500,000 men, or 1.5 percent of the labor force. In the crisis, unprecedented in gravity, in 1921, which followed the collapse of the postwar boom, unemployment reached 11.2 percent, the heaviest in our history to that date, but the figure dropped rapidly to 1.7 percent two years later, in 1923.

A 2 percent unemployment is really full employment, when we allow for seasonal unemployment, sickness, shifting of jobs, and that very considerable part of our population which is unwilling to work all the time, and prefers to rove occasionally.

The bad year, 1930, shows unemployment of 3,809,000, or 7.8 percent of the labor force. The years 1931 and 1932 were years of extreme depression with the percentage of unemployment running 16.3 and 24.9 percent respectively.

The Explanation of the Record. We have discussed the years 1931 and 1932 very fully in preceding chapters, and have seen that the extreme depression of these years traced to the extremely bad governmental policies of the Harding, Coolidge, and Hoover administrations.

Prior to 1924 we had not regarded it as a federal government function to make employment. Employment was a matter for the people themselves to work out. Beginning with the Federal Reserve purchases of government securities in 1924, we have had government policy directed increasingly toward making employment. The explanation of the good figures for employment prior to 1924, and of the desperately bad figures for employment which followed 1929, is to be found in precisely this fact. Under an old-fashioned federal government, which, in financial matters, was concerned primarily with its own solvency and with the protection of the sound gold dollar, the people themselves solved the problem of employment amazingly well. When the federal government took over and undertook to solve the problem for them, grave disasters followed.

President Roosevelt inherited a huge volume of unemployment. He did not cure it. The figures for 1933 are worse than the figures for 1932. The years 1933 to 1939, inclusive, show unemployment exceeding 10 million for three years, including 1938, and show unemployment exceeding 9 million for five years out of the seven. In only two years of the Democratic New Deal period prior to the outbreak of World War II did the annual average figure for unemployment get below 8 million. And in the best of these two years, namely 1937, the figure stood at 6,372,000, which is 12 percent of the labor force, as compared with 11.2 percent of the labor force in the year of extreme depression, 1921.

The historical record is damning. The New Deal, viewed as an economic policy designed to promote employment, is condemned by the historical and statistical record.

Retarded Technological Progress and Impaired Capital Equipment. From the standpoint of the full utilization of the productive capacities of the American people, the contrast between the old, unregulated economy and the New Deal economy may be tested by two other sets of very significant figures. The degree of unemployment does not tell the full story. The amount of slack in the industrial situation is partly a matter of unused labor, but it is also a matter of unused capital and unused technological knowledge. The New Deal policy, as we have seen, had made capital timid in the extreme and had greatly retarded the application of new technology. Obsolescence in American industrial equipment had grown to a startling extent in the Great Depression and in the early years of the New Deal. I quote the following from H. G. Moulton as descriptive of the situation in 1935:

> In many lines of industry there has been an enormous amount of "deferred maintenance" in equipment, and there has been a steadily increasing obsolescence. The *American Machinist* has made three "Inventory and Obsolescence Surveys," at five-year intervals, in the field of metal working equipment. On the basis of a survey covering 1,345,447 major items of machine tools, presses, forging machines, and welding equipment, the following trends are revealed. In 1925 the amount of such equipment over ten years of age, and hence defined as virtually obsolete, was 44 percent; in 1930 the figure was 48 percent; and in 1935 it was 65 percent.
>
> There has been almost no expansion of new plant, and there has been comparatively little replacement of worn-out and obsolescent capital structures. The amount of new capital issues for the purposes of financing new plant and equipment declined from $3,446,000,000 in 1930 to $262,000,000 in 1933. The data with reference to the decrease in the production of goods destined for capital equipment . . . also definitely point in the same direction.[2]

The revival of 1935 promised to improve this situation, but the undistributed profits tax of 1936 proved a powerful deterrent. As shown in a preceding chapter, American corporations paid out in dividends more than their total profits in 1936 and 1937, while the acute depression of 1938, even after the repeal of the undistributed profits tax, greatly reduced incentives to make large capital outlays. We came into the period of World War II with a heavy obsolescence, a large body of unused technological ideas, and a great deal of idle capital, and, as shown by the foregoing table, with 9,080,000 men unemployed, on the average, in the year 1939.

The figures from the *American Machinist*, which Moulton cites, look worse still in the year 1940. The following table shows the trend.

---

[2] H. G. Moulton, *Income and Economic Progress* (Brookings Institution, 1935), pp. 23–24.

PERCENTAGE OF METAL WORKING
EQUIPMENT OVER 10 YEARS OLD

Year	Percent
1925	44
1930	48
1935	65
1940	70

It may be said, with respect to these figures, that the year 1925 perhaps represents a somewhat better than normal situation, inasmuch as there had been, in the years 1921–23, an immense spurt in the utilization of new technological ideas and in the installation of new machinery. But the deterioration from 1930 to 1940 is very great.

Slack in American Industry, 1914 vs. 1939. Instead of the three to four percent per annum increase in industrial production which we ought to have had between 1929 and 1939, the year 1939, as shown by the Federal Reserve Index of Production (1923–25 = 100), stands well below 1929. There was immense slack in American industry in 1939, an immense amount of unused capacity in manpower, in technological knowledge, and in idle money.

Percentage of Slack in 1914. We have seen in an earlier chapter a rather precise measurement of the extent of the slack in industrial capacity in 1914 as compared with 1916, when the country was working at full capacity and straining its capacity in response to unlimited war demands from Europe. The figures given in that earlier chapter, taken from a careful study by Frederick C. Mills, are repeated on page 480.

The year 1914 was not a good year because we had a sharp knock at the outbreak of the war in August, but in that year the slack as shown in Mills' figures was relatively low. Production increased 20.6 percent in the two years following, and construction 11.3 percent. We may rest the case primarily upon the year 1916. It was, without interruption, a year when demand was pressing us to the limit of our power to produce. The years 1917 and 1918 are complicated by the withdrawal of the soldiers. The years 1919 and 1920 are complicated by the depression in early 1919 and by the crisis in the latter part of 1920. But the year 1916 has no such complication. In production it stands 20.6 percent above 1914. There was no slack in production in 1916. But this does not mean that there was in the bad year, 1914, 20.6 percent of slack, because in two years we would normally expect a substantial growth in productive capacity amounting to 3 or 4 percent per annum. The amount of slack in the subnormal year 1914 was thus not over 14 percent.

Percentage of Slack in 1939. In contrast, the slack in 1939, the year in which World War II broke out, was appalling. If we accept the new Federal Reserve Index of Physical Volume of Production (1935–39 = 100) we get an increase between 1939 and the peak year of production, 1943, from 109 to 239, or 119 percent. Subtract 3 percent per annum from this for the four years (representing normal growth for the four years), and we would still have an increase of 107 percent. This would mean a slack of over 50 percent in our utilization of our industrial resources in the year 1939.

PHYSICAL VOLUME OF PRODUCTION
AND CONSTRUCTION, 1914–22*

Year	Total volume of production	Total volume of construction
1914	100	100
1915	113.7	97.9
1916	120.6	111.3
1917	125.5	93.8
1918	124.5	64.9
1919	116.7	88.7
1920	124.5	48.5
1921	103.9	91.8
1922	121.6	139.2

* Frederick C. Mills, *Economic Tendencies in the United States* (New York, 1932), pp. 188, 191. Bases changed from 1913 to 1914.

It may be observed, moreover, in making this comparison between 1914–16 and 1939–43, that the base year 1939 was radically improved by the outbreak of the war, the latter months of 1939 showing a sharp acceleration in production, whereas the base year 1914 was sharply deteriorating after the outbreak of the war, the latter months of 1914 showing a real depression.

The contrast between the two periods is not so great as these figures would indicate. The criticisms which Gen. Leonard P. Ayres and others have made of the new Federal Reserve Index of Production, based as it is in part on man-hours rather than physical output, are valid criticisms.

How great a difference there is between production measured in man-hours and production measured in physical output is strikingly shown in an address by Andrew T. Court before the National Industrial Conference Board on September 26, 1946, published in the *Commercial & Financial Chronicle* of October 3, 1946 (p. 1677). Court, criticizing the new Federal Reserve Index of Industrial Production, says that according to this computation, July 1946 automobile production was 78 percent above the 1935–39 average. The actual production in July was about 300,000 cars and trucks compared with an average of 335,000 units for the 1935–39 period, or down 10 percent rather than up 78 percent. The government's production index is not based on the number of cars and trucks actually manufactured.

Rather, the index is estimated on the basis of the number of hours for which the employer pays. It is possible that Court's figure for physical output should be revised upward on the ground that in July 1946 the automobile accessory industry was operating at a disproportionately high level, supplying replacement parts, but no such revision could justify the new Federal Reserve index figure.

There is valid ground for thorough distrust of the new Federal Reserve index, and it should not be used. We use here instead General Ayres' figures as presented in the long chart "American Business Activity Since 1790" (17th ed., March 1944), published by the Cleveland Trust Company. This series has the advantage of giving us comparable figures for 1914–16 and 1939–43. In the figures which accompany this chart, General Ayres gives monthly figures for percentage fluctuations above or below an estimated normal. We have averaged these monthly fluctuations to get the percentage, plus or minus, for the year. The year 1914 shows an average of −5.25 percent. The year 1916 shows an average of +13.75 percent, making an increase of approximately 19 percent from the bad year 1914 to the year of unlimited demand and full production, 1916. As General Ayres' figures make allowance for estimated normal growth, it is not necessary to make any adjustment to allow for this factor, as we have done for Mills' figures and the new Federal Reserve index, above.

For the year 1939 General Ayres' figures show an average of −12 percent, and for 1943 an average of +38 percent, with respect to the estimated normal. This would mean an increase of 50 percent in production with respect to normal between 1939 and 1943, indicating an appalling slack in 1939.

A very able statistician has supplied figures based on the methods of the old Federal Reserve Index of Production (1923–25 = 100), which figures show for the years 1914–16 an increase of 30 percent and for the years 1939–43 an increase of 71 percent. Here again we must make allowance for normal growth. Assume this to be 3 percent per annum for each period. Then the 1914–16 increase would be 24 percent, and the increase for 1939–43 would be 59 percent.

Yet another computation, taken from a private index of industrial activity, adjusted for long-term growth, would show 1914 at 4.2 percent below normal and 1916 at 13.6 percent above normal, giving a percentage increase of 18.6 percent between 1914 and 1916. The same index shows 1939 at 8.5 percent below normal and 1943 at 48.6 percent above normal, making an increase during the four years of 62.4 percent.[3]

---

[3] The only figures I find which suggest that the expansion of production in World War II did not markedly exceed the expansion in World War I are those of Geoffrey H. Moore, *The Production of Industrial Materials in World Wars I and II*, National Bureau of Economic Research, Occasional Paper 18, March 1944. His study, however, is concerned with the

Three Sets of Figures Converge. Three significant sets of figures thus converge in the condemnation of governmental economic planning under the Republican New Deal and under the Democratic New Deal: (1) the table for employment and unemployment, from 1900 to 1939, inclusive; (2) the figures showing the rapidly growing percentage of metal working equipment over ten years old; and (3) the figures showing how little slack there was in the utilization of our industrial capacity in the year 1914 as contrasted with the degree of slack in the year 1939. All of these figures justify condemnation of governmental economic planning as robbing us, year after year, of the production which we might have had and the consumption which we might have enjoyed had we had the old, flexible, unregulated economy.

In 1939 we had idle men, idle money, and idle technological ideas on an appalling scale. The war set them to work, but it took the war to do it.

---

output of *industrial materials,* rather than with *total industrial production* (materials and finished products). His figures show a rise between 1914 and 1917 of about 32 percent, and from 1939 to 1942 of about 35 percent. He states that in peacetime over short periods there is a close correspondence between changes in the output of industrial materials and in total industrial production, but that it is not easy to say how close this relationship is in wartime. "Hence, it is uncertain in what degree our conclusions concerning the production of industrial materials apply also to total industrial production." His figures make no allowance for the very much greater elaboration in the working up of raw materials for war purposes than is necessary in peacetime. I think that the revised Federal Reserve index series, with its use of man-hours, greatly exaggerates this point. On the other hand, I think that Moore's figures cannot be used as an index of *total industrial production.* The estimates which I give in the text for World War II are intermediate between Moore's figures and those of the revised Federal Reserve index. It is to be observed, moreover, that the years chosen by Moore, as representative of the two periods, are different from those used in the text.

74

Alternative Explanations of the Great Depression of 1930–39

Preceding chapters have explained the Great Depression of 1930–39 as arising out of the efforts of the governments, and very especially of the government of the United States, to play God.

The trouble has come as governmental action has interfered with the markets. High tariffs following World War I, when we had changed from a debtor to a creditor nation, and when only a low tariff policy could give us a sound and normal export trade in adequate volume, made the beginning of the trouble. They created a grave disequilibrium between our export industries, notably agriculture, and the rest of our industries. Artificially cheap money, partly designed to offset this, gave us for a time a great export trade, but also created a vast fabric of debt, internal and international. As the volume of this debt grew, its quality deteriorated. The increased tariffs in 1930 further impaired the quality of the international credits, and precipitated rising tariffs and other trade restrictions all over the world, which made it almost impossible for debtor countries to pay their debts with goods. The period 1931 to March 1933 saw the progressive collapse of the unsound portions of this vast fabric of debt. The efforts of the government in 1929 and 1930 to hold farm prices artificially high, and to hold up wages and prices generally, intensified the difficulties.

Finally the failure to get out of the depression in the years 1933 to 1939 has been explained as due to the great multiplicity of New Deal "remedies," all tending to impair the freedom and efficiency of the markets, to frighten venture capital, and to create frictions and uncertainties, and impediments to individual and corporate initiative.

But there have been alternative explanations offered, which have sought to find the explanation of the Great Depression, not in the blunders of government, but in defects of industry and finance themselves, and which assert that there have been "structural changes" in industry and finance which came in the 1920s and 1930s which have made it impossible for the old free enterprise system, as we knew it before World War I, to function again. These theories come from writers who are in general hostile to the free enterprise system and who believe that the government, far from retiring from the role of God, must play God yet more vigorously. What follows will deal with certain of these alternative interpretations.

Berle's Sudden Intensification of the "Instinct for Liquidity." One theory is that offered by Adolf Berle in his book *Liquid Claims and National Wealth*, written in 1934. Berle is much impressed with the great expansion of "liquid claims" in the form of security issues, bank deposits, cash surrender value of life insurance policies, and rapidly rising security prices which took place between 1922 and 1929, moving much more rapidly than national wealth moved—and we may add, moving much more rapidly than national income from production rose. But Berle does not explain this as have the foregoing chapters. He does not see the origin of it in the unsound policy of the Federal Reserve banks, and particularly in their great purchases of government securities. He does not really know what caused it. Thus he says (p. 69), "Something happened whose cause we may only vaguely attempt to assign." Later (p. 81) he says, "Plainly, the instinct to have ready cash, either to satisfy desire or to allay fear, became in that decade an instinct requiring the satisfaction beyond all measure; and the need was considered as a necessity of life rather than the luxury of the former seeker after treasure trove, or the monopoly of the small mercantile class which really carried the load of American finance and American capitalism."

The superficiality of this doctrine—which has had wide vogue—is pretty obvious. No psychologist or biologist would accept the notion of a sudden intensification of an instinct, or the existence of an instinct of holding ready cash. The cause of the evils and abuses to which Berle refers is the excessive volume of bank credit created by Federal Reserve policy, which made a very healthy and sound financial organism go wrong.[1]

The Tendency Toward Corporate Consolidations. Karl Marx had long contended that there was an inevitable tendency toward monopoly with the elimination of small and moderate-sized businesses. The revisionist socialist Bernstein long ago gave an effective answer to this contention, but

---

[1] This writer did not have to discover this in 1934. He protested against it while it was going on, analyzed it while it was going on, and pointed out the dangers of it while it was going on, in *Chase Economic Bulletin:* "The Gold and Rediscount Policy of the Federal Reserve Banks," July 20, 1921; "Cheap Money, Gold, and Federal Reserve Bank Policy," August 4, 1924; "Bank Money and the Capital Supply," November 8, 1926; "Paper Money in National Banks Available for Rediscount with Federal Reserve Banks," April 8, 1927; "Some Major Forces in the International Money Market," October 29, 1927; "Analysis of the Money Market," June 4, 1928; "Bank Expansion Versus Savings," June 25, 1928; "Brokers' Loans and Bank Credit," October 21, 1928; "Two 'New Eras' Compared: 1896–1903 and 1921–28," February 11, 1929; "The Financial Situation—The Stock Market Crisis of 1929," November 22, 1929; "The 'Free Gold' of the Federal Reserve System and the Cheap Money Policy," September 29, 1930.

the doctrine has been revived on the basis of the phenomena of the period of the 1920s. Between 1924 and 1929 there were a great many consolidations, with a sudden cessation of consolidations after the stock market crash.

This happened once before in our history on a great scale, namely, in the years 1899 to 1902. There have been only two great periods of rapid consolidation in our history. Both of these periods were periods of cheap money and excited stock markets. The first "new era" came when, following the settlement of the gold standard question in the election of 1896, we began to gain gold on a great scale from the outside world, and, on the basis of the gold, made an expansion of bank credit in excess of the needs of trade. The surplus spilled over into the securities market and we had a big consolidation movement, as it was very easy for a holding company to put out new securities to the public and use the proceeds in purchasing the securities of individual companies which the holding company wished to dominate and consolidate. It was the period of the formation of the United States Steel Corporation and of the International Mercantile Marine. In the period 1924 to 1929 we have a good many similar things, consolidations not for industrial reasons but for stock market reasons, consolidations that would not have taken place if money had not been excessive.

Such movements are harmful and should be prevented, but they are not inherent in the nature of industry itself. The government should be alert with Sherman law prosecutions when phenomena of this sort manifest themselves, and the Federal Reserve System should prevent them from manifesting themselves by refusing to expand credit to finance a stock market boom.

For the figures with respect to financial consolidations in the United States showing the heavy concentration of such consolidations in the two periods, 1899–1902 and 1924–29, the reader may consult *Big Business*.[2]

The Fallacious Theory That Reduced Rate of Growth of the Population Narrows Investment Opportunities and Should Be Offset by Government Spending. The theory was presented by Professor Alvin H. Hansen[3] that we had a new thing in the period of the 1930s, a structural change which greatly narrowed investment opportunities. The growth of population suddenly slowed down. The population of the United States increased by 16 million from 1920 to 1930, but the rate of growth between 1930 and 1938 was perhaps half of that. The estimate is that the growth of the population in the last half of the nineteenth century was "responsible" for perhaps 60 percent of the "capital formation" in the United States. The meaning

---

[2] (New York: Twentieth Century Fund, 1927), pp. 29–33.

[3] "Progress and Declining Population," *American Economic Review* (March 1939), Professor Hansen was anticipated in this doctrine in the novels of Aldous Huxley, from whom I first learned about the theory. I thought it was not bad as a novelist's venture, but I did not expect to see an economist take it seriously!

apparently is that approximately 60 percent of the capital invested in the United States in that period was devoted to the kind of production that would supply the wants of an expanding rather than a stationary population. From this supposed decline in the opportunities for private investment, the conclusion is drawn that the government must spend greater or less amounts, depending on the state of business and the volume of the national income, for the purpose of making good the deficiencies of private investment.

There has been a long-run trend toward a higher average age in the population and toward a slower percentage growth in the population due (a) to an increasing diffusion of knowledge of birth control, (b) to progress in medical knowledge which makes for a greater length of life, and (c) for the United States, to our restrictions on immigration. But when the startling contrast is made between the 1920s and the 1930s with respect to this point, and when it is asserted that "in this shift must be sought a basic cause of not a few of the developments in our changing economy," we must raise very definitely the question as to what is cause and what is effect.

It seems clear as daylight that the sharp decline in the rate of population growth in the 1930s was effect rather than cause. The 1920s were prosperous years. Despite our restrictions, immigrants came in large numbers. Our boys could easily get jobs. Girls were happy to give up jobs and get married. Young couples had confidence in the future and had children when they wanted them. In contrast, the 1930s were years of depression, uncertainty, and fear. Immigration of aliens for several years was exceeded by emigration of aliens. Marriages were delayed. Many girls at work held their jobs after marriage. They were afraid to have children.

Taking the years 1922–28 as our base, or 100 percent, we find the number of marriages in leading cities of the United States dropping to 80 percent in 1930, to 70 percent in 1931, and to 63 percent in the gloom of 1932. But we find it also mounting rapidly again in the following years to 88 percent in 1937—only to drop sharply again to 75 percent in the acute depression of 1938.

In 1938 and 1939 we had very heavy unemployment. The average for the year 1938 was 10,099,000, or 19 percent of the working force, and the average for 1939 was 9,080,000, or 17 percent of the labor force. But with the improvement in economic opportunities which 1940 brought, marriages and babies began to increase and in 1941 both came in great volume. With our own participation in the war, following Pearl Harbor in December 1941, a new factor was added to the factor of economic opportunity—youth clinging to life and wishing to propagate more life. Young women who saw their husbands destined for foreign service wanted babies. Young men going to the front wanted to leave babies behind them.

Marriages jumped from 1,319,000 in 1938, to 1,565,000 in 1940, to 1,679,000 in 1941, and to 1,758,000 in 1942. The marriage rate, which stood at 10.20 per 1,000 population in 1938, rose to 12.60 in 1941, and to 13.10 in 1942.

Births in 1939 were 2,265,000 and the birthrate was 17.3 per thousand. In 1940 births rose to 2,360,000, or 17.9. In 1941 births rose to 2,513,000 and the birthrate to 18.9. In 1942 births rose to 2,809,000 and the birthrate to 20.9 per thousand. In 1943 births rose to 2,935,000 and the birthrate to 21.5. This birthrate for 1943 may be compared with 18.8 for 1929 and with 16.7 for 1936. The boys and girls still want to get married, and they still want babies. When they find economic opportunity, when they have even temporary good times, they quickly make an absurdity of this sudden great "structural change." The reduced growth of population in the 1930s was not the cause of depression; it was the effect of depression.

But how significant would it be from the standpoint of investment opportunity if it were true we had here a permanent change? What difference would it make? Assume that for the future we are to have less young children and more older people, and that the population is to grow more slowly. What bearing has this on the question of investment opportunities—except as any violent shift in the economic situation creates for a time a problem of adaptation? That it would mean a change in the direction of demand is quite clear. A slowly growing population with more adults and less children would demand less playgrounds and more golf courses. It would demand less milk and more whiskey.

Would it demand less automobiles? A young couple with three or four children will usually be a one-car family. A young couple with no children is more likely to be a two-car family, and the probabilities are high that they will turn in their used cars for new cars more frequently than will the one-car family with three or four children.

Will the population with less children and more adults and slow population growth make more or less demands for housing? The point is debatable. They won't need so rapid an increase in the number of separate dwellings, obviously. But if they are prosperous and have growing incomes, they will call for qualitative improvements in housing and for progressively more space per person. The young couple which is putting its increased income into more babies will be much less concerned about the newest gadgets in dwelling facilities and equipment than will the young couple with one or two children or no children. Older people, moreover, stand the stress and strain of crowding far less than younger people and children, whose nerves are quieter. They want more room, more quiet.

There is no reason at all to suppose that such a population, whose income is growing through technological progress, capital accumulation, and increased efficiency, would not offer just as great an opportunity for investment as a population which is rapidly increasing and where there are many children. The rapidly growing population would want more things of the same kind. A more slowly growing population would want better things, qualitative improvements, and a greater variety of things. It is not necessary to examine the statistical basis of the proposition that sixty percent of our capital formation in the last half of the nineteenth century was due to growth of population. Since population was growing rapidly in that period, obviously the direction of demand would be toward the kind of commodities needed in that kind of population; and capital, seeing its best opportunities for investment, would flow in that direction. If a more slowly growing population called for qualitative improvement and a greater variety in the goods it was consuming, capital investment, wisely directed, would adapt itself to that.

Related to this fallacy of Hansen's is the further fallacy that savings are excessive, that savings exceed investment opportunities, or at all events, exceed investments, and that government spending must offset uninvested private saving. This fallacy is dealt with herein, in chapter 59, "The Undistributed Profits Tax of 1936," and in chapter 60, "Digression on Keynes."

The Fallacy That Technological Progress Is Itself a Cause of Depression and General Unemployment. Economists generally agree[4] in rejecting the fallacy that technological progress is a cause of general unemployment and depression. The doctrine, of course, is old and has appeared many times, but there is rather widespread belief that a sudden intensification of technological progress in the 1920s was responsible for the breakdown in the 1930s. Part of the vogue of this fallacy emerges from the activities of the so-called Technocrats, who have given us some very extraordinary figures. In the matter of electric light bulb production, for example, it has been asserted that a man with a machine could produce nine thousands times as many electric light bulbs in 1929 as could be produced in 1914. The actual increase was impressive enough, but it was in fact only thirty-fold.[5]

We had in the nineteenth century much more impressive increases in efficiency per man in agriculture, notably with the invention of the reaper and binder, and other agricultural machinery.

The fear of technological unemployment has had many manifestations in labor policy. Thus we saw the Luddites during the Industrial Revolution in England destroying the new machines. We have seen British trade union policy and managerial policy resisting new methods both before and after World War I—which is a very important factor in explaining Great Britain's economic decline.

We have seen Sismondi, one of the precursors of Karl Marx, writing in the first half of the nineteenth century, holding that the state should attempt

---

[4] I am glad to find Professor Hansen (*op. cit.*) holding this view.

[5] *Productivity of Labor in the Glass Industry* (1927), Bureau of Labor Statistics, Bulletin 441, p. 127.

to curb production and put "a drag upon the too rapid multiplication of inventions. "[6]

Now the contention has been advanced that the period 1920 to 1930 saw a very sudden intensification in the rate of technological progress, and that the troubles of the 1930s grew out of this. The following figures, used earlier in connection with the industrial revival, 1921–23, show that there was indeed a very sharp spurt in technological efficiency between 1921 and 1923. We had not had time, under the pressure of the war years, to introduce new methods. There was a great accumulation of unused technological ideas, including the new technology of war, which was waiting for a peacetime application. In the years 1921 and 1922 entrepreneurs had both time and incentive to apply the new technology, with the result shown in the following table.

GROWTH OF MANUFACTURING PRODUCTION
IN THE UNITED STATES, 1914–23*
Index Numbers of Physical Volume of Production,
Number of Wage Earners, and per Capita Output

Year	Physical volume of production	Number of wage earners	Output per wage earner
1914	100.0	100.0	100.0
1919	127.7	124.5	102.6
1921	105.7	100.1	105.6
1923	156.3	130.3	120.0

* F. C. Mills, *Economic Tendencies in the United States*, p. 192.

There was a great spurt in technological progress and production in the two years, 1921 to 1923. The great spurt in production itself generated new purchasing power which cleared the markets of products. Production in one place gives rise to demand for products in other places.

Be it observed that the rapid spurt in technological progress came, not at the end of the great boom 1921 to 1929, but rather at the beginning of that great boom.

And be it observed that both the increase in total production and the increase in production per man that followed from 1923 to 1929 were at a decidedly slower pace.

Three different sets of figures reveal this. Mills' figures would show, as indicated above, an increase in the two-year period in manufacturing production per wage earner of 13.6 percent or an annual average increase of 6.8 percent. For the six following years, 1924 to 1929, inclusive, Mills' figures show an annual average rate of increase of 3.3 percent in production per wage earner.[7]

---

[6] W. A. Scott, *The Development of Economics* (New York, 1933), p. 258.

[7] Mills, *Economic Tendencies in the United States* (New York, 1932), p. 290.

The census of manufactures of 1931 gives the following table:

INDEXES FOR WAGE EARNERS AND
PRODUCTION, 1921 to 1929*

Census year	Wage earners	Production (quantity)	Production per wage earner
1921	100	100	100
1923	127	154	121
1925	121	158	130
1927	120	160	133
1929	128	179	140

* Biennial Census of Manufactures (1931), p. 18; bases changed to 1921.

This shows an annual average rate of increase in production per wage earner of 10.5 percent from 1921 to 1923, and of 1.9 percent from 1925 to 1929.

Finally, the study of Paul Douglas, which narrows the problem to production per man-hour in manufacturing, shows a high rate of increase between 1921 and 1923, with a drop to approximately 3.5 percent annual increase from 1923 to 1925, inclusive, which is lower than the 4 percent prevailing in the period 1900 to 1906, inclusive.[8]

Douglas' figures show that there was no increase in production per man-hour from 1915 to 1921, and the sudden spurt from 1921 to 1923 he looks upon as the making up of arrearages. He adds that "had the prewar rate of increase been maintained during the years 1913–21, when hourly output was, on the whole, stationary, the relative production per man-hour would have been approximately the same for 1925 as it was in fact." He concludes: ". . . the above data should compel those who have written about the uniqueness of the expansion of production during the last seven years to reconsider their position."[9] Professor Douglas' figures end with 1925. The two other sets of figures, coming down through 1929, strengthen the case.

We need not here go into the theory of technological unemployment. It is well-established economic doctrine, which the reader will find in the textbooks, that new inventions give rise to increasing demand for labor and that over the decades and over the centuries the standard of life for the great mass of the people with growing population has been immeasurably lifted.[10] This discussion is not concerned with the general theory of technological unemployment, but rather with the question of whether something new and startling in the application of technology to industry

---

[8] Douglas, Real Wages in the United States (Boston, 1930), pp. 546–48.

[9] Ibid., p. 548.

[10] See Chase Economic Bulletin, April 1937.

came in the decade of the 1920s, which would explain the depression of the 1930s. The answer, on the basis of the foregoing figures, is that nothing of the sort occurred.

Two "New Eras" Compared—1921–29 and 1896–1903. Some of the more serious and thoughtful adherents of the view that new and strange forces were at work in the period 1922–29 have drawn statistical materials to support this view from the elaborately worked out and careful study by Professor Frederick C. Mills called *Economic Tendencies in the United States,* in which a large number of comparisons are made between the prewar period 1901–13, inclusive, and the postwar period 1922–29, inclusive. It is due Professor Mills, since his book in referred to in this connection, to call attention to his own warning in his introduction against drawing confident conclusions from his figures: "A new cosmology is not a necessary accompaniment of every new set of observations."[11]

Moreover, as Professor Mills makes his comparisons, he is careful to make his conclusions very tentative. But some who have read the book and employed the figures it contains have gone far beyond Professor Mills' own guarded and tentative deductions. The figures for the period 1901–13 do show in many respects a slower pace than the figures for 1922–29. Certain of these contrasts are summarized by Mills himself in the following table:

	Average annual Rate of change*	
	1901–13	*1922–29*
	(percent)	(percent)
Population of the United States	+2.0	+1.4
Physical volume of production	+3.1	+3.8
Volume of production per capita of the population	+1.1	+2.4
Prices, wholesale	+1.8	−0.5
Volume of employment, manufacturing industries	+2.7	+1.0
Per capita real earnings, manufacturing workers	−0.1	+1.4
Prices of industrial common stocks	+2.8	+19.4

* *Economic Tendencies,* p. xvii.

If one be content to use Professor Mills' study as a mine of valuable and carefully worked out facts, the book is of immense value. If, however, the book is to be taken as presenting an adequate contrast between prewar and postwar tendencies (and Professor Mills makes no such claim for it), then

---

[11] Mills, *op. cit.,* Foreword, p. xx.

The New Deal in Maturity, 1933–39

an obvious difficulty presents itself at once. The two periods chosen, 1922 to 1929 and 1901 to 1913, are *unlike* periods. The later period starts with a great depression and moves with hardly any interruption to the culmination of a great boom. The period 1901–13, on the other hand, starts in the middle of a great boom, goes through a forty-five percent break in the stock market in 1903 and the major crisis in 1907, into the quieter years that followed 1909. Obviously this comparison will give us no proof that new and strange things were at work in the later period.

In early 1929, while the "new-era" philosophy still held its hypnotic power, the *Chase Economic Bulletin* instituted a comparison between the period we were then living in and an earlier "new era," namely, that from 1896 to 1903,[12] a period which, like the later period, started with a great depression and carried through into the culmination of a great boom. The earlier "new era" exhibited virtually everything to be found in the later "new era," namely, rapidly increasing physical volume of production, rapidly rising stock market prices, rapidly rising dividends, far outrunning the increases in wages, and so on. The first new era was even more brilliant on the side of physical increase in production, and spectacular enough in the matter of financial phenomena, though the palm should be ceded to the second new era in the matter of financial folly.

The Common Cause of the Two New Eras. Moreover, a common cause was at work in both of these new eras. In both new eras there was an immense flow of gold to the United States, with rapidly increasing bank reserves, with bank credit expanding beyond the needs of commerce, and with excess credit available for capital uses and for speculation. Cheap money characterized both new eras, and cheap money is the most dangerous intoxicant known to economic life, especially if it be prolonged through many years.

But the first new era was one in which the whole world was sharing in the increase in gold, in which gold was sinking in real value, and in which, as a consequence, commodity prices throughout the world were rising, whereas the second new era was one in which the United States alone had excessive gold. The first new era was a time when trade among the nations moved easily without excessive trade barriers. The second new era was one in which trade barriers were very excessive and in which the great creditor nations, and very especially the United States, could get out a large volume of exports only by giving an ever increasing volume of credit.

The reactions from the excesses of the first new era were short. The overextended credits could be liquidated as debtors sold goods at concessions in price to pay debts. As the second new era came to a close, however,

---

[12] "Two 'New Eras' Compared: 1896–1903 and 1921–27." *Chase Economic Bulletin*, February 11, 1929. A summary of the essential points contained in this *Bulletin* will be found in *Chase Economic Bulletin*, April 13, 1937, pp. 22–28.

debtor countries found rapidly rising trade barriers as they tried to sell goods and to pay debts.

The first new era, like the second new era, was characterized by an immense increase in the issues of stocks and bonds and by a growing proportion of stocks to bonds.

The first new era showed a very rapid rise in security prices, as did the second new era. And the prices of stock exchange seats rose rapidly in both periods.

Much has been made of the figures in Mills' book which show a much more rapid growth of dividends than of wages between 1922 and 1929, even though wages were advancing rapidly. It has been thought that we had here something new and startling in the postwar period, destructive of the stability of economic life and requiring a radically new social policy.

Of course dividends increase more rapidly than wages from the bottom of a depression to the top of a boom, just as dividends drop much more rapidly than wages from the top of a boom to the bottom of a depression. The stockholder is the risk bearer, the residuary claimant on the earnings of

INDEX NUMBERS OF RAILWAY WAGES
AND DIVIDENDS
Average Daily Compensation of Railway Employees*
(Simple average of ten territorial groups)

Years ending June 30	Enginemen	Firemen	Machinists	Section foremen	Dividends on common stocks paid by inter-state railways**
1894 ⎫ 1895 ⎬ 1896 ⎭	100	100	100	100	100
1897	99.9	100.3	99.4	99.8	95.4
1898	102.3	102.5	101.2	99.1	99.6
1899	102.3	103.2	101.5	99.0	107.1
1900	103.0	105.0	101.4	99.1	139.9
1901	104.0	106.0	102.5	100.6	153.7
1902	105.4	107.2	103.3	101.2	188.7
1903	109.1	110.7	109.1	103.6	203.5
1904	111.6	114.2	113.3	104.3	235.3
1905	112.7	115.5	116.0	104.8	252.3
1906	111.9	116.8	117.0	105.6	295.8
1907	116.3	122.2	125.3	111.1	345.6

* Based on *Seventeenth Annual Report of the Interstate Commerce Commission on the Statistics of Railways in the United States*, pp. 44–48, and *Twenty-first Annual Report*, pp. 48–52.

** Based on W. C. Mitchell, *Business Cycles* (Berkeley: University of California Press, 1913), p. 200.

industry. He takes what is left. But the notion that this is a new development, peculiar to the 1922–29 period, is surely negatived by the table on
page 493 comparing railway wages and railway dividends in the earlier
new era.

RELATIVE SHARES OF MAJOR CLAIMANTS IN INCOME FROM CURRENT PRODUCTION OF GOODS AND SERVICES, 1909–29*
(As percentage of total income produced)

Year	Industrial enterprisers, investors, and property holders, business savings	Employees**		
		Wages	Salaries	Total†
1909	45.6	38.0	15.6	54.4
1910	44.2	38.8	16.0	55.8
1911	43.2	39.0	16.9	56.8
1912	44.4	38.3	16.5	55.6
1913	43.5	39.1	16.5	56.5
1914	42.6	38.4	18.0	57.4
1915	45.0	37.3	16.8	55.0
1916	48.7	35.7	14.5	51.3
1917	49.7	34.6	14.9	50.3
1918	43.1	36.0	19.8	56.9
1919	44.6	36.1	18.1	55.4
1920	37.2	43.9	17.4	62.8
1921	31.3	44.3	22.5	68.7
1922	36.7	41.2	20.2	63.3
1923	37.3	42.0	19.2	62.7
1924	36.4	41.5	20.3	63.6
1925	38.3	40.5	19.8	61.7
1926	36.2	41.8	20.5	63.8
1927	35.4	41.3	21.7	64.6
1928	36.5	40.0	22.1	63.5
1929	34.9	42.1	21.7	65.1

* Based on Leven, Moulton, and Warburton, *America's Capacity to Consume* (Washington: Brookings Institution, 1934), p. 158

** "Salaries" in this table were received in 1929 by 11.5 million persons. The average salary was $1,608 a year.

† The totals include pensions, workmen's compensation, etc.

Labor's Share in the National Income. Certain doctrines currently held respecting the decade of the 1920s as compared with previous periods are, on their face, wrong. Thus, the notion that labor was getting a progressively smaller share of the total national dividend and, consequently, was progressively unable to buy an adequate amount of goods to prevent underconsumption, must be upset by the figures on page 494.

Over the decades, the interests of labor are bound up with three major factors: (1) a retardation in the growth of population through voluntary limitation on the size of families and through immigration restriction, holding down the supply of labor; (2) the accumulation of capital, increasing the demand for labor; and (3) the progress of technology. These things are overwhelmingly more important than all that labor legislation can do and all that labor unions can do. If men are scarce and dear, and capital, natural resources, technological equipment, and technological ideas are abundant, wages will be high, men will be in demand, and the worker's share in the total product of industry will be relatively great.

One Big Postwar Change—Reduced Immigration. We had, in fact, in the period following the first war, one new factor to which, strangely enough, the new economics[13] has made very little reference, namely, our radical change in immigration policy. This, in itself, accounts for not a few of the puzzling phenomena that postwar statistics reveal.

The effect of the cessation of immigration during the war and the legal restriction of immigration in the period that followed the war upon the wages of American labor is impressive. Wages shot up with great rapidity during the war, moving upward, with a lag, as prices rose, and catching up with wholesale prices in 1920. When prices fell in 1920–21, wages reacted, but not nearly so much as prices; and then, though commodity prices stayed down, wages rose again until, by 1929, they were once more at the 1920 peak.

In the period before the war, on the other hand, when, in a good year, we would bring in a million immigrants, including a very high percentage of young men and women ready to work, the wage advance was much slower. In the three boom years 1905–07, inclusive, 3,401,000 immigrants came. In the three boom years 1927–29, inclusive, 911,000 immigrants came.

With the accustomed immigration supply cut off, expanding industry in the United States in the 1920s could add to its labor supply only at the expense of other industries, once the point of approximately full employment was reached. For the United States, this meant particularly that

---

[13] I note the exception of Professor Alvin H. Hansen, whose view that a declining rate of growth of population in the 1930s as compared with the 1920s has created in the 1930s a new situation in which investment opportunities are greatly narrowed, making it necessary that the government should invest heavily, we have considered above. It is curious that Professor Hansen should find this trouble only in the 1930s and not in the 1920s. The reduction in the rate of growth of the population began with the outbreak of the war in 1914, when immigration was largely cut off.

INDEX NUMBER OF WAGES PER HOUR AND WHOLESALE PRICES, 1914-29*

Year	Wages per hour (exclusive of agriculture)	Wholesale prices (all commodities)
1914	100	100
1915	101	102.1
1916	109	125.6
1917	125	172.5
1918	159	192.8
1919	180	203.5
1920	229	226.7
1921	214	143.4
1922	204	142.0
1923	213	147.7
1924	219	144.1
1925	222	152.0
1926	225	146.8
1927	226	140.1
1928	227	143.5
1929	228	141.7

* U. S. Bureau of Labor Statistics; bases changed.

INDEX NUMBERS OF WAGES PER HOUR AND WHOLESALE PRICES, 1896-1914*

Year	Wages per hour	Wholesale prices
1896	100	100
1900	106	120.7
1905	119	129.2
1910	135	151.3
1914	148	147.1

* U. S. Bureau of Labor Statistics; bases changed.

agriculture lost labor to the cities. The farm population declined, not because it was *driven out* of agriculture, but because it was *lured into* other activities by rising wages. One consequence was increased difficulties, through higher labor costs, for farm proprietors. Agriculture and bituminous coal mining lost workers.[14] Manufacturing itself, for a period of four

---

[14] The bituminous coal miner is slower than almost any other element in our population in shifting his occupation. He, like the master craftsman at the beginning of the Industrial Revolution, has a long, specialized training, and he seems reluctant to learn a new task or to go to a changed environment.

years, had an actual decline in the number of workers, as shown by the following table, although this tendency was reversed between 1927 and 1929.

WAGE EARNERS IN MANUFACTURING INDUSTRIES, 1923–29*

Year	Wage earners (average for the year)
1923	8,778,156
1925	8,384,261
1927	8,349,755
1929	8,838,742

* *Biennial Census of Manufactures* (1931), p. 20.

Pushed Out or Pulled Out? This decline in the number of manufacturing workers during these four years has been seized upon by certain writers as evidence of technological unemployment. Were workers forced out of manufacturing, or were they lured out by other expanding occupations? Where did they go? The answer is very clear. Through the whole of this period wages rose, year by year, in manufacturing and in the general field of labor. This, in a labor market as flexible and as competitive as our labor market then was, is absolutely incompatible with growing unemployment. If the factories had excess labor that they were dismissing, they would not have been raising wages.

Where did the workers go? The answer is to be found in many things, and first in the great increase in the service industries. Our people wanted garages and filling stations. They wanted new roads built. Our women, including the working women themselves, on a great and growing scale wanted beauty parlors. Concern for the aesthetic side of life spread amazingly throughout the whole of our working population in the period that followed 1914, and, very especially, the period that followed 1923. We saw it in the development of a demand for silk stockings on the part of working women during World War I, in the widespread use of beauty parlors, in the demand for graceful lines in cheap automobiles, which culminated in the embarrassment of the Ford company when it too long resisted the popular demand for more than utility in its cars.

It manifested itself also in an immense demand for education, and one of the major places to which our people went from factory labor and farm labor was to school. The growth of the school population from 1920 to 1930 is a very striking development.

The restriction on immigration, slowing down the growth of population, led to a great increase in the wages of the individual man, and this, in turn, led to a further restriction of the labor supply, because it made possible for his children more years in school and less years in industry.

SCHOOL AND COLLEGE ENROLLMENTS IN THE
UNITED STATES, 1900–1930*

Year	Kindergarten and elementary	Secondary	College and normal
1900	16,224,784	695,903	237,592
1910	18,449,828	1,111,393	355,215
1920	20,894,171	2,494,676	597,682
1930	23,588,479	4,799,867	1,085,799

* U. S., Department of Commerce, *Statistical Abstract* (1935), p. 108.

Hours of Labor. The growing economic surplus which the accumulation of capital and the improvement of technology made through the whole of the period since 1900 manifested itself in many gains for labor. Hours of labor declined from 57.3 a week in 1900 to 49.8 a week in 1926.[15]

Child Labor. Child labor, apart from agriculture, had become virtually a disappearing problem by 1930, partly through state legislation, but even more through the increased family incomes which made it unnecessary.

NUMBER OF CHILDREN OVER 10 AND UNDER
16 YEARS OF AGE GAINFULLY EMPLOYED IN THE
UNITED STATES, 1910–30, BY OCCUPATION*

Occupation	1930	1920	1910
All occupations	667,118	1,060,858	1,990,225
Agriculture	469,497	644,174	1,427,580
Manufacturing and mechanical industries	68,266	185,652	262,123
Trade	49,615	63,724	70,789
Domestic and personal service	46,145	54,006	112,155
Clerical	16,802	79,784	70,912
All others	16,793	33,518	46,666

* Figures from *Fifteenth Census of the United States: 1930*, vol. 5, p. 346.

For children under fifteen in 1930 the figures, apart from agriculture, are very small indeed: manufacturing, 19,145; trade, 26,625; domestic and personal service, 18,676; clerical, 3,558; all others,[16] 5,727.

Recent Changes in the Work of Women. The position of women engaged in making a living improved greatly from 1910 to 1930. The percentage of women in the harder occupations tended to diminish. The number of women, for example, doing agricultural labor decreased from a total of 1,806,624 in 1910 to 909,939 in 1930. Women were relatively less

[15] Douglas, *op. cit.*, p. 208.
[16] *Ibid.*, p. 345. Between 1929 and 1932, the number of children 14 and 15 years of age receiving employment certificates dropped to about one-third of the 1929 figure (U. S., Department of Labor, *Monthly Labor Review*, December 1935, p. 1479).

important in manufacturing in 1930 than they were in 1910. In 1930, only 17 percent of the total of women workers were in mechanical and manufacturing industries, while in 1910 22 percent were so occupied.

At the same time, the growth in the number of women in the lighter, more interesting, and better paid occupations was very rapid. Office workers, such as stenographers and typists, increased from 263,315 to 775,140; telephone operators from 88,262 to 235,259. In the fields of domestic and personal service, there was a marked shift from the heavier to the lighter occupations; laundresses, for example, *decreased* from 520,004 to 336,468, while laundry operatives increased from 76,355 to 160,475. Women cooks increased only 11.3 percent in these twenty years. The most pronounced increases were in the professional and semiprofessional field. To mention only a few, trained nurses increased from 76,508 to 288,737; women authors, editors, and reporters increased from 6,239 to 17,371; women bankers, brokers, and money lenders, from 2,634 to 9,192; women in public service, from 4,836 to 17,583; and women lawyers and judges, from 558 to 3,385.[17]

Summary. There were new things in the 1920s, of course, but they were not new things in principle and they were not new things in the structure of industry. The ominous things in the 1920s have been discussed elaborately in preceding chapters. They were, first, the great expansion of credit, which meant the great expansion of debt; and, second, the strangling tariff policy of the government, which prevented the payment of international debts. The great expansion of *credit* with its accompanying phenomena we had had before, not once but many times, and notably in the period 1896–1903. But the expansion of *international* credit accompanied by high and rising trade barriers was the unique folly of the decade 1921–30. We have paid for it dearly.

---

[17] *Fifteenth Census of the United States: 1930*, vol. 5, pp. 39–49.

PART V

WORLD WAR II

75

The Outbreak of
World War II

At the outbreak of the war in 1914 sterling was immensely strong. It
rose to $7.00 in certain transactions and remained above par until
late in 1914. With the outbreak of the war in 1939 sterling broke violently
from $4.68 to $3.73, rallying upon an announcement that the Bank of
England would undertake to hold it between $4.02 and $4.04. But very
speedily the great bulk of the sterling obligations of the British banks to the
outside world were blocked. It was "official sterling" that was held at this
figure. "Free sterling," dwindling rapidly in amount because unofficial
sterling was increasingly blocked, sold at a discount from these figures.
Sterling had remained free through the whole of World War I and through
the postwar years. At its weakest, it was very strong. The world believed in
it. The world used it. But sterling promptly ceased to be an internationally
valid currency following the outbreak of the war in 1939. The reasons for
this have been made abundantly clear in preceding chapters.

The Stock Market in World War II. One of the things which makes
economic analysis such a fascinating study is the fact that it is a study of
human behavior. Human beings think and remember, and do not always
react in the same way twice under similar remembered circumstances. In
1914 the outbreak of the great war seemed to have no precedent. Business
and finance, shocked, waited to see what would happen. In 1939 they
remembered what had happened and they reacted promptly. The first
reaction in the United States was in the stock market. The stock market had
been forced to close in 1914, but in 1939 it showed great strength. There
were heavy purchases, particularly of the "war babies" of World War I.
Bethlehem Steel was bought, copper stocks were bought, and the general
list grew strong. The table on page 504 shows the behavior of the Dow-
Jones industrial averages from the outbreak of the war.

British and French Delay War Orders. The expectation which led to the
spurt in the stock market at the beginning of the war was that we should
have, as we had in 1914 and 1915, a great flood of war orders from England

and France. Such orders came, but the amount was very moderate as compared with the expectations. There was an immense inertia in both England and France. While the Germans, in the lull between the conquest of Poland in the autumn of 1939 and the invasion of Holland on May 10, 1940, were very busy preparing for the next stroke, the British and the French waited. There was a great deal of talk about war orders, but instead of giving the orders, the British and French bargained.

DOW-JONES INDUSTRIAL AVERAGES

1939	*High*	*Low*	*Close*	
Aug. 31	135.76	133.38	134.41	(War begins, September 1, 1939)
Sept. 2	139.80	136.39	138.09	
Sept. 12	157.30	151.78	155.92	
Oct. 25	155.95	153.98	155.48	
1940				
May 9	148.60	147.65	148.17	(Day preceding German invasion
June 10	114.42	110.41	111.84	of Holland)
Nov. 6	135.00	131.47	131.98	(Presidential election, November 5)
Nov. 9	138.49	136.56	138.12	
1941				
May 1	115.64	114.78	115.30	
July 28	130.37	128.65	130.06	
Dec. 6	116.87	115.74	116.60	(Day preceding Pearl Harbor)
Dec. 23	107.21	105.57	106.34	
1942				
Jan. 14	113.29	112.05	112.59	
Apr. 28	93.69	92.69	92.92	
Dec. 31	120.19	119.08	119.40	
1943				
July 14	146.26	145.08	145.82	
1944				
May	142.24	137.06	141.24	
Dec.	152.53	147.30	152.32	
1945				
Feb.	160.40	153.79	160.40	
April. 12	159.14	157.89	158.48	(President Roosevelt's death)
Apr. 16	162.76	160.57	162.43	
May 7	167.25	165.76	166.53	(Victory in Europe, May 8)
Aug.	174.29	161.55	174.29	
Sept.	181.71	173.90	181.71	(Victory over Japan, September 2)
1946				
May	212.50	200.65	212.50	
July	207.56	195.22	201.56	
Sept. 10	172.89	166.56	167.30	

The aircraft industry in the United States, especially, was bewildered, and increasingly was concerend less about the question of what business it would get and what profits it would make than it was about what was going to happen to England and France if aircraft production for their account did not speedily get under way. After the invasion of Holland had come, delays in giving orders persisted. On June 5, 1940, after the Germans were already in France, a high official of one of the West Coast aircraft companies spent five hours with a purchasing agent of the French government discussing a minor and nonessential detail of an aircraft model not yet approved.

In December 1939 a member of the British embassy stated privately that the plan was to accumulate an overwhelming mass of metal, meaning artillery, and to win the war in 1942 by the destruction of the German "west wall" with overwhelming artillery. The power of aircraft was enormously underrated.

The lethargy of the British and the French was matched by an underrating of the German military strength throughout much of Europe.[1]

It was not until the disaster in the Netherlands, Belgium, and France that England came to life. Then under Winston Churchill, who displaced Neville Chamberlain on May 10 (the day Holland was invaded), she performed magnificently and heroically.

Presidential Campaign of 1940. In the United States in 1940 we had, of course, the presidential campaign and we had the unedifying spectacle of President Roosevelt and Wendell Willkie both giving the country assurances that our young men would not have to fight on foreign soil.[2] Shall we never again have presidential candidates who will tell the people the truth?

We had a sham campaign in 1940. The Republican Party had started out courageously condemning the New Deal. The Republican candidate, Willkie, wound up giving endorsement to the Wagner Act and the wage and hour law. He doubtless expected to gain labor union votes thereby. He did not get them, and he disheartened his followers.

Following the invasion of the Netherlands there was rapidly growing

---

[1] Contemplating a trip to Europe in the summer of 1940, this writer wrote in the spring to friends in Italy, France, Belgium, Switzerland, England, and the Netherlands, inquiring if such a trip were advisable. From all these countries came the most reassuring replies. These replies came in early May and some came after May 10. One from Holland said, "Come on over, it's very pleasant here." Another said, "The Channel crossing is perfectly safe." One from Italy said, "I am entirely convinced that Italy will retain her position of nonbelligerency throughout the war." None of these correspondents, all very well informed men and all men in a position to have inside information as to the expectations of their governments with respect to the war, had any inkling of the tremendous burst of military power which Germany was about to let loose.

[2] *Commercial & Financial Chronicle,* July 13, 1940, p. 182; September 27, 1940, p. 1663.

recognition by the people in the United States that we must be drawn into the war, and the government proceeded to make preparation. Appropriations for war purposes began April 3, 1939.[3] The raising of a drafted army began on October 16, 1940. We were not formally in the war until after the Japanese blow at Pearl Harbor, December 7, 1941, but both on the side of military and naval preparation, and war economic policy, governmental action began long before this.

---

[3] *Ibid.*, March 25, 1939, p. 1730; April 8, 1939, p. 2048.

76

Our War Economic Policy

Contrasts Between Policies of Wilson and Roosevelt. The contrast between the war policy of the Wilson administration in 1917 and the war policy of the Roosevelt administration in World War II is in many ways extraordinary. Governmental measures in World War I were taken for the purpose of winning the war. They were clean-cut. They were highly intelligent. They were not complicated, in general, by political considerations. They were not mixed with the desire for the aggrandizement of governmental power. The political parties had a sort of informal truce. Ideas of social revolution or of transforming the economic life of the country were in general held down. The one "social purpose" put over was federal Prohibition, against the opposition of President Wilson, though the war was used by President Wilson for the purpose of hastening the coming of female suffrage. But this sort of thing did not enter at all into the government's war economic policy. Here there was a great singleness of purpose, and governmental wartime economic policy was directed solely toward winning the war.

In contrast, in 1940 and the years that followed, we saw the war used as a means of pushing further the New Deal program of the redistribution of wealth. The first purpose was "no war millionaires," a very grotesque demand indeed, since under our tax laws as they existed before we came into the war, a man living in New York who made a million dollars a year paid $807,000 to the federal and state governments in income taxes, and in order to have a million dollars of net income after income taxes paid in a year, a man had to make $7,140,075!

Our own government at the beginning of World War II wasted a great deal of time in giving orders for war supplies, through the closest kind of bargaining with business corporations, and subsequently forced upon these businesses complicated problems of renegotiation to squeeze out unusual profits which they might have made under the first contracts. Taxes on corporations, meanwhile, mounted to very high levels, so that if any unusual profits had been made, the government would have taken most of them anyway, and income taxes in the upper brackets, already fantastically high, rose to such high levels that wealthy stockholders would have had very little left of any corporate profits that might have been paid out in dividends.

In World War I we were much concerned about getting quick results and big results. The government honored its contracts, and counted on excess profits taxes and war profits taxes to get the greater part of extraordinary windfalls growing out of government work. The business community in World War I had far fewer distractions to contend with, and spent far less of its time and evergy with the problem of whether it could produce for the government and at the same time remain solvent.

Delay in United States War Orders, 1940. National defense expenditures ran very low in 1940 as compared with the need. The fiscal year ending June 30, 1940, shows an increase of only $450 million over the fiscal year ending June 30, 1939. And 1939 shows an increase of only $280 million over fiscal year 1937. September 1940 showed us spending only $219 million. This was a year after the President had declared a partial emergency and ordered an increase of army strength in September 1939. It was several months after the Germans had invaded Denmark and Norway (April 9, 1940) and well after the invasion of Holland (May 10, 1940), the collapse of Belgium, and the collapse of France.

The Work of Gen. Leonard P. Ayres. On September 15, 1940, Col. Leonard P. Ayres, vice president of the Cleveland Trust Company, in the distinguished monthly business bulletin of that institution, sounded an emphatic warning which woke up the country. He published a chart with two curves on army expenditures, contrasting the year 1917 with the year 1940. The government, in World War I, had moved with vigor and decision, not merely letting war contracts, but also getting war work done and paying for war work. The colonel concluded, "Our present military machine is in many ways superior to the one we had when we entered the world war—but there is one quality which our old military machine had in superabundance and which the present one has hardly as yet exhibited, and that is acceleration."

Colonel Ayres was recognized as probably knowing more about procurement of army supplies in World War I than any other one man. He had had a large part to play in organizing army statistics, and the general problem of equipping the army and getting the munitions and supplies it needed to France. The army took his criticism meekly, and called him to Washington with the rank of brigadier general, in September 1940, and he actually began active service in the early days of October 1940. General Ayres inaugurated a system of statistical *controls* for the army. It was not a system merely of statistical records. It was a dynamic thing which forecast the needs for particular kinds of munitions and supplies at particular places, which showed the volume of existing supplies of the needed kinds, and which, therefore, indicated what kinds of supplies were most urgently needed and should have priorities in production. The general also aided the navy in establishing a similar system under the highly competent management of D. R. Belcher of the American Telephone & Telegraph Company. The system was inaugurated and actively functioning long before General Ayres retired from the army to return to the Cleveland Trust Company in 1942.

By December 1940, national defense expenditures had moved up to $473,000,000, more than double the expenditures of September, and by November 1941 they had reached $1,437,000,000, nearly seven times the expenditures of September 1940. Following Pearl Harbor, of course, they moved with great rapidity, reaching $5,827,000,000 in December 1942; $7,879,000,000 in May 1944; declining to $6,948,000,000 in February 1945, with a great spurt in March (the result of the Battle of the Bulge) to $8,246,000,000—a figure nearly matched by the expenditures of May 1945 ($8,156,000,000), the month in which V-E Day came (May 8). V-J Day came September 2, 1945, in which month war expenditures stood at $5,365,000,000. By June 1946 the figure had dropped to $2,442,000,000, but still stood very high.

Cutting Red Tape. Army red tape and accounting red tape were largely cut through. The most difficult problem related to the procedure of the General Accounting Office. This had been, as we have seen, a very necessary brake on the peacetime extravagances of President Roosevelt, but the procedures of the Accounting Office could not safely be applied in war. For example, it would have been entirely impossible to have carried through in secrecy the $2 billion expenditures made in producing the atom bomb, had the usual detailed accounting required by the General Accounting Office been followed. It is amazing that the secret was kept as well as it was. Apparently nobody but the President, the secretary of war, the secretary of navy, and certain other chiefs of the armed forces knew how this was being financed, except the House of Representatives Committee on Appropriations, and this committee was obliged to disguise the appropriation in such a way that it would arouse no question on the floor of the House or on the floor of the Senate. It is greatly to the credit of this distinguished committee and of its chairman, that they took the political risks involved in giving the armed forces the $2 billion they needed for what might have turned out to be a fiasco.

The red-tape difficulties were largely overcome by the proclamation by the President of unlimited national emergency on May 27, 1941, supplemented by the Second War Powers Act, which became a law on March 19, 1942.

Army and navy officers who, at the outset, had been timid about giving orders and who were constantly changing their specifications in the early period of the war—in late 1941 there were 500 stop orders in the office of one of the great aircraft companies of Southern California—came in time to trust the businessman with whom they dealt and the businessman came to trust the army and navy officers. It took a year to a year and a half to bring this about. It had not been adequately accomplished by the time of Pearl Harbor, but after Pearl Harbor it moved rapidly.

Another great factor, of course, in bringing about the better understanding between government and business was the partial pushing aside of bureaucrats and their replacement by able men drawn from the business field. Conspicuous among these were William S. Knudsen, brought in from the General Motors Corporation, and William Martin Jeffers, from the Union Pacific System. W. L. Clayton was already on the scene when the war broke out. Numerous other men of distinguished practical experience in business and production matters gave their services, among them Lewis W. Douglas.

The $25,000 Income Limit. Even after army and navy were turned loose to spend what money was necessary to win the war, however, the President continued to push his policy of using the war to prevent individual men from making money. He asked the Congress in April 1942 to adopt legislation that would provide that no citizen should have a net income, after he had paid his taxes, of more than $25,000 a year. Congress failed to do this. Later he asked for a general authority under which he could issue many orders. But in the debate which preceded the granting of this extraordinary authority, spokesmen for the President, both in House and Senate, assured the Congress that the President would not use these vast powers for the purpose of limiting income. Almost immediately, however, the President issued an order limiting salaries, after taxation, to $25,000. The Congress was in revolt at this abuse of power and bad faith, and attached a rider to the bill raising the national debt limit, which the President had to sign, repealing the President's limitation on salaries.[1]

The Racial Social Equality Issue. The war was also made the occasion for pressing measures designed to bring about social, as well as political and economic, equality of Negroes and whites in the country—measures which aroused racial antagonism where it did not previously exist, and intensified it where it already existed.

WPA Continued Until June 30, 1943. The administration resisted changes in the New Deal legislation which efficiency in winning the war demanded. A great country, conscripting 11 million of its young men, and undertaking to be the arsenal for its Allies engaged in a desperate struggle for survival, and straining itself to the utmost to provide manpower, cannot afford such

---

[1] *Commercial & Financial Chronicle,* April 30, 1942, p. 1708; *New York Times,* October 4, 1942; March 26, 1943.

luxuries as a forty-hour week or a WPA. By December 1941, after Pearl Harbor, we had already approached full employment. The index of factory employment (1923–25 = 100),[2] which had stood at 90.9 in 1938 and at 99.5 in August 1939, had risen to 134.2 by December 1941. This same index reached its peak of 177.7 in 1943, dropping to 172.4 in 1944 and to 149.5 in 1945. Employment was very full in December 1941. The National Industrial Conference Board figures show, moreover, an unemployment of only 1,043,000 in August 1941, and a negative unemployment (excess of employment over economic labor force) of 2,678,000 in August 1942; of 7,859,000 in June 1943, and of 8,000,000 in August 1943.[3]

There was heavy pressure in the labor market in December 1941. We had already taken a large number of our young men into the armed forces and we were rapidly expanding the armed forces. Nonetheless, we continued WPA, the federal Work Projects Administration, which paid men not at work in private employment. Incidentally, we were continuing CCC and NYA.[4]

An appropriation measure was passed on June 30, 1942, appropriating $280 million for the 1943 fiscal year operations of the WPA and reappropriating $56 million from the preceding year's appropriation, making a total of $336 million available to permit an average monthly employment of 400,000 men on WPA projects.

It was not until December 4, 1942, that President Roosevelt ordered the liquidation of the Work Projects Administration. Finally on June 30, 1943, the Work Projects Administration turned back $130 million to the Treasury and went out of existence.[5]

The table on page 512 gives the wartime story of WPA.

The Forty-Hour Week Continued Through the War. In November 1941, just before Pearl Harbor, the average number of hours worked in manufacturing industries in the United States was 40.3.[6] Employers working on

---

[2] *Federal Reserve Bulletin,* December 1942, p. 1231; August 1946, p. 909. Between these two dates, the base has been changed to 1939. In the first, in the 1942 *Bulletin,* the base is given as 1923–25 = 100. Practically, this makes no difference, however, since on the earlier base, the year 1939 has an index of 99.9.

[3] National Industrial Conference Board's *Management Record,* October 1943, p. 433.

[4] When the present writer protested against this in his testimony before the Senate Committee on Banking and Currency with respect to the price-fixing bill on December 16, after Pearl Harbor, and urged that one way to hold prices down was to release the labor tied up in WPA, he was told by the chairman in open committee that the committee was not going to suggest legislation upon the subject and could not do it if it so desired. Privately he was informed by another senator that administration pressure was so great that nothing apparently could be done regarding either WPA or the forty-hour-week law. But WPA was at that moment keeping more than a million men out of the labor force.

[5] *Commercial & Financial Chronicle,* July 8, 1943, p. 110.

[6] In testimony before the Senate committee on the price-fixing bill, on December 16, this writer characterized the situation as one where, by act of Congress, we had the equivalent of a strike by one-sixth of our labor force for a fifty percent increase in wages.

WORK PROJECTS ADMINISTRATION

Year & month	Number employed*
1939	
June	2,438,255
1940	
June	1,583,242
1941	
June	1,369,728
1942	
February	1,028,577
March	963,496
April	866,723
May	786,007
June	697,819
1943	
January	288,652
February	202,568
March	135,934
April	81,860
May	45,981
June	42,437

* *Statistical Abstract of the United States* (1940), p. 358; (1941), p. 390; (1942), p. 407; (1943), p. 160.

government contracts, where the government would pay for the overtime, could afford to work labor beyond forty hours, but civilian industries in general could not, and the Congress was engaged in passing a price-fixing measure on the theory that civilian goods were growing scarce and would grow scarcer and needed to have their prices held down.

The absurdity of the forty-hour-week legislation in wartime was very widely recognized in 1941. Chairman Eccles, of the Federal Reserve Board, in testimony before the House Committee on Banking and Currency, on the price-fixing bill, had proposed, purely as a temporary matter, to make the week forty-eight hours instead of forty.[7] Even Leon Henderson, head of the as yet unauthorized price-fixing organization, made large concessions to this view, particularly for workers in the defense industries.[8]

But the whip was cracked. By the winter of 1941–42, it became increas-

---

[7] U. S., Congress, House, Committee on Banking and Currency, *Hearings on H.R. 5479*, pt. 2, p. 1247.

[8] *Ibid.*, pt. 1, p. 953.

ingly evident that the administration was determined to stand its ground on this. Men in some of the government departments devised a new theology to defend it. Forty hours was the ideal from the standpoint of productive efficiency, they maintained!

All suggestions in administration circles for abandoning the forty-hour week were quieted. Finally, in the Congress itself, men who were tremendously concerned that we should be fighting a war with one hand tied behind us by legislation of this kind, gave up the fight as hopeless when they found shortsighted businessmen with government contracts saying that it was really of no use to press the matter, that it would make labor disturbances if it were done, and that from their point of view it made no difference, since the government was paying the bill anyhow. One great senator blamed these businessmen severely. They were looking only at their own businesses. They were not concerned with the solvency of the country. "But," he said, "of course the responsibility is here in Washington."

The forty-hour-week legislation limited production in industries producing civilian goods. The business producing to sell to the civilian population could pay the overtime only if it could raise its prices radically. It could not do this under price fixing. To remain solvent, it must, therefore, have very little, if any, overtime work.

The cost of the war, great enough in any case, was greatly increased by this forty-hour-week legislation. The actual payment of overtime, great though it was, was a minor factor in the increase. The general increase in wages due to the artificial shortage of labor which the forty-hour week created was a bigger factor. The pressure on manpower would have been very much less had this legislation been abrogated for the duration of the war, and the aggregate production of the country would have been very much greater. The table on page 515 shows the average hours worked per week by all manufacturing industries of the United States for the period of the war.

Wages and Prices During the War. Partly as a consequence of the forty-hour-week legislation, and partly as a consequence of other administration policies favoring wage increases (despite the effort to retard the advance of wages under the general price- and wage-fixing policies), wages in the United States rose radically during the war. (See table p. 516.)

A "Labor Union" Government. The war was also made the occasion for powerful governmental pressure in the direction of unionization and "maintenance of membership" contracts.

It is an exaggeration to say that we had a government by labor union leaders in the United States during the war, but not a very great exaggeration.

Other Special Interest—Agriculture and Silver. Labor has not been the only organized special interest pushing special claims. Agricultural leaders have claimed very special privileges, notably "parity" and "parity plus ten percent," in connection with the price-fixing legislation. And we have had a very aggressive, highly successful, and utterly indefensible resistance by the legislators representing silver states to the use of the vast quantities of silver locked up in the hands of our Treasury, for vitally needed industrial purposes.

Government as Civilian Competes with Government as Warrior—Harry Byrd's Economy Fight. We had the spectacle too of executive resistance to the curtailment of civilian functions of government. We had the government as civilian competing with the government as warrior for needed manpower and supplies. Heavy congressional pressure, led by Senator Harry Byrd of Virginia, was able to accomplish something in reducing the ordinary expenses of government. A joint congressional committee with Senator Byrd as chairman, which included the secretary of the Treasury and the director of the budget, made some headway. But the results were very disappointing. The government continued throughout the war to employ a vastly larger number of civil servants that it had any right to employ even in peacetime—all of which contributed to the pressure on manpower and to the cost of war.

Functional Control of Prices in World War I—Limited Direct Control. Prices, as we have seen in an earlier chapter, had already risen very high in the United States before our wartime economic policy got under way in the summer of 1917. Then we checked the rise, and held prices down with real success while the war continued.

The controls were, primarily, functional controls, rather than direct controls. (1) We had a tremendous increase in taxes. (2) We borrowed from the people instead of borrowing from the banks, and as the government borrowed from the people, it took up their current income and limited their competition for goods and services. (3) We had a firm money market which held down bank expansion. (4) We had price fixing of a limited number of commodities, accompanied by a very great amount of commodity control through allocations, priorities, and rationing.

Almost Exclusive Reliance on Direct Controls in World War II. The contrast between the handling of the problem of wartime inflation in World War I and in World War II is a startling one. In the first war, we relied primarily upon functional controls. In the second war, we relied almost exclusively upon direct control. In the first war we knew that we must not let the volume of bank credit get out of hand, and that the government must not borrow from the Federal Reserve banks. In the second war we had an expansion of bank credit on an incredibly vast scale based on bank purchases of government securities, and we had direct ownership of government securities by the Federal Reserve banks on a scale for which the word *ominous* is none too strong.

HOURS OF WAGE EARNERS IN
MANUFACTURING INDUSTRIES
(Compiled by Bureau of Labor Statistics)

Industry Group	Aug. 1940	Aug. 1941	Aug. 1942	Aug. 1943	Aug. 1944	Aug. 1945	May 1946
Total	38.4	41.0	43.0	45.1	45.2	40.7	39.7
Durable Goods	39.7	42.6	45.3	46.8	46.6	41.1	39.2
Iron, steel, products	38.8	41.4	43.7	46.7	46.7	41.7	38.3
Machinery	41.2	45.1	...	...	...	...	...
Transportation equipment	39.9	41.9	...	...	...	...	...
Nonferrous metals, products	40.1	43.0	44.8	46.6	46.5	43.3	41.2
Lumber, products	39.4	41.8	41.8	45.2	44.7	40.5	40.9
Stone, clay, glass, products	37.0	38.5	40.1	43.5	44.0	41.6	40.2
Electrical machinery	...	...	46.4	46.9	46.3	41.2	38.8
Machinery except electrical	...	...	49.4	48.8	48.3	42.7	40.2
Transportation equipment except automobiles	...	...	47.3	47.0	47.4	41.9	39.2
Automobiles	...	...	45.1	47.1	45.1	33.5	35.8
Furniture and finished lumber products	...	...	41.4	44.6	44.8	40.6	41.3
Nondurable Goods	37.2	39.4	40.2	42.5	43.0	40.3	40.1
Textiles, products	34.9	38.1	40.3	41.3	41.8	38.4	39.8
Fabrics	35.7	38.9	...	...	...	...	...
Wearing apparel	33.5	36.4	...	...	...	...	...
Leather manufactures	35.8	39.2	38.4	40.0	41.2	39.3	39.6
Food, products	40.4	41.3	41.3	43.6	45.0	43.3	42.3
Tobacco manufactures	36.1	37.2	39.5	41.1	42.3	39.0	39.5
Paper, printing	38.2	40.1	...	...	...	...	...
Chemicals, petroleum, and coal products	38.7	40.0	...	...	...	...	...
Petroleum refining	35.8	38.0	...	...	...	...	...
Other than petroleum refining	39.8	40.6	...	...	...	...	...
Rubber products	36.3	39.4	42.3	44.2	45.6	41.8	39.4
Apparel and other finished products	...	...	36.2	37.8	37.7	33.1	36.9
Paper and allied products	...	...	41.2	45.6	46.2	44.0	42.8
Printing, publishing, and allied industries	...	...	38.0	40.7	41.1	40.7	40.4
Chemical and allied products	...	...	43.1	45.7	45.6	43.4	40.8
Products of petroleum and coal	...	...	39.5	46.1	46.9	46.8	39.7
Miscellaneous industries	...	...	43.7	45.8	45.1	41.8	40.9

	WHOLESALE PRICES	WAGES		COST OF LIVING	
	U.S. Dept of Labor	Natl. Ind. Conf. Bd.		Natl. Ind. Conf. Bd. •	U.S. Dept. of Labor
		Weekly earnings	*Hourly earnings*		
	(1926 = 100)			(1923 = 100)	(1935–39 = 100)
Aug. 1939	75.0	27.99	.720	84.5	98.6 (June)
Dec. 1939	79.2	28.49	.729	84.6	99.6
June 1940	77.5	28.23	.740	85.5	100.5
Dec. 1940	80.0	30.28	.754	85.9	100.7
June 1941	87.1	34.26	.818	88.5	104.6
Dec. 1941	93.6	36.8	.868	93.2	110.5
June 1942	98.6	39.52	.917	97.4	116.4
Dec. 1942	101.0	42.98	.970	101.1	120.4
June 1943	103.8	46.16	1.016	104.3	124.8
Dec. 1943	103.2	47.15	1.045	103.9	124.4
June 1944	104.3	49.30	1.069	104.4	125.4
Dec. 1944	104.7	49.91	1.086	105.7	127.0
June 1945	106.1	50.33	1.111	106.9	129.0
Percentage increase	41.5%	79.5%	54.3%	26.5%	30.8%

Data in this table are from *Survey of Current Business*, U. S. Department of Commerce.

77

War Taxation and
Expenditures

O ur Best Fiscal Achievement—Taxation. The best achievement of the government in World War II in war finance and in the functional control of prices was in the field of taxation.

Wholly Congressional Achievement over Administration Opposition. But this was wholly a congressional achievement, badly delayed by administration opposition. It was in large degree the work of the Senate Finance Committee, headed by Senator Walter F. George, although the Ways and Means Committee of the House of Representatives also showed intelligence and vigor in the matter. But the great technical skill and the great fiscal courage were in the Senate Finance Committee. The administration and the Treasury from the beginning were wholly unrealistic about taxation. They were unwilling to tax the masses of the people, where the bulk of the income was. But they were willing enough to have rates increased in the high income tax brackets where taxation had already passed the point of diminishing returns.

Treasury Discredited. The Treasury itself was rather thoroughly discredited in the eyes of the Congress in the course of the tax legislation; the financial committees of the Congress in time disregarded the secretary of the Treasury, and the Congress passed its own laws with little concern for his recommendations.

Increases in our national defense expenditures came in fiscal year 1939. We began real expenditures for national defense after Germany invaded Denmark and Norway on April 9, 1940. In fact, the President had declared a partial emergency and ordered an increase in army strength as early as September 1939. But the tax measures proposed by the Treasury in the summer of 1941 were unrealistic. The Treasury was still trying to get its main revenue out of the small part of national income that came from property ownership and business enterprise, which was already very heavily taxed, and from large salaries, already heavily overtaxed, where taking all that was left would give the government very little money. There was very little left to be taken by taxation of large incomes.

Eighty Percent of National Income Received by Those Getting Less than $5,000. There was, moreover, evidence enough that the great bulk of the income of the country was received by people having small incomes. A total of 69.10 percent of all income was received by families and individuals of $3,000 and less, and over 80 percent of the total income of the country was received by individuals and families with incomes of $5,000 and less. Over 90 percent of the total income was received by individuals and families with incomes of less than $15,000.[1]

Moreover, there was evidence enough that the most rapidly increasing incomes were the incomes of workers. The following table, taken from the *Conference Board Economic Record* (p. 597) published by the National Industrial Conference Board on July 11, 1941, shows how rapidly these incomes were increasing.

INDEX NUMBERS FOR PAYROLLS
(Base 1929)

1929	100
1936	77
1937	92.8
1938	71
1939	83
1940: January	90.4
December	110.0
1941: January	109.3
April	122.1
May	128.5

But as Late as October 1942 Treasury Still Trying to Get Main Revenue from Large Incomes. The Congress was ready to tax and would have applied vigorous taxation had there been any administration support. The administration made the reluctant concession in 1941 that exemptions for individuals might be reduced to $750, and that exemptions for married couples without dependents might be lowered to $1,500.

As late as September and October 1942 the Treasury was still fencing, and proposing a "spending tax," which turned out to be simply an additional tax on the existing body of income tax payers. This was proposed before the Senate Finance Committee on September 3, 1942, by Secretary Morgenthau and the general counsel for the Treasury, Ran-

[1] *Statistical Abstract of the United States* (1940), p. 316, cited by this writer, August 15, 1941, before Senate Committee on Finance, in *Hearings on the Revenue Act of 1941*, p. 596.

dolph Paul.[2] Paul renewed the proposal on October 7, 1942, in an address before the American Statistical Association in New York.[3]

Congress Takes Control After Election of 1942—Small Incomes Taxed. Following the congressional election in 1942, with the strong increase in conservative forces in the Congress which this election brought, the Congress felt strong enough to pass its own tax legislation. The following table will show how slow we were, while preparing for and fighting a great war, in applying real taxation to the smaller incomes.

FEDERAL INCOME TAX RATES ON SMALL INCOMES, 1939–46
Single or Married Man with No Dependents

Calendar year	Income $1,000–$1,025		Income $1,500–$1,525		Income $2,000–$2,025	
	Single	*Married*	*Single*	*Married*	*Single*	*Married*
1939	$0.00	$0.00	$14.45	$0.00	$32.45	$0.00
1940	4.90	0.00	24.70	0.00	44.50	0.00
1941	20.00	0.00	63.00	1.00	106.00	39.00
1942*	80.00	0.00	167.00	34.00	253.00	120.00
1943	80.00	0.00	167.00	34.00	253.00	120.00
1944	95.00	12.00	198.00	98.00	302.00	202.00
1945	95.00	12.00	198.00	98.00	302.00	202.00
1946	78.00	0.00	164.00	69.00	249.00	154.00

* The 1942 tax was forgiven, but 25 percent of the tax was added to the 1943 tax (except that if the 1942 tax was the greater, it became the 1943 tax with 25 percent of the originally computed 1943 tax added).

First Impressive Taxation in Fiscal Year 1944. The Revenue Act of 1940 (adopted July 25, 1940) made slight increases in the surtax of the higher brackets (individuals), and the second Revenue Act of 1940 (October 8, 1940) provided for an excess profits tax for corporations. These two acts together, accompanied by the rising volume of national income, made a modest increase in the revenues for fiscal year 1941 as compared with fiscal year 1940. But the effort was inadequate. Fiscal year 1942 brought a real increase in revenues but no adequate increase, and the same was true for fiscal year 1943. It was not until fiscal year 1944 that our tax figures look impressive. The deficit of fiscal year 1943, $55,897,000,000, was the largest deficit of the whole war period. The following table gives the story of war taxation and war deficits, with the perspective of figures running back to fiscal year 1916. The reader will note that certain captions are changed at the end of fiscal year 1941.

---

[2] *New York Times,* September 4, 1942.
[3] *Ibid.,* October 8, 1942.

UNITED STATES TREASURY RECEIPTS,
EXPENDITURES, AND SURPLUS OR DEFICIT
(FISCAL YEARS ENDING JUNE 30)
(In millions of dollars)

Year	Total receipts	Total expenditures	Excess of receipts (+) or expenditures (−)	National defense expenditures	Interest on debt
1916	783	734	+48	337	23
1919	5,152	18,515	−13,363	11,011	619
1920	6,695	6,403	+291	2,358	1,020
1923	4,007	3,295	+713	730	1,056
1929	4,033	3,299	+734	791	678
1931	3,190	3,652	−462	832	612
1932	2,006	4,535	−2,529	753	599
1933	2,080	3,864	−1,784	680	689
1939	5,668	8,707	−3,542	1,206	941
1940	5,925	8,998	−3,611	1,657	1,041
1941	8,269	12,711	−5,103	6,301	1,111
		Total budget expenditures	Deficit	War activities	
1942	13,668	32,397	19,598	26,011	1,260
1943	23,385	78,179	55,897	72,109	1,808
1944	45,408	93,744	49,595	87,039	2,609
1945	47,740	100,405	53,948	90,029	3,617
1946	44,239	65,019	21,981	48,542	4,722

Current Collection of Income Taxes. Of special significance in our war tax program was the Current Tax Payment Act of 1943, adopted June 9, 1943. This act, putting taxes on a current basis, was accompanied by withholding taxes on individuals.

It is not certain who originated this tax plan. Beardsley Ruml, treasurer of R. H. Macy & Company and chairman of the Federal Reserve Bank of New York, first offered the proposal to the Senate Finance Committee on July 27, 1942.[4] In informal interviews with the press, Ruml claimed no originality for his plan and said it had been talked about by many others. Ruml is, however, entitled to large credit for the active and effective campaign he made for the measure. The Treasury opposed the plan because it involved forgiving one year's taxes. Obviously a taxpayer could not be expected to pay two years' taxes in one year, particularly if he were in the upper brackets where his tax might run eighty-five to ninety percent of his income or more. The advantage to the government of collecting currently

[4] *Ibid.*, July 28, 1942.

the taxes on a rapidly growing national income in wartime was obviously very great, and part of the sharp increase in the revenues of fiscal year 1944 as compared with fiscal year 1943 is doubtless due to this factor.[5] The Treasury held the view that if a year's taxes were forgiven, it would be giving up "assets." But the Treasury did not carry these as yet uncollected taxes as "assets" on its books. The Treasury does not expect to be liquidated. If it had to be liquidated, matching existing assets against existing liabilities, it would, of course, be hopelessly insolvent. The Treasury's continued solvency rests on future taxes as compared with future outgo.

The immediate effect of current collection was a big increase in revenue. Over the future years as old men die, the Treasury loses the income taxes which it might otherwise collect from their widows, and as old men lose their jobs, it loses the income taxes which it might otherwise collect on their last year's incomes. On the other hand, as younger men begin to have large earnings, the Treasury begins to get large revenue from them a year earlier than would otherwise be the case. The Treasury, viewed as a long-time going concern, has no grievance, and the Treasury, financing a great war, had an immediate great gain.

The advantage to the taxpayer of having his income taxes stopped when he lost his income, and to the taxpayer's widow of not having to use her insurance money to pay taxes on her husband's last year's income when he died, was obviously very great.

A further point in favor of the measure[6] was the advantage of current collection of taxes as an antiinflation measure. The German government, in the great inflation, 1919–23, was quite helpless because it relied so largely on income taxes assessed on the incomes of the preceding year. The French government, with a much less scientific tax system, in its great inflation of the early 1920s, was greatly helped by the fact that its indirect taxes and its revenues from fiscal monopolies came in *currently,* and their volume increased currently as the franc fell and prices and governmental expenses rose. This has been discussed in earlier chapters dealing with Germany and France. Putting taxes on a current basis is a vitally necessary, even though inadequate, safeguard against both wartime and postwar inflation.

The congressional proponents of this measure were obliged to compromise with the Treasury and the President regarding the forgiving of one year's taxes. The compromise finally was that three-fourths of one year's taxes would be forgiven, and the year's taxes that should be forgiven were to be those either of 1942 or of 1943, whichever proved most advantageous to the Treasury. The provision was further made that payment of the 25 percent of taxes not forgiven should be divided between two years, meaning that 12.5 percent of the unforgiven tax was paid in each of two years.

---

[5] See table on p. 520.

[6] This writer urged this point in 1942.

RATES IN CALENDAR YEAR 1944

Amount of surtax net income	*Rate—%*	*Total surtax*
$ 0–$ 2,000	20	$ 400
2,000– 4,000	22	840
4,000– 6,000	26	1,360
6,000– 8,000	30	1,960
8,000– 10,000	34	2,640
10,000– 12,000	38	3,400
12,000– 14,000	43	4,260
14,000– 16,000	47	5,200
16,000– 18,000	50	6,200
18,000– 20,000	53	7,260
20,000– 22,000	56	8,380
22,000– 26,000	59	10,740
26,000– 32,000	62	14,460
32,000– 38,000	65	18,360
38,000– 44,000	69	22,500
44,000– 50,000	72	26,820
50,000– 60,000	75	34,320
60,000– 70,000	78	42,120
70,000– 80,000	81	50,220
80,000– 90,000	84	58,620
90,000– 100,000	87	67,320
100,000– 150,000	89	111,820
150,000– 200,000	90	156,820
Over 200,000	91	. . . . . .

For incomes in the lower brackets, this was reasonable enough. For incomes in the highest brackets, it meant that more than 100 percent of the current income was paid, in a number of cases. It meant in these cases that the income tax actually was in part a tax on capital after taking all of the income.

Taxes on Larger Incomes. In a preceding table we have seen what this war tax legislation did to very small incomes. On larger incomes, the tax rates, applicable to current incomes for the calendar year 1944, imposed tremendous burdens, not merely on incomes of $100,000 or more, but even on incomes as low as $16,000. During the war the man with a $16,000 income had no legitimate complaint. But the taxpapers have a right to demand, on behalf of the economic future of the country, a drastic curtailment of postwar expenditures, and a drastic reduction of taxes in all the brackets.

The normal tax for calendar year 1944 was placed at 3 percent for all single men with incomes as much as $500, and the surtax rate, beginning at $500, was placed at 20 percent. The table above shows the surtaxes on incomes of single men above $500.

To the surtax rates in this table should be added the 3 percent normal tax, beginning for single men at $500.

Corporation and Other Taxes. Total revenues, as indicated in our table on page 520, for the fiscal year ending June 30, 1945, were $47,740,000,000. Of this, internal revenue collections, as reported, account for $43,800,000,000, divided as follows:

INTERNAL REVENUE COLLECTIONS, FISCAL YEAR 1945*
(In thousands)

Corporation income taxes			Individual income taxes	Miscellaneous internal revenue taxes	Employment taxes, including carriers taxes	Total collections
Normal and surtaxes	Excess profits taxes	Unjust enrichment taxes				
$4,879,715	$11,147,317	$180	$19,034,313	$6,959,634	$1,779,177	$43,800,338

* I have taken these figures from *Washington Close-up,* issued by the Citizens National Committee, Inc., for August 1946, p. 7. They give as their source the *Annual Report of the Secretary of the Treasury* for the fiscal year ending June 30, 1945. These figures are more comprehensive than the figures for internal revenue collections given in the August 1946 *Federal Reserve Bulletin,* p. 907, which account for a total of only $35,062,000,000.

The miscellaneous internal revenue has, as its largest single items, the tax on alcoholic beverages, amounting to $2,310,000,000; the tobacco taxes, amounting to $932,000,000; and the manufacturers' and retailers' excise taxes, amounting to $1,207,000,000.[7]

Of the individual income taxes for 1945, $10,263,000,000 came from the withholding tax and $8,567,000,000 from the current tax payments. (These two figures for individual income taxes do not quite aggregate the $19,034,000,000 given in our table above.)

The effect of war taxes, as compared with prewar taxes, on corporation profits appears in the following table taken from *Washington Close-up* of July 1946, which in turn has taken it from the *Survey of Current Business,* April 1946.

Postwar Tax Rates in Revenue Act of 1945. The Revenue Act of 1945, passed in November after the war was over, repealed the excess profits tax on corporations, though leaving the benefits of past excess profits taxes paid as offsets to future losses.

It reduced the individual surtax rates (see p. 522) by 3 percent. It then reduced the total of individual normal tax and surtax as thus computed by 5

---

[7] The figures in this and the following paragraph come from *Federal Reserve Bulletin.*

CORPORATION PROFITS
BEFORE AND AFTER TAXES, 1929-45

Year	Profits in millions of dollars		Percentage of reduction due to taxes
	Before taxes	After taxes	
1929	9,770	8,337	−15
1930	3,225	2,348	−27
1931	−846	−1,365	−61
1932	−3,100	−3,489	−13
1933	99	−444	−548
1934	1,640	866	−47
1935	3,141	2,188	−30
1936	5,597	4,150	−26
1937	6,126	4,575	−25
1938	3,151	2,069	−34
1939	6,374	4,868	−24
1940	9,185	6,248	−32
1941	17,050	9,141	−46
1942	20,969	9,179	−56
1943	24,908	9,945	−60
1944	24,077	9,757	−59
1945	20,875	9,080	−57

percent. Taxes for 1946 remained appallingly high, and remained so high in brackets above $16,000 that they greatly inhibited the employment of venture capital, except for the very inadequate mitigating circumstance that capital gains on assets held over six months were taxed only at the rate of 25 percent.

Vast Postwar Spending. Meanwhile, despite the high rates and the enormous revenues which continued in 1946, government expenditures continued on so high a level that budget balancing could not confidently be predicted.

Civil Service—Harry Byrd. For one thing, despite the heroic efforts of Senator Harry F. Byrd and his Joint Committee on Reduction of Nonessential Federal Expenditures, the federal executive employees, apart from those in the War and Navy departments, show a net increase of 205,535 between June 1945 and June 1946. The Navy Department and the War Department decreased their civilian employees radically during that same period, but we had at the end of June 1946 a civil service of 2,748,545. Abolishment of some war agencies and cutbacks in others meant merely that many of the "displaced persons" went as refugees to other agencies apart from the War Department and Navy Department.[8]

Congressional action in the Pay Act of 1945, designed to reduce the civil service, proved entirely inadequate and was supplemented by the Pay Act of 1946. Both of these acts set personnel ceilings, and the second placed definite numerical limitations on the number of classified employees in most departments and agencies, with penalties for violations of the law. Senator Byrd was quoted as saying that "responsible government officials have professed that these provisions are 'just a gesture on the part of

EMPLOYEES IN FEDERAL EXECUTIVE CIVIL SERVICE, INCLUDING WAR AND NAVY DEPARTMENTS

1916	
June 30	480,327
1918	
November 11 (Armistice)	917,760
1920	691,116
1921	
July 31	562,252
1923	515,772
1929	559,579
1932	583,196
1934	673,095
1936	824,259
1938	
December 31	861,914
1939	
June 30	920,310
December 31	932,305
1940	
June 30	1,002,820
December 31	1,119,641
1945	
June 30	3,543,326
1946	
June 30	2,748,545

[8] Figures in *Washington Close-up,* August 1946, from Reports of Senator Byrd's Joint Committee on Reduction of Nonessential Federal Expenditures (Senate Committee Print 18, 79th Cong., 1st sess.; Senate Committee Print 29, 79th Cong., 2d sess.).

Congress.' It is my intention to see that future violators find that flouting the laws of Congress is a gesture involving penalties."

But the whole disposition of the federal government, money-drunk after living on the proceeds of bank expansion for thirteen years, was to spend, spend, spend.

It is interesting to contrast the figures, in the table on page 525, for civil service before, during and after World War I, and the years following 1929, with the present war and postwar figures.

Perspective Lost. But the spending ran far beyond the salaries for the enormously multiplied federal civil servants. Perspective had been lost. We had been urged to adopt the Bretton Woods program because it would cost us only what the war was costing us in a very short period of time, and the argument had great weight. We were pouring out vast sums to our veterans whom we love and cherish, but who are so very numerous, and who are so much an integral part of the country, that unless they themselves learn to think of themselves as citizens first rather than as a special class, they can easily wreck the finances of the country, ruining the dollar and bringing disaster upon themselves and their loved ones. We were entertaining gigantic proposals for further great taxes and further great expenditures for social security when there can be no social security in a country whose finances and currency are wrecked. We were paying out vast sums for unemployment relief in a tight labor market when employment was very easy to get. We had lost perspective.

78

Government Borrowing
in World War II

The great reason why we had lost perspective it to be found in the borrowing policy of the government. The Congress had had little to do with this borrowing policy. The Treasury asked for authority and the Treasury received it. The borrowing policy could hardly have been worse. The ideal in borrowing policy is to finance the war with long-term funded debt placed in the hands of investors, rather than commercial banks, debt which cannot come back to haunt the Treasury in a subsequent period of tight money, debt which the Treasury may in later years refund and extend in its discretion when money market conditions are favorable.

Borrowing Policy in World War I. The great bulk of our war debt in World War I was placed in this way. Investors had it. The government did not borrow from the Federal Reserve banks, and the Federal Reserve banks themselves bought government securities in modest amounts, for a few days at a time, only during the periods of the flotations of the four great liberty loans. The government did place short-term paper with the commercial banks, but as the amounts of this grew to substantial volume, the government placed funding loans with the people and sharply reduced the short-term debt. After each of the four liberty loans, the volume of short-term debt dropped drastically.

World War II Borrowing from Commercial Banks and Federal Reserve Banks. In World War II, the great reliance was on short-term borrowing, with heavy borrowing from the commercial banks and the Federal Reserve banks.

On May 10, 1945, while the war was still on, this writer prepared a memorandum for private circulation which went to the chiefs of the United States government, including the Treasury and the Federal Reserve System, appropriate members of the Congress, and to leading economists, bankers, and other responsible students of public finance. Subsequently this memorandum, with the unqualified endorsement of twenty-two other economists, and with endorsement with reservations of two others (all members of the Economists' National Committee on Monetary Policy), was sent once more to essentially the same list of people by the office of the Economists' Committee on Monetary Policy. Finally, when the war was over, the document was released to the press. It gives as clear and as compact an analysis as the writer could now make of government's borrowing policy, and it is presented here unchanged (as it would otherwise be necessary to remove the names of the distinguished group of economists who joined in the analysis and recommendations). Those endorsing without qualifications are:

Charles C. Arbuthnot, Western Reserve University
D. W. Ellsworth, E. W. Axe & Co., Inc.
William D. Ennis, Stevens Institute of Technology
Fred R. Fairchild, Yale University
Charles C. Fichtner, Wales-Strippit Corporation
Roy L. Garis, Vanderbilt University
E. C. Harwood, American Institute of Economics
William F. Hauhart, Southern Methodist University
John Thom Holdsworth, University of Miami
Philipp H. Lohman, University of Vermont
Roy W. McDonald, Donovan, Leisure, Newton & Lumbard
James D. Magee, New York University
Clyde W. Phelps, University of Chattanooga
Olin Glenn Saxon, Yale University
Carlton A. Shively, *New York Sun*
Alvin S. Tostlebe, College of Wooster
Rufus S. Tucker, Westfield, N. J.
Russell Weisman, Western Reserve University
Nathaniel R. Whitney, Procter & Gamble Company, Cincinnati
Edward Wiest, University of Kentucky
Max Winkler, College of the City of New York
Ivan Wright, Brooklyn College

The two members who endorsed the paper with reservations are:

Frederick A. Bradford, Lehigh University
Hudson B. Hastings, Yale University

MEMORANDUM ON INFLATION CONTROL AND THE TREASURY'S BORROWING POLICY
(MAY 10, 1945)

Public Debt, Bank Credit, Interest Rates. The situation with respect to our public debt, our banking system and our currency has grown extremely dangerous as a result of the unsound policy which the Treasury has been pursuing. It is essential that there be the frankest kind of discussion regarding the matter while there is still time to reverse the policy and to avoid a ruinous inflation.

We can avoid a ruinous inflation if we act promptly, but not, I believe, unless we do act promptly.

The public debt has already grown to a gigantic figure and promises to be much bigger before the war is over.

The ease with which the Treasury has been borrowing money at fantastically low rates of interest from the banks and the Federal Reserve banks has generated a false sense of financial omnipotence which is encouraging the demand for great postwar extravagances, both for governmental financing of exports to foreign countries and for unbearable governmental expenditures at home.

France in World War I and the United States in World War II. How dangerous our position is may best be revealed by a comparison of our war financing in World War II with that of France in World War I. It will be recalled that France greatly weakened her position during the war by heavy reliance upon the Bank of France and by a great increase in her banknote issue. She failed to pull up at the end of the war. In 1919 and 1920 the franc broke to low levels in the foreign exchanges. At the end of 1926 France made a *de facto* stabilization of the franc with a gold content of approximately 20 percent of the old par, and with commodity prices at 641 percent of 1913 prices.

With respect to most points we are now a great deal further along the road of inflation than France was at the end of World War I.

(1) The relation of government debt to national wealth is now worse with us. France ended the war with a national debt of 147 billion francs as against a prewar national wealth estimated at 300 billion gold francs. The debt at par was 49 percent of the national wealth. By 1926, when France pulled up, she had a public debt of 287 billion paper francs (internal), and 23 billion gold francs (external, including debts to United States and British governments). (See *Chase Economic Bulletin*, February 1927.) We had at the end of 1944, long before the war was over, a national debt of $230 billion as against a prewar national wealth not exceeding $387 billion.[1] Our national debt December 31, 1944, was thus 59.5 percent of the national wealth.

(2) The growth of money in circulation in the United States since 1939 is greater in percentage than the growth of money in circulation in France between June 1, 1914, and August 29, 1918. France had about 9 billion francs in circulation, including about 3 billion francs of gold, on June 4, 1914; 2 billion francs of this gold was turned into the Bank of France in the three years that followed, and 1 billion francs of gold disappeared from circulation. By August 29, 1918, French circulation, chiefly Bank of France notes, had risen roughly to 30 billion francs, an increase of 233 percent. This grew to 53 billion francs by June 1926. In the United States, money in circulation at the end of June 1939 stood at $7 billion and it now stands at $26 billion, an increase of 271 percent.

---

[1] This is the top figure suggested by the National Resources Committee in *The Structure of American Economy* (June 1939), pt. 1, pp. 374–76. Their top "probable" figure is $360 billion and their lower "probable" figure is $350 billion. I cannot find an estimate sponsored by the Department of Commerce later than 1922, when the figure was placed at $321 billion. Estimates both of national wealth and of national income, of course, involve assumptions, as well as facts, and the estimates for France in 1913 are, of course, less dependable than American estimates today.

(3) The percentage of national debt carried by the banks is far greater with us than with France. On December 31, 1917, the French public debt stood at 123 billion francs, of which 12.2 billion, or almost exactly 10 percent, was held by the Bank of France. But the commercial banks in France took very little of the public debt. The great banks, the Crédit Lyonnais, the Comptoir d'Escompte and the Société Générale, were badly shaken when the war broke out, and taken together, by the spring of 1918, had made virtually no expansion in their balance sheets. To some extent they had substituted government paper for commercial bills in their portfolios, but the amount was small. The only commercial bank that really expanded greatly in France during the last war was a bank of second rank, the Banque Nationale de Crédit, which expanded a few hundred millions of francs, lending both to the government and to business. At the beginning of 1918 I should estimate that not more than 12 percent of the public debt was in French banks, including both Bank of France and commercial banks.[2]

In the United States, on the other hand, at the end of 1944, 42 percent of the whole interest bearing public debt was in the commercial banks and the Federal Reserve banks combined. Leaving out that part of the public debt held by government agencies and trust funds, 46 percent of our interest bearing public debt was in the Federal Reserve banks and the commercial banks. Finally, looking only at the marketable public debt, and omitting that part held by government agencies and trust funds, 58 percent was in the commercial banks and the Federal Reserve banks.

France had very little increase in demand deposits during the war and almost all was in the Bank of France itself, where there was an increase of about 2,712,000,000 francs between June 4, 1914, and August 29, 1918. Our commercial bank demand deposits ("adjusted") plus United States government deposits stood on June 30, 1939, at $28,147,000,000. On December 31, 1944, the figure stood at $87,500,000,000, an increase of 210 percent. We have, therefore, enormously outdone France in the increase of a circulating medium, money plus demand deposits, during the war.

(4) The Bank of France steadily resisted inflationary developments, urging upon the Treasury constantly that it should borrow as much as possible from the people, and its resistance had real results. Our own Federal Reserve System seems to have surrendered its money market policy completely to the borrowing policy of the Treasury.

But we must now take account of favorable factors in our situation as compared with the French situation in the last war.

(1) We are now doing very much better than France did in taxation.

(2) Although France had a strong gold position throughout, we have what appears to be a world dominating gold position. But the outside world is gaining gold from us, and we are now apparently net debtor to the world on current account. (See National City Bank letter of April 1945.)

(3) The relation of our national debt to our national income is more

---

[2] I cannot, with the data at hand as I write, give all my French figures as of the same dates. Figures showing the classification and distribution of our own public debt at the end of 1944 will be found in the *Federal Reserve Bulletin,* March 1945, pp. 257–58.

favorable by a good deal than it was in France. The estimate for national wealth in France in 1913 was 300 billion francs, and that for national income was 30 billion francs, giving a ratio of 10 to 1. Real estate is the biggest factor in national wealth and the French capitalized their real estate on a very low yield basis in 1913. The ratio of national wealth to national income in the United States was only 5½ to 1 in 1912. It was again 5½ to 1 in 1939 if we take the figure of $387 billion given above for national wealth and compare it with the Department of Commerce estimate for national income for 1939, which was $71.8 billion.

We do not know what our national income will be in the postwar period and we are uncertain what our national debt will be.

Our Debt Largely Unfunded. In the last war we placed the debt with the people primarily and in long-term form. The government did spend for a few months funds borrowed on short term from the banks, and then issued great funding loans, in which bonds were placed with the people and out of which this short-term debt to the banks was paid down. The curve for short-term debt rose to peaks just before each funding loan, and then moved sharply down again. The banks always held some of the government debt. At the peak of the public debt they held about $4 billion but this included nearly $1 billion that they had held before the war to secure national banknotes and for other purposes. Of the war debt they held little more than $3 billion at the peak in direct ownership, and much of this was short, and they had also another $3 billion or $3.5 billion of loans secured by government bonds which they had made to their customers to help them buy government bonds.

The Federal Reserve banks owned almost no government securities during the last war, except for a few days at a time when each of the great liberty loans was being floated.

When the war was over, the debt was largely funded. The Treasury knew where it stood.

Our Treasury today cannot know where it will stand when the war is over. The debt is very badly distributed. Of the part held outside the banks, there is a great part in the hands of corporations which are carrying depreciation reserves, maintenance reserves and liquid funds for reconversion purposes in government securities, but which must turn the government securities into cash to accomplish their purposes when the war is over.

A great deal is in the form of tax anticipation certificates which will come back to the Treasury instead of cash.

The so-called war savings bonds, gigantic in volume, are in effect demand deposits. The holders can get their money at any time. These bonds have been sold in a high percentage of cases with the argument that in buying them the purchaser is buying a postwar automobile or a postwar home or a postwar washing machine. The behavior of the sales and redemptions of these bonds in fiscal year 1945, as compared with fiscal year 1944, is disquieting. The Treasury Daily Statement of April 20, 1945, shows that in fiscal year 1945 to date the Treasury has sold only $10,757,000,000 of these bonds, as against $12,612,000,000 in the corresponding period of fiscal year 1944. It shows also that in the current fiscal year the Treasury has had to redeem $3,357,000,000 of these bonds, whereas in the preceding fiscal year it redeemed only

$1,774,000,000. The net intake of the Treasury on these bonds in fiscal year 1945 is thus only $7,400,000,000, whereas in the corresponding period of the preceding fiscal year it was nearly $11,000,000,000. (Since March 1, 1945, these redemptions have included redemptions of matured savings bonds, but the tendencies indicated above were strongly in evidence before March 1.) The Treasury may have a very grave problem with these demand deposits when the war is over. It is unfunded debt. The total of these savings bonds was $40,361,000,000 at the end of December 1944 and the total of the Treasury tax and savings notes was $9,843,000,000.

Of the marketable issues, a very dangerously high proportion is in unfunded form. The total of marketable issues was $162,843,000,000 as of the end of December 1944. We may break this up as follows: Treasury bills, certificates and Treasury notes, total $69,868,000,000. To this we ought to add the Treasury bonds maturing within five years, which stood at $7,824,000,000, making a grand total of short marketable debt of $77,692,000,000. To this we should add the war savings bonds and the tax and savings notes mentioned above, making $127,906,000,000 of unfunded debt, out of a total of $230,000,000,000 of interest-bearing public debt, or 56 percent.

Of funded debt in the form of bonds maturing after five years the total is $83,761,000,000, but this funded debt of over five years' maturity is very badly held. Of this $31,672,000,000 is in the commercial banks. The part that is clearly well placed consists of $7,567,000,000 in the mutual savings banks, and $17,303,000,000 in the insurance companies, a total of $24,870,000,000 in these two classes of institutions.

The part that is held by individual investors is pathetically small. The great bulk of the public debt ought to be in the hands of the individual investors and it ought to be in funded long-term form. I cannot give the figure. It is part of $21,321,000,000 listed under the category "other," which includes business corporations, states and municipalities, educational and charitable organizations, trust funds, investment banks, brokers, and investment companies, as well as individual investors. The rates of 2 percent on ten-year bonds, and 2.5 percent on twenty-year bonds are simply too low to attract investors. The man who knows how to look at a bond table can see to what prices they would go if the rate of interest should rise, and he can look back over the history of government bond yields for the past twenty-five years and see yields exceeding 5 percent.

Diagnosis. The symptoms of pathology in the handling of the public debt are very clear in the figures given above. What is the explanation, what is the cause of the pathology? The explanation is to be found in the fantastically low rates of interest at which the Treasury has been borrowing, made possible by the artificial manipulation of interest rates by the Federal Reserve System.

The lowest interest rates in all history, at a time when the world is destroying capital on a colossal scale, and when the government of the United States is borrowing many tens of billions of dollars a year, are obviously an anomaly. Normal interest rates reflect supply and demand of capital, and rise as supply diminishes or as demand increases. There are four normal sources of capital: (1) consumer's thrift; (2) business thrift, particularly the building up of corporate surpluses out of profits; (3) direct capitalization, as where the farmer uses his spare time in building fences and barns or allows his flocks and herds to increase; (4) governmental thrift, where taxes exceed public expenditure and the government is paying down public debt.

New bank credit constitutes a fifth source of capital, safe enough when cautiously used and kept in reasonable relation to the growth of the four normal sources of capital and the growth of production in the country, but dangerous in the extreme when used to excess, as we saw in the period 1924–33.

Bank credit as a substitute for savings is particularly dangerous in wartime. It has been the typical breeder of war and postwar inflation. The classical case is, of course, that where the government leans directly upon credit from the state bank of issue, as Germany and France both did in World War I. The great expansion of banknotes is obvious. But an expansion of bank deposits is in economic essence almost identical with an expansion of banknotes. Notes and deposits alike are demand liabilities, are both media of exchange. Psychologically, the note issue is the more dangerous. We are, however, increasing both now on a colossal scale.

In World War I, between April 1917 and December 30, 1918, we expanded bank deposits by $5.8 billion and bank loans and investment by $7 billion. In the period from June 1922 to April 11, 1928, we expanded bank credit by $13.5 billion in deposits and by $14.5 billion in loans and investments. This generated our wild stock market and stock market crash of 1929 and the resulting troubles of 1930–33. In the present war, as we have seen above, as a result of the Federal Reserve cheap money policy and the policy of the Treasury of borrowing at low rates of interest from the banks, we have generated an expansion of bank credit in the United States of incredibly greater magnitude and have increased our money in circulation from $7 billion at the end of June 1939 to $26 billion.

We had already very greatly overdone cheap money and bank expansion, and government security purchases by the banks, between March 1933 and June 1939. The Federal Reserve authorities had been greatly concerned and had raised the reserve requirements of the member banks in late 1936 and early 1937 to double the minimum reserve requirements. The Treasury was concerned and created a "sterilization" fund. But presidential action compelled both the Treasury and the Federal Reserve authorities to retreat with respect to these matters in early 1938.

The Warning of the Federal Reserve Authorities. But the Federal Reserve authorities remained concerned. In a report to Congress on January 1, 1941, there was a unanimous recommendation by the Board of Governors of the Federal Reserve System, the presidents of the twelve Federal Reserve banks and the twelve members of the Federal Advisory Council urging the Congress to forestall inflationary tendencies (1) by increasing the power of the Board of Governors to raise reserve requirements of the member banks; (2) by ending the President's power to devalue the currency; (3) by repealing the power to issue $3 billion of greenbacks, and (4) by selling government securities directly to investors, rather than to the banks. The first and fourth of these recommendations looked directly toward firmer rates of interest.

Belatedly, and by action originating in Congress, recommendations (2) and

(3) of this report have been adopted or appear to be in process of adoption, but nothing has been done about recommendations (1) and (4). They seem to meet no favor in the Treasury. The Federal Reserve System, having made its protest, today lies supine. It imposes no brakes. It feeds the inflation of bank credit and currency.

Alleged Safety in New Techniques. We are told that new techniques have arisen which make the policy safe. I see very little in the way of new techniques and rather a very exaggerated use of old techniques.

We have, first, the purchases of government securities by the Federal Reserve banks, replenishing the reserves of the member banks. In World War I the Federal Reserve banks did this in connection with each of the four great liberty loans, reducing the strain in the money market for a few days, while the loans were being floated, and then promptly selling the government securities again. The magnitudes were small—for the first three liberty loans a few tens of millions, and in the fourth liberty loan, something over two hundred million—but only for a few days.

In 1924 and 1927 the Federal Reserve banks bought several hundred million in government securities and held them for a good many months, in each case generating a very dangerous expansion of bank credit, and in the second case precipitating almost unmanageable difficulties.

In the present war the Federal Reserve banks have bought government securities in terms, not of tens of millions or of hundreds of millions, but of many billions. The figure stood at $2,184,000,000 on December 31, 1940, and at $20,153,000,000 on April 18, 1945. This is no new technique, but the vast scale of its use makes one ponder.

Rediscount Rates Below the Market. In the last war Federal Reserve Bank rediscount rates were placed below the market rates to facilitate war financing. But they followed the market up as the war went on. The New York Federal Reserve Bank rediscount rate was placed at 3 percent in 1917, moved up to 3.5 percent at the end of the year, and to 4 percent early in 1918, remaining, however, below market rates. At the present time, the Federal Reserve bank rediscount rate is ½ percent for advances secured by government obligations maturing in one year or less. Here again there is no new technique, but merely an extreme application of an old one.

Reducing Reserve Requirements. The Federal Reserve authorities now have power to reduce the reserve requirements of the member banks and they have already done this as far as New York and Chicago banks are concerned. But in the last war we reduced member bank reserve requirements by act of Congress in 1917—to levels that made us great trouble in the period of the 1920s.

Unlimited Access to Federal Reserve Banks at ⅜ Percent. Finally, the Federal Reserve banks buy government bills without limit from the member banks at a fixed rate, ⅜ of 1 percent discount, with a repurchase agreement. This is designed to make the member banks look upon government bills as ready cash and to make them feel that it is not necessary to carry excess reserves. It may be granted that we have here a new technique. It is obviously a highly dangerous technique and a highly inflationary one.

Using up Ammunition Rapidly. In the process of this immense bank expansion, we have used up ammunition very fast. The reserve ratio of the Federal Reserve banks to notes and deposits combined stood at 90 percent in April

1942 and at 47 percent on April 18, 1945. Excess reserves, which stood at nearly $7 billion in early 1941, dropped below $1 billion in 1943.

Inflationary Policy in Last War. During our own participation in the last war, we held down inflation admirably. The great rise in prices in the last war came between December 1915 and July 1917, before our government war policy got into operation. Commodity prices at wholesale in July 1917 stood at 187 percent of 1913 prices. Under our war policy these prices receded to 182 percent in October 1917 and then rose slowly, under the extreme pressure of the war, to 207 percent in November 1918, after which they receded again to 197 percent in March 1919.

Our war policy in World War I with respect to prices contained four elements: (1) the sudden, very heavy application of war taxation; (2) great concern that bonds be sold to investors rather than to banks; (3) a firm money market to hold down bank expansion. Commercial paper rates in 1918 stood at 6 percent, though the government borrowed more cheaply. Rates were made, however, which would attract investors and which could look reasonable over a long period of time. The first liberty loan was issued at 3.5 percent, fully tax free, the second liberty loan at 4 percent, the fourth liberty loan at 4.5 percent, the last three liberty loans being partially tax exempt. (4) We had a limited amount of price fixing, applying to scarce essentials, and accompanied always by commodity control. We had retail price fixing only in the matter of scarce foods and fuels, and here not until after wholesale price fixing had been well established. We relied in the last war primarily on functional controls, rather than direct controls, as far as commodity prices were concerned.

Primary Reliance on Price Fixing in World War II. In the present war, building up an immense inflationary flood by the expansion of bank credit and money in circulation, we have used as our primary device for controlling inflation, price fixing, covering virtually all wholesale and retail prices and industrial wages.

Price Fixing Must End with the War. It is quite clear that these price controls cannot be tolerated if we are to have a free postwar economy. Prices have work to do. Prices are to guide and direct the economic activities of the people. Prices are to tell them what to do. Prices must be free to tell the truth.

Something may be said for the temporary continuation of price fixing, with rationing, in the case of very scarce essential commodities, but each case should be scrutinized carefully. The general idea that price fixing should be continued after the war for the purpose of preventing inflation must be absolutely vetoed. Inflation must be controlled, if it is controlled, by budget balancing and control of money and credit.

Eliminate Inflationary Money and Credit Policies Now. The existing low interest rates are made possible only by the substitution of bank credit for investors' savings. If bank expansion were to stop today, interest rates would forthwith rise. If, on the other hand, bank expansion is not stopped, we shall have a tremendous inflation. And then we shall see an immense rise of interest rates, the inevitable accompaniment of a great inflation. The choice is not between continuing low interest rates and not continuing. The choice is rather between a moderate and manageable reversal of policy in the near future and an involuntary submission to very high interest rates at a later date.

Prescription: Fund the Public Debt Now and Reduce Money and Deposits

8

6 •

Now. I believe we should act promptly while the war is still on, while we still have controlled commodity markets, and while we still have wartime motives to work with, in funding the government debt into long-term bonds at rates of interest which will attract investors' money. The vast scale of the funding operations required means that we should have to supplement the attractive yield with effective bond selling, including neighborhood pressure. I believe that if we act promptly, these rates can be intermediate between those we paid in the last war and those we are now paying.

We now have outstanding, as a result of the previous abuse of bank credit, an immense volume of idle money in circulation and an immense volume of idle deposits in the banks. If these grew active, we should have an inflation that would blow us sky high. The thing to do is to pull them in and get them invested in government bonds before they begin to work actively in other fields.

I cannot, of course, set exact figures at which investors will take long-term government bonds. Only the market can do that. But this idle cash is a market factor of first importance, tending to hold interest rates down. I think the thing to do is to increase the interest rates on new government securities forthwith to levels at which investors' money will be forthcoming. This should be accompanied by a sale of government securities by the Federal Reserve banks to tighten up the money market correspondingly.

Existing Excess of Money and Credit Tends to Hold Down Interest Rates for Refunding Purposes. Now a rise in interest rates would set in motion powerful counterforces which would tend to hold the interest rates down. With rising interest rates, savings banks and other banks would find it worthwhile to offer attractive rates on savings accounts to the people, pulling in actual cash from circulation. And commercial banks would be interested in reducing or even dispensing with service charges on demand deposits, which would pull in a great deal of money from circulation. But this money coming in from circulation would ease the bank reserve situation and tend to hold interest rates down. Moreover, investors, attracted by higher yields on government bonds, would make a market for very many of the government securities now held by the banks. As the banks sold these securities to investors, investors would pay for them by checking against deposit accounts, canceling a great deal of the inflated deposits and once more easing the money market situation by reducing the reserve requirements of the banks.[3]

Protecting the Banks When Government Bond Yields Rise. There are two main objections to the policy which I propose:

(1) That it would involve dangers to the capital structures of those banks now too heavily loaded with long-term government securities.

(2) That it would increase the tax money required to meet the debt service on the government's already enormous debt.

Let me say with respect to both these points that the problems grow progressively worse the longer we refrain from facing them.

[3] For an analogous situation, see my account of the money market in 1928. "Brokers' Loans and Bank Credit." *Chase Economic Bulletin*, October 31, 1928. See also the account of the same episode on pages 196 ff. of the present volume.

To protect the banks in this change of policy, I have proposed that the banks holding long-term government bonds be allowed to exchange them for new issues at the higher rates of interest, at a discount of, say, two percent as compared with cash subscribers, leaving them with some loss but not with losses that would ruin their depositors. The FDIC, whose solvency and liquidity are of highest importance, should have the same protection as the banks. Both banks and FDIC should be expected to take shorter maturities in making these exchanges. I have seen no other proposal for dealing with this that looks at all adequate. It cannot be solved by allowing the banks to carry these bonds at par on their books, regardless of the market. Informed depositors would simply withdraw their funds from banks whose capital structures were impaired and put them into banks whose holdings of government securities were predominantly short term. Nor do you solve any inflation problem by forcing the Federal Reserve banks to take long-term bonds from the member banks at par.

The present artificiality in the interest structure runs far beyond the regulation of member bank reserves and short-term money rates. The Federal Reserve authorities are also undertaking to regulate the long-term interest rates, by buying and selling government securities of different maturities. (For an exposition of Federal Reserve policy with respect to this matter, see *Federal Reserve Bulletin,* July 1943, pp. 590–91.) A good many bankers have come to expect a sure market for their long-term government bonds in the Federal Reserve banks themselves. This is an ominous delusion. The holders of the ultimate reserves of the country must not be investment institutions and must not be looked to, to supply long-term capital or to manipulate the bond market. When the Federal Reserve authorities are finally driven to tighten the money market in resisting a great inflation, they will not be able to protect the prices of long-term government bonds without feeding the very inflation they are trying to control.

The Interest Burden of the Public Debt. With respect to the interest burden on the government debt, let me say that this problem becomes progressively worse if we delay it. We can now fund the government debt at moderate rates of interest, as above indicated. If, however, we wait for inflation to come, interest rates will rise rapidly and the secretary of the Treasury will sweat blood as Treasury bills and certificates fall due, as people cash in their war savings bonds, and as he has to borrow money on the rapidly rising money market—or else print, which would not help the inflation.

Drastic Federal Budget Economies Essential. The notion that we can permanently hold the debt service on the public debt to a two percent rate is fantastic. The notion that we can permanently service $300 billion of public debt with $6 billion of interest is fantastic. We had best face the facts now. The facts are that our postwar budget is going to be very difficult to balance and that we face the necessity for drastic economies in the postwar period. The facts are that proposals for expanding federal expenditures after the war must be fought all along the line. We do not create social security when we endanger the dollar in which social-security payments are to be made.

Artificialities Built on Artificialities. I cannot pretend to know with confidence what is going on in the minds of men inside the government who, seeing the dangers, are still afraid to face them. But I have heard some fantastic suggestions.

One of them looks to a compulsory holding by the member banks of fixed quotas of nonnegotiable government securities as a permanent matter, at nominal rates of interest with, however, the understanding that in times of necessity they may turn these over to the Federal Reserve banks for cash. Now always in the past our government securities in the commercial banks have been looked upon as secondary reserves. Always in the past we have had a free government bond market. The liquidity of the banks, and their ability to make adequate loans to commercial borrowers and their ability to meet depositors' withdrawals, have always been greatly strengthened by their holdings of government securities. To freeze government securities in the banks is to freeze the banks. Moreover, the volume of bank deposits, which ought to be related to the needs of commerce, would then tend to be frozen, governed not by the needs of commerce, but by the Treasury's needs. Money market control with respect to the needs of trade and with respect to the need of checking inflationary tendencies would disappear under a system like this. Again the Federal Reserve banks, trying to tighten up and prevent the inflation from becoming a ruinous thing, would find themselves compelled to expand their credit as they took over government bonds from hard-pressed banks. No such artificiality will help.

I have last autumn from a man in the government's financial system, whom I do not wish to identify as he was talking with me privately, an alarming suggestion which may or may not represent a considerable body of inside thought. He told me that we had learned many things which economists had previously not known, and which made it safe to proceed along lines that we had formerly regarded as unorthodox. He said that two years ago he had been afraid of the great expansion of bank deposits and money in circulation which the Treasury's borrowing involved, and afraid of the unfunded debt, but that today he had no fear at all of inflation. It will be perfectly possible with modern techniques to control the interest rates and to control inflationary tendencies. When I pressed him regarding the methods, he said that the Nazis had developed some very good technical economic ideas. I said, "Yes, if you have enough regimentation, if you have control of all commodities and all prices, if you have control of every man's pocketbook and every man's bank balance, if you have control of the farmer's consumption of his own production, if you can control all exports and imports and foreign exchange transactions, and if you have a sufficiently powerful and efficient Gestapo, you can take great liberties with money and credit." He said that the trouble with the Nazis is that they do not have consciences.

I may add, however, that without techniques of the Nazi type described in the preceding paragraph, it is not possible to continue our present course and avoid a ruinous inflation.

I know at least one man in the Federal Reserve System who was reconciled to inflation nearly two years ago, who held that inflation always follows a great war, and that it is necessary to cover up the great war debt. To this man I would say, first, that I do not believe it. We can, by sound measures taken promptly, protect our currency from further debasement, and protect our price system from ruinous convulsive movements. Moreover, the accomplishment of the measures which I propose would still leave far more inflationary material lying around than I like to see. For one thing, we have not yet felt the main impact of the forty percent cut in the gold content of our dollar in 1934 and we have not yet seen the consequences upon the world of the rise of annual world gold production from $430 million in old gold dollars in 1930 to roughly three times that figure in new gold dollars in 1939. I would add that in any case the most hopeless pessimist would wish to have some control of the situation.

Inflation is not something that you can turn off and on like water at a faucet. Inflation and deflation are not simple terms and they are not simple opposites. There is no financial Westinghouse air brake by means of which an inflationary movement can be smoothly tapered off and brought gently to an end without a shock. Rather, inflationary forces engendered in defiance of sound financial policy may seem harmless for a long time and then suddenly break forth into great violence.

It is far better for the Federal Reserve System to act now when moderate restraining movements will accomplish a great deal, than to wait until the great inflationary movement is under way and when even violent methods of restraint may have limited efficacy. And it is far better for the Treasury to face the financial facts regarding the public debt service now, while it is possible to fund the debt on moderate terms, than to wait to face the violently rising interest rates which a real inflation always creates.

Public Debt, Bank Deposits, and Money in Circulation—Mid-1946. This memorandum describes the situation at the end of the war, and indeed in the middle of 1946, except that the figures for the debt are larger and that the figures for money in circulation and bank deposits are larger. In August 1946 the total gross direct debt to the United States government was $267,546,000,000. The figure had been high in February 1946, when it stood at $279,214,000,000, as a result of a great postwar loan in which the government borrowed more cash than it needed. Part of this cash the government has since used in reducing the public debt, despite the fact that a deficit of expenditures over revenues continued.

On June 30, 1946, the commercial banks held $83,300,000,000 of the public debt, and the Federal Reserve banks held $23,783,000,000.

Money in circulation, which had stood at $6,859,000,000 at the end of 1938, and at $26,189,000,000 in April 1945, stood at the end of July 1946 at $28,254,000,000.

Demand deposits of all commercial banks, which had stood at $28,695,000,000 at the end of 1938, and at $91,644,000,000 at the end of 1944, stood at $98,350,000,000 at the end of June 1946. This figure was $105,923,000,000 on December 31, 1945. But as a result of the Treasury's use of its deposits with the banks in buying back government securities from the banks in the first half of 1946, it had dropped to the $98,350,000,000 stated above. The connection between government securities in the banks and the volume of demand deposits in the banks is obvious and direct.

Postwar Policy of Federal Reserve Authorities. There is as yet no evidence that the Treasury and the Federal Reserve authorities have any intention of reversing policy and cleaning up the vast excess of bank deposits and money in circulation, which they have created. There was a very disheartening special report on credit policies submitted to Congress on June 17, 1946, by the Board of Governors of the Federal Reserve System.[4]

Recognize the Dangers. The report points out the inflationary dangers of the great excess of money in the hands of the people. It states:

> There can be no doubt that the country's money supply, several times greater now than ever before, is and will continue for an indefinite time to be much in excess of available goods. Under such conditions, with the heavy drains of war financing no longer existing, public policy calls for vigorous attack on the basic causes of inflationary pressures. This, in turn, requires that the government stop and reverse, if possible, the process whereby it has created bank credit. It is all the more imperative that the government reverse this process as the commercial banking system resumes its peacetime function of supplying credit to private sources whose borrowing will itself create additional funds.

After this encouraging preamble, the Federal Reserve document becomes discouraging in the extreme. It declines to reverse its low interest rate policy, giving as one reason "the Reserve Board's assurance to the Treasury that the rate of ⅞ percent on one-year certificates will be maintained, if necessary, through open market operations."

But Make Alarming, Irrelevant Proposals. Its own proposals involve the request for additional power for the Board of Governors of the Federal Reserve System to control the use of bank funds. One request is that the board be granted additional power to raise reserve requirements which, if used, would tend to raise interest rates, but as the general report indicates that they do not wish to raise interest rates, one wonders why they ask for this additional power. Another very alarming proposal is, in principle, that referred to in the memorandum of May 10, quoted above, namely, that there be compulsory holding, by member banks, of fixed quotas of nonnegotiable government securities as a permanent matter, at nominal rates of interest. The board in its June 17, 1946, report modifies this by substituting Treasury bills and certificates for the nonnegotiable government securities, but it does ask the Congress for power to compel the banks to hold a

---

[4] The relevant parts of the text of this report will be found in *Commercial & Financial Chronicle,* June 20, 1946.

specified percentage of Treasury bills and certificates as "secondary reserves" against their net demand deposits.

Now this use of the term "secondary reserves," to a man who understands banking, is an abuse of the English language which it is difficult to characterize justly in temperate words. It is an illustration of New Deal "semantics," under which the rule is to call a bad thing by a good name, as, for example, calling deficit spending "investment."

A bank's secondary reserve is made up of highly liquid assets which the bank is free to use at its own discretion. It may sell them to get additional funds to lend to its customers when they borrow. Country banks regularly accumulate them after the crop moving is over, so that they have them available when the pressure of crop making and of crop moving comes in the following year. Government securities which the banks must hold as a specified percentage against their net demand deposits are not secondary reserves, they are fixed investments available for use only in a fixed percentage as the net demand deposits go down. True secondary reserves are available for any use that the bank wishes to make: to meet runs, to meet seasonal withdrawals, to meet seasonal borrowing needs of customers, to meet any one of a multitude of special problems which may make a bank need additional funds in a hurry.

This proposal is to be denounced as one which would go far to destroy the flexibility and the usefulness of our banking system. It would be one of the Hitlerite controls referred to in the memorandum.

This document of the Board of Governors seems not to contemplate an increased placement of government securities with investors. It seems rather to visualize a shuttling of government securities back and forth between the Federal Reserve banks and the commercial banks. It proposes nothing that would operate to bring about a radical decrease in the volume of money and credit outstanding, or to meet the basic danger set forth in the first passage quoted from their report. The board indeed states, "Under a continued policy of maintaining the existing level of short-term interest rates, the principal effect of an increase in reserve requirements would be a shift of government securities from the commercial banks to the Reserve banks."

The only safety is to be found in a vast shift of the government securities now held, both by commercial banks and by the Federal Reserve banks, into the hands of investors, and the only way to accomplish this is by a rise in interest rates along the lines indicated in our memorandum above.

Figures of Debt, Not Wealth. The following table will give perspective of a disquieting sort on our swollen structure of federal government debt, bank deposits, and money in circulation. The figures show how all of these items have swollen in the period covered by the present book.

The following figures are figures, not of wealth, but of debt. They are figures for the debt of the United States government to the banks and to the

CURRENCY, DEPOSITS, AND PUBLIC DEBT, 1914–46
(In millions of dollars)

	Money in circulation	Total deposits, all commercial banks	Government securities in Federal Reserve banks*	Interest-bearing public debt**
1914, June 30	3,172	17,390	. . .	. . .
1916, June 30	. . . .	. . . . .	47	972
1918, June 29	4,195	28,011	97	11,986
1920, June 30	5,181	36,114	347	24,061
1921, June 30	4,624	32,987	302	23,737
1924, June 30	4,562	40,656	416	22,008
1928, June 30	4,510	49,215	232	17,318
1929, June 29	4,459	49,036	179	16,639
1933, June 30	5,434	31,911	1,933	22,158
1939, June 30	7,047	53,789	2,591	39,886
1941, Dec. 31	11,160	71,248	2,404	57,451
1944, Dec. 30	25,307	127,950	18,846	228,891
1945, Dec. 31	28,515	150,227	24,262	275,694
1946, June 29	28,245	143,180	23,783	268,111

* The figures for 1916 are annual averages.
** In addition to the direct debt of the United States government, there were the fully guaranteed securities of government corporations and agencies, which in June 1941 stood at $6,360,000,000. This figure had been reduced by August 1946 to $370,000,000.

people. The figures for deposits represent the debt of the banks to the people. The figures for money in circulation represent the debt of the government to the people. This debt rests on the future earning power of the people and the ability of the government to take from the people in taxes enough of their earnings to service the debt and to prevent a collapse of public credit.

Create Illusion of Grandeur. The ease with which the Treasury has been able to get money by borrowing from the banks and the Federal Reserve banks has created an illusion of grandeur. Because we have already borrowed and spent so much, it is urged that we can easily and safely borrow and spend much more. We are looked upon as the strongest financial power in the world. And doubtless in a world shattered by war, we who have not been invaded and whose physical properties have not been shattered by war, are the strongest. But we are not so strong financially as we were in 1939. Moreover, we are, as a country, rapidly increasing our debt to the outside world.

In the memorandum above, reference was made to a monthly letter of the National City Bank, published in April 1945, which indicated that we had lately become net debtor to the world on current account and that we had been losing gold. The following estimate is supplied by a great New York bank, as of July 30, 1946, of our current debt to the outside world.

On current account, it seems likely that we are indebted to the world to the extent of six or seven billion dollars. This includes holdings of U. S. currency and short-term government securities. This figure, of course, does not include our payment to the fund of $2.7 billion nor that to the bank of $3.2 billion, nor the British credit of $3.7 billion, all of which may be the equivalent of short-term debt in the near future. I take it a substantial part of the UNRRA payments amounting to $2.7 billion have already been used. On the other hand, additional loans by the Export-Import Bank may result in current drafts on us.

Our "Invincible Dollar." We think of our dollar as invincible and as the supreme currency of the world. But the same source gives the following information regarding the estimate placed upon our dollar as compared with gold in a number of outside countries.

It is true that there is a very high premium on gold in various parts of the world. Computed in dollars at current exchange rates, these premiums seem fantastically high. In India, I believe, gold has run as high as $70–$75 an ounce. In the Argentine, bars are selling in the neighborhood of $40 and coins from $60 to $70. In Syria and Egypt the price has been around $50. In Peru, a gold-producing country, no such prices have been experienced. Portugal has had quotations around $40, and even Switzerland has seen a price of about $38. Generally, it seems that these prices result largely from the extreme scarcity of gold in different localities and from our own unwillingness to grant export licenses for gold shipments abroad.

Part of the difficulty here doubtless is the reluctance of our Treasury to discredit the official exchange rates of certain foreign countries by shipping gold to sell at actual market prices in the domestic currency, and to use that domestic currency in purchasing dollars to the extent necessary for bringing the dollar to its gold parity within the country—part of it thus reflects the absurdity of the general scheme of maintaining artificial foreign exchange rates by international cooperation. These high premiums on gold as against the dollar in various foreign countries may well be regarded, however, as a warning that there are parts of the outside world, at least, which very much prefer gold to dollars. Thirty-five dollars should be able to purchase an ounce of gold (with allowances made for the cost of shipping gold) everywhere in the world. Our own people in September 1946 still had great confidence in the dollar and still have great confidence in the long-term obligations of the United States government payable in dollars. But there are limits to the abuse to which foreign and domestic confidence can be subjected—as the story of England, contained in this volume, abundantly proves.

79

Price Fixing in World War II

The original intention in the price-fixing legislation was not universal price fixing. The powers which the Congress gave were sweeping powers, but the Congress was assured by the administrator, Leon Henderson, that he intended only to fix certain prices. His most definite statement upon this point was that, whereas in World War I some thirty groups of prices were fixed, he intended to fix about one hundred.[1]

Price-fixing Edict Went Far Beyond the Law. The actual legislation gave the administrator power, when he found a set of facts regarding certain commodities, to fix their prices, but he was required to find the set of facts before fixing the prices.[2] In practice, however, the administrator, Henderson, went far beyond that. He issued an edict (April 28, 1942) fixing virtually all prices at "ceilings" based on the highest price of the month of March preceding, charged by each individual seller, without even naming the commodities and without finding any facts regarding them.

World War I Used Trade Brains in Fixing Prices and Margins. In World War I we had tried to make use of the brains of the men in the trades with respect to the actual handling of price fixing, with respect to the effect on production of a given commodity of a particular price fixed, with respect to the margins of profit that would be left, and so on. In general, trade brains were used by the government in this connection, not in blanket orders affecting all commodities, but in detailed orders affecting particular commodities. In the one case of bituminous coal, we saw that bureaucratic brains were substituted for trade brains in World War I with unsatisfactory results.[3]

[1] U.S., Congress, House, Committee on Banking and Currency, *Hearings on Price-Fixing Bill*, unrevised (1941), p. 872.

[2] Emergency Price Control Act, approved by President Roosevelt, January 30, 1942.

[3] See my address before the American Economic Association on price fixing, December 29, 1917, in *American Economic Review*, supp. (March 1918). This is reproduced as part of my testimony on the price-fixing bill before the Senate Committee on Banking and Currency, *Hearings*, December 16, 1941, pp. 466–92, 542.

In World War II, No Study Given to Individual Prices. In World War II we fixed prices without the use of any brains at all, neither trade brains nor bureaucratic brains being brought to bear upon particular prices or particular commodities. We had a sweeping overall edict. The object was to hold the price level down. The object was to offset the sweeping inflationary forces which we were creating by the borrowing policy of the government and the rapid expansion of bank credit and of money in circulation.

Price Fixing and Commodity Control. In World War I the connection between allocation, priority, and rationing, on the one hand, and price fixing, on the other, was definite and close. In general, they were in the same hands. There was far more commodity control than there was price fixing. There were separate bodies for controlling different kinds of commodities, and fixing their prices to the limited extent that price fixing was engaged in. There was recognition of the fact that prices have work to do in guiding and controlling the economic activities of men, and that when the government fixed a price, it had to undertake to do the work that a freely moving price would otherwise have done—namely, to allocate, to give priority, and to ration the supply—and that it must fix the price high enough to bring forth the needed supply. There was study of individual markets as decisions with respect to these points were made.

In World War II price fixing for virtually all commodities was done by the Office of Price Administration (OPA). Allocations, priorities, and rationing were largely in the hands of other bodies, among them the Civil Production Administration. Retail rationing of certain foods, shoes, and gasoline with coupon books was handled by the Office of Price Administration. There was doubtless interchange of opinion among the various governmental authorities concerned with these matters, but it was informal and loose.

To an extent that could not have been anticipated in advance, we had compliance during the war with the price-fixing edict from the patriotic public, and above all, from an intensely patriotic business community. We had black markets. We had a great deal of difficulty in controlling black markets. But with the war on and with almost every family having sons in the army or in the navy, our people made the price fixing effective to an unanticipated degree.

Prices During War. The price history has been interesting and startling. The index of wholesale prices for the United States (1926 = 100) stood at 77 in 1939, and moved up to 99 in 1942. Then effective resistance, so far at least as official prices are concerned, began. The figure for 1943 was 103; for 1944, 104; for August 1945, 106.

Prices were not held down as much as these figures would indicate. Black market prices were important throughout the war and the quality of goods sold at official prices deteriorated. The actual wholesale price level was undoubtedly a great deal higher than these official price indices would indicate. But the great industries respected the governmentally fixed prices. The great retail stores, on the whole, did. The organized markets in grain and in livestock and the great packing houses did. Among smaller and less responsible businesses, there was a good deal of breaking away; but even in small retail establishments, partly through patriotic motives and partly through neighborhood scrutiny, the ceiling prices were respected while the war was on, to an extent that one could not have anticipated.

Price Fixing After War. With the end of the war, however, the dam of general price fixing yielded rapidly. By June 29, 1946, the day before price fixing temporarily expired, the general index of all commodities had risen to 112.7. In July, with price fixing temporarily suspended, it rose to 124.2 on July 20, dropping to 124.1 on July 27.

But the resumption of price fixing at the end of July did not stop the price rise. On August 31, 1946, the all-commodity index stood at 128.4, four points higher than in the last week in July.

Farm products, standing at 65.3 in 1939, rose to 122.6 in 1943, and held at approximately that level through 1944. They stood at 126.9 in August 1945, then began a rapid rise, reaching 140.1 in June 1946. In July 1946, with the price control suspended, they moved up to 159.2 on July 20, dropping slightly to 157.3 on July 27. Black market prices here came out into the open. Many of the products of the farms had been sold in subterranean markets in the preceding period.

The end of August 1946, with price fixing restored, shows farm products at 157.1.

The rise in the general average of wholesale prices from September 1945 to August 31, 1946, was 22 percent in the official index for all commodities of the Bureau of Labor Statistics. It is interesting to contrast this with the postwar rise which took place between October 1918 and May 1920, amounting to 20 percent, in a period when price controls were abandoned. And it is interesting to recall in this connection the testimony of Leon Henderson in 1941, as he advocated the price control bill, in which he repeatedly spoke of a 40 to 50 percent rise in commodity prices which took place following the last war (an erroneous statement, because it was only 20 percent) and urged that price fixing was necessary in order to prevent anything of that sort after World War II.[4] Whatever may be said of our wartime price fixing, our postwar price fixing definitely failed to hold the line.

Effects of Postwar Price Fixing. Postwar governmental price fixing and wage fixing retarded the process of reconversion very greatly. Freely moving prices and wages, responding to supply and demand, are needed if

---

[4] This theme appears repeatedly in Henderson's voluminous testimony before both the House committee and the Senate committee in 1941. See U.S., Congress, House, Committee on Banking and Currency, *Hearings on Price-Fixing Bill,* unrevised, esp. p. 343.

commodities are to be produced in the proper proportions. Wages were pushed up rapidly and prices were held back, endangering profit margins, and in many cases precluding or greatly curtailing the production of parts acutely needed in the productive process. In September 1946 there was a bad unbalance in the materials and supplies which the manufacturer needs if he is to engage in capacity production. The unbalance was, of course, very greatly intensified by strikes.

It is not easy to disentangle the effects of strikes from the effects of bad OPA pricing where scarce parts were involved. Checking the matter with a number of bankers and some industrialists, one found cases of accumulation of unfinished inventory, really unfinished "work in process," requiring additional bank loans because one additional part was needed to make the product salable. In many of these cases, strikes were blamed. In other cases, the parts simply could not be obtained at OPA prices. One manufacturer was paying retail prices instead of wholesale prices to get vitally needed parts. Another manufacturer was sending men out with satchels to get the parts where they could get them. It was not easy to obtain information as to the prices he was paying! In other cases, manufacturers were refusing to pay exorbitant prices for scarce parts, but were certainly paying more than the OPA prices. There were very few industries in September 1946 that did not have complications of this kind, and very few industries where production had not been interfered with by them.

The OPA tried to fix prices from the standpoint of "just price" instead of the standpoint of functional price. Functional prices are needed to bring about and to maintain proper balance in production. And only free competitive markets can work out functional prices.

Another interesting and significant cause of accumulated inventory requiring additional bank loans was found in Los Angeles in September 1946. Fully finished goods sold and ready for shipment could not be shipped in certain important cases (a) because of the shortage of freight cars, and (b) because of strikes interfering with ocean shipping affecting goods designed for export.

It would be hard to find a more striking commentary on governmental economic planning than that revealed in the business developments from V-J Day in 1945 to September 1946, during which period we had, on the one hand, powerful national labor unions backed by the federal government, making ever increasing demands on industry and striking to obtain them, and, on the other hand, continued governmental interference with the markets and prices.

Testimony Before Congressional Committees on Price Fixing, Spring 1946. The complaints of the industries of OPA performance that appeared in the testimony before the House Committee on Banking and Currency (March 9–30, 1946) and before the Senate Committee on Banking and Currency (April 15–May 10, 1946) were detailed and impressive. The evidence presented, showing that the price increases as registered in the wholesale price index of the Bureau of Labor Statistics were wholly inadequate, when allowance was made for qualitative deterioration, was detailed and specific. For example, in the testimony before the Senate committee on May 3, 1946, Robert A. Seidel, appearing for the National Retail Dry Goods Association, gave many illustrations, among them the following: men's good grade white shirts sold at $12.80 per dozen in March 1942, but the lowest-price shipment his firm was able to obtain in November 1945 cost $21.00 per dozen. In addition, he said there was less material in the 1945 shirts and the quality of workmanship was poorer. He estimated the actual price increase in these shirts at 93 percent, while prices on boys' shirts were up 90 percent. These increases occurred under price fixing. Impressive too was the evidence that where price control was effective, there had been a radical decline in quantities produced of particular items. Evidence of black markets was conclusive.

Price Fixing Interrupted for Twenty-five Days in July 1946 and Then Resumed. General price fixing was off for the first twenty-five days of July before the compromise legislation was passed, and OPA rent and price orders that were in force on June 30, 1946, were automatically reinstated. But agricultural prices were left subject to the decisions of the new Price Decontrol Board. On August 20 the Price Decontrol Board ruled that ceiling prices should be reinstated on livestock and meats, soybeans, cottonseed products, flaxseed, and byproduct grain feeds. Dairy products and grains and livestock and poultry feeds made entirely of whole grain were left free. During July and much of August, to August 20, livestock for slaughter came to the market in great quantities. With the resumption of price fixing on meat and meat animals, the most severe meat shortage the country has ever known came in September 1946.

80

Government Versus Private Financing of War Production in World War II

First War Chiefly Private Finance; Second War, Government Finance. In 1941 a high official in the government loan organization stated privately that the decision had been made that war production should be financed by government money rather than by private money. This turned out to be the case.

In World War I the government did very little. The War Finance Corporation was created for the purpose of assisting in financing war production where private credit was not available. But by October 15, 1918, the total of all credits provided by the War Finance Corporation was $43,202,592. The rest of the money which the war industries obtained in World War I came primarily from retained profits, from the issue of new securities, and from the banks. Nonessential loans were held down, and nonessential capital issues were held down. But war production was adequately financed by

CORPORATE SECURITY ISSUES
FOR NEW CAPITAL

1923	$2,635,000,000
1929	8,002,000,000
1934	178,000,000
1936	1,192,000,000
1937	1,225,000,000
1938	873,000,000
1939	383,000,000
1940	736,000,000
1941	1,062,000,000
1942	624,000,000
1943	374,000,000
1944	646,000,000
1945	1,255,000,000

private capital and by a carefully safeguarded expansion of commercial bank credit.

New Capital Issues Low in World War II. In World War II corporate security issues for new capital stood at a low level, as shown by the preceding table.

A spurt will be observed in the year 1941, followed by a radical decline, and a spurt will be observed in 1945, but more than two-thirds of this 1945 figure came in the second half of the year after the war was understood to be over, and did not represent private capital for financing war production.

Bank Loans in World War II. Bank loans of the member banks of the Federal Reserve System, for commercial and industrial and agricultural purposes, moved as shown by the following table:

ALL MEMBER BANKS
(000,000 omitted)

Year	Commercial and industrial loans, including open market paper	Agricultural loans
1938		
Dec. 31	5,179	712
1939		
Dec. 30	5,841	730
1940		
Dec. 31	6,660	865
1941		
June 30	7,807	738
Dec. 31	8,671	972
1942		
April 1 (estimated)*	9,100	. . .
June 30	8,383	726
Dec. 31	7,387	1,089
1943		
Dec. 31	7,421	1,023
1944		
June 30	7,023	1,023
Dec. 30	7,531	1,198
1945		
June 30	7,095	1,125
Dec. 31	8,949	855

* Judging by the figures of the weekly reporting member banks, the peak figure for all member banks for commercial and industrial loans was reached in late March or early April 1942.

Bank Capital Inadequate—SEC Restrictions. With the SEC and other restrictions on the investment market and the stock exchanges, which we have discussed in connection with the stock market break of 1937, it was doubtless impossible for the private investment market to have financed the war industries adequately. The banks could do their part at the outset, and the foregoing figures show how rapidly bank loans went up in 1940–41 and early 1942. But the time came when the war industries needed such great loans from the banks that banking capital was inadequate. National banks, when lending to anybody but the government, must lend no more than 10 percent of their capital and surplus to one borrower, and the aggregate banking capital of the country for all insured commercial banks was only $6,673,000,000 on December 31, 1940, and for that matter, only $8,671,000,000 on December 31, 1945. The credit of $1,000,000,000, which was made to the General Motors Corporation by a consortium of banks, would thus have been impossible under these limitations.

But Banks Could Lend to Government Without Limit. But the banks could lend to the government without limit, and the government could use bank money in financing war industries.

Cash Advances by Treasury. Very early the Treasury began making cash advances for working capital to industries which had adequate plant and equipment, but which were suddenly called upon to do five or six times as much work as they had ever done, and had no adequate basis for bank credit in the large amounts required.

V Loans. Speedily the Treasury grew concerned about this, not knowing how to do it and not knowing whether it was done properly, and felt the need of banking minds upon the transactions, and of banking machinery in the handling of the transactions. The solution was found in the V loans, loans arranged by the commercial banks but guaranteed by the Federal Reserve banks, the latter acting as fiscal agents for the government and not putting their own funds at risk. These guarantees normally did not run above 90 percent of the loan.[1] The banks took part of the risk, though in the case of certain weaker companies, the V loans were guaranteed up to 100 percent. This was a rarity. It came when the corporation was weak and when the government desperately needed what the corporation could produce. Some V loan guarantees were only for 75 percent.

V Loans Chiefly for Working Capital. These V loans in general were not made for producing plant or equipment. They were primarily for wages and raw materials and other forms of working capital, occasionally including short-lived tools.

VT and T Loans. As the war went on, the fear of contract cancellations began to grow and VT loans came in. These were loans, guaranteed still by the Federal Reserve banks, designed not merely to facilitate war production but also to prevent a business from having its working capital frozen in

---

[1] The limitation of loans to one borrower to 10 percent of capital and surplus of the bank did not apply to the guaranteed part of these loans.

the event contracts were suddenly canceled. Finally came T loans, concerned primarily with freeing the working capital of industries producing war supplies for reconversion to peace activities.

On April 11, 1942, the Board of Governors of the Federal Reserve System announced the adoption of regulations to inaugurate the V loan system.[2] The VT loans were inaugurated in a statement released by the Office of War Information on September 1, 1943, which appears in the *Federal Reserve Bulletin* of September 1943 (pp. 849–50). The T loans appear to have followed the passage of the George-Murray bill.[3]

The table following[4] gives the statistics of the V, VT, and T loans.

It will be observed that the loans authorized at any given time far exceeded the loans outstanding on that date. For example, the General Motors Corporation received a credit of $1 billion, but the maximum use it made of this credit was $250 million. It will be further observed that the loans outstanding rapidly declined after V-J Day in September 1945.

These loans were well handled, in the opinion of many bankers, and the results have been good—able men drafted from private business and finance, working at a financial sacrifice under wartime motives, with red tape cut through, did a job which bureaucrats could never do in peacetime.

Cash advances for working capital by the Treasury continued throughout under the supervision of the army, the navy, the Maritime Commission, and other government agencies concerned with procurement of munitions, equipment, and supplies.

Throughout, moreover, the industries with good credit got regular bank loans for working capital.

Capital for Plant and Equipment. The problem of plant and equipment was solved for the most part in a different way. Tax legislation early in the war authorized rapid depreciation allowances for plant and equipment designed for war production. This was set tentatively at 20 percent a year, but the principle was that expenditures for plant and equipment should be amortized when the war was over. A great many industries used their own money first in building plant and equipment. The treasurer of one great company states that his company used $28 million in this way, which by September 1946 had been amortized down to $2.4 million.

Government Defense Plant Corporation. But when very rapid expansion of plant and equipment was called for, few industries could go far with their own funds, and with such additional funds as the very unsatisfactory investment market could provide. Government corporations stepped in. There was a Defense Plant Corporation under the Reconstruction Finance Corporation. It built plants and leased them to industries, giving the

[2] *Commercial & Financial Chronicle,* April 16, 1942, p. 1542.
[3] *Ibid.,* May 11, 1944, p. 1949; *New York Times,* August 24, 1944.
[4] *Federal Reserve Bulletin,* August 1946, p. 887.

WAR PRODUCTION LOANS GUARANTEED BY WAR
DEPARTMENT, NAVY DEPARTMENT, AND MARITIME
COMMISSION THROUGH FEDERAL RESERVE BANKS UNDER
REGULATION V
(In thousands of dollars)

Date	Guaranteed loans authorized to date		Guaranteed loans outstanding		Additional amount available to borrowers under guarantee agreements outstanding
	Number	Amount	Total amount	Portions guaranteed	
1942					
June 30	565	310,680	81,108	69,674	137,888
Sept. 30	1,658	944,204	427,918	356,677	230,720
Dec. 31	2,665	2,688,397	803,720	632,474	1,430,121
1943					
Mar. 31	3,534	3,725,241	1,245,711	999,394	1,865,618
June 30	4,217	4,718,818	1,428,253	1,153,756	2,216,053
Sept. 30	4,787	5,452,498	1,708,022	1,413,159	2,494,855
Dec. 31	5,347	6,563,048	1,914,040	1,601,518	3,146,286
1944					
Mar. 31	5,904	7,466,762	2,009,511	1,680,046	3,615,963
June 30	6,433	8,046,672	2,064,318	1,735,777	3,810,797
Sept. 30	6,882	8,685,753	1,960,785	1,663,489	4,301,322
Dec. 30	7,434	9,310,582	1,735,970	1,482,038	4,453,586
1945					
Mar. 31	7,886	9,645,378	1,599,120	1,365,959	3,963,961
June 30	8,422	10,149,315	1,386,851	1,190,944	3,694,618
Sept. 30	8,695	10,313,868	1,073,892	916,851	3,043,674
Dec. 31	8,757	10,339,400	510,270	435,345	966,595
1946					
Jan. 31	8,761	10,340,275	427,278	363,048	764,093
Feb. 28	8,766	10,341,890	357,161	302,597	477,429
Mar. 30	8,768	10,342,690	271,793	230,110	363,010
Apr. 30	8,770	10,343,018	171,036	147,164	286,701
May 31	8,771	10,344,018	116,077	100,316	147,815
June 29	8,771	10,344,018	70,267	60,214	142,617

Note: The difference between guaranteed loans authorized and sum of loans outstanding and amounts available to borrowers under guarantee agreements outstanding represents amounts repaid, guarantees available but not completed, and authorizations expired or withdrawn.

industries, in the lease contract, the privilege of buying the plant and equipment if they wished when the war was over. The government corporations played a great role in our war finance. One speaks with diffidence of the figures of the government corporations. These corporations were an unknown jungle, their number and functions were very inadequately known, and their figures were not subject to audit—until Senator Harry F. Byrd, late in the war, was able to compel disclosure of the main facts about them, and finally to bring them under the auditing system of the comptroller general. The total assets of the government corporations, as of October 31, 1939, were reported at $12,105,000,000, and the total assets as of September 30, 1945, were reported at $34,247,000,000.[5]

Government Corporations Apparently Expand over $22 Billion During War. This would indicate an expansion of $22,142,000,000 in the assets of these corporations during the war. The Reconstruction Finance Corporation shows a swelling from $1,800,000,000 of assets on the earlier date, to $9,980,000,000 on the latter date. The War Shipping Administration, which did not exist in 1939, shows assets of $8,844,000,000 on September 30, 1945. On the other hand, the Home Owners Loan Corporation, which had assets of $2,976,000,000 on October 31, 1939, had disposed of virtually $2,000,000,000 of these assets by September 31, 1945. As against this, the Federal Land Banks, which do not appear in the figures for October 31, 1939, come into the figures for September 30, 1945, with $1,279,000,000 of assets. The United States Maritime Commission, which does not appear in the figures of the first date, had assets of $3,586,000,000 on September 30, 1945. It is probably impossible to give a precise figure for the contribution of these corporations to plant and equipment of war industries or to shipbuilding or other war activities. The comptroller general may be able to do this in later years. But that their contribution to the war effort was enormous is certain. Such information as is available regarding specific transactions in which they have engaged would indicate that a very high order of intelligence and devotion to the public interest, at least where high-ranking officials were concerned, was manifest in the war work of these corporations.

Reconstruction Finance Corporation. The figures for the RFC for September 30, 1945, include Defense Plant Corporation, Defense Supply Corporation, Metals Reserve Company, Rubber Reserve Company, and Disaster Loan Corporation, which previously were affiliates, but which as of July 1, 1945 (pursuant to the Public Law 109, approved June 30, 1945), were dissolved and merged with the RFC. Also included is the War Damage Corporation, which continues as an affiliate.

The principal assets of the Reconstruction Finance Corporation on October 31, 1939, were loans and preferred stocks of $1,676,000,000, out of total assets of $1,800,000,000. The principal assets of the Reconstruction Finance Corporation on September 30, 1945, were:

---

[5] *Ibid.*, January 1940, p. 43; July 1946, p. 788.

Land, structures, and equipment $6,868,000,000
Loans receivable 1,049,000,000
Commodities, supplies, and materials 942,000,000

Prompt Settlement of Canceled War Contracts. One further point is in order with respect to the government's dealing with the industries in prompt settlement of claims and freeing the working capital of the country for the problems of reconversion. The attitude of suspicion, of slow, meticulous negotiation, which characterized the relation of government with business at the beginning of the war, gave way very largely to an attitude of mutual confidence as the war went on. The appreciation by the Senate Finance Committee, the Congress, the Federal Reserve authorities, the government corporations, the army and the navy, and other procurement agencies of the government, of the need for rapid settlement of war contracts, if industry was to do its job in reconversion, led to the working out of very expeditious measures. The treasurer of one great corporation stated in September 1946 that his company's war contracts had been terminated and settled three months before, that the war was behind them, that they felt they had been justly treated, and that they were going ahead with new things.

Information was obtained in September 1946 from representative bankers who had wide experience in dealing with companies with war contracts. All agreed that the experience of the corporation quoted above was typical. One stated that he knew no exceptions and that neither he nor his customers had any concern about the possible reopening of the settlements by the General Accounting Office. They could be reopened only in cases of fraud, and he had confidence enough in his customers to be sure that this would not occur.

Another stated that the experience was typical, but that in judging his customers as credit risks he was careful to make sure that they had completed their 1945 renegotiations and that in cases where they had not done this, he took that fact into account in determining their lines of credit. He had regularly sent to the General Accounting Office carbon copies of all contracts in which they had assigned their claims against the government to his bank as a basis for loans, and he had always waited for an acknowledgment from the General Accounting Office at Washington before he advanced the money. These acknowledgments had always come promptly and there had been very little delay in making the loans.

One of the chiefs of another bank said that he had not troubled to wait for acknowledgment from the General Accounting Office before advancing money. He too had sent the carbon copy of the contract, but the General Accounting Office had authority only of review, it had no authority to prevent the loan, and its consent was not required for the making of the loan. He had not concerned himself about 1945 renegotiations. The General Accounting Office could reopen settlements only in cases of fraud, and he knew that his customers had not engaged in fraud.

Allegations of Fraud. Cases of fraud there have undoubtedly been. So great a volume of war business could not have been financed and put through without crooks coming in here and there. Allegations of fraud and excessive profits have been made before congressional committees. The comptroller general has raised serious questions with a congressional committee regarding costs and profits. Charges of official favoritism have been freely made, and of the judgment of top armed forces officials being corruptly overriden by high civilian officials.

Charges also of great waste and extravagance have been made in connection with our wartime expenditures in foreign countries, particularly in Latin America, but also in North Africa and elsewhere.

Woodrow Wilson and Charles Evans Hughes. It is worthwhile to recall at this point the episode recorded in chapter 4 of this book. Faced with similar charges, President Wilson called upon Charles Evans Hughes, who had been his opponent in the presidential election of 1916, and asked him to make a sweeping investigation. When Hughes made his report vindicating the integrity of the government, the country was satisfied. Wilson knew that his own hands were clean and believed that the hands of his subordinates were clean. He knew also that he could depend upon the integrity and fairness of the great lawyer, his political opponent.

81

Lend-Lease, Bretton Woods, and the British Loan— England's Postwar Position

In World War I, Britain and France and their Allies were able to finance their own purchases of commodities from the outside world, chiefly the United States, from the outbreak of the war in 1914 until our entrance into the war in April 1917. This story is told in an earlier chapter. They sent us gold, they resold American securities to us, and they borrowed through bonds placed with American investors through investment banking syndicates. After we entered the war, our Congress voted them intergovernmental loans of $10 billion, of which roughly $7 billion had been taken by the time of the Armistice, in November 1918.

Financial Resources of France and England in 1939. In World War II Britain and France were weaker in their holdings of American securities and cash than they had been in 1914. The Department of Commerce, in a press release of August 29, 1939, gave an estimate which placed the total investments of Great Britain and France in the United States at between $2.8 billion and $3 billion. It estimated holdings of $2,050,000,000 in stocks, bonds, and other long-term investments, and dollar balances and other short-term funds at $850,000,000. This estimate did not include their gold held under earmark in this country. The total earmarked gold for foreign account on July 31, 1939, was $1,287,000,000. Assuming that three-quarters of this was British and French, we have $965,000,000 to add to the totals above, making an aggregate of from $3,765,000,000 to $3,965,000,000. In addition to these resources already available in the United States, we must consider the gold of the Bank of France and the recently consolidated holdings of the Bank of England and the British Equalization Fund. The Bank of France had over $2.7 billion in gold, and the British consolidated gold holdings were probably between $2.2 billion and $2.4 billion. Adding these gold holdings at home to the gold, bank balances, and investments in the United States, we get nearly $9 billion. In addition, France and England both had investments in many other countries, very substantial parts of which could be converted into cash and foreign exchange. Canada had about $1.4 billion in investments and cash in the United States.

There was another important potential source of cash for the British Empire in the current production of gold in South Africa, Canada, and Australia. As compared with World War I, when an ounce of gold made only $20.67, an ounce of gold in 1939 made $35.00. The current flow of gold measured in dollars was very much greater in 1938 than it had been in 1913, as shown by the following table:

ANNUAL GOLD PRODUCTION IN DOLLARS

Country	1913	1936	1937	1938
South Africa ..	$181,875,000	$396,768,000	$410,710,000	$425,649,000
Canada	16,598,000	131,181,000	143,367,000	165,055,000
Australia......	45,619,000	40,118,000	46,982,000	54,264,000

The Vanishing Prestige of Pound and Franc. Both Britain and France in 1914, however, had a further asset which counted for very little in World War II, namely, the prestige of the pound sterling, the prestige of the franc, and the immense credit of London throughout the world. For most of what they got in World War I they did not have to pay in cash.

They had resources in 1939 adequate for their foreign purchases for a short war, but it is clear that they felt that these resources must be husbanded. When the pound sterling was blocked, almost immediately after the war broke out, there was the thought that they might get most of what they needed from within the empire, and the timidity and delays earlier referred to on the part of both British and French purchasing agents in the United States, even after France had been invaded in 1940, may have been in part attributable to this concern about inadequate internationally valid financial resources.

German Conquest of France Leaves British Financial Resources Wholly Inadequate. Moreover, after the German conquest of France, although most of the gold of France managed to escape, that gold was blocked. Our government would not allow the Petain government of France to make use of the French gold which had come here, and no other authority was recognized as having the right to use it. England's own resources alone, on the basis of the figures given above, were thus very inadequate.

American Lend-Lease System to the Rescue. Speedily, however, our own government began to finance Great Britain, long before we ourselves got into the war. On September 3, 1940, President Roosevelt let the British have fifty overage destroyers to protect their convoys, in exchange for leases of airplane bases in the British Empire. Moreover, on March 11, 1941, we began the "lend-lease" system, under which we allowed countries fighting Germany to get money from our Treasury, not in exchange for promissory notes in dollars, but for whatever consideration the President of the United States should regard as adequate. We seemed to have learned at least one thing from the experience of World War I, namely, that governmental debts created for war purposes, repayable in cash, create incredible postwar difficulties. Gigantic sums were advanced under the lend-lease arrangements, especially after our entrance into the war, to Britain, Russia, France, China, and other countries.

TOTAL LEND-LEASE AID, BY COUNTRY*
March 11, 1941–December 31, 1945

Country	In Dollars
British Empire	30,753,304,000
USSR	11,141,470,000
France and possessions	2,377,072,000
China	1,335,632,000
Brazil	319,494,000
Other American republics	114,646,000
Netherlands	178,064,000
Belgium	82,884,000
Greece	76,838,000
Norway	37,708,000
Other countries	100,186,000
Total charged to foreign governments	46,517,298,000
Aid not charged to foreign governments	2,578,827,000
Total lend-lease aid	49,096,125,000

* Twenty-second Report to Congress on Lend-Lease Operations, for the Period Ended December 31, 1945, Table 1, p. 17.

The Growth of Blocked Sterling During the War. Britain's imports from countries other than the United States, including the Argentine, the British dominions, and India, were, in very considerable degree, not paid for but rather carried as debts in the form of blocked sterling. Part of this actually took the form of balances in British banks, but a great deal of it was simply in the form of bookkeeping entries or British government securities. The details are obscure.

	(£ 1,000s)	Date	
India	500,000	July 16,	1943
Eire	121,458	March	1943
Canada*	157,300	August	1943
Egypt	71,200	December	1942
Malaya	58,000	July	1943
Australia	64,000	May 31,	1943
New Zealand	34,000	February	1943
Argentina	17,500	December	1942

* Interest-free loan.

Blocked Sterling in India. The worst part of this, and the worst-handled part of this, appears to have been in the British relations with India. The *Economist* (London) of August 7, 1943, gave particulars for seven countries, all but one being within the British Empire, in the preceding table.

The *Economist* added that other accounts not included in the tabulation would bring the total of such sterling indebtedness easily above the one billion mark. This figure would, presumably, include the prewar balances. The *Economist* further added that the totals were growing, and that, in particular, the sterling assets piling up to the credit of the Reserve Bank of India were likely to rise by an annual increment of about £300 million.

Creates Appalling Inflation in India. Parenthetically, the *Economist* expressed great concern over the growth of the balances with India, which, it said, "is bestowing on India one of the most pronounced inflations experienced by any belligerent country." The growth of Indian balances had been held down at first by Indian use of the balances to reduce long-term Indian sterling debt, but only £12,250,000 of this debt remained in 1943, and this brake on the accumulation of sterling by India had been virtually removed. A later issue of the *Economist,* that of October 2, 1943, returns to the subject of the inflation in India, evidently very dangerous, which seems to have been intimately connected with the issue of rupee notes in India against these blocked sterling balances. Indian war finance was clearly badly handled by both British and Indian governments.

No effort is made here to give data regarding direct financial relations between the Indian government and the British government. The following figures from the Reserve Bank of India, however, show how enormously the Reserve Bank's figures for note issue have been swollen against sterling securities.

ISSUE DEPARTMENT—RESERVE BANK OF INDIA
(In rupees)

	March 1946	November 1940
Sterling securities	11,303,000,000	1,315,000,000
Note circulation	12,340,000,000	2,291,000,000

The banking department of the Reserve Bank of India had, as the two main items in its balance sheet, in May 1946, "balances abroad," 5,931,000,000 rupees, and deposits, 6,302,000,000 rupees. These two items, balances abroad and deposits, are close together in size and have risen together. The same figures in November 1940 were: balances abroad, 423,000,000, and deposits, 606,000,000. A reasonable supposition would be that the balances abroad are chiefly blocked balances in London, and that the swollen deposits of the banking department represent the exchange of blocked balances in London for deposits in India.

As the rupee was still quoted in the official exchange rates at 30.182¢ in June 1946 (a rate that continued in 1948), it is clear that we had here, in

Britain's obligations to India, vast sums. The rupee was very greatly overvalued at this 30¢ figure, and one extraordinary consequence of this was that the American dollar stood at a startling discount in terms of gold in the Indian gold market. Information from a great New York bank in August 1946 was that in India gold had run as high at $70–$75 per ounce, and this abnormality continued.

The Gigantic Total of Blocked Sterling in 1946. At the Bretton Woods Conference in the summer of 1944, Lord Keynes revealed that the British blocked balances would be $12 billion by the end of 1944. There was certainty, of course, that they would continue to increase until the war was over. Professor John H. Williams, testifying in June 1945 before the Senate Committee on Banking and Currency regarding the Bretton Woods proposals,[1] expressed the opinion that $16 billion by the end of the war did not seem to him to be too high.

The *Economist* (London)[2] stated that the chancellor of the Exchequer, in replying to a questioner, said that the "blocked sterling balances" on March 31, 1946, totaled £3.5 billion, which at $4 to the pound would mean $14 billion. The *Economist* questioned, however, whether the chancellor's information was exact, and thought that this might be a net rather than a gross figure. The *Economist* added that in the case of the Reserve Bank of India, sterling holdings had continued to increase. The *Economist* thought that there had been much worse deterioration, in the period June 30, 1945, to the end of March 1946, than the figures would indicate, because Britain had, to some extent, been covering her deficit by living on the lend-lease pipeline and surpluses.

It has been clear since the outbreak of the war, when sterling first broke violently and was then pulled up to $4.02 for "official sterling"—with free sterling increasingly blocked until almost none remained—that a free pound would go very low in the foreign exchange markets. This volume has criticized Britain's financial policy in the period of the 1920s and 1930s, but during the war, when Britain was fighting for her own life, and when for a long time she alone was fighting for us as well as for herself, there has been no reason why she should not get whatever credit she could wherever she could get it, and on whatever terms she could get it. That this involved great hardship for certain weaker countries in the British zone of influence and for India, is, of course, much to be regretted.

The Keynes-Morgenthau Plan and the Blocked Balances. It seemed right, however, to resist the effort to get a postwar situation in which all this vast blocked debt of England would be validated at the expense of the solvent countries of the world, and primarily of the United States. Particularly

[1] U.S., Congress, Senate, Committee on Banking and Currency, *Hearings on the Bretton Woods Agreements Act*, June 21, 1945, p. 332.

[2] June 15, 1946

indefensible was that part of the Keynes plan for an "International Clearing
Union,"[3] which proposed (Section 34) that the Clearing Union should
expand credit, so that countries owing these balances should be able to
regard them as liquid, while the countries which owed these balances
would have no corresponding drain on their liquid resources. And likewise
indefensible was that part of the original Morgenthau plan,[4] which appeared at the same time, that provided that the countries in the plan should
cooperate to prevent ownership of these blocked balances from being
transferred, but that the countries that owned them might sell them to the
International Fund, with the International Fund to be gradually repaid up to
eighty percent of these balances by the end of twenty-three years.[5]

Lord Keynes may not have known, when he made his original proposal
in May 1943, how big these blocked balances were, though one cannot be
sure of this because his plan was for a fund, which, as Professor John H.
Williams showed, could theoretically expand to $30 billion with a further
expansion possible to the extent that the blocked balances were absorbed.
But by the time of the Bretton Woods Agreement, Lord Keynes had
withdrawn the proposal that the blocked balances should be absorbed, and
recognized that Great Britain's figures were far too big to be handled in that
way.

Indeed, the blocked balances provisions were dropped as the Keynes-
Morgenthau plan was revised by the "Experts of Thirty Nations" in the text
released by the United States Treasury on Friday, April 21, 1944.

The Evolution of the Bretton Woods Agreements. The power of individual
governments before World War II to control currency depreciation and

[3] Text issued by British Information Services, 30 Rockefeller Plaza, New York, April 8,
1943, and reproduced in *Federal Reserve Bulletin,* June 1943.

[4] *Federal Reserve Bulletin,* June 1943.

[5] This writer opposed both plans and all subsequent modifications of them, including the
final Bretton Woods Agreement, on many other grounds as well, in the following documents:

(1) "Postwar Stabilization of Foreign Exchange—The Keynes-Morgenthau Plan
Condemned—Outline of a Fundamental Solution," an address before the Los Angeles
Chamber of Commerce, May 11, 1943. This was reproduced in full in two installments of the
Commercial & Financial Chronicle, May 20 and 27, 1943. It appears in the *Economic
Bulletin,* issued by the Capital Research Company of Los Angeles, May 11, 1943. It was
reprinted by the Economists' National Committee on Monetary Policy, running through
several editions there. It appears in full in *Vital Speeches,* June 1, 1943, and *Banker's
Magazine,* May 1943.

(2) "Postwar Foreign Exchange Stabilization Further Considered," *Commercial & Financial Chronicle,* December 16, 1943.

(3) "International Currency—Gold Versus Bancor or Unitas," address before Chamber of
Commerce of state of New York, February 3, 1944. This address appears in full in proceedings of the chamber and in *Commercial & Financial Chronicle.*

(4) "The Keynes-Morgenthau Plan as Revised by the Experts of Thirty Nations," *Commercial & Financial Chronicle,* May 4, 1944.

(5) U.S., Congress, Senate, Committee on Banking and Currency, *Hearings on the Bretton
Woods Agreements Act,* June 22, 1945; my testimony is partially reproduced in the text below.

exchange depreciation, in countries following unsound currency and fiscal policies, had, as we have seen in an earlier chapter, proved utterly inadequate in every country except Hitler's Germany. The idea arose that if the various governments would only cooperate in this matter, it would be possible for them collectively to do what they pleased with internal currency and finance, and still keep stable exchange rates. They could prevent wicked flights of capital by international cooperation. They could prevent transactions which recognized currency depreciation in terms of gold or of exchange of other countries. Countries which had overexpanded credit could continue to have easy money markets with safety. This is probably the root idea of the original Keynes plan. And Secretary Morgenthau, who had prided himself on reducing interest rates while borrowing many tens of billions a year, probably liked this aspect of the plan, and probably liked also the idea of continuing after the war the numerous controls of international transactions which had been in his hands during the war.

The Keynes-Morgenthau plan evolved through several versions. The original versions of the Keynes plan and the Morgenthau plan will be found in the *Federal Reserve Bulletin* of June 1943. There was subsequently a revision of the Morgenthau plan issued by the United States Treasury on July 10, 1943, and a new proposal was presented on October 8, 1943, by the Treasury, which proposed, as an addition or supplement to the International Fund, an international investment bank. These various proposals were subsequently revised, after a conference of representatives of more than thirty nations, in a new text issued by the United States Treasury on April 21, 1944. Finally the Bretton Woods Conference, participated in by representatives of many nations, July 1–22, 1944, culminated in an elaborate document known as the Bretton Woods Agreements.

The agreements called for an International Monetary Fund and an International Bank for Reconstruction and Development. The Fund was to be concerned with limiting variation in exchange rates, though any country was privileged to drop its exchange ten percent merely on its own initiative, and to drop its exchange an additional ten percent unless the Fund should object within seventy-two hours.

Each participating country was to put into the Fund certain amounts of gold, if it had it, and less if it did not have it, and to put in its own currency and its own securities, up to certain quotas. And each country was privileged to call upon the Fund for the currencies of other nations needed to meet its current obligations in the other countries up to a certain percentage of its quota per annum.

Participating countries were expected to remove exchange restrictions within five years after the beginning of the operation of the Fund, though Section 4 of Article 14 of the agreement on the International Fund clearly contemplates the possibility that certain countries will retain their restrictions longer than five years.

The total resources of the Fund, counting gold, and good currencies, and bad currencies, and securities all together were to be $8.8 billion, of which the contribution of the United States was to be $2.75 billion. But most of the $8.8 billion would not be internationally valid. The actually lendable part would have been about $4 billion. Of that, our contribution would be about 70 percent.[6]

The control of the Fund was to be in the hands of an international board with the United States in the minority, though the United States was to have a veto where a change in the gold content of the American dollar was concerned. This was particularly important in connection with Section 7 of Article 4 of the Fund agreement, which provided for uniform changes in the par values of all the currencies, but which required every member with ten percent or more of the total of the quotas to agree before such changes could be made.

The International Bank was to be primarily an investment institution, buying for its own account, or underwriting for sale in various markets, or guaranteeing for sale in various markets, the obligations of countries needing long-term investment funds. Here again there was international control, with the United States in the minority, although both in the Fund and in the bank it was recognized that the United States would be the principal creditor. A certain measure of protection for the United States was provided in that the bank could not sell its obligations or obligations guaranteed by it in any country without that country's consent. But this protection did not apply to the use of funds which a country might already have contributed to the bank. The subscriptions to the resources of the bank were to total $9,100,000,000, of which the contribution of the United States was to be $3,175,000,000.

Powerful Opposition to Bretton Woods Plan. Opposition to these proposals was strong and a prolonged fight was made. The United States Treasury issued a tremendous amount of propaganda for the measure, using public funds to influence congressional action in a way which was challenged as not lawful. The technical objections—and the matter was highly technical—were given little weight. The propaganda appealed to the almost universal feeling that international cooperation was necessary after the war, and made it appear that to reject Bretton Woods was to reject international cooperation. This propaganda convinced an important body of excellent people in the country, probably a majority of the able people who were not technically trained in money and banking.

Nevertheless, the powerful presentation of the case against the Fund

---

[6] See the able testimony of Prof. B. H. Beckhart before the Senate committee June 22, 1945, pp. 409–10.

before the House of Representatives Committee on Banking and Currency[7] startled the Treasury and shook the confidence of the Congress in the proposal.

But President Truman Endorsed Plan in "Honeymoon." The legislation validating the Bretton Woods Agreements would probably have been defeated but for the circumstance that President Roosevelt died in April 1945 and that President Truman, at the beginning of his "honeymoon" period, endorsed it. The House of Representatives passed the Bretton Woods Agreements bill, June 7, 1945.

The fight was continued before the Senate Committee on Banking and Currency. The following is an advance summary of the main portion of this writer's testimony before that committee on June 22, 1945, which summarizes the main points in the indictment of the Bretton Woods proposals.

The Fallacies of the Bretton Woods Plan. The great job of the government in straightening out the postwar world is political, not economic. Governments have long experience and sometimes even great skill in arms, in diplomacy, in justice and police. In the direct handling of economic life, governments are usually clumsy and ineffective. In economic life their main business should be that of traffic cop, not that of driver, and above all not that of back-seat driver.

The Congress has made an immense forward step in the passage of the Reciprocal Tariff legislation designed to help remove governmental restraints on international trade. In the great postwar emergency, we must, of course, do a great deal more than that. We must help Europe both with charity and with loans. We must not disguise charity in the form of loans which cannot be paid.

In making loans we must meet fully the great obligations of the lender to see to it that the loans are (a) adequate for the purpose; (b) not excessive; and (c) properly employed for the purpose for which they are made.

Experience After Last War. Loans to stabilize exchange rates which are not accompanied by conditions that ensure the stabilization of the weaker currencies, are wasteful and useless loans. Small loans made under proper conditions, designed to stabilize, not exchange rates, but currencies, can really accomplish their purpose. We saw this in the period that followed the last war. We wasted $6½ billion between the Armistice in November 1918 and September 1920, first in stabilizing and then in supporting the exchange rates of Europe. Our own government provided but $3 billion of this in direct loans to European governments. Private creditors put up another $3½ billion. Europe responded by buying from the United States great quantities of commodities, many of which she ought to have been producing herself and many of which she could not afford to consume. She bought finished manufactures instead of the raw materials and the industrial equipment she ought to have been buying. She bought a great many luxuries.

---

[7] Among the opponents of the measure before the House committee were Gen. Leonard P. Ayres, Leon Fraser, president of the First National Bank of New York, Prof. E. W. Kemmerer, and Dr. Melchior Palyi.

Meanwhile, continental European billigerents did nothing toward straightening out internal finances. As long as the foreign exchange markets would take their currencies the finance ministers of the continental European belligerents took the easy way. They did not tax, they did not borrow from their own people, they met every demand for expenditure and they leaned on the central bank of issue for their money. While our dollars supported that money, this process could go on.

England, the one belligerent of Europe which was getting on her feet financially, balancing her budget, joined us in this. She interposed her financial strength between us and the weak Continent. We gave her credits by taking sterling and by taking her dollar obligations and we sold her the francs and the lire and the drachmas which our exports created. We also sold her goods which she resold to the Continent. Late in 1920 we and England both had had enough of this. We pulled up and the great crash of 1920–21 came.

Must Stabilize Currencies to Stabilize Exchanges. After this costly lesson of trying to stabilize exchanges without stabilizing currency we did very much more modest things successfully. In 1923, after the Austrian crown had dropped to 14,000 to 1 in terms of gold, under the auspices of the League of Nations, a stabilization loan of about $113 million was made to Austria, placed in the investment markets of various countries, especially the United States. This was accompanied by conditions involving drastic reforms in Austria, curtailed government expenditures, increased taxes, balanced budget and definite stabilization of the currency on a gold basis. It worked.

In 1924 we did the same thing for Hungary, sending Jeremiah Smith of Boston over to sit on the lid to countersign checks and to see to it that the funds were used for the purpose indicated. Smith represented the foreign creditors. My recollection is that the Hungarian loan was about $50 million. It worked.

In 1924 we did the same thing for Germany under the Dawes Plan. This time the loan was $200 million, of which $100 million was provided by New York. This loan was accompanied by drastic conditions—increased taxes, curtailed expenses, a balanced budget and definite stabilization on gold, and foreign supervision of certain of the taxes, a foreign representative in the Reichsbank and a foreign commissioner sitting in Germany.

Those who wonder how we can ever bring continental Europe back to the gold standard may reflect upon this episode. The Dawes Plan contained a provision that Germany should come back to the gold standard, but that it was probably inexpedient to do so immediately. This last clause was reluctantly consented to by the Americans on the Dawes Committee. The French and Italians had been sentimental about it. It was not fair that Germany should have the gold standard when France and Italy could not have it. The British were not quite ready to come back to the gold standard, and their view was that Germany should go to the sterling standard and then England would take care both of sterling and Germany. But neither Washington nor New York was satisfied with this clause. Our $100 million participation was necessary for the success of the plan.

It was quietly made clear that Germany should come immediately to the gold standard if the loan was to be placed in New York. Germany did so! The big creditor is in a position to make reasonable terms when he makes a loan. But he must make his terms then—not afterward.

The effect of the restoration of sound currency in Germany was magical. They had been utterly demoralized by the deflation they had gone through. Business started up immediately. There was a strong boom and full employment. This was interrupted by a short-lived crisis in the winter of 1925–26, but full activity and full employment were speedily resumed which carried over into the international difficulties in 1929.

We did the same thing with Poland with about $72 million, sending the Honorable Charles S. Dewey over to act as representative of the creditors and to countersign checks. This worked.

Small Loans Will Do the Job. Small sums, properly used, lent country by country, will do the job. A few hundreds of millions properly used will stabilize the currencies of continental Europe. Not all of them will need it. It is not easy to see that France or the Netherlands will need it, for example. Russia has no stabilization problem at all. Her currency does not get into the foreign exchange markets. Her dealings in international trade are in terms of dollars or in the currencies of the other countries with whom she deals. Foreigners do not hold deposits in Russian banks which they can sell in the foreign exchange markets nor are the Russians allowed to throw rubles upon the foreign exchange market.

Opposes International Fund. I am opposed to the whole idea of the International Monetary Fund. It lends money without proper conditions. It gives quotas to countries which need them, and to countries which do not need them. It gives quotas to countries whose finances are deteriorating and to countries which are getting on their feet. A false analogy has been made between these quotas and lines of credit at a bank. No bank gives lines of credit this way. A line of credit is not one of a set of fixed quotas to a group of would-be borrowers, good, bad and indifferent. A line of credit is a specific understanding with a specific borrower based on the facts of his individual position, and if those facts change, the line of credit is revised. If the would-be borrower lies to the bank about his balance sheet or about his profits, or any other essential point, the bank may cancel the line of credit, and if the borrower fails to notify the bank of any essential change in his financial position the bank may cancel the line of credit. The quotas under the Fund are nothing like lines of credit.

Sound lending is a process in which the creditor makes conditions. When he is dealing with a strong borrower, he cannot make special conditions, or competing lenders will gladly take the loan, but when he is dealing with an embarrassed borrower he can, should and must, both in his own interests and in the interests of the borrower, make conditions that assure the safety of the loan. The Fund puts the debtors—the borrowers—in control of the lending. The notion that there will be any proper restraints upon the use of the funds under these conditions is absurd. The Fund has very inadequate and vague provisions in any case for restricting or withholding credits within the quotas, and these vague provisions are to be applied by a board of governors, a majority of whose members represent necessitous borrowers all of whom want to borrow more. No one of them will impose adequate restraints upon another similarly placed lest he invite retaliation when his own country is involved.

There should not be any Fund. If we stabilize the currencies one by one, the normal operations of the foreign exchange markets will keep the exchange rates stabilized and no Fund is needed.

Fund Sanctions Exchange Restrictions. The Fund is erroneously represented as an institution designed to eliminate foreign exchange restrictions. In the first place, it sanctions existing restrictions for at least five years. In the second place, it sanctions new restraints even in the countries which have free exchanges. It proposes to leave exchanges free only on current transactions and proposes international governmental cooperation to control inernational capital movements. Now this control of international capital movements is something we never talked about in the old days of free exchanges and sound moneys. The problem arises only when you have a shaky currency that people are afraid of. Then men get frightened and try to get their money out of the country. And then the government whose unbalanced budget and whose abuse of credit and currency has caused the money to become shaky, begins to blame the people who are trying to run away and begins to blame the foreigners who are trying to take their funds out of the country. The government itself created "hot" money by making their country a "hot" place for money. The way to avoid hot money is to balance your budget and redeem your currency on demand.

This plan for international control of capital movements is vicious in the extreme. It is designed to shelter unsound finance and unsound currency policies by international governmental cooperation. The plan will generate hot money. It will create new nervousness on the part of every man who has funds in a foreign country or who knows how to put funds out of his own country.

Generating Hot Money. There are two other provisions in particular that will generate hot money.

(a) The plan sanctions changes in the gold content of the various countries. They may drop ten percent merely on their own initiative and they may drop twenty percent unless the Fund makes objection within seventy-two hours. Even then, as Edward Brown has admitted in his *Chicago Journal of Commerce* article, there is no reason to expect the Fund to make effective objection when a powerful country wants to drop as much as 20 percent.

Now this possibility hanging over the markets all the time will create hot money which would not otherwise exist. Men will constantly be watching, constantly making plans to shift their funds when they face a chance of a twenty percent or even a ten percent loss on their capital. Foreign deposits paying three to four percent in banks of a country whose currency may drop ten percent with no notice, or twenty percent on seventy-two hours' notice are not attractive.

(b) The second amazing provision which will definitely generate hot money is that authorizing the Fund to declare a currency scarce and authorizing individual countries in that case to ration out the scarce currency. It is the dollar which will become scarce. What if that happens? Foreign debtors can no longer get dollars with which to pay American creditors for goods that have been shipped. No matter how many francs the French debtor may have, he cannot use them to pay. Exchange transactions, except at par, are forbidden in France and in the United States under the terms of the Fund. There is a fixed exchange *rate*, but there is no exchange *market*. In 1919 the American exporter caught with depreciating francs could at least sell his francs, take his loss and pay off his own debts. Or the French importer, obliged to pay dollars, could buy the dollars at a higher price and pay his debts. A depreciating exchange is nothing like so bad as a blocked exchange. It is flexible; it gives warning in advance. Men faced with this possibility of having their funds frozen by a declaration of scarce currencies would be constantly on the lookout ahead to get their funds out of the country where dollars are going to be scarce before the declaration comes.

The Distinction Between Current Transactions and Capital Movements Impossible in Practice. Now how can a man get his funds out of a country if capital movements are controlled and only current transactions are free?

There are a multitude of ways. Goods can be shipped out of the country and the proceeds left abroad. You do not need a foreign exchange transaction to do it. Or a business having borrowing relations with banks in New York and in Paris could pay off its New York banks and increase it borrowings in Paris which is a means of transferring capital from Paris to New York. The devices are so multitudinous that Lord Keynes admitted in his original draft of the plan for a clearing union that control of capital movements probably involves control of all foreign exchange transactions, and I would go further and say that it involves control of all borrowing and lending transactions by companies doing business in several countries and of all export and import movements, not to mention the searching of pockets and traveling bags of every traveler, and censorship of the mails. This Fund plan is erroneously represented as a plan for free international transactions.

Criticisms of the Bank. The International Bank proposed is also subject to the criticism that the borrowers dominate it. In a financial institution the lenders should control. If we are going to lend, and we should lend, let us do our own lending; let us have an American institution. Let this American institution go joint account when suitable with foreign institutions. Let it go joint account with private investment bankers. Incidentally, it is highly desirable that we use private investment funds as far as possible rather than government money in our financial aid to Europe. Moreover, it is far easier for private bankers to negotiate with foreign countries in such a way as to impose proper conditions than it is for government to do it. The banker does not make demands; he expresses his opinion as to what the investors of his country would require, with great courtesy. He raises no diplomatic issues. An American governmental financial institution could very well let investment bankers initiate and originate many propositions, then pass upon them and decide whether they wish to go joint account.

One great vice in both these plans is that the whole thing rests on new debt rather than on equity money. There is no provision for equity money. Now, if we have an American governmental institution, it could join American investment bankers in underwriting (not guaranteeing) stocks rather than bonds of European industries for sale to American investors. It is desirable that there should be American investment companies which put out their own stocks in this country, and which use their funds in buying a diversification of European stocks, diversified both by industries and by countries. Such companies should seek venture capital only. They should notify the public that their securities are not for widows and orphans. But the same thing is true of bonds in Europe under existing conditions. Bonds would be good if the countries revive. They wouldn't be otherwise. Stocks would be good if countries revive and prosper, and not otherwise.

Advantages of Equity Financing. The great advantage of the stocks is twofold: (a) with real revival in Europe, the returns would be large to American investors; (b) in bad years Europe will not have to pay any dividends. In good years she can pay large dividends. It is risk money that we are putting into Europe, and it should be put in in risk form as far as possible.

The total amounts of loans contemplated to Europe, taking into account the Fund, the bank, and other proposals, are far too great from the standpoint of Europe's ability to repay. European governments can repay to the extent (a) they can create excess of taxes over expenditures in their own country, and (b) they can transfer these back to the United States by giving us goods and services. They must pay with hams, with bottles of wine, with diversified manufactures, with shipping services, with entertaining tourists, with a multitude of services. Viewed in this way, it is clear that it is to their interest and to our interest to hold the amounts down to what can be handled, not by the printing of money, but by the movement of goods and services. To the extent that we go beyond this we are giving charity in the guise of loans, and to the extent that we do this we are inviting default, repudiation and international bitterness in the future. Let us give charity where we must. Let us lend when we can safely, but less us, above all, realize that we cannot support Europe.

The big job of the restoration of Europe is Europe's job.

I reject the absurd fear that we can't get other nations to cooperate if we refuse this plan. By the way, none of them has accepted the plan. Even the experts are not committed, except as they have agreed to refer it to their governments. But if we are prepared to lend money, the borrowers will certainly cooperate on our terms if these are reasonable.

We cannot, moreover, amend this measure adequately, even assuming that we want to go on with it in the way which this bill proposes. The bill has tried to protect the framework of the Bretton Woods proposals. The proposals themselves, even if we wish to use them, must be changed. Even the modest changes which the bill seeks to accomplish cannot surely be obtained. We put our money in first, under this bill, and then afterward ask them to change the plan. That is no way to lend money!

Other Vices of Plan. But there are further major technical vices in the measure as drawn. One which I would emphasize strongly is that the Fund proposes to use only central banks and stabilization funds in its transactions. We are to use Reserve money in making foreign loans. Our Reserve money should be the last money used for that purpose, not the first. The desirable way to make foreign loans is with investors' money, or if the government is going to do it, with taxpayers' money. Second, in foreign exchange transactions, short-run transactions, commercial banking money should be used. The worst way is to use Reserve money.

When payments are made out of the Federal Reserve bank to the Fund, the dollars come back into the reserves of our member banks, increasing our bank reserves, making our money rates easier in the United States—making it easier to lend at home because we have lent abroad. This is vicious. The other side of it is that when France borrows from the Fund, putting francs into the Fund to provide dollars for a French importer, this means payments of francs into the Bank of France from French commercial banks, tightening the money markets of France.

Every foreign exchange transaction of the Fund makes unnecessary money market complications in every country involved. This is technically vicious. If the Fund is going to operate in the foreign exchange markets, it should deal with the market as a whole, and should make large use of the deposits in commercial banks rather than of central banks.

But the whole plan is vicious, artificial, self-defeating.

In summary, I reject both the bank and the Fund. I propose instead an American institution which, cooperating where feasible with other institutions, shall make necessary loans, shall engage in necessary underwriting of equities, and, above all, shall make stabilization loans to individual countries one at a time, putting gold into their central banks on conditions of budget balancing and gold stabilization with, where necessary, supervision of the uses to which the funds are put.

Gift, with Conditions, Needed by England. It was obvious, and indeed recognized in the Bretton Woods Agreements, that the Fund could not help in Britain's great financial problem, which was the problem of unmanageable blocked balances. What was needed was a gift of three to four billion dollars to England with strings attached. The grounds for a gift were (1) that England was our partner who had spent herself in our joint life struggle, and (2) that we needed a powerful British Empire in the international picture to help us hold our own with Russia. It should be a gift rather than a loan (a) because England's ability to repay a loan was doubtful in the extreme, and (b) because the effort to pay this loan would in any case have left her less strong than our interests required her to be. But the gift should have been made with conditions. It should solve England's blocked balance problem, it should free the pound sterling, and it should stabilize the pound. The condition especially to be emphasized was that England should make compositions with her creditors on the blocked balances on terms that seemed adequate to the United States. Before we turned the money over to Britain we should have a comprehensive plan which America could approve. Part of the gift should be used in "sweetening" the settlements which England made with her creditors, giving them some immediate cash as they consented to scale down the debts, to take long-term obligations for the reduced debts and to reduce rates of interest. We should be sure that the gift really solved England's problem before we turned the money over.[8]

The Bretton Woods Plan Adopted. The fight before the Senate committee was futile.[9] The committee promptly recommended the bill and the Senate promptly passed it. The Bretton Woods Agreements are in effect, and the two institutions have been inaugurated, though Russia did not join either.

The British Loan. In addition, an American loan to Great Britain was negotiated, for a total of $4.4 billion. Of this, $650 million was to be in settlement of all lend-lease and reciprocal aid obligations of the United Kingdom to the United States, of British acquisitions of American surplus property, and of British acquisitions of the United States government's interests in installations located in the United Kingdom. The $650 million was also to include estimated supplies still in the pipelines headed for Britain after V-J Day, through lend-lease and reciprocal aid channels, less certain sums due to the United Kingdom.

The other and much larger part of the loan to Britain, $3.75 billion, was to be a line of credit extended by the government of the United States to the government of the United Kingdom, which could be drawn upon any time between the effective date of the agreement and December 31, 1951.

The American negotiant, in working out the terms of this loan, was W. L. Clayton, who had been transferred from the government loan organizations to the State Department. He did as skillful a job as was possible under the limitations which he worked. Had he been able to negotiate the terms of a gift instead of a loan, better results could have been obtained. But he worked under the necessity of making a loan, with provisions whereby the principal would be repaid and under which some interest at least would be paid. The interest rate agreed upon was two percent, but interest was not to begin until December 31, 1951. Provision was made also for waiver of interest payments in years when the government of the United Kingdom requested it, and when the government of the United Kingdom and the International Monetary Fund should make certain representations regarding Britain's international financial relations.

---

[8] This posposal was made by this writer in testimony before the Senate committee on June 22, 1945 (see U.S., Congress, Senate, Committee on Banking and Currency, *Hearings on the Bretton Woods Agreements Act,* p. 394). John H. Williams, without elaborating, had made a somewhat similar proposal in his testimony before the same committee on June 21 (*Hearings,* pp. 335–37). He personally favored a $3 billion gift under lend-lease, but, regarding this as politically impossible, he proposed a credit to England on the lowest possible terms. Professor Williams did not specify the conditions under which this special credit should be granted.

[9] A powerful case against the Fund was made before the Senate committee by Prof. John H. Williams, Allan C. Sproul, president of the New York Federal Reserve Bank, Prof. B. H. Beckhart, and Dr. Melchior Palyi. Williams, and most of the other opponents of the Fund, advocated the bank, or at least made no opposition to it.

One of the central purposes in the proposal of a gift to England was that the gift should be used in part for sweetening the settlements which Britain would make with her creditors under blocked balances. The terms of the loan agreement, however, precluded this, and the United Kingdom undertook to discharge outstanding obligations to third countries "from resources other than this line of credit."

"Free Sterling" on Current Account Within One Year. Clayton succeeded also in making arrangements that seemed to promise free sterling so far as current account transactions were concerned throughout all "Sterling Area" countries, within one year after the effect of the agreement, "unless in exceptional cases a later date is agreed upon after consultation," and that discrimination arising from the so-called Sterling Area "dollar pool" would be entirely removed, and that each member of the Sterling Area would have its current sterling and dollar receipts at its free disposition for current transactions anywhere.

The government of the United Kingdom agreed that after the effective date of this agreement, it would not apply exchange controls in such a manner as to restrict (a) payments or transfers in respect to products of the United States imported into the United Kingdom or other transactions between the two countries, or (b) the use of sterling balances to the credit of residents of the United States arising out of current transactions. Clayton was obliged to concede, however, that nothing in this part of the agreement should effect Article 7 of the agreement of the International Monetary Fund, which relates to scarce currencies—a provision discussed above in the summary of testimony before the Senate committee on the Bretton Woods Agreements.

Clayton was able, however, to bring Great Britain to agree that after one year she would not continue restrictions on payments and transfers for current transactions, and that she would not invoke the provisions of Article 14, Section 2, of the Fund agreement, which permits restrictions on payments and transfers for current international transactions.

The terms of the loan definitely contemplate restoration of multilateral trade and free exchange. But the British have succeeded in bringing in many qualifying clauses.

Both countries ratified this loan agreement, the President signing the American legislation of July 15, 1946.

Britain's Position in 1946. Britain's position, even with this loan, remained a difficult one. The British statement regarding the problem which was presented to our government in connection with the British loan agreement, a British government white paper (Cmd. 6707), appears in the *Federal Reserve Bulletin* of January 1946. It discusses the prospective financial deficits in Britain's international relations during the transitional period, "provisionally estimated at from three to five years, before internal and external adjustments can be made in the British economy adequate to restore equilibrium." The loss of the British export trade during the war was very great and this was, to a large extent, the consequence of a deliberate act of policy. The export trade must be rebuilt. The loss of shipping was very great. The loss of overseas investments was very great. The increase of overseas debt we have discussed. The loss of cash reserves was very great, though they have been, in part, rebuilt.

Britain, having survived the war with her economy still a going concern, should be able to work through these difficulties with the assistance which our loan gives her, if she will follow traditional orthodox economic and financial policies. Whether she can do this, with the large measure of governmental controls which her Labor government may be expected to continue and even to intensify, and with the cheap money policy which neither political party in England has shown any disposition to change, and with the antipathy to the gold standard and to fixed exchange rates which appears to be widespread in the British electorate, raises grave questions.

To build up an adequate export trade means that the British people must offer their products to the outside world at flexible prices which meet competition. The alternatives here are (1) that Britain develop flexible costs, including wages, and (2) that Britain engage in the process of depreciating her currency in the foreign exchanges. The latter alternative, however, is no alternative, if one is trying to build export trade. We saw evidence enough of this in the period following World War I, in the cases of Germany, France, Belgium, and Italy, the figures for which appear in preceding chapters. The use of this resource on Britain's part would invite retaliation, and could very easily break the machinery of the International Monetary Fund. Further, the use of this, or the anticipated use of this, would greatly lessen the volume of private credit in the outside world, which Britain will need.

Britain, first among all great countries, needs a large, freely moving international trade, and a large volume of internationally valid cash. It she undertakes to carry through a program of domestic reconstruction based on expanding bank credit, she speedily runs up against difficulties. A loan by a British bank to a British industry which is dependent on foreign raw materials, may have very limited efficacy in setting the industry going. The borrower can use the money in paying wages at home, but he may not be able to use the money in buying materials with which labor must work. Britain can build a great export trade again only if she can have free access on good terms to the raw materials of the world.

One very important source of Britain's income has been financial profits in financing the trade of the world. To do this she needs both cash and credit. Very short of lending power today, it would still be possible for Britain, with her great fund of knowledge of credit conditions throughout the world, and her great skill in international lending, to act as middleman in distributing credit, if her own credit in London were good. American banks would gladly go "joint account" with British banks, and would gladly take good British bills representing goods exported, say, from Brazil to France, accepted by British houses or banks, if the rate of interest were right and if the bill were looked upon as prime. But the bill could not be looked upon as prime if there were a chance that sterling might depreciate ten percent overnight, or that sterling might depreciate twenty percent in seventy-two hours, or if there were a chance that the International Fund might declare the dollar a scarce currency and permit England to ration it out instead of meeting dollar obligations in full.

A policy of cheap money in England, therefore, designed to rehabilitate England's domestic industries and designed to expand the export trade can easily be self-defeating. The danger of this becomes even greater if the British government undertakes to carry out large projects of internal improvements, and elaborate plans for social security, partly based on government money borrowed at cheap rates from British banks.

That the British government is proceeding on the Keynesian theory that cheap money and foreign exchange depreciation are essential for a full employment program is strongly indicated in the following passage from the *New York Times* of October 3, 1946: "The United Kingdom won an important concession from the governors of the International Monetary Fund today. The governors agreed that measures taken by a country to protect itself from a threat to its 'full employment' program might be considered by the Fund as coming within its authority to allow currency revaluations to correct a 'fundamental disequilibrium.' "

The National City Bank's monthly letter of November 1946 (p. 125) discusses this and seems to feel that the Fund has not made a final ruling on the point. But both the request of the British government and the provisional ruling of the Fund are disquieting. They are particularly disquieting to one who wishes to see England have large access to credit in the outside world, and one who wishes to see sterling strong enough to do its work in foreign trade and in international finance.

The nationalization of the Bank of England which the Labor government has already put through probably did not change the character of the bank. The bank had probably lost all of its independence from the government well before this happened. The legislation giving the British Treasury power,[10] on the recommendation of the Bank of England, to impose policies on the Joint Stock Banks, however, may introduce still more drastic control of general banking policy. Banking can function satisfactorily only (a) when the money market is under the limitations of gold reserves, gold exports and imports, and sound central bank policy, and (b) when individual bankers, competing with one another, are free to use good

---

[10] "Banking Under Control," London *Economist,* February 16, 1946.

banking judgment in individual transactions. Both England and the world outside need a strong fixed pound sterling, and both need interest rates in London which tell the truth regarding supply and demand of real capital as distinguished from artificially manipulated money market funds.

It may be added that the prospect of Britain's developing a favorable balance of trade, an excess of exports over imports (including both goods and services), again depends (a) on orthodox measures of sound money and natural interest rates, or (b) upon a degree of highly intelligent governmental control of the volume of exports and imports, either of which we have little reason to anticipate.

It is, of course, a hard saying that England must, in the postwar years, import less and export more goods, because she is now debtor to the outside world, whereas before the war, even with her great losses, she was still creditor. If this is understood to mean that England must import less for her people to consume than she did during the war years and than she has been doing in the troubled postwar year, 1945–46, when she still has the necessity of maintaining immense armed forces, in view of the unsettled state of the world, it would be a very hard saying. If, however, we can anticipate a real peace in the world, and can anticipate that British industry can make use of new technology and labor-saving devices, it need not be hard. Unfortunately, on this last point there is uncertainty. Union labor in England is opposed to labor-saving devices, and Britain has a Labor government. The truth is simply that she must export relatively a great deal more than she imports, comparing the postwar period with the prewar period. It is possible for the British people to do this and still have many more of the comforts and necessities of life than they had in the dark years, 1939 to mid-1946. But in order to maintain her position and in order to assure the necessary imports, it is essential that England greatly increase her exports of goods and services, including shipping and financial services, to the outside world.

Free markets, sound money, orthodox money market policy, and free banking machinery will do this automatically. If Britain is paying its external debts with tax money, it is automatically restricting the ability of the British people to consume goods by the collection of the taxes. Britain becomes a less satisfactory place in which to sell and a more satisfactory place in which to buy. If the banks are obliged to tighten their rates of discount and interest as gold moves out or foreign exchange reserves become depleted, when the British government undertakes to transfer its tax money to foreign countries through purchasing foreign exchange, less credit is available for importers and less credit is available to enable exporters to hold back goods. British exports are encouraged and imports are discouraged. The thing is automatic, and an equilibrium is reached when exports increase sufficiently and imports decrease sufficiently to bring about an equilibrium between debt payments abroad and the export balance. If, however, the British government undertakes, by control of exports and imports, to accomplish this same equilibrium, there is outcry from the British people against the restriction of imports of food and comforts, and the export of food and comforts, to which a democratic government is very likely to yield. Hitler could go far in matters of this sort. It is improbable that the British government can.

With great respect for the intelligence of the British government and with great respect for the discipline of the British people, one may well question that either the intelligence or the governmental power exists in England, or in any other democratic country, to make a system of this kind work.

Index

This book was set in the Times Roman series of type. The face was designed to be used in the news columns of the *London Times*. The *Times* was seeking a typeface that would be condensed enough to accommodate a substantial number of words per column without sacrificing readability and still have an attractive, contemporary appearance. This design was an immediate success. It is used in many periodicals throughout the world and is one of the most popular text faces presently in use for book work.

Book design by JMH Corp., Indianapolis, Indiana
Typography by Weimer Typesetting Co., Indianapolis, Indiana
Printed and bound by Edwards Brothers, Inc., Ann Arbor, Michigan
Cover design for third paperback edition by Barbara E. Williams, BW&A Books, Inc.,
    Durham, North Carolina